THE ORIGINS OF A
IN ANCIE

This is the first modern attempt to put aesthetics back on the map in classical studies. James I. Porter traces the origins of aesthetic thought and inquiry in their broadest manifestations as they evolved from before Homer down to the fourth century and then into later antiquity, with an emphasis on Greece in its earlier phases. Greek aesthetics, he argues, originated in an attention to the senses and to matter as opposed to the formalism and idealism that were enshrined by Plato and Aristotle and through whose lens most subsequent views of ancient art and aesthetics have typically been filtered. Treating aesthetics in this way can help us perceive the commonly shared basis of the diverse arts of antiquity. Reorienting our view of the ancient vocabularies of art and experience around matter and sensation, this book dramatically changes how we look upon the ancient achievements in these same areas.

JAMES I. PORTER is Professor of Classics at the University of California, Irvine. Recent publications include *Classical Pasts: The Classical Traditions of Greece and Rome* (edited, 2006), and *Nietzsche and the Philology of the Future* (2000).

THE ORIGINS OF AESTHETIC THOUGHT IN ANCIENT GREECE: MATTER, SENSATION, AND EXPERIENCE

JAMES I. PORTER

CAMBRIDGE
UNIVERSITY PRESS

CAMBRIDGE
UNIVERSITY PRESS

University Printing House, Cambridge CB2 8BS, United Kingdom

Cambridge University Press is part of the University of Cambridge.

It furthers the University's mission by disseminating knowledge in the pursuit of education, learning and research at the highest international levels of excellence.

www.cambridge.org
Information on this title: www.cambridge.org/9781316630259

First published 2010
First paperback edition 2016

A catalogue record for this publication is available from the British Library

Library of Congress Cataloguing in Publication data
Porter, James I., 1954–
The origins of aesthetic thought in ancient Greece: matter, sensation, and experience / James I. Porter.
p.   cm.
Includes bibliographical references and index.
ISBN 978-0-521-84180-1 (hbk.)
1. Greece–Intellectual life–To 146 B.C.   2. Aesthetics, Classical–Greece–History.
3. Matter–Philosophy–History.   4. Senses and sensation–Greece–History.
5. Experience–Greece–History.   6. Arts, Greek–History.   I. Title.
DF78.P76 2010
111′.850938–dc22

2010018056

ISBN 978-0-521-84180-1 Hardback
ISBN 978-1-316-63025-9 Paperback

Contents

viii *Contents*

PART IV   AESTHETIC FUTURES

Epilogue 527

Figures

Acknowledgments

Though this study had a short gestation, it belongs to a larger project with a longer history that for reasons of presentation I have been obliged to partition into three separate studies. My acknowledgments of thanks and debts must, accordingly, be partitioned as well.

I have been thinking about Greek and Roman aesthetics, in particular its materialist varieties from Democritus to Longinus, for a long while. My first encounter reaches back to my days in graduate school, which culminated in a doctoral thesis about the influence of atomism on Greek and Roman aesthetic thought. Life took me in different directions that, fortunately or otherwise, prevented me from publishing that work. Twenty-odd years and a few unrelated books later, with the experience gained in the interim, I was able to return to the question of the earliest traditions of classical aesthetics with fresh eyes. Nevertheless, thanks are due to those who guided me in the earliest stage of my career when my interest in the topic was first kindled: Tom Rosenmeyer†, Mark Griffith, Dalia Judovitz, and Phil Damon†. A long detour through Hellenistic literary criticism by way of Philodemus and the Herculaneum papyri, but also later Greek and Roman authors, permitted me to develop one aspect of this project in a series of book chapters and articles, which will form the core of a second volume devoted specifically to developments in literary aesthetics after Aristotle. Further debts to friends and colleagues will be signaled there. A third volume will treat the sublime tradition that culminates in Longinus. Down the road, I hope to treat the atomistic tradition of aesthetic inquiry in a shorter and inevitably speculative study on Democritus and his aftermath.

The present volume originated as an introductory chapter to the post-Aristotelian study, but it quickly evolved into a preliminary study with a life of its own and as a prequel volume to the later studies. It has been greatly stimulated and improved by exchanges on particular chapters or points of interest with a number of colleagues, including

Sara Ahbel-Rappe, David Blank, Armand D'Angour, Eric Downing, Jaś Elsner, John Franklin, Philip Hardie, Brooke Holmes, Gregory Hutchinson, Richard Janko, Monte Johnson, Josh Katz, André Laks, Marjorie Levinson, James Lesher, Margie Miles, Andrea Nightingale, Neil O'Sullivan, Alex Potts, Peter Railton, Ralph Rosen, Ruth Scodel, Niall Slater, Ineke Sluiter, Michael Squire, Andrew Stewart, Ken Walton, James Warren, and Tim Whitmarsh. My debts to other scholars, including any I have forgotten to name in this short list, will be evident from the pages that follow, not least from the footnotes.

Because much of this material was drafted in a condition of rapid and self-imposed exile during a year of leave during 2005–06 and then revised over the next three years, most of it did not receive the benefit of test-driving before audiences, though some of it did, largely once the MS was completed. Parts of the book were read before audiences in Paris and Los Angeles (The Getty Research Institute), and at the Universities of Pennsylvania, California at Irvine, Santa Barbara, and Santa Cruz, Michigan, Chicago, and Cambridge. An early predecessor to the final chapter was first launched as a talk with the same title at Corpus Christi College, Oxford in spring of 2003. I am grateful to all those present for their remarks at the time. Finally, a few parts of this book managed to appear in print, either as precursors, excerpts, or spin-offs. These will be signaled in the notes as necessary.

Fellowships from the National Endowment for the Humanities and Princeton's Council of the Humanities gave me the leisure I needed to press forward with my research at critical moments. The semester I spent in the Classics Department at Princeton during the fall of 2004 was particularly invigorating, and it left its mark on the opening chapter, the first that I conceived for this volume, and on parts of the final chapter. The University of Michigan, where I spent most of my professional life until recently, proved an invaluable source of support throughout, both institutionally and collegially. Release time at the University of California, Irvine during fall and spring 2007–08 allowed me to undertake the bulk of the final revisions. Maria Pantelia, my department chair at the time and now colleague, helped smooth the transition to Irvine and also offered valuable suggestions on the final draft of the MS. A succession of editorial assistants enabled me to wean out errors of all kinds, while Kevin Batton heroically constructed the index locorum, the first he had ever made. Barbara Hird generously shared with me some of the secrets of her fine art of indexing, which helped make sense of my own task as I blundered my way through the subject index. I am grateful to the members of the editorial team at Cambridge University Press – Liz Hanlon, Jodie Barnes, Jo Breeze, Tom O'Reilly, and especially Linda Woodward – for their professional expertise during the production process. Michael Sharp, my primary editor at the Press, has been exceptionally supportive of my evolving projects from start to finish, and I wish to thank him for his encouragement throughout. Needless to say, any errors that remain are solely my own responsibility.

For help with obtaining illustrations and permissions, beyond the institutions to be credited below, I would like to acknowledge in particular Alan Bowman and Charles Crowther of The Centre for the Study of Ancient Documents in Oxford, Alessia Dimartino, Alicja Egbert of The Phoebe A. Hearst Museum of Anthropology at the University of California, Berkeley, Helmut Engelmann, David Gill, Jasmine Moorehead of the Weinstein Gallery in San Francisco, Ann Sinfield of the Chazen Museum of Art at the University of Wisconsin-Madison, Peggy Sotirakopoulou, and Mark Wilson Jones. Nick Cahill kindly supplied me with readings of the Chazen vase based on rigorous autopsy at a time when my access was limited to a digital image. A grant from the UCI Humanities Center helped defray the costs of the illustrations. Special thanks go to George Castanis and his sons, Thaddeus and Gus, for providing me with the splendid cover image by Muriel Castanis, *Roman, No Arms*. It is a special pleasure to pay tribute to her artistic vision of the sublime matter of the Graeco-Roman past.

Finally, I wish to dedicate this book to my family: my mother Ellie, my brothers Bob and John, my son Gabriel, and – *in memoriam* – my father, Arthur E. Porter.

Note on translations

Where translators are given by name only, translations are drawn either from the editions listed in the Abbreviations or from the following sources: J. M. Cooper and D. S. Hutchinson (eds.) (1997) Plato, *Complete Works*. Indianapolis, IN; J. Barnes (ed.) (1984) *The Complete Works of Aristotle: The Revised Oxford Translation*. Princeton, NJ; A. H. Sommerstein (ed.) (1980–2001) *The Comedies of Aristophanes*. 11 vols. Warminster; D. A. Russell and M. Winterbottom (eds.) (1972) *Ancient Literary Criticism: The Principal Texts in New Translations*. Oxford; and the Loeb Classical Library. Further sources are noted below. Other translations are mine.

Abbreviations

Abbreviations for ancient authors and works follow S. Hornblower and
A. Spawforth (eds.) (1996) *The Oxford Classical Dictionary*, 3rd edn. Oxford
(*OCD*³); H. G. Liddell, R. Scott, and H. S. Jones, R. Mackenzie,
P. G. W. Glare, and A. A. Thompson (eds.) (1996) *A Greek–English Lexi-
con*, 9th rev. edn. Oxford (LSJ); and P. G. W. Glare (ed.) (1996) *The Oxford
Latin Dictionary*. Oxford (*OLD*). Journal abbreviations follow *L'Année
philologique*. More frequently cited works are abbreviated as follows:

AB	C. Austin and G. Bastianini (eds.) (2000) *Posidippi Pellaei quae supersunt omnia*. Milan.
Ak.	I. Kant (1902 –) *Gesammelte Schriften*, 29 vols. Berlin. (= "Akademie" edn.).
Austin	C. Austin (ed.) (1968) *Nova fragmenta Euripidea in papyris reperta*. Berlin.
CEG	P. A. Hansen (ed.) (1983–89) *Carmina epigraphica Graeca*, 2 vols. Berlin.
CIL	*Corpus Inscriptionum Latinarum* (1863 –). Berlin.
CJ	I. Kant (1952) *The Critique of Judgement*. Trans. J. C. Meredith. Oxford. (Rpt. 1982); or Paul Guyer (ed.) (2000) *The Critique of the Power of Judgment*. Trans. P. Guyer and E. Matthews. Cambridge. (*CJ* = Ak. 5:167–485; "First Introduction" = Ak. 20:195–251)
CMG	*Corpus Medicorum Graecorum* (1908–) Leipzig and Berlin.
CPR	P. Guyer and A. W. Wood (eds.) (1998) I. Kant, *The Critique of Pure Reason*. Trans. P. Guyer and A. W. Wood. Cambridge.
DK	H. Diels and W. Kranz (eds.) (1951–52) *Die Fragmente der Vorsokratiker, griechisch und deutsch*, 3 vols. 6th edn. Berlin.

FGE	D. Page (ed.) (1981) *Further Greek Epigrams*. Cambridge.
FGrHist	F. Jacoby (ed.) (1957 –) *Die Fragmente der griechischen Historiker*. Leiden.
FHS&G	W. W. Fortenbaugh, P. M. Huby, R. W. Sharples, and D. Gutas, *et al.* (eds.) (1992) *Theophrastus of Eresus: Sources for his Life, Writings, Thought, and Influence*, 2 vols. Leiden.
GG	G. Uhlig, A. Hilgard, H. Schneider, and A. Lentz (eds.) (1867–1910) *Grammatici Graeci recogniti et apparatu critico instructi*, 4 vols. in 6. Leipzig. (Rpt. Hildesheim, 1979).
GL	H. Keil (ed.) (1855–80) *Grammatici Latini*, 7 vols. Leipzig. (Rpt. 1961.)
G–P	A. S. F. Gow and D. L. Page (1965) *The Greek Anthology: Hellenistic Epigrams*. 2 vols. Cambridge.
IG	*Inscriptiones Graecae*. (1873 –) Berlin.
IGR	R. Cagnat, *et al.* (eds.) (1901–27) *Inscriptiones Graecae ad res Romanas pertinentes*, 4 vols. Paris. (Rpt. Rome, 1964.)
ILS	H. Dessau (ed.) (1892–1916) *Inscriptiones Latinae Selectae*. Berlin.
IRG	*Inscripciones Romanas de Galicia* (1949 –). Santiago.
K–A	R. Kassel and C. Austin (eds.) (1983–2001) *Poetae Comici Graeci*, 8 vols. in 10. Berlin and New York.
K–R–S	G. S. Kirk, J. E. Raven, and M. Schofield (1983) *The Presocratic Philosophers: A Critical History with a Selection of Texts*, 2nd edn. Cambridge.
LP	E. Lobel and D. L. Page (eds.) (1955) *Poetarum Lesbiorum fragmenta*. Oxford.
MXG	H. Diels (ed.) (1900) *Aristotelis qui fertur de Melisso, Xenophane, Gorgia libellus*. Berlin.
*OCD*²	H. H. Scullard and N. G. L. Hammond (eds.) (1970) *The Oxford Classical Dictionary*, 2nd edn. Oxford.
PMG	D. L. Page (ed.) (1962) *Poetae Melici Graeci*. Oxford.
Radermacher	L. Radermacher (ed.) (1951) *Artium Scriptores: Reste der voraristotelischen Rhetorik*. Österreichische Akademie der Wissenschaft, Phil.-Hist. Klasse, Sitzungsberichte 227, no. 3.

SEG	*Supplementum Epigraphicum Graecum* (1923–). Leiden and Amsterdam.
SLG	D. Page (1974) *Supplementum lyricis Graecis: Poetarum lyricorum Graecorum fragmenta quae recens innotuerunt.* Oxford.
SVF	H. von Arnim (ed.) *Stoicorum veterum fragmenta*, 3 vols. Leipzig.
TrGF	B. Snell, R. Kannicht, and S. Radt (eds.) (1971–2004) *Tragicorum Graecorum Fragmenta*, 5 vols. Göttingen.
TLG	*Thesaurus Linguae Graecae*®. A Digital Library of Greek Literature, University of California, Irvine (www.tlg.uci.edu).
U–R	H. Usener and L. Radermacher (eds.) (1899–1904) *Dionysii Halicarnasei quae exstant opuscula*, 2 vols. Stuttgart. (Rpt. 1985; 1997.)

Introduction

This book forms part of a larger project on the origins and evolution of ancient aesthetic inquiry, which will appear in three loosely connected and progressively narrowing installments. In the first and present volume, I trace the origins of this inquiry in its broadest manifestations across a range of art forms and discourses as these evolved from before Homer down to the fourth century and then into later antiquity, albeit with an emphasis on Greece in its earlier phases. A second installment, *Literary Aesthetics after Aristotle*, will cover the history of this development after Aristotle down to the Augustan age, again mainly in the Greek world, but with a special emphasis on literary criticism, theory, and aesthetics. A third volume will examine the emergence of the sublime in antiquity and its eventual theoretical expression in Longinus' treatise, *On the Sublime*.[1]

The accent in the present study is emphatically placed on sensualism and materialism, as opposed to the formalism and idealism that were enshrined by Plato and Aristotle, and through whose lens most subsequent views of ancient art and aesthetics have typically been filtered, including our own today. One aim of my approach, then, is corrective. Aesthetics as a term and in its root meanings points us to the sensuous experience of art. Treating aesthetics in this way can help us perceive the commonly shared basis of the diverse arts of antiquity, namely their common foundation in a shared set of experiences, which the various languages of the day sought to capture in different ways and in different disciplines or pre-disciplines. And so too, reorienting our view of the ancient vocabularies of art and experience can dramatically change how we look upon the ancient achievements in these same areas.

---

[1] A separate study, tentatively titled *Atomistic Aesthetics: A Speculation*, will have to wait for another occasion, though to be sure the spirit of atomism may be felt in various places below.

Existing accounts of ancient art and its theory are ill equipped to analyze these phenomena in their manifold expressions for a simple reason: they follow a modern division of the senses and the labors of form. Art history is equated with visual art; musical history and theory exclude poetry; history of philology excludes all of these; philosophy is a sideline occupation at best; and so on. Aesthetics as a unifying disciplinary marker is rarely invoked. Larger categories like beauty, the sublime, the sensuous, the palpable, or the rhythmic occur adjectivally, but only rarely do they occur as legitimate nouns in modern studies. Finally, contemporary perspectives on ancient art and aesthetics are dominated by those that attained canonical status in the fourth century BCE with Plato and Aristotle and then were enshrined in subsequent millennia, first at Alexandria and later during the Italian Renaissance. Contemporary perspectives – not simply on aesthetics, but also governing the very way the disciplines of classics are conceived and carried out – are dominated, in other words, by two mutually reinforcing views: formalism, which may provisionally be defined as any attention to the purity or ideality of form, structure, or design (principles which are thought to organize matter or material); and a kind of Platonism, which for present purposes may be defined as a repudiation of the senses.[2] This is the perspective that reigns whenever the capacity for higher-order reflection on art and aesthetics is not being denied altogether to the ancients, a denial that is represented above all by Paul Oskar Kristeller and by others in his wake, but that (thankfully) is a minority position within classical studies, though not outside the discipline.[3]

The aim of this study, in contrast, is to furnish a new and I hope in ways revisionist account of the development of aesthetic theories in

---

[2] One need only recall Plato's admiration for "the beauty of forms" or "figures" in the *Philebus* (σχημάτων κάλλος, 51c1) – forms that are explicitly denied any phenomenal richness (for instance, color or mass), and that ultimately stand in for Forms that elude sensation altogether. See further Ch. 2 below. On aesthetic form in the sense defined here and on Plato's contribution to it, see Eldridge 1992; further, Bruns 2008, 226, on form "in the classic Aristotelian sense of an artifact reposing in the unity, integrity, and harmony of its disparate elements," and what Adorno, for example, refers to as "the arrangement of sensuous elements" (ibid.), where the accent lies on arrangement, not sensuousness. For a useful critique of form and formalism in aesthetics, see Summers 1989. For some examples of the linkage of Platonism, formalism of design, and classical Greek art in contemporary art history, see Ch. 1, n. 62 below. *Formalism* is often used to signify something further, namely, an "exclu[sion] of the cognitive from the realm of the aesthetic" (Saito 2007, 10, n. 1). I do not use *formalism* in that sense here, as it too easily ends up being conflated with the materialist positions I wish to discuss. Finally, on the exclusion of materiality from the conduct of classical studies, see my essay, "The Materiality of Classical Studies" (Porter 2010b).
[3] There are innumerable difficulties with Kristeller's argument, which will be touched on in Chapter 1 below.

antiquity from a more historically and philosophically complete perspective than is currently available, in part by attending to some of the neglected margins of ancient sources of the kind signaled just above. These latter are to be viewed as part of a larger aesthetic discourse that in turn reaches into the very foundational problems of meaning and value in antiquity. And so, while the perspectives offered up by this study are comprehensive, they are not exhaustive, and in some ways they are emphatically partial. It is not my purpose to offer a complete survey of aesthetic criticism in antiquity, its history, or its sources. Rather, my book presents something like a general account of the *missing* history of these fields, and then offers a particular slice (or slices) of this history, which hopefully can serve as a stimulus to future studies in its wake.

The structure of the book follows a simple logic. Foundational and historical questions about larger concepts are treated in Part I: aesthetics, form and formalism, matter and appearances. The belief in matter as a constituent of experience and reality was strongly rooted in Greek thought, but also highly contested. The implications of this belief for art and aesthetics alone were immense, though they remain underestimated. The purpose of Part I, accordingly, is to detail the emergence of the Greek concepts of matter and materiality, their expression in appearances, and their rejection or qualification through the counter-concepts of form and the immaterial. Aesthetics has a unique history in relation to all of this that needs to be told. Indeed, the very possibility of a history of aesthetics, understood in part as a history of the senses and of the thoughtful reflection on their deliverances, hangs in the balance. Part II traces the rise of aesthetic reflection from the sixth to the fourth centuries BCE across a variety of fields: rhetoric, philosophy, music, the visual arts.[4] As treated here, these conventional labels quickly give way to less recognizable themes that deliberately cut across familiar boundaries – for example, componential systems of analysis (based on the *stoicheion*, or smallest determinable unit of analysis), the aesthetics of the voice (whether written or heard), pleasure in materials, the roles played by touch and sight, the mutual evocation of sensory experiences (synaesthesia), the vivacity of sensation. The third and final part is a chapter unto itself, and it encompasses a wider mix, but above all a blending and tension, of arts, media, and discourses on art: inscriptions, lapidary metaphors in poetry, actual

---

[4] Medical writers, while represented in places below, are not investigated in any depth; more work remains to be done to bridge this field with others.

architecture and "verbal architecture," the sublime and "sublime matter." I will have more to say about the specific realignments that come with shifting one's focus from form and idealization to matter and sensation later in this Introduction. Suffice it to say for now that attention to the most basic questions of sensation and perception in aesthetics permits a far more inclusive approach to the commonalities in experience that were shared across media and to the languages that sought to capture these.

This book's argument starts from concepts and problems and moves towards particulars and solutions. It builds slowly, but surely. In historical terms, one could say that my study is about the discovery, as concepts and names, of matter and appearances and then their deployment in the reflection on art in ancient Greece. The aim here is to unearth the materialist and sensualist predecessors to Plato and Aristotle in the theory of art and aesthetics – no easy task, but essential for getting, as it were, behind the back of these two formidable presences in the evolution and transmission of ancient aesthetic thought. The flip side of this approach is to ask who it was that Plato and Aristotle were reacting to when they laid down their influential views. Neither thinker can be fully comprehended except as responding to this somewhat submerged background. Accordingly, one sub-plot of the present study is a re-consideration of aspects of both thinkers' views on aesthetic theory, above all Aristotle's, whether in their own right or as opening a window onto their predecessors. In more elemental terms, my study maps out a theory about how aesthetic encounters must proceed, from the experience of matter (in some form or other) to the assignment of aesthetic values. Thus, to some extent and in places, the study is intended as a contribution to aesthetic theory or its modern history, though this is by no means its primary purpose. In disciplinary terms, the book's contents move from philosophy to art and culture, which is to say, from theory to practice. But, again, these are boundaries whose firm distinctions it is among the book's goals to contest.

THE AESTHETICS OF EXPERIENCE

The starting point of my project is the intuition, which ought to be uncontroversial, that a productive way to approach ancient art, or any art for that matter, is through the realm of experience. Focusing on experience helps bring attention back to the root meanings of aesthetics, and therefore to the root experiences of *aisthēsis*, or sensation and perception. Driving aesthetics back to the level of sensation, but without halting there, has the virtue of putting the act of attending back in touch with matter and materiality, the senses, and experience. Seen in this light, the terms of my title map out a logical *progressus* for ancient aesthetic subjects that corresponds to one of the guiding assumptions in this study: a subject confronts *matter* (hard and resistant bodies, objects, things, their materials, or their properties); he or she has a perceptual *sensation*; the *experience* of matter (and in particular, of matter's materiality[5]) gives rise to *aesthetic* perceptions, whether pleasure or pain, beauty or sublimity, or else some smaller-scale qualitative apprehension concerning an object's sensuous features, be this its roughness or smoothness, its mass or dimensional qualities, and so on; these aesthetic perceptions or experiences, in turn, give rise to some larger, categorical judgment that often engulfs the whole of the object in question: "This thing is [aesthetically speaking] X," where the bracketed expression need only be implied and X expresses some kind of aesthetic evaluative labeling.

To describe the process in this way is not to presume that a confrontation with bare matter can give rise, as if by magic, to aesthetic experience. Bare matter (if such a thing ever existed; this will be discussed in Chapter 3 below) is transformed *in its very apprehension* – first when it is apprehended *as* (bare) matter or material, and then again when it is apprehended as capable of containing, releasing, or just triggering aesthetic properties, perceptions, or experiences. The not-so-hidden premise of my argument, in other words, is that to have an aesthetic perception is to have an empirical – phenomenal, material, sensual – encounter with that object, the experience of which *can never be shed* subsequently.[6] To think along

[5] Roughly understood as the material nature of matter or the subjective sense or feeling one has of this. By contrast, matter can be said to have non-material (formal) properties, such as shape, contour, or arrangement. Whether these are truly non-material remains to be seen. (I doubt it.) One can also appeal to the (formal construction of the) idea of matter as its "materiality," which is, however, not what I have in mind by the term.

[6] See the similar premise of Frank Sibley in a well-known article from the 1960s, "Aesthetic and Non-Aesthetic": "It is of importance to note first that, broadly speaking, aesthetics deals with a kind of perception. People have to *see* the grace or unity of a work, *hear* the plaintiveness or frenzy in the music, *notice* the gaudiness of a color scheme, *feel* the power of a novel, its mood, or its uncertainty of tone.... Unless they do perceive [these qualities] for themselves, aesthetic enjoyment, appreciation, and judgment are beyond them. Merely to learn from others, on good authority, that the music is serene, the play moving, or the picture unbalanced is of little aesthetic value; the crucial thing is to see, hear, or feel" (Sibley 1965, 137; emphasis in original). This view is common enough today among theorists of art and aesthetics (see, e.g., Arnheim 1986, esp. 678), perhaps because it speaks to an inevitable component of all aesthetic activity. I would only qualify Sibley's remark by adding that the qualities in question need not be objectively part of the work, but only objectively part of the experience. The music need not be really frenzied; I need only hear it that way for the perception to be "mine," while social conditions will more or less guarantee that my perception is (more or less) shared.

such lines is to enhance one's view of aesthetic experience; and it is to enlarge the scope of lived experience, thereby enriching it, drawing it out, extending its dimensions. Indeed, aesthetic and empirical experience go hand in hand, as they only can. Recognizing that they do helps enlarge the scope of inquiry to anyone interested in broadening the frames of reference concerning aesthetic questions in antiquity on offer today.

Currently, approaches to aesthetics as a legitimate domain of thought and inquiry in antiquity are virtually non-existent, and the reason has to do with the limitations of modern perspectives alone, not with the ancient capacities for art and reflection on art. Access to the domain of aesthetics is restricted by pre-established routes of entry that inhibit a more encompassing vision. In place of wide-angled views, one finds piecemeal visions, determined and overdetermined by disciplinary sightlines. History of art (understood by convention to mean plastic and visual arts), music, poetry, philosophy (which can include theories of art but also analyses of the senses), history of philology, studies of popular and other views of pleasure and pain, not to mention cosmological, natural, or antiquarian description, barely come into contact with one another. The question of how these various fields of study interact is rarely addressed, let alone the equally decisive issue of how the *spheres of experience* they variously encompass interact. As a result, the charge that ancient vocabularies for discussing or appreciating art are impoverished is frequently heard, nor is the blame laid only on the lack of source materials (an admittedly lamentable but not insuperable handicap).

But the charge can be turned around if we begin to notice that the languages for expressing pain, pleasure, form, shape, surfaces, luminosity, hues and colors, rhythm, sounds, aromas, palpability, the very sense of time, or any aesthetic category you please (the beautiful, shapely, pleasing, ugly, or sublime) are both in good supply in the ancient world and found in places where art is not directly discussed. What *is* being discussed whenever such topics are on the table is, on the other hand, a matter of experience, which is to say, *what passes through the mind and senses in the face of vivid phenomena – the primary features of sentience.* As it turns out, these same features mark the languages of art in antiquity, and not only those of everyday experience. And here, there is no trace of impoverishment, but only a richly shared vocabulary of languages that cut across boundaries, defying narrow scholastic categories and enabling a richer analysis by us today. In broadening our view of what counts as evidence for aesthetic experience, we are at the same time acknowledging that aesthetics is fundamentally a question of experience, which is to say, of sensation and perception. In a word, we are acknowledging that *arts are genres of experience*, while at the same time expanding our conception of what I occasionally refer to below as the – ever-changing and ever-adapting – *aesthetic public sphere* of antiquity.

In sum, my study is conceived as a plea in the name of aesthetics. By *aesthetics* I understand everything that can conceivably fall under this term, from sensation and perception to all imaginable forms of art in antiquity. But by the study of aesthetics I also understand something more, namely a unifying approach to the various realms of ancient art by way of the commonalities of experience (and not only vocabularies) those arts can be shown to have shared. Secondly, this study proposes a reconstruction of ancient aesthetic thought and inquiry that lies outside the mainstream of Platonic and Aristotelian speculation on art, with roots traceable to fifth-century BCE phenomenalism and materialism and the nascent languages of aesthetic criticism in poetics, music, and the visual arts, but also earlier, in the reflexive statements of poets and other artists. In a sense, the study constitutes an extended commentary on and a historical critique of Aristotle's (eventually canonical) formalistic aesthetic theory (by tracking, as it were, anti-Aristotelianism before and after Aristotle), as well as what might be termed an anti-Platonic aesthetics that originates prior to Plato and persists long after him. It also constitutes a reflection on the ideological shapes that aesthetic value assumes in antiquity. Thirdly, this study hopes to offer, by way of an alternative, a glimpse of the materialist traditions in aesthetics which originated in ancient Greece. In doing so, I will be inverting the standard biases of histories of art and aesthetics which have reigned supreme since Winckelmann (who was, however, himself of two minds on the subject).[7]

AESTHETIC MATERIALISM

Any book that sets out to discuss the relationships between matter, sensation, experience, and aesthetics in antiquity immediately begs several large and probably unanswerable questions about the meaning of its own terms. Accordingly, I must begin with a disclaimer. I have no intention of defining in some final way these concepts in the pages that follow, though

---

[7] On Winckelmann's ambivalences, see esp. Potts 1994. On the suppressed Epicureanism (viz., materialism) behind Winckelmann's apparent Platonizing aesthetics, see Porter 2007a, 109–10. Modern biases in art often reflect this vacillation in their double endorsement of idealism and sensuality, though their approaches tend, I would hazard to guess, towards a formalistic analysis of their objects.

I will be providing some frameworks by which one may grasp the presence
and values of these terms, or what they point to, across a relatively wide
sampling of aesthetic reflection in Greek and (to a lesser extent) Roman
antiquity. Nor, as I said earlier, is it my intention to provide an exhaustive
account, historical or otherwise, of the aesthetic traditions of Greece or
Rome.

The more modest aim of this study lies somewhere between the goals of
suggestion and remapping. I doubt that any reliable understanding of
ancient aesthetics can be possible in the absence of a thorough treatment
of either materiality or sensuous experience, even if this is not the standard
view. And so, one of my aims in what follows will be to stake out the
presence of these notions (even more than the terms that roughly name
them) in the ancient traditions. Another aim is to offer, within a limited
compass, a comprehensive overview of the history of ancient aesthetic
speculation unlike those found in available accounts and of the sort that
more or less automatically results from including the terms *matter, sensation,* and *experience* in one's historical and critical lexicon.

The departure point will be constituted, as I mentioned, by the
sensuous dimensions of aesthetic experience, which are typically demoted
to minor significance in what may be called, for want of a better umbrella
term, the dominant idealist and formalist traditions of criticism in
antiquity and in the modern accounts that mirror these biases. My
counter to this tendency is threefold: that to attend to these repressed,
sensate dimensions in the ancient sources is to tease out something like
the materialist urges of aesthetic thinking in antiquity; that if you pull on
this thread hard enough you will find that materialism is an essential
component of aesthetic reflection in antiquity from its earliest origins
to whenever one chooses to date the end of these traditions; and finally,
that this materialist strand of thought threatens, in places, to break free of
the ancient traditions and to define a tradition of its own.

The history of this countertendency is utterly neglected in the available
accounts, and it is one that the present study seeks to restore. Even so,
characterizing the precise object of my study is not easy. On the one hand,
I am tracing the emergence, in ancient Greece, of the languages of
aesthetic description and analysis *simpliciter* – in a word, of Greek
aesthetics and some of its afterlives in Rome. On the other, I am characterizing in my own language and in a language borrowed from the
ancients an element that is inescapably common to all aesthetic perception (sensuousness), and noting the marks it left wherever it appeared.
In doing so, I am consolidating the markers, so to speak, of aesthetic

materialism (or materialist aesthetics)[8] in antiquity and demonstrating their prevalence across a wide range of areas. Because all these ways of attending to objects and of reflecting upon them – labeling their features, describing their qualities, their impact, their feel, and so on – build upon one another historically, they can be rightfully said to add up to a tradition of sorts, regardless of how these different vocabularies and discourses were finally put to use. That is, materialist aesthetics, as a way of capturing certain features of aesthetic objects and of aesthetic experiences, is an instrument of cultural expression that can be put to a myriad of uses, be they civic, private, religious, class-based, gendered, ethnic, or any other number of further ends beyond aesthetic enjoyment for its own sake (examples of which abound). Having said this, there is probably something wrong with dividing up the work of aesthetics and its application in a given context, since in reality the two are closely integrated and, in the heat of the moment, indistinguishable. The felt properties of a votive object (its colors, shape, and sheen) merge into the activities in which that object is dynamically inserted. Under the right circumstances, the vocal intonations of a text when read aloud take on the aura of classicism and may be used to support that form of ideology (say, in the classroom). How can we separate these out? We can, because the ancients did. And they did so in the shared experience and languages of ancient aesthetic description. It is thanks to their accounts that we can tell these elements of their experience apart. That there is no third language for describing the fusion of aesthetic features and, as it were, utility values – something like an aesthetics or materialism of useful practices – is not a deficiency of aesthetic thought in Greece: we are guilty of the same deficiency today.

My account is intended as a partial precursor to other historical studies in which the empiricist tendencies of art reflection and inquiry are well established, or at least where a case for their presence has been convincingly made, likewise against prevailing counter-views, whether in the Byzantine, medieval, Renaissance, or early or later modern periods.[9] So common and consistent are the sensual allures of art, one is tempted to say that art and aesthetics, at every moment in time, have been shadowed, if not outright driven, by materialist tendencies as much as

[8] I am not sure I see any significant difference between these two designations, which are in any case modern, not ancient (though one could easily stipulate a difference for them). In what follows, I will use both terms more or less interchangeably.
[9] See Ch. 1, n. 17 below.

they have been propelled by opposing factors that value a transcendence of the sensory given alone. The tensions between these two opposing but not infrequently overlapping and even collaborative developments, as significant as they may be, are too complex to detail here beyond a number of suggestions. More urgently needed, at least in the area of classics, is the kind of corrective and recuperative work that can lay the foundations for such studies in the future.

The outstanding trait of the perceptions and viewpoints I will be tracing, which only in modern accounts figure as non-canonical, is the emphasis they place on works of art as phenomenal and material objects, that is, as palpable and sensuous objects of experience. And while a kind of native sensualism and materialism were everywhere in evidence from Homer down to the fifth century, it seems apparent that there was an increasing focus on the empirical and material dimensions of art during the fifth century in the wake of the Presocratics (especially the pluralists), an era that also happens to correspond to the formative years of art theory. Though Plato and Aristotle write largely in response and in opposition to these developments (a fact that is itself too little heeded), they do not succeed in displacing them. That is, Plato and Aristotle are not the beginning of aesthetic inquiry in antiquity by any means; they are merely one of its more prominent *derailing* moments. After Aristotle, proponents of a sensuous aesthetics stand out not least by the way they diverge from the canons of taste and criticism enshrined in the Museum at Alexandria, which is to say, the official, institutional, and academic style of criticism that set the standard for so many of the arts during the Hellenistic period and beyond.

These counter-views, grounded in aesthetic materialism as they are, frequently stand in a critical relation to established norms. Aesthetic materialism can highlight problems of conventional value in striking ways. If aesthetic criticism implies a discussion of cultural biases, norms, and values (from morals to meaning), criticism in a materialistic vein – criticism that is centered on the phenomenal experience of art as registered through the pleasures of the body (as disseminated through the eye, ear, touch, and other senses) – can be intensely critical of conventional values, and especially of the conventions of nature that underpin them. By these latter, I have in mind the naturalistic and naturalizing assumptions so common in antiquity, according to which the appropriateness, say, of signifiers and signifieds (images or sounds and meanings), or of kinds of musical rhythms and ethical behaviors, or of bodily postures and bodily decorum, were felt in some quarters to be justified. So conceived, materialist aesthetics touches, as it were, the very heart of valuation – the conditions that determine the value of values – in a way that non-materialist aesthetics does not. The latter view of art, by contrast, works to elide the origins of value by rendering them either natural or obligatory.

In its critical function, aesthetic materialism points directly to the contingency of one's own frameworks of meaning and understanding, owing in no small part to the way in which these have conventionally been erected on the back of things. For if it is true that matter, sensation, and experience have habitually been taken for granted or, worse, debased and disgraced in Western regimes of meaning (and not only there), then bringing these categories back into view again, in a kind of return of the repressed, inevitably involves challenging the privileged status of meaning over mere matter, with two contrasting effects – sometimes negating meaning, sometimes heightening and deepening it by reawakening or revitalizing it, but in any event always altering it. The very encounter with matter and with materiality presents artists and viewers with a challenge, with a risk (lying as it does at the limits of intelligibility and expression), and with an opportunity. The best of art seems to know how to harness these conditions and to convert them into grounds for further thought and reflection. Matter never leaves meaning untouched. The ethical value of materialism in art lies in the recalibration of one's sense of meaning that the experience of the senses necessarily requires.

Though sensation and perception will in this book be taken to furnish the root experiences and activities of aesthetics, it is not my contention that all of aesthetic sensibility in antiquity was concerned with the sensuous surface of material objects or with felt appearances. It is my contention, though, that sensuousness is a salient element of a good deal of ancient aesthetic sensibilities, and that in cases – and more frequently than one might suppose – one even finds an exclusive interest in this aspect of aesthetic experience at the expense of, say, attention to meaning, morals, or religion. And pure attention to sensuous detail often could have no other apparent purpose than aesthetic pleasure for its own sake. Pliny relates a telling anecdote in this regard. It is the story of a contest between two master painters towards the end of the fourth century BCE. According to Pliny (and the story may be apocryphal, but that is irrelevant if the story was believed or merely widely told), Apelles of Cos traveled to Rhodes to meet Protogenes and to behold his work. Not finding Protogenes at home, Apelles left a calling card in the form of a panel painted with a single brushstroke consisting of an extremely fine line in a single color. When Protogenes returned, he immediately recognized the brushwork as Apelles', for no one else, he declared, could have produced such a finished and self-contained (*absolutum*) work (*opus*). In reply (or revenge), he painted a still finer line on top of the first in another color, and instructed his attendant to show it to Apelles in the event he should return. Apelles did return and, ashamed to be outdone, he proceeded to paint an even finer line on top of the existing lines with a third color, in the process "leaving no room for any further display of minute work (*subtilitati*)." Protogenes admitted defeat and handed the panel down to posterity, "a wonder for everyone, and above all for artists." But that is not all. Pliny's conclusion is itself a marvel of description, as the object was a truly minimalist work from antiquity: "its vast surface contained nothing but the almost invisible lines (*lineas visum effugientes*), so that among the outstanding works of many artists it looked like a blank space (*inani similem*), and by that very fact attracted attention and was more esteemed than any masterpiece."[10] Lines, themselves fleeing the gaze, against a background void – and that was worth more than any masterpiece of art!

What is further remarkable about this story is how painters like Protogenes and Apelles were capable of putting pigments and surfaces above all else. As telling as the anecdote is about ancient professional rivalries, it is no less telling for what the rivalry had to do with in this particular case: artistic skill, sheer technique, marvel at surfaces, appearances, and finish – but nothing more. Painters like Protogenes and Apelles were capable of putting pigments and surfaces above all else, and this is significant in itself. The sheer ability to produce a finely traced line, a singular and inimitable specimen of its kind, blazoned forth in its own material presence – that is all the anecdote is about. This is also why Apelles was famous for the proverb, "No day without a line" – in other words, no day passed when he didn't practice drawing a line.[11] And if painters could be so attentive to the bare materials of their art and their art's sensuous properties, so must have been their audiences, as indeed Pliny's anecdote confirms. Indeed, whether in inscriptions or in literary documents, with the frequent mention of the kinds of materials from which objects were made in antiquity, be this wood, metal, clay, stone, glass, or other precious or semi-precious materials, there automatically comes an attention to the material properties of the objects that were made of these same materials.[12] And comments of a theoretical nature attested

---

[10] Pliny *HN* 35.81–3; trans. Rackham, adapted.

[11] Ibid., 35.84.

[12] Examples to be given below. But witness the many Hellenistic inscriptions that bear the formula εἰκόνα χαλκέαν (votive or dedicatory "image made of bronze," e.g., *IG* IV² 1:66, Epidauria, 74

from before Pindar to the sophists to Aristophanes and on to a host of post-Aristotelian literary critics to a smattering of later art historians only confirm the popular impression that the materiality of aesthetic objects in all media were a matter of considerable importance in antiquity.

To admit this much is already quite a lot. But it would be wrong, I believe, to go on and confuse sensuous absorption with aesthetic autonomy. Consider once more the anecdote from Pliny. For all its emphasis on the simplicity of materials and their mere apprehension, no one in the story is making any claims about the autonomy of art generally or about the aesthetic autonomy of the putative work of art produced jointly by the two painters locked in professional competition, nor even about the autonomy of sensation itself. The only claims being made are paradoxical ones – about how a plank of wood is turned into an *opus*, about the near inconspicuousness of the art and its absolute recognizability for what it is (attesting to indisputable masterwork, genius, and excellence). There is a collision going on here in this account between the sensible and the insensible, between the visible and the invisible, between the diminishing scale of brushwork and the ascending scale of aesthetic merit, between connoisseurship and the fleeting and fugitive nature of the object being beheld.

We might say that a canon of tastes and values is being formed, and not merely confirmed, at the intersection of these differently clashing planes. And implicit in the idea and the practice of any canon of tastes and values is the shared system of pleasures that keeps this system afloat, which gives us two further reasons why aesthetic autonomy fails to capture the richness of any account of aesthetics that is grounded in the senses. First, aesthetic pleasures of the senses are directly – and immediately – related socially to the pleasure one takes in non-aesthetic objects. To experience aesthetic pleasure in antiquity was (and still is) to be caught up within a circuit of valuation, of value-production and value-consumption, a system – implicit, to be sure – that ran through the entire fabric of society, and within which all social agents were implicated. To enjoy things aesthetically was to participate in a social process. And to do this was to participate in an entire series of norms, rules, and conventions that ran through all areas of society at once.

BCE), or earlier Attic inscriptions bearing the formula φιάλε χρυσε̄ ("golden bowl," e.g., *IG* I³ 297, 429/8 BCE); cf. *CEG* 351, Corinth, 458/7 BCE. A bronze discus dedicated in *c.* 530–525 BCE (Cephallenia) bears an inscription in the form of a spiral that mentions the bronze material of the discus (μ' ἀνέθεχε ... | χάλχεον) and recalls the circular shape of the object at one and the same time (*CEG* 391), apparently a common practice (see Jacobsthal 1933).

Thus, there was no such thing as an autonomous artistic pleasure that could be sundered from other kinds of pleasures in antiquity, any more than there is on any reasonable theory of art today. Secondly, and for the same reason, aesthetic sensuousness was intimately tied into the shapes that sensuousness enjoyed in the contemporary cultures of the day – shapes that were distinctive of those cultures and distinct from, say, those of Jonathan Richardson's London or Immanuel Kant's Königsberg. I will have more to say about the shared nature of sensation and experience in relation to art's materials below.

THE DISGRACE OF MATTER AND THE SENSES: A CORRECTIVE

Why bother with materialism at all? one might well ask. Materialism in aesthetics is capable of bringing out much that non-materialist aesthetics, which is to say, any aesthetics predicated on the suppression – the *disgrace* – of matter and sensuousness, is not. Reversing time-honored biases such as these in the areas of intellectual history and the history of material and cultural practices is bound to throw the all-too-familiar into a new light. And the familiar here is unfortunately itself the victim of an idealizing prejudice, not least in the area of ancient aesthetics.

Classical aesthetics, as it has been inherited and constructed over the millennia, has given us a partial view of ancient art and its aesthetic perceptions. It is the view that the Winckelmann of the handbooks would hold dear – of objects bathed in brilliant light, bleached white by the clear sun, displaying firm lines and bold contours, but otherwise colorless, cool to the touch, pure and remote. The classical imagination is an unsensuous one, or rather one that has been shaped by a displaced, imaginary sensuousness. Architectural objects appear as plastic, but not as animated. Polychromy is non-existent, and forbidden. Paintings are of secondary interest. Music, sound, and motion are often no more than attributes of stationary objects, for instance, sculptures moved at best by the mind, or temples registering at most visual rhythms, but unpopulated, and preferably unroofed (nobly half ruined). Vases sit obediently on museum shelves, "unravish'd bride[s] of quietness," their decorations suggesting much commotion and sound, but "not to the sensual ear" (Keats). Textures, layers, traces of the hand or tool, attention to the way in which materials curve and bend and thereby elude the distinction of their own form (do they even have one?), sound patterns detached from sense, the rise and fall of the dancer's foot, enjoyed for their rustle and self-serving cadences – these are not the concerns of a classical aesthetics. And so, to this extent the aesthetics that will concern us in what follows will not be the canonically classical aesthetics, though it will be fully representative of classical antiquity, broadly conceived. To see how this larger representation is warranted, one has to look outside the narrow confines of the canonical, classicizing tastes and prejudices that take their cue from Plato and Aristotle.[13] One has to go back to the very root conditions of aesthetic experience, which were widely available at all periods of antiquity, as can be easily attested.

To attend to aesthetic questions in antiquity is to attend to the ways in which the world was perceived, sensed, and grasped. That is, aesthetic questions, whether posed by us or by the ancients, cannot be hewed off from the most basic questions about how antiquity appeared to its inhabitants, as if these latter questions, concerning a sentient antiquity, were merely so many accessories to the ancient world. Tracing these primary forms of attention will be one aspect of the present study. Another will be reconstructing the kind of reflection on aesthetic experience that results from such protracted attention to the material and sensuous dimensions of art. I am calling such attention a form of *aesthetic inquiry*, and I believe it lies at the origins of every inquiry into art. On the other hand, whenever this deliberate attention to matter, to sensuous details, and to the palpable appearances of art later evolved into a self-standing theoretical articulation of art, it would occupy much, though never the entirety, of later art theory. And though aesthetics in antiquity was, to be sure, rarely *exclusively* materialist, nevertheless one has to ask, When was aesthetics in antiquity *not* in some sense predominantly materialist (attentive to matter, the senses, and palpable detail)? My answer to this question is, emphatically, never. Indeed, can ancient idealism and formalism possibly be reconceived as a sensuous aesthetics in sublated or sublimated guise? Very likely, they can. Consequently, even though upholders of senuous aesthetics may appear to be non-canonical when measured against Plato and Aristotle, in point of historical fact it is the canonical authors like those just named who were in the minority as taste-makers in the ancient Greek world.

How far back in time can we trace aesthetic inquiry, so defined? And how did the inquiry evolve? Intuitively, one wants to say that for as long as

---

[13] Cf. Lloyd 1979, 135–38 for a quick survey of some of the anti-empiricist tendencies of early Greek thought, which culminate in Plato and carry over into Aristotle. (Aesthetics is not discussed.)

there was art there was an implied aesthetic sensibility among both producers and consumers of art. More than that, there must have been available on both sides a kind of theory, or proto-theory, of aesthetic experience, which would have derived from and overlapped with an, as it were, naturally evolving aesthetics *of* experience. Recovering any portion of these buried assumptions is both possible and an urgent task. Indeed, establishing the validity of this claim about the deeply rooted nature of aesthetics and experience in culture is one of the largest aims of the present study. I further assume that talk about sensation in ancient sources gives us a unique and privileged access to what we may call, following the lead of Raymond Williams, "structures of feeling" in antiquity. These latter, which closely resemble Bourdieu's concept of *habitus*, are socially conditioned and historically variable modes of relating to institutions and ideologies, but at a level that lies below the threshold of articulable knowledge.[14] While structures of feeling change over time and they do give us a unique insight into the minds of historical actors, we should not assume that when an ancient source discusses feeling and sensation we are therefore being given direct access to the immediate reality of some physical sensation as it existed at the time even for an agent. Sensations are not only highly subjective; they are also socially shared objects of communication – the very opposite of private and internal states of affairs. For this reason, sensations when they appear to agents are not direct empirical imprints of some outer material reality. They are prismatic reflections of the languages of sensation whose acquisition is a prerequisite to social life. They are thus highly complex events. What is more, aesthetic objects are congealed products of socially collaborative labor: they index their own material production, and so they cannot fail to be expressive of social relations in their material character, a point that has been repeatedly made from Karl Marx to Michael Baxandall to David Summers, to name just these.[15] The ultimate challenge to anyone interested in piecing together a fuller picture of aesthetic inquiry in antiquity is to trace in the history of sensations and of characterizations of objects a history of cultural transformations.[16] Reconstructing the languages of materialism in aesthetics is, accordingly, a daunting task. If I have not always paid

---

[14] On both concepts, see Porter 2006b.

[15] See Summers 1989, 397–98 (stressing *facture* and materials, as well as the manufacturing and labor process).

[16] For example, it might pay to ask how inherited views of matter might have influenced ancient experiences of material objects (ruins, topographies, collections, artifacts, cult objects). Xenophanes could easily have paved the way forward with his inquiries into fossils and geology (DK 21A33),

sufficient heed to the social and cultural pathways by which developments in aesthetics were being channeled at every moment (including in religion and politics), this, too, remains a challenge for the future, and for others.[17]

REALIGNMENTS

A word on realignments is in order, for these are bound to result from any study that reconceives its subject matter not according to customary disciplinary markers but by following the cues and the languages of the senses. My project is attentive to larger contours while recognizing that there is a marvelous specificity to its source materials that is as compelling as the picture taken as a whole. That is, my project is meant to be both synthetic and highly detailed. Much of my discussion is, accordingly, intended to contribute fresh readings of the diverse subject matter at hand, whether this is formed by individual passages from any number of ancient sources or by general readings of, say, Aristotle's *Poetics*, aspects of Plato's treatments of beauty, the Presocratics conceived as precursors to aesthetic inquiry, early traditions of music, the early and later histories of the voice (an especially fruitful way of realigning evidence from various quarters – in poetry, rhetoric, inscriptions, and so on – as opposed to dividing these practices up by genres and areas of application), the theory of the *stoicheion* (element) as a part of a componential and compositional method in several (proto-)disciplines, time as a way of dividing materials and rendering them into perceptual durations, the self-reflexive dimensions of *facture*, the aesthetics of verse inscriptions, and the sublime and the monumental in visual and verbal art, in addition to several brief, revised accounts of modern aesthetic traditions that speak to questions of matter, form, and experience, from Immanuel Kant to Alois Riegl, the Russian Formalists, the first-generation American Pragmatists, and

though Homer puzzles over physical ruins to poetic effect too (*Il.* 2.811–14; *Il.* 23.331–32). The question remains an open one, and with it a whole area of study. Contemporary approaches ("thing theory," phenomenologies of materiality), some of it derived from antiquity and much of it flourishing outside of classics (in anthropology, archaeology, and cultural studies [see Ch. 3, n. 16]), would be relevant tools to apply here.

[17] Most recently, Stewart 1997, Elsner 1998, Steiner 2001, Tanner 2006, and Platt forthcoming tackle these problems, each with different methodologies and outcomes. The classic gauntlet thrown down in the field of art history remains Gordon 1979, though he may err in turn by overaccentuating the religiosity of Greek art objects at the expense of their aesthetic character (on the assumption of the incompatibility of the two categories). As Karen Bassi suggests (*per litt.*), one aim of an approach such as mine is "to historicize the history of aesthetics, to defamiliarize its lexicon, and to understand that lexicon as part of wider social and political structures and beliefs" – admittedly, all lofty goals which not even the present study may succeed in attaining.

the New Critics – not to mention the skepticism that has been voiced around the question whether art and aesthetics have any meaning at all when applied to antiquity (encapsulated by the question, "Is Art Modern?"). I will show why such skepticism is unfounded, despite the surprising degree of unanimity this view has enjoyed in twentieth-century scholarship.

One major turning point to be mapped out in this study is the "invention" – the nomination – of matter and appearances by the so-called Presocratics. My thesis is that once these entities were named as such, they became available in all their manifold forms for use (for probing, exploration, palping) by artists, and then eventually, and increasingly, by more technically minded theoreticians, critics, and systematizers of the arts. Individual case studies fill out this picture (Lasus of Hermione, Aristophanes, Gorgias, Alcidamas, and Aristotle, alongside briefer accounts of minor, ancillary, or simply less well attested figures, such as Licymnius of Chios, Hieronymus of Rhodes, or the Philodemean *kritikoi*). Thematic chapters, organized around music, the voice, visual experience, and sublime monuments, round out the remainder. However disparate these various components may sound, they are in fact intimately bound up by threads that tie them together from end to end.

For example, some of the realignments to be proposed along the way involve reconstructing centuries-long traditions or else clusters of associations over this same length of time. As in other cases, these new groupings result from reorganizing our view of the ancient arts according to aesthetic principles. Hence, by tracing the materialities of voice and stone *à la* Jesper Svenbro's probings into *la parole et le marbre*, or *à la* Jan Assmann's (somewhat) parallel thematics of *Stein und Zeit* in ancient Egypt, one can flesh out the history of literary and other aesthetic inquiries and practices in a new way, particularly by tying together traditions that are normally treated as disjunct. Thus, a direct line can be shown to connect Homeric quasi-inscriptions, archaic (especially sepulchral) verse inscriptions, the *epitaphioi logoi*, inscribed poems (real and notional), what might be called "the epigraphic turn" in fifth-century authors, the rise of the "poem as object," *oggetti parlanti*, the archaic Greek lyric poets' so-called rivalries with immobile plastic art forms (sculpture and monumental architecture), extensions of the same in the later rhetorical tradition (for example, in Gorgias, Alcidamas, and Isocrates), and then Hellenistic extensions: epigrams, objects in poetry (for Hellenistic poetry is frequently object-oriented, even object-obsessed), ecphrastic poetry, and the literary-critical tendency towards euphony, which resumes and incorporates features from all these art forms. A recurring thread in these various historical strands is the superimposition of contrasting motifs – the collision of durability and transience, of loss and permanence, of tangibility and evanescence, of stone and voice, of matter and appearance – that typifies so much of materialist aesthetics in antiquity.

The roots of classicism and the forms that classicism assumes after Aristotle are to be found in these kinds of encounters (dialectical, oxymoronic, paradoxical) with the material dimensions of aesthetic experience – the very kinds of experience that will be demoted in the traditions hostile to matter and its appearances, namely, what one can palpably see, hear, and feel in art.[18] As a consequence, while there are perhaps two primary aesthetic traditions in antiquity – the one "materialist" and the other "immaterialist" or "idealist" – both originate in the same phenomenal moment, defined by an encounter with materiality, and both converge or even flip over onto each other at the nether ends of their respective trajectories. Thus, along with the naming of matter and appearances, an event that can be pinpointed historically, came their instant repulsion or subversion, whether through an initial negation, for instance by the Eleatic monists (chief among them, Parmenides), keen as they were to demote material reality to a mere apparition or illusion, or else through a refinement and sublation, which not even the most avid exponents of materialism could resist. The materiality and phenomenality of matter are elusive entities, as will be seen, and they lead as much in the direction of the intangible and the evanescent as they do in the direction of hard and resisting realities. Why, after all, did the atomists and other pluralists go off in search of the ultimate constituents of physical being in the realms of the *unseen* and the *unapparent*? In ways, the Presocratics seem to have discovered the sublime *en route* to discovering matter.

Similarly, Plato's experience of Forms borrows, precisely, from the realm of experience, and it is conveyed, after all, in language. For all its transcendental yearnings, it remains marked by its origins in the empirical, phenomenal, and material realms. Its asceticism and anorexia in the face of the senses are, oddly (and betrayingly) *insatiable*. In contrast to the Presocratics, who revel in matter, Plato's response to the encounter with brute matter is to recoil from the experience and to take flight in an idealized realm bereft of matter, the senses, surfaces, and tangibility of all kinds, and to discover a beauty (or sublimity) *in this very deprivation of*

---

[18] I say "*palpably* see," not least with a view to the tactile character of ancient visual experience, which will be gone into at greater length in Ch. 8 below.

sensuality.[19] Note, too, how the convergences mount. For, materialism can
appear to shed all traces of its origins in matter at the unrivaled heights
of its experience *of* matter. Consider the materialist aesthete closing
his eyes in rapture before a painting or statue, numbed into a sensory
blur by the sheer profusion of appearances, or conveyed into ecstasy by
sounds that cannot be heard (and euphony in its purest form is in fact an
aural fantasy and a utopia of sounds, as any *kritikos* would acknowledge).
The tradition of sublime monuments (the topic of Chapter 9) is ambivalently drawn both to concrete built structures and to a *kleos* that is
imperishable and everlasting. *The very precariousness of sensuous experience
can itself be productive of intense aesthetic experiences* of the sort that
in antiquity could be described as sublime. Beauty rarely achieves this
kind of distantiation, though it sometimes can – ancient examples are
hard to find, but one thinks of the Aestheticists' pleas in the name of
"material beauty" and of a subversive "art of the senses" during the
second half of the nineteenth century, or of Roland Barthes' unruly
jouissance, its latter-day extension (perhaps Lucian's aesthetic writings
would qualify here).[20]

Be that as it may, this study is not primarily concerned with the
aesthetics of the sublime, but rather with aesthetic inquiry *tout court,*
and above all its materialist expressions, starting from sensation pure
and simple. Indeed, at times I have been tempted to dispense with all
such inheritances as beauty and sublimity and to speak instead of some
more neutral gradient, for instance aesthetic values and intensities[21] –
though I have not done so in the end. Whatever labels we choose to
apply, the fact remains that matter, sensation, and experience are
inescapable elements of aesthetic experience which can never be quite
dematerialized, and that idealizing tendencies in art and aesthetics are a
disavowal of this fact. All aesthetic experience owes its origins to

---

[19] This is what I would call an "immaterial" sublime, to contrast it with the "material" sublime. I plan
to develop the distinction and the underlying connections between these two sublimities in my
future discussion of the sublime.
[20] W. Rossetti 1866, 27; Pater on W. Rossetti (brother of D. G. Rossetti) in Ward 1883, IV:637;
Prettejohn 2005, 127–28; 194. The aesthetic formalism of Clive Bell is tellingly opposed to "material
beauty" ("*e.g.* the wing of a butterfly") and champions instead "significant form" and "pure form"
(Bell 1981, 43). Bell felt that he was reacting to aestheticism (ibid., 52), though he was perhaps in
ways perpetuating it. An earlier echo might be Winckelmann's "sensuous beauty" (e.g.,
Winckelmann 1985 [1755], 37), on whom Pater devoted a chapter in his *Studies in the History of
the Renaissance* (1873). See below on Lucian.
[21] Cf. also Gumbrecht 2004, 98–100.

materiality, and no form of it, not even the immaterial kind, can erase its material origins.

Hence, the starting point laid out above remains valid: aesthetics arises out of the bare – often violent, always arresting – confrontation with matter, and it never sheds this attachment (or stain), even as it effloresces into the various discourses and categories of art and judgment. To ignore this initial convergence and eventual divergence is to overlook a significant proportion of much ancient aesthetic reflection and practice. To acknowledge these is to alter the way we look at aesthetic thought in antiquity.

PART I

Foundations: Aesthetics, Formalism, and Materialism

CHAPTER I

Aesthetic thought in antiquity

Anyone who wishes to rediscover the potentials of aesthetic thought, experience, and reflection in antiquity must first come to terms with the various available meanings of *aesthetics* today. Two problems immediately stand in the way of such an undertaking. First, the word *aesthetics* was unknown in Greece and Rome, nor do any obvious equivalents come to mind. The question of anachronism, or at the very least of a disparity between modern analytical frameworks and ancient objects of analysis, inevitably looms large. Secondly, the discipline of aesthetics, being a modern invention, has come to shape, and to a large extent limit, how we conceive of aesthetic subject matter. How can we hope to think our way past our contemporary blinkers about what counts as art and aesthetics? But this last constraint can be turned to our advantage if we work backwards, mindfully and critically, starting with modernity and then moving into the past. In fact, assessing the history of the emergence of aesthetic inquiry in the modern world is the only way to surmount, or at least to acknowledge, these modernizing constraints. But there is yet a third problem lurking in the background. For the desire to rediscover aesthetics in the classical past can be misguided if this means simply relabeling what we have always done – the study of ancient art, music, literature, the assessment of beauty, style, inspiration, and the like – as somehow "aesthetic." What is needed is not merely a question of relabeling or reclassifying what is known, but a thoroughgoing coming to grips with the problems that determine the very nature of aesthetic reflection, however we decide to understand these. And the only way to get at these is by starting from the known and proceeding to dismantle or to reconceive it, even at the risk of stumbling upon the unknown. So with all of this in mind, let us take up what we know about aesthetics in its modern senses and work our way from there back into antiquity. Modern aesthetics may prove to be a less familiar entity than it is usually thought to be.

Aesthetics in the modern era has covered a wide and sometimes baffling range of meanings since the discipline of aesthetics was coined by Alexander Gottlieb Baumgarten in the middle of the eighteenth century and formalized by Kant towards the end of that century.[1] In its academic senses, *aesthetics* has run anywhere from the science of beauty in art and nature to the philosophy of art and (aesthetic) experience (the vagary of the parenthesis is crucial, as we shall see) or of sensuous perception. But in a narrower, disciplinary sense, aesthetics is perhaps best understood as allied with the philosophical project that "accounts for the [regularity and] translatability of different modes of perception and representation and ensures that this process is unarbitrary."[2] Elsewhere, the term has been more or less parasitic on these academic uses, and its colloquial derivative, *aesthetic,* is often merely synonymous with *beautiful, pleasing,* or *conforming to taste.* Aesthetics today is a contentious field, one that is mined with unsolved problems, for instance: Are there aesthetic properties? Does aesthetics properly speaking pertain to nature or to art, to experience or to the objects of experience? And what are the limiting conditions, if any, of art and the aesthetic? Aesthetics has also evolved into a highly specialized subfield of philosophy, at times a formidably analytic one.[3] But the root questions of aesthetics remain valid and of interest nonetheless, and not even the more serious charge that "the modern system of the arts" as applied to antiquity represents an anachronism, as Paul Oskar Kristeller once held in a still widely influential essay from 1951–52, can stand in the way of exploring aesthetic problems in Greece and Rome.[4] His view merits a closer look given the issues it raises, some of them prejudices, others misunderstandings, not least because it represents a particularly distilled version of the premise that aesthetic reflection is a modern and not an ancient pursuit.[5]

I IS ART MODERN?

What was the first man, was he a hunter, a toolmaker, a farmer, a worker, a priest, or a politician? Undoubtedly the first man was an artist . . . .

---

[1] See Baumgarten 1954 [1735] for the coinage, esp. §116 ("the science of perception, or aesthetics"). That science is developed in his *Aesthetica* from 1750. Kant would call his aesthetics *The Critique of Judgment* (1793). See below on the contribution of the British empiricists.

[2] Mitrović 1993, 66 (taken somewhat out of context).

[3] For a good snapshot of the field, see Levinson 2003.   [4] Kristeller 1990.

[5] The following section represents a much telescoped version of Porter 2009a and Porter 2009b.

Man's first expression, like his first dream, was an aesthetic one. (Barnett Newman[6])

Consider the famous anecdote about Sophocles in Ion of Chios (*FGrHist* 392F6). At a dinner-party on Chios the presence of a very handsome young male slave prompts Sophocles to quote a phrase from Phrynichos, to which a literal-minded schoolmaster takes exception, and Sophocles flattens him by citing instances of poetic licence in the use of colour-terms from Simonides and Pindar.... There is abundant evidence that in preliterate cultures the composition of songs is a process in which discussion and criticism, often passionate, play an important part – and inevitably so, because any aesthetic reaction implies preference, and preference implies criticism. Is anyone prepared to say that the conversation described in Ion fr. 6 was impossible in the Bronze Age? I, for one, am not. (K. J. Dover[7])

By "modern system of the arts" Kristeller understands "the irreducible nucleus" of five art forms that together comprise the Fine Arts (*beaux arts*): painting, sculpture, architecture, music, and poetry. Decorative arts, engraving, gardening, dance, theater, opera, "and finally eloquence and prose literature," were added as an afterthought, historically speaking; these, in any event, never won universal consensus, unlike the five previous arts, which did, or so he claims. The point is that the Fine Arts so constituted are set off from crafts, sciences, "and other human activities": they enjoy relative autonomy, are freed from utilitarian objectives, and are guided by no moral agendas.[8]

This separation is supposed to have occurred in the eighteenth century. The ancients, by contrast, and despite all claims to the contrary as voiced by the likes of Newman and Dover above, had no such unified conception of art or beauty. A series of negative comparisons ensues. The ancients did not separate moral beauty from beauty in art. They did "not treat music or the dance as separate arts but rather as elements of certain types of poetry, especially of lyric and dramatic poetry." The "emancipation of instrumental music from poetry" occurred only late in the day. The social and intellectual prestige of painting, sculpture, and architecture "was much lower than one might expect from [the] actual achievements" that were made in these areas. "No ancient philosopher ... wrote a separate

---

[6] Newman 1947, 59.   [7] Dover 1993, 33.

[8] Kristeller 1990, 165. While Kristeller does not use the expression "aesthetic autonomy," he does invoke the concept through synonyms and through functionally identical ideas, such as the "separation" or "distinction" of the arts from "other human activities" (ibid.), especially from "morality" (199), and not least of all through the invocation of "(modern) aesthetics" as a self-standing discipline (165, and *passim*), which he takes to represent this very separation.

systematic treatise on the visual arts or assigned to them a prominent place in his scheme of knowledge."[9] In short,

we have to admit the conclusion, distasteful to many historians of aesthetics but grudgingly admitted by most of them, that ancient writers and thinkers, though confronted with excellent works of art and quite susceptible to their charm, were neither able nor eager to detach the aesthetic quality of these works of art from their intellectual, moral, religious and practical function or content, or to use such an aesthetic quality as a standard for grouping the fine arts together or for making them the subject of a comprehensive philosophical interpretation.[10]

Accordingly, he concludes, or rather begins, for this is the premise of his essay,

"aesthetics"... and ... the subject matter itself, the "philosophy of art," [were] invented in that comparatively recent period [the eighteenth century] and can be applied to earlier phases of Western thought only with reservations.[11]

Plainly, if Kristeller is right, then any exploration of aesthetics or its subject matter, the philosophy of art, in the historical periods before their "invention" (*c.* 1750) can only be a futile exercise in anachronism.

Kristeller is far from being alone in his disparagement of the ancients' capacity for aesthetic reflection. The kernel of his historical thesis derives from Julius Schlosser's *Die Kunstliteratur* (1924), while his philosophical assumptions are derived at least in part from R. G. Collingwood.[12] Another early exponent of the same view is Schlosser's contemporary, Erwin Panofsky, who accuses Plato of failing to think aesthetically because he was unable to separate metaphysical from aesthetic questions. Accordingly, Plato was incapable of contributing to art theory.[13] This conclusion about Plato is later assented to by Eva Keuls on grounds that would, moreover, exclude Kant from the history of aesthetics – for instance, given Plato's failure to privilege artistic beauty over natural beauty.[14] To be sure, Plato in particular has not lacked his advocates, among them

---

[9] Kristeller 1990, 174.   [10] Kristeller 1990, 174.   [11] Kristeller 1990, 163.

[12] Schlosser 1924 (see Kristeller 1990, 174 n. 79, etc.). Collingwood 1938, esp. 1–56 (see Kristeller, ibid., 164 n. 3; 166 n. 12). A striking predecessor to Kristeller is Tatarkiewicz 1937, who denies outright that any sort of aesthetics based on "the standpoint of ... the spectator or hearer and their aesthetic perceptions" was available in antiquity at all (371). This "lack" resulted in the arts' being disjointed, and it "left nothing but a heterogeneity of the arts" behind (ibid.).

[13] Panofsky 1924, 2. Ernst Cassirer holds a similar view (Cassirer 1998 [1924], esp. 137), as does Lukács (Lukács [1920] 1971, 26), voicing an obviously widely held romantic view of the Greeks.

[14] Keuls 1978, 56, and *passim.* Cf. Sibley 2001, 135, who dates the rise of art-centered aesthetics not to the eighteenth century, *pace* Kristeller (who is not mentioned), but to Hegel: prior to then, nature claimed as much aesthetic attention as art.

Bernard Bosanquet, Edgar Wind, Pierre-Maxime Schuhl, Bernhard
Schweitzer, and, from an unsuspected quarter, Erich Auerbach in his book
on Dante from 1929, each of whom produced powerful appreciations of
Plato's aesthetic theories.[15] Nor has Kristeller's view gone unchallenged
here and there, though the nearly otherwise unquestioned orthodoxy that
it has enjoyed is astonishing.[16] And yet, as if in another, parallel universe,
histories of art and aesthetics from the classical period to the Renaissance and
beyond proceed apace, blithely indifferent to Kristeller's astonishing claims
about the impossibility of aesthetic theory and philosophy prior to 1750,
yet also for the most part unaware of the deeply layered traditions of
aesthetic inquiry that stretch back into early Greece. The aesthetic cultures
of ancient Mesopotamia and Egypt, to name just these, are worlds unto
themselves, albeit not without links to the aesthetic cultures of Greece and
Rome, and they likewise present forbidding challenges to the Kristellerian
viewpoint, even if the aesthetic theories from the ancient Near East are more
often than not to be found embedded in practices rather than in surviving
treatises. Kristeller's most basic claim is that art precedes the theory of art and
the concept of aesthetics. Yet as Barnett Newman, K.J. Dover, and others
have insisted, it is not even clear why art should be considered logically or
historically prior to the concept and experience of aesthetics at all.[17]

I believe that Kristeller is wrong, but that is not the main point. What
makes Kristeller's argument of interest are the sorts of issues it admits
and especially those it omits from its purview. It is hostile to a view of the
arts as interactive, that is, as borrowing across their own closed boundaries. It is art-centered – and therefore lacks any notion of the experience
of aesthetics. It has a reductive and monolithic view of the "modern"
(and so too of its antithesis, the pre-modern). And it ignores the formative
role of the senses. In all of these respects, his position is very like the

[15] Bosanquet 1956, e.g., p. 1: "But the thing ["Æsthetic"] existed before the name"; Wind 1983 [1932]
(thanks to Stephen Halliwell for this reference); Schweitzer 1953, esp. 13; 29 (Plato is the first Greek
"*Kunstkenner*"); 88; Schuhl 1952; Auerbach 1929, 8–15.
[16] Kristeller's view is adopted by Murdoch 1978, 6–7, who claims to be following Bosanquet, and it is
developed at book length in Shiner 2001. Elsewhere, it is widely cited as established orthodoxy
(see, for example, Nehamas 1999). For three differently critical views of Kristeller, see Halliwell
2002, 7–9; Martindale 2004, 31–33; and Leszl 2004. (I am grateful to Stephen Halliwell for the
reference to Leszl.)
[17] Mesopotamia: Winter 1995 (cf. "theory," which must be embedded, not a modern attribute, p. 2572);
Winter 2002; Egypt: Assmann 1991; classical Greece: Tanner 2006; Byzantine: James 1996; Pentcheva
2002; James 2004; James 2007; medieval: Eco 1970; Eco 1994; Renaissance: Panofsky 1924; Summers
1990 (with an excellent survey of Plato's and Aristotle's views on sensation); Townsend 1998, 355–57;
early modern: Barnouw 1993; Townsend 1991, 358–59; Townsend 1998. On the logical and probable
historical priority of aesthetics to art, see the excellent arguments in Sibley 2001.

dominant views, or rather presuppositions, in current studies of the arts of Greece and Rome. Alternative views to Kristeller's are possible – as they are concerning antiquity too.

There are difficulties with Kristeller's picture, starting with its historical validity. Is it even true as a description of the state of the arts and their classification in the eighteenth century? This depends on where one looks. Clement Greenberg gives a radically different picture of the same era in his equally renowned essay from 1940, "Towards a Newer Laocoon." In his view, the arts were dominated by a single art form by the time the seventeenth century arrived in Europe – namely, literature. "A confusion of the arts" resulted, whereby each art sought to assimilate itself to the dominant literary form, "pretend[ing] to conceal their *mediums* [so] as to annihilate [these] seemingly in favor of *illusion*."[18] Greenberg's analysis of the situation of the arts in the seventeenth and eighteenth centuries is remarkable for the polar contrast it makes with Kristeller's historical picture, but also – strangely – for its striking similarities with the situation of the arts of antiquity as depicted by Kristeller. Greenberg locates not only a "confusion" but also a "fusion" of the arts during this period, whereby, for instance, "painting [could] imitate sculpture, and sculpture, painting, but both could attempt to reproduce the effects of literature."[19] All this he considers to be a sign of the "decline" of the arts at the time, and it is not until well into the next century that he sees any signs of recuperation. (The Romantic revival only marked a worsening, not an amelioration, of the confusion of the arts.[20]) Indeed, it is only with the debut of the avant-garde, dated by Greenberg to Courbet's new realism and the rise of Impressionism in his wake, that the arts finally asserted their autonomy. By this self-assertion of the arts Greenberg means the assertion of their independence from literature (understood more broadly as "subject matter") and their discovery of intensified expressive forms and media (subserving no single art form in particular, and always in the name of "experience" alone).[21] What is more, and of particular relevance to the present study, the breakthrough of the new, as it were, system of the arts

---

[18] Greenberg 1986–93 [1940], 1:24; emphasis in original.
[19] Greenberg 1986–93 [1940], 1:24–25.   [20] Greenberg 1986–93 [1940], 1:26.
[21] "There is a common effort in each of the arts to expand the expressive resources of the medium, not in order to express ideas and notions, but to express with greater immediacy sensations, *the irreducible elements of experience*" (Greenberg 1986–93 [1940], 1:30). With this last italicized phrase contrast Kristeller's mantra, "the irreducible nucleus of the arts." And with Greenberg's celebration of the expansion of the expressive resources of media and their sensuous surfaces, compare below on Lasus of Hermione and elsewhere.

in the late nineteenth century happened to coincide with a new, studied pursuit of "materialistic objectivity," "a new flatness" (Greenberg's aesthetic rallying cry in the 1940s and 1950s, and even later), a new, "almost complete absorption in the very physical quality of [the] medium," a new engagement with ever "more immediate and more powerful sensations," and, finally, "a new confusion of the arts," as each art form sought to borrow "the procedures and effects of some other art," whether this was music seeking coloristic effects in Impressionism, or painting returning the favor with its moods and rhythms, or poetry imitating painting and sculpture (for example, through imagism).[22] So much for Kristeller's theory about the indissoluble nucleus of the fine arts, early and late. On Greenberg's picture, there was no such nucleus in the eighteenth century, and none in the nineteenth either. But that is not the end of the story.

If we look elsewhere, a third historical picture looms into view, generally compatible with the second but not all that compatible with the first. On this view, the rise of modern aesthetic theory was due not to an obsession with formal purism, disinterestedness, disembedded contemplative perspectives, and (what amounts to the same thing) questions of autonomy, let alone to successful or failed classificatory schemes, but to the rise of empiricism and sensualism during the Enlightenment. That is how we are to understand Alexander Gottlieb Baumgarten's treatise on the science of sensate perception (*sensa*) and sensate representations (*representationes sensitivae*) from 1735 (*Meditationes philosophicae de nonnullis ad poema pertinentibus*) and his *Aesthetica* from 1750, to take just these two instances, which are usually cited together as the single founding moment of modern aesthetic theory, though opinions vary, and British empiricism has an equally rightful claim to the honor.[23] If this is right, and it is a fairly commonplace view today, then aesthetics was engaged from the first with a mapping of the senses, while it remains an open

---

[22] Greenberg 1986–93 [1940], 1:28–31. For a confirmation (and condemnation) of this same trend, see Baudelaire 1962, 104 (from an essay published posthumously in 1868, "L'Art philosophique").

[23] See Stolnitz 1961, 131: "The British did not invent and never use[d] the words 'aesthetic' or 'aesthetics,' but it is simply frivolous to allow this to decide who 'created' aesthetic theory. The British were the first to envision the possibility of a philosophical discipline, embracing the study of all of the arts, one which would be, moreover, autonomous, because its subject matter is not explicable by any of the other disciplines." Here, the obvious candidates are Locke, Richardson, Hogarth, Hume, Burke, Addison, Priestley, and others. There are, to be sure, further ways to date the onset of modern aesthetics. Auerbach 1967, 177 labels Vico "the actual founder of modern aesthetics." For a survey of different narratives to this same history and yet another proposal (the idea of the freedom of the imagination as the major historical catalyst), see Guyer 2005, ch. 1.

question whether the modern system of the arts (so-called) was the fruit of this activity or not.[24]

Whatever the case may be, if we take this last historical approach, then Kristeller's focus comes up short, for it presents the problem of Enlightenment aesthetics as one of a rational containment, when in fact what seems to have been at stake was, in Jacques Rancière's terms, a "distribution of the sensible."[25] Nor is the system of the fine arts much of an issue on the empiricist view. Baumgarten ignores it, and so do Hume, Burke, Lessing, and (for the most part) Kant.[26] On this alternative picture, modern aesthetics, true to its name, comes about with a sudden attention to empirical sensation. Sensation is eventually rationalized and the philosophical discipline is born, though over time the need for a renewal of the senses is felt and another surge in the direction of materialism occurs midway through the nineteenth century.[27] Hence the reassertion of materialism in art with the later avant-garde as described by Greenberg, and the "*new* confusion of the arts" which this refocusing of the sensible brings in its train, the arts being prone to sensual conflations by their very promiscuous nature. Much the same occurs at different moments in Greco-Roman antiquity too – a tendency that, in Kristeller's eyes, would disqualify antiquity from entertaining deeper thoughts about the nature of aesthetics. To be sure, pinning the rise of any complex assemblage of ideas on any simple set of factors is a hazardous enterprise. The new interest in empiricism cannot by itself account for the rise of the modern study of aesthetics. On the other hand, there is something attractive, even intuitively right, about reconfiguring the entire history of aesthetics and aesthetic theory according to shifts in attentions to the sensible (which may prove to have been less dramatic than I have

---

[24] For the general thesis about the concurrence of the rise of empiricism and materialism and the rise of aesthetics, see Stolnitz 1963; Eagleton 1990, ch. 2; Ferry 1990; Townsend 1991; Barnouw 1993; Korsmeyer 1999, ch. 2. Of course, this leaves aside the earlier contenders (see n. 17 above), some of which can be empiricist or sensualist in part if not in whole.

[25] Rancière 2006.

[26] Kant knows about the fine arts (*CJ* §§51–53). But he measures them according to their approximation to the free beauty of nature as received by the imagination; and they are invariably deficient.

[27] Cf. Eagleton 1990, 32–33: "The proto-materialist impulse of [early German aesthetics] soon surrenders to a full-blown formalism; indeed no sooner has sensation been ushered into the court of reason then [sic] it is subjected to a rigorous discrimination." But the pendulum eventually swings back the other way again, starting with the second half of the nineteenth century, as the accounts by Greenberg, T. J. Clark (e.g., Clark 2001), and others make abundantly clear – though the swings in either direction may in fact have been less radical than this summary suggests, and materialism may have been more of a constant presence in the arts.

depicted). And upon closer examination, it might turn out that the regard for sensuousness never completely vanished at any moment in the modern era. Thus, for example, Wilhelm von Humboldt's sensualist classicizing aesthetics has to be weighed against Kant's anti-sensualist, and anti-classicizing, formalism.[28] And in classics, Humboldt's views were at least as dominant, if not more so, than Kant's. Whatever the case may be, by worrying about walls and ladders (hierarchies and classificatory schemes) and not about experiential forms, not to mention broader historical considerations, Kristeller puts the emphasis in the wrong place.[29]

It is questionable whether the distinctions sought after by Kristeller were ever actually achieved even in the eighteenth century. Indeed, I doubt that the modern system of the arts, in the form that Kristeller wants us to imagine it, ever existed at all.[30] Part of the problem is that Kristeller is conflating the so-called modern system of the arts with claims to aesthetic autonomy. Again, while no one would doubt that the concept of the fine arts exists at this time, the claim about their belonging to a system and its relationship to aesthetic autonomy remains highly doubtful (despite Kristeller's assurances to the contrary).[31] And the conclusions about antiquity that Kristeller draws from this argument are intolerable. For once it is established that, unlike the moderns, the ancient Greeks and Romans lacked a concept of autonomy of art and aesthetics in some pure or abstract sense, any number of asymmetries can be shown to follow. This is not to deny the existence of historical differences, but only to suggest that if one wants to postulate a blank rupture with the antique past, it is not going to come in the form of the very idea of art or aesthetics. The Greeks had access to both. So just what is it that modernity after 1750 enjoyed that the world lacked prior to then? One answer, perhaps, is a *differently shaped* set (or better yet, competing and discordant

---

[28] See Humboldt 1960–81, II:13–14; 30–31; 49–57; 68–69; Porter 2000, 186–93; 268.

[29] Hence, grouping together the arts into an autonomous systematic unity, which (allegedly) encouraged theoretical reflection on art in the form of aesthetic philosophy proper, is for Kristeller a privilege that was unknown to, indeed unthinkable in, antiquity, which instead struggled at "attempts at a classification of the more important human arts and sciences" (Kristeller 1990, 172). That such a grouping and classification are a prerequisite to aesthetic thought is an unproven and unwarranted assumption. Similarly too concerned to locate the ancient essence of art according to its classifications, this time in Kristeller's wake, is Tatarkiewicz 1963. Contrast Stewart 1979, III: "That the Greeks had no word for 'art' or 'artist' has clearly little or no bearing on the problem at hand, for the appearance of the artist as an autonomous creator well after the codification of Greek aesthetic terminology for art was simply the result of an historical accident."

[30] See Porter 2009a.

[31] Kristeller 1990, 165.

sets) of aesthetic sensibilities and theories. But beyond this, I can see no
occult or other property that would account for modernity's magical
difference with the past in the areas of art and aesthetics.

Historical arguments aside, a clean break between aesthetic qualities
and the rest (intellectual, moral, religious, and practical function or
content) is difficult to maintain in any context, a point that has been
repeatedly made from Dewey to Eagleton to any number of contemporary philosophers of art. Indeed, the very assertion of this kind of break is
itself typically the sign of some sort of ideological or other non-aesthetic
pressure that is being brought to bear.[32] Hutcheson, Hume, and Kant –
three figures named by Kristeller in connection with the purported
separation of beauty from morals – in fact establish the opposite of
Kristeller's point: all three sought a common grounding of aesthetics
and morals in the more basic domain of human sensibility (the *sensus
communis*). The mere admission of causality as a source of beauty or
aesthetic value, which can be found in both Hutcheson (*An Inquiry into
the Original of our Ideas of Beauty and Virtue*)[33] and Aristotle (*Poetics,
passim*), though not quite in Kant, already reveals how (apparently)
morally neutral and autonomous aesthetic values can disguise moral and
other values (here, rationality, as a prerequisite of a moral subject).[34]
Normative stipulations about aesthetic pleasure are not innocent: they
also make normative stipulations about the nature of the human mind.[35]
And for the same reasons, they are a far cry from supporting claims about
aesthetic autonomy understood in an unrestricted sense (affirmations of
beauty, say, when it has been surgically removed from its contexts), which
are probably incoherent in any event, though aesthetic autonomy – in
effect, pure self-reference – is what Kristeller would have the modern
closed circuit of the arts achieve. The idea that the *discipline* of aesthetics
might enjoy autonomy is defensible if it is taken to mean that it sets its

[32] Adorno 1970; Bürger 1984; Eagleton 1990; Guillory 1993; Eagleton 2003. See further at n. 37 below.
[33] Hutcheson 2004 [1725; 2nd edn. 1726], 58, Treatise I, Sec. v, §XIX.
[34] On Kant, see Porter 2009b, 176–77; and Guyer 2005. The same holds for Shaftesbury, who has a
fair claim to having founded modern aesthetics in the first decade of the eighteenth century (so
Stolnitz 1961 and others after him). But if so, then he did so on the premise that morals and
aesthetics are nearly "indistinguishable" (Stolnitz 1961, 133).
[35] Cf. Hutcheson 2004 [1725; 2nd edn. 1726], 80–81 (Treatise I, Sec. VIII, §II.5): beauty's utility and its
moral value lie in its capacity to help focus the mind. What stands revealed to the mind in this state
is the world's rational and "Benevolent Design," which "gives [the beholder] the Pleasures of
Beauty" (Hutcheson 2004 [1725; 2nd edn. 1726], 57; Treatise I, Sec. v, §XVIII). For further
complicating arguments, see Paulson 1996, ch.1 ("Aesthetics and Deism").

own criteria in its own domain. But this is quite different from a vaguer notion of aesthetic autonomy as applied to objects and experiences.[36]

Complete autonomy cannot be even imagined, for what would it mean? Even the negation of relation to a given sphere (culture, religion, morals) involves a necessary entanglement in what is being refused. While it may not in fact be the distinctive feature of eighteenth-century theories of art or experience that it is all too widely imagined to be, aesthetic autonomy is a chimera that has held a powerful sway over the modern imagination nonetheless, and it reappears whenever anyone pursues, say, the separation of art from life, of form from content, or of sensuousness from other kinds of value.[37] In fact, Kristeller's own view about the unquestioned separation of the fine arts and of aesthetic value from all other spheres since the eighteenth century may owe as much to a movement he repudiates as it does to Kant, whose formalism inspired that movement: aestheticism. Kristeller's problem is that he cannot point to a moment when the modern system of the arts and its corresponding stabilization of the aesthetic ever quite take hold. Not even Kant provides a good purchase for Kristeller's purposes. His third *Critique, The Critique of Judgment*, is least of all a "theory of beauty *and the arts*":[38] Kant famously scants the arts in his treatise, which constitutes a theory of nature, and ultimately a theory of mind. And as soon as the aesthetic (never) does take hold on Kristeller's story, it crumbles away again. Thus, once we enter into the nineteenth century,

the traditional system of the fine arts begins to show signs of disintegration. Since the latter part of the nineteenth century, painting has moved further away from literature than at any previous time, whereas music has at times moved closer to it, and the crafts have taken great strides to recover their earlier standing as decorative arts. . . . The excesses of aestheticism have led to a healthy reaction which is yet far from universal. The tendency among some contemporary philosophers to consider Art and the aesthetic realm as a pervasive aspect of human experience rather than as the specific domain of the conventional fine arts also goes a long way to weaken the latter notion in its traditional form.[39]

Whether or not any of these claims about the relations among the arts is true (and it seems to me that they are all questionable), one has to wonder whether the epithets *traditional* and *conventional* have really been

---

[36] A mistake not made by Stolnitz 1961.
[37] For examples of the repudiation of aesthetic autonomy among contemporary aestheticians, see Walton 1993; Scarry 1999; Bohrer 2000; Stewart 2005, 15–27; Saito 2007. See also Wind 1983 [1932]; and n. 32 above.
[38] Kristeller 1990, 223; emphasis added.   [39] Kristeller 1990, 226.

earned. Much depends upon the historical yardstick by which one chooses
to measure things.

In the last sentence from the long quotation above, Kristeller footnotes
the source of the idea he is paraphrasing here: John Dewey's landmark
book *Art as Experience* (1934), which is in some ways a direct heir to Kant,
and in others an exponent of a vitalist tradition that has immediate roots
in nineteenth-century German philosophy.[40] Dewey's book articulates
what will in fact be one of the central theses of the present study, namely
that aesthetics denominates an element of human experience that is ill
captured by individual art forms, and, indeed, by the domain of art
generally. As Dewey says, "If art is an intrinsic quality of activity, we
cannot divide and subdivide it."[41] Moreover, art as an experience is, for
Dewey, indivisible from all other forms of activity and experience.

Dewey makes it quite clear that art and experience lie on a continuum
that is organic – he suggestively calls this continuum "the stream of
living" – and that renders distinctions between common experience and
aesthetic experience fruitless.[42] The very idea of "the fine arts" is, consequently, anathema to Dewey's theory of art. Indeed, his book is a sustained
attack on the notion, from its first pages to the last. There are no "fine" arts
that can be cut off as an autonomous domain from the utilitarian arts,
let alone from daily life.[43] The view that they can is the product of a
capitalist culture in the service of nationalism and militarism (his terms)
and of a museum culture in the service of all three.[44] "The factors that have
glorified fine art by setting it upon a far-off pedestal did not arise within
the realm of art nor is their influence confined to the arts."[45] The criticism

---

[40] E.g., Dewey 1989 [1934], 226: "The separation of architecture (music, too, for that matter) from
such arts as painting and sculpture makes a mess of the historical developments of the arts." Cf.
ibid., 235: "something architectural is found in every work of art...". Dewey might contest his
inheritance of the Kantian legacy: he certainly is no fan of Kant's cordoning off of "the esthetic
from other modes of experience" (ibid., 257). But that is all a matter of how one reads Kant on
experience, as I hope to show. Dewey's vitalism is incontestable, and at times he sounds
Nietzschean, but that is another story.

[41] Dewey 1989 [1934], 218. Cf. ibid., 181: "the common element in all the arts ... is organization of
energy as means for producing a result" – a rather Nietzschean point. See previous note. Similarly,
Clark 2001, 100–01 (in very Deweyan language): "the aesthetic is part of the stuff of life ... [,] and
the world ... is unthinkable save as a texture and structure of phenomena, of sensate 'experiences.'"

[42] Ibid., 12.

[43] Cf. ibid., 33: "It is customary, and from some points of view necessary, to make a distinction
between fine art and useful or technological art. But the point of view from which it is necessary is
one that is extrinsic to the work of art itself. The *customary distinction* is based simply on acceptance
of certain existing social conditions" (emphasis added). On Diderot's prescient critique of this
distinction, and Richard Sennett's recent rehearsal of the same critique, see Porter 2009b, 175, n. 14.

[44] Dewey 1989 [1934], 14.   [45] Ibid., 12.

is a good one, and for two reasons: it recontextualizes the very premise of the fine arts, which Dewey's theory insists must be seen as radically embedded (his term again) in the processes of society, life, and history;[46] and it democratizes art as an experience that is available to anyone and virtually everywhere. Thus, Dewey insists – echoing, to a surprising degree, some of his eighteenth-century empirical and commonsense philosophical predecessors – that art can be found in the work of the intelligent mechanic, in the "casting and playing" of an angler seeking fish, in the experience of a thought, in all "qualities of sense, those of touch and taste as well as of sight and hearing," in actions considered as completing processes and experiences, in "any impulsion toward organization of material," and in the very "practice of living." Indeed, "any practical activity will, provided it is integrated and moves by its own urge to fulfillment, have esthetic quality."[47] Dewey is even prepared to entertain the key point that Kristeller will later deny, namely that the Greeks were capable of "fram[ing] a generalized conception of art."[48] Small wonder that Kristeller should have been puzzled by Dewey's theory and all that it represents. Dewey's book is a refutation *avant la lettre* of Kristeller's entire thesis, which it completely anticipates and even renders obsolete by two decades.

Glossing Dewey and his contemporaries (whoever these may have been), Kristeller comments:

All these ideas [about the uncertain boundaries between art and non-art, and between art and experience] are still fluid and ill defined, and it is difficult to see how far they will go in modifying or undermining the traditional status of the fine arts and of aesthetics.[49]

Traditional or modern – or illusory? Kristeller appears to have come full circle, and to have returned us to a premodern lack of definition – in Greenberg's terms, "confusion." Dewey's theory of aesthetics points to changes that Kristeller's vision cannot even anticipate: "these contemporary changes," Kristeller continues, "may help to free us from certain conventional preconceptions and to clarify our ideas on the present status

---

[46] Ibid., 16.
[47] Ibid., 11, 16, 33, 45, 46, 84, 87, 126. Thomas Reid (1710–96) found beauty to be "common to the thought of a mind, ... the form of a piece of matter, to an abstract theorem, and a stroke of wit," insofar as pleasure is tied, universally, to the contemplation of excellence of all kinds. Hence, "there are beauties of speech and beauties of thought; beauties in the arts, and in the sciences," etc. (Reid 1846, 498). Elsewhere he adds "moral and intellectual qualities" to the list (ibid., 453). For comparable insights into the aspectual reach of the meaning of "beauty" according to the context (*l'emploi*), see Diderot in the *Encyclopédie* (1751), s.v. *Beau* (2:176).
[48] Dewey 1989 [1934], 31.   [49] Kristeller 1990, 227.

and future prospects of the arts and of aesthetics," as well as a better understanding of their "historical origins." But Dewey is not predicting changes in art or its prospects; he is offering a changed view of what art *is*, one that applies as much to the past as it does to the present, which is to say, one that ought to change our descriptive historical accounts of the past (which, in Dewey's hands, it does, as we just saw – at least concerning the ancient Greek past).[50]

The problem is that art *may have no determinable boundaries* today – no specificity and no essence – and it may never have had any in antiquity, or in the Renaissance, or in early modernity either. What may have changed since antiquity are not the boundaries that delimit art, but the spheres of activity that fail to do so cleanly. The question is of capital importance. It affects how we can claim to know and understand a culture from the remote past. Consider the following word of caution from the introduction to a recent collection of essays entitled – on its own terms, dangerously – *Art [sic] and Text in Ancient Greek Culture*.[51]

As Richard Gordon has argued at length, the later [viz., modern] associations of the word "art" and "artist" are inappropriate for the pots and potters who provide most of the source material for Greek imagery. The general term "art" also tends to obscure the very different frames in which the images of Greek culture occur. It may be of major importance – even for "identification" – whether an image is found on a temple – public, state-funded, religious display – or on a cup designed for the male world of private drinking parties; or on a perfume flask for male or female use. How images are framed affects recognition. There is a danger in using the general word "art" in that significant nuances of contextualization may be effaced.

The point is Kristellerian again, as a glance back at my first set of quotations from Kristeller's essay above (pp. 27–28) will show: both positions hold that a separation of the arts in antiquity is impossible to conceive on our current understanding of art, so much so that the term *art*

---

[50] A further irony of this revision of art's definition is that Shiner, looking ahead but in Kristeller's wake, predicts the overthrow of the modern system of the arts in favor of a new system of the *sensuous* arts in the conclusion to his study (Shiner 2001, 303–07). Three points: (a) this was the thrust of Dewey's own argument; he insists upon art as a sensuous phenomenon; (b) the sensuousness of art is nothing new in art, but part of its constituent definition, not only during, say, the nineteenth century, as a painter like Eugène Delacroix (1798–1863) illustrates in words and in paint throughout his career (see Hannoosh 1995), but even in the way the modern definition of aesthetics came to be determined starting in the eighteenth century, as we've seen; (c) the turn to modern sensualism is a *return* to the origins of ancient Greek sensualism, as I hope the present study will make amply clear.

[51] Goldhill and Osborne 1994, 7.

risks misleading us into a false identification of the nature of ancient aesthetic production altogether.[52] Is it really the case that the ancients had no conception of art comparable to ours? Can we ever hope to approach their art on its own terms? Or worse still, in order to gain access to ancient culture, must we abandon all hope of approaching it through what we used to call its art?

Putting the problem in this way may lead to unwarranted desperation, and probably (as I suggested) to an overinflated estimation of the autonomy of art and aesthetics today. More interesting than the problem of how we might discover the proper autonomy of the arts is the problem of how we can discover the arts' properly embedded contexts and interrelations in any age.[53] Reflecting on the nature of aesthetics can, I believe, show us a way forward, even as it will lead us to other, more challenging problems.

While it is true that art is always embedded in cultural and social practices, it is also true that practices do not obtain except insofar as they are experienced. And *qua* experienced, they carry aesthetic features that are susceptible of analysis, in ways that are at least as meaningful as the analysis of art cut off from these features. Indeed, the pleasure one takes in these experiences *qua* experiences constitutes a first and indispensable level of analysis. Such a pleasure, being reflective of aesthetic value, is an aesthetic experience.[54] It is for this reason that aesthetic questions

[52] The view, which I believe seriously misrepresents Richard Gordon's, whom the authors cite for support of their own (see Gordon 1979, esp. 23–24), is practically a cliché and widely held (e.g., even by Eagleton 2003, 75), so much so that one might be tempted to assent to it out of a kind of intellectual *akrasia* – which would of course be an error. If to speak of ancient *art* is anachronistic, then what are we to make of Kristeller's assertion that the ancients were "confronted with excellent works of art and quite susceptible to their charm" (Kristeller 1990, 174)? The term *art* here must be both an abbreviation for "fine art" (as on the same page and ibid., 168, where the phrase is rightly put in scare quotes) and (therefore) an anachronism: for, whose criteria are being used here to assign the label of "art," let alone "aesthetic quality" or "excellent"? Surely, these are modern, retrospective judgments, and illicit ones at that, as they all rest on a presumption about (purely) aesthetic judgment that is being denied to the ancients themselves – and indeed, to anyone before the mid-eighteenth century. Such thinking in terms of ruptures is pernicious, and is hardly restricted to aesthetics. Witness the wide scatter of claims about modern inventions – of sexuality, literature, the self, the body, the will, justice, race, class, etc. All such claims are "Kristellerian" in spirit.

[53] Panofsky's bracing study of French Gothic architecture and scholasticism (Panofsky 1957) is a good example of this latter approach.

[54] See Walton 1993, e.g., 505: "Let's define *aesthetic pleasure* as pleasure which has, as a component, pleasure taken in one's admiration or positive evaluation of something; *to be pleased aesthetically is to note something's value with pleasure.* This makes aesthetic pleasure an intensional state.... One takes pleasure *in* something: the pleasure attaches in part to one's awareness of something," not only in, say, "[a hot] shower or [a] walk [around the block]" or Beethoven's C# Minor Quartet, "but also in one's experience of admiring it, in one's judging it to be good," where goodness means

are, I believe, our best bet for gaining access to the problems of art in antiquity – not because art is the ultimate resting point for such an inquiry, but because it represents a relay to something else: it is a window onto modes of sensory experience, onto modes of attention generally, onto perceptual habits and cognitive styles, and, therefore, onto the social relations that are embedded in things. For as Michael Baxandall and others have so well shown, the arts are "deposits of social relationships," as are, indeed, the worlds inhabited by the senses.[55] To view art in this way is to view it as an aesthetic phenomenon of the richest kind imaginable. By attending to aesthetic questions in antiquity, to the way in which the world was perceived, sensed, and grasped – not in some unmediated way, but always through the conditioning filters of a given culture and its historical features – we can reach into the very foundations of meaning and value in antiquity. Aesthetics, narrowly conceived, opens onto aesthetics more broadly conceived. Indeed, it is doubtful that access to the one (art and aesthetic experience) can be gained in the absence of the other (sensation and perception).

In addressing itself to the field of aesthetics rather than to this or that medium, or to literary or art criticism proper, my study will be seeking to transcend the barriers between the various art forms and their contemplation or analysis and to arrive at what they share in common. The very presence of the term *aesthetic* in the title of my book is an appeal to this commonality. The inclusion of the term also has a certain polemical intent: it is meant as a call to revisionism.

2 AESTHETIC QUESTIONS

Prior studies of art and literary criticism typically ignore the wider implications of aesthetics, let alone those of aesthetic materialism. Nevertheless, the field is ripe for change. Materiality, sensation, and experience in the contexts of art must first of all be understood not as categories of nature but as categories of aesthetic thought and perception that have a history to them and that, once identified (inevitably, to some extent by our own lights), can be shown to have an application even when they are

---

no more than being marvelous, suitable (to its task), or valuable (second emphasis added). At a more basic level, the pleasurable responsiveness of the senses to their objects of sensation will also qualify as aesthetic by the same criteria, as Aristotle knew full well (see below).

[55] Baxandall 1980, ch. 6; Baxandall 1988. See now also Turner 2006 on the collaboration of a wide array of non-aesthetic and aesthetic languages in another predisciplinary world, Elizabethan England.

not explicitly named as such.[56] To view the past through such categories as these is not merely to document a history that simply needs to be revealed. It is to begin to undertake a speculative reconstruction of tastes, habits, and perceptions, in collaboration with the ancient theories or understandings, and to some degree independently of them. It is, in the last analysis, to participate in the ancient reflections on aesthetics, and not merely to recover them.

Current accounts of the ancient traditions of the arts and especially of reflection on the arts suffer from three principal weaknesses, which are undoubtedly the result of disciplinary histories more than anything else, and which I hope the present study, playing the part of a cheerful trespasser, will begin to remedy. First and most obviously, there simply are no comprehensive views of ancient aesthetics available. Instead, with rare exceptions, aesthetic phenomena and ancient speculation on aesthetic problems are parceled out according to modern disciplines, with minimal conversation across their boundaries.[57] Whether as a result or cause,

---

[56] For the same reason, it is no contradiction to affirm that the categories just named are necessary (inevitable) constituents of aesthetic experience, or at least the bulk of it: the necessity lies not on the side of nature but on the side of the aesthetic process. But arguing the point here would take us too far afield.

[57] Two current exceptions to this last caveat are the work by Andrew Stewart and Jaś Elsner, which travel freely between art and text and often broach issues of central importance to aesthetics, for the most part while working out the pragmatics of art or viewing. Hellenistic literary analysis has recently seen a small boom in aesthetic inquiry, in large part out of its sensitivity to the eclectic learning and allusiveness of Hellenistic authors. See also the remarkable observations about the various Greek and Roman arts, rigorously viewed under – practically subordinated to – their "sensory" and experiential (i.e., aesthetic) aspects, in Scranton 1964, who poses astonishing parallels throughout, many of which effectively ruin the neat distinctions among the arts, and who poses correspondingly hard but fundamentally useful questions, as on p. 9: "[In music,] the sound corresponds to the light of a painting; the question is whether there is in music anything that corresponds to the pigment in painting" – thus surpassing Plato's own inquiry (*Rep.* 6.507c–e): "Do hearing and sound need another kind of thing in order for the former to hear and the latter to be heard, a third thing in whose absence the one won't hear or the other be heard? ... You don't realize that sight and the visible have such a need? ... I mean what you call light" (trans. Grube; rev. Reeve). Similarly, sculpture Scranton defines as "an art of the sense of touch" (ibid., 18), a point that could be expanded, if one so wished, by connecting it to Greek optical theories, for which vision was an extension of the faculty of touch, or also to a theory of art like that of Alois Riegl's (see below), who considered the "haptic" dimension to be central to the early stages of Greek art. (Incidentally, the contrast with Hegel's disembodied view of classical sculpture, to be discussed at n. 120 below, could not be any greater.) See further, Webster 1939; Grassi 1962; Webster 1964; Fowler 1989; Goldhill and Osborne 1994; Zeitlin 1996; Steiner 1998, esp. 124–37; Benediktson 2000; Steiner 2001; Leszl 2004 and Leszl 2006; Tanner 2006, esp. on the (for him, multi-sensory) archaic period; Thomas 2007. See also the short but excellent encyclopedia article on "Beauty" in antiquity by Most 1992 (with further references to secondary literature), followed up now by Büttner 2006. Tatarkiewicz 1970 juxtaposes primary texts from a variety of ancient sources with informed commentary and concludes with an interesting discussion of Plotinus. Older works, such as Walter 1893, Bosanquet 1956 (1st edn. 1892; 2nd edn. 1904), and Gilbert and Kuhn 1953, are not

fundamental problems of aesthetics, concerning the language of aesthetic description and the basic component questions of aesthetic apprehension (What is art? What is aesthetic perception? What is criticism?), too often go unasked, never mind answered. But such questions were asked in antiquity, and they drove much of the literature that survives in the areas of grammar, rhetoric, criticism, history of art, and so on, even where all we have are documents of practical or applied rhetorical criticism. They were implicit in ancient practices and in the habits of consumption at an intuitional level, in what might today be termed ancient "folk theories."[58] And they were often spelled out or (more often) implied in ancient discourses on art in a wide range of arenas. As was mentioned in the Introduction above, recovering these buried assumptions is possible, and an urgent task.

Secondly there are considerable gaps in existing accounts. The Hellenistic period has yet to be integrated into an overall picture of the evolution of literary and aesthetic thinking from the fifth-century sophists (or earlier) to Longinus. And later developments not obviously connected to aesthetics but obviously connected to cultural shifts – for instance, the history of Atticism and linguistic purism (*hellēnismos*) – are poorly accounted for. More broadly, non-canonical sources in all periods are marginally represented, and as a consequence what appear to be minor points of interest in relation to the monuments of criticism (Plato and Aristotle) tend to be written out of existing narratives. Yet these neglected sources invariably played their part in a rich history, to which the more familiar names are either responding or tributary. Worse still, our modern views of ancient aesthetics are still very much shaped by the views of Plato and Aristotle, which became canonical already in antiquity,[59] and which we might call idealist or formalist in tendency, inasmuch as they valorized either ideal Forms or abstract formal properties and relations, for instance,

---

without interest, but they are dated, and their discussions of antiquity are inevitably sweeping, given their character as surveys. Carpenter 1959 (1st edn. 1921), promising in its title (*The Esthetic Basis of Greek Art of the Fifth and Fourth Centuries B.C.*), will be dealt with separately below, as will further works. At some point, the modern lines of inquiry can be traced back through Hegel to Winckelmann and then to the Renaissance art historians. Consequently, one way to attack the problem is through the construction of classicism (see Kuhn 1931; Jaeger 1931, more a symptom than an analysis; Porter 2006c). More recently, Martindale 2004 is eager to reclaim aesthetics as a valid field for inquiry into classical antiquity, albeit restricting himself to literature and only with a view to Kantian beauty.

[58] See Walton 2007, 153–56.

[59] Though not to the point of automatically casting competing trends into a non-canonical corner: that is a modern distortion of an originally much more colorful and variegated field, as a quick glance at Athenaeus or any other ancient anthologizer will serve to remind us.

design and arrangement. As a result, our views are severely distorted by theirs.[60]

Rhys Carpenter's influential study, *The Esthetic Basis of Greek Art of the Fifth and Fourth Centuries B.C.* (1921), is still entirely characteristic – for instance, in its presumption that fifth-century " 'idealism,' the 'classic restraint,' the 'omission of non-essentials,',... are all traceable to the attempt to put into material guise an almost metaphysical abstraction, a type-form which should satisfy the reason in its quest of perfection and ... the supersensual"; in other words, in its exhibition of Platonic Forms. Matter, plainly, is but a transparent and passing guise for ideal forms. Carpenter feels that his claim is justified on the basis of his own thinned-out version of Winckelmann (who for all his Platonism was far more of a sensualist than Carpenter). Here is Carpenter:

> The Greek intellectuality (partly because of the extreme atmospheric lucidity under which the world of sense was presented to it?) was not 'cloudy-minded' and 'unearthly,' but markedly observant of the external world and analytic of its phenomena. [Hence] it will seem natural that such a race, highly intellectualized in the direction of observation and analysis, and immersed in a sense-world of highly accentuated outlines but rather diminished tactile and plastic values, should imagine its concepts as visual linear forms. Not the mass, not the material constitution, not the physical behavior, but *the seen appearance*, was for them the essential. To know what a thing is, they must know the *look* of it. The material might be comparatively irrelevant, since objects can be of different substance, and yet have the same look; and matter changes so illusively (as when food turns into flesh and blood), while the form is abiding and amenable to the understanding.[61]

The injustice of these remarks when they are measured against the very art that is used to support them ought to be manifest. Little has changed: art history and much literary criticism too remain trapped by Plato or Platonism. It is time for a correction.[62]

---

[60] See Pl. *Rep.* 6.487e–488a for the foundational notion of the ideal (*paradeigma*), viz., "the idea of an image constructed from many exemplars, which becomes such a topos in later art-criticism" (Halliwell 2000, 107, n. 21). As Halliwell notes, this idea was in circulation prior to Plato and it had a lasting afterlife in antiquity (see at Ch. 5, n. 82 below), while Plato's own view of it gave it an immaterial character that also had its own afterlife (see Panofsky 1924).

[61] Carpenter 1959, 95; 108; emphasis in original. Plato is mentioned in the next sentences, and the visual character of Platonic Forms is argued for on p. 107.

[62] For an updated version of the same theory, see Pollitt 1999, e.g., p. 6: "Greek artists tended to look for the typical and essential forms which expressed the essential nature or classes of phenomena in the same way that Platonic 'forms' or 'ideas' expressed essential realities underlying the multiplicity of sense perception. A geometric statuette of a horse is an attempt to get at the 'horseness' which lies behind particular horses. ... Consistency and limit are characteristics of order; diversity is more

Finally, literary criticism and theory and developments in aesthetic theory or description in non-literary media (painting, sculpture, architecture, music, and rhythmical theory) tend to be treated in isolation from one another. This is *prima facie* odd, given how these categories tended to be thought together in antiquity. To take just one example, Aristotle's theory of color, especially in *On Sensation,* is conceived in terms of ratios of mixed or superimposed pigments. But this conception appears to be grafted onto a pre-existing theory of musical harmonies in mathematical ratios (proportions). The application of one theory to another may be original with Aristotle, but it may have had precedents, possibly among the Pythagoreans or their followers. While the heritage of the conceit is impossible to demonstrate, the mere fact of this confluence of ideas is what matters, and it remains underexplored.[63] Furthermore, the language of visual color is rich in musical terminology (*tonos, harmogē*), and occasionally the reverse is true (*chroai,* "colorations" – think of "chromaticism"). The two sets of terminologies frequently appear in accounts of language itself, whether in rhetorical writings or in the writings of poets and literary critics whenever they are seeking to capture something like the musical or visual effects of words. Such combinations will frequently crop up in the discussion that follows.

I suspect that the cause of this last-named condition is not so much the increased specialization of the modern-day disciplines that have parceled out tracts of antiquity, as it is the fact that the idea of the aesthetic seems to have no weight and no presence in contemporary discussions of antiquity. This, again, seems to derive from a narrow and, one is tempted to say, philological reasoning. The term *aesthetics* and its accompanying discipline are, to be sure, eighteenth-century coinages. But even if aesthetic reflection – reflection on commonalities shared across various art forms, whether pertaining to judgment or to qualities or properties of objects (beauty, excellence, gracefulness, sublimity) – was not formalized until the age of Baumgarten and Kant, it does not follow that aesthetic reflection went unpracticed prior to then. We can be certain that reflection on art as an aesthetic phenomenon reached a high level in archaic and

often a characteristic of chaos"; ibid., p. 6, locating the same features of Greek art in its "purely formal qualities of design"; cf. Pollitt 1974, 26 on classical Greek beauty conceived as "an invariable conceptual reality [a kind of ideal entity] underlying the structure of all physical objects" and as "a unity behind all apparent diversity." Similarly, Laporte 1947; Sörbom 1966, 48–51; Schweitzer 1953, 15. Contrast Snell 1980, 206; also, Cassirer 1998 [1924], 140.

[63] See Sorabji 1972; Rouveret 2006, 21–22. Empedocles makes for an intriguing predecessor, but is far from a clear source; see Ierodiakonou 2005, 7–8, and Ch. 3, §5 below.

classical Greece just in virtue of the nature of choral and lyric performances, which involved a simultaneous display of forms (music, song,
dance), as is attested, for instance, by Pindar, whose language would be
plundered by later critics and theorists of the arts:

> The garlands placed like a yoke on the hair exact from me payment of this sacred
> debt: to blend together properly (συμμεῖξαι πϱεπόντως) the lyre with her
> intricate voice, and the shout of oboes, and the placing of words (ἐπέων
> τε θέσιν).[64]

> Lyre of gold!... to you the dancers listen, as they begin the celebration; and
> singers obey your signals, each time you fashion (τεύχῃς),
> on your quivering strings, the opening notes of the preludes.[65]

If Pindar's language would pass seamlessly into that of later treatise
writers, it is because he was their obvious forerunner. His contributions
to ancient musical theory will be discussed in Chapter 7 below. Being the
self-conscious artist that he was, and working in the complex medium that
he did, Pindar could not help but achieve a high level of aesthetic
sophistication. Did he have his own system of the arts? Put it this way:
under the purview of which discipline today ought the performance of a
Pindaric victory ode to fall? Poetics? Musicology? Choreology? The point
is that in its lived moment, "the entire experience" of Pindar's verses
engaged the eye and the ear together, just as the performance of his odes
will have engaged an entire range of performers and several genres of
craft in such a way as to "blend them together properly." But deprived as
we are of the totality of that experience and left with nothing beyond
the text of his poems, we naturally mistake the part for the whole and
focus on the isolated words of what was originally a larger and more
complex phenomenon.[66] The ancient literary-critical sources do not for
the most part make this same mistake, even if they had to operate under
many of the same constraints that limit our approach to the ancient
materials today. And as Aristotle says in another context, "if you are
speaking of [the words] *sound* and *color*, [the word] *seeing* (ἰδών) is not
common to them, but *perceiving* is" (τὸ δ' αἰσθόμενος κοινόν).[67] Or
consider Aristotle's theory of "common sensibles," which he develops in
his psychological works. These are the sense objects that can be perceived
commonly through the different sense faculties (e.g., movement, rest, number,

[64] Pind. *Ol.* 3.6–9; trans. Thomas 1992, 118.   [65] Pind. *Pyth.* 1.1–4; trans. ibid., 118.
[66] See Thomas 1992, 118 (quotation: "the entire experience"), and *passim.* An important precursor is
the conception of "song culture" elaborated in Herington 1985.
[67] Arist. *Rh.* 3.1407b.20–21; trans. Kennedy.

shape, size, and time). More to the point, they are qualities that are invariably co-perceived, for instance, color and size: if we perceive one, we perceive the other.[68] What this theory points to is the intrinsic complexity of all aesthetic perception, even if the nature and location of the faculty of "common perception" (κοινὴ αἴσθησις) in Aristotle is a matter of dispute today.[69] In other words, even if *aisthēsis* does not quite mean *experience* in Greek (*empeiria* does),[70] it is *the* word to describe the commonality of aesthetic experiences, and it does this in a way that no other Greek term can. Our term *aesthetics* perfectly captures this common realm in turn.

To take another example, one that has recently been adduced by Rosalind Thomas, inscribed writing has a visual impact that tends to be overlooked today, thanks once again to the isolation of texts in modern editions, which simplify or ignore the original layout of texts and thus eliminate from view "the aesthetic handling of writing." This latter was in fact artistically diverse, site-specific, and calculated (or so one can infer), at least in the case of archaic inscriptions, to be decorative and shapely, as much a drawing as the representation of a word, and, in the case of public inscriptions from the high classical period, designed to be at once "highly ornamental, impressive, and monumental."[71] The very difficulty of assigning a phenomenon like this, interestingly labeled by Thomas as the "irrational use of writing," to any one discipline, is further proof of its value to many. Why assume that only the epigraphist should care about the impact of lettering and not, say, the student of orality and literacy, or the student of visual cultures, or the student of aesthetic phenomena generally?[72] That all these should so care is well shown, *inter alia*, by the intricate reading by Anne Carson of Simonides' epigram to Harmodius and Aristogiton, which was inscribed on the monument erected in their honor by the Athenians either in 480 or in 477/6. There, lettering and sound reenact the syncope of the two heroes' murder with a power that

---

[68] Arist. *An.* 3.1.425b9; id., *Sens.* 1.437a9. See also Summers 1990, 78–109, 322–35; Thomas 2007, 207–10.

[69] Hamlyn 1959, 13–15; Gregoric 2007.

[70] On the other hand, much depends on where one turns. In Aristotle, for example, *aisthēsis* captures a range of activities, including "perception, objectively understood," viz., "the objective perception of qualities and other sensory features of the natural world," as well as subjective "awareness, feeling or reflexive consciousness," viz., "the 'raw feel' of perceptual experience" and "empirical consciousness" (Kahn 1992, 364–65).

[71] Thomas 1992, 78, 88; cf. Carson 1999, ch. 3; Steiner 2001, 257.

[72] See also McLuhan 1962, 61–67 on *caelatura*, viz., relief engraving, as engaging both the tactile and the visual senses – a very Rieglian insight. (Thanks to Fred Bohrer for this reference.) The aesthetic function of writing on vases is better studied. See, e.g., Osborne and Pappas 2007; Ch. 4, §8 ("Stoicheia and Perception") and Ch. 9, §2 (on stoichedon) below.

Carson suggestively calls "sculptural."[73] As it happens, the aesthetic impact of writing ought to be of deep interest to anyone who reads ancient literary critics, who are in turn prone in places to visualize writing on a page as precisely a kind of inscription on stone. But as the visualization of writing is of little obvious immediate interest to literary criticism narrowly conceived, its appearance in a treatise on style passes for a mere metaphor. Its potential relevance to visual aesthetics properly speaking is all the less likely to be brought out, even if the origin of the metaphor lies, as we just saw, in a visual practice.

Aesthetic questions are in different ways undisciplined questions, and that is their virtue. They obey few rules, and they tend to fall out of line whenever anyone wishes to muster them into closed ranks. It is on this tendency to refuse to be pinned down to a single place that a larger, more capacious view of aesthetic inquiry can best capitalize. But they are not utterly irrational, and they do follow patterns. Aesthetic questions arise whenever questions of how one experiences phenomena arise. Perception and sensation are their immediate ingredients; imagination, feeling, emotion, and the like are closely allied. Aesthetic pleasure is but a special kind of pleasure; its value probably cannot be grasped by an aesthetic subject unless she also has a sense of some larger economy of pleasures into which they fit and without which they will not register. Whether looking from without or standing within, to engage in aesthetic speculation one has to know in the first instance what qualifies as a pleasure generally, and then how pleasures are valued *en bloc* and ranked. The same holds for the various senses, their relative worth and dignity, and the ways in which they can or cannot be traded in for one another – and similarly the various media in which the arts find expression (whether plastic, verbal, musical, visual, performative, and so on).

Language has a cultural function that is captured by a certain (and often not so certain) set of experiences, as do, in their own ways, music, buildings, and writing on stone. Any account that tells us anything about these phenomena will be valuable simply for filling out the cultural milieux in which each of these objects has resonance – a potential for meaning or significance. Echoes across the various spheres of culture need to be listened to attentively. Aesthetics can be found anywhere that culture

---

[73] Fr. 1 *FGE* = *CEG* 430; Carson 1999, 90–93 (quotation at p. 93). As Meritt 1936, 356 notes, the first couplet contained sixty-six letters and was written entirely on one line of the inscription; the (audible) elegiac verse rhythms thus create a tension with the (legible) inscribed form, which adds a dimension to Carson's reading.

exists, which is to say, anywhere that culture is lived and felt. And culture provides the background in which these forms of experience can be brought to the level of language and can be named and expressed as such – with mute or inarticulate (felt) presence counting for just as much as any articulated naming of the experience. *The experience of culture is itself an articulation of culture*, perhaps not quite at the level of language or names, but assuredly at the level of attention, whenever phenomena are apprehended and dwelt upon. It is one of the valid ways in which cultural forms are objectified and shared.

3 AESTHETIC PERCEPTIONS

Beauty? It seems to me that beauty is an example of what the philosophers call reification, to regard an abstraction as a thing. Beauty is a series of experiences. It is not a noun. People have experiences. If they feel an intense aesthetic pleasure, they take that experience and project it into the object. They experience the idea of beauty, but beauty in and of itself does not exist. To put it another way, experiences are sorts of pleasures that involve verbs. The fallacy occurs in taking the experience "I like X" and referring to "X" as beauty. The process is similar to what T. S. Eliot said of Wordsworth, "Wordsworth found in stones the sermons he had planted there." In fact, beauty is only a mystified expression of our own emotion. (Louise Bourgeois[74])

Beauty, without relation to the feeling of the subject, is nothing by itself. (Kant[75])

In connecting cultural life, experience, and aesthetics, I am consciously giving the idea of aesthetics a broader reach than it has among many contemporary academic aestheticians, who are fussy about policing the boundaries between aesthetic experiences (sometimes typified by appreciations of nature) and experiences of works of art, or between aesthetic properties (beauty, ugliness) and non-aesthetic properties (neutral qualities such as size and shape). Without engaging with these views here, suffice it to say that academic aestheticians do not own the field; they are not the only voices to pronounce on what should or should not count as aesthetic inquiry. Thinkers as diverse as Theodor Adorno, Raymond Williams, and Elaine Scarry, not to mention a philosophical tradition that arguably runs from Spinoza to Nietzsche and into the past century, especially among the Russian Formalists and the Prague Linguistic Circle

---

[74] Bourgeois 1998, 331. Cf. Dewey 1989 [1934], 135: "[Beauty] is properly an emotional term.... Unfortunately it has been hardened into a peculiar object."
[75] *CJ* §9, p. 103; trans. adapted; Ak. 218.

in Europe and the Pragmatists and the first-generation New Critics in America, have done much to enrich the scope of aesthetic inquiry beyond a formalistic pursuit in a Kantian vein, at least as Kant is usually read (see below for a divergent reading). In this alternative tradition, aesthetics is no longer cut off from the most vital of everyday activities – living, breathing, taking in and responding to the world of sensations.[76]

Here I need only recall the words of the Prague linguist, Jan Mukařovský, from 1936: "The aesthetic function embraces a much wider area of activity than does art by itself.... There is no definite borderline between the aesthetic and the extra-aesthetic." Each of these two statements is true for Mukařovský, given his more basic view that "any object and any activity, whether natural or human, may become a carrier of the aesthetic object," in virtue of the fact that aesthetic value resides not in objects but in perceptions. In effect, Mukařovský's aesthetic function is no more than the mere possibility of possessing aesthetic value, however fleetingly this possession may last. This is a remarkable expansion of aesthetics. The aesthetic function, so conceived, is the function of a socially shared perception and experience; it is of immediate focus whenever it is had, and is always "only instinctively felt," being a "vital" experience that is at once completely absorbing and utterly "intimate" as well; and it touches, indeed "is saturated" by, "the entire area of human affairs."[77] The same thought can be found in other writers on aesthetics – for instance, those mentioned above (Adorno, Williams, Scarry, Walton, and Dewey above all), but also William James, Dave Hickey, Alexander Nehamas, and others.[78]

---

[76] Some specific examples include Prall 1929, whose aesthetics of the sensuous surface is largely forgotten today, and Berleant 1964, who echoes both Prall and Dewey, and, in anticipation of Sontag 1966, affirms the sensuous (and the erotic) over against the formal, logical, and moral strictures on art and aesthetics. An earlier effort to bring high art history down to the level of everyday perceptions and experience is the exemplary work of Riegl 1927 (which it would be wrong to identify with the history of the decorative arts). Riegl has, however, almost next to nothing to say about the nonvisual arts. And there are problems with his reconstruction of the (ideal) beholder, who turns out to be little more than a reflex of the stylistic expression of objects, but that is another matter.

[77] Mukařovský 1970 [1936], 1; 70; 82–83; 90; 96.

[78] See Prall 1929, 26–29; Dewey 1989 [1934]; Sibley 1959; Sibley 1965; Berleant 1964, 186: "every perception is potentially aesthetic"; Nehamas 2004, 30: "perhaps no experience is completely unaesthetic." Nehamas (ibid., 60) quotes from Hickey 1993 to the same effect; Walton, n. 54 above. Addison held a similar view (*Spectator* no. 413 in Addison 1856, 6:334: "almost everything about us [has] the power of raising an agreeable idea in the imagination"), as did Thomas Reid, the eighteenth-century Scottish common-sense philosopher (see Reid 1846, 453; 498; quoted at n. 47 above), and James (see next note).

Surprisingly, a little-noticed source of this modern tendency whereby aesthetics permeates the whole of life's experience is none other than Kant, who himself acknowledges a primordial link between aesthetics and the conditions of experience in general.[79] This, after all, is the justification he offers for his third *Critique* as a necessary complement to his prior two critiques of theoretical and practical reason. For, as he says in the Introduction to the third *Critique*, though judgment is part of the "family" of higher cognitive powers that mediates between reason and understanding, an even stronger reason for introducing a critique of judgment as "mediating the connection of the two parts of philosophy to [form] a whole" is the more primitive fact that "the soul's powers or capacities" can be redescribed as comprising, at a more basic and irreducible ground, "the *cognitive power* (*das* Erkenntnisvermögen), the *feeling of pleasure and displeasure* (*das* Gefühl der Lust und Unlust), and the *power of desire* (*das* Begehrungsvermögen)."[80] Each of the three higher faculties (reason, understanding, judgment) is, so to speak, in charge of these lower faculties, which collectively urge the mind to do its business; they are its prime movers. Thus, understanding governs the cognitive power, reason the power of desire (which is typically, Kant claims, a desire for freedom), and judgment the feeling of pleasure and displeasure. Their interlocking roles, both by threes and by twos (the triads, divided into higher and lower faculties), guarantee a coherence to the whole mental system. But more importantly, it is the presence of judgment, in particular aesthetic (reflective) judgment, and so too its connection with pleasure and displeasure, that effectuates a linkage all its own. But this does not emerge until several pages later.

In section six of the same Introduction, Kant makes it clear why pleasure plays so central a role. His reasoning is simultaneously shrewd and pragmatic. It is that nothing comes about, in mental life, without the accompaniment of pleasure. Indeed, there are no mental experiences at all

---

[79] *Pace* Dewey, who is unfairly hostile to Kant, unlike his contemporary fellow pragmatist William James, who saw himself as realizing certain potentials made finally possible by Kant (James 2003 [1912], 3). James, even more than Dewey, would allow that there is a fundamental singular basis to all experience. See James, ibid., 76, and compare his notion of "pure experience" (e.g., ibid., 2–3, virtually a monistic view, or better yet, a homoeomerous one: ibid., 56) with its essential "aesthetic factor" (ibid., 146); and cf. 107: "harmoniously" (a nice Kantian touch). Similarly, Carroll 2001, 36, critiquing Monroe K. Beardsley's isolation of "aesthetic experience" via its unique features (object directedness; felt freedom; sense of intelligibility and wholeness, etc.): these, on the contrary, "are simply garden-variety elements of any act of absorbed attention, whether to aesthetic objects, artworks, newspaper articles, philosophical treatises, and so on." But Carroll remains critical of both Kant and Dewey.

[80] *CJ*, p. 16; Ak. 177; emphasis as in original.

without pleasure – no desires, no cognitions, and ultimately no mental activity of any kind. The pragmatism of Kant's position is shrewd, but so too is the way in which he slips in the presumed naturalness of the assumption. You can desire something, but you cannot realize your desire unless you experience the pleasure of having done so, if only in anticipation. For (and here Kant never sounded more like Freud) "the attainment of every aim (*Absicht*) is combined with the feeling of pleasure." "And if," Kant goes on, "the condition of the former [sc., reaching the aim] is an *a priori* representation ... then the feeling of pleasure is also determined through a ground that is *a priori* and valid for everyone." So perhaps even to desire something gives pleasure, even if the incompleteness of the aim is at the same time a source of displeasure.

Further, pleasure is so basic to our interchange with the world that even "the most common experience (*die gemeinste Erfahrung*) would not be possible without it." Kant's view of the mind is a profoundly optimistic one. It presumes a few basic things: that the world appears to the mind in a harmonious condition, ordered, fitted together (coherent), and seamlessly fitted to, and so agreeing with, our mental faculties; and that in apprehending the world, so formed, our minds respond spontaneously (and, Kant suggests, for the most part unconsciously[81]) with a feeling of pleasure. This essential congruence of the mind and its objects could not obtain without the mediating services of the faculty of aesthetic judgment, which provides the framework within which the harmonies on both the subjective and objective sides of the equation are allowed to mesh. Indeed, another name for this congruence, viewed in and of itself, is "beauty."

In other words, Kant's position is that *our fundamental posture towards the world, and the world's posture towards us, is aesthetic.* That this is so guarantees that we, as it were, grope our way meaningfully through the world before we come to know and understand it, and that we can never fully grasp (know or understand) the grounds by which we do so. We feel, in the experiential sense, our way through the world, which is not to say that we have a mere sensation, or *Empfindung*, of the world. We do not experience bare sensation, because for Kant experience is directed at the form of appearances, not at appearances as such, while both are in fact problematical in his eyes and, as he would say, not a possible object of experience.[82] The distinction between appearances and the form in which

---

[81] Kant, *CJ*, p. 27; §VI, Ak. 187: "We no longer notice any decided pleasure ..." (*Zwar spüren wir ... keine merkliche Lust mehr ...*).

[82] *CPR* B34.

they are given is crucial, and it will be of use to us below, where we will find that *aisthēsis* in Greek can point to a similar ambiguity. In more up-to-date terms, and without being put off by the presence of the term *form*, we can say that our experiences are in a sense *pre-formed*: they are conditioned by the frameworks that allow us to have and to recognize experiences at all. In very contemporary parlance, one could say that our experiences are constructed, though this leaves hanging all kinds of crucial determinants – constructed by what, exactly? – and it suppresses one factor that Kant would wish to involve: the co-determinant of human nature.

At any rate, to be in this posture or state is to be what Kant calls a subject, or if we like, an aesthetic subject.[83] And as he later adds, in the section on Beauty, to be this is to be, quite simply, *alive*. For the pleasure we feel whenever we take in the world (whenever we have an experience) consists in a "feeling of life," a *Lebensgefühl*, which more broadly speaking is the capacity for pleasure and unpleasure.[84] Pleasure and aesthetics are deeply rooted, indeed seemingly hard-wired, in our very experience of things, at least for Kant. And the upshot of this deep strand in Kant's thought is that we do not have to worry about straying too far from the roots of the tradition of aesthetic speculation if we decide to treat the category of experience as prior to the categories of either art or nature and as common to both. As it happens, the roots of Kant's view are to be found in antiquity itself. Consider two instances.

In the *Eudemian Ethics*, Aristotle draws a distinction between higher and lower pleasures and pains, which we may characterize, following Kant, as aesthetic and sensual pleasures and pains. One the one side, there is the experience of the *sōphrōn*, or the temperate individual, and on the other that of his opposite, the intemperate individual, but also that of his kindred in spirit, the brutes of nature, animals. The distinction is crude, and it follows the fairly predictable line of the Golden Mean. And while it leads, equally predictably, to a privileging of sight and hearing over taste and touch, it also happens to lead to some unpredictable results.

---

[83] "That subjective aspect (*Dasjenige Subjektive*) in a representation *which cannot become an element of cognition at all* is the *pleasure* or *displeasure* connected with it [sc., that representation]" (*CJ*, Introd. VII, p. 75; Ak. 189; trans. adapted).

[84] *CJ* §1, p. 90; Ak. 204. Cf. Kant 1997, esp. 1068–95, for Kant's earlier (1781/82) but related views. There, Kant's view, which is somewhat Stoicizing, is that our capacity for pleasure, and our *Lebensgefühl*, are directly proportional to our capacity for and experience of pain.

On Aristotle's account, animals and intemperate individuals share an incapacity to appreciate the objects of the higher faculties of sight and hearing, and so remain insensible to harmony or beauty,

for they obviously have no feeling worth mentioning *at the mere sight* (αὐτῇ τῇ θεωρίᾳ) *of the beautiful or the* <*mere*> *hearing* (ἢ τῇ ἀκροάσει) *of the harmonious*, except, perhaps, in some marvellous instances. And with regard to pleasant and disagreeable odours it is the same, though all their senses are sharper than ours. They do, indeed, feel pleasure at certain odours; but these gladden them accidentally and not of their own nature (καθ' αὐτάς).... The odours enjoyed for their own nature are such as those of flowers (therefore Stratonicus neatly remarked that these smell beautifully, food, etc., pleasantly).[85]

If we look past the objectionable prejudices, what we find in Aristotle is in fact an interesting claim about pure aesthetic pleasure, and one comparable in ways to Kant's. It is a claim that wants to isolate the simple, unadorned act of aesthetic contemplation by itself, abstracted from all other impinging wants and desires – and, Kant would add (nor does Aristotle seem to disagree), absent any act of conceptualization. Thus, "*if one sees* a beautiful statue, or horse, or human being, *or hears* singing, without any accompanying wish for eating, drinking, or sexual indulgence, *but only with the wish to see the beautiful and to hear the singers*, he would not be thought profligate any more than those who were charmed by the Sirens."[86] The aesthetic contemplation of a beautiful object is a pure act in a twofold sense: the object is enjoyed for its own sake, in and of itself (*kath' hauton*), and, as Aristotle would say in his *Nicomachean Ethics*, the enjoyment is the purest (unimpeded) actualization of the faculty that is involved, whether this is the eye or the ear or the more abstract faculty of contemplation itself.[87] In fact, there, in the *Nicomachean Ethics*, Aristotle could not be more explicit about the aesthetic nature of perfected activity if he wanted to be:

Since every sense (αἰσθήσεως) is active in relation to its object (πρὸς τὸ αἰσθητόν), and a sense which is in good condition acts perfectly in relation to the most beautiful (τὸ κάλλιστον) of its objects (for perfect activity seems to be ideally of this nature; whether we say that *it* is active, or the organ in which it resides, may be assumed to be immaterial), it follows that in the case of each sense the best activity is that of the best-conditioned organ in relation to the finest of its objects. And this activity will be the most complete and pleasant.[88]

[85] *EE* 3.2.10.1231a2–12; trans. Solomon.   [86] Ibid., 1230b31–35; emphasis added.
[87] *EN* 10.4.1174b14–23; *Protr.* fr. B87 Düring.   [88] *EN* 10.4.1174b14–20; trans. Ross.

But lest we should be distracted by the admittedly puritanical strains of Aristotle's position, we should also note that Aristotle in the earlier passage is talking about a wish, or rather a desire, as well as a pleasure: there is an immediate pleasure in the seeing or hearing and an auxiliary pleasure of wishing and wanting to see and to hear, and presumably the further desire for the continuation of the activity and its prolongation. And, after all, pleasures have a seductiveness of their own, much like Sirens: they are absolutely compelling, and they absorb us into their activity, ideally without remainder, to the point that the pleasure and the activity become nearly indistinguishable.[89] Similarly, Kant finds it impossible to distinguish the consciousness of formal purposiveness from the pleasure taken in the contemplation of an object.[90] But because this consciousness seems to be just what the contemplation is, pleasure and the activity of contemplation must, as in Aristotle, be identical or nearly so. In point of fact, *aisthēsis* in Aristotle can bear both meanings.[91] Kant likewise notices our tendency to "linger (*weilen*) in our contemplation of the beautiful," whereby this lingering contemplation (*Verweilung*) "strengthens and reproduces itself."[92] The idea is a partial calque, though no doubt an unintentional one, on Aristotle.[93]

The temptation, in both cases, is to deduce from these accounts an attempt to isolate beauty in its pure form, which is to say, a conception of beauty as autonomous and self-contained. But that would be to misjudge the thrust of the two accounts. For both philosophers, aesthetic contemplation at its broadest is a pleasure that comes not from the aesthetic domain conceived as distinct from the rest of life, but from the bare fact of living understood in its essential definition, which includes as its primary ingredient the sheer fact of being (in Kant's language) an aesthetic subject. Thus, for Aristotle, "the pleasure that comes from living . . . is the pleasure we get from the exercise of the soul; for that is true life," which is to say,

---

[89] *EN* 10.5.1175b33.   [90] *CJ* §1; Ak. 204.

[91] E.g., Arist. *De an.* 3.2; *EN* 9.9.1170a29–b4. See Kahn 1966; Kosman 1975, esp. 508, 515–19; cf. 519: "It is by virtue of being sensitive that we are aware of our lives, and not vice versa."

[92] *CJ* §12, p. 107 (trans. adapted); Ak. 222; cf. *CJ* §35; Ak. 287 ("*belebend*," "*Beförderung*").

[93] "Philosophy," the culmination of true pleasure, "is thought to offer pleasures marvellous for their purity and their enduringness" (τῷ βεβαίῳ) (*EN* 10.7.1177a25–26; trans. Ross), though *bebaios* is perhaps better rendered with "firmness" or "certainty." There is a slight circularity here, seeing how the pleasures are firm and certain thanks to the power of contemplation, which in fact gives rise to the pleasures. Goethe would later pick up the Kantian theme in his famous line from *Faust* (ii, 5), "Verweile doch! du bist so schön!" ("Tarry a moment! You are so fair!"), where the sought-for moment of prolongation comprehends both the object of beauty and its contemplation by a subject, as would Hegel, in the ultimate, Romantic transformation of this formula: "tarrying with the negative" ("bei ihm [sc., dem Negativen] verweil[en]"; Hegel 1970, 36).

contemplation.[94] Aristotle's aesthetic creatures are not only "good" at living; they are also lovers of life. But they are the one insofar as they are the other: "For in loving life they love thinking and knowing; they value life for no other reason than for the sake of perception (διὰ τὴν αἴσθησιν), and above all for the sake of sight (διὰ τὴν ὄψιν); they evidently love this faculty in the highest degree because it is, in comparison with the other senses (αἰσθήσεις), simply a kind of knowledge."[95]

The second point of comparison with Kant comes from a more unexpected corner, though the Aristotelian points of view will have paved the way for the comparison, both for us and in antiquity. It comes from Epicurus' philosophy of experience or feeling, which contains within it, I believe, an implicit aesthetics or theory, or simply a recognition, of beauty. The example, briefly, works something like this.

One premise of the Epicurean philosophy of nature is that experience is either pleasurable or painful. Presumably, such experience will be similar to the experience of beauty or ugliness: pleasure and beauty draw us in, pain and the ugly repel. Skipping several steps, we arrive at the conclusion that the experience of beauty, *qua* the most pleasurable experience there is, will be an experience of intense perceptual awareness. It is clear, immediate, sensuous, uniquely suited to our perceptual apparatus (it is naturally affined to us: σύμφυτον or συγγενικόν); it has, in other words, all the attributes of a clear grasp of the sensible world (*enargeia*). In fact, it just is the sensation we have whenever we have a clear grasp of the sensible world. And that is available to us all of the time – not in the form of a painful sensation, but in the form of a pleasurable one, because as a hedonist Epicurus is willing to wager that on balance our experience of the world will lead to pleasure and not pain (however we end up deriving the sensation; for Epicurus, a correction of false beliefs is required to arrive at this "truth" about human reality).

If this is right, then we can conclude that for Epicurus our primary orientation towards the world is not only a pleasurable one, but also an aesthetic one. It is a perception of the world as a beautiful thing, in the same way that the gods, who represent the most perfect of beings, are simultaneously the most beautiful beings there are, just as living well, the moral ideal, is in an extended sense a dwelling in beauty (τὸ καλῶς ζῆν).[96] Another, clearer, and more powerful way of making the same case, which still reads like an analogy rather than an identification between

[94] Arist. *Protr.* B89–90 Düring.   [95] Ibid., B73.
[96] Cic. *Nat. D.* 1.47–48 (gods); Epicur. *Ep. Men.* 126 (τὸ καλῶς ζῆν).

beauty and pleasurable experience, would be to say that for Epicurus the experience of beauty and the purest form of experience (ataraxy) differ in no way at all because *they are indistinguishably the same experience*, which is to say, they give the same quality of pleasure and the same degree of clarity about the world that they bring to our minds, bodies, and souls (or their union). Nor should we forget for a second that in Epicureanism the vehicle of this conveyance is sensation, just as the world that all our experiences report on is the sensible world. As with Aristotle and Kant, so too with Epicurus: the experience of pleasure, which we can dub aesthetic in the root sense of the term (a nomenclature Epicurus will not have objected to, even if he might have chafed at our relabeling his philosophy of experience and sensation a philosophy of beauty), is arguably the pleasure we take in experience *tout court*. It is a basic pleasure that attaches to a basic experience of the world. It is, arguably, the pleasure of living.[97] In Augustine's later thinking, it would be the pleasure taken in being, and in all that is.[98] An atomist might concur, but would add a caveat: any pleasure taken in all that is will result from viewing reality as it exists "for us," that is, from a first-personal (phenomenological) perspective. This is so, because for an atomist the world is not the source of pleasure, meaning, or value when it is viewed from a third-personal perspective (that of physics).

4 AESTHETIC VOCABULARIES AND THE LANGUAGES OF ART

With Epicurus we have arrived at an admittedly extreme example of a larger rule. But the rule holds nonetheless. The point is simply that if the aesthetic vocabulary of antiquity seems deficient when measured against current standards, there is in fact a surfeit of descriptions of aesthetic phenomena from antiquity. We need only look for these in the right places, which may not always be the most obvious places. Here, then, is a first suggestion: that we consider the arts in antiquity to be *genres of experience* rather than self-standing, autonomous or semi-autonomous realms marked off by processes and products that obey conventional generic categories (usually, modern ones). A second suggestion is that we pay some heed to the philosophical background noise that is audible even in non-philosophical discourses from antiquity. Philosophers, after

---

[97] See Porter 2003 on this thesis about Epicurus, and also on the possible relationship between Epicurus and Aristotle's *Protrepticus*.

[98] August. *Ep.* 3.18: *omnis pulchritudinis forma unitas est.* Cf. Riegl 1927, 395.

all, debated the very terms that will be of interest to us in what follows – terms like *appearances, size, dimension, quality, quantity, clarity, obscurity, particularity* (encapsulated by indexicals like "*thisness*" and "*hereness*"), *judgment, distinctness,* and so on; and they also helped to develop a vocabulary for framing the very kinds of problems that contemporary artists and critics had to deal with, each in their own ways. The languages of ancient philosophers ought in principle to bear directly on any inquiry into aesthetic speculation in antiquity, especially given the relative (or alleged) poverty of the technical vocabularies for artistic description, and the correlative eagerness shown by the ancients to share and borrow terminologies and concepts as these evolved, a phenomenon not uncommon in other arenas – for instance, between medicine and philosophy.[99]

While we are on the subject, a brief word about the question of linguistic impoverishment or richness is needed. The technical language of aesthetic description from antiquity is notoriously in short supply. This dearth of attested vocabularies may be owing in part to an underlying paucity of surviving treatises on the individual arts, though it may also point to the circumscribed vocabulary of those materials, which might not grow appreciably even with new discoveries of primary sources. The very existence of shared vocabularies is often taken as further evidence of their collective impoverishment, though the fact that an aesthetic lexicon is shared could just as easily lead to the opposite inference about ancient capacities to reflect on art, as I will attempt to show. At any rate, this alleged poverty goes a long way towards explaining why moderns have so often been disappointed with the level of aesthetic sophistication and judgments from Greco-Roman antiquity, and why views like Kristeller's above are possible, effectively denying to the ancients any interest in aesthetics. D. A. Russell, despite being one of the most sensitive scholars of ancient literary criticism today, nevertheless cannot conceal his disappointment, nor is he alone, when he writes: "We find [the ancient critics] often inadequate and unsatisfactory, if we compare them with our own responses to the same texts." "Bewildered, disconcerted, perhaps disappointed," he is disturbed to see "little or no attempt to delimit the critic's field, to fence it off against his three neighbours: the scholar, the moralist and the teacher of rhetoric." Indeed, he suspects "that sensitive readers in antiquity, had they chosen to make their responses articulate, would have seemed wiser and more sophisticated than their

---

[99] For a parallel problem-*cum*-solution, that is of apparently impoverished aesthetic vocabularies discovered to be richer from surprising sources, see Baxandall 1988, 37, and *passim.*

teachers and theorists."[100] The lesson, alas, is that modern histories of literary criticism are in general the wrong place to look if one wants to find out how the ancients crossed boundaries and thought in general terms about art.

Such histories won't be of much help with a passage like chapter 4 of the *Poetics*, where Aristotle, defining the centrality of mimesis to the whole of human activity, discusses the pleasures of aesthetic viewing, harmony, and rhythm, all of which he says are natural to us, but none of which, he also says, is of any importance to his theory of literature, though they are to theories held by others. Unfortunately, Aristotle does not report these competing theories. Yet, the very fact that he mentions them is itself a significant clue to a much wider field of debate than is normally presumed. Nor will most modern histories be of much help with Plato's claim in the *Phaedo* that *harmonia* belongs to *all* the crafts: "harmonies [are] found in music and all the works of artists" – in Greek, the *dēmiourgoi*, which can include painters, sculptors, architects, but also shipbuilders and other kinds of makers.[101] Or his glossing, in the *Republic*, of poets as "sound-artists" or, if one prefers, "auditory imitators" ([οἱ μιμούμενοι] κατὰ τὴν ἀκοήν).[102] Or his casual hendiadys for aficionados of art and beauty: "lovers of sights and sounds" (φιλήκοοι καὶ φιλοθεάμονες), who "like beautiful sounds (φωνάς), colors (χρόας), shapes (σχήματα), and everything fashioned out of them," even though "their thought is unable to see and embrace the nature of the beautiful itself."[103] Modern histories of literary criticism will be of little use, first because they tend to be focused on some narrow sense of *literary*, and secondly because they tend to ignore the strands that get pushed aside by Plato and Aristotle. Thus, too, they will generally be of little use beyond reminding us, briefly, of the all-important fact that *mousikē* in Greek "covers music and poetry together, because in the ancient world you

[100] Russell 1981, 1; 7.
[101] Pl. *Phd.* 86c; trans. Grube. Cf. *Gorg.* 503e. Cf. Plin. *HN* 35.29 on blending and transition of colors as *harmogē* (a closely, and etymologically, related concept). Further, Schuhl 1952, 13–14, n. 5. Similarly, the rhythm of the dancing body is "a feature shared with the movement of the voice" (Pl. *Leg.* 2.672e). What is aesthetically of interest here is not only the shared feature of rhythm, but also the very description of the voice as a *movement* (κίνησις). Aristoxenus' *Elements of Harmony* is based on this exact premise: it is a treatise on "the movement of the voice" (*Harm.* 3.5–6 da Rios; numeration after Meibom). The premise is derived ultimately from physics and from Pythagoreanism. Cf. Democr. DK 68A135(59); Hippasus, *ap.* Theo Sm. 59.4–21 (= DK 18A13); [Arist.] *De audib.* 803b26, b30; [Arist.] *Pr.* 11.16.900b27, 11.35.903b2–4, 19.35.920b2–4; Xenocr. fr. 87 Isnardi Parente (= Porph. *In Ptol. Harm.* pp. 30.1–31.21 and 32.23–33.4 Düring); etc.
[102] Pl. *Rep.* 10.603b5–6. [103] Pl. *Rep.* 5.476b4–8; trans. Grube; rev. Reeve.

usually hear them together, as song."[104] Yet music is rarely investigated alongside literary criticism, let alone other art forms. And the neighboring fields respond in kind, keeping an all too polite distance from areas usually deemed borderlands rather than homelands.

Both Plato and Aristotle attest to the existence of attitudes and at times even full-dress theories of art and aesthetics that run counter to the formalism and anti-sensualism of their own. Why should we take our bearings from these two philosophers whenever we reconstruct the history of ancient aesthetic inquiry? Confirmation that Plato and Aristotle do not tell the whole story comes from many places, but at times where one least expects it, for instance, in Quintilian: "The musical theorist Aristoxenus divides what concerns sound into rhythm and melody, the former comprising the 'modulation,' and the latter the tone and the quality of the sound. Now are not *all* these essential to the orator?"[105] That is, Quintilian takes for granted what Plato and Aristotle openly reject. The bulk of ancient opinion follows Quintilian, and we ought to do so too.

But even this only begins to scratch the surface. Individual terms tell their own stories, which can be followed like clues. Leaving aside the wide resonance, and not just applicability, of terms like *poiēsis*, *technē*, or *mimēsis*, which point to the largest roles of art, no matter what the medium, as a form of making, technique, or representation – or more simply, as a form of production and reproduction[106] – consider how *euschēmosunē* (gracefulness) cuts across various art forms in addition to personal deportment (what we would call *habitus*): "Fine words (εὐλογία), harmony (εὐαρμοστία), gracefulness (εὐσχημοσύνη), and rhythm (εὐρυθμία) follow goodness of character (εὐηθία)."[107] Terms like *harmonia* (fittingness), *poikilia* (variety), *diathesis* or *dispositio* (arrangement), *rhuthmos* (rhythm, shape), *charis* or *gratia* (charm), *megethos* or *pondus* (grandeur or weight), *sklēros* or *durus* (hard, severe, rough), are commonplaces that run through all the domains of ancient art. The overlap of terms suggests that in matters of art boundaries are thought together, not apart. At times, causal connections are evident, as in the quotation above, which is from Plato, who is following a logic that specifies a functional dependency between character and music or poetry. (He, or rather Socrates, claims to have inherited this notion from Damon

---

[104] Burnyeat 1997, 222.   [105] Quint. *Inst.* 1.10.22; trans. Russell.

[106] The opening pages of Aristotle's *Poetics* are a primer in such boundary-crossing, but he is resuming earlier usages, not innovating.

[107] Pl. *Rep.* 3.400d–e; trans. Grube; rev. Reeve; adapted. Cf. *Tim.* 47d–e, which adds *rhuthmos* to the list. On the polymorphic utility of *rhuthmos* in ancient aesthetics, see Petersen 1917.

of Oa, though the basis of this conceit is popular and widespread.)
At other times no causal connections need be implied. But what *is* implied,
I would suggest, is a commonality of experiences: what one notices not only
in a painting but also in one's own response to it, and what eventually
comes to be labeled *harmony*, is comparable to what one notices in the face
of scales heard in music, or in the way that shapes fit together in a three-
dimensional object, each of which is likewise known in Greek as *harmony*.

But if existing histories of art and criticism tend to fare badly with such
crossovers, neither do they cope well with the astonishing news that "the
Elder Pliny's 'Chapters on the History of Art' in fact form part of what is
for us an entirely different topic, the taxonomy and technology of metal
and stone in books 34–36 of his *Natural History*. But so to muddle
chemistry, metallurgy, mining, pharmacy, domestic hygiene and the
history of Art is simply incomprehensible to us."[108] The usual response
to this fact is not necessarily the best one: "Scholars have obligingly
removed the embarrassment by publishing the 'art history' abstracted
from the rest: which imperceptibly generates an assumption that the
ancient world enjoyed something called 'Art History.'"[109] Another, possibly better response is to consider that art has an irreducibly material
dimension to it in antiquity, and that the best way to approach ancient
reflection on objects of art is through their physical nature: works of
art for Pliny are composed of natural elements, the way "some colours are
somber and some brilliant, the difference being due to the nature of
the substances or to their mixture," or the way "dark purple ... is produced
by dipping silversmith's earth along with purple cloth ... the earth
absorbing the colour more quickly than the wool."[110] The lines have an
Empedoclean ring. The possibility is less outlandish than it might first
appear (see Chapter 3 below), even if there is no proof of direct influence.

As it happens, some of the best modern indicators of the range of
aesthetic vocabularies in Greece and Rome exist neither in discussions of
literature and criticism nor in histories of art, but in the form of handbooks and source books, mainly within the art-historical tradition:
Overbeck's *Die antiken Schriftquellen zur Geschichte der bildenden Künste
bei den Griechen* (1868), Jex-Blake, Sellers, and Urlichs' *The Elder Pliny's
Chapters on the History of Art* (1896), Schlikker's *Hellenistische Vorstellun-
gen von der Schönheit des Bauwerks nach Vitruv* (1940), and most usefully
and recently, Pollitt's *The Ancient View of Greek Art: Criticism, History,
and Terminology* (1974), which is as much about the vocabulary of Roman

[108] Gordon 1979, 7.   [109] Gordon 1979, 7.   [110] Plin. *NH* 35.44; 35.30.

art as it is about Greek art. Just to turn their pages is to learn a good deal about the dazzling richness of ancient aesthetic description. Whether they are focused on plastic arts, architecture, history of art, or simply art, what these handbooks collectively highlight is best called an aesthetic core of the ancient arts, or else of the ancient sensibilities to the arts.

One could speculate in different ways about the reasons why the ancient arts shared so much descriptive and critical vocabulary. Indeed, I have begun to do so above. Impoverishment is a poor answer. Presumably, it was noticed that features in objects across media (harmony, gracefulness, and so on) were similar to one another, and that their experiential correlates were likewise similar (the feeling one has before an object displaying harmony or gracefulness), and that this convergence alone sufficed to justify the adoption of a unified vocabulary in the realm of the arts. To do so made the experience of aesthetic contexts more coherent. Or rather, *the uniformity of aesthetic terms brought out the seeming natural coherence of aesthetic experience itself.* This brings us to a potential criticism one could direct at the handbooks just mentioned: not that they cover too much ground, vaguely gesturing at the visual arts in different, or (in cases) in all domains, but that *they do not go far enough.* What they fail to do is to mark the extraordinary diffusion of the very same language into non-visual arts: the arts of language, whether poetry or prose (rhetoric), but also of music (instrumental or vocal), and dance. Nor should we forget that many of the arts were contiguous, if not also multifaceted: buildings and sculpture were painted; choral performances required music, dance, song, and lyrics, functions that were frequently discharged by the self-same performers;[111] drama intensified these requirements further still, adding the appurtenances of stagecraft (masks, costumes, scenery); even "simple" pots required a practiced eye that could take in many of the foregoing elements in their visual aspect. Winckelmann was probably not far off when he suggested, with moist lips no doubt, that *gumnasia*, or "naked places," provided an ideal setting for artists and philosophers to study bodies in motion and in poses.[112]

In sum, a comprehensive study of aesthetic terms and, what is of even greater interest, of aesthetic concepts and domains in the Greek and Roman arts still awaits us. One can be sure that the result would not be

---

[111] Auletes conducting dithyrambs may have danced as well. See D'Angour 1997, 342 n. 71, for the suggestion.

[112] Winckelmann 1985 [1755], 35. One could even "study physical outlines or the contour of the body in the impressions left by the young wrestlers in the sand," a point freely borrowed from Aristophanes' *Clouds* (975–76).

impoverished but voluminous, and also immensely enlightening. And there are further possible extensions one could venture for some, though not all, of the terms – into the languages of adjacent sciences (philosophy, medicine, physiology, astronomy, or mathematics) and, where we can glean this, popular forms of expression,[113] which leads one to suspect that a combination of factors are at play in the rise of these vocabularies, including:

(i) A shared analytical core of terms and concepts which evolve, and which are eventually ransacked by nascent fields or disciplines as the need arises. For instance, there is the language of componential analysis, which sees complex totalities being constructed out of smaller constituent parts, such as *stoicheia*, or elements, which in turn may or may not be divisible, analytically speaking. More speculatively, consider the influence of medical physiology on sculpture and, less speculatively, on the verbal arts.[114] Other areas contributing to this shared pool of aesthetic terms and concepts would include optics, acoustics, mathematics, physics proper, and so on;

(ii) A shared developmental factor, whereby languages of description and analysis in different areas evolve in coordinated ways, feeding off and into one another in a series of transformations, both together and sequentially over time – for instance (but with only rough claims for the historicity of the example), poetry into music into visual art, and architecture into criticism and into poetry again;

---

[113] By "extensions" I do not mean to imply anything about the actual derivations of terms. On the contrary, it may frequently transpire that adjacent disciplines are the source of literary-critical, musical, or other aesthetic terminology. (For the case of medicine and literary criticism, see Griffith 1984, 290.) A further complication is that once boundaries are recognized to have been fluid, sources become tricky to pin down. To take an example, analyses of the physiology of sound leave deposits in various fields of literature, rhetoric, and music, but under what aegis were they originally conducted? Medical? Anatomical? Philosophical (viz., as part of "physics")? Or as independent offspring of these within the more aesthetically oriented disciplines? The answers may vary at different historical moments, and they may be unanswerable today. Mathematics and aesthetics converge around questions of measurement, symmetry, and scale (as in architecture or sculpture; see below); on issues of scale in Hellenistic aesthetics, see Porter 2010a; on symmetry, see Hon and Goldstein 2008.

[114] For sculpture, see Métraux 1995 (leaning heavily on Leftwich 1987; Leftwich 1995 is a revision of the same) who demonstrates, if nothing else, how difficult it is to establish this connection, as intuitive as it ought to be: there are simply no smoking guns, unlike in the case of Greek drama and rhetoric, where lexical items provide a good clue to borrowings or affiliations. The most promising and probing work to date connecting Greek medicine and literature around the question of the body is Holmes 2010. A useful survey of Galen's aesthetic thought and vocabulary may be found in Gourevitch 1987.

(iii) And, at least in the more properly aesthetic domains, which by no means excludes philosophy, an intense and shared interest in accounting for (describing and analyzing), not so much qualities of objects *per se*, as qualities of experience in the face of objects as they are perceived.

It is in this last-named step that the relatively rich language of value terms – aesthetic terms – comes into being: *pleasurable, painful,* but also *beautiful, ugly, grand, sublime, awesome, terrifying, luminous, charming, dry, elegant, sweet,* and so on. These are merely the most obvious experientially based value terms in aesthetics, though a case could be made that even objective descriptions such as *order, hardness, smoothness,* or *perfection,* which seem most to apply to features of objects, also imply a subjective experiential correlative: each term or concept has a distinctive "feel" for a beholder; but more importantly, each feature of the object picked out by such terms exists *for* a beholder – the features are meaningless except as the objects of a beholder's gaze.[115] Gombrich calls this "the beholder's share."[116]

It is precisely at this level of description and on the order of what is experienced, which is seemingly a basic level of operation in the arts (a common denominator of sorts – not only lowest but also highest), that the barriers between one art form and another break down, or else those between all the art forms and the kinds of experience that lie outside of art. Even if the idea of comparing a temple and a piece of music as aesthetic objects might seem either absurd or improbable, surely their aesthetic experience can be meaningfully compared. The pleasure you take in a temple and the pleasure you take in a musical tune will be hard to distinguish qualitatively (in part owing to the imprecision of the idea we have of pleasure, or else of the proportional symmetry or harmony that we feel underlies each object and its experience). Circumstances may make such distinctions all the harder if, say, the pleasures are phenomenologically associated (as they would be in, for example, a ritual context), in which case they may be compounded, made more complex, or simply unified into a third kind of pleasure – say, the associative pleasure of enjoying the temple's design while enjoying a melody's harmony. But if we heed Kant, or Aristotle (at least in the passages quoted earlier, but not in his *Poetics*), or the hedonist Epicurus, it may prove hard to distinguish any of the so-called higher forms of pleasure from one another at all.

---

[115] For a similar point, see Nick Zangwill in Levinson 2003, 331.
[116] Gombrich 2000, Part Three.

And if these pleasures are raised to a certain pitch of intensity – for instance, one of rapt absorption and sheer mental or perceptual focus, to the point that all that is left is a sense of marvel, astonishment, or wonder (as in the sublime), or else merely a quiet but intense tranquility (of the sort that comes with any intense form of attention) – it is likely that the pleasure one takes in the experience will prove a mismatch with respect to any formal accounting of the experience, regardless of its source. We might say that at this point, pleasure has tipped over into some other state that lies beyond pleasure. Both Aristotle and Epicurus would argue that the pleasure achieved here is, on the contrary, a perfection of pleasure, not its supersession: it is pleasure in its highest and purest form, corresponding to the richest possible grasp of a moment; and the same would have to hold for the experience that is this grasping and that fills this moment. Indeed, these two entities – the pleasure and the grasp of the moment – would be one and the same thing.

At such moments, two things can occur, according to the evidence of the ancients. Either a deeply satisfying lucidity sets in (as with Epicurean ataraxy) or else a cognitive and affective confusion arises (I experience the "colors" of the tune and the "harmonies" of the building). Either way, familiar boundaries break down. And whenever they do, new juxtapositions suggest themselves. Synaesthetic descriptions, analogies (for instance, between words and visual media running in either direction), metaphors, the collapsing of boundaries between art and life, are only the most spectacular breaches of decorum between domains. And yet, such breaches may turn out to be the operative conditions of aesthetic experiences, not their extreme cases. Boundaries are artificially constraining in any event, and it is only when we *start* with the assumption of their existence that their ruptures will appear strange.

"A visual event may reproduce itself in the realm of touch (as when the seen face incites an ache of longing in the hand, and the hand then presses pencil to paper), which may in turn then reappear in a second visual event, the finished drawing."[117] There is nothing strange about such translations from one medium to the next, let alone from one sensation to another. Pleasure and pain (the most primitive of aesthetic responses) are perhaps the least obtrusive signs of shared limits, because they belong to workaday appearances. More marked valuations, aesthetic and moral, which occupy a middle ground in terms of their relative scarcity and therefore salience, are also communally shared, even if it seems obvious

[117] Scarry 1999, 4.

that proportionality in architecture need have nothing to do with proportionality in music, apart from the shared assumption that the two kinds of judgment must at least be minimally commensurable in some way or other. When we move to other areas, such as the ways in which architectural structures not infrequently resonate to voices or instruments, whether by accident or by design, or to the incidental sounds of ritual spectators and visitors (all of which can be classed under the more general rubric of "sound sculpture"; see Chapter 9 below), we involve ourselves in a deeper, if more ambiguous, form of mixed aesthetic and sensory perception, one that likewise has a reflex in the perception of one- or two-dimensional objects as three-dimensional ones, whether as architectonic or resonant structures or occasions (examples will be discussed below as well).[118]

Aesthetics is a dangerous area precisely because it is considered to be a contact zone between the primitive levels of sensation and the higher, more cultivated levels of taste. Negotiating this zone of contact can be a tricky business. It is not clear that the so-called primitive aesthetic responses can be completely rendered irreducible to (can be severed from) aesthetics in the narrowest of its meanings, that is, rendered into a mere sensation rather than a function of art. Sensation is typically held to be too impoverished to account for the complexity of aesthetic response. But accepted aesthetic labels often fare little better. Never mind such determinate labels as *spectacular, gorgeous,* or *beautiful,* or those indeterminate stand-ins which are like – or simply are – so much grasping at straws, the *Oohs* and *Ahs* and *je ne sais quoi*'s. The term *pleasure* is *in itself* an impoverished label for positive aesthetic experiences – and this is as much a fact of modern usage as it is of Greek or Latin. The pleasure you take in a statue or a vase is in its own way irreducibly complex, and the experience of each ought to be in principle irreducibly unique – not confined to their origins in the optic nerve, but not independent of these either. Compare what John Dewey has to say about visual pleasure in *Art as Experience*, which, as the title suggests, chimes with the approach I am presenting here:

When we perceive, by means of the eyes as causal aids, the liquidity of water, the coldness of ice, the solidity of rocks, the bareness of trees in winter, it is certain that other qualities than those of the eye are conspicuous and controlling in perception. And it is as certain as anything can be that optical qualities do not

---

[118] Tilley 2004, *passim*, and esp. 14–16 ("Synaesthesia: The Fusion of the Senses").

stand out by themselves with tactual and emotive qualities clinging to their skirts.... Any sensuous quality tends, because of its organic connections, to spread and fuse."[119]

It is the same rich insight into perception that led Hegel to proclaim, in a rare lapse into sensuous insight, that Greek classical statues consist of "congealed light."[120] At such moments, it is questionable whether the experiences in question are a matter of synaesthesia – if by this we understand the false effect of a transfer of sensations or a metaphoric turn of language – or whether, on the contrary, they simply designate the complex manner in which aesthetic pleasure, channeled through the senses, is taken in: differentially, variously (from one occasion to the next), and at the limits of language.

Before surrendering the question to modern psychologists, biologists, or even philosophers to sort out, we might also remember that accounts of the senses in antiquity varied considerably too. In some schools, vision was considered a haptic sense organ, as much a matter of touch as of sight, while in other schools other theories reigned (Aristotelian optics, resisting the conflation of sight with touch, is one of these).[121] The point is simply that epistemologies can impinge unexpectedly on phenomenologies. Nor can we, from our perch in the present, decide in advance how or where to draw the lines around spheres of experience. We have to approach such questions with open minds. What is more, in our attempt to approach aesthetic attitudes from antiquity we need to be alert to the aestheticization of social and political ties, which are merely a further extension of the crossover effects we have been surveying above. For instance, there is the sort that we find in Lucian when he speaks of "a lover of Greek learning (*philomathēs*) and of beauty (*philokalos*) in education and culture," and so touches on a *topos* that reaches back to the age of Pericles.[122] Or there are the easy ambiguities of being *philokalos*, loving beauty or loving higher things, of the sort that follows from being well born, noble, and virtuous, such as we find in Aristotle.[123] Or there is the kind of transformative rapture caused by Athenian civic ideology that is mocked by Socrates in the *Menexenus*, in a way that recalls Marx's critique of bourgeois vanities in his manuscripts of 1844. For whenever

---

[119] Dewey 1989 [1934], 129.   [120] Hegel 1975, II:706.
[121] See Arist. *De an.* 2.7; *Sens.* 2. For a survey of ancient theories, see Simon 1988.
[122] Lucian *Merc. Cond.* 25: φιλομαθὴς τῶν Ἑλληνικῶν μαθημάτων καὶ ὅλως περὶ παιδείαν φιλόκαλος; Thuc. 2.40.1: φιλοκαλοῦμέν τε γὰρ μετ᾽ εὐτελείας καὶ φιλοσοφοῦμεν ἄνευ μαλακίας.
[123] Arist. *EN* 10.9.1179b9.

Socrates listens to a grand funeral oration praising the war dead, an annual event in Athens by the end of the fifth century, something remarkable happens to him:

[The speech-writers] do their praising so splendidly that they cast a spell over our souls (γοητεύουσιν ἡμῶν τὰς ψυχάς), attributing to each individual man, with the most varied and beautiful verbal embellishments (κάλλιστά πως τοῖς ὀνόμασι ποικίλλοντες), both praise he merits and praise he does not, extolling the city in every way, and praising the war dead, all our ancestors before us, and us ourselves, the living. The result is, Menexenus, that I am put into an exalted frame of mind (γενναίως πάνυ διατίθεμαι) when I am praised by them. Each time, as I listen and fall under their spell, I become a different man – I'm convinced that I have become taller and nobler and better looking (μείζων καὶ γενναιότερος καὶ καλλίων) all of a sudden. It often happens, too, that all of a sudden I inspire greater awe in the friends from other cities who tag along and listen with me every year. For they ... think the city more wonderful (θαυμασιωτέραν) than they thought it before. And this feeling of dignity (ἡ σεμνότης) remains with me more than three days. The speaker's words and the sound of his voice (ὁ λόγος τε καὶ ὁ φθόγγος) sink into my ears with so much resonance (οὕτως ἔναυλος) that it is only with difficulty that on the third or fourth day I recover myself and realize where I am. Until then I could imagine that I dwell in the Islands of the Blessed.[124]

Each of these three cases (Lucian, Aristotle, Socrates) is an example of popular and widespread sentiments. They serve to illustrate how aesthetic qualities can permeate the very fabric of civic life, and not just one quarantined aspect of that life where we would normally look to find aesthetic experiences (whether in the theater or in the face of monuments or other objects of art). Indeed, to revert to the language from above, all talk of aesthetic subjects assumes an unexpectedly literal meaning in such cases – to the point that it becomes difficult to detach the two realms of subjectivity and aesthetics at all: to be a subject (a politically constituted subject) is to be invested in a set of aesthetic values, and it is to reflect those values in the very core of one's self-image.

Recent scholarship has increasingly grown attuned to the nexus of aesthetics and ideology in Greece and Rome.[125] It pays to remind ourselves of this connection, which is in fact inextricable, and for all the reasons that I have discussed so far. Aesthetic perception is a highly charged social event. The mere designation of an aesthetic feature –

---

[124] Pl. *Menex.* 234c–235c; trans. Ryan, slightly adapted; cf. Marx 1964, 167–69.
[125] E.g., Bérard 1989; Stewart 1997; Habinek and Schiesaro 1997; Habinek 1998; Porter 1999; Wohl 2002; Porter 2006b.

whatever it is that earns the label of excellence or pleasure or their opposite – is socially conditioned, but also, for the same reasons, often the most hidden element in this kind of judgment. Frameworks of judgment are the least visible factors of aesthetic labeling. Judgments of aesthetic value, accordingly, appear to be spontaneous and self-evident; and they seem to belong properly to the subjects who hold them, even if those subjects are, to degrees they can never fully be aware of, "held" by them, as Socrates pretends to be in the passage above. Pleasure is a delicate social event before it becomes an individual feeling. At issue in any act of aesthetic judgment is a movement from outside to within: the problem for an aesthetic subject is not in the first instance to decide whether this or that object is pleasurable, but rather to decide how one should appropriate ideological pleasures as one's own.

What all of the foregoing discussion means, if I am right so far, is that a whole new expanse of territory opens up to view whenever we wish to explore aesthetic attitudes and postures in antiquity. In place of an embarrassing dearth of aesthetic vocabulary, we run the risk of discovering an embarrassing overflow of evidence: once we have eliminated the artificial boundaries between the aesthetic and the non- or extra-aesthetic, no text and no artifact will be immune to plundering for its indexical value to the newly expanded category of the aesthetic. Correlatively, no aesthetic object or aesthetic vocabulary, conventionally speaking, will be immune to being read for its social and political resonances, or its more broadly connotative aesthetic resonances, and indeed for its conditioning factors – and not only in the seemingly direct carry-overs from aesthetics into politics or vice versa, as in the case of Critias, who appears to have adopted "a Polykleitan term, ἔμμετρος ('well balanced'), in the title of one of his political treatises."[126] But, once again, the study of the language of politics and the political aesthetic subject, while undeniably rich, is an avenue that is too broad to be fully pursued in the pages that follow. No doubt, compelling intersections with recent studies in the field of cultural poetics could be found, a field that has already begun to elaborate on a number of areas of ancient aesthetic inquiry, above all in the realm of performance.[127]

---

[126] Stewart 1998, 273–74. The title, "Well-Balanced Constitutions," is preserved by Joannes Philoponos; see DK 88A22.

[127] E.g., Dougherty and Kurke 1998; Kurke 1999a; Easterling and Hall 2002; Dougherty and Kurke 2003; Murray and Wilson 2004.

To summarize, then: aesthetics involves, from start to finish, the sphere of sensation and experience. Its immediate (albeit always culturally mediated) objects are sensuous, material things. Together, these describe a valid field of inquiry in antiquity. But how does form fit into the picture? And what is the role of formalism in ancient aesthetics, viewed generally and as a sensualist pursuit? These questions will be the topic of the next chapter.

CHAPTER 2

Form and formalism

While terms like *form* and *formalism* are deserving of our attention in ancient aesthetic contexts and often so used, it is not self-evident why this should be so. After all, there are no obvious equivalents in Greek or in Latin for either term, and it is not even clear that formalism marks out well-defined schools or tendencies of thought in the ancient world. Surely *mimesis, inspiration, instruction, performance, beauty, symbolism,* and *allegory* are better suited to making sense of ancient reflection on the arts, if not the phenomena of the arts themselves.

Well, yes and no. There are many ways to approach problems of aesthetics in antiquity, and each has its virtues and limitations. In defense of exploring the terms *form* and *formalism*, we may summon the following arguments: (i) the terms are commonly invoked by modern scholars in connection with antiquity already; this being so, then any further clarity we can gain about these terms can also help us clarify our own nomenclature and its potential relevance to the ancient sources; (ii) formalism (and its implied antithesis, materialism) does not name a sharply defined school of art or criticism in modernity either, but only a tendency or aspect of practices that can in fact be shown to have striking parallels in antiquity, once these have been correctly identified; mapping these parallels is a worthy enterprise in and of itself; (iii) though the present study is not strictly concerned with formalism, one of the best ways to understand the historical emergence of the concepts and categories of matter and materialism is to consider what may be called "the formalist reaction" to them.

As will soon become evident, what matters to me are less the terms themselves or their abstract reifications (*matter*, and above all that most suspect of entities, *form*) than the practices and the acts of attention that the two opposed tendencies, materialism and formalism, tend to evoke in the face of aesthetic objects – attention, that is, to the sensuous and palpable dimensions of works of art (their matter) as opposed

70

to everything that eludes this description but is claimed nonetheless to inhere in art works and to provide them with internal coherence (their form). This distinction may have a slightly stipulative ring to it, but it also has a pedigree that is traceable to the very kind of terminological divisions that are in question here. Rather than arguing for this inheritance, I will simply make do with it, and then attempt a few refinements and historical comparisons. But I should also warn the reader that in what follows I will be offering more like a *materialist critique of form* than an objective account, let alone defense, of form. As I hope to show, form is suspect, not least because it is intrinsically vague as a concept, and hence unlocatable in concrete works of art or their experience. Form's unlocatability is often one of its strategic strengths for adherents of form or formalism.

I FORMS OF FORMALISM

Perceptual form and "pure form"

Defined narrowly, formalism in aesthetic contexts consists in the isolation of form, as opposed to matter or content, in works of art. On this view, form can provisionally be understood to refer to "the perceptual elements of an artwork and to the relationships holding between them."[1] Even this provisional rendering, which Kant did much to popularize, is unsatisfactory, in part owing to its ambiguities.[2] As we shall see, conventional understandings of formalism have in fact tended to place less value on the act of perception itself and its objects than on what are felt to be the qualities of aesthetic perception, which in turn are drawn towards various realms of the immaterial. Thus, in Roger Fry's terms, "pure form ... sets free a pure and as it were disembodied functioning of the spirit," while in Clive Bell's terms, "the nature of the focus [of 'pure aesthetics'] is immaterial," which is to say, emphatically *non*-material, because its object is what "significant form" evokes: an emotional content (a kind of

---

[1] Krukowski 1997, 213.

[2] Thus, while Kant speaks about judgments of "pure form," their defining characteristics tend to be cast in negative terms: they are made without reference either to empirical sensation or to conceptual content (see, e.g., *CJ* §14; Ak. 224–25) – but why are they judgments of *form*? (The answer is partly to be sought in his first *Critique*.) Then there is "purposive form" and "purposiveness without purpose," as well as "the form of an object (of intuition)," "the form of (the subjective) finality of (or in) an object" or "in the representation" of the object, "the form of the presentation of a concept," and so on.

objective correlative) divorced from meaning and reference, but also from "the chatter and tumult of material existence."[3] (In point of fact, the content of aesthetic emotion, on Bell's deliberately circular definition, is the emotion felt at the perception of form, which in turn echoes the state that caused a corresponding emotion in the artist's mind and which ultimately echoes "the formal significance of material things," metaphysically speaking – namely, their "latent reality."[4])

Conventionally, understandings of formalism have further tended to place a high value on the relationships among the objects of perception – the formal properties, as they are often called – of works of art or their synthesis in the mind. Bell's "significant form" is a case in point: this he defines as "*relations* and combinations of lines and colours."[5] Nevertheless, empirical perception is an ineluctable element of aesthetic form, as is the material resistance (the opacity) and the sensuous materiality of the object perceived. "Form cannot be the form of nothing," Santayana once wrote, stating an easily forgotten but obvious fact.[6] Thus, to the degree that formalism strives to minimize the significance of the empirical perceptual element in art, a tension enters into the concept of form that makes itself felt in its various manifestations: is formalism staked on the empirical perception of objects, on the imperceptible qualities of perception, or on the (formal) relations among perceived objects?

To this precise extent, formalism, so defined, which also happens to capture its basic tendency in modern art and aesthetics, is a *defense against* the perceptual nature of the aesthetic act – its very own. This self-imposed contradiction leads to all kinds of confusions, both for the exponents of formalism themselves and for anyone who would attempt to describe the formalists' tendencies. One result is that formalism in some quarters comes to be confused with its opposite, namely the apprehension of sensuous properties *simpliciter* (for instance, line, shape, and color, regardless of their formal arrangement).[7] But nothing could be further from the truth. Formalism in its modern tradition, which may well stem from Kant, if not earlier from Frances Hutcheson, works against the fact of the embodiment of aesthetic properties in what we may call the *matter* of art, following the imperative that Hegel would later identify as the gradual

---

[3] Fry 1990, 169; Bell 1981, 17; 52; 55. [4] Bell 1981, 54
[5] Bell 1981, 17–18; emphasis added. [6] Santayana 1988 [1896], 51.
[7] As in Zangwill 1999, 611: "formal properties are those aesthetic properties that are determined solely by sensory or physical properties." Zangwill goes on to invoke abstraction in art, and then Bell and Fry. For a start at a corrective, see Davis 1997.

"dematerialization" of art over historical time.[8] Thus, in Hegel's grand narrative of art, painting, with its two-dimensional surfaces, inevitably overtakes sculpture, with its volumetric plastic forms – as do music and poetry, the realms of formal and ideated abstraction: aesthetic experience is in this way gradually spiritualized (dematerialized). As art progresses historically, matter is cleared away, leaving form to manifest itself in all its conspicuous presence.[9] The result is a *minimizing* of the perceptual spectrum, its reduction to a non-distracting range and a bare minimum of sensuousness:

Now it follows from this that *the sensuous* must indeed be present in the work of art, but *should appear only as the surface and as a pure appearance of the sensuous*. For in the sensuous aspect of a work of art the spirit seeks neither the concrete material stuff ... nor the universal and purely ideal thought. What it wants is sensuous presence which indeed should remain sensuous, but *liberated from the scaffolding of its purely material nature*.... Consequently the sensuous aspect of art is related only to the two theoretical senses of sight and hearing, while smell, taste, and touch remain excluded from the enjoyment of art. For ... these [latter] senses cannot have to do with artistic objects, which are meant to maintain themselves in their real independence and allow of no *purely* sensuous relationship.[10]

In Hegel's view, the tendency of art is not towards a greater integration of form and content in the work of art (for that was achieved in classical sculpture, albeit on the sensuous surfaces of sculptural forms), but rather towards a *deeper* integration of form and content, whereby form gives expression to a richer, if ever more enigmatic and subjective, content – that of inner Spirit itself. If this tendency comes out in Hegel's narrative looking like a drive towards conceptual abstraction, the drive is also towards formalism, in the sense that form increasingly takes itself as its own content, and thus no longer stands in opposition to content, pure and simple. Formalism in modern art and criticism, expressed as aesthetic autonomy, is very much in Hegel's spirit.[11] What is form from one angle is palpable material from another.

---

[8] For the term, which is not Hegel's (*pace* Krukowski 1997, 213) but is Hegelian in spirit, see Pippin 2002, 2. Hegel speaks, rather, of the "spiritualization" of the sensuous aspect of art, whereby the spirit appears in a sensuous form (Hegel 1975, 1:39). Bakhtin 1990, 305 endorses a similar thought: "Form is dematerialized."

[9] E.g., Hegel 1975, II:810.   [10] Hegel 1975, 1:38–39; all but last emphasis added.

[11] See Pippin 2002, esp. at 3 n. 2. To the extent that for Kant the content of an aesthetic judgment of beauty is nothing other than the formal (non-sensuous) determination of a unified manifold of subjective perceptions, the same could be said to apply to Kant (as Clement Greenberg never tired of insisting).

Formal abstraction

So much for formalism construed narrowly as "form" and opposed either to matter or to content. More broadly speaking, formalism can be said to consist in the mere abstraction of categories and structures that are themselves slices of works of art, mere aspectual distinctions that exist separately only in the mind but not in the concrete work of art (examples of which include structure, the arrangement of parts, content, but also materiality – as opposed to matter – and appearances). These in turn supply criteria for the analysis and often for determining the essence of art and, accordingly, its value. In one sense, formalism represents the becoming-autonomous of these elements, of which literary form is only the most obvious example, but perhaps also the most problematic, for reasons I want to consider next.[12]

The "form" of a work, in the sense of its organizational principle, is notoriously difficult to point to and inevitably a matter of interpretation and argument.[13] A given work can be said to harbor any number of forms. Form is a "plural concept that comprise[s] many regions and many orders within the same work.... In any work, form ... cover[s] several layers and scales of structure, expression, and representation. Line, mass, space, color, dark-and-light constitute different orders in painting, as do words, actions, characters, and the large sequence of narrative in a play or story." So writes Meyer Schapiro, in a stimulating essay entitled "On Perfection, Coherence, and Unity of Form and Content" (1966) that offers many valuable insights into aesthetic perception, while also attacking the "vagueness" of the form/content unity and distinction.[14] I want to take Schapiro's insight further and argue that form is less a plural phenomenon than a heuristic postulate of interpretation (that is, it is itself an "ideal hypothesis"), and every bit as vulnerable to the uncertainties and contingencies of reading (which is the actual thrust of his essay) as are attempts to localize the plural instantiations of so-called form(s).[15] But one could press Schapiro's results still further and ask how

---

[12] For a useful, if tendentious, anatomy of form, see Bakhtin 1990, to be discussed briefly below. Zangwill's defense of "moderate formalism" (Zangwill 1999) conflates "formal properties" with "aesthetic properties," confusingly. For sharp critiques of form and formalism, see Isenberg 1973 [1955]; Wollheim 2001. The formalism I've just described would overlap with what Wollheim calls "Latent Formalism."

[13] See esp. Schapiro 1994 [1966].   [14] Schapiro 1994 [1966], 43.

[15] Ibid., 43. Schapiro uses "ideal hypothesis" to refer to "the unity of form and content," not to form alone – perhaps because he seems to think that form is on the whole less problematic to locate in works of art than content is (cf. ibid., 45–46), though it may simply be that he finds the

serviceable the idea of form is. How abstractable is form, in fact? Even to point to a work of art's apparently least disputable formal features, whether metrical or other, is not clearly to point to something we can call its segregatable form. Rather, it is to point to the division of the *material* in a work. Thus, Aristoxenus of Tarentum, in his *Elements of Rhythm*, could say that rhythm divides time and then arranges the divisions into a shape:[16] rhythm is, in this case, the "form," if you like, but it is palpable, something heard and felt in the very arrangement of the intervals of quantities of time dispersed over a work and supervening on the materials – be these musical notes, dance elements (movements), or words – and competing for attention alongside any other number of formal, or (better yet) organizational, systems in a given work.

Palpable form: Russian Formalism

The literary theorists from the early part of the twentieth century known as Russian Formalists drew attention to form in order to bring out, precisely, its material and palpable qualities, and indeed its deformations. They were mislabeled *formalists* by their adversaries, and the name, which was pejoratively meant, somehow stuck, despite the protestations of the original members of the group.[17] The most radical and unpredictable of these was Victor Shklovsky. (A collection of his essays is entitled *Knight's Move*, which captures nicely the defiant zigzags of his thought.) As if appealing to Baumgarten's definition of aesthetics as the science of sensate perception (*sensa*) and representation (*representationes sensitivae*) and then literalizing this definition, Shklovsky made a powerful case that art exists in order to awaken and renew our sensations – both our empirical sensations and our sensation of life. Shklovsky is in fact renewing one of the deepest strands of aesthetic inquiry, which was signaled above in Chapter 1, namely the insight into the connection between aesthetic activity, the feeling of life, and the vivacity of sensation.

His theory, encapsulated in an essay from 1917 entitled "Art as Technique," is addressed in part as a critique of modern industrial life and its routinizations:

Habitualization devours works, clothes, furniture, one's wife, and the fear of war. "If the whole complex lives of many people go on unconsciously, then such lives

---

conjunction of the two more complex than analysis allows (while some works' original meanings, viz., their content, are irretrievable today).
[16] Aristox. *Rhythm.* 2.5–6.   [17] See Erlich 1975, 11.

are as if they had never been" [Tolstoy]. And art exists that one may recover the sensation of life; it exists to make one feel things, to make the stone *stony*. The purpose of art is to impart the sensation of things as they are perceived and not as they are known. The technique of art is to make objects "unfamiliar," to make forms difficult, to increase the difficulty and length of perception because the process of perception is an aesthetic end in itself and must be prolonged. *Art is a way of experiencing the artfulness of an object; the object is not important.*[18]

Here, Shklovsky announces his famous doctrine of "defamiliarization" (*ostranenie*), which would later be adopted by Brecht and transformed into the theory of *Verfremdungseffekt*, or alienation effect. Shklovsky's point is that form is worth isolating in order to pick out particular objects of attention or effects, all of which contribute to making art, then life, palpable. *Form*, so conceived, picks out what one feels and experiences, sensuous or empirical detail, the technique of art, artfulness, and the act of perception itself. Thus, to focus on form is a strategic gesture, the aim of which is not only to advance the perception of certain elements or aspects of art (or rather of perception itself), but also to *exclude or postpone* an opposed set of items in one's perceptions: questions of content or meaning, reference, knowledge, and cognition. Whence, he adds, "the meaning of a work broadens to the extent that artfulness and artistry diminish."[19] On the other hand, defamiliarization can apply to reference and meaning as well as to form, so that to defamiliarize the habitual content or meaning of an expression is sometimes to make palpable its conventionality, and sometimes it is simply to bring its reference startlingly back into view, the way Tolstoy describes marriage with a question: "Why, if people have an affinity of souls, must they sleep together?"[20]

To defamiliarize language in this way does not obliterate reference. It recreates reference as though it were being seen for the first time, "as if [it] were unfamiliar."[21] Nevertheless, defamiliarization, so conceived, is a far cry from a poetics designed to foreground, and hence to serve, the demands of referentiality or meaning. Nor does defamiliarization quite turn the thing in question or the language used to express it into a piece of matter or a physical object. It does, however, impede the habitual perception of the idea that is being expressed and the conventions that are typically used to express this idea. Defamiliarization *does* act upon language by bringing out a kind of materiality. Only, the materiality it brings

---

[18] Shklovsky 1965 [1917], 12; emphasis in original.   [19] Shklovsky 1965 [1917], 12–13.
[20] Cited in Shklovsky 1965 [1917], 17.   [21] Shklovsky 1965 [1917], 17.

out does not lie on the level of reference (which in the case of Tolstoy happens to be spiritual) or even on the level of linguistic materiality, but rather in the vivacity of perception, in the strangeness that results from seeing something afresh. What is attended to is not the thing itself but the shock of attending to it (the shock that comes from noticing the gap, say, that separates our habitual perception of marriage from its renewed present perception). And this awareness is what gives the perception its aesthetic dimension. Defamiliarization is thus a lot like putting a window, or rather a frame, in front of an object we normally see without one, and then seeing the object through that medium. Only, what we see is not the object but the difference between the two kinds of seeing, our habitual seeing and this new strange seeing (which now involves a second-order, reflexive dimension), while the pleasure we take lies in that perceived difference.[22] And so, while reference and meaning are not necessarily obliterated, they are not at the center of the aesthetic experience: the shock and pleasure of perception are. To this extent, Baumgarten's oxymoronic injunction to "know sensately," an otherwise promising gambit for any materialist aesthetics, is no longer being adhered to but is being taken to task: feeling and perception overwhelm cognition in Shklovsky's scheme.[23] Thus, the purpose of whatever attracts our attention in art "is not to make us perceive meaning, but to create a special perception of the object – *it creates a 'vision' of the object instead of serving as a means of knowing it.*"[24] In fact, in place of cognition, art provides a space for "nonrecognition."[25]

To what extent is Shklovsky even a formalist? We can say that he is a formalist to the extent that he isolates an imaginary entity that he calls *form*. But once we examine the features of Shklovskian "form," we will doubtless be, so to speak, estranged by his selection. While form for Shklovsky is opposable to content in the conventional sense, it is not opposable to matter, and if anything it finds a new home there. Indeed, Shklovsky typically uses the word *material* to describe what form minus

---

[22] Thanks to Eric Downing for helpful discussion on this point.

[23] That is, assuming that Baumgarten is a factor in Shklovsky's mind, which is not at all inconceivable. One possible explanation may be that Shklovsky was reacting to the Russian Symbolists' imagistic theory of poetry, the premise of which was that "art is thinking in images" (Shklovsky 1965 [1917], 5), while Baumgarten's theory of aesthetics is partly based on a theory of images (Baumgarten 1954 [1735], §§28–30; 55; 68, etc.), and partly is just not sensuous enough to suit Shklovsky's tastes, being too concerned as it is with the logical status of content (e.g., §71). For a similarly minded approach to form as a matter of perception likewise exclusive of content, see Dewey 1989 [1934], 222.

[24] Shklovsky 1965 [1917], 18; emphasis in original.   [25] Shklovsky 1965 [1917], 20.

"the automatism of perception" becomes.[26] This is striking, but also significant. Form is deformed, and radically so. When it is made sensuously palpable, whether through a technical feat by the artist – which is to say, made salient (palpable) through contrastive, "roughening" devices – or else through an act of attention by the observer (and Shklovsky appears to countenance either route as a way of producing, or isolating, the phenomenon of form's palpability), form returns to its natural state of matter. This is how form becomes "unfamiliar" again – "again," because it once was unfamiliar, or so Shklovsky's theory must postulate, before it became automatic and habitual: alienated in her perceptions, the viewer sees and hears things as if for the first time. All of this – the making perceptible of art – is what Shklovsky means by "making forms difficult." Form is artistically significant when it becomes an object of experience in its own right, a material for sensation and perception. But because form in art is a *conventionally inherited structure* that routinely exists in order to enable meanings, form must be deformed if form is to become the material of a perception again: its existence has to be foregrounded and made palpable, and its enabling function *qua* conveyer of meanings has to be disabled. And so, Shklovsky reasons, form has to be *made difficult to perceive* so that it can provide perceptual pleasure: its perception must be "impeded" in order that its perception will require greater and longer attention.

With this last term ("attention"), Shklovsky's project can be seen to conjure up a traditional set of aesthetic concerns. On the one hand, he appears to be approaching Kant's position that aesthetic perception is a matter of attending to an object without attending to its cognitive content. As we saw in the previous chapter, Kant's term for this kind of attention was the loaded Romantic notion of *Verweilen*, or "tarrying." The similarities between "tarrying" in this sense and Shklovsky's idea that aesthetic perception involves a deliberate prolongation of the observer's gaze are indeed quite close: aesthetics requires a delicious "lingering" over an object, which is to say, an experiencing of experience itself. On the other hand, Shklovsky takes this Kantian insight to a truly paradoxical conclusion: if the aim of art is to draw attention to itself, then *the aim of form is to impede its own perception*:

A work is created "artistically" so that its perception is impeded and the greatest possible effect is produced through the slowness and "roughness" of the perception. As a result of this lingering, the object is perceived not in its extension in

---

[26] As at Shklovsky 1965 [1917], 22 (whence the quotation).

space, but, so to speak, in its continuity. Thus "poetic language" gives satisfaction. According to Aristotle, poetic language must appear strange and wonderful . . .[27]

By the same token, Shklovsky consequentially, if a bit perversely, defines poetry as "*attenuated, tortuous* speech" ("the language of poetry is . . . a difficult, roughened, impeded language"), and he defines rhythm, whether in poetry or in architecture, as the "disordering of rhythm." The example he offers is once again taken from antiquity: "not a single column of a Greek temple stands exactly in its proper order," an allusion to *entasis* (swelling) or the off-center leaning of columns, which is to say, to the dissonance in harmony that animates even the heaviest and sturdiest of Greek architectural forms.[28]

Provocatively, we could say that meaning is merely the effect of a retardation enacted upon or through form, just as one of Shklovsky's most acute students, Roland Barthes, would define suspense – "the thrilling of intelligibility" – as "the threat of an uncompleted sequence," only to go on to add that "'suspense' accomplishes the very idea of language."[29] But in that case, meaning and "material" in Shklovsky's sense of the term would have merely been assimilated to each other. Perhaps they have indeed been assimilated to each other, given the way in which matter and the palpability of form have been so approximated on Shklovsky's view. Hence, too, Shklovsky's championing of what he called "trans-sense (*zaum*) language," a notion he borrowed from contemporary theorists who were reaching back to earlier Russian Romantic poetics in search of theories of inarticulable meaning, which is to say, aesthetic meaning and ultimately aesthetic pleasure that can be found only in the experience of sound and "sensual tonality."[30] It was in this context that Shklovsky declared that "words in a poem are not chosen for their meaning nor for their rhythm, but *for their sound*."[31] Roman Jakobson would reinforce this idea in his famous "Closing Statement" (1960) by defining the "poetic function" as proneness of attention (*Einstellung*) towards the verbal sign as such in its material "palpability."[32]

We seem to have encountered a sharp inversion of Hegelian formalism, according to which form and content are one (as with Hegel), but with

---

[27] Shklovsky 1965 [1917], 22.   [28] Shklovsky 1965 [1917], 22; 24.   [29] In Sontag 1982, 290.
[30] Shklovsky 1985 [1916].   [31] Shklovsky 1985 [1916], 17; emphasis added.
[32] Jakobson 1960, 356: to focus on the message itself, which is the criterion of the poetic function, is to focus on "the palpability of signs." Jakobson likewise held that "equivalence in sound . . . inevitably involves semantic equivalence," but not the other way round (ibid., 368).

form taking itself for its own content (*pace* Hegel). *The form of art, understood as the perceptible aesthetic surface, just is its own material.* Perhaps the Russian Formalist view is in ways Nietzschean: "One is an artist at the cost of regarding that which all non-artists call 'form' as content, as 'the matter itself' (*die Sache selbst*). To be sure, then one belongs in a topsy-turvy world: for *henceforth content becomes something merely formal.*"[33] The Russian Formalists could only have agreed. But they would have stressed that the aim of art is not to make content merely formal, but to make form materially palpable again. I want to suggest that their view of art points us back, promisingly, to another way of looking at art and aesthetic reflection on art in ancient Greece and Rome. Indeed, their emphasis on the palpability of art finds a genuine resonance in antiquity.

Their name notwithstanding, which is in fact a misnomer, I have been arguing that the Russian Formalists were advocates of a kind of aesthetic materialism.[34] For a confirmation, we may compare the later critique of Russian Formalism by Mikhail Bakhtin, who writes in a supplement to *Art and Answerability*, entitled "Content, Material, and Form in Verbal Art," "At one time, a class slogan ... asserted, in effect, the *primacy of the material* in artistic creation, for it is precisely material that separates the arts." Bakhtin continues, "It is in the soil of the natural sciences that a tendency is nourished to understand *artistic form* as the *form of a given material* and nothing more, as a combination achieved within the bounds of a material in its natural-scientific and linguistic determinateness and regularity .... We shall call that conception – *material aesthetics.*"[35] Though no identifying reference is given here, it seems clear that he has the Russian Formalists squarely in view, and sure enough they crop up a few pages later as the obvious intended targets.[36] Bakhtin turns his nose up at the "primitivism" and "hedonism" of their crude vision of aesthetics. But polemics and labels aside, we can happily find in Bakhtin's account a confirmation of the very sort of aesthetic tendencies that can be documented both among the Russian Formalists, such as Shklovsky, and in ancient Greece and Rome, as will be shown.

Bakhtin's response is useful in a further way: in defending a narrow, parochial formalism of a purist cast, it is typical of the formalist reaction

---

[33] *The Will to Power* §818; trans. Kaufmann and Hollingdale; emphasis added.
[34] See at n. 17 above.   [35] Bakhtin 1990, 261–62; last emphasis added.
[36] The Russian Formalists are finally named on p. 265 and again on p. 273. I am grateful to Brooke Holmes for pointing me to this work by Bakhtin.

against materialism in art, which in its extreme versions tends to overreact in two ways – first by labeling all materialist aesthetic tendencies reductionist, and secondly by foreswearing, as it were *e contrario*, all contact with the materiality of works of art. Thus, "the aesthetic component (we shall call it for the present an image) is neither a concept, nor a word, nor a visual representation, but a distinctive aesthetic formation which is realized ... with the help of the word, and ... with the help of ... material, *but which does not coincide anywhere with the material or with any material combination.*"[37] The imprecision of this definition, which refuses to locate "the aesthetic component" anywhere along a spatio-temporal continuum, is matched only by its absurd allergy to matter: the aesthetic object cannot be touched "anywhere" by matter; it cannot even, seemingly, be conceived as existing in a material form, and hence cannot be touched in any way at all. Needless to say, this view represents a complete regression from the positions held by the Russian Formalists, and is worth citing for its contrastive value alone.[38] A similar reactive tendency will be demonstrated when we come to Plato and Aristotle below.

Much later, another of Shklovsky's distant students would take up the crusade "against interpretation" and symbolism, likewise in the name of "a vocabulary of forms." What Susan Sontag sought to champion in 1964 were various elements of art as technique, and ultimately "the sensuous surface of art" and "the sensory experience of the work of art" in its "material plenitude." Sounding a rallying cry against the numbing routinization of modern life, much as Shklovsky had done half a century earlier, Sontag makes a brave appeal to the vivacity of experience and the ultimate value of the senses in her essay "Against Interpretation":

What is important now is to recover our senses. We must learn to *see* more, to *hear* more, to *feel* more.

Our task is not to find the maximum amount of content in a work of art, much less to squeeze more content out of the work than is already there. Our task is to cut back content so that we can *see* the thing at all.

The aim of all commentary on art now should be to make works of art – and, by analogy, our own experience – more, rather than less, real to us ...

In place of a hermeneutics we need an erotics of art.[39]

[37] Bakhtin 1990, 300. Bakhtin's text is all in italics; I have left only the final portion in italics for emphasis.
[38] The final words of the essay have to do with the "alien" and "mediating foreign bodies" through which the "material" of art must pass as it is transmuted from a form into an aesthetic content. A bizarre essay, indeed, though in its spiritualist urges and in other respects it shares some similarities with the formalism of Roger Fry and Clive Bell.
[39] Sontag 1966, 14.

New critics and form

Consciously or not, Sontag was echoing a generation of American critics from the 1940s who had rallied around the sensuous particulars of poetry. From T. S. Eliot's retrieval of "the feeling for syllable and rhythm, penetrating far below the conscious levels of thought and feeling, invigorating every word[,] sinking to the most primitive and forgotten," to Monroe C. Beardsley's focus on the "texture" of structure and form, there is a strain of materialism and sensualism that runs undeniably throughout the formalism of New Criticism even in its more structurally attuned varieties.[40] Like the Russian Formalists, who were wrongly branded as forerunners of formalism, the first-generation New Critics have been gravely misinterpreted: they were rebellious, counterestablishment thinkers who championed the senses, not organic meaning.

One of the more vigorous champions of a sensuous aesthetics from this era was the poet and critic John Crowe Ransom, the spiritual founder of the New Criticism. On the surface, Ransom could appear to represent the balanced tendency of the New Critics, for instance in his critical *aperçu*, "A poem is a *logical structure* having a *local texture*."[41] But Ransom was himself more interested in texture than in structure.[42] Thus, in a daring critical essay from 1941, "Wanted: An Ontological Critic," Ransom wrote, "Poetry intends to recover the denser and more refractory original world which we know loosely through our perceptions and memories." His plea was for a new kind of "ontological critic," namely one who grasps the "objectivity," or rather the objectality, of the world through the materiality of poetry as an object in its own right; "iconic signs," poems exist as an order of rhythms and sounds: they are "contingent and unpredictable," saturated with particular aesthetic qualities (richness, fullness, color, immediacy, concreteness, vividness), filled out by "the body of language," and occupying an "ontological density which proves itself by logical obscurity."[43] Poetry appeals to the senses, not the mind. In an interesting move, on the last page of the essay, Ransom aligns himself with the Presocratic "pluralists" against the Eleatics.

---

[40] Eliot 1986 [1933], 111; Beardsley 1981.   [41] Ransom 1941a, 110; repeated in Ransom 1941b, 280.
[42] Cf. Ransom 1943, 287: "I should still prefer my own two terms, however ...: where the prose indicates a *structure*, an operation working with proper member materials, but the materials demand an attention in their own right when they exhibit their private quality or *texture*."
[43] Ransom 1943, 281; 285; 293; 300; 335.

Is form concrete or transcendent? Beyond form and formalism

To be sure, art has always made similar appeals: art is forever sensuous, directing attention to its surface features, begging to be "read" in a tactile way, seductive and erotic in its appearances. But art theory has not always responded to art's vocations, nor has formalism always been a hospitable locus for an aesthetics of the seductive surface to flourish in. *Formalism* is a plastic term with a checkered history that has run the full gamut of possible stances, from the rejection of materialism to its embracement. Part of the reason for this vacillation lies in the incoherent aspirations of formalism, and above all the underlying desire of a great many of the critics associated with formalism to reify form. Form made concrete is virtually a material thing – and then again it is not. For, no sooner is form located in an aesthetic object than it is banished again into remote abstraction. Formalism is truly of two minds. Thus, while modern aesthetic formalism has sometimes conjured up what its name would seem to imply (structures without any appeal to sensual content, "setting free a pure and as it were disembodied functioning of the spirit," in Roger Fry's words quoted earlier), it has just as frequently drifted towards a full-bodied aesthetic materialism ("pure form" is "almost nothing else except sensuous," according to Clement Greenberg, and so it relentlessly pursues "materialist objectivity").[44] Much the same kind of fluctuation holds for the ancient varietals of formalism, two canonical instances of which will concern us next (Plato and Aristotle). Perhaps no thought of form can be had in the abstract (form must, after all, be of *something*, as Santayana reminded us earlier, in near exasperation) – all of which considerations may, on balance, give us good grounds to cast away *form* and *formalism* in favor of a more productive set of terms, for instance those that were mentioned above (material, texture, sensuality, palpability, tactility, and the rest).[45] But let us first turn our attentions to the main traditional repositories of form in antiquity.

2 FORM AND THE FORM OF BEAUTY IN PLATO AND ARISTOTLE

Above, I described how formalism in one sense consists in the abstraction of categories and structures or aspectual distinctions that exist separately

---

[44] Fry 1990, 169; Greenberg 1986–93 [1940], I:31–32; I:29. On this drift towards aesthetic materialism, see Kelly 1998, II:213–25, s.v. *Formalism.* Further, Prettejohn 2005, ch. 4, for a useful overview of twentieth-century formalist art criticism from Fry to Greenberg.

[45] On the indiscernibility ("indiscriminability") of form, see Wollheim 2001, 133 and *passim.*

only in the mind but not in the aesthetic object (for example, form, arrangement, content, materiality, or appearance), which in turn supply criteria for analyzing and often for determining the essence of art and its value. Formalism in this sense is a tendency, not a clear-cut position expressly taken in antiquity. Plato may well have inaugurated the distinction between form and content when he reduced what a poet can know and mean to either uninformed knowledge (ignorance, opinion) or falsehoods (myths). Poetry for Plato has no true content, and at the extreme it has no content at all.[46] As he puts it in the *Ion*, "a poet is a light, winged, holy creature, and cannot compose until he is possessed and out of his mind (ἔκφρων), and his reason is no longer in him" (ὁ νοῦς μηκέτι ἐν αὐτῷ ἐνῇ).[47] A poet is literally mindless, and so too his verses are meaningless. Given its deficiencies in content, poetry for Plato is effectively all form, and illegitimate at that. Hence his association of the non-semantic features of poems (music, harmony, and rhythm) with empty utterances in the *Ion*, and, in the next breath, his paradoxical praising to the sky of Tynnichus of Chalchis, "who never composed a poem worth remembering except the paean, which everyone sings, perhaps the most beautiful of all lyrics, a real 'windfall of the Muses,' as he says himself."[48] Poetry's form and its content, defined through mimesis, renders poetry ontologically and technically deficient. It is a travesty of true and original form, which has a metaphysical grounding beyond the material world.[49]

Aristotle's reply in his *Poetics* is that all that matters in tragedy, which for him is the consummate poetic genre, is its rational form, namely the unfolding action of a play (the *muthos*) in its internal logical unity and consistency. What counts on this view is not the poet's intention or meaning (or anything resembling "poetic content"), let alone poetry's correspondence with fact, but only poetic intelligibility insofar as this is embodied in literature's internal unity and consistency: its rational form (poetry's formal and final causes). Plato's complaints against poetry's harmfulness are thus neutralized.

Together, Plato and Aristotle built up a powerful argument for formalism that neither philosopher could quite control. In isolating (if only to disparage) the formal techniques of poetry, such as *mimēsis*

---

[46] Pl. *Ion* 530b–c (see p. 94 below); *Rep.* 2–3, 10.   [47] Pl. *Ion* 534b3–6; trans. Russell.
[48] Pl. *Ion* 534d.
[49] Plotinus would draw out the implications of his philosophical ancestor even more explicitly, as in *Enn.* 5.8.2: "Is not [true] beauty everywhere form (εἶδος) . . . [viz.,] the forming principle which is not in matter but in the maker, the first immaterial (ἄυλος) one . . . ?" (trans. Armstrong).

and *diēgēsis*, Plato paved the way for their independent analysis, and thus earned a place for himself in the history of literary theory. Aristotle refined Plato's insights, in part extending them and in part reversing them. A further powerful distinction the two philosophers of the fourth century made is more easily overlooked. It consisted in abstracting, aspectually, the sensuous dimensions of poetry. Only here, the contrast is no longer between form and content, but between form and *matter*. In order to examine each of their approaches to this question, which are surprisingly similar, it will be essential to take them up in turn.

Plato's formalism

Plato singles out, so as to restrict, the expressive elements of verbal artworks (rhythm, harmony [that is, mode or tuning], and movement), as, for instance, in *Republic* 3, where he discusses two kinds of expression:

"In one of them, the variations (μεταβολάς) are not great. If you give the expression its appropriate mode (ἁρμονίαν) and rhythm, a correct speaker is able to deliver the piece practically in one and the same mode – the variations are small – and in very much the same rhythm."

"Quite so."

"The other performer's type, on the other hand, needs the very opposite – all modes and all rhythms – if it is to be delivered appropriately, because of the manifold forms of its variations (παντοδαπὰς μορφὰς τῶν μεταβολῶν)."

"Certainly."[50]

Plato's preference obviously goes to the first performer, the "correct speaker" with the more restricted range of expressive possibilities. As elsewhere (for example, in the *Ion*), Plato is following a form/content distinction in which matters of form – modes of expression, such as harmonic mode (tuning)[51] and rhythm – are to be subordinated to meaning (*logos*).[52] Whether we reckon these features as form or matter makes little difference in the end, because what counts either way is the restriction that Plato puts on them both: *mimēsis*, and by extension all forms of art, must be as "unmixed" (ἄκρατον) as possible.[53] By this, he means that *mimēsis* must be pure and restricted in its expressive forms, uncontaminated by plurality and modality, change and alteration, shape-shifting, and plurivocality (in every sense of the word). Colors and

---

[50] Pl. *Rep.* 3.397b6–c6; trans. Russell, adapted. Cf. *Rep.* 3.399e8–10.
[51] On the modes, see Barker 1984, 163–68.   [52] *Rep.* 3.398d8–9.   [53] *Rep.* 3.397d5.

shapes are a bedazzlement to the senses and a distraction from the harder, cooler lines of truth:

"Similarly, we can say that the poet with his words and phrases lays on the colours of every art [with his specious imitative knowledge of alien spheres of learning], though all he understands of it is how to imitate it in such a way that other people like himself, judging by the words, think it all very fine if someone discusses cobbling or strategy or anything in metre, rhythm, and harmony. These have by their very nature such immense fascination (κήλησιν). I imagine you know what the content of poetry (τὰ τῶν ποιητῶν ... λεγόμενα) amounts to, stripped of the colours of music (γυμνωθέντα γε τῶν τῆς μουσικῆς χρωμάτων), just on its own (αὐτὰ ἐφ' αὑτῶν). You must have seen it."
"I have."
"It's like a pretty but not beautiful face, isn't it, when youth [literally, 'its bloom,' τὸ ἄνθος] has departed from it?"
"Exactly."[54]

The phenomenal and sensual aspects of art are like so many lures and distractions. Once these are stripped away, art uninformed by philosophy stands nakedly revealed and empty-handed. It has nothing to show, no beauty and no attractions: there is nothing left to see, or worth seeing. Philosophically informed art does not need the distractions of the sensual to reveal its beauties: they shine through for what they are. What is worse, the allurements of the sensual are intrinsically dangerous. For that reason, they are not only unnecessary, but also unwanted.[55]

That is why in Book 3 of the *Republic* Plato insists on an austere standard of purity in art. Not only are Homer and the other canonical poets banished from Callipolis, the ideal city, dirges and other songs of lamentation must also be eliminated along with their musical modes, the Mixolydian and the Syntonolydian, and others of the same kind. The Lydian and Ionian modes are likewise too "slack," too soft and convivial, and so too they must be banished, which leaves only two: the severe Dorian and Phrygian modes. Multi-stringed instruments and all polyharmony must likewise go, along with their kindred spirit among the wind instruments, the *aulos* (being "the most 'many-stringed' of all," presumably because it is capable of the greatest number of tonal inflections[56]), leaving the simpler lyre and the cithara, and the shepherd's

---

[54] *Rep.* 10.601a4–b8; trans. Russell.
[55] Cf. *Phd.* 100d (quoted at n. 74 below); and *Symp.* 211e (at n. 75 below).
[56] Cf. Pind. *Pyth.* 12.23, where the *aulos* is said to produce a "many-headed strain" (κεφαλᾶν πολλᾶν νόμον). Plato's strictures against the *aulos* are more comprehensible when read against the cultural history of the instrument, on which see Wilson 2003 and p. 323 below.

pipe. These are all capable of producing unimaginable variety (*poikilia*) – and whatever is *poikilos* is "never the same as itself."[57] Then Socrates pauses: "By the dog, without being aware of it, we've been purifying (διακαθαίϱοντες) the city we recently said was luxurious." "That's because we're being moderate." "Then let's purify (καθαίϱωμεν) the rest." He then turns to regulations on rhythm and meter, paralleling those that were established to govern modes and the rest.[58]

Plato's word choice, *purify*, is not haphazard. It is an essential component of his aesthetics, which is an aesthetics of rigorous and austere limits, indeed an aesthetics of purity. And that is virtually an oxymoron, because it presses the question of just how so narrow a range of objects and features could ever deliver an aesthetic experience at all. Platonic aesthetics is a minimal aesthetics. It is grounded in the most intense perception of the least amount of variability and fluctuation (or becoming) and in the greatest degree of changeless, unwavering, and unadulterated essences. As a consequence, it is unfriendly to the senses: it strives for an apprehension that is least contaminated by sensory interference. Matter and the body must be removed from view to the greatest possible extent so that Being in its translucent essence can shine through most purely – untarnished and untainted.

This is the tendency we have been observing in the *Republic*. And the tendency is even more pronounced in the *Philebus*, which is thought to be one of Plato's last works, and which contains one of his richest aesthetic (or rather anti-aesthetic) reflections.[59] There, he develops a notion of "unmixed pleasures" (ἄμεικτοι ἡδοναί) – the echo with the "unmixed *mimēsis*" of the *Republic* is unmistakable – pleasures which are "true," and which contain nothing of their opposite (pain), but which obtain only under limited and limiting circumstances. Unmixed pleasures arise in the face of "so-called" beautiful shapes and colors and other sensible properties, by which Plato understands those "*neither of living creatures nor of paintings*" (a rather firm limitation on art!)[60] but rather of geometrical figures, for instance, lines, circles, plane figures generally, and solids, drawn with mathematical precision and by instrument – or else whiteness, the color he names (for it is "the most perfectly clear" of all),

57 Pl. *Rep.* 8.568d. Cf. *Rep.* 3.399e, tilting against "great variety in meter," where the same term is used.
58 *Rep.* 3.399e (trans. Grube; rev. Reeve); 3.398e–399e.
59 Pl. *Phlb.* 50d–53c; *pace* Frede 1997, 299–300 (her special pleadings for Plato here fail to take into account his statements on art's severe limitations elsewhere in his writings, consistent with those in *Phlb.*).
60 *Phlb.* 51c.

which is to say, not so much the color but rather its essence, pure white, namely the very whiteness of white: white *in its whiteness*.[61]

Plato appears to be echoing Parmenides, who in his great poem took a firm line against phenomena generally and against color (and change) in particular: "Therefore [true Being] has been named all the names which mortals have laid down believing them to be true – coming to be and perishing, being and not being, changing place and *altering in bright colour*" (διά τε χρόα φανὸν ἀμείβειν).[62] Color is objectionable – not a property worthy of true Being – *because it just is an alteration of the visible spectrum*, unlike white, which represents visuality in its purest, most limpid, and unchanging condition. Plato would doubtless have approved of Hegel, who took the next logical step and freed color from its physical contingencies to the fullest possible extent, "dematerializing" it, and reducing it to its minimal precondition, that of pure, disembodied, and colorless *light* (which he evidently did not conceive of as a physical entity, at least not in its aesthetic aspect)[63] – though whiteness borders on the brightness and brilliance of colorless light already.[64] In the same passage from the *Philebus*, Plato also names "smooth and clear [or 'bright'] sounds" heard singly as individual notes ("issuing forth a single pure *melos*") and untrammeled by harmonies, relations, or aural decay.[65] In fact, all the aesthetic objects commended by Plato are not "beautiful relative to anything else (πρός τι), as other things are. On the contrary, they are forever beautiful in and of themselves (καθ᾽ αὐτά) by their very nature (πεφυκέναι), and they are possessed of proper pleasures" (ἡδονὰς οἰκείας).[66] Such pleasures are, like their objects, "pure" (καθαραί and εἰλικρινεῖς), in contrast to all others, which are

---

[61] *Phlb.* 53a–b, pursuing the question, "What would *purity of whiteness* [viz., pure white] be for us?" (πῶς οὖν ἂν λευκοῦ καὶ τίς καθαρότης ἡμῖν εἴη;) "*Plainly it will be the most perfectly clear color.*" (τὸ μάλιστ᾽ εἰλικρινὲς ὄν.) "You are right." *Leukos* seems to have even less substance than *white* in Greek. It denotes *shining, bright,* or *pale.* See Platnauer 1921, 156; Sorabji 1972, 294.

[62] DK 28B8.38–41; trans. K–R–S.

[63] Hegel 1975, ii:810: "Light as such remains colourless, the pure indeterminacy of identity with itself. Colour, which in contrast to light is something relatively dark, entails something different from light, a murkiness with which the principle of light is united, and it is therefore a bad and false idea to suppose that light is compounded out of different colours, i.e. out of different darkenings." Cf. Schuhl's apt phrase for Plato's vision, in the *Phaedrus*, of a "paysage immatériel, sans couleur et sans forme, mais baigné d'une pure lumière" (Schuhl 1952, 42). The allusion is to *Phdr.* 250b–c, esp. the words ἐν αὐγῇ καθαρᾷ, where a final revelation of Beauty is described: "pure was that light that shone around us," etc. Cf. also *Symp.* 210d3–8 on "the great sea of beauty" upon which one "gazes," which turns out to be "knowledge, the knowledge of such beauty"; and *Rep.* 6.507b9–508b4, in praise of light, which makes sight "the most sunlike of the senses." More seemingly tolerant of the color spectrum is the account in *Phd.* 100d–e – only a myth, to be sure.

[64] See n. 61 above.   [65] *Phlb.* 51d6.   [66] *Phlb.* 51c–d.

"impure" (ἀκάθαρτοι).⁶⁷ By "all others" we may understand phenomenal pleasures, because Plato's pleasures here are *barely* phenomenal, and indeed they are more akin to the pleasures of learning than to anything else.⁶⁸ Their object, after all, is eternal. They are beautiful, but only in a manner of speaking (τὰ καλὰ λεγόμενα).⁶⁹ They are glimpses of Forms.⁷⁰

They are glimpses of Forms, and not only of formalist aesthetic objects, which is why the following comment on the passage is misleading: "As an aesthetician Plato favors non-objective art; he would enjoy the work of Mondrian or Bauer."⁷¹ (figs. 2.1 and 2.2) This cannot be right. Paintings are explicitly ruled out by Plato, as we just saw.⁷² But Plato's objection is aimed not only at paintings, but at *paint.*⁷³ Elsewhere, in the *Phaedo*, he scoffs at "bright (εὐανθές) color, shape, or any such thing," all of which he finds "confusing" (ταράττομαι).⁷⁴ And he betrays a similar antipathy

---

⁶⁷ *Phlb.* 52c–d.
⁶⁸ *Phlb.* 51e7. "Barely," but still clinging, nonetheless, to a phenomenal "skin," which they cannot ever quite shed. Does Plato ever really *want* them to shed their ties to materiality? His erotic investment in Forms, which goes beyond protreptic seduction, speaks against this possibility, at least in places, as do other features of his metaphysics. See Carpenter 1959, 107, Morgan 2000, 182–84, and Nightingale 2004, 79–83 on this stubborn persistence. And see the acute remark by Merleau-Ponty 1964, 200: "Disons seulement que l'idéalité pure n'est pas elle-même sans chair ni délivrée des structures d'horizon: elle en vit, quoiqu'il s'agisse d'un autre chair et d'autres horizons. C'est comme si la visibilité qui anime le monde sensible émigrait, *non pas hors de tout corps, mais dans un autre corps* moins lourd, plus transparent, comme si elle changeait de chair, abandonnant celle du corps pour celle du langage, et affranchie par là, *mais non délivrée, de toute condition*" (emphasis added). It is in their ambivalence to matter – attaching themselves to it while also straining to break free from it – that ideals attain their own degree of (material) sublimity.
⁶⁹ *Phlb.* 51b3.
⁷⁰ So, too (or nearly so), Schuhl 1952, 42. The question whether Plato in this late dialogue is still contemplating Forms is fraught, and the literature is divided. Geometrical shapes are said to be divine at 62a–b, and much else besides points to a source of knowledge and truth that exceeds human limits, which is all that "glimpses" here need indicate. Plotinus certainly got the message right. See *Enn.* 1.6.5, describing the ecstasy of lovers in the face of "inward beauty," which is patently immaterial and also permeated with Plato's language of Forms: the source of their ecstasy is "not shape or colour or any size, but soul, without colour itself and possessing amoral order without colour and possessing all the other light of the virtues...." (trans. Armstrong); cf. Pl. *Phdr.* 279b9: "inward beauty"; ibid., 247c6, describing Forms as being "without color or shape."
⁷¹ Davidson 1990, 378. Cf. Murdoch 1978, 16, likewise, and interestingly, ruling out the paintings of Mondrian and Ben Nicholson, "which might be thought of as meeting [Plato's] requirements."
⁷² *Phlb.* 51c2–3: "neither living creatures nor paintings."
⁷³ "Paintings" (ζωγραφήματα) implies this alone. Cf. Pl. *Crat.* 431c, where the same term is now linked to "color." This is true despite the sprinkling of comments elsewhere which might appear to indicate an interest on Plato's part in painting (so, for example, Halliwell 2000) – an interest that can at best be described as a (cautious) blend of "ethical expression, idealization and beauty" (ibid., 113). Halliwell's closing comment is closest to the truth: for Plato "philosophers are ... painters in a different medium," and ultimately "interpreters of a cosmic work of art" (ibid., 115).
⁷⁴ *Phd.* 100d; trans. Grube. Plato's immediate point is that the cause of beauty in things is their participation in Beauty, not their phenomenal properties. Cf. ibid., 79c for closely similar language used to depict the material world of the senses.

Fig. 2.1 Piet Mondrian, *Composition.* 1921. Jacques and Natasha Gelman Collection, 1998. Metropolitan Museum of Art.

in the *Symposium*, where he speaks of "the Beautiful itself, absolute, pure, unmixed, not polluted by human flesh or colors or any other great nonsense of mortality."[75] Rather, Plato would have approved of the fetching prospect of Goethe's neoclassical Altar of Good Fortune in his garden at Weimar (1777), which consisted of a plain stone sphere and

---

[75] *Symp.* 211e; trans. Nehamas and Woodruff. Plato's purist language is striking, and severe: αὐτὸ τὸ καλὸν ἰδεῖν εἰλικρινές, καθαρόν, ἄμεικτον; cf. ibid., 211a–b: beauty never takes on a bodily or material appearance, but "itself by itself with itself, it is always one in form" (αὐτὸ καθ᾿ αὐτὸ μεθ᾿ αὑτοῦ μονοειδὲς ἀεὶ ὄν). I suspect that his language is inflected with Anaxagorean attributes of Mind, which is said to be "mixed with nothing" (or "with no matter" or "appearances": μέμεικται οὐδενὶ χρήματι; see Rivier 1956, 59 at n. 3), "the finest of all things and the purest" (λεπτότατόν τε ... καὶ καθαρώτατον), and "all alone by itself" (μόνος αὐτὸς ἐπ᾿ ἑωυτοῦ ἐστιν) (DK 59B12 = Simp. *in Ph.* 156.13–15, 19–20; trans. K–R–S). Nicholas Denyer (*per litt.*) adds that "the insistent repetitions of *kalon* and *aischron* in *Symp.* 210e–211b are reminiscent of Anaxagoras stylistically also." In the same way, Plato's hostility to color and motion appear to be further derived from, or at least in harmony with, Parmenides (DK 28B8.38–41). Additional echoes in a similar vein: Pl. *Tim.* 33c–d: the Demiurge made the world perfectly self-contained (πάντα ἐν ἑαυτῷ καὶ ὑφ᾿ ἑαυτοῦ).

Fig. 2.2 Rudolf Bauer, "Prison Drawing." 1938. Private collection.

a plain stone cube, both colorless, the former representing the labile desires, the latter stable virtue (fig. 2.3).[76] The *Timaeus*' limited, abstract geometries essentially confirms this[77] (see fig. 2.4). Art and phenomena in their sensuous appearances are simply uninteresting to Plato. What appeals to him is something that lies well beyond appearances, a world uninhabited by matter or even people, a "place beyond the heavens [which] none of our poets has yet sung" or "shall sing worthily ... It is there that true Being dwells, without colour or shape, [and] cannot be

[76] See Rosenblum 1967, 150–51 for an account of Goethe's creation, esp. 151: "Such a complete purification, however, was more of an exercise in symbolic geometry than a creative work of sculpture or architecture."

[77] See *Tim.* 33b–34b on the formal perfections of the sphere, and the rest of the dialogue on other basic geometrical solids. Perhaps we should say that if Plato were to appreciate Mondrian's paintings, it would not be *qua* their being colored but *qua* their being geometric, outlined, with bare lines describing bare shapes, and so on, that is, for their purely abstracted form. For an interesting later echo, see Arist. *Metaph.* I. 2, which locates a host of formal purities, expressed in terms of formal "unities," in the following objects or features: the color white, the melodic quarter-tone, the vowel among letters, and the triangle among rectilinear figures. Further on, Aristotle adds, in this seemingly Platonizing mood, "Other things, if they have a quality that is *in form one and the same* (ἐν τῷ εἴδει) – e.g. whiteness (τὸ λευκόν) – in a greater or less degree, are called like *because their form is one*" (ibid., I. 3.1054b9–10; trans. W. D. Ross). Thanks to Gregory Hutchinson for drawing this obscure connection from Aristotle to my attention.

Fig. 2.3 Goethe's *Altar der Agathe Tyche* (*Altar of Good Fortune*). 1777. Weimar.
Conceived by Goethe, and designed by Goethe and the architect Adam Friedrich Oeser
for Goethe's garden in Weimar, where it still stands.

touched; reason alone, the soul's pilot, can behold it," for it is the locus of
metaphysical truth and knowledge.[78] Attempts to rescue from Plato's
writings a Platonic theory of visual art in some positive form, rather than
seeing in the momentary concessions to the arts made in the dialogues a
series of rich attestations to contemporary and historical attitudes, are
overly optimistic, if not somewhat desperate.[79]

Plato has other ways of attacking the substance of art, in particular
poetry. Here, he creates what we might today call a form/content distinction, though on closer inspection that division amounts to something

[78] Pl. *Phdr.* 247c; trans. Hackforth.
[79] For the former, see Halliwell 2000 (who does not confront the passages quoted here); contrast, e.g.,
Steiner 2001, 63–78. For the latter approach (Plato as sourcebook), see Rouveret 1989. To be sure,
Plato's works represent much more than a set of testimonia: he offers an exciting reaction to
contemporary views and a new synthesis of his own.

Fig. 2.4 Nicoletto da Modena. *Apelles.* 1500–22. Engraving. New York, The Metropolitan Museum of Art. Apelles is shown contemplating pure geometric forms and a framing square, the tools of a draftsman, not of a painter.

like a matter/content distinction, or if one prefers, one between appearances and value or truth. (Plato will, of course, nullify both halves of the distinction whenever poets are at issue.) A case in point is to be found in the *Ion*, where Socrates claims to envy the lot of rhapsodes, who dress up in fancy robes and "look as handsome as possible" in order to occupy themselves with the finest of poets, "and Homer above all, the best and divinest of all, and [in this way, rhapsodes] learn not only his words (τὰ ἔπη) but his meaning" (τὴν διάνοιαν).[80] By "words" (or "verses") Plato plainly has in mind not only the text of Homer learned by rote and reproduced "mindlessly" by rhapsodes in performance, but also the aesthetic qualities of the verses, such as harmony and rhythm, which are irrelevant to the core meanings of the poetry and do not carry over in the course of their being rendered into prose – the very features of verse that make it a perfect conduit for inspiration and possession (its "pretty face," as Plato puts it in *Republic* 10).[81]

What Plato says of epic poets also applies to lyric poets, because "every individual poet can only compose well what the Muse has set him to do": "Just as Corybantic dancers perform when they are not in their right mind, so the lyric poets compose these beautiful songs when they are not in their right mind (οὐκ ἔμφρονες); once involved in harmony and rhythm, they are in a state of possession."[82] When Plato says that poets are possessed and "not in their right mind," we need to understand this in a quite literal sense: because the god has "taken away their mind" (their νοῦς), the poets haven't got a thought in their heads, which are instead filled with rhythmic impulses flowing from a divine source that lies beyond all art (τέχνη) and about which they are helpless to comment on intelligently (whence Ion's hapless condition).[83] They are all form (or rather empty show, performance, or appearance) and no content. Their only modality is one of *aisthēsis*: "[they] keenly perceive (αἰσθάνονται ὀξέως) only the tune (τοῦ μέλους) that belongs to the god."[84] Or so Plato would have us believe. Plato's reduction and dismissal of the two components of poetry, its words and its music, is extreme and parodic. His gesture builds on earlier developments in the critical traditions to be discussed below, both among the sophists (Gorgias and his pupil Licymnius spring to mind), but also among the poets and the musicians themselves. Thus, in driving a wedge between meaning and its trappings, Plato is not innovating – that conceptual division was achieved earlier (as we shall see). He is merely radicalizing and in a sense emptying out those earlier gestures, leaving poets and critics alike with next to nothing to work with, and above all with no positive motivations for wishing to do so.

---

[80] Pl. *Ion* 530b–c; trans. Russell.   [81] *Rep.* 10.601b6 (quoted on p. 86 above).
[82] *Ion* 534c2–3; 533e8–534a3.   [83] *Ion* 534c8; 533d–534c.
[84] *Ion* 536c3; trans. adapted. Strictly, Corybants are meant, but poets are included by analogy.

Where does this leave Plato as a "formalist," aesthetically speaking? A comparison with Kant can be illuminating. Appearances notwithstanding, Plato is no Kantian: he is not enamored of pure forms for the sake of their formal *aesthetic* purity. Quite the contrary, the two philosophers differ entirely on the role and primacy of experience in aesthetics. The point is worth underscoring briefly. Kant, for example, treats simple colors and tones as in themselves a synthesis of a manifold of sensations, which is to say, as a "formal determination" of a complex event,[85] whereas for Plato metaphysics short-circuits sensuous perception. Moreover, Kant views the purity of colors and tones not as intrinsically valuable, but as a spur to a more enhanced appreciation of the "form" of the presentation of the object of the sensation: empirical properties direct the mind more concertedly to the object they inhere in, and they sustain attention to it, though what counts in the end is not anything in the object but only its presentation to the subject, which is to say, its aesthetic perception.[86] In this respect, Kant's view is closer to Aristotle's, though in one respect all three thinkers converge: Aristotle, like Plato before him and like Kant later on, favors clear (formal) outlines over (sensuous) colors and textures. Comparing plot to the situation of a painting, Aristotle writes, tellingly, "the most beautiful colours (τοῖς καλλίστοις φαρμάκοις), if smeared on at random, would give less pleasure (εὐφραίνειν) than an outline picture of something in black and white (λευκογραφήσας εἰκόνα)."[87] The obvious implication is that a plot just is this outline in its formal essence, its *ousia*, which is being defined in this very section, and the way it is later described – for instance, in chapter 17 of the same work, where what one "sees" is the universal form ("this is what I mean by 'seeing in general terms'" [θεωρεῖσθαι τὸ καθόλου]), not its particular, materiate embodiment.[88] Needless to say, such "seeing" is hardly phenomenal in character.

---

[85] *CJ* §14; Ak. 224.   [86] Ibid.

[87] Arist. *Poet.* 6.1450b1–3; trans. adapted. Cf. Plut. *Mor.* 16B–C for the alignment of color with sensual (and deceptive) stimulation and line drawing with rational plausibility.

[88] Arist. *Poet.* 17.1455b2–3. Colors, by contrast to bare (minimal) plot-outlines, are analogized in the earlier passage to speeches expressive of character and well composed in reasoning and in diction (1450a29–30), as the commentaries note too. *Leukographia* may denote a preliminary sketch for a painting, though the exact procedure Aristotle has in mind is unclear (white background or white markings); see Lucas, ad loc.; Keuls 1978, 93. The sense of preliminariness fits well with ch. 17; Aristotle's interest in color is secondary and negligible, as at *Poet.* 4.1448b19. Cf. Kant, *CJ* §14, p. 110; Ak. 225: "In painting and sculpture, indeed in all the pictorial arts ... the *drawing* (*Zeichnung*) is what is essential, in which what constitutes the ground of all arrangements for taste is not what gratifies in sensation but merely *what pleases through its form*. The colors that illuminate *the outline* (*Abriß*) belong to charm; they can of course enliven the object in itself for

Aristotle's formalism: his theory of beauty in the Poetics

Now to Aristotle. Like Plato, Aristotle tends to scant the material, sensuous, and phenomenal aspects of poetry (song, dance, spectacle, meter, and language as expression [*lexis*]). Unlike Plato, he favors poetry's formal and discursive aspects: action, character, as revelatory of action and functionally subordinated to action, thought, as revelatory of character – but *not* as revelatory of poetic "meaning," let alone of the poet's meaning, neither of which has any relevance for Aristotle. For Aristotle, poetry's "content" just is its final form, but it is *nothing other than* this final form: take away the form of a tragedy, and nothing will be left over – this, in contrast to Plato's more conventional view that formal properties are the dressing to a removable content, albeit one that in the case of poetry turns out to have little to recommend it.

In making these distinctions in his *Poetics*, Aristotle is doing more than simply outlining a theory of tragedy or of poetics. He is developing a theory of aesthetic perception. Just as Plato "use[s] painting . . . as a synecdoche for the figurative arts as a whole," so too, one suspects, "tragedy" is covertly doing double duty for literature in its essential and perfected form for Aristotle: for tragedy culminates the progression of literary history from epic, and it surpasses every other genre in poetic mimesis.[89] By the same token, Aristotle's theory of poetics is a way of elaborating a more general theory of aesthetics (roughly, the experience and perception of works of art), one we would not be far off the mark in calling formalist – with the caveat that nothing strictly corresponds to "form" in his treatise, and that the label is, as it were, more for our benefit than it is for Aristotle's.[90]

The first point about literature is not terribly hard to make. The treatise is after all titled *On Poetics*, not *On Tragedy*, and the first line of the work singles out its focus: "poetry itself," or rather "the poetic [art] itself" (περὶ ποιητικῆς αὐτῆς), where the intensive pronoun does the work of abstraction, immunizing it from other kinds of consideration, at least initially. Above all, introducing the category "itself" protects the focus of the *Poetics* from the kinds of critique that Plato, Zoilus, Protagoras, and

---

sensation, but they cannot make it worthy of being intuited and beautiful, rather they are often even considerably restricted by what is required by *beautiful form*, and even where charm is permitted it is ennobled only through the former" (emphasis added).

[89] See Halliwell 2000, 103 (on Plato).

[90] In defense of the label, one could always invoke the (too-little explored) parallelism between tragedy's essence (οὐσία) and the equivalence of essence and εἶδος (form) in other of his writings, e.g., *Metaphysics* Z.

others had lodged against poetry, whether on the grounds of morality, representation, or grammar, and which Aristotle can now dislodge as lying "outside the art" and thus beyond the proper purview of poetry (as in chapter 25), or as we would say today, literature (there being no Greek term for literature, as Aristotle laments[91]). This by itself constitutes a move in the direction of an aesthetic reading of poetry. Indeed, the whole of the treatise sets up the conditions by which a properly poetic, or aesthetic, judgment of poetry (in the guise of tragedy) can be passed, whereby tragedy seems to offer the most auspicious conditions for fulfilling the aesthetic experience of poetry: here, poetry can be experienced in its purest and most concentrated form.[92]

Whence the focus on formal unity, but also its surveyability – the one (formal unity) pertaining to the object, the other (surveyability) to its apprehension by us (the beholder's share). But in establishing these conditions, Aristotle occasionally crosses the line that would divide poetry from aesthetic objects generally. The criterion of excellence in both is quite explicitly the criterion of a successful aesthetic *experience*, and this turns out to be beauty. Consider the following from chapter 7 of the *Poetics*:

It is not enough for *beauty* (τὸ καλόν) that a thing, whether an animal or anything else composed of parts (ὃ συνέστηκεν ἐκ τινῶν), should have those parts well-ordered (τεταγμένα); the thing must also have amplitude (μέγεθος) – and not just any amplitude. For *beauty* consists in amplitude as well as in order (ἐν μεγέθει καὶ τάξει), which is why a very small (πάμμικρον) creature could not be *beautiful*, since our view (ἡ θεωρία) loses all distinctness (συγχεῖται) when it comes near to taking no *perceptible time* (τοῦ ἀναισθήτου χρόνου γινομένη), and an enormously ample one (παμμέγεθες) could not be *beautiful* either, since our view of it is not simultaneous (οὐ γὰρ ἅμα ἡ θεωρία γίνεται), so that we lose the sense of its unity and wholeness as we look it over (οἴχεται τοῖς θεωροῦσι τὸ ἓν καὶ τὸ ὅλον ἐκ τῆς θεωρίας); imagine, for instance, an animal a thousand miles long. Animate and inanimate bodies, then, must have amplitude, but no more than can be taken in at one view (εὐσύνοπτον); and similarly a plot must have extension (μῆκος), but no more than can be easily remembered.[93]

Aristotle here is a far cry from repeating Plato's analogy between the literary whole and an organic totality (an animal, a ζῷον, with a beginning, middle, and end).[94] Much as Aristotle subscribes to this notion of the objective totality of a work of art, here his interest lies, for once, in the

---

[91] *Poet.* 1.1447b9–10.
[92] See *Poet.*, ch. 26; "more concentrated" (ἀθροώτερον): ibid., 1462b1. Similarly, Else 1938, 194–95.
[93] *Poet.* 7.1450b34–1451a6; trans. Hubbard, adapted; emphasis added.
[94] Pl. *Phdr.* 264c.

modalities of aesthetic *appearances* – not unity and wholeness (τὸ ἓν καὶ τὸ ὅλον), but these qualities as they exist in the eye and the mind of the beholder. Nor is this all. Aristotle's conception of beauty in this passage seems to include *two* distinct but equally necessary perceptions. There is the perception of the object, and there is the perception of the time it takes to perceive the object. This latter element is crucial: the time of an aesthetic perception must *itself* be aesthetically perceptible (*aisthētos*). If a perceptual object requires no perceptible time to be taken in, the aesthetic perception as a whole, Aristotle says, will be marred.[95] *Beauty*, in other words, *cannot be glimpsed*: it must be perceived, and it must be perceived *as such*, almost in a second-order fashion. That is, beauty must be the object, if not of a glimpse, then at least of a self-contained *look* with a certain, palpable amplitude. Here, Aristotle puts us in mind of Shklovsky's emphasis on perceptual lingering and vivacity – only so can one have a truly aesthetic perception, which involves not just an experience of an object, but also an experiencing of the experience itself. As Shklovsky adds in the same essay ("Art as Technique"), "the technique of art is to . . . increase the length of perception because the process of perception is an aesthetic *end in itself* and must be prolonged."[96] And yet, Aristotle insists, stretch the look beyond the boundaries of a manageable, eusynoptic totality, and the conditions of beauty will be spoiled once again, this time in the other direction. If we sense in Aristotle an argument against Plato, we are probably not far wrong. Indeed, as if making a *reductio ad absurdum* of the analogy to organic wholes in Plato, Aristotle adds, with a kind of petulancy that is rare, "imagine, for instance, an animal a thousand miles long!," the point being a good one: in itself, symmetrical totality – the mutual correspondence of parts within a self-enclosed whole[97] – is insufficient to render an object aesthetic (that is, the object of aesthetic perception and experience).

Aristotle, to be sure, has a long list of additional features that render a tragedy aesthetic, or rather a consummate instantiation of its genre, and these have to do with its conditions of intelligibility (the logical inter-weaving of probability and necessity in the plot) and its fulfillment of its proper end. But here, in chapter 7, he is concerned with *to kalon* (beauty).[98] The term *kalos* appears twenty-one times in the *Poetics* in

---

[95] It will also lack a basic and defining trait of phenomenal sensation. See n. 109 below.
[96] Shklovsky 1965 [1917], 12; emphasis added.
[97] τεταγμένα (Aristotle); πρέποντα ἀλλήλοις (Pl. *Phdr.* 264c5; cf. πρέπουσαν ἀλλήλοις, ibid., 268d5).
[98] Which would go far to account for the far greater complexity of this definition of *eusynoptic* as compared with that offered in *Rh.* 3.9 (1409b1) or *Rh.* 3.12 (1414a12).

different forms, but only seven or (doubtfully) eight of these occurrences
have a narrowly aesthetic meaning, as opposed to their being used in a
normative sense (for example, as applied to a "well-" or "better-made" or
"best" tragedy).⁹⁹ Four of these "aesthetic" uses appear in the passage just
quoted. Of the rest, two occur in the context of painting – the first in
chapter 6, in a discussion of "pretty" (viz., colorful) paints daubed "at
random" on a surface,¹⁰⁰ and the second in chapter 15, where Aristotle
notes that tragedians imitate characters "better" (βελτιόνων) than ourselves, while painters, appearing to paint likenesses of individuals, in fact
render them "more beautiful" (καλλίους) than they really are.¹⁰¹
The seventh occurrence is in chapter 22, where it has to do with the
aesthetic quality of a verse; its contrasting quality is εὐτελές, "tawdry" or
"unimpressive."¹⁰² The last occurrence, which is also the earliest, is
overwhelmingly sociological: καλὰς πράξεις, "noble [viz., fine] actions,"
even though we have to allow that such categories can take on aesthetic
qualities too.¹⁰³

Plainly, some other consideration than that of Aristotle's operative
model in most of the remainder of the treatise is at work here in
chapter 7.¹⁰⁴ Elsewhere, Aristotle's overriding concern is with tragedy's
conditions of intelligibility, which are linked to its formal organization
(its plot or *muthos*), but never to its beauty. Indeed, the overall absence of
any concern for beauty in the *Poetics*, with the one concentrated exception
of the present passage, is striking – and something of an anomaly in the
history of Greek aesthetic thought. To put the matter most simply,
tragedies are not essentially beautiful for Aristotle. Beauty is not part of their
final goal, let alone part of their definition (*Poetics*, chapter 6).¹⁰⁵

---

⁹⁹ I am assuming a simple distinction between normative and descriptive (aesthetic) uses of the term
for the sake of the argument. To be sure, in practice no such rigid distinction ultimately exists, but
nothing prevents Aristotle (or us) from pretending that it does. When he writes of epic that "its
reasonings and expression must (δεῖ) be fine" (ἔχειν καλῶς) at 1459b11–12, the obligation to
fineness is a perfect case of the distinction having been blurred – though not so blurred that "must
be beautiful" could be deemed an adequate rendering for δεῖ ... ἔχειν καλῶς. On the contrary,
καλῶς ἔχειν means "be of an appropriate level of aesthetic refinement and quality for the genre,"
its commonest meaning in the *Poetics*.
¹⁰⁰ *Poet.* 6.1450b1–2.   ¹⁰¹ *Poet.* 15.1454b8–11.   ¹⁰² *Poet.* 22.1458b21–22.
¹⁰³ *Poet.* 4.1448b25. At 25.1461a14 καλῶς (occurring twice) has a clear moral sense.
¹⁰⁴ This difference escapes Halliwell 1986, 97–99, who is concerned only with conditions of
intelligibility in the passage.
¹⁰⁵ This is true, even if (and especially if) Aristotle is capable of expressing the notion of formal and
final causes in terms of beauty, as in *Part. an.* 1.5.645a22–26): "Each and all [kinds of animals in
nature] will reveal to us something natural and something beautiful (τινὸς φυσικοῦ καὶ καλοῦ).
Absence of haphazard and conduciveness of everything to an end are to be found in nature's works
in the highest degree, and the end for which those works are put together and produced occupies

And yet, given this passage from chapter 7 of the *Poetics*, we would nonetheless have to say that tragedies *are* in some basic sense beautiful even for Aristotle: they fulfill all the conditions of the aesthetic experience outlined there. It is just that tragedies must do all of this and much more; and this "much more" is what gives them their distinctive and essential quality. Thus, the passage from chapter 7 is interesting precisely because it brings to the fore a more general set of aesthetic criteria, one that we can assume underlies all perceptions of beauty in Aristotle's eyes. Those criteria are in keeping with another key pronouncement by Aristotle, this time from the *Metaphysics*, where he singles out "order, symmetry, and definiteness" as the three main constituents of beauty: "The chief forms (εἴδη) of beauty are order and symmetry and definiteness (τάξις καὶ συμμετρία καὶ τὸ ὡρισμένον), which the mathematical sciences demonstrate in a special degree."[106] But while the passage from chapter 7 of the *Poetics* is consistent with this somewhat traditional definition of the elements of beauty from the *Metaphysics* (traditional, to judge from the only explicit contemporary theoretical statements we have and can use to compare, those of Polyclitus and Plato),[107] the *Poetics* passage spells out a far more demanding standard of beauty, one that involves time, perception, considerations of magnitude or dimension, and of the relativity of magnitude or dimension to time and perception.[108]

The concession to beauty in chapter 7 is nonetheless brief and out of character given the general tenor of the *Poetics*, and Aristotle quickly retreats from his momentary phenomenalism[109] in order to reassert the priority of the true essence of tragedy *qua* art (τέχνη) over its realization in

the place of the beautiful" (τὴν τοῦ καλοῦ χώραν εἴληφεν) (trans. Ogle, adapted). It can be no accident that in both passages Aristotle is talking about animals. (There are other parallels too.) The two passages are still very different, as they focus on different kinds of perception.

[106] Arist. *Metaph.* M 3.1078b1–5; trans. Ross.

[107] Pl. *Soph.* 235e–236a; *Tim.* 87c–d; *Phlb.* 64e–65a. On Polyclitus, see Ch. 3, §9 and Ch. 5, §1, below.

[108] Indeed, in rejecting the sufficiency of order (τάξις) as a criterion of beauty, the *Poetics* passage supersedes the *Metaphysics* passage. Symmetry has no clear place in the *Poetics* passage, while definiteness is being given a clearer meaning.

[109] Such phenomenalism is what his requirement about the time of perception amounts to emerges most clearly from *Sens.* 6.446b1–13: "Now, even if one always hears and has heard – and, in general, perceives and has perceived – at the same time (ἅμα) . . . yet . . . the local movement takes place in the space between," involving a lag in time between the source and the experience of the sensation. "For certainly it is not true that the beholder sees, and the object is seen, in virtue of some merely abstract relationship between them, such as that between equals" (trans. Beare). That is, phenomenal perception (of actually perceptible magnitudes) takes time. *Aesthetic* perception, as defined in *Poet.* 7, flourishes in this gap in between; it is a *tarrying* over an object and a luxuriating in the perception – an experiencing, we might say (along with Shklovsky and others) of the experience. (But see Ch. 1 at n. 91 on Aristotle's notion of perceiving that one is perceiving.)

"performances (ἀγῶνας) and perception" (αἴσθησιν) on the stage – indeed, he does so in the very next breath in the same chapter. What Aristotle is observing is in fact a tension between the demands of performance on stage on the one hand and the formal demands of "the art itself" or else – what amounts to the same thing – "the very nature of the matter" (κατ᾽ αὐτὴν τὴν φύσιν τοῦ πϱάγματος), which is to say, the plot, on the other.[110] The latter criteria are not fundamentally determined with an eye to their being taken in by the senses, but only with a view to their being understood intellectually and remembered: hence, they must be "clear" (σύνδηλος) and "easily remembered" (εὐμνημόνευτον), and the like.[111] Aesthetics is not "aesthetic" for Aristotle, at least not in the initial sense of "sensuous perception" that I am trying to establish in this study.[112]

His momentary digression into beauty notwithstanding, Aristotle is and remains a staunch formalist. The mere separation, in theory, of the material and formal causes of poetry is itself a formalistic gesture. *Formalism consists in this very abstraction.* It generates aspectual categories, effectively identifying the "essence" of poetic works with the fulfillment of aspectual, and ranked, duties. One tendency of formalism is to lapse into essentialism (as here, in the case of Aristotle). Plato had already ventured in this direction, setting to work his powerful logical invention, the distinction between relatives (πϱός τι) and absolutes (καθ᾽ αὐτά), as we saw.[113] Aristotle follows suit, but changes the values. For Aristotle, the isolation of the essence of poetry yields a recognition of the fundamental poetic quality of poetic works: isolated is what he calls "*the poetic art itself*" viewed "*in and of itself*" (καθ᾽ ἑαυτήν); a work of art is to be judged *per se* (αὐτὸ καθ᾽ αὑτὸ κϱῖναι), not with respect to extrinsic criteria, which oddly enough include, in the case of tragedy, the conditions of performance, the work *qua* performed in public ([τὰ] πϱὸς τὰ θέατϱα) as opposed to its being read in private.[114] This last point deserves further emphasis, as it is a central if rarely appreciated feature of Aristotle's theory of tragic form. Aristotle's theory is constructed around a series of rather

---

[110] Arist. *Poet.* 7.1451a6–15.   [111] Arist. *Poet.* 7.1451a5; a10.
[112] See also Else 1967, 295, n. 31: "One factor, undoubtedly, is [Aristotle's] tendency to equate aesthetic experience with αἴσθησις, which he has ruled out ([*Poet.* 7.1451]a7) as a serious criterion." Cf. Grassi 1962, 141, for a different explanation of this deficiency (one I find dubious): the kind of beauty described briefly in *Poet.* ch. 7 is fundamentally architectural, not poetic, a "rendering palpable of ontological beauty, which cannot be given in [poetic] art." Aristotle's minimally acceptable "perceptions" (*aisthēseis*) would also apply at *Poet.* 15.1454b15–16.
[113] On this tool, see Owen 1957 and Fine 1995.   [114] Arist. *Poet.* 4.1449a8–9.

outré assertions that must have struck his contemporaries with at least as much force as they ought to strike us today. I will call these Aristotle's "heresies" and will merely list them with a minimum of commentary.[115]

Aristotle's heresies

Contra Aristotle, who assigns spectacle (ὄψις) and song (μέλος) only to the garnishings (ἡδύσματα) of tragedy – and thereby sanctions the *Lesedrama* already. (Nietzsche)[116]

The following remarks by Aristotle give us clues to the essential character of tragedy:

§1 Anatomical impossibility (a horse represented with both front legs thrown forward) is not the error *of the poet*. "Error *in the art of poetry itself* is of two sorts, (a) error in *the art itself* (καθ᾽ αὑτήν), (b) error by coincidence (κατὰ συμβεβηκός)."[117]

Related to this is Aristotle's de-emphasis, throughout the *Poetics*, on the individual contribution of the poet relative to the autonomous or intrinsic functioning of the work itself, which takes logical precedence, as in "[recognitions] made up by the poet";[118] contrast solutions to the plot that arise "*from the plot itself*" or effects arising "*from the structure of the incidents itself*."[119]

§2 Without action a tragedy cannot exist, but *without characters it may*.[120]

§3 The potential of tragedy exists even *without a performance and actors*.[121]

---

[115] Translations are from Janko 1987, with occasional adaptations. Janko is more literal in these sections than Hubbard.

[116] Nietzsche 1988, VII:78 (1869/70).   [117] *Poet.* 25.1460b15–16.

[118] αἱ πεποιημέναι ὑπὸ τοῦ ποιητοῦ (*Poet.* 16.1454b30–31).

[119] ἐξ αὐτοῦ τοῦ μύθου; ἐξ αὐτῆς τῆς συστάσεως τῶν πραγμάτων (*Poet.* 15.1454a37; 14.1453b2–3). I originally discussed **§1** in Porter 1992, 77–80. See further Rosenmeyer 1973.

[120] *Poet.* 6.1450a23–25. Halliwell 1986, 57 and 163–64 seeks to blunt the sharp edges of **§2**. While one can say (ibid., 163) that "Aristotle notes the possibility of dispensing with tragic characterisation, [but] does not recommend it," it is just as true that Aristotle never softens his claim or retracts it (cf. *Poet.* 6.1450a25–29 contrasting Zeuxis and Polygnotus on the same question). The *Poetics* is sprinkled with such startling counterintuitions. And these stand, despite any mitigating considerations we might come up with (see Janko 1984, 228–29, on *opsis*; but *ibid.*, 230–31, on *ēthos*). Another example, not far removed from the present case, is Aristotle's claim that among Aeschylus' innovations was making speech – not characters – into a "protagonist," viz., he gave it the leading role (καὶ τὸν λόγον πρωταγωνιστεῖν παρεσκεύασεν; *Poet.* 4.1449a17–18) – a pun, no doubt, but with point as well.

[121] *Poet.* 6.1450b18–19.

For the same reason, the *Poetics* declares off-limits all discussion of delivery (ἡ ὑποκριτική), "since it belongs to another field and not to poetry."[122] Technically, this is correct if one understands ὑποκριτική in the narrow sense of rhetorical delivery. But as the synonymy of *hupokrisis* already suggests, the two areas of acting and delivery were closely connected both genetically and in actual practice, as will be shown in Chapter 6 below. Compare further Aristotle's remark that a length of time that "stands in relation to the *performance* and *perception* (τὴν αἴσθησιν) *is not 'of the art itself,'* " viz., is not determined by the nature of tragedy but by extrinsic considerations.[123] And compare *Poetics* chapter 26, where *aisthēsis* is associated again with popular and debasing perceptions: "Assuming that the spectators will not take notice (ὡς γὰρ οὐκ αἰσθανομένων) unless [each actor] adds something himself, the actors use a lot of movement...."[124] Sensation (a lower faculty in this context) and sensationalism are closely affined for Aristotle in the *Poetics*.

§4 Tragedy can produce *its own* [sc., *effect/function*] even *without movement*, just as epic does.[125]

"Movement" is a broad category that encompasses gesture, action, and dance. Compare chapter 26: epic is a noble form, because it does not require gesture to get its effects across, while only inferior tragedies and actors stoop to the level of gesture to make an impact (cf. §3).[126] And compare chapter 19: "These [effects] should be apparent (φαίνεσθαι) *without an explanation* [viz., by the speaker; or perhaps: 'without dramaturgical instruction' (διδασκαλίας)], but those dependent on speech should be produced by the speaker and arise from speech."[127] Tragedy achieves its effects, ideally, without resorting to the orders of movement or speech (see §8).

---

[122] *Poet.* 19.1456b10, 18–19.   [123] *Poet.* 7.1451a6–7.   [124] *Poet.* 26.1461b29–30.

[125] *Poet.* 26.1462a11–12.

[126] *Poet.* 26.1462a2–10. The "immobility" of tragedy is written into its very evolution, away from choric (satyric) dancing: see *Poet.* 4.1449a22–24: "At first [poets] used the tetrameter, because the composition was satiric and mainly danced; but when [spoken] diction came in [i.e., took prominence and supplanted dance], nature itself found the proper verse-form," namely, the iambic trimeter.

[127] *Poet.* 19.1456b5–7. διδασκαλία is perhaps best taken in its technical sense, *pace* Lucas' comment ad loc. and *pace* Else's wish to view Aristotle's remark as an endorsement of method acting (Else 1967, 565), and should in any case be linked to §3 above. (Cf. the identical contrast in the sequel remark in §8.) Here, as everywhere in Aristotle, the emphasis falls on the events *qua* structured plot as necessary cause of the tragic effect, ἐκ τῶν συμβαινόντων (§5), not on the contingency of their staging.

§5 The plot should be constructed in such a way that, *even without seeing it,* someone who hears [from reading] about the incidents will shudder and feel pity at the outcome, as someone may feel upon hearing the plot of the *Oedipus*.[128]

Aristotle has substituted for "phenomenal viewing" a *non-phenomenal, "theoretical viewing,"* akin to the poet's "setting out the universal" (θεωρεῖσθαι τὸ καθόλου).[129] In the place of vision, he substitutes the self-fulfilling "transparency" of a successfully constructed work of art (cf. §4: "These [effects] should be apparent").

§6 It is obvious (φανερά: *"self-apparent"*) *from reading* [tragedy] what sort it is, [sc., what its nature is].[130]

(This claim is contradictory, to be sure, as the reading in question would have been performed aloud, thus restoring at least the acoustic elements of performance that Aristotle is so keen to demote under the rubric of *melos*: rhythm, meter, tonality, song, etc.[131])

§7 The [tragic] poet must be the *maker of plots rather than of meters*.[132]

Meters (and rhythms) are the material of language (*lexis* in its conventional sense, not *qua* conveyer of an agent's rational choices); they therefore fall under the purview of another art.

§8 (sequel to §3) What would the speaker's function be, if the element [viz., the character's reasoning, or the result aimed at by a speaker] were apparent [or: "if the plot's function were apparent in the way it needs to be"] even *without* [*the use of*] *speech?*[133]

As if regrettably, Aristotle must somehow, nonetheless, address the problem of *lexis*. Here in chapter 19 (introductory to the chapter on *lexis*), he contemplates, just for a second, a way round this hindrance. The question he asks may be rhetorical, but in his intense focus on the formal criteria of tragedy and driven by the logic of his position, Aristotle is broaching an idea that not even he can ward off. The result is yet one more paradox. Aristotle's commentator, D. W. Lucas, expresses his own perplexity, "It remains obscure how *dianoia* is expressed if not in speech."[134] Aristotle,

---

[128] *Poet.* 14.1453b3–6. [129] *Poet.* 17.1455b2. [130] *Poet.* 26.1462a12–13.
[131] As is rightly noticed by Smith 1997, 85–86. See below.
[132] τὸν ποιητὴν μᾶλλον τῶν μύθων εἶναι δεῖ ποιητὴν ἢ τῶν μέτρων (*Poet.* 9.1451b27–28).
[133] τί γὰρ ἂν εἴη τοῦ λέγοντος ἔργον, εἰ φαίνοιτο ἡ ἰδέα (Madeus: *idea* Lat.: ἢ δέοι Vahlen) καὶ μὴ διὰ τὸν λόγον; (*Poet.* 19.1456b7–8).
[134] Lucas 1968, *ad Poet.* 19.1456b7–8.

serenely, can always reply: in the same way that you can have tragedy
without *ēthos* (but not without *praxis*).

§9 If [a poet] puts in sequence speeches full of character, well-composed in
diction and reasoning, he will not achieve what was [agreed to be] the function of
tragedy; a tragedy that employs these *less* adequately, but has a plot (i.e., a
structure of incidents), will achieve it far *more*.[135]

Perhaps by "far more," Aristotle is conceding the unreachable ideality of
his formalism (it has a force similar to κατ᾿ εὐχήν in the *Politics* ["the
most desirable" constitution, one "answering our prayers," hence, "ideally
suited"]).

§10 He himself [sc. Orestes] says what the *poet* wants, not what the *plot*
[wants].[136]

Euripides has therefore blundered. Poets are agents of their plots, and
utterly subordinated to them.

What licenses these extreme sounding claims, which in every other
respect are perfectly in keeping with Aristotle's theoretical agenda in his
Poetics, is the rigor with which he sunders the different elements, or
aspects, of tragedy. Tragedy consists of six "parts": plot, (the imitation
of) character, verbal expression, (the imitation of) thought, spectacle, and
music.[137] But these parts stand in a ladder of subordinations, in fact in the
same order that Aristotle's list, reproduced here, endorses. "Subordination" is perhaps not strong enough a term, because all six elements of
tragedy derive whatever value they have in relation to the formal and final
telos of tragedy: the higher up the ladder a given element stands, the more
essential the element and the closer its relation to this *telos* will be. And as
it turns out, the farther removed from the *telos*, the less essential and the
more accidental an element will be (as we already saw in **§1**). But plot, the
mimesis of an action, is the soul of tragedy (ch. 6). The remaining
elements stand virtually apart from plot, not only subordinate but also

---

[135] *Poet.* 6.1450a29–33; trans. slightly adapted.
[136] *Poet.* 16.1454b34–35. For a remarkable reversal of this insight, see schol. Eur. *Phoen.* 1710:
"[Sophocles and Euripides] arrange their plays in the way they want" (ὡς βούλονται γὰρ
οἰκονομοῦσι τὰ δράματα).
[137] *Poet.* 6.1450a9–10. While plot is one of the six parts of tragedy, technically it ought to be
considered *prima inter pares* and not even a part in the same sense as the others at all. To use
an Aristotelian refinement, "'part' is used in several senses" (*Metaph.* Z 10.1034b32), and *muthos*
ought logically to be more like the formal identity of a whole (a *pars pro toto*, perhaps) than a part
of a whole. But there is no need to press the point here.

qualitatively distinct from it.[138] One could try to salvage Aristotle's distinctions by saying that he has merely isolated the essential elements of tragedy, those that make it most purely itself, as opposed to those it shares in common with other arts (see *Poetics*, chapter 1).[139] If so, then Aristotle has either done a singularly poor job in the attempt (the essential elements of tragedy singled out by him do not by themselves, *qua* elements, distinguish it from epic or comedy),[140] or else he has merely demonstrated once again his biases about what constitutes the essential nature of tragedy.

The radical but also anomalous nature of Aristotle's value system needs to be underscored. In a way, he has virtually turned his face against Greek culture, and not only against the reality of the phenomenon he has set out to analyze. "Th[e] musical element," placed at the bottom of the scale by Aristotle, "was by no means merely incidental to classical drama, but an important factor in its total impact."[141] Less politely, "ancient Greek theater was a fundamentally musical experience," which is to say that music was fully integrated into every aspect of drama, right down to "the rhythmical and musical quality" of spoken dialogue.[142] Not even the conservative reaction to the New Music at the end of the fifth century could justify Aristotle's demotion of music in tragedy: the usual response, first audible in Old Comedy, was to pine nostalgically for the purer,

---

[138] *Pace* Sifakis 2001, 54–71, who attempts to show that music – and performance generally, including spectacle (*opsis*) – is essential to Aristotle's definition of the tragic *telos*. One crucial leg of his argument is the controversial claim that ἡδυσμένῳ λόγῳ in *Poet.* 6.1449b25 carries a heavy burden of instrumental meaning, which it is rarely taken to do, and rightly so. *Contra*, Halliwell 1986, 337–43; Taplin 1995; Smith 1997. A good survey of the issues is to be found in Janko 1984, 225–29.

[139] Thanks to a reader for this suggestion.

[140] That is, unlike lyric, music, and painting, tragedy, epic, and comedy all share plot (the mimesis of an action), until plot is more closely defined, in addition to character, thought, and language. Moreover, plot may well be the principal formal feature of epic too (*Poet.* 26.1462b10–11).

[141] West 1992, 17, with some telling arguments to back up his point, which looks to be leveled against Aristotle, even if Aristotle is not mentioned by name. These arguments include how Phrynichus "was remembered with affection two generations after his death not for the power of his plots but for the sweetness of his melodies and the resourcefulness of his choreography," how Aristophanes "in his critique of Aeschylus and Euripides in his *Frogs* devotes special attention to their music," and finally how Athenian soldiers saved their lives after the Syracusan debacle of 413 BCE "because they were able to sing portions of Euripides." For the same point, see Bernays 1970 [1858], 53 n. 1, concerning how "essential" an element of tragedy the chorus is (not to mention staging, *das Scenische*) in the "normal" Greek view and how remote Aristotle's criteria are from the standards of his day.

[142] Wilson 2002b, 39 and *passim*. It is noteworthy that even on this point Aristotle sought to minimize the presence of music, stressing that the spoken parts of tragedy in iambics were closer to everyday speech (*Poet.* 22.1459a11–13). For the contrasting view, see Dion. Hal. *Comp.* 11 on "the melody of spoken language."

morally upright music of the classical era and to bemoan the decadent
hedonism of the musical present.[143] That Aristotle was not alone is clear
from one precious piece of information that comes to us via Duris of
Samos, namely that the fourth-century historian Ephorus of Cyme, who
also wrote on literature and the history of writing (*On Lexis* and *On
Inventions*), held strong views about aesthetic seductions: he was opposed
to mimesis and to literary pleasure (ἡδονὴ ἐν τῷ φράσαι) and to the
performance of literature, probably on similar grounds to his suspicion
that music originated in deception and magic. Literature was best taken in
as a *written* text; he had no truck with oral literature (αὐτοῦ τοῦ γράφειν
μόνον ἐπεμελήθησαν). The view was shared by Theopompus.[144] I suspect
that Aristotle is laboring under influences like these, in addition to that of
Plato's aesthetic and metaphysical purism, while the very reactionary stance
of both suggests, *e contrario*, the existence of opposed strands of aesthetic
thinking in the period leading up to the fourth century.

Plato is himself a first-rate witness to these opposed strands, as, for
instance, in his *Hippias Major*, in a passage that resists the intuitive claim,
to which Hippias readily assents, that "beauty [or 'the fine,' τὸ καλόν] is
what is pleasant (ἡδύ) through hearing and sight":[145]

"If whatever makes us be glad (χαίρειν), not with all the pleasures (τὰς ἡδονάς),
but just through hearing and sight (διὰ τῆς ἀκοῆς καὶ τῆς ὄψεως) – if we call
that fine (καλόν), how do you suppose we'd do in the contest? Men, when
they're fine anyway – and everything decorative, pictures (τὰ ζωγραφήματα)
and sculptures (τὰ πλάσματα) – these all delight (τέρπει) us when we see
them, if they're fine. Fine sounds (οἱ φθόγγοι) and music altogether, and
speeches and storytelling have the same effect...."
"This time, Socrates, I think what the fine is has been well said."[146]

Such clues to pre-existing counterviews are strong, but they are admittedly
not the same as treatises in sensualist aesthetics, which sadly have not
survived. There are hints from the remains of the so-called Presocratics
which suggest that some philosophers did experiment in writings, or at
least in comments, of this sort (more will be said about the Presocratics in
the next chapter). And some of the sophists are likewise good candidates

[143] Ar. *Av.* 1373–1409 (attacking Cinesias), *Ran.*, *passim* (favoring Aeschylus and lambasting Euripides); Pl. *Leg.* 2.669c–670a; 3.700a–701b; Ath. 14.632a–b = Aristox. fr. 124 Wehrli; [Plut.] *De mus.* 1141c–1142b. Further, West 1992, 369–72; Franklin 2002 (for revisionist arguments, and the useful reminder that Aristophanes was guilty of New Musical indulgences himself).
[144] *FGrHist* 76 F1 (Duris) = 70 T22 (Ephorus) and 115 T34 (Theopompus).
[145] Pl. *Hp. mai.* 298a6–7; trans. Woodruff.
[146] Pl. *Hp. mai.* 297e5–298b1; trans. Woodruff.

for literature in the same vein – for instance, Hippias himself. But in case the simple existence of the tragedies and the few tatters of their surviving scores – not to mention the visual evidence from vases – aren't enough to contradict Aristotle's verdict, which has become nearly canonical (even despite Nietzsche's valiant plea that we attend to the totality of the tragic experience in all of its sensuous fullness – and prior to him, that by Jacob Bernays[147]), we can, thankfully, turn to a handful of later texts for counterarguments.

One of these is the *Life of Aeschylus*, which credits Aeschylus with innovations in the very same areas that Aristotle abhors:

Aeschylus was first to enhance tragedy with highly heroic effects and to decorate the stage and to astound his audience's eyes (τὴν ὄψιν) with visual splendour (τῇ λαμπρότητι), through pictures (γραφαῖς) and devices (μηχαναῖς), with altars and tombs, trumpets, phantoms (εἰδώλοις) and Furies. He equipped the actors with gloves and dignified them with long robes and elevated their stance with higher buskins.[148]

Though of late date, the *Life* is in fact derived from earlier material, some of it from Aristophanes' play *Frogs*, and some of it from Aeschylean dramaturgy itself and inferred from the plays.[149] Evidently, for ancient audiences and *pace* Aristotle, "being present at a tragedy [was] 'an outstanding aural and visual experience,'" as Plutarch would later confirm.[150] Quintilian is of the same opinion. In a section on *hupokrisis*, or delivery, he writes that "productions [of stage actors] give us infinitely (*infinito*) more pleasure when heard than when read, and at the same time they secure an audience even for some of the poorest, so that authors for whom the libraries have no room may often find a place on the stage."[151] And a scholiast on Sophocles' *Ajax* notes how the appearance of Athena on stage (ἐπὶ τῆς σκηνῆς) "would certainly be pleasing to the spectator" (χαρίζεσθαι ... τῷ θεατῇ).[152] So much for tragedy by the book, whether

---

[147] See n. 141 above. For the somewhat slim and difficult evidence from vase painting, see MacDowell 1982, 25; Green 1991; Taplin 1992; Csapo and Slater 1994, 53–78.

[148] *Vit. Aesch.* 333.6–11 Page; trans. Lefkowitz 1981, 159, adapted. Cf. ibid., 332.4–5: "He used visual effects (ταῖς ὄψεσι) and plots (καὶ τοῖς μύθοις) more to frighten and amaze than to trick his audience," a comment that seems to be aware of its transgression of Aristotelian canons of judgment in its balancing out the two criteria.

[149] See Lefkowitz 1981, 73–74. The comment about buskins is an anachronism (Easterling 2005, 28, whose analysis is, however, generally too reliant on Aristotle as a touchstone for early tragic performances).

[150] Plut. *Mor.* 348c; Hall 1996, 297.

[151] Quint. *Inst.* 11.3.4; trans. Russell.

[152] Schol. Soph. *Ajax* 14. See Falkner 2002, 345 for this and other similar examples. See also Schol. Eur. *Phoen.* 1710 in n. 136 above.

in one's study or in a library! Even Aristoxenus, whose general Peripatetic leanings are beyond doubt, strays from the party line: he wrote a treatise comparing tragic, comic, and satiric forms of *dance*.[153] And the later grammarian, Aristophanes of Byzantium, must have followed suit he wrote a study on dramatic masks; his enthusiasm for drama, visible in his Menandrian scholarship and in his collection of tragic and comic hypotheses, is well established.[154]

The next text in my list to contradict Aristotle happens to be by Michael Psellus or some other Byzantine author (*Oxon. Barocci* 131 fol. 415[r-v]), though its first editor, Robert Browning, detects in it "the débris of Hellenistic literary theory."[155] This is undoubtedly correct, given the striking echoes that are to be found in tragic scholia deriving from Hellenistic scholarship.[156] Nonetheless, it is quite likely that the substance of some of the views expressed in the treatise reach back further still, even if its rhetoric has been shaped in response to Aristotle, as we shall see, and even if the treatise is in other ways typical of the Byzantine revival of materialist aesthetics that can be found elsewhere, including in Psellus himself.[157] The treatise bears the title *On Tragedy*, and, as this implies, its aim is to define the nature and essentials of tragedy. A mere eighty-odd

---

[153] Frr. 103–12 Wehrli. The treatise is variously titled according to the ancient sources (*On Choruses, On Tragic Dancing, Comparisons*), unless there were several treatises. Perhaps Aristoxenus felt two conflicting impulses here: his own musicology combined with Peripatetic literary history would have dictated his interest in the chorus, while Aristotle's theory of poetics would have discouraged it.

[154] *On Masks* (Ath. 14.659a); Pfeiffer 1968, 190–96; Falkner 2002, 346, with bibliography, and speculating that Hellenistic performance culture was a vital ingredient in this Alexandrian interest – as, e.g., the hypothesis to Eur. *Or.* appears to bear out: τὸ δρᾶμα τῶν ἐπὶ σκηνῆς εὐδοκιμούντων.

[155] Browning 1963, 68, without specifying which theory he has in mind. One suspects this is a mere guess based on Browning's disbelief that the ideas expressed in the treatise could have originated prior to Aristotle. Perusino 1993, who for the most part follows Browning but takes no stand on this particular question, though he does note that the bulk of the author's views go beyond Aristotle's in various ways (cf. "superamento": ibid., 18) – but in what sense "beyond"? Cf. also Glucker 1968, 268: "It is possible that in late Hellenistic and Imperial times, when tragedy developed more and more into some form of 'musical,' ... the musical side of the production came to be considered as a more and more essential part of the director's tasks," etc. Oddly, Glucker finds that the author of the treatise has "misunderstood" Aristotle (ibid., 271), only to throw up the alternative possibility that some Peripatetic author, possibly leaning hard on lost portions of Aristotle's *Poetics*, is the ultimate source of the treatise (ibid., 271–72). For more concrete suggestions about Hellenistic revivals, see Easterling 2005, 26–27, based on the hypothesis to *Agamemnon* and other scholia, which pick up on motifs similar to those highlighted in the text under consideration here (*ekplēxis*, the use of the *ekkuklēma*, and other visual effects).

[156] An excellent summary is to be found in Falkner 2002. Some parallels will be indicated below.

[157] Byzantine aesthetic materialism is increasingly well documented. See, e.g., James 1996 (on color); Pentcheva 2002 (on the sensuous phenomenology of icons); James 2004 (on the senses); many of the essays in James 2007; and Papaioannou forthcoming (on Psellus). To be sure, Riegl led the way here.

lines long, it is a kind of *Poetics* in miniature. But from the word go, its polemical stance towards Aristotle is, or ought to be, as obvious as are its debts to that philosopher. Shadowing the ideas of the *Poetics*, *On Tragedy* subtly erodes them as well.

This is evident from the opening cascade of tragedy's elements, where the means by which tragedy performs its two mimetic functions are listed, namely the imitation of "sufferings" and of "actions": plot, thought, *lexis*, meter, rhythm, song, "and then in addition to these," spectacle, staging, *topoi* (a word of disputed meaning), and movements. The list should raise eyebrows: Aristotle's original six constitutive elements have been expanded into *ten*. "The classification here is more detailed, and presumably later." So the editor, who adds, in desperation: "A possible ultimate source is the *Poetics* of Theophrastus."[158] This cannot be. The expansion of the list is polemical, not faithful as one might expect of a disciple. It runs directly counter to Aristotle's aims, as the rest of the treatise will soon bear out. Let us simply note for now where the extra elements have been added, namely in the very areas that Aristotle most wished to suppress: rhythm, staging, *topoi* (stage directions? place indications? *tupoi*? ["poses"?]; *tropoi*? ["musical styles"?][159]), and movements. Then comes, in the next paragraph, the first crushing blow to Aristotelian tragic theory: "Sufferings are more mimetic than actions." The claim stands Aristotle's theory on its head. Once again, the original editor tries too hard to reconcile the treatise with its (anti-)model: "Implicit in Aristotle's *Poetics* but nowhere stated."[160] The claim is nowhere stated in the *Poetics* because it goes right against the grain of that work, according to which actions (*praxeis*) are the heart and soul of tragedy; indeed, the imitation of action is constitutive of tragedy's formal essence (*Poetics*, ch. 6).[161] *On Tragedy* sees things differently, however. "For the protagonistic element in all tragic dramas is *pathos*. Tragedy is also imitative of what is called character, and especially in the stasimon songs.... But *praxis* [action] *is harder to imitate than suffering*."

---

[158] Browning 1963, 68.

[159] Cf. Perusino 1993, 40. *Tupoi* was proposed by Borthwick (Browning 1963, 72); Glucker 1968, 268 considers vocal terminology (*topoi*, *tropoi*).

[160] Browning 1963, 73.

[161] Aristotle does claim at *Poet.* 14.1453b36–39 that tragedies in which the agents have all the ingredients for tragic action (knowledge and intention) but then fail to act are "untragic, because they lack *pathos*," viz., tragic outcomes (i.e., suffering or death). But this is hardly the same as saying that suffering (*pathos*) is more mimetic than action, which would be an absurdity for Aristotle.

This last claim is nothing short of a shocking howler in Aristotelese, while the business about stasimon songs being imitative of character can claim *no* precedent in Aristotle, even as it hints at the fundamental disaccord between the two approaches to tragic drama that is being staged in this document.[162] Aristotle may mention music, but music receives no analysis in the *Poetics* whatsoever. *On Tragedy* is accordingly standing Aristotle's approach to tragedy on its head in at least two distinct ways. First, it approaches tragedy *as staged drama*, which involves *visible* suffering.[163] And secondly it looks to *music* and *dance* as a special source of tragic style and tragic pleasure. Simplifying, we could say that *On Tragedy* appeals to the *eye* and to the *ear*. Simplifying still further, we could say that the treatise revives the *phenomenal character* of tragedy that Aristotle (and Plato) sought to eliminate from the genre's idea. As if on cue, the next section brings out this very difference for us. The *ekkuklēma*, the device used for wheeling out and displaying gory victims in tragedy, is praised for being a "dramatic requirement for *making* events within the house *appear*" (αἴτημα δραματικὸν τοῦ φαίνεσθαι),[164] and then other devices for making gods and heroes *appear* (φαίνονται) on stage are mentioned. The author is plainly interested in tragedy's appearances, or to revert to our terminology from above, in its "phenomenality."[165] Finally, a whole paragraph is devoted to *melopoiia*, or musical composition. The language is relatively technical, and it has no parallels in the *Poetics*. And from here to the end, which is to say, for the length of the second half of the treatise, the discussion is taken up with the particulars of strophic composition, meters, rhythms, song, acting, dance (movement), and musical instruments. The treatise finally comes to a close in a way that would be unthinkable to Aristotle: "Both Euripides and Sophocles made use of the cithara in their tragedies, and Sophocles made use of the lyre in the

---

[162] This and other indications speak against the suggestion of Glucker 1968, 271–72 that the original source of the treatise may be a Peripatetic after Theophrastus.

[163] Suffering, however, is the hallmark of the (Hellenistic) tragic scholia, which may point once more to the immediate source of this document. See Heath 1987, 10: "they regard emotion, *pathos*, as the defining quality of the genre." Correctly on this point also Glucker 1968, 268.

[164] See Browning 1963, 73 and Perusino 1993, 48 for the meaning of αἴτημα. Papaioannou (*per litt.*) compares Eust. *Od.* 1.396.23 and *Il.* 3.824.21.

[165] Cf. schol. Aesch. *Eum.* 64: "And next there is a display (φαντασία), for the device [sc., the *ekkuklēma*] is turned around (στραφέντα ... μηχανήματα) to reveal (ἔνδηλα ποιεῖ) the situation in the shrine. And the spectacle is tragic (ὄψις τραγική). Orestes still holds the bloody sword, and they guard him in a circle" (trans. Falkner 2002, 349). Cf. further schol. Soph. *Aj.* 346, where the *ekkuklēma* is praised for "bringing heartrending things in full view" (τὰ ἐν τῇ ὄψει περιπαθέστερα) and thus contributing to astonishment (*ekplēxis*); trans. Falkner 2002, 354.

Thamyris." A remarkable slap in the face designed to set to rights the much slighted tragic Muse.[166] Here, tragedy, unlike Humpty Dumpty, is put back together again.

As these counterexamples indicate, Aristotle's approach to tragedy, in its radical reduction of tragic essence to form at the expense of matter and appearance, is anything but standard practice in ancient aesthetics. This reductionism follows from a trait that is commonplace in Aristotle's thought, which we might call conceptual *chōrismos*, or separation: divining the essence of tragedy, Aristotle is convinced that this essence can be grasped in and of itself, independently of its surrounding characteristics. The move is in ways Platonic. What is more, there is a continuity of the deepest kind across the various branches of Aristotle's thinking, though this is hardly ever discussed. What does it mean to call the plot the "soul" of tragedy? For one thing, Aristotle makes no bones about the logical separability of soul *qua* the formal principle of intelligibility and the essence of an animate body. In *On the Soul*, the soul *qua* active intellect is "what it is" – which is to say, is precisely defined – "only when separated" (χωρισθείς).[167] In other words, "the 'active intellect' has no corresponding bodily potentiality."[168] This is in answer to a view of an earlier chapter from the same work: "if there is anything *idion* [proper] to the soul's actions or affections, the soul will admit of separation" (ἐνδέχοιτ' ἂν αὐτὴν χωρίζεσθαι).[169] Clearly, by the later chapter Aristotle has isolated that *idion*, the soul's proprietary and defining aspect.[170] To these considerations, let us add Aristotle's claim that soul, so defined, stands to the rest of an organism as *technē* stands to *hulē*, or art to material.[171]

This should resonate even more deeply in the *Poetics*. *Muthos* (plot) may be the "soul" of tragedy, but then soul has to be understood in its non-"aesthetic" and "actively intellectual" functions. Like soul, *muthos* is separable in definition (χωριστοῦ ... κατὰ λόγον),[172] the principle in virtue of which alone, viewed *per se*, a tragedy is "what it is" (καθ' ἣν ἤδη λέγεται τόδε τι; αὐτὸ καθ' αὐτό);[173] and this is because *muthos* is the

---

[166] Nor is it the solitary text of its kind from the period. See Psellus' essay on Euripides and George of Pisidia, in Dyck 1986. The emphasis on tragedy as performed is all the more striking given the dearth of theatrical productions in the Byzantine era, especially those of a classical stamp (La Piana 1936; Irmscher 1981; Puchner 2002). But the tradition associating Sophocles with lyre-playing runs through the Sophoclean *Life* as well (indeed, the last tag about the *Thamyris* is a direct echo from the *Life*, §5).

[167] Arist. *De an.* 3.5.430a22–23.

[168] Long 1982, 35. Cf. Robinson 1978, esp. 117–24; form as the principle of intelligibility is hinted at on 122.

[169] *De an.* 1.1.403a10–11.

[170] On its probable Platonic and Academic origins, see Vlastos 1991, 256–65.

[171] *De an.* 3.5.430a12–13.

[172] *De an.* 3.4.429a11–12.

[173] *De an.* 2.1.412a8–9; *Poet.* 4.1449a8.

principle of a tragedy's intelligibility *and* the criterion of its identity as well.[174] And while it is true that Aristotle's efforts are directed, ultimately, at the synthesis of matter with form (resulting in so-called "enmattered" form), in reaction to the Platonic "separation" of Forms,[175] at least as much effort is spent in the Aristotelian corpus at isolating that which within these compounds (or predicated of them) gives them their essence and identity. In making these sorts of moves, Aristotle is unsparingly formalistic: essence is logically divorced *from* matter (ἄνευ ὕλης).[176] And the trait of logical separatism is deeply ingrained.[177]

In the very same way that Aristotle can hold in the *Metaphysics* that "bronze is a part of the compound statue, but not of the statue as form (εἴδους)," which is to say, is a part of the statue's constituent matter but not part of its formal essence (which is in any case partless),[178] so too it can be said that chapter 6 of the *Poetics* defines the "essence" (οὐσία) of tragedy (the *sunthesis* of actions or events) over against its "matter" (spectacle [which includes movement, gesture, and dance], song, diction, the *sunthesis* of meters), even though Aristotle offers no corresponding umbrella term in the *Poetics* for the non-formal, material aspects of poetry or art. His biases are evident enough – and, it needs to be underscored again,

---

[174] *Poet.*18.1456a7–8.

[175] As stressed brilliantly by Owen 1965. "*Idion*" is Aristotle's way of making form inhere again.

[176] *Metaph.* Z 7.1032b14.

[177] In rendering a distinction between form and matter in this sense, Aristotle can be assumed to be reverting to a distinction *within* matter of the kind that is highlighted in the *Metaphysics*. "If a line is divided and destroyed into halves, and a man is destroyed into bones, sinews (νεῦρα), and bits of flesh, it does not follow that these compose the whole as parts of the substance (οὐσίας), but only that they compose it as its matter (ὕλης). They are parts of the compound (συνόλου), but not of the form (εἴδους), which is what the account is of; that is why they are not included in accounts either" (*Metaph.* Z 10.1035a17–22; trans Irwin 1988, 241). In the wake of this kind of distinction, Irwin (ibid.) usefully makes a distinction between "proximate matter" and "remote matter," the former belonging to the definition of the formal hylomorphic totality of a definitional entity (the essential man), whereby form actualizes the organic matter of an entity, the latter constituting the "chemical" (what I am calling "material") components that comprise that entity as a physical thing and that survive its destruction or death (here, form and matter are truly sundered in their functionality). The former compound is what Irwin (ibid., 243) calls "a formal compound," the latter "a material compound." Both senses of matter are plainly at work in Aristotle, and they sometimes overlap, as it were materially, but never definitionally. Interestingly, the matter of a formal compound will not be perceptible in any physical sense, whereas the matter of a material compound will be. You cannot "see" the form of a statue or a tragedy (whence the "theoretical viewing" tragedy requires), whereas matter in the latter sense (bronze, costumes) is "part" of a compound precisely "*qua* perceptible matter" (ὡς ὕλη αἰσθητή) (*Metaph.* Z 7.1035a17). In the philosophical tradition inspired by Aristotle, matter's connection to material (physical) sensation is hardly its selling point, and is even its downfall, not only philosophically (Frede 2004), but also aesthetically speaking.

[178] *Metaph.* Z 10.1035a6–7; trans. Ross, adapted.

they fly in the face of both Greek tragedy and Greek culture generally.[179] What counts in tragedy is its formal essence. The rest is mere sweetener, or relish (ἡδύσματα): these other elements exist "to give pleasure," but not to furnish the proper pleasure of the plot: they are the minority causes of the literary work's *raison d'être*.

Incredibly, speech (λέξις) for Aristotle is simply part of the matter of tragedy, a vehicle for giving voice to the form. It is this, but it is also less, for the aesthetic function of language is to give patterned expression to the form, much like an optional accessory, and this is written into the formal definition of tragedy: "tragedy is a mimesis of a high, complete action having [a certain] amplitude (μέγεθος), by means of speech pleasurably enhanced (ἡδυσμένῳ λόγῳ), the different kinds of [enhancement] occurring separately in separate sections [viz., iambic verses in dialogues and lyric songs in choral passages]," etc.[180] Differently put, the aesthetic pleasure of language is not tied in any essential way to the proper pleasure of tragedy. It is a mere "sweetener." Then comes an explanatory gloss, echoing Gorgias: "by speech pleasurably enhanced I mean one that has rhythm and harmony, or song."[181] A further gloss a few lines down makes the same point in a more technical vocabulary: "By verbal expression (λέξιν) I mean the composition of the [spoken] meters itself" (αὐτὴν τὴν τῶν μέτρων σύνθεσιν), which is to say, the way in which the spoken verses are joined.[182] As for the rest of the "sweeteners," after verbal expression "song-writing (μελοποιία) is the most important, while spectacle (ὄψις), though attractive (ψυχαγωγικόν), has least to do with art (ἀτεχνότατον), with the art of poetry that is."[183] Spectacle is a mere "adornment" or external arrangement (κόσμος),[184] in contrast to the inner essence of tragedy.

Taken together, these adjuncts at most contribute to the vivid apprehension of pleasure. But there is nothing necessary about them: the imagination activated by reading can arrive at an equal degree of vividness

---

[179] To take the example of music alone, consider again the chastening words of M. L. West (who seems to have Aristotle in mind): "The musical element was by no means merely incidental to classical drama, but an important factor in its total impact" (West 1992, 17; quoted earlier). On the place of music in Greek life generally, see ibid., ch. 1.

[180] Arist. *Poet.* 6.1449b24–29; trans. Hubbard; final bracketed supplement mine.

[181] λέγω δὲ ἡδυσμένον μὲν λόγον τὸν ἔχοντα ῥυθμὸν καὶ ἁρμονίαν καὶ μέλος (ibid., 1449b28–29). καὶ μέλος was bracketed by Tyrwhitt (followed by Kassel). The phrase is retained and construed as epexegetic by many scholars; see Janko, ad loc.

[182] *Poet.* 6.1449b34–35.

[183] *Poet.* 6.1450a15–18.

[184] *Poet.* 6.1449b33.

on its own without the crutches of visual and aural display – or so Aristotle claims.[185] Whether he can get away with the claim is another question altogether. It is doubtful that an intense imaginative experience of a tragic action, whether induced from reading or even simply from recollection, can avoid the very sorts of features that Aristotle's hierarchy of elements ranks below the level of plot, namely the expressive, phenomenal, and sensuous dimensions of drama. If Aristotle claims to be able to experience fear and terror (and therefore pity and possibly catharsis) merely from reading *Oedipus the King*, or from hearing it read, then it is surely because in his mind's eye he is hearing the voices, the screams, the choral antiphonies, the verbal rhythms, the staccatos and stichomythias, is visualizing the staging and scenery, the stumbling of the blinded king, and so on, just as the poet had done when he composed the drama to begin with.[186] That is, imaginative experience can be fully sensuous, and it can import all that is had through direct empirical experience. Indeed, at times the imagination can be even more intense than direct experiences. Modern aesthetic theory is firm on this point.[187] If Aristotle denies all this, then he is either wrong or he is being self-contradictory or both.

Whatever the case may be, Aristotle isolates, or claims he can isolate, the essential function of tragedy, its *idion, ergon,* or *telos.*[188] Yet this kind of isolation, which at bottom is nothing more than the identification of an aspect and its abstraction from a totality as such, has powerful historical implications that go well beyond what Aristotle ever imagined. For once this essentializing and functionalist move is made, nothing prevents it from being co-opted for other ends. Thus, once it is determined that poetry can be defined in terms of some property *F,* then *F* can be filled in with something besides a principle of intelligibility (Aristotle) or of unintelligibility (Plato). Why not make the *material* cause the essence of poetry? Or why not make a *particular* kind of intelligibility the essence of poetry, such as allegory, the way later writers would attempt to do?[189] Thus, the historical irony of formalism is that it gives conceptual tools,

---

[185] *Poet* 26.1462a17–18.

[186] Cf. *Poet.* 26.1462a17–18; 17.1455a22–26.

[187] See Prall 1929, 28 and Dewey 1989 [1934], 37; 263 (both on "sensuous imagination"); Collingwood 1938, 139; 147–51; 306–07 ("imaginative experience is a sensuous experience"); 308; Walton 1997b, 73–80; Walton 1997a; Currie 2005, 341–44.

[188] *Poet.* 4.1449a8–9; 6.1450a30–31; 13.1452b29, 33; 25.1460b21, 24–25; 26.1462a11.

[189] On this tradition of allegoresis, see Ramelli and Lucchetta 2004.

if not quite license, to its antagonists – for instance, to exponents of a materialist poetics. The proto-euphonist critic from the third century BCE Neoptolemus (of Parium, presumably), whose theory is preserved by the Epicurean philosopher Philodemus of Gadara (early to mid-first century BCE), is a good example of such aspectualism gone awry from an Aristotelian perspective.[190] In the wake of Neoptolemus, the euphonists' isolation of the category of "the poem *qua* poem" (τὸ ποίημα καθὸ ποίημα), which is to say, the poem as a texture of sounds independent of its meanings, is a further evolution of the same idea.[191]

The same holds for another of the euphonist critics' most cherished distinctions. The *sole* preoccupation of poets, according to these Hellenistic critics, lies in what is *idion* to their poetic productions, not in what is common to all other poems or what can be found "outside" their art (by which they mean meaning, diction, plots, and even, presumably, moral content) – whence the phrase that is used to designate this extraneous material, ἔξω τῆς τέχνης, that which lies "outside the art" of "the poem *qua* poem."[192] The phrase is striking for the way it recalls Aristotle in the *Poetics* (ἔξω τοῦ δράματος, ἔξω τοῦ μύθου)[193] and Aristotle's strictures on Plato's censure of the art of poetry narrowly conceived "in and of itself." It is no less striking for the way it departs from Aristotle's own criteria of what counts as essentially poetic.

Equally astonishing is the occurrence in their writings of the term *chōrismos*, notably in the following passage from Philodemus' *On Poems*, which discusses the "particularity" (the *idion*) of poetic sound, using the example of Homer:

So one must observe, in Homer's [verses] too, the sound in itself (τὸν ἦχον αὐτόν), *separated* from the underlying meanings ([τῶν ὑ]ποτεταγμένων | [ἀποσπ]άσαντα), as it has the supremacy (ἡ`γ´εῖ|[ται]) over the words [or: "over

---

[190] See Porter 1995b, 102–18, and *passim.* Neoptolemus represents an Aristotelian point of departure for the euphonist critical program (ibid.).

[191] Porter 1995b, 130; cf. ibid., 102 on the characteristic euphonist claim that "the composition *in and of itself* (καθ' αὑτήν) produces *psuchagōgia*" through the sound that the composition yields (*P. Herc.* 1676 col. 7.7–17). Of course, a similar twist was arguably given by Aristotle to Plato's (inherited) notion of things "beautiful in and of themselves" (καθ' αὑτά). Aristotle deontologized this aesthetic, decoupling it from a conception of beauty in the process, as we saw, while making it depend upon formal criteria alone. The euphonists next transferred the criterion of "in itselfness" over to sensuous properties (or effects).

[192] Phld. *De poem.* 1 cols. 132.27–133.3 Janko; trans. adapted: "But <Crates> says that 'the arguments and [all the] meanings lie outside the art'" (ὁ δὲ "ἔξω || τῆς τέχνη[ς" φησὶν εἶναι "τοὺς] | λόγους καὶ [πάντα τὰ διανο]ήματα").

[193] Arist. *Poet.* 14.1453b32; 17.1455b8. Cf. ἔξω τῆς τραγωδίας (ibid., 15.1454b7), and also the rhetorical equivalent, ἔξω τοῦ πράγματος (*Rh.* 1.1.1354a15).

everything"].... One can see from birds too that the voice is a sovereign [principle] (ἀρχηγόν). For in their case, as *separable* sound (χωριστοῦ ... ἤχου) emerges [viz., as devoid of sense and palpable in and of itself], precisely a kind of articulated voice (ἔναρθρος φωνή) is produced.[194]

The mere separation or detachment of sound, first *as sound* ("the sound itself"), and then of sound from sense (these really amount to the same thing), is a commonplace of the euphonist dogma that is being retailed. The usual term for this act of separation, which is purely mental and aspectual (it is a diverting of the mind from one thing towards another), is *apospan* or *perispan*, and it implies a certain tearing and even violence. As Janko notes (ad loc.), the rare application of the term χωριστός in the present case does indeed look like an Aristotelianism.[195] Only, if so, then this is Aristotelianism being turned upside down. Future poets, critics, and theorists in antiquity would seize upon the same logic – for instance, Ausonius in his *Technopaegnion*, who explicitly eschewed sense in favor of another kind of verbal interplay and coherence.[196]

Plato, for his part, had helped poetic materialism articulate its program merely by dividing poetry into two conceptual halves – form and content, or better yet: surface features and underlying meanings – and then by casting strong aspersions on both sides of this division. The division was helpful inasmuch as it gave a sharper articulation to a conceptual schism that was being explored by poets and theorists already (these predecessors will be discussed in later chapters). Aristotle's achievement was of a different order altogether. Utterly original and powerful, Aristotle's refinement of Plato opened the door to entirely different criteria of poetic value from even those that Aristotle approved of, for example poetry's material causes, and thus to other critical preferences, such as poetic materialism (which in its own way is a kind of formalism, in the sense of isolating an aspect or aspects of works of art and promoting these at the expense of all others). One of the historical ironies of this development, already mentioned, is the apparent transformation of Aristotelianism into the celebration of the euphonic phenomenality of the "poem *qua* poem."

---

[194] Phld. *De poem.* 1 col. 114.10–25; trans. Janko.
[195] An influence from the side of Neoptolemus of Parium may be suspected. See above.
[196] See Ausonius' first preface to the *Technopaegnion* (text after Green, Auson. xxv): "Quae lecturus es monosyllaba sunt, quasi quaedam puncta sermonum, in quibus nullus facundiae locus est, *sensuum nulla conceptio*, propositio, redditio, conclusio aliaque sophistica, quae in uno versu esse non possunt, sed cohaerent ita, ut circuli catenarum separati." Further such examples, characteristic of later antique literature, may be found in Roberts 1989.

Nonetheless, formalism in the narrow, Aristotelian sense, which focuses upon rational, logical, and self-reflexive properties (structures of meaning, though not meaning *per se*, plot organization, art [so understood] "in itself"), and all of the associated cognitive emotions (including intellectual pleasure), dominates ancient literary theory and criticism, albeit in varying degrees of strength. The Peripatetic influence is most strongly felt in professional circles, thanks to its diffusion by Theophrastus[197] and then the Alexandrian Museum, which inherited and institutionalized Aristotle's main literary assumptions. Thus, the so-called Aristarchean maxim, "explain Homer from Homer," and the justification of criticism as a clarifying of poetic intention, are in fact attempts to lay bare the formal, unifying properties in a work in the way that the work is claimed to lay them bare (or to instance them) itself. Formalism is not unique in requiring self-evidence for its principles. But the insistence on the integrity of the work's inner logic and coherence, mooted already in Plato's organic metaphors for poetic totality,[198] is the hallmark of Aristotelianism in criticism, and a powerful precursor to modern intuitions about literary wholeness and coherence. A final caveat is warranted, however.

Ancient formalism here shows itself to be a precursor to modern intuitions about literary wholeness and coherence – but not about *form*. Modern formalists might seek an ally in Aristotle, but if so they won't have looked hard enough at his treatise. Aristotle's logic of the poetic whole has to do with a synthetic unity, a compound that is made up of parts. The idea of form as "a discriminable . . . isolable element in or aspect of" a work of art that one can point to, never mind as the dominant pattern of a work, is entirely foreign to his thinking – thankfully so, as no such entity exists in the world.[199] (Plot, as we shall see in a moment, is not form in this sense.[200]) When the Russian Formalists turned form into a kind of material palpability, claiming that the "awareness of the form [comes about] through its violation," they were acknowledging this very fact: forms exist only in the negative contrast between two disparate sets of

---

[197] Cf. fr. 78 FHS&G (= Ammon. *in Int.* 65.31–66.2).
[198] Pl. *Phdr.* 264c.
[199] Wollheim 2001, 133.
[200] That is, Aristotle may be a formalist, not because he believes that plot gives the form of tragedy, but because he attributes causal power to the essence or definition of tragedy, which is its true "form," and which is not reducible to the shape of events, but which is reducible, rather, to their logic.

materials, or else between two perceptions.[201] Differently put, form has no positive existence, but is rather salient only when two complexes of materials stand in relation to each other.[202] The experience of this relation is what gives the sense of aesthetic palpability to what is in every other respect a mere gap in matter and perception.

Two lessons follow from this. First, we should beware of modernizing Aristotle on this central tenet of his poetic theory, at least not as the Roger Frys and Clive Bells of the world might do. The point is not just that, though plots may have a shape and trajectory of sorts, plots are more often than not the object of endless debates rather than an objective part of a work. It is that Aristotle's idea of a tragic whole and its unitary character is not always dignified in his treatise in the way that one might expect literary form to be – whether as "a disembodied function of the spirit" or as a "significant form." Quite the contrary, *praxis* (plot) can be molecular, kinetic, and even medical, as in *Poetics* chapter 8: "a plot ... should be so constructed that, when some part is transposed or removed, the whole is disrupted (διαφέρεσθαι) and disturbed" (κινεῖσθαι).[203] There is little scope here for the modern ghost of "form." Secondly, and closely related to this first point: Aristotle's conception cannot help but revert to a kind of materialism, despite his best intentions. With the backbone of tragedy – its soul – emphatically defined as a *sustasis* or *sunthesis*, or aggregate of parts, albeit of immaterial parts (actions, the ingredients of *muthos*, viewed as conveying a logical action),[204] Aristotle is dipping into the conceptual vocabulary of his predecessors who were following a materialist model of physical elements (*stoicheia*) joined into a compound unity. That model is ultimately derived from atomism, as I will show in Chapter 4.

To be sure, Aristotle would seek to downplay this kind of connection. One small clue that he has done so comes from the very evidence, which is faint but indisputable, that the theory of plot was in existence long before Aristotle decided to revamp it late in the fourth century. There is even some evidence that plot was originally called a *sustasis* prior to Plato,[205] and that as such it had strongly material connotations that could

---

[201] Shklovsky 1965 [1921], 31.
[202] See Lotman 1977 on what he calls "minus devices."
[203] *Poet.* 8.1451a31–35; trans. Janko. On the medical and surgical echoes in this passage, see both Lucas and Else, ad loc. Further, Ch. 5 at n. 136 below.
[204] E.g., ἡ τῶν πραγμάτων σύστασις (*Poet.* 6.1450a15); ἐξ αὐτῆς τῆς συστάσεως τοῦ μύθου (ibid., 10.1452a18–19); λέγω γὰρ μῦθον τοῦτον τὴν σύνθεσιν τῶν πραγμάτων (ibid., 9.1450a4–5; cf. 13.1452b31).
[205] Pl. *Phdr.* 268c5–d5. On this prehistory, see Ch. 4, nn. 264–65 below.

be expressed in different ways. To give an example: one of the equivalent expressions for plot found in Aristophanes' *Frogs* appears to be "the nerves [or "sinews"] of tragedy."[206] It is only natural that Aristotle would wish to replace a corporeal metaphor like "nerves" or "sinews" with the metaphor of the "soul," the latter being for him a decidedly non-corporeal and non-composite entity, all his hylomorphism notwithstanding.[207] ("Sinews" [νεῦρα] are explicitly excluded from the formal matter of essences elsewhere by Aristotle, inasmuch as they belong to the physical matter of organic bodies.[208]) But Aristotle would also have been reluctant to reform the language of poetics altogether. Saddled with the terms *sustasis* and *sunthesis*, he was likewise saddled with their vestigial physical associations.[209] He doubtless could conceive of the concrete and embodied "form" of tragedy in no other way, and neither could any other ancient, so far as I am aware.

---

[206] Ar. *Ran.* 862: τἄπη, τὰ μέλη, τὰ νεῦρα τῆς τραγῳδίας. See Ch. 4, n. 265. A bizarre echo in this connection is Plato's description, at *Rep.* 3.411b, of the way music can emasculate a healthy individual, cutting out "as it were the very sinews of his soul" (ἐκτέμῃ ὥσπερ νεῦρα ἐκ τῆς ψυχῆς); trans. Shorey.

[207] On Aristotle's much-disputed hylomorphism, which is the view that the soul cannot function apart from its enmattered condition in a substrate (a body), see Nussbaum and Rorty 1992. My points about the soul being nowhere defined by Aristotle as a *sustasis* or a *sunthesis* still hold. See *De an.* 1.5.410a18–21 and 1.5 *passim*, rejecting the language of Presocratic predecessors who took the soul to be a material *sustasis*; and ibid., 2.1.412a17, rejecting the corporeality of the soul.

[208] As in *Metaph.* Z 10.1035a19 (see n. 177 above).

[209] The same is true of Aristotle's theory of language, which is likewise inherited, and likewise inflected with corporeal associations (e.g., *arthra*, "joints," "articles"; *sundesmoi*, "sinews," "ligaments," "conjunctions"; and not least, *phōnē*, "voice"; cf. Belardi 1985, 10–20; Zirin 1980; Lo Piparo 1999, 126–29; Sluiter forthcoming. Nor should we omit the fact that "structure" has an architectural, hence physical, sense that is occasionally felt even today – though perhaps not by structuralists. (More on verbal architecture in Ch. 9 below.)

CHAPTER 3

Matter and appearances

What is called matter in the arts is not in the first instance what form
is caught in, what it can be applied to. It is what dumbfounds form,
and summons it: it is the occasion, the touch.

J.-F. Lyotard[1]

The truth of the matter is that what is form in one connection is
matter in another and vice-versa.

J. Dewey[2]

Having explored the concept of form it is now time to turn to the – rather
intractable, but ever fascinating – concept of matter, which, as we saw, the
very idea of form cannot help but evoke and at times incorporate. The
congener of matter is appearance, for that which makes matter aesthetic is
the way it offers itself to sensation and experience: appearance is matter's
face. As we shall see, the two go hand in hand, a virtual pair. But in order
to get to grips with materialism in ancient aesthetics, one has to compre-
hend the emergence of the idea of matter and how that idea could have
first been made available to artists in all media and to anyone who wished
to reflect on art. To do this, I want to suggest, means reaching back to the
Presocratics, whose contribution to ancient aesthetic inquiry will be the
focus of this chapter. I want to begin, however, with some general
reflections on matter as a stigmatic category of thought, before offering
a brief sketch of the history of this stigma among philosophers, from Plato
to Sartre. Then I will take up one of the very rare examples of an
aesthetician (Alois Riegl) who sought to think through the evolution of
ancient art from Greece to Rome by reference to some of the more
interesting challenges presented by art's materialism. That approach,
while promising, did not prove sufficiently searching: its focus was limited
to visual art, and its timeline began far too late. This is where the

---

[1] Lyotard 1991, 27; trans. adapted.   [2] Dewey 1989 [1934], 133.

121

Presocratics come in. But first to the prejudicial views of matter, the examination of which will help explain why a materialist history of aesthetics and art, or if one prefers a historical aesthetics of materialism in art, is lacking today.

Mary Douglas points out the striking truth, apparently first enunciated by Lord Palmerston, that dirt is matter out of place.[3] Imagine a fried egg on your plate and now on the floor, a bar of soap in the shower and then in the garden, dirt in the garden and then in your bath tub, your spoon in your mouth and then in mine. What each of these examples illustrates is the fact that dirt is a relative notion. Its qualities are perceived rather than intrinsic, so much so that what counts as dirt will vary from one setting to another. To a child none of the examples named may count as dirty, however much you or I might protest the fact. These examples or others like them might be contested across cultures. The relativity of dirt is thus found at home and abroad. The variations can extend over time and not only across space: what once counted as dirt often no longer does, and vice versa, just as the frameworks for labeling dirt change. Science has introduced the specter of microbial pathogens. Religion's purifying powers have largely receded.[4]

Not only is dirt relative to place, but there is also a relativity to dirt itself. Not all category violations disturb in equal measure (assuming this could be measured), and we can speculate about a reason why this might be so: in slipping out of place, objects approximate themselves to matter, and some of these approximations are more troubling than others – presumably because they more closely *resemble* matter and assume its imagined traits.[5] But what the examples imply is that dirt is both an ineluctable category (the very definition of "place" depends upon an exclusion that constitutes "dirt") and an indispensable one, an

---

[3] Douglas 2002, 44 (unattributed, except as "the old definition"). The "celebrated" phrase, "Dirt is matter in the wrong place," is attributed to Palmerston in different forms throughout the nineteenth and early twentieth centuries (e.g., by Dickens in *All the Year Round,* 4 April 1868, p. 390), though Palmerston seems to have been citing someone else: "Now, gentlemen, I have heard a definition of dirt. I have heard it said that dirt is nothing but a thing in a wrong place" (*The British Farmer's Magazine,* 22 [1853] 137).

[4] Douglas 2002, 44.

[5] For some partial criticisms and revisions of Douglas, see Miller 1997, e.g., 38–59.

all-purpose way of dividing up and labeling, or relabeling, the world according to our wishes and whims (for what can never count as dirt in some circumstance?). What they further imply, and I take this to be one of the more intriguing upshots of Douglas' insight, is that *matter itself can be a relative notion*, visibly itself in some contexts and properly and invisibly itself in others. That is, in some contexts, indeed in a wide array of contexts in our culture (though not in all), there may well be something fundamentally "dirty" about matter viewed in isolation and from close range. The reason has to do with the way in which the concept of matter came to become a contested site of value (or disvaluation) in Western culture in certain circles, notably in philosophy (above all in the field of metaphysics) and in aesthetics.

The point is *not* that matter is intrinsically stigmatic or dirty taken by itself, but only that it came to appear so wherever it was so labeled and once the values that attached to matter became fixed and, indeed, ossified. Just as the cultural category of "dirt" is the by-product of a system of contrastive pairs, such as the pure and the impure or matter and spirit, in the same way the idea of matter for the philosophers or aestheticians is typically produced as a dirty element in a system of opposing elements. In the latter cases, the elements tend to include not only matter and spirit (or intelligence), but also categories like matter and form. Douglas' definition – "dirt is the by-product of a systematic ordering and classification of matter, in so far as ordering involves rejecting inappropriate elements"[6] – can, in other words, be extrapolated a step further to include symbolic systems of a more abstract kind. Dirt is not only a feature of ritual and behavior practices. It is also a feature of one of their rarified extensions: *conceptual* practices. The point of making this extrapolation here is to be able to account for defilements that occur in all domains of perception, or at least in all domains of concept-formation, whether or not their underlying assumptions succeed in rising to the surface sufficiently to survive inspection.[7]

In the same essay ("Secular Defilement"), Douglas is at pains to elucidate how dirt is "a residual category, rejected from our normal scheme of classification."[8] It is rejected because dirt is not something we readily contemplate as an active ingredient of our valuations: dirt, we

---

[6] Douglas 2002, 44.
[7] Thanks to both Mary Douglas and Charles Stewart for helping me see what was unclear about an earlier formulation of this last set of ideas.
[8] Douglas 2002, 45.

might say, is itself a dirty category of thought, as abject as dirt itself. To be sure, there is a subtle hypocrisy involved in this stance of ours towards dirt, which does in fact play a steady role in our classifications, even as the category of dirt repugns. But mental categories are often more a matter of habit than reflection, and it is far easier to denigrate things than to reflect on the act of denigration as we go about our daily business. Denigration denied is dirt in the mind. On the other hand, all of our classificatory schemes are, in fact, so deeply lodged in our minds and behaviors that bringing them up for inspection is a difficult chore. One might have thought that simply to inspect a category of classification is to bring attention to the fact, and the facticity, of the classification, if not of classification itself. Beauty, we might wish to believe, is best taken in the way one inhales the perfume of a rose, but not when beauty is examined too closely – for instance, as the product of a system of ideas or habits. So why should we expect the category of dirt to be an exception?

Dirt may not be exceptional at all in this respect. But just as Douglas is moved to ask, "Can we even examine the filtering mechanism itself?,"[9] so too it may be that whenever we bring our filtering categories into view for inspection we risk sullying them, moving them out of their assigned place, and exposing their delicate nerves. To examine a pattern of thought or a value is to concretize a formal abstraction: it materializes a category. Turning something into dirt, then, perceptually speaking, is a way of turning it into matter, irrespective of whether in question is beauty, a flower, a poem, or a joke (all these are notoriously hard things to analyze without murdering). Matter and dirt here are not quite synonymous things, but for the most part in our culture matter just is a kind of dirt, end of story. Yet their status is probably disguised rather than determined by the logic of being-out-of-place. Would we say that dirt is *form* out of place, or that it is *abstraction* out of place? It would seem nonsensical to do so. But we can say without absurdity that form and abstraction out of place – placed like an egg on a plate for embarrassing inspection – are these things made material. Matter is the dirtiness of form, and it is visible whenever form's function becomes the object of perception instead of the mechanism that filters and guides perception. So perceived, form becomes palpable and aesthetically apprehensible. This is what the Russian Formalists sought to expose through their revisionary aesthetics during the early part of the twentieth century, as we saw in the previous chapter.

[9] Douglas 2002, 46.

If dirt is, as it were, the most recessed of the already concealed categories of our perception, then matter is dirt's nobler relation. Matter can at least be named, and it has a philosophical pedigree, whereas dirt does not. Matter (in Greek *hulē*, in Latin *materia*) is a recognized and indispensable metaphysical category even among non-materialist philosophers like Plato and Aristotle (though these latter tend to produce or adduce the category in order to banish it again). And yet matter, too, is something we tend to take for granted in life as in thought: its assigned role is to reside quietly in the background and never to obtrude itself into the foreground. Matter, we might say, has its place in being placeless. It is a part (or aspect) of everything around us, but its job is to be imperceptibly placeless, while other categories, so to speak, see to it that matter does its job. Its being recessive is *actively* enforced in a way the recessiveness of other categories is not: these are simply taken for granted, like Kant's notion that pleasure in experience is so obvious as to be forgotten, whereas matter by contrast and convention is jealously guarded against: it is stigmatic, brutish, and pathological. There is a vehemence to the way matter and materiality are driven into the background of things. And in the history of thought, this vehemence is even more evident and more vehement than it is in daily life.

Matter and materialism have traditionally been driven into abjection, made into "a residual category" of their own, and indeed into the locus where all residues must reside, virtually repressed from view. That they have been this is fairly clear from the backlash of materialism which took place during the Enlightenment, with Helvétius and d'Holbach leading the charge, and which gathered momentum over the next century. A good index of the revival of philosophical materialism is to be found in Friedrich Albert Lange's *Geschichte des Materialismus* ([*History of Materialism*], 1866; 2nd edn. 1873), a work that sought to marry Kantianism to psycho-physiology, and which had an enormous impact in Germany, from Nietzsche to the Frankfurt School. Lange's direct inspiration was Democritus, and his greatest rival was a tradition that in turn drew its inspiration from Platonism. Plato's antipathy to Democritus and his materialism was apocryphal already in antiquity.[10] Plato's third-century CE successor, Plotinus, leaves little doubt about his own views on the question – for instance, in his discussion of the soul in its (literally disgraceful) commerce with matter and the body:

---

[10] See Ch. 4 at n. 117 below.

[A soul drawn to matter is] impure, I think, and dragged in every direction towards the objects of sense (τὰ τῇ αἰσθήσει προσπίπτοντα), with a great deal of bodily stuff mixed into it, consorting much with matter (τῷ ὑλικῷ πολλῷ συνοῦσα) and receiving a form (εἶδος) other than its own it has changed by a mixture which makes it worse; just as if anyone gets into mud or filth he does not show any more the beauty which he had: what is seen is what he wiped off on himself from the mud and filth; his ugliness (τὸ αἰσχρόν) has come from an addition of alien matter, and his business, if he is to be beautiful again, is to wash and clean himself and so be again what he was before. So we shall be right in saying that the soul becomes ugly by mixture and dilution and inclination towards the body and matter.[11]

As J. M. Rist writes of the Plotinian conception, "since matter is sheer negativity, it is utterly destitute of sense, virtue, beauty, strength, shape, form and quality, and must be called the complete ugliness, the absolute evil."[12] And as Plotinus' own language betrays, the ancient disgrace of matter, even in outwardly metaphysical contexts, may amount to little more than an *aesthetic* preference.[13]

A latter efflorescence of materialism directed against idealism was the "radical empiricism" espoused by William James at the turn of the twentieth century. In James's impassioned words, "the greater sublimity traditionally attributed to the metaphysical inquiry ... entirely disappears" when one embraces the pragmatic empiricism of experience. "The mere abstract inquiry into causation's hidden nature is not more sublime than any other inquiry equally abstract. Causation inhabits no more sublime level than anything else. It lives, apparently, in the dirt of the world as well as in the absolute, or in man's unconquerable mind."[14] Similar thoughts may be found in James's pragmatist contemporary and successor John Dewey, who lamented the way in which "the attempt to connect the higher and ideal things of experience with basic vital roots [is] so often regarded as betrayal of their nature and denial of their value," and how as a result of "repulsion" by and "contempt for the body, fear of the senses, and the opposition of flesh to spirit ... sense and flesh get a bad name."[15] More recently, materialism has made a radical resurgence, perhaps with more insistence in anthropology than in aesthetics, as well as in some areas of cultural studies, for example

---

[11] Plotinus, *Enn.* 1.6.5; trans. Armstrong. Cf. ibid. 5.8.   [12] Rist 1967, 128.
[13] See also James 1987, 527 (*Pragmatism* [1907], Lecture 3), characterizing the conflict between materialism and spiritualism as "little more than a conflict between æsthetic preferences." He continues: "Matter is gross, coarse, crass, muddy; spirit is pure, elevated, noble," etc.
[14] James 2003 [1912], 97–98.   [15] Dewey 1989 [1934], 20; 26–27.

so-called thing theory.[16] Classical studies have yet to catch up with this return to matter and materialism, and if anything they are constitutionally resistant to it, having been founded on the exclusion of materiality from the conduct of their studies (this is what might be called their guiding *operational* aesthetic). The study of the classics has by definition been classicizing, which is to say idealizing, purifying, and rarifying, despite the fact that its evidentiary base is undeniably material. The chemical bleaching of the Elgin marbles is just one, sadly typical, example of this tendency.[17]

Against the prevailing negative views of matter and materialism, above all in classical contexts, a different tack is warranted. We might begin by considering when the concepts of matter and materiality first entered the Western tradition and how they did so. In this chapter, I will suggest the following historical picture. In Greek antiquity, matter was first named by the Presocratics. Prior to then, materiality existed, but intuitively. Homer's world is densely material, crowded with things; his art is marked by a pleasure in materials. Bodies, objects, things, and their properties furnish a sense of materiality (of what is hard, resistant, or malleable; subject to agency, alteration, and destruction). Notably lacking is any sense of the immaterial and the incorporeal (gods are fleshly; souls are bits of breath). Homer is therefore arguably the first materialist in the West, albeit an intuitive one. Over the next few centuries, a new sense of materiality gradually emerged, in tandem with a growing sense of the immaterial (the rare [*araios*]; the incorporeal [*asōmatos*]; the empty [*kenos*]), and eventually of form as an immutable substance or essence (Parmenides: *eukuklos sphaira*; Plato and Aristotle: *ideai*; *eidos*).[18] The earliest philosophers sought to explain the natural, sensible world in terms of its physical constituents or principles, often reductively so (water, the unlimited, air, fire, infinitely divisible stuff, indivisible atoms, and other *archai*, or principles), not infrequently

---

[16] See DeMarrais *et al.* 2004; Meskell 2005; Miller 2005 (three collections featuring the term "materiality" in their titles). Anthropological histories of the senses are also starting to abound (see Howes 2003 and Howes 2005, and the book series "Sensory Formations" published by Berg), though Nietzsche was a forerunner (see Porter 2000, 150, on Nietzsche's abandoned project on "the history of sensation"). For thing theory, see Brown 2001 (and ibid., 2, on the various "returns of the real" in historicism, contemporary art, and object-oriented studies generally); Brown 2003. The Birmingham School's resort to Marx and to modern Marxisms (e.g., Gramsci, Althusser) produced various inquiries into materialism, some more culturalist, some more aesthetic (R. Williams, T. Eagleton, Coward and Ellis).

[17] See St. Clair 1999; Jenkins 2001; Porter 2010b.

[18] Parmenides, DK 28B8.43–49 (on the perfect sphere of what is); Pl. *Phd.* 103e; Arist. *Metaph.* Z.

pressing matter towards the limit of the material. Just as their theories clashed, so did their vocabularies: no consensus term for matter emerged until after Aristotle (*hulē*). Stoics and Epicureans perpetuated the earlier Presocratic materialist traditions, while Peripatetics and Neoplatonists refined Aristotle and Plato's essentialism.

And yet, what seems to have brought the concept of matter into existence was the thought of its opposite, the immaterial. As we shall see, the gradual refinement of matter (its reduction, so to speak, to itself) brought about something like an increasing sublimation of matter, practically its de-materialization (in Democritus' terms, it underwent a progression *epi leptoteron*, to an ever finer degree). A parallel development can be detected outside of philosophy. Atthis' absent lover communicates her thoughts mentally from Sardis to Lesbos, while Sappho imagines (makes sensuously present) the absentee lover in turn (fr. 96 LP);[19] poems outlast their first empirical occasion (Pind. *Nem.* 5.1–5); musical notes could be recorded differently from the way they were heard (Pythagoras; Lasus; Epigonus); geometries described patterns that could, like music or writing, be abstracted from their objects, whether in architecture, mathematics, or art.[20]

Could the dynamics and the cognitive challenges of writing have contributed to the sense of the immaterial, and thus to the concept of matter? While impossible to prove, the speculation is worth entertaining. Writing, or more broadly any recording system used for encoding objects, would have made graphic the distinction between the physicality of an object and its concept, which would in turn have helped to solidify the very idea of matter and the immaterial in at least two ways: first, the concept could be represented even in the absence of the object; and secondly, through its visual and tactile character, the very medium of notation reinforced the idea of materiality; writing had a texture and

[19] The poem is all about transcending empirical limits, thereby illustrating how communication occupies the interval between two limits. The first two lines read: "... in Sardis ... often sends her thoughts here" ( ] Σαρδ.[| πόλ]λακι τυίδε [ν]ῶν ἔχοισα); line 20, possibly the poem's last, reads: "... is very noisy *the space between*" ( ] πόλυς | γαρύει [..(.)]αλον[.....(.)] τὸ μέσσον); trans. Damon (adopting τῷ ap. LP). See Damon 1961, ch. 2, 272–80, esp. 277: "the sweep of moonlight across the sea objectifies the power of memory and fidelity to transcend physical separation" in a way that is not found in Homer; further, ibid. 279.

[20] It is unclear whether Theodorus of Samos made use of the same sorts of devices as are found in the later metrological reliefs at Samos, Salamis, and Didyma (see Ch. 8 at n. 110 below), but it is not inconceivable that he did in his treatise on the Temple of Hera on Samos (Vitr. 7. praef.12). Likewise, it is not known whether Polyclitus used diagrams to illustrate his *Canon*, but he may have. Mathematical geometry is plainly attested by the mid-fifth century with figures like Hippocrates of Chios.

immediacy that were palpably other than those of its *representata*.[21] From here, it was but a short step to a break in the chain of materiality and to a recognition that notation encoded not sound or objects, but ideas or conventions, and to the realization that these latter had no obvious material correlates in nature. Hence, it was all but assured that when matter was discovered as a concept, so was its contrary, the immaterial. The two emerged, full-born and consciously formed, as antagonists in a dynamic tension that would never vanish, but would merely change shapes in the centuries and millennia to come.

My suggestion is not that the Greek concept of matter was produced by the introduction of writing, but that the concept was first affirmed through its rejection by the early philosophers of the immaterial (Parmenides and his Eleatic succession), and, more speculatively, that writing helped to pave the way for the emergence of both. Once matter was coined as a concept, it was here to stay. Henceforth, matter could only be *disgraced*, but not erased.

Exactly when the tide turned against philosophical materialism is hard to say, but it would not be wrong to look to Plato as one of the decisive moments. Prior to Plato, Presocratic thought had been divided between a materialism of sorts, championed by the natural philosophers (including the Milesian monists, who viewed the world as consisting of one kind of stuff: Thales, Anaximander, Anaximenes; Xenophanes, a pluralist; the Ionian pluralists, who viewed the world as consisting of various kinds of stuff, e.g., Anaxagoras and Empedocles; the atomists; and, somewhat earlier, Heraclitus, nearly unclassifiable), and materialism's polar opposite, the greatest proponent of which would have been Parmenides of Elea, who denied the existence of the material world and thus paved the way for Plato. Starting with Parmenides, the very concept of matter was thought to be weak, philosophically speaking, and this weakness could in turn be seen as one of matter's primary rebuffs.

Plato took up Parmenides' challenge and then made it philosophically hegemonic, at least for a century. For Plato, matter, or rather material particulars, are debased, contingent things, fragile, constitutionally deficient in perfection, given to change, wandering, and annihilation, or as he says of the body in the *Phaedo*, "mortal, multiform, unintelligible, soluble, and never consistently the same as [themselves]," in contrast to the soul, which is "most like the divine, deathless, intelligible, uniform,

---

[21] See McLuhan 1962 and Ong 1982 on writing systems generally; and Netz 1999, esp. 13–67, on mathematical (lettered) diagrams.

indissoluble, [and] always the same as itself."²² In Plato's wake, Aristotle viewed matter in its "primary" quality as lacking all essential features and therefore all definition and knowability, apart from its being featureless in itself and receptive to form (in Aristotelese, it embodies pure potentiality and is devoid of all actuality); as such, matter is generative of composite bodies, while primary substance, the essence of things, can be conceived, though it cannot exist, "without matter."²³ The Hellenistic schools, dominated by Epicureans and Stoics, would reinstate materialism, but never with quite the same force as it had enjoyed in the days prior to Plato.

Both Plato and Aristotle were working off the intuition that matter is connected somehow to the notion of a material (physical) body, which is to say, a three-dimensional object extended in space. But just what satisfies the definition of a material body, like that of matter itself, is far from clear and constantly changing over time and across theories. Democritean atoms are miniature versions of visible bodies (they can be hook-shaped, spherical, and so on). But their spatial extension combined with impenetrability (solidity) has not withstood the test of time as a criterion of matter, even if they roughly anticipated the idea of mass, though not of energy. Modern-day physicists have revised the idea of matter, locating ever smaller constituents within it or of it, from atoms to protons, neutrons, and electrons (endowed with solidity but also with wavelike properties), to finer subatomic particles (quarks, leptons, and bosons), to (more speculatively still) their constituent strings, which is to say, infinitesimally small objects defined by vibrational states.

While matter remains an elusive notion, it is at least partly this to the extent that the assumption of its reality appears forever to be in advance of its absolute evidence. Matter is for this reason a paradoxical entity and concept – or as Bertrand Russell once memorably put it, "the name of a problem."²⁴ Berkeley was not far off when he chastised "the materialists" (by which he meant modern-day avatars of Lucretius as well as Newton, Locke, and their offspring) for postulating matter "only for the sake of supporting accidents," namely "colour, figure, motion, and the rest of the sensible

²² Cf. Pl. *Phd.* 80b1–5; trans. Grube, adapted. As is well known, matter as such is not Plato's primary concern until the *Timaeus* (e.g., 52a–c), though material composites are (and they do not fare well in his hands).
²³ Arist. *Metaph.* Z 10.1036a8–9 (unknowable); ibid., Z 7.1032b14 (essence without matter). Cf. Code 1982 and Bostock 2006, 30–47, esp. 34–35; for further refinements, see Lewis 2008.
²⁴ "The word matter is, in philosophy, the name of a problem" (Russell 1900, 75). Russell then goes on to detail five different senses of the word in the Leibnizian system alone.

qualities."[25] There does indeed seem to be something wildly counterintuitive to the endless hunt for a material reality behind the veil of perception. Isn't matter just its appearances, or at least to be found *in* them? Berkeley's conclusion that matter, being in the view of his contemporaries "an inert, senseless, unknown substance, [and] entirely made up of negatives," is therefore but a figment of the mind ("it follows that we have no longer any reason to suppose the being of *matter*"), may seem unwarranted, but it is also part of a longer tradition of attacks on the reality of matter that begins in the West with Parmenides.[26]

To take up a materialist stance is not necessarily to endorse empirical reality naïvely. Some of the more daring materialist positions, both ancient and modern, not only counter this assumption. They also revel in the paradoxes of matter, thereby flaunting its problematical status. Democritean atoms incorporate Eleatic features in their microscopic nature, adding insult to injury: each little pluralistic atom represents a quantum of monistic Parmenidean Being. Worse still, atoms cannot be described, let alone imagined, in anything but phenomenal terms, as we saw, though this is an illicit move: strictly, atoms ought to be devoid of all phenomenal features apart from size, weight, and position.[27] At another extreme, consider how Sartre chooses to close the final chapter of *Being and Nothingness* (1943) when he launches into a lengthy ode to viscosity, or as the English version would have it, to *sliminess*. Poised ambivalently on the verge between being and its annihilation, viscosity stands, in Sartre's imagination, for certain characteristics of matter (it is "the revenge of the In-itself," matter turned nightmarish), and therefore represents challenging new possibilities for the mind. Viscosity is both inviting and repellant, a source of fascination and of horror. Neither solid nor liquid ("the viscous is the agony of water"), it threatens to absorb everything into its illimited self, including ourselves – and never more so than when we plunge our hands into, say, a pot of sweet honey and lose ourselves in its "tactile fascination." Viscosity represents, among other things, the repugnant materiality of matter in concentrated form, but also the smearing of the boundary between subject and object (it "outlines a kind of continuity of the slimy substance in myself"). Sartre absolutely revels in the

<hr>

[25] Berkeley 1999, 56 (*Principles of Human Knowledge*, §§73–74).
[26] Berkeley 1999, 54; 56 (*Principles*, §§68, 73). For a contemporary and somewhat reckless attempt to "expel matter out of Nature" (Berkeley), see Robinson 1982.
[27] See O'Brien 1981; Porter 2000, 85–86; 88–89.

ambiguities, and the agonies, of matter, which for him are central to his peculiar form of existential materialism.[28]

So much for the intractabilities of matter's definition, which owe as much to the resistances that matter commonly presents in phenomena (matter is often intelligible as being essentially no more than the source, within objects, of their resistance in the world) as to the opacities of its ultimate composition and definition. In what follows, I will generally restrict my use of the term *matter* and its congeners to sensuous phenomena, for the simple reason that sensuous phenomena occupy the level at which objects are accessible to aesthetic sensation.[29]

2 MATERIALISM IN ART

Materialism in art is a difficult category to define, not least because it is barely established in contemporary theories and especially histories of aesthetics, despite the perpetual interest and even fascination with the materiality of art objects. Perhaps no more eloquent an account is to be found than in a recent remark by one of the leading exponents of aesthetic materialism today, T. J. Clark:

Painting is material. Materialism, for it, is not one view of the nature of the world among others, but the view – the felt reality – it cannot help but inhabit. Courbet used to enjoy upsetting the serious neo-Catholic disciples of Ingres by sticking his stubby hand in their faces and saying: "La peinture, c'est ça!" But there is no need to be an atheist or a positivist for it to be one's life's work to place a viewer in the here and now. Poussin was neither, but his world is as earthly and creaturely as Goya's or Masaccio's. One thing that seems to follow naturally from painting's material nature is that it sees its task as always turning on the human body – the body conjured up immediately and substantially. But the human animal is not painting's whole subject (here is what marks it off from sculpture, to say nothing of dance). For painting is also convinced, in the way of no other art but architecture, of the reality of space. And it thinks that painting is uniquely equipped to give us

---

[28] Sartre 1956, 603–15 (= Sartre 1943, 695–708). See esp. the last few pages on childhood sexuality and on eating, which replay the dialectic of being and nothingness in terms that consciously evoke "Parmenidean" *materialism* (Sartre 1956, 613 = Sartre 1943, 705) and finally abandon "ontology" altogether. Hence, too, the (foundational) centrality of the body in the generation of the *pour soi*, or the domain of human consciousness, perception, and ethics (Sartre 1943, 392).

[29] The words of Clark 2001, 99 are worth recalling here, especially given their art-historical (i.e., aesthetic) context: "No wonder we can never be sure where materiality ends and phenomenality begins. Each thrives interminably on the other's images and procedures. An account of matter will never be rigorous enough, or vivid enough, to seal itself against the other's metaphorical world." Or, as he puts it more simply and starkly (ibid., 93), "Color comes out of a tube into the eye."

this space, to contain and articulate it – to show its specific shape and pressure. The world in painting is one of bodies, but bodies in surroundings.[30]

Painting is material, but (as Clark would readily agree), so too are other art forms, whether dance, music, sculpture, poetry, gemstone carving, jewelry making, or architecture, all of which depend upon felt reality, the body, the here and now, the reality of space (each in their own way), all of which exist in embodied materials, are received in vivid sensations and perceptions that register these elements, and all of which issue in higher-level evaluative labels – labels that may or may not reflect their sensuous origins ("luminous" does; "innovative" does not).

To be sure, the arts are material in this sense, and they can be more than this, but all of them are this at a minimum – at a very big minimum. What is surprising, then, is why the obvious fact about art's materiality, or the materialism of art, should need to be stated at all. Art is material, and has always been material. It cannot *help* but be material, given the very nature of its media. And the same holds for reflection on art, which has always been a form of – has always been grounded in – materialism. By reflection, I mean an activity that runs up a scale of elaborateness: first, in the basic sense of empirical observation; then, in the slightly elevated sense of minimally self-aware reflection on this experience – say, perceiving that one is perceiving (or experiencing that one is experiencing) the materiality of art or the sensuousness of art objects, leaving aside for now the definition of what such objects are, and provisionally accepting the intuitive appeal that materiality (the fact and reality of art's material nature – *c'est ça!*) and sensuousness (its felt reality) enjoy; and finally, in the higher-order sense of organized reflection on a level approaching theory about art and experience. Of course, some forms of reflection on art close off this process by rejecting their origins in sensuous perception. This does not make them any less materialistic; they are merely forms of disavowal put into practice. Unfortunately, reminders of the obvious like Clark's are necessary today because the traditions of disavowal have assumed such a dominant lead in the Western traditions of aesthetics. What statements like Clark's forget to mention is that aesthetic materialism is neither a timeless stance nor an invention of modern painting. On the contrary, it has a rich history that can be traced in the remotest corners of Greek antiquity (and earlier, and elsewhere). But one can do a bit more than simply trace the forgotten history of aesthetic materialism.

---

[30] Clark 2008, 3.

A preoccupation with works of art as phenomenal and material objects – as palpable and sensuous objects of experience deriving their interest from their empirical and sensible properties – is a continuous strand of ancient Greek and Roman theories of art, poetry, and rhetoric, the prejudices of Plato and Aristotle notwithstanding (as discussed in Chapter 2 above). Poetry, we should never forget, was produced in order to be performed, seen, heard, and sung, and the same holds, *mutatis mutandis*, for all other forms of ancient art.

If we are looking for a quick label to cover all the arts and to offer a materialist view of art at the same time, we can say that art existed, and exists, in order to be *sensed* and *experienced*. To be sure, art also exists to be mulled over and to be remembered: it has an immaterial extension both in the present and into the future. But even the most rarified conceptual and abstract art depends for its existence on a material support. As the American minimalist Robert Ryman said in an interview from 1971 about painting, the aim of the art for him meant "getting the paint across":

That's really what a painting is basically about, whether you talk about figurative painting or abstract painting ... I wanted to point out the *paint* and *paint surface* and not so much the objectness. Of course, they are always objects ... *You can't get away from that.*[31]

Ryman's point is not so surprisingly reminiscent of Shklovsky's: both are taking up materialist perspectives on art. One of the keenest observers of ancient art, Alois Riegl, shared this view, and he went so far as to coin a name for artists in their aspect as guardians of the senses: *Kunstmateria-listen*, or "art-materialists." To look at art in this way is to view art as a concerted effort to cater to the senses. It is to notice that "mankind wanted to see sensuous appearances placed before its eyes in planes or in space, in outline and color, at different times and in different ways."[32] Riegl's theory, as it is laid out in his *Late Roman Art Industry* (*Die spätrömische Kunstindustrie*), is worth recapitulating briefly, as it is one of the rare attempts to focus on the materialist tendencies of ancient aesthetics (albeit from within the visual arts only).[33]

---

[31] From an interview by Phyllis Tuchman with Robert Ryman, *Artforum*, May, 1971, in Lippard 1973, 27; emphasis added.

[32] Riegl 1927, 392.

[33] Thanks to Jaś Elsner for recommending this text several years ago, and to Eric Downing for recently reminding me why I needed to read it. The following is but a brief response to both of these stimuli.

In the evolution of art from Egypt to the Byzantine era a pattern can be traced, Riegl argues, one that follows the evolution of an aesthetic sensibility from a direct apprehension of objects to an indirect apprehension of them. Riegl famously names the earlier modality *taktisch* (and later changed it to *haptisch*), occasionally dubbing it *plastisch*, and the latter *optisch* or *malerisch* (or *koloristisch*). The one appeals directly to the sense of touch, the latter fulfils this same aesthetic imperative by way of the eye, in an "optical" or "painterly" and "coloristic" fashion.[34] The key points here are that aesthetic apprehension begins in a desire to grasp objects in their impenetrable materiality and individuality (*Undringlichkeit, Stofflichkeit*). *Touch* is the sense that most closely yields up this grasp of things, but it does so punctually, pointillistically, and it requires repeated graspings to cover any ground. Gradually, the idea of a *surface* is generated, but one that is depthless (for in question is an object that is impenetrable, virtually an atomic *sensum*) – whence comes into being the initial aesthetics of the surface in two dimensions, lacking all depth, that typifies Egyptian and then Greek art. At this earliest stage, aesthetics is all a matter of matter – of material, the senses, and appearances. Riegl speaks of "material appearance" (*materielle Erscheinung*), which emanates from the surface of things, and to which corresponds, in a beholding subject, a "pure material viewing" (*rein materielles Schauen*).[35] After the so-called classical period (a label whose privileged bias Riegl's study is in effect designed to contest), aesthetic sensibilities and stylistic sensibilities evolve in an increasingly three-dimensional, "optical," and "dematerialized" direction (Riegl speaks at one point of "*Entstofflichung*").[36] He does so most famously by tracing a history of the ornament, which is in itself a counter-classical art historical project. But there is much more to his study than a change in art objects and values.

The history of this shift is fascinating, but one that lies beyond the historical reach of the present study. Suffice it to say that what Riegl observes is the discovery of *gaps* in the material surface of aesthetic objects that rupture the continuities of the face of matter – most innocently and intriguingly of all in the invention of windows in architecture, or in the perforations (drilling) of statues (in the eyes or in curls of hair) and dimplings (*Punzierungen*) of metal work, but also in what Riegl sees as

---

[34] Riegl 1927, 27–28; 32 (asterisked note), 69; 73; etc. The distinction seems to have been anticipated by Anselm Feuerbach, and may even be derived from this source (though Riegl gives no hint of this in his work). See Feuerbach 1855 (1st edn. 1833).
[35] Riegl 1927, 33; 39; 122; 126; 174; 211; 254.   [36] Riegl 1927, 39; 122–23.

a new sensibility to a rhythmic patterning of space through intervals generally. In line with this notion of dematerialization, the introduction of the interval as an aesthetic factor is registered, Riegl believes, as a *negative substance*, and so it forms a stark polar contrast to the starting position of the evolution that his study, so misleadingly titled, traces: the arc passes from *impenetrable matter* to *emptiness*. At the end of the trajectory, what one discovers is "the ungraspable, the immaterial, the formless, the empty, not-being," or in St. Augustine's terms (since at this point Riegl is drawing some of his vocabulary and inspiration from there), a privation (*privatio*).[37] More positively, what is at stake is "the emancipation of the interval, of the ground [in contrast to the figure], and of space."[38] Either way, the active component in the construction of aesthetic space and perception is a (volatile) gap of space.

As exciting and logical as this progression sounds, there are a few complications, one foreseen by Riegl and one not. The first, echoing my claim from the Introduction (pp. 5 and 20) that matter is inescapable and cannot ever be quite dematerialized (in Ryman's words, "you can't get away from that"), lies in the fact that the progression, while on the surface tracing a neat polarity, is in fact underlain by a tension, one that Riegl is eager to hold on to. Aesthetic apprehension may begin, historically speaking, in a wished-for sense of objectivity, or better yet objectality, being immersed in tactile immediacy, but it is constantly betrayed, as it were, by its instinct to synthesize the data of sensation, first through the imaginary construction of a surface, and then in other ways. "An inner opposition was latent" from the very beginning, "and in this latent opposition simultaneously lay the seed of all later developments."[39] Nor does the opposition – or rather tension – ever resolve. Once we reach the other end of the evolutionary scale, it turns out that the aim of the eye, almost its *secret* aim, is to produce for itself a sense of tactility and of the haptic. This is, after all, one reason why the optic sensibility is permitted to supersede the haptic sensibility. Vision can accomplish the *same* goals as touch. Only, it can do this more efficiently, whether independently of, or else in conjunction with, the haptic sensibility. "The eye multiplies the individual perceptions far more rapidly than the faculty of touch.... Where the eye perceives a coherent patch of color belonging to a single stimulus (*Reiz*), in the same place, thanks to the experience, there also arises a perception of the palpably impenetrable

---

[37] Riegl 1927, 399.   [38] Riegl 1927, 398.   [39] Riegl 1927, 28.

surface of a closed-off material entity."[40] And anyway, the discovery of
the third dimension of depth lies beyond the capacity of both.

It is in this final stage, with the discovery of the third dimension of
depth, or rather its illusion, and the breakthrough into the immaterial,
that Riegl's own apparatus becomes a bit wobbly. On the one hand, he
insists on the dyadic nature of his scheme even as the evolution he traces
has, by his own reckoning, exceeded the framework of this pairing. Thus,
when "insubstantial nothingness" arrives on the scene, it does so in the
form of a "purely optical-coloristic" phenomenon.[41] The apparent incon-
sistency (the introduction of color into the void of nothingness) is partly
to be explained by the "rhythmical" generation of contrasts, mentioned
above, which renders intervals aesthetically perceptible at all, as in the
contrast between light and shade, or between the presence and absence of
matter in a form. Another way of stating this is to say that the tension
between the tactile (haptic) and the optical sensibilities never really goes
away, but merely changes shape and styles. After all, even after the age of
Constantine we are having to do with an effort in the arts to "render
sensuous the spatial nature of individual figures."[42] And so, while the
object of the aesthetic focus has changed (space, rather than materiality
per se), the goal has not; it remains what it always was: the rendering
sensuous, and thereby the individuation, of a perception. Such a goal may
even be the primary directive of the aesthetic impulse itself in antiquity on
Riegl's reckoning, which remains firmly dedicated to the materiality of art
despite its apparent interest in tracking the function of empty space in
aesthetic matter, or else the rhythmic flashes of aesthetic perception in the
intervals of matter.[43] (One term that is conspicuous by its absence in
Riegl's study is *form*.) The introduction of the blank, immaterial interval
seems to mark the outer limit of that materialistically inclined sensibility
from antiquity.

At least it does on Riegl's scheme, though why it should – why that
scheme should pass from matter to the immaterial as a historical development – remains puzzling. A further question is whether there is any
historical validity to the idea to begin with. Riegl himself concedes that
"the introduction of the process [of "the emancipation of the interval"]
reaches far back into the pre-Constantinian period," and he points to a
passage from Cicero's *De oratore* that draws on interval theory from music

---

[40] Riegl 1927, 29.   [41] Riegl 1927, 49; cf. 35.
[42] "... *die Versinnlichung der Räumlichkeit der einzelnen Figuren*" (Riegl 1927, 223).
[43] Riegl 1927, 30–31; 211.

to describe prose rhythms.[44] As we shall see below, the aesthetics of the interval or gap was far more developed than Riegl's scheme allows, far more ancient and far more integral to more strands of aesthetic speculation in antiquity than he assumes. Finally, his attempt, a few pages later, to align the (on his scheme) primitive notion of impenetrable, punctual, material, and individual sense objects with the conceptual framework of ancient atomism (an inevitable move, it would seem in hindsight),[45] naturally invites a second look at the, as it were, *Schattenseite* of his scheme, namely "the ungraspable, the immaterial, the formless, the empty, non-being." Didn't the atomists have a name for this too: τὸ κενόν, or Void? That they did points to the very antiquity of the idea that Riegl's aesthetic history names as its culminating or, better yet, postponed evolutionary consequence. Which brings us to the Presocratics and their possible contribution to ancient aesthetics.

3 PRESOCRATIC MATERIALISM, 'EN ROUTE' TO THE SUBLIME

Prima facie, the Presocratics ought to occupy an important place along the pathway that leads from the embedded reflections on art of the archaic era and earlier to the explicit reflections on art from the mid-fifth century during the so-called Age of Enlightenment and leading up to Plato and Aristotle. Surely these early philosophers formed an integral link in the chain. Even so, reconstructing Presocratic aesthetic thought is a dicey affair. As with so much else before the fifth and fourth centuries, the evidence is sparse. In the case of the Presocratics, the situation is perhaps worse: it is not even clear that these intellectuals, whose label is more of a modern convenience than a reflection of any ancient reality,[46] were particularly concerned with aesthetic thought in our sense of the term. "Presocratic Aesthetics" is by any measure an unpromising topic for a scholarly treatment of any length, which probably accounts for the near absolute dearth of studies on the topic. No Presocratic philosopher – with the apparent exception of Democritus – pronounced on what we would call aesthetic theory, and in some quarters historians would argue, and have argued (as we saw in Chapter 1), that aesthetics, as a recognizable category of organized theoretical inquiry, is an invention of the eighteenth century. Accordingly, a word or two of caution is in order.

---

[44] Riegl 1927, 398; Cic. *De or.* 3.186.   [45] Riegl 1927, 402; 403.
[46] See Long 1999, 1–21; Laks 2002; Frede 2004; Laks 2006.

To begin with, instead of tallying the – in any case meager and piecemeal – contributions of individual Presocratics to the problems of aesthetic inquiry in antiquity, I will be taking a more considered tack in what follows, one that I hope will be more useful in any case. My aim will be to locate aesthetic reflection, understood in the broadest possible sense, in Presocratic thought. To this needs to be added the painfully obvious fact that Presocratic philosophy is a treacherous business and an academic minefield of conflicting opinions. What is more, speculation is a necessary evil here, given the nature of the sources. Most of the claims that have been made about the Presocratics are no more certain than the available evidence for those same claims. My treatment of these philosophers will be no different in this respect from any others in the available literature.

In the opening chapter I suggested that aesthetics, narrowly conceived (having to do with art), opens onto aesthetics more broadly conceived (having to do with experience). The best aestheticians have wrestled with the relationship between these two domains, whose boundary-lines are never entirely clear. The problem before us now is, how far back in time can we trace this narrower kind of inquiry? And how did the inquiry evolve? We know that aesthetics in some sense had to be alive in archaic and classical Greece just in virtue of the nature of choral and lyric performances, which involved a simultaneous display of forms (music, song, dance), as in the case of Pindar, whose language would be raided by later critics of the arts, especially in music, literature, and rhetoric. Pindar is himself a kind of proto-aesthetician, as we shall see in Chapter 7, and the same is true of much poetry before Aristophanes' *Frogs*, which is typically considered the first document of ancient literary criticism. As we saw from just a few snippets of Pindaric verse in Chapter 1, aesthetic activity even at this early stage could be highly complex. And it existed in a highly self-conscious form long before Socrates and Plato came along largely to dismiss it as theoretically naïve. If we are going to talk about a Presocratic aesthetics, we are going to have to do justice to this kind of archaic art, which is in its own way "Presocratic." But what was the specific contribution of that motley assortment of philosophers known today as the "Presocratics"?

The little that has been written on this subject is either too broad or too narrow in reach to give much of an answer. The confines are usually taken to concern poetry, not aesthetics, and when such studies do not try to canvass every conceivable meta-comment about poetry before Plato, whether by poets or philosophers (as in Lanata's *Poetica pre-platonica* [1963]), they are typically limited to the stray comments we have (most often petulant criticisms) by Presocratic philosophers on (mainly) individual poets: Homer, Hesiod, or Archilochus.[47] More rarely, one finds a study of the poetic practices *of* the Presocratics (who frequently wrote in verse, and were praised, or blamed, for writing "poetically" in antiquity).[48] Wider intellectual studies that attempt in various ways to account for the evolving "Greek mind" or Greek mentalities in relation to changes in Greek culture inevitably confront the Presocratics, who are looked upon as a historical watershed. Occasionally, the Presocratics are conceived as indirect contributors to aesthetic developments more broadly conceived, and according to one influential art historical account they were formalists and even proto-Platonists, insofar as they sought to locate "an invariable conceptual reality" – a kind of ideal entity – "underlying the structure of all physical objects."[49] Artists followed suit, according to this mental map of the age, and produced a limited set of ideal entities of their own, virtual Forms or ideas of objects, representing such things as "horseness" rather than horses, and so on.[50] This view does little justice to the variegated nature of the phenomena in art that it seeks to describe, and above all it does little justice to them *as* phenomena, which is to say as phenomenal works of art.[51] A very different view of these developments will emerge from the pages that follow.

Nonetheless, even once we widen our focus, we encounter genuine obstacles, some of them unexpected. Anaxagoras (500–428 BCE) ominously wrote that "every *aisthēsis* [is accompanied] by pain" (μετὰ πόνου).[52] Aristotle confirms the view, seemingly adopts it (though he ultimately rejects it), and then generalizes it to all the Presocratics: "The animal nature is always in travail (ἀεὶ γὰρ πονεῖ τὸ ζῷον), as the [early] students of natural science (οἱ φυσιολόγοι) also testify, saying that sight and hearing are painful (λυπηρόν); but we have become used to this, as they

---

[47] Lanata 1963; e.g., criticisms: Xenophanes DK 21B1.19–21; B11; Heraclitus DK 22B42; B56; praise: Xenophanes, B10; B6; Heraclitus, B56; Anaxagoras, DK 59A1.

[48] See Most 1999; DK 22A1a: ποιητικῶς (Heraclitus); DK 10A1 (Anaximenes); DK 12A9 (Anaximander); Aristotle fr. 70 Rose (= D.L. 8.57), *Mete.* 357a24–25, *Rh.* 3.5.1407a34–35; DK 31B84: ποιητικῶς (Empedocles). For reflections on Presocratic views of the visual and plastic arts and beauty, see the brief remarks in Philipp 1968, 56; 57; 59–60.

[49] Pollitt 1974, 26. Cf. Pollitt 1972, 5–6.

[50] Pollitt 1972, 6. Similarly, Laporte 1947; Sörbom 1966, 48–51; Schweitzer 1953, 15. Contrast Snell 1980, 206; also, Cassirer 1998 [1924], 140, for a very different reading of the Presocratics' view of nature. And see Neer 2002, 28 for a critique. See further next note.

[51] Different stories of the same developments can be told. For an alternative that does place the accent on the phenomenality of art, see Vernant 1991, 151–85.

[52] DK 59A94 = Aet. 4.9.16. Cf. Theophr. *Sens.* 29: μετὰ λύπης.

maintain."[53] Not a very promising beginning for a theory of aesthetics! In the hands of one modern interpreter, Aristotle and the Presocratics come out sounding rather Schopenhaueresque: "Life as such is burdensome. . . . It is simply the struggle of the very process of living, the 'pain of living.'"[54] But whereas Schopenhauer at least saw in aesthetic pursuits a momentary (if illusory) relief and distraction from the pain of existence, in the case of the ancients the position might appear stronger and more hopeless still: if the very condition of aesthetic pursuits – *aisthēsis* (perception and sensation) – is painful in itself, how can one ever hope to overcome this pain through art?

Quite apart from their appearing to be relatively indisposed towards *aisthēsis,* if we wish to put any trust in Aristotle's assessment of them (which, frankly, seems bizarre), there is the further obstacle that I hinted at when I began: no Presocratic seems to have addressed the problem of aesthetics in our sense of the term. As Hanna Philipp sums it up rather tersely in her study of Preplatonic visual arts, "The question about beauty in and of itself (*das Schöne an sich*) was not yet formulated" until, probably, Plato and Aristotle[55] (though Polyclitus' controversial definition of beauty might deserve to count as a possible exception). But once formulated philosophically, the problem of aesthetics seems to offer little scope for flourishing. Plato's strictures on beauty are so severe as to exclude its physical perception altogether, or at least tendentiously so: it is hard to derive much sensuous enjoyment from staring at a square or at a patch of whiteness. Plainly, Plato's views about the constitution of reality are reflected in his views about art and aesthetics, and these subsequently became widespread, albeit in a diluted fashion (we find these in pleas on behalf of untouchable ideas, as in Cicero's ideal orator and elsewhere).[56] A strong Platonic bias is palpable in Aristotle. And together, their views reigned supreme for centuries to come. Indeed, as I will be arguing throughout this study, we are still very much in their grip today.

Unlike Plato, Aristotle does admit of aesthetic pleasures, though the way he does so is telling. He puts huge constraints on these, rendering them fairly ascetic in their range and quality, more or less following Plato's cues, as we saw: sensuous perception accounts for the least essential aspects of aesthetic objects in Aristotle's *Poetics* (in tragedy, these are the

---

[53] *EN* 7.15.1154b7–9; trans. Ross. Cf. ibid., 1154a27–28: "owing to the excesses of pain that men experience," though pleasure can "expel pain" and act as its curative.

[54] Merlan 1960, 7–8; the embedded quotation is from H. H. Joachim's commentary ad loc., where it appears as a paraphrase of Aristotle's argument, in scare quotes.

[55] Philipp 1968, 60.   [56] See Panofsky 1924, 5–16.

outward – formal and material – features of language, song, and spectacle). And if Aristotle on one or two occasions briefly concedes that beauty is a function of appearances, he quickly retreats from this momentary phenomenalism and returns to Plato's side, without, however, accepting Plato's premises about the ultimate metaphysical status of beautiful objects. For Plato, beauty is grounded in an ideal Form; for Aristotle, the aesthetic value of the experience of tragedy is instantiated in the logical and formal structure of action. In this one respect, then, Plato and Aristotle join hands in being staunchly opposed to the phenomenal and material or embodied aspects of art, and even to the phenomenalism of beauty itself, whose existence, allurements, and dangers they are nonetheless keenly aware of and to which they even occasionally fall prey.

I want to suggest that the Presocratics paved the way for this radical push away from materialism into form and formalism (so understood) by the two grand philosophers of the fourth century, and that they did so in a few different ways. First, by virtue of the kinds of conceptual lines they knew how to draw, the Presocratics produced, and so made it possible to isolate, the two categories of matter (the realm of substances) and phenomena (the realm of appearances), which were unknown as such in prior mythological and mystical thinking. Henceforth, one could conceptualize matter and phenomena, and one could either embrace them (in a reductive materialism, as with the pluralists) or vilify them (in a spiteful antimaterialism, as in the case of the Eleatic monists, and above all Parmenides and Zeno). There were intermediary positions, of course, and there was plenty of room for profound ambivalence too. But on the whole, ambivalence does not seem to have been the dominant mood. And as for the Presocratics' having regarded sensation and perception as a source of pain, this is a red herring. To begin with, the claim (in one of its forms) was not that every sensation is dominated by pain. Aristotle himself concedes that even if pain is always present in sensation, we are no longer conscious of it out of habituation. And Anaxagoras' point, which he must be paraphrasing here, was similar: the pain that accompanies sensation, which results from the contact of like with unlike, only "becomes evident either from too long a duration or from an excess of sensation."[57] Surely anyone who has sat through the Ring cycle or trudged

---

[57] DK 59A92; trans. K–R–S, adapted. Alternatively, one might speculate that life is in a perpetual state of pain and "disquiet," but that these pains and their perception "are too small to be perceptible (*apperceptibles*)" (so Leibniz 1965 [1704]), 151, in response to Locke's *Essay Concerning Human Understanding*, book 2, ch. 21, § 29). See Heller-Roazen 2007, 196–99.

through one museum exhibit too many will be inclined to agree with this conclusion, if not with the premise. Excessively bright lights or loud noises can also cause pain, Anaxagoras adds in the same fragment, but this, too, is uncontroversial.

In other respects, Anaxagoras appears to have held a moderate form of hedonism, as did other Presocratics, when he did not, in fact, aspire to an absolute form of hedonism.[58] He also showed a fairly intense interest in visual phenomena and even in optics and aesthetics. He and Democritus were jointly held responsible in antiquity for the optimistic slogan of empirical inquiry, "Appearances are the sight of things unseen," and for the earliest mathematical theories of perspectival illusion to be applied to tragic scene painting. Given these known interests, it would seem *prima facie* odd if Anaxagoras simply turned his back on the faculty of vision because it was the source of ineliminable pain.[59] Indeed, as both these last examples, or rather counterexamples, would seem to suggest, Anaxagoras' interests lay precisely in the ameliorative possibilities of vision, that is, in the ways in which vision could overcome some of its physical handicaps – empirical limitations, proneness to illusions – and could reap both benefit and even enjoyment from them.[60] This tendency likewise conforms with Anaxagoras' generous pluralism, which borders on an exuberant vitalism and a celebration of sensory plenitude, as the beginning of one of his fragments preserved by Simplicius makes abundantly plain: "And since these things are so [i.e., given the infinite divisibility of matter, and so on], we must suppose that there are many things *of all sorts* (παντοῖα) in everything that is being aggregated, seeds of all things with *all sorts* (παντοίας) *of shapes and colors and tastes*" (ἡδονάς).[61] Reality presents a large canvas of appearances that exist to be taken in by the senses and enjoyed. Nor is Anaxagoras unique among the Presocratics in assuming this stance towards the world.

---

[58] Anaxagoras: A94 (Aspas.); B4; Diogenes of Apollonia: DK 64A19.43 (pleasure is natural, pain is unnatural); Democritus (*passim*). Absolute hedonism is the (doubtless unreachable) goal of Anaxagoras according to Arist. *EE* 1215b11–14. For relevant discussion and a defense of Anaxagoras, see Warren 2007.

[59] DK 59B21a ∼ DK 68A111; DK 59A39 ∼ DK 68B15b = Vitruv. 7.praef.11.

[60] Another way of stating these empirical limitations would be to say that the senses are too "weak" (ἀσθενεῖς), for the most part, to penetrate empirical data (appearances) and to assess (κρίνειν) their underlying truths, as DK 59B21 puts it. This needn't conflict with the claim, "Appearances are the sight of things unseen" (B21a). It merely qualifies it, paving the way for alternative routes to judgments of empirical fact (mental, logical, analogical, etc.).

[61] B4 = Simp. *in Ph.* 34.29–35.3; trans. K–R–S.

But the Presocratics did more than simply produce the concepts of matter and phenomena. They also took an aesthetic or proto-aesthetic attitude towards these things, as the last fragment from Anaxagoras already demonstrates. One immediate way in which they did so was by treating matter *as* phenomena, and vice versa. In other words, their tendency was to take up a *phenomenological perspective on matter*. On this view, matter was something to be perceived; it was an object of *aisthēsis*, and so it automatically had primary aesthetic qualities that could be attended to, experienced, and described. As we shall see, many of these qualities are poetic-sounding, and sometimes they are couched in the traditional language of the poets, a natural reference point and one still vested with canonical authority in the sixth and fifth centuries, when the Presocratics were most active.

But beyond the registration of matter as phenomena, something quite curious happens among the more committed materialist Presocratic philosophers in their accounts of matter. Matter begins to proliferate. It spreads into the indefinite reaches of the universe (in their favored terminology, εἰς ἄπειρον, *ad infinitum*). And as it does so, it transfixes the beholding gaze and becomes more than mere matter: it becomes increasingly refined, less *crudely* material, more and more sublimated – in a word, it becomes sublime. At the extreme, the Presocratic pursuit of matter turns into the pursuit of something like *sublime matter*, a sheer and sometimes purer form of materiality by way of matter's hyperextension into infinity. One early example is Anaximenes' introduction of air as a candidate for the original substance and basic form of matter, replacing Anaximander's principle of the *apeiron*, or the indefinite-infinite. Anaximenes took air to be "one and infinite ... not undefined as Anaximander said but definite"; it produced changes in nature through rarefaction and condensation: "being made finer (ἀραιούμενον) [air] becomes fire, being made thicker (πυκνούμενον) it becomes wind, then cloud, then (when thickened still more) water, then earth, then stones" (λίθους).[62] While air is empirical and visible, it is also "close to the incorporeal" (ἐγγὺς ... τοῦ ἀσωμάτου), or at least so it would appear to a later writer (Olympiodorus).[63] The comment seems justified. The proof lay in air's "infinity," and in the fact that gods "arose from air," along with the heavenly bodies.[64] In short, air was just about as close to the immaterial as matter could possibly be.

---

[62] DK 13A5; trans. K–R–S.   [63] B3 = Olymp. *De art. sac. lap. phil.* 25.
[64] B3; A9–10; A7.2; A7.5.

In this, Anaximenes was following a characteristic tendency of many of the materialistically minded Presocratics, for whom matter naturally gave way to a thinning out of its own substance and even to a state of near-evacuation altogether, resulting in such concepts as those of the (barely material) divinities or the empty Void. The necessary pertinence of these latter entities to the materialist systems suggests that they are extreme elaborations of matter, not yet its betrayal. On the one hand, they are conceived as elements of the physical universe and not as existing outside it. On the other, void, understood either as empty space or as not-being (as in atomism), is an insult to pure, immaterial cosmologies, the more so as it remains an ambiguous form of being (a "negative substance," in the words of one modern commentator) – which would help to explain why true idealists, from Parmenides to Plato, have no truck with void, nor does Aristotle find void a coherent concept.[65]

As it happens, this trajectory from matter to the sublime – that is, from matter to its sublimation in aesthetic experience – more or less maps out one underlying trajectory of the present study. My suggestion is that the pattern is already being traced in its rudiments among the Presocratic thinkers, who thus constitute an essential stage in the history of Greek and Roman aesthetic thought, and who ought to be acknowledged as having discovered an incipient – or if one prefers, primitive (that is, root) – aesthetic sense of the sublime in their very elaboration of the (ontological) ideas of matter and materiality. That is, I wish to argue that the Presocratics invented two concepts at one and the same time: first, they discovered matter, and they discovered this as an aesthetically attractive category – as palpable and phenomenal, as engaging the physical senses; and secondly, when they discovered matter, they also discovered the sublime, that is, whenever they pressed the concept of matter to its limits, especially its physical and cosmological limits. This, at least, is what the next pages are intended to show. But before going any further, it will be essential to ask a preliminary question: How justified are we in labeling the majority of Presocratics *materialists?* The rubric normally designates philosophers who believe, roughly, in that "inert, senseless substance, in which extension, figure, and motion, do actually subsist," as Berkeley would put it (paraphrasing Locke, polemically, while branding Locke one

---

[65] See Sedley 1982, 175–76 ("negative substance"), and *passim* on Aristotle's objections (which appear in *Ph.* 4.6).

of "the materialists"). But so stated, this is a notion that, I believe, was available to the ancients, even if there are no corresponding equivalents in the ancient philosophical vocabulary.[66]

Consider the following well-known passage from Plato's *Sophist*, a contest between two philosophical camps which is glossed by its translator, F. M. Cornford, as a battle between "materialists" and "idealists," not without some justification:

ELEATIC STRANGER: What we shall see is something like a Battle of Gods and Giants going on between them over their quarrel about reality (τῆς οὐσίας).

THEAETETUS: How so?

ELEATIC STRANGER: One party is trying to drag everything down to earth out of heaven and the unseen, literally grasping rocks and trees in their hands, for they lay hold upon (ἐφαπτόμενοι) every stock and stone and strenuously affirm that real existence belongs only to that which can be handled (ἐπαφήν) and offers resistance to touch. They define reality as the same thing as body, and as soon as one of the opposite party asserts that anything without a body is real, they are utterly contemptuous and will not listen to another word.

THEAETETUS: The people you describe are certainly a formidable crew. I have met quite a number of them before now.

ELEATIC STRANGER: Yes, and accordingly their adversaries are very wary in defending their position somewhere in the heights of the unseen, maintaining with all their force that true reality consists in certain intelligible and bodiless Forms (νοητὰ ... καὶ ἀσώματα εἴδη). In the clash of argument they shatter and pulverize into little bits (κατὰ σμικρά) those bodies which their opponents wield, and what those others allege to be true reality they call, not real being, but a sort of moving process of becoming. On this issue an interminable battle is always going on between the two camps.[67]

The actual identity of the two warring camps in this philosophical parable by Plato is never disclosed, and it would perhaps be as futile to

---

[66] Berkeley, *Principles of Human Knowledge*, Part I, §§ 9; 18. Cf. Frede 2004, 14: "from the very beginning [of Greek philosophy] philosophers in the first instance were concerned to give an account of the sensible, natural, material world and its prominent features," and only later introduced "immaterial principles" to account for aspects of the physical world "that are not themselves perceptible or material." See also ibid., 27: "philosophers naturally started out to try to explain things in terms of the material components of these things" and their properties. Further, Broadie 1999, 209, on Xenophanes' interest in "the fundamental material of things"; the literature on Xenophanes cited below; and Graham (n. 83 below). Cf. Arist. *Metaph.* A 1.992b24–25.

[67] Pl. *Soph.* 246a–c; trans. Cornford, slightly modified.

seek out specific targets as it would be to dismiss as nil the evidentiary value of the passage altogether.[68] At the very least, Plato's divisions attest to a sensibility on his part, if not on the part of others, to a contest over ways of perceiving reality. On one view, reality is tangible or resistant. It is comprised of bodies – probably macroscopic bodies to judge from the parable ("little bits" feature only after matter is destroyed). But we needn't look for detailed nuances in Plato's imagery, which in its boldest outlines could as easily accommodate an atomist as it could an Empedocles or an Anaxagoras.[69] On the other view, which points towards Plato's own, reality is intangible, invisible, incorporeal, static rather than in motion, and a thing of the mind. It is inhabited by Forms, measured against which all so-called bodies vanish into immateriality. Plato is plainly aligning himself with the Eleatic monists against the pluralists, and assigning the latter to the camp of affirmers of the body, or in modern terms, materialists of a sort.[70]

4 WERE THE PRESOCRATICS REALLY MATERIALISTS?

The question whether the Presocratics were materialists hangs in part on the question of how we understand materialism and matter. Now, it is a well-attested fact, and one apparent even to Aristotle, that the majority of the Presocratics just *were* materialists of a sort: they made principles of matter into the underlying causes of all things: "Most of the first philosophers (τῶν πρῶτον φιλοσοφησάντων) thought that principles in the form of matter (τὰς ἐν ὕλης εἴδει ἀρχάς) were the only principles of all things."[71] True, Aristotle's claim is notoriously controversial. Taken to the letter, his observation from *Metaphysics* A 3 is a distortive and reductive one, and at the very least tendentious.[72] No Presocratic would have understood most of his terms (*matter, form,* or, probably, *principles; philosopher* was rare enough until the late fifth century), and it is doubtful that any of them would have accepted his

---

[68] Commentators allow that the so-called materialists may cover both philosophers (including Presocratics) and average folk (Cornford 1957, 232; Bluck 1975, 89–91; Rijk 1986, 100); but philosophers seem better suited to being labeled "formidable."

[69] See DK 68A119 (= Arist. *Sens.* 4. 442a29) on the centrality of touch to Democritus' theory of sensation. Similarly, Empedocles, DK 31A86 (= Theophr. *Sens.* 15); Anaxagoras, DK 59A92 (= Theophr. *Sens.* 29).

[70] For a similar, if vaguer, allusion to "bare" materialism, cf. *Leg.* 10.886d–e, where the Athenian Stranger ridicules scientists for claiming that bodies in the sky "are simply earth and stone, being entirely incapable of taking heed of human things."

[71] *Metaph.* A 3.983b6–8; trans. K–R–S (§85).   [72] See Cherniss 1935, 219–20.

reduction of material elements to a permanently subsisting substrate (ὑποκείμενον), which is the basis of his hylomorphic construction, and which lies behind the concept of matter in the passage just quoted.[73] Nonetheless, there is a recognizable core of truth to Aristotle's claim, once it is stripped of his own metaphysical overlays. We might compare *Metaphysics* A 8, where he defines the meaning of ὕλη ("matter") more closely, and more sensibly – and, incidentally, in a way that recalls the requirements he puts on phenomenal beauty in chapter 7 of the *Poetics* – as "corporeal matter ... having spatial magnitude" (καὶ ταύτην σωματικὴν καὶ μέγεθος ἔχουσαν).[74]

Aristotle knew very well that matter was a tricky concept. In his own terms, it was a πολλαχῶς λεγόμενον, something used in several senses. Thus, in a compound of matter and form, "the matter is in a sense called part of a thing, while in a sense *it* is not, but only the elements of which the formula [the *logos*, or definition] of the form consists."[75] The reason for this complexity of definition is that matter has at least two senses for Aristotle: there is proximate matter, which is what is actualized by the form and comprising the organic parts of a totality; and there is remote matter, which is what "corporeal" matter is just above (the chemical constituents, as it were, of a thing, which subsist irrespective of that thing's essential functions).[76] Thus, when Aristotle states that "bronze is a part of the compound statue, but not of the statue as form" (εἴδους), he is describing the physical stuff, bronze.[77] When he wants to, Aristotle can disambiguate the two kinds of material by referring to corporeal matter as *hulē* and to proximate matter as functionally related to a thing's *ousia* ("substance"),[78] which suggests that his failure to do so is willful, not sloppy, while his ability to name stuff whenever he wants to do so very likely reflects a co-optation of the predecessor concept for matter, something corresponding to mass or stuff (like Thales' water or Anaximander's *apeiron*), though one that very possibly had no single overarching name, such as *matter*. This is likelier, I believe, than the alternative explanation, according to which his ascription of matter to his predecessors and rivals is a simple back-projection and an unwitting (or willful) anachronism.[79]

---

[73] Cf. *Ph.* 2.1.193a9–28; *Metaph.* Δ 4.1014b36–37, with Cherniss 1935, 243 n. 114. ἀρχή is a possible but contested exception (Kirk *et al.* 1983, 108–09).

[74] *Metaph.* A 8.988b22–27. See Frede 2004, esp. 13 and 39.   [75] *Metaph.* Z 7.1035a2–3; trans. Ross.

[76] For the distinction, see Ch. 2, n. 177 above.   [77] *Metaph.* Z 10.1035a6–7; trans. Ross, adapted.

[78] As in *Metaph.* Z 7.1035a20. See Irwin 1988, 241–42.

[79] For well-considered arguments against anachronism on Aristotle's part, malicious or other, see Frede 2004. Further, Mansfeld (next note).

That Aristotle may be consciously and carefully oversimplifying is another question, and certainly possible.[80]

Aristotle's exception above ("*most* of the first philosophers") surely excludes the Eleatic monists, the precursors to Plato who may have denied the reality of the phenomenal world, and to some extent the Pythagoreans, who endowed number with reality, though as Aristotle recognizes, reality in this case still meant material reality.[81] Finer distinctions can be made in the case of other philosophers whose principles (change, Love and Strife, the Indefinite or Mind) will not have interfered with their materialist or physicalist ontologies.[82] Indeed, as has recently been argued, by introducing an umbrella term for matter, Aristotle was merely helping the Presocratics out to a concept that they were already on the way to grasping.[83] But my point from above still holds even in the case of the clear-cut exceptions, which is to say, the non-materialist Presocratics. In segregating the features of phenomenal reality, even if only to denigrate them, the Eleatics and others managed to denominate and to bring further attention to the very dimensions of reality that later proponents of a sensuous aesthetics, or proponents of sensualism in any kind of aesthetics, would be concerned to name and to attend to as well. Indeed, it is likely that in this the Presocratics were merely extending earlier habits of thought, of the sort that can be found in Homer, Hesiod, and later archaic writers. Without pressing this last point too far, we might consider the findings of Robert Renehan's remarkable article on the origins of the ideas of incorporeality and immateriality in Greek thought: in Homer and in "the early Greek view of reality" he represents, "the world and all that was in it was more or less material. There are no immaterial beings. The gods themselves are corporeal and normally anthropomorphic, indeed severely so; they can even be wounded by humans. The souls of the dead are so literally material that an infusion

---

[80] For this suggestion, see Mansfeld 1985b.

[81] Arist. *Metaph.* A 5.986a17; cf. Ross ad loc.: "Like all the pre-Socratics, they had not reached the notion of non-spatial reality."

[82] Cf. again *Metaph.* A 8.988b22–27, which rightly stresses the materialism of, e.g., an Anaximander or Empedocles, regardless of any immaterial or transcendent principles they may have postulated. (Ross 1924, 1:147 takes Empedocles' principles to be "material things." Cf. Arist. *Ph.* 3.5.204b22, squarely identifying Anaximander's Indefinite with body: τὸ ἄπειρον σῶμα.) Whether or not Thales is a materialist *monist*, a claim the passage from *Metaph.* A 3 quoted earlier serves to introduce (*contra*: Kirk *et al.* 1983, 90–91, 93–4; *pro*: Barnes 1982, 9–11), is irrelevant to the larger question.

[83] "Aristotle will finally co-opt a word originally meaning 'wood' or 'building material,' *hylē*, for matter – a concept the early Greek philosophers deal with constantly without being able to refer to abstractly" (Graham 1999, 172).

of blood will restore temporarily their wits and vitality," and so on.[84]
Aesthetic correlatives to these materiate things, not explored by him but
touched on by others, will be discussed in later chapters.

If this is indeed the background against which Presocratic thought
emerged, and I think it is a plausible scenario, then my point ought to
be plausible too: it is that the Presocratics came along to articulate the
intuitions that were taken for granted in the widespread materialism of
their culture. What is more, thanks to the Presocratics, the background
assumptions of the archaic age will have been thrown into sharper relief,
whether this articulation of ideas was carried out in the spirit of critique or
out of a desire to enforce in a positive way pre-existing conceptions of
matter and materiality.

Instances of this kind of positive attention will be adduced below in the
case of Xenophanes and Heraclitus, but let's consider for a moment the
harder case of somebody like Zeno the Eleatic, renowned for his puzzles
about monism and pluralism. Ostensibly in defense of Parmenides,
though his aim may rather have been to point up vulnerabilities in
Parmenides' logic, Zeno "*proves*," according to Simplicius (who is paraphrasing Zeno here, but adopting his terminology), "*that what has neither
magnitude* (μέγεθος) *nor solidity* (πάχος) *nor bulk* (ὄγκος) *would not
even exist.*"[85] To the common man, this glorious proof no doubt would
have seemed like pushing at an open door, but in philosophical circles it
must have been the equivalent of establishing the logical status of the
number 1 in the *Principia mathematica*. For what it is worth, all of Zeno's
entertaining antinomies and paradoxes have to do with existing *bodies*,
whether at rest or in motion (the stadium, the arrow, Achilles and the
tortoise, the moving rows). The formidable logician Zeno was thus in fact
a logician of the material world. He was as firmly grounded in material
reality as any of his more materialistically minded peers, even if his
intentions were to establish the antinomies of matter, not to verify its
legitimacy. The example of Zeno illustrates that even an aggressive stance
against materialism involves an affirmation *ex hypothesi* of matter prior
to its refutation, whatever its existence or value may be supposed to be.
Anti-materialists among the Presocratics could thus in the long run prove
to be materialism's secret allies, above all in the conceptual articulation
of matter's many faces.

[84] Renehan 1980, 108. I owe this reference to Brooke Holmes.
[85] B2; trans. K–R–S (= Simp. *in Ph.* 164.17–20); emphasis added.

Parmenides (born *c.* 515) is undoubtedly the odd man out. A forerunner of an extreme, ethereal idealism of sorts, he looks like the contradiction of all materialism and empiricism. His philosophy seeks to show that what is exists in an ungenerated, unmoving, monistic, and unchanging state of perfection that is conceivable only with the mind, in contrast to the world of plural becoming, which is revealed to us by the faulty senses and by untrustworthy belief. When he sought to deny the evidence of the senses in the first half of his great poem (though not in the second), he was taking up a self-consciously counterintuitive stance.[86] He was thus sharpening up, *e contrario*, a commonsense belief about the nature of phenomenal reality and turning it into a philosophical instrument – one that would later be wielded against him. For as it happens, Zeno's arguments pierce even the Parmenidean One, which at a minimum enjoys spatial extension just like the plural existents that Zeno sought to target.[87]

5 PRESOCRATIC AESTHETICS: PAINTING THE 'PHAINOMENA'

In most other cases, there was less embarrassment and more of a whole-hearted embracement of matter and matter's appearances among Socrates' predecessors. In casting their vote in favor of the phenomenal world and its underlying entities, the Presocratic philosophers would have only been fortifying the attention to art's appearances that artists had been cultivating in their own ways and that poets had been articulating since Homer (more on which below), however much the philosophers might seem to have run into conflict with either the artists or the poets. Yet, even here, these conflicts are more superficial than they first appear: they are more like glancing blows *en route* to other, larger goals, and often wrapped up in contests of authority, rather than indices of principal concerns held by the philosophers. Thus, Heraclitus' criticism of Homer, preserved in a mention by Aristotle, is an assertion of his own philosophical program at the expense of the poet's (innocent) "misuse" of the word *strife* (*eris*): "Heraclitus blames the poet who wrote 'may strife perish from among gods and men' [*Il.* 18.107]; for (says Heraclitus) there could not be harmony without the low and the high note, nor living things without

---

[86] "Clearly a shock to his contemporaries" (Kirk *et al.* 1983, 195).
[87] DK 28B8.42–49 (Parmenides): Being is "like the mass of a well-rounded sphere" (εὐκύκλου σφαίρης ἐναλίγκιον ὄγκῳ), a vulnerable view; see Kirk *et al.*, 269.

male and female, two opposites."[88] The criticism *pro domo sua* does not prevent Heraclitus from showing off a little musical knowledge, knowledge that famously colors his philosophy of blended harmonies without, however, being its primary object in any way. Xenophanes (*c.* 570–*c.* 475) famously criticized Homer and Hesiod, a move that influenced Heraclitus and established a veritable trend in Greek thinking. But this was in the area of morals and directed against mythological thought.[89] Elsewhere, Xenophanes makes light of the capacity of mimesis to capture the reality of divinity: if oxen, horses, and lions could paint images and make statues, their gods would be portrayed in their own forms;[90] and Empedocles of Acragas (*c.* 492–432) is said to have quipped that the Acragantines lived large as if they were going to die on the morrow, but they built homes as if they were planning to live forever in them.[91] But again, the former *aperçu* is best understood in the context of religion, not as a contribution to mimesis-theory, while the latter quip is an ethical judgment, not an observation about monumental architecture.

The imagery of painting and the language of beauty, on the other hand, do occasionally feature positively in the Presocratic remains, but incidentally and typically by way of metaphor. The most famous and extended of these occur in Empedocles. In one fragment, we find an analogy between natural genesis and painting:

Moreover he added a clear model of the way different things come from the same: "As when painters (γραφέες) are decorating offerings [i.e., votive tablets, ἀναθήματα], men through cunning well skilled in their craft (ἀμφὶ τέχνης ὑπὸ μήτιος εὖ δεδαῶτε) – when they actually seize pigments of many colours (πολύχροα φάρμακα) in their hands, mixing in harmony (ἁρμονίῃ μείξαντε) more of some and less of others, they produce from them forms resembling all things (εἴδεα πᾶσιν ἀλίγκια), creating trees and men and women, beasts and birds and water-bred fish, and long-lived gods, too, highest in honour: so let not deception (ἀπάτη) overcome your mind and make you think there is any other source of all the countless mortal things that are plain to see, but know this clearly, for the tale you hear comes from a god."[92]

---

[88] Arist. *Eth. Eud.* 1235a25–29 = DK 22A22; trans. Solomon.   [89] See n. 47 above.
[90] DK 21B15.
[91] DK 31A1.63 = D.L. 8.63. Neither this nor the previous quotation earn a mention in Lanata 1963, nor does any of the other fragments discussed in the present chapter. True, Lanata is interested narrowly in poetics. But her exclusion of broad aesthetic questions is characteristic of current approaches to ancient literary criticism, with very few exceptions, which is to say, characteristic of an excessively narrow understanding of "poetics" today.
[92] B23; trans. K–R–S.

Empedocles shows more than a passing familiarity with the technical aspects and the language of painting. He knows, for instance, that colors are generated through a process of mixing, by which he appears to mean not the blending of pigments, a process that evolved only starting with Apollodorus in the late fifth century, but the combining of a small palette of pigments either through their juxtaposition and arrangement or else through their superposition over a wash (what would later be known as *harmogē*).[93]

Empedocles would have had a vested interest in these processes for several reasons. For starters, he had developed his own theory of color perception, and indeed was one of the first Greek philosophers to do so. Naturally, the practices of the painters would have attracted his attention: their processes contained a kind of embedded theory of color. But the mere fact that Empedocles chose to speculate about color is significant in itself: it attests to his keen interest in the colors of the world. As Katerina Ierodiakonou has shown, Empedocles' stakes were polemical. Parmenides had denied that color was a primary feature of reality.[94] And he had inveighed heavily against phenomenal change, and in particular against changing colors in the phenomenal world ("*alteration in bright* [or '*appar-ent*'] *colour*," διά τε χρόα φανὸν ἀμείβειν).[95] "Against Parmenides, Empedocles took it upon himself to explain both how it comes about that objects in the world actually are colored," as all worldly objects for him are, "and how, in consequence, it is that they appear to us as coloured."[96] Color is both a material property and a phenomenal property of empirical objects.

The colorful nature of reality was grounded in Empedocles' theory of cosmogony and physics. The four roots, or elements, of nature combine at the origin of the world to produce primordial forms and colors:

And if, concerning these things, your conviction is in any way wanting as to how from the combining (κιρναμένων) of water, earth, aether, and sun the forms and colours of mortal things might come to be, which have now come to be, fitted together (συναρμοσθέντ') by Aphrodite ....[97]

---

[93] In this, I am following Ierodiakonou 2005, esp. 4–8 and 18 (on the juxtaposition of colors as discussed in Arist. *Sens.* 3.439b20: παρ' ἄλληλα τιθέμενα).

[94] DK 28B8.41.   [95] Ibid.

[96] Ierodiakonou 2005, 2. Empedocles' powerful interests in color and in painterly practices suggest that he could well have had an impact on later color theory, including that of the painters (on which, see Pollitt 2002, who, however, doubts this kind of connection).

[97] B71; trans. as in Ierodiakonou, ibid., 4.

The process by which the discrete physical elements combine is one of "fitting" or "joining together," as in brick laying, gluing, or the mixing of paint pigments.[98] Here, Empedocles' interest in painting and in color theory is conjoined with his interest in physics. And with his model of parts and wholes, he shows himself to be a forerunner of the materialists who, from the latter third of the fifth century on, will adopt a model of elements joined in combination, to be described below as the componential analysis of material parts, or *stoicheia* – a term not yet available to Empedocles, who instead speaks of *rhizai*, or "roots," though Aristotle says that Empedocles was "the first to speak of four material *stoicheia*."[99] In essence, this model is one in which discrete elements aggregate into larger patterns or wholes, which in turn produce larger-scale effects greater than and often different from those that the individual parts are capable of producing on their own. In some versions, the elements lie below the threshold of sensation, and the effects they give off are emergent or, if one likes, supervenient. In a further subset of this same model, the elements lack phenomenal features (they cannot be seen, heard, felt, tasted, and so on), and only their combined qualities possess such features. In Empedocles' version, the elements have phenomenal features but are imperceptible to the senses (there are, say, black and white microscopic constituents of objects in the world), while their combined effects are various and striking: in different proportions and under different conditions (for instance, given varying degrees of moisture), the particles within things generate different colors and eventually the full spectrum of visible colors, thus variously coloring the objects in which they inhere.[100] What is extraordinary is how deeply ingrained this model is; how well suited to expressing material processes it is; how varied its applications are (from the most primary cosmic elements to paint pigments to the letters of the alphabet, and on and on, seemingly without end); and what a long and illustrious pedigree it enjoys, from the Presocratics to the fifth century, and from there well into later antiquity.

---

[98] A34; A43; B23: ἁρμονίη μείξαντε; B71.4: συναρμόζεσθαι; B96.4: Ἁρμονίης κόλλῃσιν ἀρηρότα (cf. B34); B96 test.: Arist. *De an.* 1.5.410a1–2 (cf. ibid., 7–8): τὰ στοιχεῖα … λόγωι τινὶ καὶ συνθέσει; B107: ἁρμόζεσθαι.

[99] Arist. *Metaph.* A 4.985a32 (trans. Ross): τὰ ὡς ἐν ὕλης εἴδει λεγόμενα στοιχεῖα τέτταρα πρῶτος εἶπεν.

[100] So Ierodiakonou 2005, a plausible picture. Cf. DK 31A94 (Arist. *Sens.* 4.441a5) on Empedocles' theory of flavors in their various kinds, which are "imperceptible (ἀναίσθητα) owing to their minuteness."

So far, we have two reasons why Empedocles would have shown a strong interest in painting analogies: his pursuits in optics and his physical model of combining elements. A third is perhaps the most diffuse but hardly the least negligible, and it underpins the other two: he was keenly interested in the variegated and changing nature of phenomenal reality. Like Xenophanes, who could project a persona that was dazzled by the senses and who expressed himself in poetic verses rivaling Homer's, Empedocles was a philosopher-poet who chose to write in an epic trad-ition *à la* Homer and Hesiod and whose verses are bursting with colors and light in different hues. Compare a famous set of verses from his cosmogony, oft-quoted even in antiquity:

And kindly earth received in its broad melting-pots (χοάνοισι: "channels" or "receptacles")[101] two parts of the glitter of Nestis (Νήστιδος αἴγλης) out of eight, and four of Hephaestus, and they became white bones, marvelously joined by the gluing of Harmonia (Ἁρμονίης κόλλῃσιν ἀρηρότα θεσπεσίηθεν).[102]

Whiteness here is a *color*, unlike in Plato: it glitters and gleams, marvel-ously. Elsewhere, rain is said to be "black," water is "silvery."[103] Things are generated, and they never cease their process of (re)generation. In doing so, they present themselves to the senses in a rich panorama – the world is intrinsically "phenomenological": "there are just these [the two cosmogonic principles, Love and Strife, but also implicitly the four elements], but running through each other they assume different appearances (γίνεται ἀλλοιωπά); so much does mixture change them."[104] Elsewhere, Empedo-cles speaks of "all the countless [or "marvelous"] mortal things that are plain to see" (ὅσσα γε δῆλα γεγάκασιν ἄσπετα).[105] An elaborate lamp meta-phor describes the function of the eye. The image is itself aglow:

As when someone planning a journey through the wintry night prepares a light, a flame of blazing fire (πυρὸς σέλας αἰθομένοιο), kindling for all sorts of winds a linen lantern, which scatters the breath of the winds when they blow, but the finer light leaps through outside and shines across the threshold with unyielding beams: so at that time did she [sc., Aphrodite] give birth to the round eye, primeval fire confined within membranes and delicate garments (λεπτῇσίν ⟨τ'⟩ ὀθόνῃσι λοχάζετο) .... [106]

---

[101] On the erotic connotations of this word, see Mourelatos 1986, 175.   [102] B96; trans. K–R–S.
[103] B111.6; B100.11.   [104] B21.13–4; trans. K–R–S.
[105] B23.10. For a different rendering, see Mourelatos 1986, 179, who rightly stresses the phenomenological character of this and similar verses.
[106] B85 (part); trans. K–R–S, slightly adapted.

Empedocles' celebration of the birth of vision is not merely a baroque metaphor. It is at the same time a defense of the senses. This position in favor of the authority of the senses is one he programmatically assumed early on in his poem,[107] again in the teeth of Parmenidean objections. Knowledge through sensation is not only possible, but also essential to human existence. And it is secure. Indeed, its objects are "clear" (δῆλα).[108]

Here, in his account of sensation, the analogy to painting has one further application. Limited though the senses are, being partial and fragmentary, they nonetheless "[can] transcend their fragmentariness and help to achieve the synthetic grasp that [Empedocles makes] the distinctive mark of his thinking."[109] Thus, the senses collaborate and in concert produce a unity of knowledge. But in order to appreciate the full significance of this kind of synthesis, we have to return to Empedocles' cosmogony.

Elemental synthesis, as in the mixing of paint pigments, is the governing model and mechanism of the Empedoclean universe. Cosmogony is a plural act of creation, passing from many to one to a diversified plurality again, which finally reunites in a grand synthesis of the divine:

All ... things come together to be one only, not suddenly, but combining (συνιστάμενα) from different directions at will. And as they mingled (μισγομένων) countless tribes of mortal things poured forth; but many remained unmixed, alternating with those that were being mixed.... And as they mingled countless tribes of mortal things poured forth, fitted with forms of all kinds (παντοίαις ἰδέηισιν ἀρηρότα), a wonder to behold (θαῦμα ἰδέσθαι).[110]

It would be a mistake to downplay the miraculousness and the pure visual splendor of the world contemplated by Empedocles here. The Homericism, "a wonder to behold," drives home the poetic character of Empedocles' insight, but also its philosophical and materialistic pluralism: Empedocles is envisaging the world in all its spectacular variety. What is more, each individual act of perception, by virtue of its combining the manifold of sensory appearances into a graspable unity, rehearses the world's first synthesis: sensing (like knowing) is in more than a mere manner of speaking the coming into being of a world for a perceiving subject. Thus, as André Laks observes, "whether sensation or thought, every cognitive act is the anticipation, within the limits of human life, of

---

[107] Probably just a single poem (Osborne 1987; Inwood 2001, 14–19).   [108] B2; B3; B23.10.
[109] Laks 1999, 262 (citing B3).   [110] B35.5–8; trans. K–R–S.

the ultimate fusion of the elements in the unity of the divine Sphere. These are acts of love, and this is why they are linked to pleasure."[111] One need only add that this seductiveness of the universe is aesthetically pleasing too.

Small wonder, then, that another particularly seductive set of verses by Empedocles exemplifies the language of beauty, combined with its perennial co-characteristic in Greek aesthetic thought, desire:

But come, look upon the witnesses to this former discourse of mine, should beauty (μορφῆι) have been lacking in it earlier: the sun, hot to see and dazzling all over (λαμπρὸν ἀπάντη); all the immortals that are bathed in heat and brilliant rays (ἀργέτι αὐγῆ); rain in all things dark and chill; and from the earth pour forth things rooted and solid. In Anger all are of different forms and separate, but in Love they come together and are desired (ποθεῖται) by each other.[112]

Lucretius would later be drawn to these verses, particularly in his hymn to Venus in the opening book of *On the Nature of Things*. There, he celebrates the erotics of nature, cast (with a certain poetic license) as brimming over with procreative urges: "so surely enchained by delight (*capta lepore*) each [creature] follows you in hot desire (*cupide*) whither you do hasten to lead it on (*inducere pergis*). Then through seas and mountains and tearing rivers and the leafy haunts of birds and verdant plains do you strike fond love (*blandum per pectora amorem/efficis*) into the hearts of all, and make them renew the stock of their races in hot desire (*cupide*), each after its own kind."[113] But Lucretius' imagery is also carefully balanced by the philosophical materialism of his own poem, whereby all the vivid bustling and colorful burgeoning described in the preamble is ultimately to be viewed against the blank backdrop of a featureless void containing myriad atoms, themselves devoid of phenomenal features.

Empedocles' verses likewise blend matter with beauty and desire. Indeed, they celebrate the beauties of matter as something that is *saturated* with desire. They merely do so without any hint of the featureless reductionism that will come to mark the atomist worldview. And though Empedocles, like the atomists, is himself a pluralist, he renews the suspicion, first mooted by Parmenides, that the phenomenal world is a

[111] Ibid., 267.　[112] B21.1–8; trans. K–R–S.

[113] Lucr. 1.15–20; trans. Bailey, adapted. Further direct Empedoclean echoes in the proem are detected by Sedley 1998, 23–26, who suggests that Empedocles' poem may have opened with its own hymn to Aphrodite.

world of deceptive appearances, as is any account of it: "so let not deception (ἀπάτη) overcome your mind...."[114] Indeed, his notion of the emergence of perceptual complex properties out of combined simples, whether through optical fusion or by means of similar processes in other regions of sensation, naturally leads to the suspicion that sensation is the dupe of its objects, and that perceptions, consequently, are no better than illusions.[115] This was a risk that affected all the pluralist Presocratics.[116] Gorgias would later trade on all these associations, both in his aesthetic theories and in his critiques of metaphysics and language (see Chapter 5 below).

6 SUBLIME MATTER: A PRESOCRATIC INVENTION

So far, I have been making a case for the Presocratics as conceptual innovators. We can now sharpen up this insight. For what is most significant about the Presocratics' contribution to aesthetic thinking is not only that they, as it were, dub matter or materiality categories of thought and occasionally find beauty in this realm, but also that they construct these categories as existing in infinite expanses, farther than the eye can see or the mind can grasp, whether proliferating endlessly into this one world or else (as in the case, for example, of Anaximander, Xenophanes, Anaxagoras, and the atomists) into infinite parallel or successive worlds. Thus, what stands out as endowed with an immediate and arguably intrinsic aesthetic value is the sheer *profusion of matter* that so many of the Presocratics countenance in their systems. There is something overwhelming and breathtaking about this kind of postulate, which is in its own way sublime (a term that does not seem to have occurred to the Presocratics, though it is occasionally used in later descriptions of their thought).[117] Xenophanes' description of the heavens, filtered by Hippolytus, is a good example of this kind of thinking:

The sun comes into being each day from little pieces of fire that are collected, and the earth is infinite (ἄπειρον) and enclosed neither by air nor by the heaven.

---

[114] B23.9; cf. Parmenides, DK 28B8 (with n. 158 below).
[115] This same idea is raised, and dismissed, by Mourelatos 1986, 178–87.
[116] For Heraclitus, see at n. 194 below.
[117] Cf. "Your thoughts go higher than the air" (φρονεῖτε νυν αἰθέρος ὑψηλότερον) (Adesp. *TrGF* 2.127 = Diod. Sic. 16.92.3), which can be connected to the sublime thoughts of the natural philosopher whose mind dwells in the heavens. And cf. Pl. *Phdr.* 270a, connecting "ethereal speculation" (μετεωρολογία), in the context of Anaxagorean cosmology, with "loftiness of mind" (ὑψηλόνους). Further, Capelle 1912; Quadlbauer 1958, 58; Dover 1968, lxvii–lxviii; Pucci 2006. Cf. further *P. Herc.* 1788 fr. 3 (see n. 139 below).

There are innumerable (ἀπείρους) suns and moons, and all things are made of earth (τὰ δὲ πάντα εἶναι ἐκ γῆς).[118]

The heavenly bodies, for Xenophanes, seem to have been made up either of a concentration of fiery particles or of ignited clouds, and scholars sometimes worry about this divergence in the testimonia.[119] But an even greater divergence ought to be felt in the claim that the sun is made of fire but "all things" are made of earth.[120] The contradiction can perhaps be resolved if we assume that fire, too, is made of earth, or else that *earth* is Xenophanes' way of expressing *matter*, and that fire is a form of matter. Alternatively, earth is not a constitutive element but a local source ("all things *come from* earth").[121]

Whatever the case, the world so viewed is a pretty place, and it is filled with matter. And so too, faced with a verse like *Iliad* 11.7 (a description of Agamemnon's corselet inlaid with snakes, which are compared in their sheen to rainbows), Xenophanes, according to the scholia, responded in kind: "What they call Iris [rainbow], this too is cloud, purple and red and yellow to behold" (πορφύρεον καὶ φοινίκεον καὶ χλωρὸν ἰδέσθαι).[122] This is a nice point. To make it requires the eye of a careful reader capable of penetrating several levels into an embedded simile in order to retrieve a tiny glittering detail, in addition to that of a natural scientist. The point is also poetically expressed. The Homericism, with ἰδέσθαι in final position, seems calculated to bring to mind, or rather to the ear, two epic formulas: εἰς ὦπα ἰδέσθαι ("to look X in the face") and especially θαῦμα ἰδέσθαι ("a wonder to behold"). There is thaumaturgy in the natural wonders of a secularized nature too.[123] Empedocles, discussed a few pages ago, would later show himself vulnerable to identical impulses, perceptual and poetic – or, in a word, aesthetic.[124]

The same holds for another fragment from Xenophanes, this time one that is more obviously cast in poetic form (hexameters):

γαίης μὲν τόδε πεῖρας ἄνω παρὰ ποσσὶν ὁρᾶται
ἠέρι προσπλάζον, τὸ κάτω δ' ἐς ἄπειρον ἱκνεῖται.

---

[118] DK 21A33.3; trans. K–R–S.   [119] Kirk *et al.* 1983, 173.   [120] Cf. DK 21A32.

[121] So, e.g., Lesher 1992, 124–28 (*ad* B27). Lesher, *per litt.*, suggests another alternative for resolving the problem, namely, "that when Xenophanes mentions earth, he means to include moisture as part of the earth (cf. B29)." This last idea, like Fränkel's remark, "of course, the sea must be counted as earth" (Fränkel 1974, 119), to be discussed below, is compatible with the suggestions named above.

[122] DK 21B32; trans. K–R–S.

[123] Similarly, Lesher 1992, 143, who refers to *Od.* 6.306, 13.108 ("purple, a marvel to behold") and to the fact that in Hesiod Iris is the daughter of Thaumas (*Theog.* 265–66).

[124] See above on Empedocles, B96.

Of earth this is the upper limit which we see *by our feet,*
in contact with the air; *but its underneath continues indefinitely.*[125]

These verses are remarkable for a few different reasons. First of all, they
reiterate the theme of the *proliferation of matter ad infinitum* witnessed
above. But they do so in a dizzying, vertiginous way. Or rather, they
bring out what was vertiginous in the theme already quoted. Only now,
they reproduce this endlessness, the infinite expansiveness of matter in
all directions and even (perhaps, though this is contested) into other
worlds, in the form of an *abyss* of matter – one that takes place right
beneath your very own feet.[126] Xenophanes' conceit is no doubt framed
as a deliberate paradox. Though, as it were, on the surface seemingly
designed to demonstrate the solidity of the earth, the fragment in effect
points up the opposite of this geophysical feature. How stable, conceptually, is the ground on which we stand? That is, what determines
where the line gets drawn between where we stand and the infinite
space of earth below? The conceit is for the same reason sublime, or so
it would appear to later tradition – for instance, to Longinus, in his
account of Tartarean abysses, to which Xenophanes' text has likewise
been thought to allude.[127] The question is whether it was not already
felt to be sublime in the sixth century BCE. The evidence in favor is
strictly inferential, as it can only be. The Presocratics, after all, are
primarily natural philosophers, not aestheticians, with the sole exception
of Democritus, who wrote on just about everything (as Aristotle attests) –
but whose work in aesthetics is known mainly from his preserved titles.
(We will return to Democritus provisionally in the next section and then
again in a later chapter.)

One more testimony deserves a brief mention in this context:

Xenophanes said that there are many suns and moons according to regions,
sections and zones of the earth, and that at a certain time the disc [i.e., the sun] is
banished into some section of the earth not inhabited by us, and so, as it were
(ὥσπερ), treading on nothing [lit., "treading on emptiness": κενεμβατοῦντα],
produces the phenomenon of an eclipse. The same man says that the sun goes
onwards *ad infinitum* (εἰς ἄπειρον), but seems to move in a circle because of
the distance.[128]

[125] B28 = Achilles *Isag.* 4.34.11 Maas; trans. K–R–S.   [126] Cf. Mourelatos 2002, 335.
[127] On the hint of abyssal depths in the Xenophanean passage ("'indefinite' or 'indeterminate' depths")
and its possible allusions to earlier poetry, see Lesher 1992, 130–31; for Empedocles' reaction to it, see
DK 31B39 (on which see below); for Longinus (*Subl.* 9.6), see Porter 2007b, 168, etc.
[128] DK 21A41a (= Aet. 2.24.9); trans. K–R–S, adapted.

We are in the same ambit of multiplied phenomena, heavenly bodies, of bodies proliferating into infinity. Once again, the abyssal implications of this hyperextension of matter are brought out in a hyperbolic extension of thought and language, tempered only by the qualifier, "as it were" (ὥσπερ). The passage has elicited no small amount of puzzlement among commentators. Kirk, Raven, and Schofield find it "bizarre." Trying to make rational sense of the conceit, they propose the following: "That the sun continues westward indefinitely looks like a deliberately naïve statement of the anti-scientific viewpoint.... It is possible that the segments of the earth were regarded as hollow depressions," etc. Then, out of desperation, they try another tack: "Whatever is the true explanation, it is clear that Xenophanes permitted himself a certain degree of fantasy here (and possibly, judging by the expression 'treading on nothing', of humor). Perhaps there was some kind of irony, too."[129] This looks like grasping at straws. It is unlikely that Xenophanes tolerated a concept like void: on the contrary, his worldview is *stiflingly* filled with matter, so much so that Hermann Fränkel was moved to produce the remarkable but in some sense true observation, "für ihn gab es ja keinen Himmel" ("for [Xenophanes] there simply was no heaven").[130] What seems undeniable, on the other hand, is that in the present case, as elsewhere, Xenophanes is inviting us to think beyond the limits of matter into its absence, here in the form of a void (the "empty"). It is as if the very "sublimation" of matter by way of its pluralization (here, into "many suns and moons") produced the thought of its opposite – a pattern we will occasionally witness in the pages to follow. Here, *les extrêmes se touchent*, and matter meets the sublime.[131]

It is worth noting that the idea of the visible world as existing in the form of a limitless expanse is as ancient as Greek literature itself. Tartarus in Homer and Hesiod is the *locus classicus* for an immense, and sometimes seemingly bottomless, subterranean expanse,[132] and "towering" Ida (Ἴδη ὑψηλή) or a perch "on top (ὕψου) of the highest summit of timbered Samos" provide an ideal eyrie from which to take in all the world below

---

[129] Kirk *et al.* 1983, 174–75.
[130] Fränkel 1993, 381. To this one might as well add the thought that for Xenophanes "we are all created of earth and water" (B33): his materialism touches even our human nature, and so too does the threat of claustrophobic limits. In other words, the infinitization of matter moves not just outwardly, but also within.
[131] For the Lucretian, Longinian, and Kantian aftermath, see Porter 2007b. See also Else 1930, 175 (on Schopenhauer), a reference I had missed.
[132] *Il.* 8.16; *Theog.* 720. For the troubles with the notion of chasm in our inherited text, see West 1966, *ad* v. 740.

and the skies above for "far-seeing" Zeus (εὐρύοπα Ζεύς).[133] But there
were other poetic symbols evocative of infinite and sublime stretches,
including Strife, whose feet touch the ground but whose head strikes
heaven, and who would later inspire a breathtaking passage in Longinus,
in an account of literary expanses that evoke immense cosmic spaces,
including Tartarean depths.[134] A characteristic of endlessness is its indeterminacy (the root meaning of *apeiron*, or *infinite*). Chaos in Hesiod is
another such *apeiron*. The expression used by Xenophanes above, ἐπ'
ἀπείρονα, "serves to designate large expanses lacking observable boundaries or borders (Herodotus: 'a boundless (ἄπειρον) plain stretching as
far as the eye can see,' etc.)."[135]

Empedocles later seems to have ridiculed Xenophanes' claim about the
earth extending εἰς ἄπειρον below:

> If indeed the depths (βάθη) of earth and abundant aether are unbounded
> (ἀπείρονα),
> as is poured out in a vain stream
> from the tongues in the mouths of many, *who have seen little of the whole*.[136]

Yet the counterargument, if that is what it is,[137] does nothing to diminish
the power of the original insight, and if anything it confirms it, as the
italicized portion of Empedocles' language shows. Empedocles, like
Aristotle who preserves this fragment,[138] is chiding Xenophanes for
making an unwarranted empirical claim, but he is not disputing the force
of the claim itself. In postulating a whole that exceeds the grasp of the
visible, Empedocles has created another excessive infinity of his own. If
Empedocles meant to expound a theory of a determinate totality as
opposed to a regressive infinity or indefinite expanse, he nevertheless
has preserved the tension that exists for a subject in sheer phenomenological terms: grasping the whole lies beyond reach, while the mere
prospect of a successful or defeated grasp of this whole can be sublime.[139]

---

[133] At *Il.* 15.146–47, there is even a significant word-play on *Ida* that brings out this connection: "Zeus
wishes / both of you to go to him with all speed, at Ida (εἰς Ἴδην); but when you have come there
and looked upon Zeus' countenance (εἰς ὦπα ἴδησθε), . . ." (trans. Lattimore 1951).

[134] *Il.* 5.770–72; *Subl.* 9.5–8.

[135] Lesher 1992, 130 (*ad* B28); Herod. 1.204.1; cf. Snell *et al.* 1955–2010, s.v. ἄπειρον.

[136] DK 31B39; trans. Inwood; emphasis added.   [137] So, e.g., Lesher 1992, 130.

[138] *Cael.* 294a21–28.

[139] More work might be done to pursue the thematics of height and transcendental claims in
Empedocles, especially in the later parts of his poem, which at times sound rather Zarathustran
in a Nietzschean vein (though the reverse is more likely to be true). Cf. *P. Herc.* 1788 fr. 3.3–6,
which combines the adjective *hupsos* with a quotation from DK 31B112.4 ("I am an immortal god,

One last note on Xenophanes is in order, which an insightful comment by Hermann Fränkel will help to clarify:

There is in [Xenophanes'] scheme no vaulted distant heaven over men's heads (A33.3); nor is there some deep ocean or infernal bottom into which the earth's roots extend. In his view, the two massive bodies [earth and sea] on whose mutual boundary we lead our lives alone suffice to occupy the All to its full extent.

In the next breath, Fränkel corrects himself by adding, "Of course, the sea must be counted as earth."[140] The correction is somewhat opaque (in exactly what sense must the sea be counted as earth?), but we can take Fränkel's remark as supporting the view I suggested earlier, namely the identification of earth with matter. The point has to be understood in its largest context. There is a kind of reductive materialism and empiricism at work in Xenophanes, especially vis-à-vis inherited mythology. The net effect of this reduction of all that is (the All or universe) to the horizon of the visible can be felt either as stifling or liberating, depending on one's perspective. I suspect Xenophanes meant his picture of the universe to be liberating from a rational point of view, and perhaps stifling from a mythological point of view (for anyone in search of transcendental perspectives, that is). By foreclosing the mysterium of heaven and hell, he radically confronts mankind with empirical phenomena.[141] On Xenophanes' revision of cosmology and phenomenology, there is in the world *nothing but matter* (earth), which must be conceived as an *endless surface, even in its depths* – for these are but endlessly receding surfaces of (ever more) earth (matter). That is, there is nothing but matter to confront humankind, our gaze, our senses, and our minds. Materialism is here made oppressively – or else, exhilaratingly – omnipresent, and quite literally so.

---

no longer mortal"). The missing substantive to which *hupsos* belongs is unclear, and the candidates on record are "philosophy," "thought," and "Etna" (one might add two more: "poetry" or "language"). But this is admittedly just a word in a fragment, and no more than that (though the presence of other Presocratics in the two earlier columns, including *inter alios* Leucippus and Democritus – plus their works, the *Megas Diakosmos* and the *Mikros Diakosmos*, respectively – and Gorgias, and of the word *poet* in fr. 7, is tantalizing). The papyrus is very likely a relic of Philodemus' *Syntaxis philosophorum* on Presocratic philosophers. For the papyrus text, see Crönert 1906, 147. For the text's identification and its context, I am indebted to Obbink 2005, an unpublished paper.

140   Fränkel 1974, 119.

141   See the author of *On Ancient Medicine*, who on epistemological grounds rules out of bounds the postulate of "the mysteries of heaven (τῶν μετεώρων) and of the regions below" (τῶν ὑπὸ γῆν) (*VM* 1.3 = 1:572 L.; quoted in Fränkel 1974, 129, who sees a Xenophanean influence here).

Xenophanes' physical picture represents quite a novel approach to the world, even if it is tendentially in line with some of the other early Presocratics' thinking – for instance, that of Anaximenes, who saw the universe as coming into its present form through a process of condensation (πύκνωσις) of air into earth, and then again of rarefaction (ἀραίωσις) of earthly exhalations into astral bodies. And so, too, for the inherited sublime effect of the vaulted ceiling of the sky and the abyss of Tartarus familiar from the fictions (πλάσματα) of poets,[142] Xenophanes substituted the sublime prospect of *unlimited surfaces of matter*, and so too an unlimited field for human exploration and knowledge (and ignorance) – a sterling instance of "the material sublime." Or rather, on Xenophanes' revisionist view, there is nothing in the world that matters to us beyond the limits of the visible earth, which is to say beyond the limits of human experience, nothing, as Empedocles' criticism observes (albeit too late, because it was already anticipated by Xenophanes), that we can register with our faculties. For beyond those limits lies god, who is now rendered more absolute than ever before: numerically one, greatest of all (μέγιστος), non-anthropomorphic, unmovable but all-moving, fully sentient, yet seemingly set off from all earthly matters by an inconceivable chasm ("not at all like mortals in body [δέμας] or in thought"), or else by a chasm of inconceivability, standing as he does like a pure conceptual limit or puzzle[143] – that is, when he wasn't taken to be utterly immanent to the world, as Aristotle, for instance, understood him to be.[144] So there is world, and there is god. And yet, even god seems to be possessed of a *kind* of corporeality, because he enjoys spatio-temporal location and is endowed with physical powers, though what kind of corporeality he has remains unclear.[145] Perhaps god is composed of a sublime matter, unless he is just composed of *the sublimity of matter* itself? If so, then his job, philosophically speaking, is to designate the divinity of reality.[146]

---

[142] B1.17.
[143] B23–26; the quotation is from B23. Fränkel 1974, 130, Reinhardt 1959, 118, and Lesher 1992, 117–18 all assume a version of this claim about an absolute divide between human and divine perspectives (albeit with sometimes differing views on how to fill in the nature or purpose of Xenophanes' divinity). Rivier 1956, 58–60 and *passim*, finds this kind of claim anachronistic, but at the cost of selling short, it seems to me, the archaic capacity for contradiction.
[144] Arist. *Metaph.* A 5.986b21–25, a contentious reading; see Algra 1999 (who endorses it) 60 with n. 31.
[145] See Kirk *et al.* 1983, 170; Lesher 1992, 100, 106.
[146] "The divinity of reality" is a phrase employed by Kirk *et al.* 1983, 397, not quite to capture Xenophanes' doctrine, but rather to capture one of its implications as this could have been derived by Melissus. The idea it renders is felicitous.

The same pattern will repeat itself in Anaxagoras, though with slightly different emphases. Matter here is made to proliferate, only not along the axis of the surface as in Xenophanes, but in a more pointillistic and more abstract way. In Simplicius' paraphrase, "*Neither is there a smallest part* (τὸ ἐλάχιστον) *of what is small* (τοῦ σμικροῦ), but there is always a smaller (ἔλασσον ἀεί). . . . Likewise *there is always something larger* (μεῖζον) *than what is large*" (τοῦ μεγάλου).[147] Matter proliferates endlessly into two directions on this view, into the infinitely microscopic and towards the ever-receding macroscopic. *The two infinities* of Anaxagorean matter thus contrast with *the prolific expanses* of Xenophanean matter, but ultimately they both serve a similar end. More could be said about Anaxagoras, whose system is intricate and full of implications that would only lead us astray. Suffice it to say that Anaxagoras formed a conceptual bridge between the Eleatics and the atomists, to whom we may now turn.

7 THE AESTHETICS OF ATOMIC MATTER

The atomists were masters of the infinitesimally small and of the infinitely large, but they also arrested the movement of the infinite regress that Anaxagoras had installed in his ontology. Henceforth, atoms were the smallest elements of material substance, with no sub-divisible physical parts to them, while their number (and potentially their size) was infinitely large. Aristotle captures some of the peculiarity of this logic well in labeling them "atomic [or "partless"] *magnitudes*" (ἄτομα μεγέθη).[148] What he means is that atoms are bodies with extension, not extensionless points.[149] But what his phrasing points too is a further fact about atoms, namely that they are sheer *quanta*, which is to say they are not qualitied: they are featureless. As such, they represent magnitude in no particular dimension at all; that is, they represent the bare possession of magnitude. And this is what the atomistic conception invites us to do: namely, to abstract the material of an atom from all comparisons and to view it in all of its brute materiality, as a dimensionally inert *quantum* (what the atomists sometimes called an *ogkos*). So viewed, a bit of *material* is

---

[147] B3; trans. K–R–S; emphasis added. [148] Arist. *Phys.* 1.3.187a3 (DK 29A22).

[149] Cf. Arist. *Gen. corr.* 1.2.316a–b. Elsewhere, he makes a similar kind of claim: "[Democritus] makes his magnitudes, the atoms, substances" (τὰ γὰρ μεγέθη, τὰ ἄτομα, τὰς οὐσίας ποιεῖ; *Metaph.* Z 13.1039a9 = DK 68A42). The term μεγέθη is in this sense unattested in the fragments. It is a curious fact that though there are a handful of attestations in which atoms are understood as μεγέθη, these appear only in the Aristotelian tradition.

reduced to a bit of *matter, something* is reduced to a nondescript *thing*. And behind matter – something – lies the threatening abyss of Void – nothing. Here, the reduction to pure matter seems to be finally complete.

But there is a flip side to this material reduction. For once it is so reduced, matter can be – or rather, *always is* – reinvested with traits it does not properly have: it is sublimated. In atomistic terms, matter becomes a bit of *onta*, which means it becomes invested with Parmenidean traits of Being: impassiveness, eternality, oneness, uniformity of nature, and so on. In terms of the present study, matter becomes aesthetically interesting, and potentially sublime. Consider Democritus' accounts of atomic motions, which are often livelier than his accounts of palpable experience: atoms, little *sōmata* (bodies), have rough or smooth edges or hooks, they rush through space in graceful arcs, they quiver, and so on. (Strictly speaking, atoms have three properties, which may or may not be relational: *rhuthmos, diathigē,* and *tropē,* or rhythm [motion], touching, and turning, terms that are misleadingly rendered by Aristotle as *schēma, taxis,* and *thesis,* or shape, position, and order. Weight is sometimes counted as a fourth.) Perforated by void and pieced together again by aggregation, matter and materiality take on a new and strange significance. Further paradoxes ensue, some of which were mentioned earlier.[150] In a word, the cosmic spectacle of matter jostling in the void is unsettling in the extreme. But it also happens to lend itself to poetic description (as Lucretius further attests). Later onlookers confirm this insight. Friedrich Nietzsche stood in awe of the "sensuous clarity and comprehensibility" of the accounts that Democritus could give to natural events, and that is the source of the former's gushing, and no doubt calculatedly shocking, commentary on the "poetic" quality of the Democritean physical landscape itself.[151] Both Nietzsche and later Bergson would find the mere spectacle of atomism moving to the point of being sublime.[152] The atomists', and especially Democritus', contributions to aesthetic thinking in antiquity would deserve a study unto itself,[153] and I will summarize these briefly when I turn to one area characteristic of late fifth-century aesthetic method in

---

[150] See §1 above; also Porter 2000, 87–88.
[151] Nietzsche 1933–42, IV:59; IV:82. See Sedley 1982, 181, on the atomists' linguistic innovations; von Fritz 1938, on the vivid character of their language, which includes aural characteristics as well as visual ones (ibid., 29); Dion. Hal. *Comp.* 24.
[152] Nietzsche 1933–42, III:332; Bergson 1884, 23 n. 7 (*ad Lucr.* 1.945). See further Else 1930 on Lucretius' "aesthetic attitude," which he rightly ties, *inter alia*, to the poem's sensuousness and vivid perceptual alertness.
[153] See my Introduction above.

the next chapter. The contribution of early atomism to the ancient awareness of the sublime will have to wait for another occasion.[154] Of interest to us here is the atomists' culmination of the Presocratic views of matter and its appearances, whether these latter were conceived as legitimate objects of the senses or as surreptitiously inferred and visualized by the mind.

8 PRESOCRATIC EMPIRICISM: PERCEPTION AND EXPERIENCE

If we seem to have passed from matter to perception, that passage is inevitable: matter cannot be thought, let alone grasped, except by way of its phenomenology. And so it should come as no surprise if, by the same token, sensation and perception, *to aisthēton*, went the way of matter, though not all the way. For the Presocratics (and here, in the interests of space, I will need to simplify things even more than I already have), whatever existed in a material sense also existed in a phenomenal sense, at least potentially if not actually so. Even atoms would reveal minimal phenomenal properties if one had the equipment to register these. ὄψις τῶν ἀδήλων τὰ φαινόμενα: "appearances (phenomena) are the sight of things unseen" – so Anaxagoras, and so Democritus,[155] though the same principle was operative for other Presocratics too. The idea cuts two ways: phenomena are the gateway to truth, and therefore a screen to be removed; but they are also the mirror or analogue of truth, and for that reason worthy of exploration in their own right.[156] Even Parmenides and Heraclitus, for all their seeming anti-empiricism (more so, to be sure, in Parmenides' case), showed a remarkable curiosity and, what is more, a strong theoretical interest in the contribution of the senses to human thought.[157] And as was mentioned earlier, it is thanks to Parmenides and his Eleatic cohort that the very notion of appearances became a discussable item, something to be objectified in thought and contested in argument, however much it might have been derided as a source of

---

[154] On its later relation, the Lucretian sublime, see Porter 2007b.

[155] Anaxagoras, DK 59B21a; Democritus, DK 68A111.

[156] Fränkel 1974, 123; Rivier 1956, 59: "[Les 'phénomènes'] ne sont pas là pour manifester autre chose qu'eux-mêmes.... Ce sont des χρήματα ... (c'est à dire littéralement 'des choses à quoi on a affaire')"; Vernant 1991, 180–81. For χρήματα in the sense of matter and material things, see Anaxagoras, DK 59B12.

[157] On Heraclitus' empiricism, see Barnes 1982, 57–81; Hussey 1999 89; 99–100; on Parmenides, see Fränkel 1974, 131; Williams 1981, 220, on "the touching and seeing models"; further at nn. 167–69 below.

delusion among men. Not even Parmenides could contest the existence of appearances (what he calls "the way of Seeming"); all he could do, or chose to do, was to contest their epistemological worth.[158] A backlash was inevitable, the full force of which would not be felt until the middle of the fifth century at the height of the sophistic era. But already among non-sophistic Presocratics anti-Parmenideanism had set in.

Xenophanes was concerned with "all that reveals itself to the view of mortals,"[159] and then some, as we have already seen. His empiricism is a powerful element of his thinking, which explains why his thought hews so closely to appearances. Distrustful of appearances, Heraclitus is famous for apothegms such as, "An unapparent structure (ἁρμονίη) is stronger than an apparent one,"[160] and relatedly, "Nature likes to conceal itself."[161] But he also argued for inquiry through the deliverances of the senses, knowing full well that these give us our reality: "[Those who seek wisdom, φιλοσόφους ἄνδρας] must be inquirers (ἵστορας) into a good many things,"[162] and, "All of which the learning is seeing and hearing (ὅσσων ὄψις ἀκοὴ μάθησις) [or: 'All that lends itself to learning, seeing, and hearing']: that I value most" (προτιμέω).[163] He further mocked ignorance as a trait characteristic of "those of no experience" (ἀπείροισιν).[164] For André Rivier, the whole of Heraclitus' method is founded upon "a lived experience" in which the unity of world and thought is "consummated," or else, in Bruno Snell's less abstract language, *embodied*.[165]

An interesting feature of the original form of Heraclitus' rivers fragment, "Upon those that step into (ἐμβαίνουσιν) the same rivers different and different waters flow," is that the perceiving subject must literally

---

[158] See Parmenides, DK 28B8.38–41 (quoted in Ch. 2 at n. 62 above); id., B8.50–56, on the Way of Seeming, where appearances are captured with such general terms as μορφαί and δέμας, viz., outer visible shapes. Cf. Williams 1981, 225: "For even if men are deluded by the senses, and appearances conceal rather than reveal reality, at least it is true *that there are appearances*, and any full account of what actually exists must include the actual existence of (misleading) appearances" (emphasis in original). This "must" is what is historically relevant.

[159] ὁππόσα δὴ θνητοῖσι πεφήνασιν εἰσοράασθαι, B36: trans. Fränkel 1974, 123.

[160] ἁρμονίη ἀφανὴς φανερῆς κρείττων, B54; trans. K–R–S, adapted.

[161] B123.   [162] B35. On *historiē*, see Snell 1924, 59–71; Thomas 2000, 161–67.

[163] B55; trans. Hussey 1999, 89. The bracketed alternative rendering is by Diels in DK.   [164] B1.

[165] Rivier 1952, 16. Cf. Snell 1926, 356, on B12 (cited by Rivier, ibid., 16 n. 17): "Nicht ein kühler Beobachter hat diese Bewegung [sc., the flux of things] gesehen, sondern der ganze Körper hat sie gespürt." Snell's paraphrases are full of the language of *Empfindung* and *Erlebnisse* (ibid., 357, 361, 363), which is doubtless in part a reflex of his neo-Romanticism (evident, too, at Snell 1924, 69–70, which leans heavily on W. von Humboldt), and in part an echo of something that can be heard in Heraclitus.

wade into the phenomena of which the rivers are an emblem.[166] Direct immersion into matter could not be any clearer than this. Parmenides, for his part, wrote, "Nor let custom born of much experience (ἔθος πολύπειρον) force you to ply along this road an aimless eye and echoing ear and tongue (ἄσκοπον ὄμμα καὶ ἠχήεσσαν ἀκουήν | καὶ γλῶσσαν), but judge by discourse a much-contested testing spoken (ῥηθέντα) by me."[167] He was thereby conceding that "the senses might well be 'good witnesses'"[168] – wisely so, since he could not deny, except on pain of self-refutation, that his own discourse was "spoken" and thus an object of experience – much as Heraclitus had done, and as Empedocles would later urge his disciple Pausanias to believe, in language pointedly echoing that of Parmenides:

> But come, observe (ἄθρει) with every power in what way each thing is clear (δῆλον), without holding any seeing (ὄψιν) as more reliable compared with hearing, nor echoing ear (ἀκοήν) above piercings of the tongue (τρανώματα γλώσσης); and do not keep back trust at all from the other parts of the body (γυιῶν) by which there is a channel for understanding, but understand each thing in the way it is clear (δῆλον).[169]

Plainly, the very *medium* of early Greek philosophy was calling attention to the act of perception by which its first principles – about the materiality of the world and the lively nature of sensation – must be grasped.

9 AESTHETIC DEVELOPMENTS IN THE WAKE OF EARLY PHILOSOPHY, AND EARLIER

Once matter and appearances were separated out from the constituents of reality to the extent that they could be named, sought out, probed, and analyzed, the way was paved for an exploration of the matter and appearances of art in a new, supercharged technical language. The contribution of the Pythagoreans consisted in mathematical formulae that could in turn be applied to phenomena, chiefly in music, though probably not

---

[166] B12; trans. K–R–S. Rivier's belief that ἐμβαίνουσιν is an interpolation by later Heracliteans, albeit one made in an authentic spirit, makes no difference to this reading of the fragment, and if anything indirectly supports it: "on voit qu'elle [sc., Heraclitus' own philosophy] invitait ses lecteurs à insérer dans le fragment l'idée de ce sujet sentant *qui devait prendre corps* avec le participe ἐμβαίνουσιν" (Rivier 1952, 39) – especially if the invitation was always on offer from the beginning.

[167] B7.3–6; trans. Laks 1999, 261.   [168] Laks 1999, 262 (inverting Heraclitus B107).

[169] B3.9–13; trans. Laks 1999, 262. For somewhat similar arguments about Parmenides' empiricism, see Fränkel 1974, 131; Williams 1981, 220.

in visual and plastic art (but this is admittedly disputed, and there are adherents of the thesis in the modern field of architecture).[170] Until recently it was thought that Polyclitus' *Canon*, or theory of beauty (originating around 430), was modeled on Pythagorean doctrine, and this would have given us the single most prominent example of a direct link between early philosophy and art. Diels and Kranz even assign Polyclitus a section in their anthology of Presocratic philosophical fragments. But Carl Huffman has now demonstrated that Polyclitus owes nothing to the Pythagoreans; he merely developed a mathematical procedure for calculating what he deemed to be aesthetic perfection in the manufacture of statues.[171] This finding should not be taken to downgrade the significance of Polyclitus' achievement, which does after all represent another technological transfer across "disciplines," this time from mathematics (whatever the source may have been – the use of mathematics was already widespread) to sculpture. Polyclitus' theory of beauty is based on a demanding rigor of numerous calculated proportions or ratios and a symmetry of (bodily) parts that miraculously come together in a successful outcome (τὸ εὖ, εἰς ἕνα καιρὸν ἡκόντων) equivalent to artistic perfection, albeit "just barely" (παρὰ μικρόν).[172] The last two words (Huffman's rendering) are Polyclitus' way of advertising the difficulty of the achievement without undermining its attainability, just as the notion of the *kairos* signals an attainable end, not an irrational ingredient marking what lies beyond calculability, or so it would follow on Huffman's argument, which I find compelling.[173] An indirect confirmation that this is so may be found in Longinus' apparent preference for the "failed Colossus" over the perfectly achieved and rational beauties of Polyclitus' *Canon* (the Doryphorus): one can stare in amazement all day long at the attained perfections of art (ἐπὶ μὲν τέχνης θαυμάζεται τὸ ἀκριβέστατον), but sublimity lies in something incalculably greater than that (ἐπὶ δὲ τῶν φυσικῶν ἔργων τὸ μέγεθος).[174]

In most other cases we can only speculate about the connections between philosophy and the arts. It can be imagined, for instance, that

[170] Cf. DK 58A15 (= Aet. 1.3.8); Barker 1989, s.v. "Pythagoras"; Barker 2007, 305–07 for a brief but useful summary of the tradition, especially of its founders, Philolaus (who "seems to have been uninterested even in the nature of the niche occupied by sounds in the world of matter and movement") and Archytas (who did turn to physical acoustics in his pursuit of a mathematical study of harmonics). On Pythagoras' possible influence in southern Italian architecture, see the brief notice in Ch. 7, §1 below.
[171] Huffman 2002.   [172] DK 40B2; Plut. *Mor.* 45c.
[173] On this latter disputed question, see Schulz 1955; Stewart 1978, 126–27.   [174] *Subl.* 36.3.

Anaxagoras' "contention that 'phenomena are a sight of the unseen' invited one to look for hidden structures and meanings in the world."[175] It can equally be imagined that the same contention invited artists and viewers to pay even greater heed to the phenomenal properties of art. The resistance to this kind of attention, palpable in some quarters, may be taken as proof of the trend, as for instance in the following exchange between Socrates and the painter Parrhasius from Xenophon's *Memorabilia*. Socrates is attempting to explain why painting is a deficient art:

SOCRATES: Would you say, Parrhasius, that painting is a likeness [or "representation"] of the visible (γραφική ἐστιν εἰκασία τῶν ὁρωμένων)? You painters represent with your pigments and copy hollows and heights, darkness and light, hard and soft, rough and smooth, young bodies and old ones.

PARRHASIUS: That's true.

. . .

SOCRATES: Well now, do you represent the character of the soul, which is the most attractive and pleasing and appealing and desirable and lovable part of us? Or is it not a subject of representation at all (ἢ οὐδὲ μιμητόν ἐστι τοῦτο)?

PARRHASIUS: How could it be, Socrates, when it has neither shape nor color nor any of the other qualities that you mentioned just now, and is not even visible at all (μηδὲ ὅλως ὁρατόν ἐστιν)?[176]

In denying the power of painting to capture the invisible, Socrates is implicitly denying the philosophical maxim, "phenomena are the sight of things unseen." Could he possibly be *alluding* to this maxim and annulling it with his countermaxim, "painting is a likeness of the visible"? Whatever the case, existing popular currents naturally fed into the ongoing exploration of the material sign, and not only in visual art, but also in poetry, from the major poets to the *carmina epigraphica* to anonymous folk poetry, this last now mainly lost. That they did will be the contention of the concluding chapter of this study.

In a sense, existing sensibilities towards art were already materialistic (and decidedly non-formalistic). Beholders didn't have to wait for theorists to remind them that the sensuous surfaces of things at times shone with a radiance that was all compelling. Xenophanes was hardly the first to marvel at the embossed snakes whose sheen Homer likens to rainbows. If anything, the very fact that Xenophanes isolated this detail for philosophical commentary shows that he was counting on the verses'

---

[175] Stewart 2008, 113.   [176] Xen. *Mem.* 3.10.1–4; trans. Tredennick and Waterfield, adapted.

familiarity among his readership. Consider another conspicuous detail
from the *Iliad*, which is repeated in the *Odyssey*:

> Lifting one from the lot, Hecuba brought it out [sc., a Sidonian robe]
> for great Athena's gift, the *largest, loveliest,*
> *richly worked, and like a star it glistened,*
> deep beneath the others.
> τῶν ἕν' ἀειραμένη Ἑκάβη φέρε δῶρον Ἀθήνῃ,
> ὃς κάλλιστος ἔην ποικίλμασιν ἠδὲ μέγιστος,
> ἀστὴρ δ' ὣς ἀπέλαμπεν· ἔκειτο δὲ νείατος ἄλλων.[177]

Or consider the verse from Pindar: τίς ὁ ῥυθμὸς ἐφαίνετο; "What
rhuthmos [pattern, rhythm, movement] displayed itself to the eye" in
the design of the third temple of Apollo?[178] Then there are the archaic
inscriptions of the "περικαλλὲς ἄγαλμα" ("exceedingly fair dedication")
kind, to be discussed in Chapter 9. Indeed, there is no shortage of
examples attesting to this powerful interest in art's, as it were, native
materialism – a fact that has encouraged some scholars, such as Christos
Karusos and Hanna Philipp, to speak of an unalloyed "pleasure in
materials" (*Lust am Material*) in the popular tradition (here, with reference to inscriptions, whether votive or funerary).[179]

Nikolaus Himmelmann takes their argument a stage further. While the
focus (say, in epic poetry) on material detail can bring about a kind of
reality effect, which is to say, an enhancement of reference at the expense
of art, attention to such a level of detail can in fact have the opposite
effect: the beholder fastens onto the artistry that is involved, the more so
since so many of the objects in question are themselves simulacra of the
artistic process itself; accordingly, "an unthinking identification of image
and reality is out of the question."[180] Himmelmann's point is that
"reflection" on artistry – self-consciousness by the artist, heightened
awareness on the part of the beholder – involves, or has as its immediate
index, a reflection on the materiality of the work of art: Homeric narrative
"ties admiration [for the qualities of a work of art being described] to its
reference to the material [of that same work of art]" – a Shklovskian point.
Materiality and technique go hand in hand, aligned neatly on the one side

---

[177] *Il.* 6.293–95 ~ *Od.* 15.106–08.; trans. Fagles.   [178] Pind. *Pae.* 8.67.
[179] Quotation from Philipp 1968, 24; cf. ibid., 5–20 on the materiality of epic poetry. See Karusos
1972 [1941] esp. 92–93: "Beauty cannot be severed from the material, nor can it be understood as a
separate feature of the work." A neglected precursor is Pater 1914 [1895], 192–223.
[180] "Von einer unreflektierten Gleichsetzung von Bild und Wirklichkeit [kann] keine Rede sein"
(Himmelmann 1969, 24).

of production, against the demands of naïve and unreflective aesthetic consumption.[181] Indeed, the very language of description is inflected with sensuous detail. Initially formulaic and endowed from the beginning with a certain materiality of its own (it is the language of "thick description," after all), the language used to describe intricate objects grew increasingly elaborate, conventionalized, and richer over the centuries.

Philosophy, in other words, could be the beneficiary and not only the motor of aesthetic speculation. It would be wrong to ignore the impetus from the side of the practicing artists. We have already seen how aesthetic practice, with its embedded theorization and high orders of sophistication, could make an impact on philosophy, as in the case of Empedocles and the painters. And we have seen cases in which philosophy modeled itself on poetic precedents, for instance in the verses of Xenophanes, and not only at the level of metaphors, but also in his adoption of a proneness to observational wonder, and of the sort that could be found in Homer. A more speculative example is the case that has recently been made for Anaximander and the architects. Hippolytus, in his *Refutations*, records how Anaximander likened the earth to "the drum of a column," whereby he seems to have envisioned a round section.[182] From this and other bits of evidence, it has been speculated that Anaximander was influenced by contemporary architects of monumental temples, while both had in their sights something like a "cosmic architecture."[183] While this is an attractive hypothesis for any number of reasons, it rests on the barest shreds of evidence, on some very heavy extrapolations from architectural proportions, and on some questionable assumptions about the symbolic – cosmically charged – meaning of sacred spaces in Greek temples. Nevertheless, Anaximander must have known about column drums, and if so, he must have known something about architectural construction as well. The influence, whatever its nature was, clearly came from the side of art here, and it left its imprint on his prose and his thought.

Eventually, as aesthetic speculation took off in all quarters in the final third of the fifth century, Presocratic philosophers contributed directly to these developments, and not just indirectly as before, at times merging their interests with those of contemporary sophists and technicians of the

---

[181] Ibid. Cf. Steiner 2001, 26–27; and the apt account in Langdon 2008, 12–16, e.g., 14: "Homer takes us from the shield's conception in a hot, sweaty workshop to its final presentation to Achilles, a path that deepens the object's biography." Such a biography includes material manufacture and social (and divine) circulation, all of which, so to speak, "stains" the object with material traces, and so too adds to its luster, value, and capacity for description.

[182] Hipp. *Ref.* 1.6.3 = DK 12A11; cf. A25; B5.   [183] Hahn 2001; Hahn 2003.

various arts. Chief among these later writers stands Democritus, whose list of titles (nearly all that remains) spans a broad range of subjects, from rhythm to music, painting, poetics, and euphony.[184] Thanks to Vitruvius, we can add to this list perspectival theory, an interest that Anaxagoras apparently also shared.[185] Whatever else these inquiries contained, one can speculate that the interest of a Presocratic philosopher like Democritus would have been to test the general validity of his concepts of matter, appearance, and sensory experience, and only secondarily to care about distinctions among art forms, genres, and the like. (This very insouciance towards formal distinctions is shown by his later intellectual descendants, both Nausiphanes of Teos, the last of the atomists, and by the Hellenistic euphonists.[186]) And because for a materialist form is merely the arrangement of matter, all these distinctions would have amounted to mere differences at some epiphenomenal level in any case (as we know, say, from Philodemus, but also from Aristotle and Cicero).[187] It was one of the hallmarks of Democritus' theory, and of those of his peers generally, that they set out to explain a variety of phenomena from a limited set of unifying first principles. Kristeller's worry about the systematic unity of the arts (see Chapter 1 above) would have been instantly nipped in the bud on any view of aesthetics modeled on Presocratic precepts.

Once again, I suspect that the Presocratics' view, and Democritus' in particular, would have resembled in at least one important respect that of John Dewey in his book *Art as Experience*. Dewey was reacting to formalism. The Presocratics may well have provoked its rise. For Dewey, not only is it the case that "every product of art is matter and matter only," but it is also the case that experience is an unbroken continuum that includes aesthetics and art, which are to be conceived not as isolated realms, but as integral parts of the sensuous domain.[188] In a profound way, *all* experience is aesthetic on this view.[189] The same is true for Kant, whose position, as we saw, is that our fundamental posture towards the

---

[184] These are arranged under τὰ μουσικά, or "Writings on Art," in the Thrasyllan catalogue of Democritus' writings (D.L. 9.48 = DK 68B15c–26a). See pp. 210–11 below; Porter 1986a.

[185] Vitruv. 7.praef.11. The exact nature of this interest is unclear, but it is the attestation that matters most here.

[186] On Nausiphanes, see Porter 2002, 147–49; on the euphonists, see Porter 1989, 171 at n. 119; Porter 2001a, 329 n. 47.

[187] Arist. *Gen. corr.* 1.1.315b6–15; Cic. *Nat. D.* 2.93.   [188] Dewey 1989 [1934], 195.

[189] That is, it is either aesthetic in character or else it contains an aesthetic core; see ibid., 11, where Dewey recommends "going back to experience of the common or mill run of things to discover the esthetic quality such experience possesses."

world is aesthetic. And it is also true for more recent writers, such as Alexander Nehamas, who holds that "aesthetic terms [and qualities] are part of the texture of our life," hence "nothing is in principle excluded,"[190] while John Armstrong writes that "the experience of beauty . . . consists in finding a spiritual value (truth, happiness, moral ideals) at home in a material setting (rhythm, line, shape, structure) and in such a way that, while we contemplate the object, the two seem inseparable."[191] One might sharpen up this last remark by stressing that beauty (or whatever aesthetic value is in question) is nothing more than, or apart from, the experience through which beauty (or this value) eventually comes to be named – beauty and its experience are inseparable. (Beauty, however spiritual it may appear to be, will always be *embodied*.[192]) And a materialist would, of course, want to stress that the actual source of any aesthetic experience lies in its material "home."

On the materialist view, beauty and experience are inseparable, but not in the way that Hegel would claim they are when he defined beauty as the manifestation of the Idea in its appearances. That makes of beauty a hypostasis, rendering it an outer object of experience, rather than the inner content of experience. Rather, beauty (or the aesthetic, more broadly) and experience are inseparable in the same way that the veil painted by Parrhasius in the late fifth century could not be detached from its appearances: his rival Zeuxis sought in vain to tear the veil away from the canvas on which it was painted, while the painting concealed nothing more than the fact that the veil had nothing to conceal.[193] This notion of appearances that are enjoyed for their own sake and that frustrate the search for something that lies beyond themselves was one of the logical outcomes of the Presocratic inquiry into *phainomena* (apparent things). Such was the lesson of the riddle of the lice, for example, in the parable that Heraclitus gives, which is much more than a put-down of the great wise man, Homer. For when lice-bearing children deceived Homer by declaring, "All that we saw and got we left behind, but what we didn't see or get we brought with us," they were illustrating the principle that where knowledge of visible and obvious things (τὰ φανερά) is concerned, deception (ἀπάτη) is the rule. In other words, mankind is most easily duped by the most self-evident of things. This, at least, is how Heraclitus

---

[190] Nehamas 2007, 50–51. Cf. ibid., 51: "Aesthetic terms are everywhere because everyone uses language aesthetically all the time."

[191] Armstrong 2004, 163.   [192] Dewey 1989 [1934], 34.   [193] Plin. *HN* 35.65.

introduces the tale.[194] Against the idea that appearances are embodied in material reality and conceal nothing, because they just are part of this reality itself, the formalist reaction of Plato and Aristotle would set in. And within this framework, with its installation of invisible realities lying well beyond the reach of the senses, the rest of the history of aesthetics would unfold.

---

[194] B56: ἐξηπάτηνται, φησίν, οἱ ἄνθρωποι πρὸς τὴν γνῶσιν τῶν φανερῶν, κτλ. See Hölscher 1974, 231: the secret is manifest; ibid., 233: it "reveals and hides itself at once." To be sure, Heraclitus' riddle turns on a verbal pun, "to get": the children were killing lice; those they "got" they left behind; those they didn't get, they brought with themselves. See on Heraclitus B123 above ("Nature likes to conceal itself" – perhaps by *exposing* itself?).

PART II

The Nascent Aesthetic Languages of the Sixth to Fourth Centuries BCE

CHAPTER 4

The rise of aesthetic reflection in the fifth century

The first three chapters have laid the groundwork for a study of alternative strands of ancient aesthetic speculation. It is now time to begin a historical study of the earliest phases of aesthetic reflection proper. These do indeed take shape in the fifth century, as standard accounts have it, though there are clear predecessors from the previous century and even earlier, typically transmitted in the form of names or less, mere shadows that can just barely be glimpsed through the sources. Accordingly, while Chapters 5–7 will focus on specific developments between the sixth to fourth centuries BCE and within literary criticism, rhetoric, and music, the present chapter will take up developments at a more general level within the nascent aesthetic languages in the wake of the Presocratics during the age known as the Greek enlightenment, and in ways that may prove somewhat uncustomary in existing studies on art and criticism. Treacherous as it may be (the sources are sparse and fragmentary, they are frequently prejudiced by hostile witnesses, and so on), the territory is far from having been exhausted. One immediate reason why this is so is that the terms of inquiry so precious to the present study tend to be neglected in others: sensualism, phenomenalism, materialism, and empirical experience, understood as preconditions to forming judgments about beauty and pleasure (aesthetic value) in any medium whatsoever. It is here that the fifth-century thinkers made huge strides, and it is here that we most stand to learn from them in turn. But first we will need to glance back at some of the roots of aesthetic inquiry and of aesthetic reflection prior to its formalized inquiry. Then we will be in a position to return to the fifth century, its cultural situation, and its intellectual ferment.

I REFLECTING ON ART AND AESTHETICS: FIRST BEGINNINGS?

When did reflection upon the arts and aesthetic experience begin in the Greek world? The question is an involved one. We can start by asking the question about literary criticism, where the evidence is best attested, and by searching for the first literary critic. Theagenes of Rhegium, the shadowy figure from the late sixth century who experimented in allegorical defenses of Homer and who is said to have developed a theory of Greek style (*hellēnismos*), is one candidate. The ancient grammarians, at least, thought so: they placed him first in the succession of Homeric scholars.[1] A second frequently adduced candidate is the Presocratic philosopher Xenophanes (*fl.* second half of the sixth century),[2] though here the label would appear to stick only if we understand by *critic* a stinging critic of Homer in the line of Heraclitus, Protagoras, Zoilus, and Plato. (Theagenes may well have been provoked to his defense of Homer by this elder philosophical contemporary.) Xenophanes and Heraclitus were discussed in the previous chapter. Yet a third candidate is the poet Simonides of Ceos (*fl.* early sixth century BCE): "Simonides is Western culture's original literary critic, for he is the first person in our extant tradition to theorize about the nature and function of poetry" (so Anne Carson).[3] But if so, then literary criticism in the West was born, remarkably, of an interaction between art forms, for as Carson also notes, Simonides was keenly aware of the visual implications of poetry and its rivalry with painting and the plastic arts. In that case, literary criticism arose inseparably from visual criticism.

That it did is not so far off from the truth. The languages of the visual arts, and indeed of other arts (music and dance), appear to have developed in parallel with those of the verbal arts. T. B. L. Webster's still valid sketch from 1939, "Greek Theories of Art and Literature down to 400 B.C.," makes this point well at least for literature and for visual art (he is silent about other art forms). One of Webster's most significant findings, beyond this pairing, is that the evidence for theoretical self-reflection on art, while admittedly meager and hard to track, shades off imperceptibly into the very beginnings of the arts themselves, and that the strongest exponents of theory down to the end of the fifth century remain the artists. The first treatises on art emerge clearly with the invention of prose in the sixth century and are often written by practitioners – among them, Theodorus of Samos, the architect, sculptor, and metalworker from the end of the sixth century, who wrote a book on his sanctuary to Hera at Samos; Lasus of Hermione, the poet and contemporary of Simonides, who wrote on music; Hippodamus the town-planner, born around

---

[1] DK 8A2 (schol. B *Il.* 20.67 = Porph. 1.240.17 Schrader): πρῶτος. Cf. 8A1a (on *hellēnismos*), and Pfeiffer 1968, 11; 158.
[2] Webster 1939, 166, following Diels 1969 [1910], 12–13.   [3] Carson 1999, 46.

500, who wrote on his craft; Parrhasius the painter, active before 450, who wrote on painting, as did Euphranor and Apelles later. But while it is true that treatises and techniques evolve hand in hand and new technical vocabularies are being forged all along, the concepts and practices and even modes of self-reflection that are exhibited during this period of evolution and even afterwards can be seen to extend farther back to the earliest forms of art.

A good example is one of the key terms Webster sets out to track in his article: *mimēsis*. As a term of art, *mimēsis* and its verb forms are late in coming: they "do not seem to have been applied to art and literature before the fifth century." "But," Webster adds, "vocal imitation has a much longer past."[4] The Delian *Hymn to Apollo* contains the earliest known instance of *mimeisthai* (to imitate),[5] "but Helen already possesses the accomplishment in the *Odyssey*."[6] Even more significantly, the term is a poor clue to the presence of the theory, as Webster shows. References to statues seeming to be alive, terms for likeness or seeming, captions on vases in the genitive implying an elided subject or a likeness, and so on, all count as much as any of the *mimēsis*-cognates. And these likewise reach much farther back in time than the vocabulary of imitation.[7]

Webster insists on dating "the *mimēsis*-theory" to the third quarter of the sixth century, by which he means a tight, and ever tightening, conjunction of the demands of imitation with those of realism. But this shouldn't prevent us from acknowledging that the theory of the arts in classical antiquity is the province of the artists from the start, their best kept secret. By *theory* I mean self-conscious reflection on art. In fact, simply to clear the board from the beginning, I might as well state the obvious, namely that art just is a self-reflexive medium, virtually by definition. The question of when self-reflexivity in Greek consciousness begins, so often fought over in various domains (chiefly in philosophy, where questions of personal identity arise, but also in poetics and in art history), is meaningless when confronted with this simple truth.[8] From Homer's depictions of bards, which act like virtual *mises en abîme* – and,

---

[4] Webster 1939, 168.   [5] *Hom. Hymn Ap.* 163.   [6] Webster 1939, 168.
[7] Halliwell 2002, 18–22 revisits some of the same evidence and arrives at more or less the same conclusions as Webster about the nature and early dating of *mimēsis*.
[8] The Russian Formalists were clear enough on this. See Shklovsky 1965 [1917]; Jakobson 1960. The Russian Formalists tended to press the question of art's essence to an extreme by asking for definitions of art *qua* art and literariness as such. Such chimeras are difficult to pin down under any circumstances, and not only when one is faced with the problem of art in a religious context like that of Greece.

to be sure, self-advertisements – of the rhapsode's own performing situation, to Pindar's allusions to his craft,[9] to the chorus' query in *Oedipus the King*, "Why should I dance?"[10] to Sophocles' (lost) treatise on the chorus and Polyclitus' (likewise lost) treatise on the *Canon*, which his identically named statue was meant to illustrate, to the self-designating treatment of floral patterns in archaic and classical vases, which violate the boundaries of art and nature,[11] not to mention other framing devices in vase painting (and especially their absence, or rather their replacement by the vase's own contours),[12] there runs a straight and unbroken line of reflection on artistic practice – and, what is more, such reflection gives rise to a richly cross-pollinated discourse among the various art forms.

Artists were constantly looking to one another for ideas and inspiration. And many of the art forms individually involved more than one medium (for example, music and poetry, or both of these and dance), or else were joined by shared physical settings (architecture providing an obvious example, whether in the form of public theaters, temples, and music halls or in that of private dining rooms).[13] Specialized reflection in art, music, and literature by professional critics is a much later development (see below). Historical retrospection comes first, virtually as a natural outgrowth of the earlier, often local, traditions of poets' and musicians' lives, and then blends indistinguishably into criticism and evaluation, as may be shown by *The Contest of Homer and Hesiod* in its oldest strata (those that can be inferred from the surviving document, at least), or the lost *Epidemiae* (*Visits*) by Ion of Chios, of which only anecdotal traces survive.[14] Another example, to be discussed in Chapter 7 below, is the

---

[9] Cf. Richardson 1981, 8 n. 31, on Pind. *Nem.* 7.14, "where song itself is ἔργοις δὲ καλοῖς ἔσοπτρον ['a mirror of fine deeds']": "Here, as so often, Pindar anticipates the language of later literary criticism," specifically Alcidamas in his *On Sophists* (to be discussed in Ch. 6 below).
[10] Soph. *OT* 896.   [11] See Hurwit 1977; Hurwit 1992; Neer 2002, 27–86.
[12] On this, especially on so-called spot-light vases, see Neer 2002, 65–77; and Ch. 8 below.
[13] On bards in Homer, see Segal 1992; further, Scodel 2002, arguing that Homeric conventions are themselves conventionally – viz., self-consciously – adhered to. On the tragic chorus, see Prins 1991; Henrichs 1995.
[14] Art history (at least in painting) probably begins with Duris of Samos (two titles are preserved, *On Painting* and *On Sculpture*: fr. 32 Wehrli = Plin. *HN* 34.61; cf. Podlecki 1969, 126–27) and Xenocrates of Athens, a generation after Lysippus (Schweitzer 1932, 5), even if Democritus may have discovered the historicity of art (ibid., 8). On Alcidamas' *Museum* as a proto-history of literature, prior to the various works by Heraclides of Pontus (e.g., *On Poetics and On Poets*, D.L. 5.88), see Richardson 1981. For Ion of Chios' earlier work on poets' lives, *Epidemiae*, evidently the first of its kind and spliced with poetic questions and, *en passant*, stylistic commentary, see DK 36; Blumenthal 1939; Leurini 2000 (editions); and Bowra 1940, 386; O'Sullivan 1992, 16; and now Jennings and Katsaros 2007 (discussion). For Stesimbrotus of Thasos, see the fragments of his book on Homer (*FGrHist* 107 F21–5); and Pfeiffer 1968, 35; Dover 1988, 8–9; Dover 1993, 36. These last

literary history of sibilancy (the *s*-sound) as traced by Pindar in his second *Dithyramb*. But prior to everything comes poetic (and other) introspection, a kind of native reflection on art and its intricate processes.

Only at a much later date, with boundaries fluid and expertises up for grabs, fifth-century sophists played the part of professors, competing with poets, musicians, and philosophers. Thus did the earlier, original tendencies to interactive criticism – a healthy "confusion" of the arts, if one will – persist into a later age. Many of the sophists, polymaths that they were, discoursed and wrote on several art forms separately and resorted to comparisons and analogies among the arts whenever they felt the need to do so (which is to say, frequently).[15] Philosophers were rivals first of the poets, quarrelling from early on (as Plato observes and exemplifies in his own person), and then of the sophists, and they momentarily usurped the genre of criticism, at least by the fourth century, keeping it under their wing, and under the close supervision of rational method and purpose. Thereafter, the boundaries become murky again. By the Hellenistic era, the exact status of a critic is unclear (in our terms, is he a poet, a grammarian, or a critic?) and a thing of contention (in their terms, is he a *philologos*, a *grammatikos*, or a *kritikos*?), as would emerge especially in the case of Crates of Mallos and those in his vicinity, but not only there.[16] Later on, the hard-won category of "critic" lost currency to the encyclopedist, the grammarian, and the antiquarian, with no firm line being drawn between these (Aulus Gellius is a bit of each), while the sophist was revived in the imperial era as a literary-cultural critic and roving pedagogue-*cum-littérateur* and rhetor-showman.[17]

The uncertainties that inhabit these traditions are part of what made them so fertile. And behind everything lies the abiding fact that mutual dialogue amongst the arts was intense, cultivated, openly acknowledged, and deemed thoroughly appropriate by the cultures of antiquity, as the following chastening reminder from Quintilian can serve to show. We should bear in mind that Quintilian here is merely defending the broad reach of a single art – his own – in his massive work from the end of the

---

two figures (Ion and Stesimbrotus) could well have furnished the Peripatetics with a template for their *Lives*. Aristoxenus of Tarentum in the fourth century follows the Peripatetic habit of constructing a prehistory of failed (musical) efforts leading up to his own. On ancient *Lives* generally, see Lefkowitz 1981. Local histories and genealogies provided a supporting context for these fledgling aesthetic histories.
[15] See Richardson 1975, the single best overview.   [16] See Pfeiffer 1968, 156–59.
[17] Gellius has recently attracted a good deal of attention. See Holford-Strevens 2003; Gunderson 2009; Keulen 2009. On the second-degree sophists, see Gleason 1995; Swain 1996; Goldhill 2001b; Whitmarsh 2001.

first century CE, *The Orator's Education*. What is more, his lessons could be multiplied, *mutatis mutandis*, across all the other known arts from antiquity in equal measure (oratory is, after all, an exemplification of the widely adopted Roman ideal of *enkuklios paideia*, or liberal education):

> It is not enough just to read the poets. Every type of literature must be thoroughly combed, and not only for learned information but for words, which often get their legitimacy from the great authors. Again, *grammatikē* [the study of language and literature] cannot be complete without music, because it has to discuss metre and rhythm; nor can it understand the poets without a knowledge of astronomy, since (to mention nothing else) they so often use the risings and settings of constellations as indications of time; nor again should it be ignorant of philosophy, both because of the numerous passages in practically every poem that depend on intricate points of natural science, and indeed because of Empedocles among the Greeks, and Varro and Lucretius among the Latins, all of whom have expounded philosophical doctrines in verse. Eloquence too is needed, and in no small measure.... This should make us less tolerant of people who criticize *grammatikē* as trivial and jejune.[18]

Later on, Quintilian makes good on his promise about astronomy, adding to the requirements of oratory nothing less than an understanding of *geometry*, not least of all because "geometry also soars higher, to the very system of the universe (*tollit ad rationem usque mundi*)."[19] The older pretensions of the first sophistic seem to be very much alive and well under the emperor Domitian, and even capable of striving after a modest degree of sublimity.

As long and rich as the traditions were, it is undeniable that a new watershed was reached in the fifth century BCE in Greece. An age of intellectual ferment, the fifth century saw a general flourishing of discourses on art and aesthetics, and these developments were often closely linked. Investigations into the nature of music, rhythm, and the visual arts (and illusions) took place alongside inquiries into language, in some cases conducted by the same thinkers (such as Hippias of Elis, who wrote or lectured on music, rhythm, painting, and sculpture)[20] – which ought to put us on our guard against the older catch-all phrase for such linguistic speculations, "the origins of philology."[21] That is too convenient a mirror

---

[18] Quint. *Inst.* 1.4.4–5; trans. Russell. Cf. ibid., 1.10.1; 12.11.21–4; Vitr. 1.1.12 on *enkuklios paideia* or *disciplina*; and Phld. *De poem.* 5 cols. 1–5 Mangoni.
[19] Quint. *Inst.* 1.10.46; trans. Russell.
[20] DK 86A2 (= Philostr. *VS* 495). The point, at least as regards visual art, has recently been reinforced by Halliwell 2000, esp. 100–01 with nn. 3–6.
[21] Diels 1969 [1910] and, to a lesser extent, Pfeiffer 1968.

of modern philological inquiry, and too narrow a rubric to capture the spirit of the ancient inquiries. Critical and descriptive vocabularies were shared, and analogies between art forms came naturally (hence the wide applicability of such staple and enduring terms as *eurhuthmia, summetria,* and *phantasia*): art theory in the sense we would recognize it today was born of this cross-fertilization. The convergences that obtained were not due to any deficiencies in the then contemporary theories. Indeed, the overlaps appear to reflect a more basic overlap in the experiences that could be had of the different art forms just named, or at least such is the thesis of this study. They all existed in, and were expressive of, a larger, public sphere of shared experiences.

Perceptions and discourses were mutually determining, and the effects were lasting. The imprint of this collective experience is visible in the shared vocabularies of the discourses on art. Thus, for example, *eurhuthmia* (orderly flow, proportionality) and *summetria* (balance, commensurability), are used in musical, poetic, sculptural, and architectural contexts throughout antiquity to capture – not always identically conceived but nonetheless suggestively parallel – aesthetic properties of objects or their perception, while *phantasia* enjoys an equal latitude in labeling a range of subjective processes, from mere appearances to their coalescence in a unified sensory or else imaginary impression. To take the least obvious of these applications: poets, Isocrates says, "bewitch (ψυχαγωγοῦσι) their audiences with their shapeliness and symmetries alone" (αὐταῖς ταῖς εὐρυθμίαις καὶ ταῖς συμμετρίαις), that is, *even absent compelling ideas* (τὰς διανοίας), an insight that recalls Gorgias (and later Plato), but which is nonetheless dressed in terminology that may have been borrowed from the visual arts.[22] With its momentary exclusion of cognitive appreciation and its foregrounding of aural pleasures, this view plainly belongs to that strand of aesthetic appreciation in antiquity that I am calling sensuous and materialist. Is musical theory another influence here? *Eurhuthmia* does not appear in any preserved musical writing, though *eurhuthmos* does appear in musical contexts prior to Isocrates (thrice in a treatment of dance by Aristophanes), and several times afterwards, starting with Aristoxenus,[23] as does *summetria*, the latter only after Isocrates, whereas *summetria* is famously featured in

---

[22] Isocr. 9.10.
[23] Ar. *Thesm.* (411 BCE) 120–22: "And Leto, and the strains of the Asian lute, out of time and in time to your step (ποδὶ παράρυθμ' εὔρυθμα), at the beck of the Phrygian Graces"; ibid., 985: "Wheel about with rhythmic step!" (ἀνάστρεφ' εὐρύθμῳ ποδί); trans. Sommerstein. Similarly, Ar. *Plut.* 759. Aristox. *Rhythm.* 2.7, etc.; Aristox. *Fr. Neap.* 11 (in Pearson 1990); Psell. *Rhythm.* 3 (Aristoxenian).

Polyclitus' *Canon*.[24] *Eurhuthmia* is likely to have occurred in sculptural contexts too, given that it appears so prominently in the discussion of Pistias' corselets in Xenophon's *Memorabilia* in a treatment of visual beauty and proportions: "Some bodies are well proportioned (εὔρυθμα) and some badly" (ἄρρυθμα).[25]

Musical and linguistic analysis form another (or just better attested) confluence after Aristoxenus, as the writings of Dionysius of Halicarnassus establish beyond a doubt (he himself defers to Aristoxenus). Compare chapter 11 of his technical treatise, *On the Composition of Words*:

Now that the difference between music and speech has been shown, a few remaining points may be made. If the intonation of the voice (lit., "the music of the voice," τὸ μὲν τῆς φωνῆς μέλος) – not in song but in ordinary conversation – has a pleasant effect upon the ear, it will be called "song-like" (lit., "melodious," εὐμελές) rather than "singing" (lit., "melodic," viz., not breaking formal rules of harmony, ἐμμελές).[26] So too the measured arrangement (συμμετρία) of the words according to their quantity, when it preserves the lyrical form, is rhythmical (εὔρυθμος) rather than in rhythm (ἔνρυθμος).[27]

Though much of the evidence for this interaction between musical and linguistic analysis comes after Aristoxenus, there are clear hints of activity in this area prior to him, which make it quite likely that musical thinking had influenced the theory of the voice as early as the sixth century (Lasus of Hermione is a key figure here, as will be discussed in Chapter 7 below), and then during the height of drama, when actors turned to specialists for tips on how to improve their vocal skills (see Chapter 6 below). Quintilian picks up the same thread in the late first century CE, understanding yet another, related sense of this broadly connotative term: "Moreover, an apt and becoming movement of the body – what the Greeks call *eurhythmia* – is essential, and cannot be obtained from any other source. A large part of the subject Delivery depends on this." He goes on, in a similar vein, to

---

[24] For Polyclitus, see p. 265 below. *Summetros* appears in physical contexts, some of which are not far off from aesthetic ones, as in Gorgias DK 82B4 (= Pl. *Men.* 76d): "Color is the effluence of things [or "shapes"] which is commensurate with (σύμμετρος), and perceptible to (αἰσθητός), sight" (trans. Gagarin and Woodruff 1995, 209).

[25] Xen. *Mem.* 3.10.11; trans. Tredennick and Waterfield.

[26] ἐμμελές has a technical ring, especially if one compares Aristoxenus, the likely source of the term – though Aristoxenus contrasts "the melodic" (τὸ ἐμμελές) with "the non-melodic" (τὸ ἐκμελές), e.g., at *Harm.* 37.2 (see Barker 2007, 234). Cf. Xenocr. fr. 87 Isnardi Parente = Porph. *In Ptol. Harm.* 32.29 Düring: "notes that are soothing and smooth are ἐμμελεῖς," where the term overlaps with εὐμελές in Dion. Hal. and thus fails to give the precise contrast he is seeking. (In fact, εὐμελ- appears in none of the musical writers, while the contrast τὸ εὐμελές/τὸ ἐμμελές appears only in the present passage.)

[27] Trans. Usher.

add music to the orator's quiver of tools: "Again, will not the orator, as a priority, take trouble about his voice? What is so specially the concern of music as this?"[28] Such crossovers as these, which are only among the most explicit of their kind, remain underexamined – inexplicably, because literary theory, the most intensively studied (and best attested) theoretical region of ancient aesthetics, arose out of this cross-pollination, and it never cut its ties to its sister arts. Other, subtler interactions among the various art forms and their analyses will be discussed below – for instance, between conceptions of space and built environments, or between acoustics and architecture, or between sound and painted forms. They are, in ways, the most telling of all.

Philosophy continued to feed into the discourses of art throughout the Hellenistic era and beyond, and the discourses of art continued to borrow from one another. Their separation, often epitomized by the contrast between Aristarchus' Alexandria and Crates of Mallos' Pergamon, which is to say, as a stand-off between literary criticism (or philology) and philosophy (or theory/allegory), is a modern-day myth.[29] Similarly, it is our error but not the ancients' that literary theory is viewed as radically distinct from musical or art-historical theory. To stick with the example of music: Aristoxenus of Tarentum, the fourth-century Peripatetic music-ologist, perpetuated and renewed a tradition of interaction between musical and literary theory that was represented by the late fifth-century "harmonicists" (*harmonikoi*), but that had roots in the previous century (Lasus of Hermione, Pindar, and Pratinas). Aristoxenus also wrote a treatise comparing tragic, comic, and satiric forms of dance, interestingly disobedient with regard to the preserved practice of Aristotle.[30] But in a real sense, the object of Aristoxenus' musical studies was not music, dance, or the voice. It was *time* – the arrangement of time, its rhythms and articulations – in various media. He actually wrote a treatise on the subject, *On the Primary Duration*, of which only a fragment is preserved. The treatise concerns the basic unit of time measurement (the *prōtos chronos*, or "primary duration") in the analysis of rhythm.[31] But time, temporal measurement, and the inter-relationship of temporal durations is basic to Aristoxenus' other writings – for instance, his *Elements of Rhythm* – and it is built into his analysis of rhythmical composition in

[28] Quint. *Inst.* 1.10.26–27; trans. Russell.   [29] See Porter 1992.
[30] Frr. 103–12 Wehrli. See Ch. 2, n. 153.
[31] The fragment is preserved in Porphyry's commentary on Ptolemy's *Harmonica* and conveniently reproduced and translated in Pearson 1990, 32–35.

his *Elements of Harmony*. And the same holds for all musical thinking within and beyond the musical tradition narrowly conceived, and not only after Aristoxenus. We will turn to one case study in this interaction in a later chapter.

Or to take another case, likewise to be explored below, rhetoricians developed a theory of acting and performance (*hupokrisis, actio*), with choreographed gestures and carefully orchestrated delivery that was taken over from actors, who in turn were developing a theory of the voice that must have shared features in common with the theory and practice of singers. Often we have only the slightest hints and traces of these affiliations, mere titles and mentions (apart from the abundant self-reflexive allusions drawn, for instance, by playwrights). Some of these point to a lost literature, to manuals and other kinds of writings whose contents we can only begin to speculate about. Such precious clues as we have nonetheless indicate a powerful nexus of concerns that a thinly textualizing history of antiquity, one that reduces the phenomena of the past to our experience of them through texts, can never even imagine.[32]

2 MATERIAL ECONOMIES OF ART AND AESTHETICS

The second half of the fifth century BCE is an exciting time for anyone interested in the history of ancient aesthetics. As artistic production in Athens and elsewhere in the Greek world took off at a remarkable pace, it achieved heights never before dreamt of, and in every conceivable realm. Cultural developments across a range of intellectual domains grew apace. Literacy came into its own, and prose became a lively medium of expression. Athens made itself "the center of the world" (Aristides, echoing earlier generations),[33] and it left a heritage in words and objects that would assure itself a glorious place in world history for ever more. Having attained a newborn consciousness of itself and its purpose, Athens began making itself classical.[34]

The reasons for this sudden profusion of art and culture are hard to pin down. Surely one factor will have been the transfer to Athens of the Delian League treasury in 454, which contributed to the injection of funding for the arts which had already been set in motion a quarter

---

[32] See Ch. 1 at n. 66 above. For an excellent recent corrective that focuses attention on the all-too-neglected non-visual dimensions of spectacle, see at n. 51 below.

[33] Aristid. *Or.* 1.14–16; cf. *Anth. Pal.* 7.45 = *FGE* 1052 [Thuc.].

[34] I use the term *classical* advisedly. See Porter 2006a.

century earlier. The so-called Periclean building program (roughly 449–431, so designated according to approximate dates of conception rather than completion) was the direct beneficiary, but the subsidiary effects in the immediate world of arts and crafts must have been equally momentous.[35] Plutarch describes the bustle surrounding the construction of new monuments in Athens in the wake of their destruction by the Persians. (New dedications had in fact already begun in 479, a year after the Persian War ended, but the major rebuilding effort took place under Pericles.) Plutarch's account suggests just how deeply engaged the artistic community of Athens was at the time:

Now that the city was sufficiently supplied with the necessities for war, [Pericles maintained that] they ought to devote the surplus of the treasury to the construction of these monuments, from which, in the future, would come everlasting fame, and which, while under construction, would supply a ready source of welfare by requiring every sort of workmanship and producing a wide variety of needs; these in turn would call into service every art, make every hand busy, and in this way provide paid employment for virtually the entire city, thereby ornamenting it and sustaining it at the same time.[36]

The huge sum of 5,000 talents was appropriated for outlays, and the public debts were not fully paid off until a decade after the Parthenon was completed in 432. The quantities of money and materials used are staggering. They were also controversial, even scandalously so, at the time.[37] Similar construction projects at Olympia and Bassae, as well as distant echoes at such places as Selinus and Syracuse in Italy, will have had an equivalent impact in those regions,[38] though nothing could equal the Athenian building program in its sheer scale and ambition. The Parthenon was quite simply "the largest and most sumptuous building that had ever been constructed on the Greek mainland."[39] A general stimulus in the economy of the arts throughout the Greek world ought to have been as generalized as it was inevitable, given the flow of monies and energies and the gathering together of the best artists available in the day. The only difficulty for anyone interested in tracing this impact is that

---

[35] For the contested dates of this building program, see Hurwit 1999, 157–99; 206. On the diversion of the Delian League treasury to the building program in relation to existing sources of funding, see ibid., 310.

[36] Plut. *Per.*12.4; trans. Pollitt.

[37] Cook 1984, 9–16. Cf. Plut. *Per.* 12.1–6, 14.1–2, 31.2–5; Boersma 1970, 65–81; Hurwit 2004, 79–81, 96–97, 112–14, 116–17. Cf. the inscriptions in Meiggs and Lewis 1988, nos. 54, 58–60 (440–433 BCE).

[38] E.g., Miles 1998 (Selinus); and see further Ch. 8 at nn. 25–27 below on Syracuse.

[39] Hurwit 2004, 117.

there is no hard evidence for this kind of general connection between economics and art at the time. Or rather, the only evidence we have is the art itself. The point is significant, as it helps to bring out yet another way in which materiality and aesthetics are deeply intertwined in antiquity. It also helps to add urgency and edge to what we already know about the mutual co-implication of art forms and of the languages of art at certain key moments of their profusion and diffusion. Communication amongst the vast communities (and armies) of artists in such situations is no longer a matter of mere speculation. It was a prerequisite to getting the job done.

Knock-on effects were unavoidable. In the past, the founding or reorganization of religious festivals had been the occasion for intensified musical innovation and activity – for instance, at the Pythian festival (founded in 586 BCE), which was made memorable not least of all by the striking innovations of the solo aulete and nomist Sacadas of Argos (about whom more will be said in a later chapter), but also at the Thargelia in Athens and elsewhere – and the case was no different here. Religious festivals such as the Panathenaea and the procession at the start of the annual City Dionysia would have taken on new life against the richly redecorated backdrop of Athens. The Odeion, or indoor Music Hall constructed under Pericles (and said to have been personally supervised by him), was built on the south slope of the Acropolis and was used during the Panathenaea to stage *kithara* and *aulos* competitions, probably the very same kind as are depicted in the Parthenon frieze.[40] Soon afterwards, the Odeion became the venue where dramatists would offer sneak previews of their upcoming offerings for the City Dionysia, in an event called the *proagon*. Other kinds of contest followed suit.

Vases testify to this. "A sudden surge in depictions of musical contests and victors about 440" suggests that "whatever Pericles did" – and ancient written evidence indicates that he either introduced, reintroduced, or simply reorganized musical contests (*mousikoi agōnes*) such as those at the Panathenaea – he "made these contests more visible and more popular with the Athenian audience than they had been at any time since before the Persian wars."[41] Restorations of buildings and cults inspired dramatic renderings of the same process, as with Aeschylus' *Eumenides* (458) or, even more aptly, Euripides' *Erechtheus* (late 420s), which was performed while the Caryatid temple identified as the Erechtheion was being built (or planned) and which seemingly alludes to the construction of that

---

[40] Hurwit 2004, 214.
[41] Shapiro 1992, 57–58; Plut. *Per.* 13.5–6. See also the excellent pages in Csapo 2004, 207–16.

building: "I command you to build a precinct in the middle of the city with a stone enclosure."[42]

Indeed, architectural viewing and imagery run throughout Euripidean tragedy on an unprecedented scale, as if reflecting a new visual *habitus* of the age. The chorus of the *Ion* (*c.* 410) pay homage to the posture of a touristic voyeur in the parodos of that play as they approach the temple of Delphi and marvel at its sculptural decorations:

> Not only in holy Athens after all
> Are there courts of the gods (αὐλαὶ θεῶν)
> With fair columns (εὐκίονες), and homage paid
> To Apollo who protects the streets.
> Here too on this temple
> Of Leto's son shows
> The bright-eyed beauty of twin façades (διδύμων προσώπων
> καλλιβλέφαρον φῶς).
> Look, look at this (ἰδού, τᾷδ' ἄθρησον): Zeus's son
> Is killing the Lernaean Hydra ...
> Look there (πρόσιδ' ὄσσοις) ...
> My eyes dart everywhere (πάνται τοι βλέφαρον διώκω).
> See (σκέψαι)! The battle of the giants on the marble walls.
> Yes we are looking (δερκόμεσθα).[43]

The scene is a veritable declension of verbs for (ecphrastic) seeing.[44] The stimulus, again, can only have been the excitement of the new visual landscapes of Athens, rather than Delphi, which must have heightened the appreciation for sightseeing – in Greek, *theōria* – at home and abroad.[45] The chorus here are in effect reinforcing the *habitus* of a touristic gaze newly awakened by the recent construction at home ("Oh, the sights are *just like in Athens!*"). The prologue of *Hippolytus* likewise plays on the crossing of vision and architectural urges and displays – as the genre demands, fatally: Hippolytus came to Athens to see (ἐς ὄψιν) the mysteries, Phaedra saw (ἰδοῦσα) Hippolytus, and, love-struck, "founded (ἐγκαθείσατο) a temple of Aphrodite near the rock of Pallas [i.e., on the south slope of the Acropolis] in view of this land" (κατόψιον γῆς

---

[42] ... σηκὸν ἐν μέσηι πόλει | τεῦξαι κελεύω περιβόλοισι λαΐνοις (Eur. fr. 65.90–91 Austin = *TrGF* 370.90–91). See Austin 1967, 17 and 59 for the suggestion, and Hurwit 2004, 163–68, 174 for discussion.

[43] Eur. *Ion* 184–208 Diggle; trans. R. F. Willetts.

[44] See Zeitlin 1994, 147–65, the classic analysis.

[45] On the transformations of this term's significance, see Nightingale 2004.

τῆσδε).[46] And all of this visual activity is being troped, or drilled in, once more by being enacted on the stage for a viewing audience.[47]

Surprisingly, the Theater of Dionysus, for all its centrality to Athenian culture, appears to have undergone only modest renovations in sheer monumental terms.[48] On the other hand, changes of a technical and dramaturgical nature were constantly being made, for example to the stage and its associated machinery,[49] while the grandeur of the theater would have been enhanced by virtue of its being nestled on the south slope of the Acropolis with the temple towering above and behind — precisely "near the rock of Pallas in view of this land." Theater was a powerful collection point for the arts. As Froma Zeitlin says, in one of the most trenchant discussions of the co-efficiency of the various visual art forms in the latter half of the fifth century, "Not only can the construction and conception of a framed space such as the theatre be added to other architectural achievements of the period, but the development of the figurative arts themselves (sculpture, reliefs, painting) is more or less coextensive with the evolution of dramaturgical techniques and concerns."[50] And as others have more recently noted, no doubt encouraged to a degree by Nietzsche's once maligned first book, *The Birth of Tragedy out of the Spirit of Music* (1872), the arts of song, music, and gesture were an integral part of the new mixture, which produced a veritable *festival* of sensuous appearances and pleasures.[51]

At about the same time these changes to the public face of Athens were taking place, a sudden efflorescence of speculation about the arts began to leave its traces in the writings from this period or in the notices about it. It is tempting to try to connect up these intellectual changes with the material changes and other related cultural upheavals of the time. How could they be unrelated?[52] Even so, several factors forbid certain knowledge. Again, we lack clear evidence that would make the links for us and that would enable a fuller grasp of the nature of the intellectual changes

---

[46] Eur. *Hipp.* 25–31.

[47] For further intimations of visual culture in Euripidean theater, esp. in *Helen* and *Iphigeneia among the Taurians*, see Zeitlin 1994; Zeitlin 1996; also Eur. *Androm.* 1086–87 (yet another conflation of touristic and aesthetic voyeurism on the one hand and civic and religious *theōria* on the other). See further the interesting pages in Barlow 1971, 9–16; 147 n. 71, on Euripides' interest in light and color, possibly reflecting the work of contemporary painters.

[48] Hurwit 2004, 216–18.   [49] Mastronarde 1990.

[50] Zeitlin 1994, 139.   [51] See Easterling and Hall 2002.

[52] Cf. Zeitlin 1994, 140: "The sheer profusion of public artistic monuments, painted pottery, and votive offerings attest to this broader trend [viz., the emphasis on 'visual perception in the cultural life of the city'], as does the marked theoretical interest in dramatic and artisanal techniques, the mathematics of optics, and the issue of mimesis itself."

themselves. What is needed is more than an account of the rise of "naturalism," expressivism, rational control over media, new technical achievements, and so on – for such stories tend to be told in a teleological, celebratory, often Whiggish fashion, and they are invariably told under the spell of retroactive classicism.[53] Something in between a technical history and a stylistic history would be needed – something more than a history of art and closer to *a history of the senses* (rather than a history of the body), documenting how the Greeks learned, over the course of the fifth century, to see, hear, and generally to sense their environment in new ways, and to express all of this in a new, self-descriptive, and to varying degrees self-conscious vocabulary.[54] The next sections are intended to furnish the barest outlines of such an approach.

3 THE RISE OF AESTHETIC REFLECTION IN A NEW AESTHETIC PUBLIC SPHERE

Let us return to our initial question about the origins of reflection upon the arts and aesthetic experience in Greece, only now with our focus trained on developments in the fifth century. The details are sketchy, but the overall picture seems clear enough. Across the arts, whether verbal, visual, or musical, writers were groping for a language by which to describe the new achievements of their culture. From Pindar and Aeschylus to Aristophanes and then on into the fourth century, the languages of aesthetic description began to take off, keeping pace with the public works and monuments, the statues, vases, and paintings, the songs and dances, and the dialogues and speeches that were all just coming into public view. I say *languages*, though I might well have said *language* for the simple reason that the vocabulary of art and aesthetics seems to have been a shared phenomenon. Sculptors, architects, painters, musicians, and wordsmiths turned to this vocabulary and helped to enrich it so as to render an account of their own productions and to proclaim the truths of their discoveries as theories, often in the form of public manifestos. Competition among the various media was a factor in the take-off and subsequent growth of these media, as were local and regional rivalries, though these latter were tempered by

---

[53] For two critiques of such narratives, see Neer 2002, esp. 1–8; 27–86; and Porter 2006a.
[54] Nietzsche once contemplated a "history of (rhythmic) sensations," which would have been broadly cultural and philosophical in scope, but based on ancient rhythmical theory. See Porter 2000, 142–43; 147; 166.

growing Panhellenic sentiments and by the desire to communicate styles and ideas across the Aegean and into the West. Diversity and convergence are the two dominant traits of the era in this realm, and they are held together in a productive tension.

The boundaries between theory, self-description, and performance were fluid and permeable, being drawn as they were in a competitive environment in which polemics and publicity were inseparable. At times, description came after the fact; at times, it accompanied the performance; in rare cases, works were designed to illustrate the theory. Ictinus wrote a treatise on the Parthenon he helped to design.[55] Gorgias, from Sicily, enunciated his theory about the poetics of language in the same breath as he performed it. His two longest preserved set pieces, the *Encomium of Helen* and the *Defense of Palamedes*, are not actual speeches but only theoretical speeches, in every sense of the word. As Eduard Norden noted long ago, Gorgias' aim was "to establish how the theory [of the ancient theoreticians of prose style] looks when it has been put into practice," which is to say, his aim was to model theory in practice or to practice theory, which is not quite the same thing as simply practicing or simply theorizing. Consequently, his works resulted in far more challenging objects for his audience, and us, to analyze.[56] Polyclitus, from Argos, took the unusual step of first describing his theory of proportions in a treatise called the *Canon* and then of illustrating – literally, embodying – the treatise with a statue. The treatise is now lost, but the statue, which was named *Canon* after the treatise, survives in Roman copies, if it was indeed the famed *Doryphorus*.[57] The early musical theorists known as the *harmonikoi* demonstrated their theories of harmonics by playing their instruments in public performances.[58] Tragedians had their choruses describe the movements and rhythmical patterns they were dancing or the sounds of their accompanying instruments or of their own singing in its various emotional timbres, as in: "You are beating out fearful things in song (μελοτυπεῖς), in unutterable clamour (δυσφάτῳ κλαγγᾷ) and high-pitched *nomoi* (ὀρθίοις ἐν νόμοις)," or, "I can hear something: by the river a nightingale sits.... She is at her music-making task (ὑμνεῖ) with her many-stringed (πολυχορδοτάτᾳ) voice," or finally, "I

---

[55] Vitr. 7.praef.12.   [56] Norden 1971 [1909–18], 1:50.
[57] For the attribution, see Stewart 1990, 1:160. This is not to deny that Polyclitus' treatise seems to have been designed to theorize and justify prior works by him, which would also have embodied his theory of proportions.
[58] *P. Hibeh* 1.13. See Barker 1984, 184–85.

am too sad, I cannot set up choral dances (χοϱούς) I with the Argive maidens I or beat the tune (κϱούσω) with my whirling foot."[59]

While the economies of art must surely have been a contributing factor, helping to intensify not only the sheer quantity of art but also its collaborative nature during the later fifth century, I want to suggest that a heightened sense of self-reflexivity could have also resulted from a further factor: an expansion of a public fund of perceptions that were being communicated and developed like so many languages. The self-descriptive languages of music, poetry and prose, visual representation, philosophy, mathematics, optics, and so on gravitated towards one another, or else arose out of a common source – for instance, a common pool of experiences. The very public nature of those languages as well as their novelty and incipience helps to explain this mutuality. But there is also a shared fascination palpable across the various realms of aesthetic endeavor, as though artists and intellectuals were looking back over their shoulders at their peers, whether out of curiosity or competition, but in any case were eager to lay claim to the powerful experiences that everyone was undergoing in the new vibrant arena of what might be called a new aesthetic public sphere. Surely some of the most striking examples come from the poets whenever they cast an eye at their sister arts in the visual realm, as with Simonides' comparison of poetry to painting and to the plastic arts a generation earlier, or Aeschylus' later account of the lifelike qualities of plastic art, or finally Euripides' vivid description of temple friezes in the prologue to the *Ion*.[60]

Some of the fascination and its power lay less in the particulars of the experiences than in the bare fact that such experiences were being had at all. That is, one element of the experiences was of a second-order nature: it is one thing to be affected by an aesthetic object and quite another to notice that the experience is not yours alone but is crucially shared. A tension between particularity and universality inaugurated itself, and then came to be the object of contestation in the culture at large. Thus, some of the competition we find in antiquity is often over the question of who has a rightful claim to define the nature of the experiences that are on offer in the aesthetic public sphere. Yet aesthetic reflection by its nature,

---

[59] Aesch. *Ag.* 1152–53; Eur. *Rhes.* 547–48; Eur. *El.* 175–80. The first two translations are from Barker 1984, whose chapter on fifth-century tragedy is full of such examples. The last translation is from Henrichs 1995, 89, after E. Vermeule.

[60] Simon. *ap.* Plut. *Mor.* 346F; cf. ibid., 18A; Simon. *ap.* M. Psellus *De operatione daem. dialog.* 821B Migne = fr. 190b Bergk; Aesch. *Ag.* 242 (see Fraenkel, ad loc.); id., *TrGF* 78a, col. 1.5–8.

like experience itself, has an intensely private side (or feel) to it that can never be completely suppressed or ignored. Whence the ambiguous appearance, from our point of view today, of ancient aesthetic experience. How private and how public aesthetic experience is can never be easily determined. But we can be sure that aesthetic reflection is in the first instance a reflection about the nature of aesthetic experience, which is to say that it is first viewed from the perspective of the observer and of the immediate effects of that experience on the observer (who begins the process of self-inquiry in the fashion of a Protagoras with such questions as, "How does the experience strike *me*?"), and only then is it about the productive sources of that experience. Concerned as it is with how art *appears*, aesthetic reflection of this kind is in many ways insistently *superficial*. But it is by the same token ineluctably circular. For the language through which experience is expressed, and the very frames of reference through which experience is allowed to appear at all, can never be private, but can only be publicly shared, because it is culturally given. Private experience cannot be simply given; it must be *taken* – assumed, appropriated, made personal, attached to a subject as distinctively his or hers – even if these frameworks are often the least visible and least conscious of all.

4 PROTAGORAS AND THE NEW ROLE OF EXPERIENCE

To risk a broad generalization about the development of thought from the Presocratics to the age of the fifth-century sophists, we may say that if the Presocratics ushered in the "birth of metaphysics," as Bernard Williams once wrote, they also gave rise to the categories of phenomena (what Vernant suggestively calls "the birth of images," meaning "appearances") and of matter, as well as to speculative inquiry into the realms of sensation and empirical reality, as was suggested in Chapters 2 and 3.[61] If so, it next fell to the sophists to radicalize the incipient empiricism and phenomenalism of the Presocratics, in large part simply by challenging the virtues of metaphysical speculation altogether, which had never ceased to accompany inquiry into the phenomenal reality of appearances. The result was a marked thinning of the speculative terrain, which was henceforth reduced to the surface planes of matter and sensation, to what one could palpably

---

[61] Williams 1981, 216; his next chapter heading (p. 223) is titled "Appearance and Reality"; Vernant 1991, 164–85 (in effect, tracing the evolution "from apparition to appearance," ibid., 167).

see, hear, touch, taste, and smell. This opened the door wide to what William James would later call "radical empiricism."[62]

Empiricism in its broadest sense is the philosophical belief that knowledge derives from experience, with the latter most often understood as sensory experience emerging from the realm of phenomena. The privileged central terms here, translated into Greek, would be *aisthēsis, phain-* words, *empeiria* and its cognates, and, in the absence of a more abstract technical terminology, words that correspond to sensory and phenomenal qualities (colors, motions, sounds, smells, tastes, and the like).[63] With the exception of *empeiria*, all these are precisely what one finds in great concentration in the language of the intellectuals known, for good or ill, as the sophists (a label they chose for themselves, nor was it pejorative in its origins: it simply meant "wise men"), whether or not they do in fact constitute a uniform group of thinkers.[64] Contemporary with the last generation of the Presocratics (Anaxagoras, Empedocles, possibly Zeno, Melissus, Philolaus, Democritus, and Diogenes of Apollonia – even Parmenides may have died around 450 BCE), the sophists are sometimes classified with them. They are reported to have rubbed shoulders with the Presocratics, sometimes studying in their circles, often contesting their teachings. However one views it, Presocratics and sophists belonged to the same world, even if that world was changing. Unlike the earlier philosophers, the sophists tended to locate in the new regional superpower and cultural magnet of Athens and to hire themselves out for exorbitant fees, lecturing, competing in the new intellectual marketplace, promoting themselves theatrically – part philosophers, part rhetoricians, part schoolmasters, part gurus. Their names are familiar enough: Protagoras, Gorgias, Hippias, Antiphon, Prodicus, Thrasymachus, along with a supporting cast of countless extras (the Poluses, the Lycophrons, the Euthydemuses, and others of the same standing).

The eldest member of their "circle" is usually considered their most typical representative: Protagoras (*c.* 490–*c.* 420 BCE). A colorful figure who knew Democritus (a fellow Abderitan) and crossed swords with Socrates, Protagoras may have been the first to label himself a sophist.

---

[62] James 2003 [1912].

[63] One might also add *historiē*-words (words for empirical inquiry), which first appear in Herodotus and in the Hippocratics. On these, see Thomas 2000, 163–67.

[64] Lloyd 1987, 93 n. 153; Nightingale 2004, 30. For the possibility of applying empiricism "in a suitably broad sense of the term" as a way of describing the commonalities among the sophists, see Bett 1989, 169. Cf. Pater's charge against the sophists: "With them art began too precipitately, as mere form [i.e., materialism] without matter [i.e., content]; a thing of disconnected empiric rules, caught from the mere surface of other people's productions ... – art from one's own vivid sensation or belief" (Pater 1893, 105; quoted by Martindale 2004, 58).

He is perhaps best known for the celebrated dictum "Man is the measure" (*homo mensura*). The full statement, which we have on Plato's authority, reads, "Man is the measure (μέτϱον) of all things, of the things that are that [or "how"] they are, and of the things that are not that [or "how"] they are not."[65] Sextus Empiricus, who also quotes the saying (and names its original seat, a work entitled *The Downthrowers* [*Kataballontes*]), suggests that by *measure* Protagoras meant "criterion" of truth and "standard of judgment," which is confirmed by Plato a little further on in his own dialogue.[66] Plato's discussion throws more light on Protagoras' position, which it is essential to repeat here. Protagoras, we shall see, set a new standard for epistemology, one that held significant implications for aesthetics, even if he did not draw those implications himself.

First, Protagoras explained how the process of measurement took place according to subjective appearances: "He puts it something like this, that as each thing appears (φαίνεται) to me, so it is for me, and as it appears to you, so it is for you – you and I each being a man."[67] From this it follows that whatever anything may be in and of itself, hot or cold, sweet or sour, what it is for you or me is just how it *appears* to you or me – whence the radical subjectivism with which Protagoras is frequently associated. A bit further on, *appears* is glossed with *perceived to be*: "But this expression 'it appears' means 'he perceives it'" (τὸ δέ γε 'φαίνεται' αἰσθάνεταί ἐστιν;)? "Yes it does." And in the next breath, abstract nouns are substituted for the verbs: "The 'appearing' of things (φαντασία), then, is the same as perception (αἴσθησις), in the case of hot things like that?" "Yes, that seems right."[68]

One question is how faithful these glosses are to Protagoras. Much hangs on the issue. Diels and Kranz treat the verbs for appearing in this passage as part of the original language of Protagoras' treatise, and indeed as part of the fragment. The most recent Oxford Classical Text (1995) treats *phainetai* as a Platonic gloss on a Protagorean idea.[69] But we can be fairly certain that the language is authentic, especially given a new

---

[65] DK 80B1 (= Pl. *Tht.* 152a); trans. Guthrie 1971, 183.

[66] Sext. Emp. *Math.* 7.60 (DK 80B1); cf. Sext. Emp. *Pyr.* 1.216 (DK 80A14); Pl. *Tht.* 178b. See Guthrie, 1971, 183.

[67] DK 80B1 = Pl. *Tht.* 152a; trans. Levett; rev. Burnyeat. Text after the OCT of 1995.

[68] Ibid., 152b.

[69] That is, where DK offer the first occurrence of *phainetai* as part of the fragment and print the Greek with *Sperrung*: "φ α ί ν ε τ α ι, τοιαῦτα μὲν ἔ σ τ ι ν ἐμοί," the OCT prints the text with no quotations (and no *Sperrung*, of course). φαίνεται is further emphasized at 152b10 in DK, but not treated as a quotation in the OCT, etc.; and when it is printed with emphasis at 152b12 in DK, it is done so as if the word were being quoted from Protagoras, whereas the quotation marks around the term in the OCT signal a reprise of Socrates' earlier use of the term a moment ago.

Protagorean fragment attributed to Didymus the Blind (discovered in 1941 and first published in 1968). The crucial portion reads:

Protagoras' followers come to a different opinion – Protagoras was a sophist. He says that (i) "for things that are, being lies in appearance" (τὸ εἶναι τοῖς οὖσιν ἐν τῷ φαίνεσθαί ἐστιν). He says that (ii) "When you are present, I appear to be sitting" [or: "I am manifestly sitting"]; but for someone who is not present, I do not appear to be sitting [or: "I am not manifestly sitting"], <and> it is unclear whether I am sitting or not sitting" (φαίνομαι σοὶ τῷ παρόντι καθήμενος· τῷ δὲ ἀπόντι οὐ φαίνομαι καθήμενος, ἄδηλον εἰ κάθημαι ἢ οὐ κάθημαι).[70]

It has taken scholarship time to digest this papyrus text and to accept the fragment as Protagorean. Nevertheless, the first of the two reported claims does have a strongly Protagorean ring to it: truth ("being") is in appearances, and nothing that is not apparent can be declared true or false for a witnessing subject. This much agrees well enough with the man-measure doctrine and with Plato's testimony too (and with that of others, including Aristotle's in *Metaphysics* book 4). Therefore, we can safely say that appearances were lodged at the center of Protagorean philosophy. One upshot is, as Paul Woodruff neatly puts it, that "Protagoras would have balked at the existence of an ἄδηλον," that is, of anything he couldn't grasp with his senses.[71] The second claim is a straightforward application of the first. You and I both know that I am sitting if you are in the same room as I am in (and if I am sitting), but unless some third party is also in the same room, she won't know for a fact whether I am sitting or standing (or even if I am in the room at all): it will not be evident to her. The Greek plays on the two conjoined senses of φαίνομαι here: I am "manifestly" sitting, because my sitting is "apparent" to anyone present.

Protagoras' radical subjectivism has, by the same token, earned him the label of being a radical relativist, someone who was utterly indifferent to the existence of objective values. Whether or not that label is merited,[72] there is little reason to doubt that his position entails some kind of phenomenalism that is consistent with claim (i) above, and furthermore that his position is decidedly relativist insofar as it is bound up with some kind of subjective perspectivism. On this view, reality is conceded (is relevant) only insofar as it *appears* to a *perceiving* subject: if I cannot

---

[70] Trans. after Woodruff 1985, 485, modified; punctuation after Mansfeld 1981, 52.
[71] Woodruff 1985, 487.
[72] See Bett 1989 for a useful sketch of kinds of relativism and a denial of relativism in a "deep form" to Protagoras (and to all remaining sophists). Similarly, Luther 1966, 166.

perceive an object with my senses, that object does not exist for me. Consequently, gods don't fare well in Protagoras' view of things (he is an agnostic),[73] nor do sounds that cannot be heard[74] or geometers' theoretical curved and straight lines[75] – nor would, presumably, atoms.[76] He would have taken issue with the claim, championed by Anaxagoras and Democritus, that "phenomena are the sight of things unseen" (τῶν ἀδήλων) – if the Didymus fragment above isn't a sign of this polemic already. Nor was Protagoras alone. There was at least one contemporary with similar views, namely Hippo, the materialistically minded Presocratic from either Samos or Rhegium (b. 480 or 470), who held that nothing existed except what could be perceived by the senses, and was judged on that basis to be an atheist (DK 38A9, a late report).

There are two ways of construing Protagoras' philosophical claims, one hard, one soft. To state the gist of Protagoras' doctrine of *homo mensura* in terms of appearances and perception (*phainomena* and *aisthēsis*) is in one sense to accentuate the mechanisms by which "man" takes the measure of reality. It is to put the emphasis on the physical interaction between the subject and his world. But if we recall the contrast with Protagoras' predecessors, and in particular with the Eleatics like Parmenides, who replaced appearances and sensations with metaphysically reliable entities closer to gods than to men, we can also note the striking promotion of man to the center of things in Protagoras' doctrine. His view is tantamount to claiming that truth and knowledge are not metaphysically grounded in unseen entities outside the realm of human experience, but instead are "grounded in human experience and relative to human concerns."[77] On this view, the accent falls less on the mechanics of sensation than on its subjective impact and on the world it creates for a subject – the world of experience.[78] The term *experience* has no exact equivalent in Protagoras' language, the way it does, for instance, in his contemporary Democritus, who could hold that "it is from their wealth of experience that men have learned to perform the things they do."[79] Indeed, words built from the πειρ-root (ἔμπειρος, ἄπειρος or πειράω), all denoting experience or its lack, are remarkably rare in Presocratic and sophistic

---

[73] B4.   [74] DK 29A29 (on Zeno and Protagoras).   [75] B7.

[76] On Protagoras' likely relation to atomism, see Mejer 1972; Woodruff 1985, 493–97.

[77] Farrar 1988, 48, echoing earlier views, for instance that of Versenyi 1962, 184.

[78] See also Mansfeld 1981, 49. But for Mansfeld, such a world excludes rich or interesting views about sensation and empirical reality in Protagoras' case.

[79] DK 68A171 Nachtrag (vol. II: 423), a translation of Galen from the Arabic; it would be good to know the original term for *experience* here, but that is not given in DK, which has only the English.

writings, a fact that is all the odder given how experience is the new watchword of the age, starting with Herodotean historical inquiry (where the term ἔμπειρος does, in contrast, appear with some frequency).[80] On the other hand, as invisible as the individual term *experience* may be in Protagoras' preserved traces, the concept is written directly into the relational grammar of his propositions: it exists in the invisible threads that tie subjects and objects, in the adjectival nature of the perceptions that are had, in the prepositions that govern the verbs of sensation – in a word, in the circumferential reach that man's measure draws around himself and his world.[81]

Empirical experience – sensory experience of the material and phenomenal world – was already a powerful component of the pluralist Presocratic tradition, as we saw in the previous chapter. What is radically new with Protagorean empiricism is its bold centrality and its virtual self-sufficiency: *empirical experience is practically all there is* to Protagorean philosophy. That is, sensory experience goes all the way down for Protagoras; and once it gives out, nothing is left to take its place. Unlike the Presocratics, Protagoras has no developed physics, no cosmology, no theology, and no cosmogony. This is true even if "he held that the soul is nothing apart from its sensations" (τὰς αἰσθήσεις), as Diogenes Laertius reports, or if he located the soul in the chest. Such statements encouraged Kerferd to talk about Protagoras' "physical doctrine of the soul," whereas they may at most point to a semi-developed view about the soul as the seat of sensation.[82] Whatever the case may be, Protagoras' world is one that has been reduced to a world of sensory apprehension and nothing more: it is a flat surface, not of matter (as with so many of the Presocratic pluralists we witnessed in the previous chapter), but of appearances. It may be that on this scaffolding Protagoras erects a wide-reaching analysis of human endeavors that extends over the realm of law, society, politics, and virtue. But if so, those inquiries are conducted on a "what-you-see-is-what-you-get" basis: there are no infinities, no depths, and no beyonds to behold here, in marked contrast to the Presocratics (for instance, Xenophanes or Anaxagoras). Whether his epistemology had any

---

[80] On Herodotus, see Meyer 1962. πειϱ-words also enjoy currency in the Hippocratic writers, in Thucydides, and in Antiphon, and among poets (Pindar) and dramatists.

[81] The language of experience in connection with Protagoras is highlighted in Mansfeld 1981 and Farrar 1988, 48–58. It appears to derive from Fritz 1971, 222–23 (see Mansfeld 1981, 49 n. 35).

[82] DK 80A1 = D.L. 9.52; DK 80A18; Kerferd 1981a, 110. Whatever else the report from Diogenes establishes, it does show that the soul is inconceivable, and possibly nonexistent, once it is removed from its sensations.

other role than that of a leveling one, demolishing ("downthrowing") metaphysical pretensions and constructing a common (albeit agonistically styled) meeting ground for human agency and action, is hard to say.

To what extent was Protagoras a materialist? That individual sensations on his theory were intensely unique and "enmattered" is indisputable (see below). On the other hand, matter as such does not seem to have been a concern of Protagoras'. It was, quite possibly, too abstract an entity, too caught up in metaphysical reflection, to be of any interest to him. After all, he might well have objected, and not without some reason: you can touch a table or chair, but can you touch *matter*? In doing so, he would have drawn the approval of William James, for whom "there is no original spirituality or materiality of being, intuitively discerned" – these are too high-flown, or else too primordial, for intuition – "but only a transloca-tion of *experiences* from one world to another." James has in mind the so-called primary qualities of atoms, which are irrelevant phenomeno-logically speaking. "Time itself," he adds, "is subjective" according to some schools of thought, of which the atomists were one.[83] Only the effects of material atoms matter to us, for these can be felt. Resembling a latter-day Protagorean, James holds that "what actually *does* count for true to any individual trower, whether he be philosopher or common man, is always a result of his *apperceptions*."[84] Consequently, James prefers *real* to *true* as the ultimate pragmatic criterion of being; for reality "is *just what we feel it to be*": it is palpable in its effects.[85] By the same token, if appearances for Protagoras simply seem to appear, as it were from nowhere, that is because they are being taken by him at their face value, less for their own sake than by way of attesting to a subject's measurable relation to the world. Better yet: appearances just are the measure of any subject's relation to the world.

For the same reason, perhaps, if Protagoras had any aesthetic inclin-ations, these are not hinted at, or else are only barely hinted at, in the record he left behind.[86] At any rate, sheer absorption in sensory qualities

[83] James 2003 [1912], 77; emphasis added.
[84] James 2003 [1912], 107; emphasis in original. Cf. ibid., 109: "Material facts, taken in their materiality, are not *felt*, are not *objects of experience*, do not *get reported*." Such caveats notwithstanding, James at times seems prepared to count himself a materialist in respect of physical reality, as in the claim just quoted (cf. also ibid., 19; 104–05). If so, he would wish to count this as one further instance of "ambiguity." ("Soul, life, breath – who can make a precise distinction between them?"; ibid., 117; on ambiguity, see the discussion at n. 239 below.)
[85] James 2003 [1912], 97.
[86] In Aristotle's rendering of the man-measure doctrine at DK 80A19 (= *Metaph.* K 6.1062b13–19), the items surveyed by Protagoras include "beauty [or 'the fine,' τὸ καλόν; cf. *Dialex.* 2] and its opposite."

does not seem to have detained him in any way. Nor does the most prominent exception, his conduct in the face of Simonides' Scopas ode in Plato's *Protagoras*, inspire much confidence, if it is a reliable index at all. There he limits his interpretive activity to discovering contradictions in the poet's alleged claims.[87] And in Aristotle's *Poetics* we learn that Protagoras "criticized" Homer for confusing prayer with command: Homer *commanded* the Muse to sing of the wrath of Achilles when he meant to *pray* to her to do so![88] Aristotle excludes this interpretive activity from poetics proper, but at stake is probably not only the linguistic classification of sentence-types based on verb forms (what today are known as perlocutionary acts) but also intonation and delivery, as modern commentators on the passage note. And these latter activities would, in fact, belong to the art of poetry, just not to poetics as Aristotle confines its definition (which would further explain Aristotle's exclusion). Even so, how seriously Protagoras meant the criticism, which looks to be as facetiously irreverent as the blundering verse in Homer it singles out for chastisement, is another question altogether.

None of this is to deny that Protagoras could easily have cleared a path for others in his wake in the spheres of art and aesthetics. What kinds of connections might there be, one wonders, between Protagoras and, say, Polyclitus' *Canon*, which from one angle looks like a physical embodiment of the man-measure doctrine? J. J. Pollitt locates in Greek sculpture from the period, and in particular the sculptural program of the Parthenon, "a tendency toward subjectivism in the design of sculptural form, that is, a tendency to think of sculptures not only as hard, 'real' objects known by touch and by measurement but also as impressions, as something which is in the process of change, a part of the flux of experience, bounded not by solidity and 'hard edges' but by flickering shadows and almost undiscernable transitions," as well as "a kind of general anthropocentrism," all of which can be approximated to Protagorean ideas.[89] The notion of "flux" aside (which is a contamination from the side of Plato, who conflates Heracliteanism with Protagoreanism in the *Theaetetus*), and

---

[87] Pl. *Prt.* 338e–339e. Socrates follows suit. See ibid., 344b, where the demonstration of the poem's artful construction (ἀποδεῖξαι ὡς εὖ πεποίηται) is rapidly dismissed as extrinsic to the matters at hand, which merely makes explicit what was painfully obvious all along: only the poet's paraphrasable meaning and intention have been at issue.

[88] Arist. *Poet.* 19.1456b15–18: Homer imagined (οἰόμενος) he was praying to the divinity, but he blundered and commanded her instead.

[89] Pollitt 1999, 69, explicitly citing Protagoras in a section entitled, "Man and the measure of all things."

arguably that of "softness" too, the idea has its attractions. Flux and softness scarcely apply to Protagorean subjectivism: the lines demarcating my appearances from yours are firm and immovable, not soft and fuzzy. The kinds of qualities that are ever in question are meant to be starkly contrastive, mutually exclusive, and incorrigible, not flickering and indiscernibly bounded at the edges – cold *or* not cold, bitter *or* not bitter, correct *or* incorrect, sitting *or* not sitting.[90] Protagoras was for the same reason a master of opposing arguments.[91] Nevertheless, subjectivism in some form *is* increasingly a feature of the visual arts from the middle of the fifth century into the next, and Protagoras was well placed to lead the way by articulating and validating this newly aroused interest in phenomenalism and appearances.

Protagoras' achievement, by any measure, was immense. An imposing figure in his lifetime, he clearly stamped the sophistic era in incalculable ways. There may be some truth to the claim that "the correct understanding of [the] meaning [of *homo mensura*] will take us directly to the heart of the whole of the fifth-century sophistic movement."[92] That movement was of course diverse, and its members are not easily typified. But after Protagoras, sensuous experience was here to stay. It might be challenged and contested (Plato was its fiercest opponent), or modified and even doubted, but henceforth it was a permanent fixture in the landscape of philosophical argument. Indeed, anyone coming after Protagoras would be faced with an interesting challenge. Appearances from this point on had a bracing materiality to them. Rooted in some sensible reality, they were resistant to metaphysical co-optation (that is, to being derogated to metaphysical irreality). And in Protagoras' hands, sensible reality simply *was*, while he was unwilling to speculate about its exact nature, lest he become ensnared in airy metaphysics again.[93]

We might compare Sextus Empiricus' record of Protagoras' doctrine of appearances, assuming it preserves some degree of fidelity to the original: "He says that the *logoi* of all the appearances subsist in matter, so that matter, so far as it depends on itself, is able to be all those things which

---

[90] See B1 (= Pl. *Tht.* 151e, 152a); cf. Pl. *Tht.* 166e; etc.; and the valuable discussion in Kerferd 1981a, 85–92.

[91] A21; B5; C2.   [92] Kerferd 1981a, 85–86.

[93] See Mejer 1972, who argues that Protagoras remained agnostic about deep philosophical questions, but not about matter itself, e.g., p. 178 on Protagoras' "minimal ... requirement to [*sic*] matter: that it must be such as to make all sense impressions possible.... I am convinced that Protagoras must have believed in the existence of matter." Kerferd's notion of the physical doctrine of the soul (see above) could perhaps be rewritten in this same minimalist spirit, in line with what I suggested earlier. *Contra*, Mansfeld 1981.

appear to all."[94] Protagoras' position is neither entirely objectivist nor subjectivist, but a disconcerting blend of both. It coyly posits a material substrate while refusing to speculate further on the exact nature or essence of this substrate. Indeed, the role of matter seems to involve two, somewhat self-canceling features: (i) it enjoys self-subsistence as an objective reality; (ii) but it enjoys this only insofar as matter can in turn ground disparate appearances for individual subjects. The neo-Kantian F. A. Lange put it well:

> Protagoras, the sophist, is the first [in the history of philosophy] to take the decisive step from the *object*, from nature, to the *subject*, as his point of departure.... He taught that *the foundations of all appearances are present in matter, so that matter, so far as it is concerned, could be whatever appeared to anyone*. One can regard this principle as the cornerstone of the transition from materialism to sensualism.[95]

Rephrasing Lange slightly, one could say that what we have in Protagoras is something more like a materialistic sensualism combined with a high tolerance for individualized perspectivism. Henceforth, to confront an appearance, in all its depthlessness, was to confront something hard, reluctant, incorrigible, and tangible, insofar as it was rooted in some material reality. It belonged definitively to this world of sensation, not to some remote and untouchable world of truth beyond appearances. Never before had sensible reality been so powerfully affirmed.[96]

5 PROTAGORAS' PEERS

The fruits of this kind of thinking, we may speculate, were immediately to be felt. I have already mentioned the possible links with the visual and plastic arts. Elsewhere, we are on firmer ground. Fifth-century phenomenalist and materialist thinking was particularly influential in articulating the dimensions of literary experience. Democritus, Gorgias, Prodicus, Hippias, Thrasymachus, and their disciples (for instance, Licymnius and Alcidamas) all explored the aural and musical qualities of poetry. Offering

---

[94] DK 80A14 = Sext. Emp. *Pyrh.* 1.218; trans. Kerferd 1981a, 107–08.

[95] Lange 1866, 14–15; emphasis in original. These remarks are altered in the second edition from 1873 (in many ways a less radically conceived work). Lange sought to blend Kantianism with materialism. It is therefore remarkable to see what a significant place he accords to Protagoras in his *History of Materialism* – an even greater place than that which he accords to Democritus.

[96] Not even among the Presocratics, who, while often blurring the line between matter and appearances, tended, in their allegiance to natural science, to commit themselves to matter (ontology) over appearances (phenomenology). Hence, the unique transitional value of Protagoras.

literal "analyses," they brought attention to the composite – the compositional and systematic – nature of language and of linguistic products (*suntheseis*) and to their epiphenomenal and often illusionary effects, starting with the smallest analyzable elements of language (letters representing sounds) and progressing up the ladder to higher levels of organization (syllables, words, rhythmic cola, sentences). Analogies to music, corporeal rhythm, and the visual arts were ways of promoting a richer appreciation of language, but also of underscoring the difficulties of the attempt to do so. Such parallels across media point, in any case, to a more basic and unified, or just culturally imprinted and shared, set of assumptions about aesthetic experience, broadly conceived. Inquiries into the physical, at times violent, processes attending the perception of poetry were also in vogue and were expressed in medical or mystical idioms (*ekstasis, enthousiasmos*), without necessarily implying endorsement. Illusions of all kinds were part of the same picture, and an inevitable extension of any account of appearances: the passage from appearance to illusion is a subtle one (*phantasia* covers both meanings in Greek). Theory here, sometimes in the guise of naturalism, shades off into cultural description and, finally, into cultural critique. But more on all this below.

A further possible resonance is to be found in an unlikely quarter: medicine. Consider how a Hippocratic writer from around 400 BCE makes the following, now famous (and famously controversial) claim about medical methodology (the claim comes from a heavily polemical context):

One must aim at attaining a certain measure (μέτρου τινός στοχάσασθαι), and yet there is no measure – neither weight (σταθμόν) nor any other calculation (ἀριθμόν) – which can serve as a criterion of accuracy (πρὸς ὃ ἀναφέρων εἴσῃ τὸ ἀκριβές), unless it be the sensation of the body (τοῦ σώματος τὴν αἴσθησιν). Therefore, it is hard to gain knowedge so accurate (οὕτω καταμαθεῖν ἀκριβῶς) that one errs only a little this way or that. Perfect accuracy (τὸ δὲ ἀτρεκές) is rare.[97]

The remark is astonishing for any number of reasons: its studied disregard for abstract, rational calculation, at a time when such rational criteria were being all but fetishized in the various arts and sciences; its rejection of complete accuracy, when accuracy was likewise a catchword of the intellectual elite; its celebration of the body, sensation, and perception (or

---

[97] *VM* 9.3–4 = 1:590 L. See Lloyd 1979, 135 on this, and ibid., 129–38 on the larger context into which the treatise fits, viz., the contemporary debates for and against empiricism; further Schiefsky 2005, 13–16; 185–202; 361–74.

feeling) as a countermeasure, the accuracy of which is left teasingly uncertain, fleeting, almost ungraspable – yet this alternative standard of feeling, the author suggests, is the only measure that is to be had in medical affairs, and probably the only reasonable standard of accuracy as well.[98] And as if reinforcing the uncertainties of sensation, there is an unresolved ambiguity in the passage, one that has led to endless controversies among scholars from the nineteenth century onward – namely, whether the sensation described is to be located in the body of the patient or in the hand of the physician. (One possibility is that both scenarios are meant.[99])

Be that as it may, the attitude displayed here – of going all in for *aisthēsis*, of elevating the sensate body over *logos*, and turning to both as a basis of scientific inquiry into the *phainomena* without the aid of any abstract or mathematical calculus – is not an isolated position by any means during the second half of the fifth century, as we have already seen. It is here, I would suggest, that a meaningful parallel to Protagoras is to be found, not in the latter's relativism (which has been the most contested and unresolved point of contact between the two thinkers), but in his empiricism.[100] In fact, the same author's denial of the relevance of whatever cannot be witnessed by the senses as a criterion of truth brings him even closer to Protagoras than the secondary literature has acknowledged. But if the passage from *Ancient Medicine* seems to have taken us rather far from aesthetics in the sense that concerns us in the present study, there may be more of a connection than first meets the eye. For the passage brings to mind (at least, to my mind) what the Augustan literary critic Dionysius of Halicarnassus will later call the "irrational criterion" of aesthetic judgment, which rests on the same faculty or sensitivity as the Hippocratic doctor was addressing, merely developed now to different ends.

---

[98] Cf. the programmatic statement from *VM* 1.3 (= 1:572 L.), a blanket denial of any criteria of precision in science apart from the visible and apparent, which (as has been noted; see the commentaries ad loc.) closely echoes Xenophanes DK 21B34, and thus points to a return to an earlier, Presocratic empiricism: "Concerning [invisible and doubtful things (τὰ ἀφανέα τε καὶ ἀπορεόμενα)], one has to resort to a hypothesis if one attempts to say anything about them, for instance about things in the sky or under the earth; and if anyone should explain them and understand how these things are, it would be clear neither to the speaker nor to the audience whether this was true or not; for there is no criterion to which one could refer in order to have clear knowledge of the matter" (partially quoted earlier at Ch. 3, n. 141).

[99] So Holmes 2010, 167–69 in her discussion of the passage.

[100] See most recently Schiefsky 2005 for discussion and references. (Schiefsky, however, does not admit a Protagorean influence in the quoted passage.)

As with all other arts and realms of beauty, Dionysius writes, one discovers the intangible qualities of excellence through the senses and not through reason (αἰσθήσει καὶ οὐ λόγῳ):

> The advice which teachers of music give to those wishing to acquire an accurate sense of melody and thus be able to discern the smallest tone-interval in the musical scale, is that they should simply cultivate the ear (τὴν ἀκοὴν ἐθίζειν), and seek no more accurate standard of judgment (κριτήριον) than this. My advice also would be the same to those readers of Lysias who wish to learn the nature of his charm: to banish reason from the senses and train them by patient study (μακρᾷ τριβῇ) over a long period to feel without thinking [lit., "to train the irrational faculty of perception together with irrational feeling" (καὶ ἀλόγῳ πάθει τὴν ἄλογον συνασκεῖν αἴσθησιν)].[101]

By *aisthēsis*, the Hippocratic author has in mind a sensitivity to medical symptoms. Dionysius has in mind a developed perceptual faculty for language,[102] with language understood as an enriched phenomenon that is capable of registering multiply enhanced aesthetic effects (musical, visual, and other). The underlying principles are really quite similar. What both of these views yield is not so much knowledge as a kind of intimate connoisseurship, less a matter of sense than one of sensation, and less a grounding of measure than a kind of commensuration (of one body with another). Dionysius was drawing on a long tradition that, as he acknowledges, runs back through Aristoxenus and his own appeals to the unrivaled powers of *aisthēsis* in the realm of phenomena – musical, acoustic phenomena.[103] The same principle must surely have driven earlier research among the sophists and Aristoxenus' other predecessors in music and rhythm (whether in music proper or in the musicality of language) – but also elsewhere in other arts. As I hope is clear by now, with the present study I have been interested in tracing the origins and evolution of this sensibility, this awareness of the phenomenally apparent, which plainly runs counter to the aesthetic investments of Plato and Aristotle, and which has evident ties to an intellectual attitude that lies outside of aesthetics proper. That sensualist and materialist urges ran through antiquity and in formative ways ought by now to be apparent. More could be said about the contribution to this tendency by the medical tradition, but the general drift should be evident enough.

---

[101] Dion. Hal. *Lys.* 11; trans. Usher.
[102] Cf. *Comp.* 22: οἱ μετρίαν ἔχοντες αἴσθησιν περὶ λόγους.
[103] Aristox. *Harm.*, *passim*. Cf. Barker 1978, e.g., 16: "what counts [as musical, and so on] are, on [Aristoxenus'] own principles, determined directly by αἴσθησις, by ear, not by any abstract mathematical considerations."

6 GORGIAS

Gorgias of Leontini (*c.* 485–*c.* 380) was the premier sophist, one of the very few to have been honored by Plato with a dialogue in his own name. Plato mocks him there as a doddering old fool, but this disguises the enormous respect that Gorgias earned for himself in antiquity, which was both lasting and widespread. Even more so than Protagoras, Gorgias forms a bridge between the Presocratics and the sophists. (Protagoras in many respects seems to have *burnt* every bridge to his Presocratic predecessors.) He was said to be a pupil of Empedocles, and his treatise *On Not Being; or, On Nature* (preserved in the later compilation, *De Melisso Xenophane Gorgia* and also paraphrased by Sextus), shows a direct engagement with Eleatic philosophy, the premises of which lead, or so he is keen to demonstrate, to intolerable consequences. While Gorgias' language and thought are sprinkled with materialistic touches throughout, it would be too simplistic to say that he is a materialist thinker pure and simple, as it is commonplace to do. On the contrary, it is preferable to view Gorgias as an opportunist who deploys materialist-sounding arguments when it advances his cause, while his final objective is not to adopt this or that strategy but simply to comment on the nature and especially the pitfalls of human persuasion and conviction. Nevertheless, along the way and, as it were, *en passant* Gorgias does contribute to the evolution of materialistic thought in the areas of art, language, and sensation. But at the same time, Gorgias also offers something like a prescient critique of materialism, as will be discussed in detail in the following chapter. And he is uniquely positioned to do so, straddling as he does the various arts and sciences of the day, committed to none and free to comment liberally on them all. From what we can see, Gorgias seems to speak his mind even more freely than his other sophistic contemporaries. If this is right, then Gorgias can provide us with a rare insight into just how far materialistic thinking in art and aesthetics had advanced by the second half of the fifth century. But before turning to Gorgias (see Chapter 5), we will need to look at some of his more dedicated materialist contemporaries and to throw a quick glance at the contribution that Democritus made to aesthetic thinking as well.

7 DEMOCRITUS, HIPPIAS, AND PRODICUS: THE COMPONENTIAL AND COMPOSITIONAL METHOD

Let us turn, then, to some of Gorgias' peers in order to assess the status of aesthetic understanding in its earliest phases after Pericles. A good deal of this material is sometimes referred to as "the origins of philology," but a redescription of the same subject matter from the perspective of aesthetic inquiry is equally valid and yields a somewhat different picture altogether. The sophistic thinkers Prodicus, Hippias, and Protagoras all worked in the same ambit as Gorgias, while the atomist Democritus (*c.* 460–*c.* 385) towered in their midst. If Democritus' interests in aesthetics are the most pronounced among his peers, this is in no small part because he had a robust theory of perception into which to insert them. But that cannot be all there is to it, because Democritus left a uniquely impressive series of titles on art and aesthetics behind, above all those preserved in the catalogue of his works assembled by the polymath Thrasyllus (*fl.* mid-first century CE) and transmitted by Diogenes Laertius.

The relevant titles ascribed to Democritus make up two tetralogies under the general heading of τὰ μουσικά, or "Writings on Art," which suggest a remarkable interest in poetry and its study: *On Rhythm and Harmony, On Poetry, On the Beauty of Words, On Euphonious and Harsh-Sounding Letters, On Homer,* or *On Orthoepeia and Glosses,*[104] *On the Bard, On Words,* and *Onomastics.*[105] Diogenes records the further title *On Painting,* which may or may not have been linked to Democritus' study of perspective.[106] Democritus was reputedly prompted to engage in this last-named study, along with the philosopher Anaxagoras, in the wake of Agatharchus' advances in illusionistic scene decoration (*scaenographia*) "when Aeschylus was presenting a tragedy," whether we are to understand by this that Agatharchus was active during the staging of the *Oresteia* in 458 BCE or else that he was active during a revival of the great tragedian around the middle of the fifth century.[107] There are other well-attested indications to support this long list of Democritean titles (for which no fragments beyond the titles themselves have survived), or at least to support the notion that Democritus commented explicitly on art and aesthetics, for instance, his comments on the inspirational sources of poets (which he doubtless would have traced to physiological causes) or on

---

[104] Did *orthoepeia* cover "correctness of *diction*" (so LSJ) or "correctness of *pronunciation*" (so Dion. Hal. *Ant. Rom.* 1.90.1; Quint. *Inst.* 1.5.33; Ael. Herod. and Hdn. Gr. *Orth.* s.v. = *GG* 3.2:561 Lentz)? Its earliest attested usage at Pl. *Phdr.* 267c is hardly illuminating. Perhaps the term was fundamentally ambiguous (as at, e.g., Dion. Hal. *Dem.* 26).

[105] D.L. 9.48 = DK 68B15c–26a (with further fragments).

[106] D.L. 9.48 = DK 68B28a. Cf. Vitruv. 7.praef.11.

[107] Vitruv. 7.praef.11. For the first possibility, Rouveret 1989, 114; the second suggestion is by T. B. L. Webster: see Keuls 1978, 64. Rouveret 1989, 113 points out that Agatharchus is not reported by Vitruvius to have painted but only to have manufactured (*fecit*) a *scaena tragica*. If so, then there is no compelling reason to align Democritus' work *On Painting* with his geometrization of perspective, which would, in turn, yield two separate spheres of aesthetic inquiry for Democritus.

Homer having "constructed a manifold world of words" or "verses" (where the emphasis on synthetic construction is palpable again).[108] And if we scan his more properly physical titles, we can find still others that slot neatly into those already mentioned: *On Colors*,[109] *On the Different Rhythms* [or *Shapes*],[110] *On Sensations* [or *On the Senses*],[111] and *On Sounds*.[112] In addition, there are attestations related to these latter physical inquiries, which prove that the recorded titles are not figments of the doxographical tradition, as well as a further series of fragments on the nature of language and meaning. The totality of all these works, both literary (or musical) and physical, point to a cohesive bundle of interests.

The list is indeed impressive. Yet, if any one thing stands out in Democritus' views on art, it has to be his keen interest in the *generation* of aesthetic features – features available to the senses – *as distinctively subjective effects*, but also as effects arising *from distinctively non-subjective material origins*, be these colors arising (presumably) from the combination or superposition (*sunthesis, mixis*) of pigments blended together in an image or simulacrum in the eye,[113] or sound qualities, rhythms, and harmonies arising from phonic materials, or the configuration of appearances on a picture plane as these present themselves to the eye and mind of the beholder (πρὸς τὴν φαντασίαν):[114]

Following from [Agatharchus'] suggestions [who wrote a treatise on *scaenographia*, which must have been the first of its kind], Democritus and Anaxagoras wrote upon the same topic, in order to show how, if a fixed centre is taken for the outward glance of the eyes and the projection of the radii, we must follow these

---

[108] B17–18; B21: ἐπέων κόσμον ἐτεκτήνατο παντοίων ("hat einen wohlgeordneten Bau mannigfaltiger Verse gezimmert").

[109] Περὶ χροῶν (B5h).

[110] Περὶ τῶν διαφερόντων ῥυσμῶν (B5i). These are probably "of atoms," but the interest in *rhuthmos* would have carried over from the atomic to the phenomenal level.

[111] Περὶ αἰσθησίων (B5f).

[112] Literally, *Causes of Sounds*, or better, *Researches into the Causes of* [*Human Vocal* (?)] *Sounds* (Αἴτιαι περὶ φωνῶν, B11f), included among the *Asuntakta*, or *Unassigned* titles, which reflects the exigencies of Thrasyllus' straightjacketing tetralogy scheme; on a different grouping, this title could conceivably fall (or did fall) under *Ta Mousika*. How these titles originally appeared, for instance as subtitles of an all-inclusive work such as *The Great* or *Small World-System* (B4b–c), is anyone's guess.

[113] That Democritus would have been interested in pigment combinations is an inference based on the evidence of Empedocles (DK 31B23) and Anaxagoras (DK 59B4; B21), as well as Plato (*Crat.* 424d and *Tim.* 67c–68d). See Keuls 1975; Keuls 1978, 63–72; 128; Rouveret 1989, 39–49; 103–06. The other half of the inference, about visual images, flows from Democritus' theory of vision.

[114] This last tag appears in another context, that concerning the appearance of color, in A125 (= Aët. 1.5.8; cf. A29; cf. also Pl. *Tim.* 67c: πρὸς αἴσθησιν), and also in the same context of *scaenographia*, but not where Democritus is named (Damian, *Opt.* 27.16 Schöne: πρὸς φαντασίαν; 27.19: πρὸς ὄψιν).

lines in accordance with a natural law, such that from an uncertain object, uncertain *images* (*imagines*) may give the *appearance* (*speciem*) of buildings in the scenery of the stage, and how what is figured upon vertical and plane surfaces can *seem to recede in one part and project in another*.[115]

It is this unique combination of intense interest in both subjectivism and materialism that distinguishes Democritean atomism, and that must have lent its special stamp to Democritean aesthetic inquiry as well.[116] The long-term impact of this brand of inquiry in aesthetics is literally incalculable (examples would include Lysippus' phenomenal idealism, to be discussed in Chapter 8 below, and the radical euphonist theories of the Hellenistic era, to be touched on in the next section), just as the contrast it makes with the aesthetic biases of Plato and Aristotle could not be any greater. As was noticed even in antiquity, Plato suppressed all mention of Democritus' name, and was even reported to have wished to destroy Democritus' writings by fire.[117] And Aristotle, though he pays all due respect to this major Presocratic, nonetheless is keener to refute or assimilate his predecessors than to report their views at any great length (especially in aesthetics), nor is Democritus any exception. We have already had occasion to note how Aristotle in his *Poetics* pays scant heed to the role of whatever stands in relation to perception in drama (πρὸς τὴν αἴσθησιν), and how he places relative disvalue on the most sensuous elements of the genre (sonorousness of diction, music and melody, and the visual).[118] This is not the place to attempt a wholesale reconstruction of Democritean aesthetic theory, which would be a speculative undertaking in any case. Instead, let us simply note a few of what would have been its hallmark features and which arguably are detectable in contemporary (fifth-century) and later inquiry into the various arts.

---

[115] Vitruvius 7.praef.11; trans. Granger; emphasis added.

[116] In this light, Democritus' fragment on enthusiasm (B18: "Whatever a poet writes under the power of enthusiasm and divine inspiration [μετ' ἐνθουσιασμοῦ καὶ ἱεροῦ πνεύματος] is beautiful") could be understood not as a sign of his embracing the traditional poetics of inspiration but as paralleling his critique of religion, or at least as his acknowledgment that the sources of inspiration are purely phantasmal, entirely lacking in any material reality, or to quote from Momigliano 1929–30, 97, "provocata da un impulso interno, a cui non corrisponde nulla di reale all'esterno." Democritus' theory might thus be best called a *poetics of the phantasmal*. Of equal note in the same fragment is its emphasis on *pneuma*, or breath. A materialist understanding of this fragment would bring out the connection of breath to speech (phonation) and to sound, something that would have fallen under Democritus' attested interests in euphony and that never ceased to be linked to euphonism (see Porter 2000, 95–106, and below).

[117] D.L. 9.40. The anecdote was transmitted by Aristoxenus.   [118] See Chapter 2, §2.

8. 'STOICHEIA' AND COMPONENTIAL ANALYSIS

The first and most significant of these is what I will call the *componential analysis of material parts*. The easiest way to explain this method is to begin by quoting a passage from Plato's *Cratylus*, which throws a telling light on the contemporary scene. Socrates is asking how best to approach language systematically:

Since an imitation of a thing's being or essence (τῆς οὐσίας) is made out of syllables and letters (γράμμασιν), wouldn't it be most correct for us to divide off the letters or elements (τὰ στοιχεῖα) first, just as those who set to work on [speech(?)] rhythms first divide off the forces or powers (τὰς δυνάμεις) of the letters or elements (τῶν στοιχείων), then those of syllables, and only then investigate rhythms themselves?[119]

What we have here is a merger of Platonic and pre-Platonic terms and concepts: Socrates is plainly overlaying a search for essences onto existing grammatical, rhetorical, or musicological criteria and methods (these distinctions are nearly irrelevant in the predisciplinary world of fifth-century Athens).[120]

Without a doubt, one of Plato's inspirations in the passage just quoted is the sophist Hippias of Elis (late fifth century), whom we find deploying a similar elemental and incremental analysis, likewise in a Platonic context. As Pfeiffer says, "Hippias seems to have been the first 'literary' man, not a musician, to treat language together with music, distinguishing 'the value (δυνάμεως) of letters and syllables and rhythms and scales (ἁρμονιῶν)'" in a sequence that runs from the smallest discernible units to ever larger combinations, and that finally culminates in harmonics, which is to say, the largest-scale arrangement of sounds in a sentence.[121] The sequencing clearly anticipates the lessons of a schoolmaster in a classroom: the progression mimics the way one learns one's ABCs. Pfeiffer's wording ("language together with music," "traditional Greek unity of word and 'music'") can be made more precise: Hippias was not only combining linguistic and musical analysis; he was also attempting to

---

[119] Pl. *Crat.* 424b–c; trans. Reeve, adapted.

[120] Still immensely useful on the overlaps between rhetoric and music is Kroll 1907, esp. 95–97.

[121] περί τε γραμμάτων δυνάμεως καὶ συλλαβῶν καὶ ῥυθμῶν καὶ ἁρμονιῶν (Pl. *Hp. mai.* 285d = DK 86A11; cf. A12 = Pl. *Hp. mi.* 368b); Pfeiffer 1968, 53; cf. ibid., 60. "Scales" are sometimes taken to imply "accentuation," and Arist. *Rh.* 3.1.1403b31 is named in support (e.g., O'Sullivan 1992, 18 n. 87). But the incremental sequence of Hippias' analysis, passing on to ever larger units, speaks more in favor of larger harmonic or compositional shapes; cf. Dion. Hal. *Comp.*, *passim*, and e.g., ch. 2 (p. 7.16 U–R); ibid., ch. 18 (p. 79.2 U–R); *Subl.* 39.4.

discover a *single* model for capturing *the music of language* whenever it is sung, set to rhythm, accentuated with pitches, and so on.

The key term, *dunamis* (value) – called *potestas* among Latin grammarians – designates the audible, aesthetic, and prosodic value or quality of *stoicheia* once they are "realized" in a given context.[122] That this is the case can be surmised from the early uses of *dunamis*, but also from later direct parallels, such as are found in the grammatical scholia to Dionysius Thrax: "*Dunamis* is the <sound (φωνή)> that results from and completes the *stoicheia*." It "completes" them inasmuch as it gives them their material realization (phonation). Dionysius of Halicarnassus, in the first century BCE, is a crucial link in the same tradition: "It is from this number of letters (γραμμάτων), with the properties described (δυνάμεις τοιαύτας ἐχόντων), that are formed what we call *syllables*."[123] The language of Hippias, but also that of his later heirs, is identical to that of the *Cratylus* passage quoted earlier. A Democritean influence is to be suspected.[124] But the trend also seems to have been widespread. Plato speaks of "experts" in *stoicheia*, while Aristotle can resort to the analogy casually as a well-established and by now familiar model.[125]

Now, suppose you take away the *dunameis*: what does that leave you with? The answer is, quite simply, *stoicheia* without *phōnē*. But what are these? In the *Cratylus* passage above, and indeed wherever the term occurs in linguistic contexts, *stoicheia* is the neutral, scientific, and colorless equivalent of *grammata*. The label converts the twenty-four letters of the Greek alphabet into the potentially more numerous, but in any case smallest components of a systematic whole, into units that themselves can no longer be divided.[126] While *stoicheia* and *grammata* are often interchangeable in common usage, strictly speaking and in their more technical designation, linguistic *stoicheia qua* purely systematic entities are themselves soundless: they are arrived at by mentally subtracting the *dunameis* (breathings,

[122] *Potestas*: e.g., *GL* v:548.3 Keil; *GL Suppl.*, clxxxi.23–clxxxii.2 Keil–Hagen.
[123] Schol. Dion. Thrax 197.29 Hilgard; Dion. Hal. *Comp.* 22.   [124] Cf. Pfeiffer 1968, 60.
[125] Pl. *Cr.* 424c7; Arist. *Metaph.* B 3.998a23–25: "the primary constituents (στοιχεῖα) of a thing ... like the elements (στοιχεῖα) of sound/voice (φωνῆς)"; cf. Xen. *Mem.* 4.2.20 (μάθησις καὶ ἐπιστήμη ... τῶν γραμμάτων).
[126] "More numerous," because as later grammatical theory reveals, the number of *stoicheia* escalates to huge proportions if a *stoicheion* is understood as the potential carrier of a sound-quality (in modern terms, as a phoneme; see next chapter). Debates over the number of *stoicheia* raged among the grammarians, in part owing to a lack of clarity over the exact nature of what a *stoicheion* was. For a sample, see schol. Dion. Thrax 30.25–47.31 Hilgard, and see further below. For a parody and critique, see Sext. Emp. *Math.* 1.99–121.

pitches, accents, and so on) that give voice to letters (*grammata*).[127] By the same token, a linguistic *stoicheion* can be made to resound and be linguistically recognizable (and "readable") only in the context of a system and (in the predominantly oral culture of antiquity) in the environment of sounds. Only so do they become phenomenal. They are activated by the system of sounds. But they also are that system. Let me explain.

Linguistic *stoicheia* in many ways resemble the current-day phoneme.[128] Phonemes do not *have* a sound, because they *represent* the *potential for* sound. For this reason, phonemes are conventionally written today in such a way as to distinguish them both from alphabetic letters (e.g., /a/, /l/, /p/, /h/, /a/, /b/, /e/, /t/)[129] and from phonetic transcriptions of the alphabet (e.g., [ælfəbet]). The idea of a theoretical entity such as the phoneme would have made intuitive sense to any late fifth-century Greek interested in discovering the foundations of language, precisely at a time when the conditions of orality and literacy were undergoing a dramatic revolution.[130] The rise of linguistic reflection at this time, and in particular the theory of the *stoicheion* as the foundational element in the new sciences of language, can only have been a reflex of this larger change, possibly even a causal effect of that change. The theory of an intrinsically meaningless building block of meaning is further tied to the concept of language as a system, without which the individual *stoicheion* (element) has no place nor does it make any "sense."

Language as a system: atomistic origins

Consider the table below, which is designed to clarify the ancient componential and compositional system of the Greek language as I am interpreting it here.

---

[127] Cf. schol. Dion. Thrax 175.21–22: "it is impossible to phonate without modulation [pitch] ... and tonality [or accentuation]" (ἀμήχανόν ἐστι φωνὴ δίχα τάσεως ἀποτελεσθῆναι· ... οὐκ ἂν εἴη φωνὴ δίχα τόνου); cf. ibid., 198.19–23. That *stoicheia* in the abstract lack all δύναμις is what the formulation of the *Cratylus* already hints at.

[128] The argument is controversial. See Lüdtke 1969, contesting the resemblance. For a similar suggestion about the Aristotelian *stoicheion* of language, see Zirin 1980; Belardi 1985, 91–97; Ax 1986, 136.

[129] This is not a genuine phonemic transcription of the word "alphabet," but only an illustration *exempli gratia*. There are several competing systems available for both counting and then transcribing phonemes in (American) English, but IPA, modeled here, is the most widely accepted.

[130] On this larger cultural revolution and its implications, see most recently Thomas 1989; Thomas 1992; Yunis 2003. None of these studies links the revolution in literacy to the nascent sciences of language (a topic that would deserve a study of its own).

PHENOMENALITY	GREEK TERMS	LINGUISTIC CATEGORIES (TRANSLATED)	COMPLEXITY
Non-phenomenal	*stoicheia*	indivisible and irreducible elements	*least complex*
Phenomenal	*grammata/phōnē*	letters of the alphabet/voice	
	dunameis	audible, sonorous features of *stoicheia*	
	sullabē	syllable	
	onomata, rhēmata, etc.	nouns, verbs, etc.	
	sunthesis	compositional unit (word, colon, sentence, etc.)	
	logos	speech act/sentence/discourse	
Non-phenomenal	*sustēma*	totality of the language system	*most complex*

Fig. 4.1 Hierarchy of constitutive elements on the componential/compositional model of the Greek language.

The atomistic analysis provided a suitable model, not just analogue, for this line of grammatical analysis, which involves a "phenomenalization" of the constituent elements of speech. Atoms, the building blocks of the universe (its *stoicheia*), lie beneath the threshold of sensation; joined together in compounds (*suntheseis*) they produce visible phenomena: sounds, colors, smells, and so on.[131] In fact, it seems likely that atomism was the source of this original fissuring into system and sonority. A few factors point this way. First, while the distinction between phenomenal and real, conjoined with the componential model, was widespread among any number of Presocratics, Democritus in particular showed a deep interest in the analysis of language, sound, music, and poetry, far more so than, say, Empedocles or Anaxagoras. Secondly, a number of testimonia beginning with Aristotle explicitly link the atomists to developments in the analogy between *stoicheia* (physical elements) and language, which is generally thought to have originated with them. Thirdly, the concept of the atom *qua* smallest indivisible element, and even the term *atomos* itself, continued to attach to the concept of the *stoicheion* in later versions of the componential model. Fourthly, atomism was uniquely suited to express the concept of linguistic matter in a way that the four-element system of "roots" in Empedocles, let alone his two-element system of Love and Strife, or the homoeomerous system of Anaxagoras (which lacked a smallest divisible term), were not. Atoms are featureless, non-sensible,

---

[131] See Arist. *Metaph.* A 4.985b4–19 and, e.g., DK 68A37.

and the smallest divisible elements of a greater whole. Infinite in number yet all of one nature, they combine mechanically into complex assemblages, and in combining they produce larger macroscopic and ultimately sensible and differentiated qualities (sounds, colors, degrees of hardness, tastes) which the elements can be said to "cause" (they are for this reason called the *aitia* of phenomena).[132] The analogy between the elements of nature and the elements of language might seem strained, but it is not so very far-fetched (and it was encouraged by the atomists). Language after all does have a structure that is invisible to the eye or the ear: its elements comprise a *sustēma*, or total system of relations. Just as that structure is phenomenally indifferent and inaccessible, so too are its elements. Yet, both are capable of producing an infinite number of appearances (an endless array of sounds or letter shapes), as is nature itself.[133]

Leucippus and Democritus seem to have drawn an analogy between the combinations of atoms and those between letters of the alphabet.[134] Other clues suggest that the atomists played a crucial role in linking the two models, or rather in propagating the one model across the two domains of physics and language, even if they inherited the compositional model of mechanical change from their Presocratic peers under the various guises of *mixis, krasis, sugkrisis, sunthesis,* or *harmogē* (all different names for combination). Because the basic model was simple, its variants, its implications, and its applications were both many and complex. As a result, the label *stoicheion* (or its equivalents) could be applied to any element of any systematic whole, be it in language, music, architecture, painting, astronomy, mechanics, or, more abstractly, a theoretical system of rules, as in harmonics or in mathematics, where *stoicheia* are simply "elementary" or "first" "principles." Such is the beauty of the model, its endless extensibility and its unifying effect across disciplines. Examples outside of language, for instance in sculpture (Polyclitus' *Canon*) and in Aristoxenian rhythmic theory will be touched on below. For now, I want to limit the discussion to the best attested application of what we might call the *stoicheion*-model of analysis, which happens to have taken place in the area of language theory.

---

[132] Arist. *Metaph.* A 4.985b13–15.

[133] A further indication of the non-phenomenal character of the *stoicheion* is to be found in Greek harmonic and rhythmical theory, which takes as one of its minimal elements a literal gap (*diastēma*) between notes or proportional rhythmic groupings. Such a gap, while literally a temporal silence, does have a palpable (audible) consistency, but only in the overall composition or *sustēma* in which it appears, which is to say, retroactively and, as it were, in silhouette.

[134] Arist. *Metaph.* A 4.985b4–19.

A *stoicheion*, wherever it occurs, including in the analysis of language, is a kind of methodological "atom." It is literally "partless" and "indivisible" (ἀμερής, ἀδιαίρετος, ἄτομος, *atomos* in Latin), "the smallest part" – here – "of vocal sound" (φωνῆς μέρος τὸ ἐλάχιστον), and the building block upon which is built, successively, the various analytical parts that conspire to make up the composite entity under examination (universally called a *suntheton*) – in the present case, the sounds, syllables, rhythms, words, or so on of a linguistic utterance (whether spoken or sung).[135] Thus, in chapter 20 of Aristotle's *Poetics* we find a summary of earlier grammatical and linguistic knowledge that rests on the *stoicheion*-model:

Verbal expression as a whole (τῆς δὲ λέξεως ἁπάσης) has the following parts: element, syllable, linking word, articulatory word, noun, verb, termination, statement (στοιχεῖον συλλαβὴ σύνδεσμος ὄνομα ῥῆμα ἄρθρον πτῶσις λόγος). An element is an indivisible sound (φωνὴ ἀδιαίρετος), not any sound, but that capable of producing intelligible utterance (ἀλλ' ἐξ ἧς πέφυκε συνθετὴ γίγνεσθαι φωνή [lit., "from which composite [viz., articulated] sound can arise"]).[136]

Similarly, when Dionysius of Halicarnassus speaks of "the elements (στοιχείων) out of which (ἐξ ὧν) an argument" is constructed, he is reverting to the language of methodological atomism. In the very next breath, he talks about the "differences" (διαφοράς) that exist between the parts, "down to the smallest cut" ("the last detail," Usher; ἄχρι τῆς εἰς ἐλάχιστον τομῆς). Beyond that point, the constitutive elements, being the partless "atoms" of the argument, exist no longer.[137] The idea that (imperceptible) elements combine to make perceptible (phenomenal) differences derives from the atomists themselves.[138]

Implicitly, elements belong to a complete whole, in the present case to the whole that constitutes language itself. That they do lies behind the very idea of the *stoicheion*-model, which in fact derives not from linguistic analysis but from Presocratic physics, though it would take some time

---

[135] Cf. Arist. *Poet.* 20.1456b22; schol. Dion. Thrax 316.24–30 Hilgard; ibid., 300.1; Sergius in *GL* 4:475.9 Keil (*atomos*). For *stoicheia* as the "elements" of musical composition, viz., (the primary) notes, see Pl. *Tht.* 206a–b.

[136] Arist. *Poet.* 20.1456b20–23; trans. Hubbard.   [137] Dion. Hal. *Lys.* 15.

[138] See Arist. *Metaph.* A 4.985b11–16. A recent trend has been to trace biological metaphors in ancient grammar, especially in Aristotle (see the scholarship cited at Ch. 2, n. 209 above). I suspect, however, that the original inspiration behind the *stoicheion* model is mechanical, not biological and organic, just as some of the examples that have been adduced in favor of this thesis are not clearly biological in character.

before the idea of language as a totality was fully articulated (or else simply attested) in ancient linguistics. We might compare Plato in the *Timaeus,* where he speaks about "the ABC of everything," which is to say, of the universe (στοιχεῖα τοῦ παντός), and contrasts these elements with those that comprise the "syllables" of words.[139] Whether or not Plato calqued the physical sense of *stoicheion* onto the pre-existing grammatical term,[140] he did not invent the model of elements combining into a whole: that was derived from the *phusikoi.* That elements belong to a complete whole is further implied by the very definition of element as "smallest part" which is itself "indivisible," as in Aristotle's inherited usage in the *Poetics* passage above.[141] For, at the other end of the scale lies not simply a syllable or a word, but the entire realm of combinations of articulated voice (συνθετὴ φωνή), which, while in principle infinite in its expressions, in another way is finite: when elements are combined, the threshold of recognizable utterance is attained. Language is the theoretical sum of all such possible utterances. Whence the phrase τῆς λέξεως στοιχεῖα, "elements of expression," found first in Plato's pupil Xenocrates of Chalcedon (one of Aristotle's forerunners in the *Poetics* passage just cited) and then in the Stoic Diogenes of Babylon, though, oddly, no satisfying single equivalent for the abstract concept of language ever quite emerges in antiquity.[142] (*Logos* sometimes carries this meaning, but not consistently or unequivocally.) And if a language is the theoretical sum of all possible utterances within that language, implicitly the reverse ought to be true, at least for Aristotle, if not for others: the individual constituents (*stoicheia*) of language are themselves recognizably linguistic, not extra-linguistic.[143] Finally, though this is a slightly different way of stating the previous point, but important nevertheless, the *stoicheion*-model works in two directions at once without residue. It is componential because it is compositional, and vice versa, building up to a whole and reducing back down into its constituent parts again.

The physical origins of the componential/compositional model of language more or less guaranteed the idea that language, to which the elements belong and which they jointly comprise, is a totality. The elements were originally the material constituents of the universe, as in

[139] Pl. *Tim.* 48b8–c2; trans. Taylor 1928, 306.   [140] Crowley 2005, 381.

[141] Cf. also *Metaph.* Δ 3.1014a26–34.

[142] Xenocrates: fr. *120 Isnardi Parente (= Sext. Emp. *Math.* 10.253); Diogenes: D. L. 7.56.

[143] Even the atomists were pointing to an analogy, not to a reductionist model of language. But behind that analogy stood the idea (or threat) of a reduction of language to matter itself (see below).

Empedocles and the atomists, and later Plato (as we just saw).[144] It matters little if the term *stoicheion* in the sense of *letter* does not appear before the fourth century with one exception, known through a reference by Aristotle to the sophist Euthydemus of Chios, because it is the model and not the terminology that matters:

There is also the argument that one who knows the letters (τὸν τὰ στοιχεῖα ἐπιστάμενον) knows the whole word (τὸ ἔπος οἶδεν), since the word is the same thing [as the letters that compose it] (τὸ γὰρ ἔπος τὸ αὐτό ἐστιν).[145]

Euthydemus' point has further bite if *epos* refers not to *word*, but to *epic*:[146] what if the whole (say, the *Iliad*) is nothing beyond the sum of its constituent parts – here, the letters that make it up, or for an atomist, the atoms that comprise its sounds?

From the start, the componential model has a reductionist and materialist tinge that it never sheds, likewise an inheritance from physics.[147] Language cannot be reduced to an irrational residue, at least in anti-materialist quarters. Aristotle will express this worry in a *reductio* when he insists that the syllable "ba" is something else (*heteron ti*) besides "b" plus "a" – otherwise it would be a mere "heap," a σωρός. Presumably, this something-more has to do with the formal nature of the syllable *qua* linguistic entity.[148] And Plato will marshal similar arguments in the *Philebus* when he notes that what unifies language is not the mere succession of the alphabetical letters, but the grammatical knowledge that collects them in their totality and allows us to recognize any given letter *as a letter* at all.[149]

The materiality of the stoicheion

The examples from Plato and Aristotle illustrate just how advanced thinking about the systematic nature of the *stoicheion* had become by the fourth century. Both authors rely upon the concept of language as a

---

[144] Arist. *Metaph.* A 4.985a32 (Empedocles); ibid., 985b4–19 (atomists); *Timaeus*, see above.
[145] Arist. *Rh.* 2.24.3.1401a28–30.
[146] Burkert 1959, 179. Opinions remain divided between a fifth-century origin for the term *stoicheion* in the atomists or sophists and a fourth-century origin in Plato (see Burkert 1959, esp. 179 on Euthydemus of Chios and the circle around him; ibid., 193 on Hippocrates of Chios, the mid- to late fifth-century geometer; Pfeiffer 1968, 60–61; 281–82). But the concept and its aesthetic application predate Plato, as Plato is the first to admit (*Crat.* 424c7, deferring to "specialists in these matters," οἱ δεινοὶ περὶ τούτων; cf. ibid., 424c1).
[147] Cf. Cic. *Nat. D.* 2.93.   [148] Arist. *Metaph.* Z 17.1041b11–33. See further Porter 1996.
[149] Pl. *Phlb.* 18c–d; see below.

systematic totality. Implicit in this model is the principle that the *stoi-cheion* could point to some invisible element of language that has every-thing to do with its structural operations. As Walter Burkert notes, "the thoroughly palpable difference between *gramma* and *stoicheion* is not a question of sound versus letter .... What distinguishes them is precisely their relation to rational analysis; it is precisely the meaning of 'elem-ent.'"[150] But that is true only because sounds and letters are both outward manifestations of *stoicheia* (elements). In fact, the same *stoicheion* could be manifested by either a spoken sound or a written letter.

That the linguistic *stoicheion* appeared when it did was no historical accident. With the introduction of writing to ever more numerous spheres of private and public life, the eye became highly sensitized as never before to the physical appearance of texts: texts had a materiality that one could actually touch and see. But what about the same texts when they were sung or read aloud? Or speeches? Or seen or heard in the mind? What kind of materiality did these have? The concept of the *stoicheion* was a partial answer to questions like these. It at least provided a uniform basis, in theory, to the various manifestations of language. And if the term *stoicheion* (or the concept behind it) did in fact arise out of the context of *phusiologia*, or natural philosophy, then it also carried the suggestion of being a material or at least quasi-material entity. This uncertain origin would have sufficed in itself to provoke doubts and some consternation should anyone have chosen to press the issue of the status of the *stoicheion* as an entity: was it a concept, a thing, a bit of matter, or an abstract element of language conceived as a system of relations? Was it audible or not, visible or not?

Irrespective of this inheritance from natural philosophy, linguistic science necessarily would have faced a kind of impasse whenever it confronted the issue of written versus oral expression: how could the same elements account for the two very different phenomenological experiences of language associated with these two different realizations (materializa-tions) of *logos*? One possibility was already mentioned: *stoicheia*, insofar as they are distinct from *grammata*, are phenomenologically neutral, which means that they are *neither intrinsically visual or oral*, but are rather *potentially both*. They are also susceptible of *multiple* possible realizations.

---

[150] Burkert 1959, 172; 173. He might have added irreducibility to the defining features of the *stoicheion*, which defines its systematicity (as Vollgraff 1948, rightly points out, esp. at p. 91), but strangely he does not, seemingly taking issue with this idea in one place (ibid., 168; *contra* Vollgraff), but not in another (where he speaks in favor of the inherent "atomism" of this conception; ibid., 179).

This is a view one might expect a linguistic conventionalist to hold, such as Aristotle, who writes in the *Metaphysics*,

> not even every kind of letter (τὰ στοιχεῖα πάντα) will be present in the *logos* [the formula, or essential definition] of the syllable, e.g. particular (ταδί) waxen letters or the letters as sounds in the air [i.e., letters in written or spoken material form]; for these also are part of the syllable only in the sense that they are its perceptible matter (ὡς ὕλη αἰσθητή).[151]

In other words, the *only* letters present in the formal definition of a syllable are those that have *no phenomenal characteristics*. Such is the economy, even parsimony, of *stoicheion*-based definitions. The same view can be demonstrated for the Hellenistic period (witness the grammarians to be discussed momentarily) and beyond.[152] But even a naturalist could be seen to succumb to this view's charms, no doubt owing to the recognition that to reduce the Greek language to the twenty-four letters of the alphabet is a mere contrivance and an impoverishment of the reality: after all, sound, being a continuum (a fluid sound-stream), is infinitely diverse (φωνὴ ἄπειρος).[153] Thus, even for Socrates in Plato's *Cratylus*, who construes *stoicheia* as sound values and not as phonically neutral, the values of a given *stoicheion* are not fixed on a one-to-one basis: *rho* imitates motion in some contexts and hardness in others, and "we must here remind ourselves that each letter is assumed to have multiple imitative powers" that are contextually variable and therefore differently realized in different settings.[154]

In its most rigorous form, the elements would simply *be* the relations that make up the system; their identity would be completely exhausted in their relations to one another (just as phonemes are today: /a/ is defined as not /b/, /c/, /d/, etc.). We get hints that this notion lies behind the concept of the *stoicheion* as a systematic entity in various places, which is to say, as constituting an element of a *sustēma*, or totality, but perhaps no earlier or more explicitly than in Plato's *Philebus*, where the mythical figure of Theuth is invoked to explain the discovery of language as a system. Theuth noticed that in the unlimited stream of the vocal sounds that comprise language he could discern rational divisions, which he called *stoicheia*. "And as he realized that *none of us could gain any*

[151] Arist. *Metaph.* Z 7.1035a14–17; trans. Ross.
[152] See Vogt-Spira 1991, 326–27 on the Roman grammarians.   [153] Pl. *Phlb.* 18b6.
[154] Pl. *Crat.* 434c; Sedley 2003, 129–30; 146 (quotation). Cf. *Tht.* 202e6: τὰ τῶν γραμμάτων στοιχεῖά τε καὶ συλλαβάς, "*letters* – the elements of language – and syllables" (trans. Levett; rev. Burnyeat; emphasis added), where written signs are meant.

knowledge of a single one of them taken by itself without understanding them all, he considered [knowledge of] that to be the one link that somehow unifies them all and called it the art of literacy."[155] The thought has striking parallels with the theory of the musical note and the elements of rhythm known from the harmonicists and later from Aristoxenus (see below). In both cases, the entities in question must be read (recognized) against the system of relations that mark them out as such.

A later expression of this same insight comes from Crates of Mallos in the second century BCE. His theory of the *stoicheion* is preserved in a short paragraph from the scholia to Dionysius Thrax that is astonishingly modern-sounding:

Crates defines the *stoicheion* thus: "[It is] the smallest part of ordered [voice]." He called it the "smallest part" *inasmuch as it stands in relation to the entire system* (πρὸς τὸ ὅλον σύστημα) of voice capable of being articulated into letter-sounds. Aristotle [defines it] thus: "simple and indivisible voice." Others define it in the same way.[156]

A further definition is given in a treatise attributed to the great second-century-BCE grammarian Dionysius Thrax, but which is now commonly thought to postdate him by several centuries. While the treatise probably contains a blend of authentic and later material, the following is very likely of Hellenistic origin:

Grammata are the twenty-four letters of the alphabet from *alpha* to *omega* .... The same entities are called *stoicheia* due to their occupying some "place" (*stoichos*) and position.[157]

Synthesizing, we can say that whereas *grammata* stand for the twenty-four letters of the alphabet, *stoicheia* are clearly the same items viewed now

---

[155] Pl. *Phlb.* 18c–d; trans. D. Frede; emphasis added. A similar formulation is the vexed passage at *Tht.* 201e–202b, which concludes, "Thus, *stoicheia* are unaccountable and unknowable (ἄλογα καὶ ἄγνωστα), but they are perceivable" (αἰσθητά). About this passage, Burnyeat 1990, 135 writes, "the claim [and its argument] is a mystery as dark as anything in the dialogue." But one possibility would be to fill out the claim as follows: "*stoicheia* <viz., the theoretical constituents of a system,> are unaccountable and unknowable <in and of themselves, though not in relation to the whole>, but they are perceivable <when embodied in their physical counterparts and so recognized>."

[156] ὁρίζεται δὲ τὸ στοιχεῖον ὁ μὲν Κράτης οὕτω· "φωνῆς μέρος τὸ ἐλάχιστον <τῆς κατὰ σύνταξιν". "μέρος ἐλάχιστον" δ' εἶπεν ὡς πρὸς τὸ ὅλον σύστημα τῆς ἐγγραμμάτου φωνῆς>. ὁ δὲ Ἀριστοτέλης οὕτως· "ἁπλῆ καὶ ἀδιαίρετος φωνή" [ ]· ἄλλοι οὕτως, κτλ. [< > transposed by Mette, following Hilgard, from [ ]] (fr. 52a Mette = fr. 95 Broggiato = schol. Dion. Thrax 316.24–27 Hilgard).

[157] γράμματά ἐστιν εἰκοσιτέσσαρα ἀπὸ τοῦ ᾱ μέχρι τοῦ ῶ [....] τὰ δὲ αὐτὰ καὶ στοιχεῖα καλεῖται διὰ τὸ ἔχειν στοῖχόν τινα καὶ τάξιν ([Dion. Thrax] *Ars Gramm.* §6; Περὶ στοιχείου, p. 9.25–32 Uhlig). See Lallot 1998, ad loc. on the dating of this material.

from a different perspective and according to different criteria: they are the same signs regarded, not for their property of following one another in an established sequence, but simply for their property of occupying a position in that sequence at all. To be a *stoicheion* is not to possess any particular value but just to be a placeholder for particular values in a system. Crates' innovation, if it was one, was to bring out what was implicit in the componential model all along: the systematic character of the *stoicheion*. Hence, he defined it as "stand[ing] in relation to the entire system (πρὸς τὸ ὅλον σύστημα) of [linguistic] voice." That is, *stoicheia* are abstract, differential units, which is to say, purely relational entities that are defined by two aspects: (i) according to their differences from one another rather than according to any positive features they carry intrinsically (for this reason, *stoicheia* have no sound: they are, by definition, intrinsically featureless); and (ii) according to their position within the system or totality of language. The *stoicheion*, in other words, is very much the relative of the modern-day phoneme, however much the latter notion may be contested among contemporary linguists.[158]

If the later grammarians accepted the systematic nature of language, Plato was worried about its cognitive accessibility: how could we gain knowledge of the parts without first knowing the whole to which they belonged? A related but differently framed problem would haunt Aristotle. In *Metaphysics* Z 17 he worries over the genuinely difficult issue of what it is that gives a compound (a *suntheton*) its unity, as we saw.[159] The "cause" of a syllable cannot be reduced to the mere juxtaposition of the letters: that yields a heap (σωρός), whereas what he is looking for is something else, a *heteron ti*, which might mark out their linguistic essence or form. The legibility of letters as such, he decides, is thanks to a theoretical and psychological grasp of a formal and conventional principle – not quite of meanings *per se*, but of the "form" of language.[160] Does a meaningful syllable, then, cease to be a mere sound? Perhaps not, but henceforth it becomes impossible to distinguish the sound (*psophos*) from its being voice (*phōnē*), even if a syllable carries no meaning by itself, like "ba," or else the syllable (collection of sounds) "oice" from "voice" (his example is "υς" from μῦς).[161] So powerful is Aristotle's theory of language, it effectively precludes the possibility that linguistic sounds

---

[158] See n. 128 above.   [159] Arist. *Metaph.* Z 17.1041b11–33.
[160] For Aristotle, rational considerations inhabit even the source and locus of linguistic utterance: "voice is made by an animal, *and not with any chance part of his body*" (*De an.* 2.7.420b13–14).
[161] Arist. *Int.* 4.16b31–33.

("voice" or *phōnē*) can be reduced back again to their materiality as *psophos*. They remain always potentially semantic, even if they are actually "only voice" (which for him is not quite the same thing as sound).[162] Consequently, aesthetic properties, which naturally have to do with sound, are optional for Aristotle: they can be *added* to words (τοῖς ψιλοῖς λόγοις), as in Gorgias,[163] but they cannot be derived by *subtracting* meaning from them or from their consideration, through a mental effort of inattention, as the Hellenistic euphonists would later hold – unlike Gorgias.[164] Gorgias provokes the question of materialism, and he explores its possibilities (as we shall see in Chapter 5), while the later euphonists hold a far more potent version of it: they are unabashedly and reductively materialists whenever they train their focus on sound. Aristotle, meanwhile, stands far removed from linguistic materialism, a term that requires explanation.

For present purposes, I am taking linguistic materialism to be one of two things, one weaker, one stronger. On the weaker view, (a) all language is expressed in meaningless matter (whether in sound or script or in the materials associated with both), so that one must have a theory of the interrelation of meaning, form (or organization), and matter if one wishes to have a linguistic theory founded in the materials of language: this is the ineluctable materialism of language. On the stronger view, (b) linguistic expression (including meaning) is decisively determined by, and in the extreme case reducible to, the properties of some non-linguistic physical substrate. I don't know if any ancient took the second view. The first-generation atomists presumably did, since the atomistic analogy between linguistic and natural compounds points in this direction, and Aristotle's worries about linguistic heaps seem to confirm the impression.[165] Moreover, the early atomists would have analyzed linguistic sounds into streams of atoms whose clusterings we conventionally associate with meaning, whereby meaning is itself reducible to a state (*diathesis*) of the mind's physical make-up (what is conventionally called thought). But the atomists are unique among the ancients in holding such a view,

---

[162] Arist. *Int.* 4.16b31–32: οὐδὲ γὰρ ἐν τῷ μῦς τὸ υς σημαντικόν, ἀλλὰ φωνή ἐστι νῦν μόνον; *Poet.* 20.1457a3–6.

[163] Arist. *Rh.* 3.2.1404b11–14; Gorg. *Hel.* §9.

[164] Meaning does not cease to exist for the later euphonists: it simply doesn't matter, aesthetically speaking. They speak of the ear being "distracted" from the meaning to the sound and then lingering there. Their own practice suggests a willful distraction on the part of the critic and an equally willful neglect of semantics in favor of the aesthetics of sound.

[165] Aristotle goes on to address Democritus a page or so later in a related discussion (*Metaph.* H 3.1043b4–12).

and not even their heir Epicurus would accept (b), though no one could escape the implications of (a).[166]

Be this as it may, Aristotle's view of language had direct implications for aesthetics. Henceforth, one could speak of "aesthetic heaps." Cicero would do just this, seemingly repeating Aristotle's critique of Democritus, with an eye now to Latin verse:

> I cannot understand why [anyone who believes in the principles of atomism, and especially in the theory that atoms (*corpora quaedam solida atque individua*) by colliding fortuitously together "produced[d] this very elaborate and beautiful world"] should not also think that, if a countless number of copies of the one-and-twenty letters of the alphabet, made of gold or what you will, were thrown together into some receptacle and then shaken out on to the ground, it would be possible that they should produce the *Annals* of Ennius, all ready for the reader. I doubt whether chance could possibly succeed in producing even a single verse![167]

Aristotle himself supplies a version of the same point in the *Poetics*: the brute, sequential arrangement (ἐάν τις ἐφεξῆς θῆ) of the parts (μέρη) of a tragedy – all its speeches, full of character as they may be, even well composed in *lexis* and *dianoia* – would constitute a mere "heap" and no unity in the absence of a supervenient principle, that is, the intelligible synthesis (σύστασις) of the organizing plot.[168] Instead of a causal chain ("one thing because of another," τάδε διὰ τάδε), such a play would exhibit all the defects of history: it would consist in "one thing after another" (τάδε μετὰ τάδε).[169] But this is so only because Aristotle claims to have identified what it is that gives an aesthetic whole its unity.

Stoicheia *and perception*

Analysis by way of *stoicheia* has further implications for the perception of objects in ancient thought. Componential analysis creates a *double articulation*: to every abstract, methodological entity there corresponds an embodied material equivalent, be this a proportional body length, a

---

[166] Oddly enough, Plato's theory of etymology (if it is his) in the *Cratylus* could be reckoned a kind of linguistic materialism if viewed from an angle from which it is not usually seen: not from that of the derivation of names, but from that of the limitation that sounds create for linguistic expression.

[167] Cic. *Nat. D.* 2.93; trans. Rackham. Cf. also Procl. *in Ti.* 1:59.19–21 Diehl for the same metaphor, this time using Epicurean atoms (though, I would argue, premised on a worry prompted by the first-generation atomists).

[168] Arist. *Poet.* 6.1450a29–33.

[169] "ἐφεξῆς suggests not disorder, but absence of an ordering principle" (Lucas ad loc.).

building unit (such as the architectural *embatēr*, or "module" [*modulus*], which seems to have had a sculptural application, if not origin),[170] a slice of time (in rhythmical theory, a *chronos prōtos*, or primary duration),[171] or a part of the color spectrum (on the theory of mixture alluded to as early as Empedocles; see Ch. 3, §5 above). In the realm of language or music, to discover the materiality of the entities in question one normally has to seek out *stoicheia* in the dimension of *sound*, for it is *as sound* that the productions in language and music strike the sensorium (following the principle enunciated above concerning the subjective impact of aesthetic impressions). Thus, for Aristoxenus the primary elements (durations) of rhythm act on bodies (bodies made rhythmic, whether hands, feet, or vocal apparatus), which in turn carve up time into segments (that is, into minimal and indivisible time-lengths): "the object made rhythmic (τὸ ῥυθμιζόμενον) must be capable of being divided into recognizable parts, *by which it will divide time.*"[172] Supervening on its objects as a division of time, rhythm is at once sensuous and abstract; it is "made perceptible to the senses" (γνώριμον ... τῇ αἰσθήσει), but it is less a sensation than the shape of one: what supervenes on objects made rhythmic is in fact a system of relations (ratios of time-lengths, or durations [χρόνοι]), literally a structure of signs, the pattern of which becomes available (recognizable) only retroactively.[173] Aristoxenus' predecessors, the *harmonikoi*, sought out the smallest musical measure, an interval or gap (σμικρότατον [or ἐλάχιστον] διάστημα), of which a whole system of relations (melodic systems, συστήματα or ἁρμονίαι) were composed and through which these same systems could be analyzed.[174] The proportional *embatēr* in architecture or the Polyclitean canonical measure may have worked in a similar fashion, the elements and their patterns emerging synthetically, *a posteriori*, from the visual experience of objects – with one possible difference: the first model may have been more inductively oriented, given that musicologists were not typically musicians, while the latter two models may have been geared more towards

---

[170] Vitr. 1.2.4; 4.3.3. On its possible adaptations in sculpture (e.g., Polyclitus' system of proportions), see Schlikker 1940, 56–61; on the archaic roots of this exchange between the two art forms around the *embatēr*, see Wilson Jones 2001, 698–99.

[171] The primary duration is a time-atom; see n. 201 below.

[172] Aristox. *Rhythm.* 2.6; trans. Pearson, adapted; emphasis added; cf. ibid., 2.9.

[173] Ibid., 2.16.

[174] Pl. *Rep.* 7.531a7 (σμικρότατον διάστημα); Aristox. *Harm.* 28.5 (ἐλάχιστον διάστημα), 7.20–34, 36.15–37.7 (melodic systems).

construction (architects and sculptors being more closely involved in the production of their own artifacts, as well as their first observers).[175]

Now, as a rule one has to look for *stoicheia* at their point of articulation on the body or within the material that gives rise to their expression and appearance: they exist to be embedded there. In spoken language, this means looking to the sources of sound, be this "according to the shape of the mouth," "the place of contact <of the lips and teeth>" (Aristotle)[176] or in the gaps and spacings and clashings or blendings amongst the letter-sounds. Though Aristotle attests to the antiquity of the tradition, one might compare Dionysius of Halicarnassus in his *On the Composition of Words*, who adds a subtle factor, namely the element of time: "The process of the mouth's altering from one shape (σχηματισμόν) to another, that is neither akin to it nor like it, entails a lapse of time (χρόνος), during which the smoothness and euphony of the arrangement is interrupted" (διίσταται).[177] Harshness of sound merely brings to the fore what euphoniousness serves to conceal: *sunthesis* produces an *effect* of harmony *where none in fact exists*. In other words, *language is intrinsically cacophonous*, and Dionysius is well aware of the fact.[178] He knows, for instance, that euphony in its pure form exists in only three open vowels – *alpha, ēta*, and *omega* ("because they are sounded for a long time, and do not arrest the strong flow of the breath") – and that in practice these rarely or never occur except in combination with other letters that, by contrast, are *not* euphonic.[179] The job of *sunthesis* is to create an appearance in the ear – that of an aural illusion:

> It sets out to blend together and interweave its component parts, and to make them convey as far as possible the effect (ὄψιν) of a single utterance. This result is achieved by the exact fitting together of the words, so that no perceptible interval (χρόνον αἰσθητόν) between them is allowed. In this respect the style [in question, viz., the smooth style] resembles a finely-woven net, or pictures in which the lights and shadows melt into one another.[180]

While Dionysius is discussing only the smooth style of composition in this passage, a more general lesson emerges that holds good for all compositional styles, but which can be transferred beyond the realm of language: sound effects supervene on the *sunthesis* of the elements as its

---

[175] On Polyclitus, see Chapter 5, §1 below. I discussed the Vitruvian system in Porter 1987.

[176] Arist. *Poet.* 20.1456b31–33; the addition in angle brackets is supplied by the Arabic version (see Gudeman 1934, ad loc. and in his app. crit.). For relevant parallels, cf. Arist. *Hist. an.* 4.9.535a28–b1 (on the pharynx, larynx, lungs, tongue, and lips); *De an.* 2.8.420b26–29 (on the trachea).

[177] Dion. Hal. *Comp.* 22; trans. Usher.   [178] See Porter 2001a.   [179] Dion. Hal. *Comp.* 13.

[180] Ibid., 23.

secondary qualities and as its "appearances." The same is true of colors and shapes supervening on patches of paint or notes and time-lengths in combination. (Dionysius' resort to *opsis*, or "visual effect," for "aural effect" may attest to a further correspondence between these two theories.) Another lesson is that aesthetic effects are directly correlated to the time of perception, as Shklovsky would later note: the longer the perceptual duration, the more palpable an object's sensuous qualities will be (or appear to be). Time intensifies aesthetic perception. Even Aristotle seems to have made this observation, as we saw earlier in a discussion of his theory of beauty in the *Poetics*.[181] Time, when it is made into an object of sensation in its own right, can in turn affect aesthetic characterizations. Shklovskian "roughening" would best apply to the ancient grand style, with its pronounced clashes of sound, heightened difficulties in pronunci-ation, retardations, gaps in structure, imbalances between clauses and periods, grammatical solecisms, and the rest, all of which render the time of perception itself most intensely palpable (not least by manufacturing mini-pauses, *chronoi*, to attend to), and which thus "prevent the ear from gaining the impression (φαντασίαν) of one continuous clause" or of other sorts of patterns.[182] This is an interesting finding by itself, as it suggests that the grand style, and the sublime in particular, may have less to do with grandeur *per se* and more to do with an increased sensory contact, on the part of the beholder, with the various dimensions of any given aesthetic object. *That is, the sublime may have more to do with an intensification of aesthetic experience than with some of the more conventional factors of sublimity.* I happen to think this is right, but I do not want to press the point here. Similar arguments could be made, in reverse, about the smooth and lighter styles.

One way in which we can conceive of Shklovskian roughening in Dionysius' terms is to notice how in the grand style (what Dionysius calls the austere style) the elements of language and the mechanisms of style are gradually pulled apart and exposed to view. In contrast to the blurring effect of the smooth style, where "lights and shadows melt into one another," here all the materials stand exposed, in part thanks to the slow-motion effects of the thickening and stuttering of rhythms and sounds. Individual letter-sounds protrude; combinations break down; the illusory mechanisms that once produced *phantasiai* grind to a halt. In Shklovsky's terms, complementary to his language about thickening, the "technique" of the verbal artistry is laid bare. But so too is the basic

---

[181] Ch. 2, §2.   [182] Ibid., 22.

structure of language itself. For what stand exposed now are the individual *stoicheia*, their *suntheseis*, and the euphonic effects they no longer produce (though they of course continue to produce further aesthetic effects, albeit of an opposite but still positive nature).

It is here that critics come to an appreciation of the *technē* of literary composition, but also to disagreements about the sources of literary effects: are these to be found in the *stoicheia*, in the *sunthesis*, or in the sound that appears on the surface of the *sunthesis*? And for parallel reasons, grammarians begin to wonder about the sources of sound working behind the scenes: they know very well the difference between the symbol α, the name for the symbol (*alpha*), and the variable phonic expressions of the same (long, short, rough, smooth, acute, grave, circumflexed, and then all of these in every permissible permutation) – whence the disagreements that arise over the number of letters in the alphabet, which suggest that the *stoicheion*, when it was considered as part of a systematic whole and not as a *gramma*, was in fact being treated as the equivalent of the modern-day phoneme: viewed as a *stoicheion*, it had no sound.[183] Here, one might be obliged to speak of a *triple articulation* that bears upon: (i) the linguistic material; (ii) the resulting sound; and (iii) the abstract entities (phonemes) lying behind both. This unresolved ambiguity is the source of endless disputes among the euphonists reported by Philodemus, who seem unable to agree whether the criterion of good poetry is to be sought for in the *sunthesis* (the combination of letters/elements) or in the euphony that results from the letters and finally reaches the ear. That is, they cannot agree on how to articulate, in theory, the division of labor between the elements of language (*stoicheia*) and the effects these elements collectively produce.

It is a fair question whether the componential method of analysis actually *creates* the material equivalents it presupposes (or implies), since it is evident that letters, syllables, and rhythms do not exist by nature but only by convention (at least on some ancient views of sound and voice, including the atomistically inspired models), and thus that these entities are not so much found in the world as they are brought into existence by theories about the world. The sound spectrum is naturally fluid yet arbitrarily divisible (at least most of the time in antiquity): so why is *tau* (the symbol τ, or rather the theoretical entity /t/) a *stoicheion*, while the word-sounds *to* or *tau* (τό, ταῦ) are not? As we have begun to see, a sound is not a *stoicheion* at all, whereas only its theoretical

---

[183] See nn. 126 and 127 above.

counterpart is. And this divergence – and in actual occurrences, this momentary convergence – between contingency and materiality can lead to interesting consequences. For example, the indivisibility of a *stoicheion* is not a property of being a letter (*gramma*), but its sonic and phonic qualities are, once the *stoicheion* has been singled out as such in this or that instantiation of itself.[184]

The same can be said of its visual qualities. After all, a *stoicheion* names, abstractly, what its graphic realizations do. Here, the *stoicheion* would in modern terminology be labeled a *grapheme*. The marked fascination of sixth- and early fifth-century vase painting with writing for writing's sake, sometimes taking the form of "pseudo-inscriptions" or pure non-sense inscriptions (strings of letters which seemingly exist to represent the fact and the materiality of writing but which combine into no known lexical items), could well serve to capture the (new) strangeness of writing itself, rather than serving a purely calligraphic, decorative function, as is sometimes thought (see fig. 4.2).[185] These stochastic sequences of letters could, that is, be an attempt to capture something of the surdity of written language, its opaque otherness (its brute materiality) – the more so if the norm in painted vase inscriptions was to read them out to one's peers in social settings, for instance at *sumposia*.[186] What better way to express the otherness of writing in visual terms than by reducing words to decorative strokes or meaningless sequences of letters? If "inscriptions inherently emphasize the nature of the surface *as* surface,"[187] nonsensical and calligraphic inscriptions inherently emphasize the materiality of inscription and of language generally.[188] They present visual strings of *stoicheia*, at once luring and congesting the eye. Here, we would have a parallel to the "thickening" of sound perception noted above in the case of euphonistic criticism, where questions of meaning dissolved before the sheer attentiveness to sound as a perceptual phenomenon. The fact that inscriptions are banished from vases starting in the fifth century strongly suggests that a waning fascination with these properties of writing as script, rather than

---

[184] This is what I mean by their "double articulation": *stoicheia* are both contingently abstract (systematic) and corporeally material (phonetic) entities.

[185] Cf. Boardman 2003, 112 at n. 9.

[186] See Snodgrass 2000. Nonsense inscriptions would make superb challenges at contests, of course.

[187] Hurwit 1990, 192.

[188] This is true even if it is also true that (some?) decorative nonsense inscriptions can help to articulate the visual patterns they interact with (so Osborne and Pappas 2007) – for the writing in this case is effective not as semantic but as one aesthetic element playing off another. To be sure, drawing a hard and fast line between "purely decorative" and "purely nonsensical" inscriptions, viz., between aesthetic and nonaesthetic uses, would be a parlous business.

Fig. 4.2 Detail from side A of White-Ground Footed Mastoid Skyphos *c.* 515 BCE.
The song of an elderly poet is represented by nonsense letters flowing from the poet's mouth
like a fountain. The letters are somewhat crudely and illegibly drawn, and some of them
only approximate to actual letters, vaguely mimicking rather than consisting of letters.

the incipient rise of illusionism, is to blame for the demise of this most
intriguing of phenomena.[189]

---

[189] See Snodgrass 2000, 31 for a retabulation of Immerwahr's data; and Hurwit 1990, 193, for the view
that "the word was a casualty of illusionism." Hurwit adds as another factor the changing dynamics
of orality and literacy (ibid., 193–97), but this does a better job explaining the appearance of normative
writing on vases than it does explaining the stranger appearances of letters on vases (pseudo-
inscriptions) or the disappearance of both. Snodgrass (ibid., 32–33) offers up a further suggestion:
the introduction of the "synoptic" technique of visual narrative. But this is a weak parallel, related
to painted inscriptions by chronology only. At the far end of the literary tradition lie the
Hellenistic *carmina figurata* (shaped poems), which present the diametrical (and graphic)
opposite phenomenon: verses made "surd" (or nearly so) *qua* images. In fact, such poems retain
a semantic function. A curious genre, they may derive from inscribed vases, and they do strain to
become visual objects again. On this visual-verbal genre, see Strodel 2002; Ford in Yunis 2003, 18;
on its possible early origins, see Lissarrague 1987, 59–65; 119–33; Hurwit 1990. A famous instance of
an ancient puzzle that plays on the ambiguities of *graphai* and *stoicheia* is Callias' *Letter Tragedy*
(post *c.* 421 BCE), as transmitted in *On Riddles* by Clearchus of Soli, a pupil of Aristotle's, and
reported by Athenaeus (see most recently Smith 2003).

Fig. 4.3 Nonsense inscription. Attic black-figure kylix, sixth century BCE.
Detail from side A. Berkeley 8–358. The inscription reads: *epoiuepoiuepoiunsunesu*,
stuttering on the word *epoiei*, "He made."

It has been suggested that nonsense inscriptions give the deliberate
"illusion" of literacy's functions, inasmuch as they were "written by
literate painters who felt that the scenes [depicted on the vases] should
have inscriptions even where no precise information was to be transmitted. . . . [Nonsense inscriptions] give the illusion that the story is also told
in words and show that the painter can write, even where he lacks the
precise words or the time to put them on."[190] Perhaps. It is true that such
inscriptions often recall real words, as in the frequent reminiscences of
epoiēsen ("so-and-so made"), for example, the stuttering *epoiuepoiuepoiunsunesu* (fig. 4.3),[191] or as in the reminiscence of *kulix* in *uilkuliailiu*.[192]
Barely self-referential – that is, referring to themselves as objects and
unable to refer to anything else – these texts create two simultaneous
walls, one of visuality and another of sound (much like tongue-twisters),
as well as a barrier between these two competing levels of perception.
They recreate, in other words, the effects of *illiteracy in literacy* or *at
the margins of literacy*, which is to say, the condition of alienation from
Greek that only a child or a foreigner (or a drunkard) could experience
towards his or her language in its written form. Tongue-twisters (so-called

[190] Immerwahr 1990, 45.   [191] Berkeley 8/358.   [192] New York 41.162.72.

chalinoi; lit., "bits and bridles") were a recommended pedagogical staple in the ancient rhetorical schools, and this practice will be discussed below.[193] A further possible influence from the side of contemporary sepulchral verse inscriptions, where a similar emphasis on surface materiality is in play, cannot be ruled out either (see Chapter 9 below).[194]

At any rate, *stoicheia* raise interesting problems about nature and convention. Indeed, the language of this contrast – *phusis* and *thesis* – breaks down as soon as one realizes that *stoicheia* stand in mutual "positional" arrangements (they are organized θέσει), however "natural" they are conceived to be: *thesis* is thus imported into the very heart of *phusis*.[195] To revert to the example of Dionysius of Halicarnassus from above, what is "natural" in language needn't describe some deep metaphysical foundation; it merely captures how letters behave in language, their "nature," even their conventional nature, just as today we speak of a syllable's quantity being long by nature or by position. But on a Stoic theory of language, as on a Cratylean theory, matter and meaning would be bound together by a non-contingent nature that flows from Nature itself. In later theory, and possibly already at the end of the fifth century, *stoicheion* captures this relation between matter and convention in the system of signs that make up intelligible wholes the way no other term can. Not even Aristotle can escape the grip of this powerful conceptual tool, as we saw at the end of Chapter 2. His concept of plot is modeled in its own way on the componential system. Plot is a compound (σύστασις, σύνθεσις) of parts (μόρια), though to be sure of immaterial parts, which combine into a larger, wholly rational unity whose texture is the sort that only a logical coherence can have. These parts are of a decidedly unparticular ("universal" or universalizing) cast, and are visible to the mind's eye alone. As we also saw, Aristotle's theory of plot was inherited, and not uniquely his own. In its earlier variants, from the little that we can tell about them, the model had a more material cast – which is *not* to be

---

[193] Ch. 6, §9.

[194] For a catalogue, with analysis, of nonsense inscriptions, see now Immerwahr 2007.

[195] See Democritus DK 68A45; A64; A135 (79): atoms, which are all of "one nature," nonetheless are distinguished from one another, *inter alia*, by position (θέσει). Democritus' stance must have resonated in the *nomos/phusis* controversies of the day, but this is not the place to explore the problem. The carry-over into linguistic analysis, if it is one, is evident in, e.g., Dionysius of Halicarnassus, who sets out to discover the *phusis* of *sunthesis*, which is defined positionally as ποιά τις θέσις παρ' ἄλληλα τῶν τοῦ λόγου μορίων, ἃ δὴ καὶ στοιχεῖά τινες τῆς λέξεως καλοῦσιν, as "a certain process of arranging the parts of speech, or the elements of diction, as some call them" (*Comp.* 2), a statement with general validity, though it seems limited here to grammatical categories. Composition among literary critics like Dionysius is, generally speaking, a matter of habit and convention, not of nature.

confused with an earlier naïveté. Leucippus and Democritus may have pioneered or at least suggested this kind of analysis of plot as *sunthesis*. This follows from the suggestiveness of their basic letter-atom analogy alone. But the impression is strengthened by the fact that they appear to have carried their analogy over into the realm of the composition of tragedy and comedy (or at least so Aristotle implies).[196] In contrast to Aristotle, on the atomistic model the difference between the two genres is epiphenomenal to their underlying arrangements: whether the aggregate looks like one or the other kind is strictly a matter of how things *appear* to a subject at a macro-level.[197] Thus, any atomist theory of tragic and comic genres would have been rigorously phenomenological and anti-essentialist, in the same way that the early atomists would deny that colors were in any way real.[198] The model obviously survived down to the time of the grammatical scholia. And while the transformation from physics to language was never forgotten, the atomistic origins of this model would never be fully explicit again.[199]

Musical and literary sunthesis

Once it lands in the territory of the musicologists, the componential-compositional model evolves, and then, as if given a new lease of life, it becomes available for further reappropriation by students of literature. Thus, Aristoxenus gives us the first clear attestation of this analogy between the two kinds of *sunthesis*, musical and linguistic (which Theophrastus and others would later sometimes call *harmonia*), though he was probably preceded by Hippias and others:

[196] Arist. *Gen. corr.* 1.1.315b14–15 (= DK 67A9), with Joachim 1922, ad loc. Further, Diels 1899; Burkert 1959; Wismann 1979; Ferrari 1981; Steiner 1994, 116–26.

[197] "Owing to the changes of the compound, the same thing seems different to different people ... and appears utterly other by the transposition of a single constituent" (ὥστε ταῖς μεταβολαῖς τοῦ συγκειμένου τὸ αὐτὸ ἐναντίον δοκεῖν ἄλλῳ καὶ ἄλλῳ ... καὶ ὅλως ἕτερον φαίνεσθαι ἑνὸς μετακινηθέντος) (Arist. *Gen. corr.* 1.1.315b12–14; trans. Joachim). Cf. Arist. *Poet.* 8.1451a31–35: "a plot ... should be so constructed that, when some part is transposed (μετατιθεμένου) or removed, the whole is disrupted (διαφέρεσθαι) and disturbed (κινεῖσθαι); for if it makes no visible difference (μηδὲν ποιεῖ ἐπίδηλον) whether a thing is there or not, that thing is no part of the whole" (trans. Janko and Hubbard, adapted).

[198] Democritus' heir, Nausiphanes of Teos, took a similarly nonchalant stance towards discourse genres (see Porter 2002).

[199] But see schol. Dion. Thrax 506.25 Hilgard: ἄτομα. See at n. 219 below; Porter 1986a; Porter 1989. Oddly, the transformation may already have been forgotten by the time of the *Timaeus*, if Plato is indeed translating *stoicheia* in a grammatical sense back into a physical sense again, as he seems to be doing at 48b8–c2 – unless it was Plato who coined the physical sense of *stoicheion* (so Crowley 2005, 381).

The nature of continuity in melody seems to be similar to that which in speech relates to the putting together of letters (οἴα καὶ ἐν τῇ λέξει περὶ τὴν τῶν γραμμάτων σύνθεσιν). For in speaking it is natural for the voice, in each syllable, to place some one of the letters first, others second, third and fourth, and so on for the other numbers. It does not place just any letter after any other: rather, there is a kind of natural growth in the process of putting together (τῆς συνθέσεως). In singing, similarly, when the voice places intervals and notes (τά τε διαστήματα καὶ τοὺς φθόγγους) in succession, it appears to maintain a natural principle of combination (σύνθεσιν), and not to sing every interval after every other, either when the intervals are equal or when they are unequal.[200]

The idea of notes arranged in a *sunthesis* is a commonplace of the treatise. Still, there are huge differences between the musical and linguistic models, the most immediate being that whereas the linguistic/grammatical model operates with combinations of letters that represent *sounds*, the musical/harmonic model operates with combinations of notes and *soundless intervals*.[201]

Aristoxenus was famous in antiquity for having changed the face of musical theory and rendering it more systematic and scientific than ever before. But he is equally aware, or so it seems, of developments outside of music prior to himself: his entire compositional approach is indebted to precursors in music and in linguistic science. The porosity of the boundaries between the two fields and their mutual serviceability emerge as soon as Aristoxenus begins to describe the phenomena of "voice" generally, including its "movements": he speaks of the voice's "relaxation," "tension," "pitch," and so on.[202] These properties all fall within the realm of the *dunameis* familiar from Hippias, and in fact Aristoxenus avails himself of the same term (*dunamis*) to capture the higher level "melodic functions" or perceptual "characteristics" of the notes or voice as it appeared within larger harmonic structures (for instance, scales). Unfortunately, the surviving parts of the *Elements of Harmonics* do not elaborate with any clarity the meaning of this key term.[203]

---

[200] Aristox. *Harm.* 27.18–32; trans. Barker. Cf. ibid., 37.3–6; *Rhythm.* 2.8, 4.27–30 Pearson: "We are familiar with what happens in combinations of letters of the alphabet (τὰ περὶ τὴν τῶν γραμμάτων σύνθεσιν) and combinations of musical intervals (τὰ περὶ τὴν τῶν διαστημάτων). We know that we cannot combine letters at random in speech or musical intervals in singing," etc. See also Theophr. fr. 691 FHS&G, quoted at n. 213 below.

[201] In the *Elements of Rhythm*, intervals are the smallest "elements" of time (time-atoms, as it were): "it is clearly necessary that there exist some durations that are smallest (τινας ἐλαχίστους χρόνους), in which the singer will locate (θήσει) each of the notes" (*Rhythm.* 2.11; trans. Barker). For the "atomistic" conceit, see Aristid. Quint. 1.14: "A primary duration is one that is indivisible and minimal" (πρῶτος μὲν οὖν ἐστι χρόνος ἄτομος καὶ ἐλάχιστος); trans. Barker.

[202] Aristox. *Harm.* 3.5–6.   [203] See Barker 1989, 122.

Here, too, Aristoxenus is not exactly innovating, nor should we expect him to be doing so: the goal of his science, after all, was to lead up, in a dramatically new way, to the familiar effects of music and harmony. And even if Aristoxenus would be the last to acknowledge this, there was a long prehistory that paved the way to the sciences of language and music with their componential and compositional methods. An early case is *Prometheus Bound*, attributed to Aeschylus, which celebrates, *inter alia*, the invention of writing: "I discovered for men the putting together of letters" (ἐξηῦρον αὐτοῖς γραμμάτων τε συνθέσεις).²⁰⁴ Palamedes could make a similar claim, and in similar up-to-date terminology, as in a fragment from Euripides' lost *Palamedes*, which consciously alludes to, and even outbids, the passage from *Prometheus* just cited: "putting together unvoiced and voiced letters into syllables, I discovered a way for men to know writing" (ἄφωνα καὶ φωνοῦντα, συλλαβὰς τιθείς, | ἐξηῦρον ἀνθρώποισι γράμματ' εἰδέναι).²⁰⁵ I have already mentioned the sophistic interest in the constructs, and construction, of language, which both plays doubtless mirror. And when Thucydides expressed his famous canon of history, that it should be "composed (ξύγκειται) as a possession for all time, rather than as a declamation (ἀγώνισμα) composed for the moment of hearing," he was expressing himself in the very same compositional language.²⁰⁶ To write was to put letters together and to make a composite "thing" (*ktēma*).

The terminology is found in all quarters. Thus, at the turn of the century, Alcidamas speaks of "composing every phrase (τὰ ῥήματα συντιθέναι) with precision and rhythm."²⁰⁷ Aristotle's *Rhetoric* (*c.* 340–335 BCE, but possibly begun as early as 358 BCE) is no stranger to this kind of language: "selecting, one combines" (ἐκλέγων συντιθῇ).²⁰⁸ His *Poetics* (of uncertain date) mentions "the *sunthesis* of meters."²⁰⁹ It also speaks of the "*sunthesis* of words" and of linguistic construction at a still lower level of analysis: that of compound letters (*stoicheia*) "composed" of two sounds, one of which is *s*, namely *psi* (*ps*) and *xi* (*ks*).²¹⁰ And elsewhere, for instance in *On the Parts of Animals*, Aristotle defers explicitly to predecessors in the metrical science, the way Plato had done before

---

²⁰⁴ Aesch. *PV* 460. Cf. Aesch. *Sept.* 468: βοᾷ δὲ χοὗτος γραμμάτων ἐν ξυλλαβαῖς.
²⁰⁵ Eur. *Palamedes TrGF* 578.2–3 (= Stob. 2.4.8). ἄφωνα καὶ φωνοῦντα codd.: ἄφωνα καὶ φωνῆντα Hemsterhuis: ἄφωνα φωνήεντα Nauck. συλλαβὰς τιθείς codd.: συλλαβάς τε θείς Hemsterhuis.
²⁰⁶ Thuc. 1.22.4.   ²⁰⁷ Alcidamas *Soph.* 16.
²⁰⁸ *Rh.* 3.2.1404b25. For the dating, see Kennedy 1991, 299–305.
²⁰⁹ *Poet.* 6.1449b34–35. For the date, see Halliwell 1986, Appendix 1.
²¹⁰ *Poet.* 22.1458a28; 21.1458a9 (ὅσα ἐκ τούτου [viz., *sigma*] σύγκειται).

238 *The rise of aesthetic reflection in the fifth century*

him: "Vocal speech consists of combinations of the letters. . . . But what are the differences presented by these . . . and the nature and extent of such differences, are questions to which answers must be sought from the metricians" (δεῖ πυνθάνεσθαι παρὰ τῶν μετρικῶν).²¹¹ By the time that Aeschines could insult Demosthenes in public for exploiting vocal modulations (ὁ τόνος τῆς φωνῆς) and verbal *sunthesis* or arrangement (τὴν τῶν ὀνομάτων σύνθεσιν), the technical language of linguistic and musical science could already be flung about the courtroom with the ease of a cliché. This was in 330 BCE, several years ahead of Aristoxenus' treatise on harmonics.²¹² Theophrastus is reflecting both traditions when he writes, "There are altogether three means by which grandeur (τὸ μέγα), dignity (σέμνον) and impressiveness (περιττόν) are achieved: the choice of words (τῆς ἐκλογῆς τῶν ὀνομάτων), their melodious arrangement (τῆς ἐκ τούτων ἁρμονίας) and the figures of speech in which they are set."²¹³ The phrase "composition [or 'arrangement'] of words" as found in Aeschines above (ἡ τῶν ὀνομάτων σύνθεσις) would later give the title to Dionysius of Halicarnassus' great treatise on style, which ransacks the Aristoxenian tradition for musical terms and concepts, but also draws on earlier forebears, not all of them named. As Dionysius recognizes, "the science of civil oratory is, after all, a kind of musical science, differing from vocal and instrumental music in degree, not in kind."²¹⁴ And as Philodemus' works on music and poetics show, the appropriation of the musical tradition was alive and well a half century earlier, and indeed during the Hellenistic period generally.²¹⁵

In reaching back to earlier tradition, Dionysius of Halicarnassus marks one difference from Aristoxenus, and so too he can be shown to be reaching, as it were, behind the back of "the musician," as Aristoxenus came to be known in later antiquity, in order to connect up with earlier sophistic and other models. When Aristoxenus talks about *stoicheia*, what he has in mind are not the componential units that combine into larger synthetic entities, as his predecessors had used the term. Rather, he seems to be

---

²¹¹ Arist. *Part. an.* 2.16.660a2–8. Cf. Arist. *Poet.* 20.1456b33–34; Pl. *Crat.* 424b–c (discussed earlier).
²¹² Aeschin. 3.210; 3.142. See Barker 1989, 119 on the date of the *Harmonics* (Aristoxenus did not arrive in Athens until after 330.)
²¹³ Theophr. fr. 691 FHS&G (= Dion. Hal. *Isoc.* 3).   ²¹⁴ Dion. Hal. *Comp.* 11; trans. Usher.
²¹⁵ Cf. Phld. *De mus.* 4 col. 22.35–38 Neubecker (= col. 136.35–38 Delattre), conceding – begrudgingly, to Diogenes of Babylon, the Stoic grammarian – a certain similarity between the art of music and that of language: both are susceptible of written recording (κατὰ μέντοι τὸ γρά-[φεσ]θαι | καὶ ἀνταποδιδόναι τ[ὸ] μέλος ἔστω τι παραπλήσι[ο]ν αὐλ[τ]ῆς [sc., τῆς μουσικῆς] καὶ τῇ γραμματι[κῇι]). And the *kritikoi* reported by Philodemus draw heavily upon the musical tradition in their own euphonistic criticism (see Porter 2001a).

referring to the methodical principles or axioms according to which his science of music unfolds.[216] Thus, the *Elements of Harmony* and the *Elements of Rhythm* are named after these axiomatic, logical entities which have shed their material connotations – in fact, they have nothing at all in common with the corporeal *stoicheia* we have encountered so far. And yet, Dionysius of Halicarnassus continues to use the older componential system in his analysis of the aesthetics of verbal composition (what he likewise continues to call *sunthesis*), and in this he is typical of later grammatical tradition:

Thus I maintain that beauty in literary arrangement (τὸ καλὸν ἐν ἁρμονίᾳ λέξεως) must be pursued by the aid of all those elements that constitute (ἐξ ὧν) attractiveness (τὸ ἡδύ). Here as before, the cause (αἰτία) resides in the nature of the letters and in the phonetic effect (δύναμις) of the syllables, from which the words are woven together (ἐξ ὧν πλέκεται).[217]

"Letters" (γράμματα), he adds at the start of the next chapter, are also called *stoicheia*, owing to their systematic character: for "every vocal sound originates in these in the first place and is ultimately resolved into them" (πᾶσα φωνὴ τὴν γένεσιν ἐκ τούτων λαμβάνει πρώτων καὶ τὴν διάλυσιν εἰς ταῦτα ποιεῖται τελευταῖα). The language of genesis and corruption, used to describe the *phusis* of the sound elements,[218] reminds us of the distant origins in natural science of this model for systematizing the aesthetics of sound.[219]

9 "RADICAL EMPIRICISM" AND THE RADICAL AESTHETICS OF THE PARTICULAR

One last point needs to be made about the *stoicheion*-model before we move on. The progression it describes might appear to mark a progression towards beauty. This is the impression Plato gives in his account of the

---

[216] See Aristox. *Harm.* 1.18, 29.1; Barker 1989, 146 n. 121.

[217] Dion. Hal. *Comp.* 13; trans. Usher, adapted.

[218] τῶν δὴ στοιχείων τε καὶ γραμμάτων ... φύσις (Dion. Hal. *Comp.*14).

[219] The language is conventional and technical, not literary critical. Cf. Arist. *Gen. corr.* 1.2.316b13–14 (= DK 68A48b), where Aristotle shows himself to be baffled at the atomists and attempting a *reductio ad absurdum* of their theory: πῶς εἰς ταῦτα διαλύεται καὶ γίνεται ἐκ τούτων, "[If I cut into wood,] how is the wood dissolved into such constituents and how does it come-to-be out of them?," sc., atoms or magnitudes, though here he is thinking of their polemical counterpart, the theoretical "points" into which matter can, *ex hypothesi* and absurdly, be divided *ad infinitum*; and cf. the comparable language in Simpl. *in Cael.* 242.23–25 (= DK 67A14) on the generative combinations of atoms: οὕτως τὴν τῶν συνθέτων γένεσιν ἀποτελεῖσθαι. Later, the scholia to Dionysius Thrax, reflecting earlier tradition, draw frequent parallels between linguistic *stoicheia* and "cosmic" elements, whether conceived as atoms (ἄτομα) or as the four Presocratic natural elements. See schol. Dion. Thrax 197.28–30; 299.38–300.2; 317.24–28 Hilgard. Further, Porter 1989.

model in the *Cratylus* (resuming his seeming inquiry into the *dunameis* and rhythms of language, discussed earlier):[220]

So mustn't we first divide off the vowels and then the others in accordance with their differences in kind, that is to say, the "consonants" and "mutes" (as I take it they're called by specialists in these matters) and the semivowels, which are neither vowels nor mutes?... Similarly, we'll apply letters to things, using one letter for one thing, when that's what seems to be required, or many letters together, to form what's called a syllable, or many syllables combined to form names and verbs. From names and verbs, in turn, we shall finally construct something important [lit., "large"], beautiful, and whole (μέγα ἤδη τι καὶ καλὸν καὶ ὅλον). And just as the painter painted an animal, so – by means of the craft of naming or rhetoric or whatever it is – we shall construct sentences [or "our speech," τὸν λόγον].[221]

But before we saddle Plato with some form of linguistic materialism and an aesthetics to match it, we should beware of his procedures. Just as we saw earlier, Plato is again merging borrowed terms and concepts with his own. Sensuous beauty may have been the goal among some of the sophists whenever they were bent on exploring the music of language, but not so for Plato. Beauty is for Plato a rational whole; it is shot through with *logos* (or its equivalents).[222] It is not clear that Plato has even "heard" the lesson of Hippias and his peers, for at the end of the day there is no obvious place for rhythm or harmony on the view of completed beauty that Plato is offering. The sentences he is contemplating are soundless; they lack all *dunamis*. Plainly, this is a distortion of the aesthetics he is partially retailing and otherwise co-opting. Recall how for Hippias "beauty [or 'the fine,' τὸ καλόν] is what is pleasant (ἡδύ) through hearing and sight."[223]

In contrast to Plato, for Democritus, for Hippias and other sophists, and later for Dionysius of Halicarnassus, there is a beauty to be found *at each level of analysis*, whether amidst the individual elements taken in isolation, in their initial combinations (syllables), or in their larger aggregates, first as rhythms, then as larger complexes set to harmonic scales (melodies) or simply in their larger, complexive totality (as prose). In this latter conception of aesthetics, beauty is not an aggregate value, and it is not a teleological one either. On the contrary, it exists in the immediate apperception of a sensory datum, in the mere physical quality of a given

---

[220] See Pl. *Crat* 424b–c quoted (in part) at n. 119 above.   [221] Pl. *Crat.* 424c–425a; trans. Reeve.
[222] Cf. Pl. *Symp.* 211c–d; *Grg.* 465a: only art, *technē*, not *empeiria*, can provide a *logos* of itself; and Ch. 2, §2 above.
[223] Pl. *Hp. mai.* 298a6–7; trans. Woodruff.

sound, whether that sound is simple or complex. We can express this theory in ancient and in modern terms as follows.

In the language of the Hellenistic euphonists, who are working in the same tradition and are preserved by Philodemus, aesthetic value is an *idion*, which means that it is a directly apprehensible, concrete, and localized feature of a perception, matched by some singular feature of an object:

> The composition [alone, being *idia*], is the object of elaboration. And it stands as [engraved] in [stone] for all the *kritikoi* that euphony, which appears on the surface [of the composition], is to be considered *idion* [specific to a poem or its being heard], while the meanings and phrases [sc., the diction] must be considered external and common [or: universal, *koina*]; but this idea is manifestly silly, as my previous comments show.[224]

What Philodemus is saying, or rather restating, is nothing less than the core of the euphonists' poetic program. The value of poetry for these critics lies not in what poetry means but in the way it sounds – its "musicality." They are euphonists, but with a vengeance. Poems on this way of thinking are aggregates of sound – whence their favored term, *sunthesis*, which has to be taken literally: it stands for a *sunthesis* of the *stoicheia*, the elements or letter-sounds that make up, like building blocks, the *sullabai* (syllables) of the *lexeis* or words (or more rarely, rhythmical "times" or "durations," *chronoi*). Poems so conceived are indeed no more than sound effects arising (in their own striking terms) "epiphenomenally" or "on the surface" of poetic compositions,[225] thanks to the technical artistry (the *technē* or *exergasia*) of the poet, while the sounds are themselves ephemeral and, logically, specific to each audition (or reading): such radical contingency is what is meant by being *idion*. In this way, these critics, unconventional by any standard, arrive at a theory about what might be called *the absolutism of the poetic particular*. A poem's specificity, which is elusively of the moment and punctual, is grounded in its material coordinates: *this* sound *here*. Hence, the property of being *idion* captures

---

[224] *P. Herc.* 1676 col. 6.1–11 (text after Janko 2000, 125 n. 1 [part]): σύνθε[σιν μόνον ἰδίαν] | ἐργάζεσ[θαι,] καὶ τὸ τὴν μὲν| [ἐπιφαι]νομένην [ε]ὐφωνίαν ἴδιον [εἶ]ναι, τὰ δὲ νοή|ματα καὶ [τ]ὰς λέξεις ἐκτὸς| εἶναι καὶ κοινὰ συνάγεσ|θαι δεῖ[ν, πα]ρὰ πᾶσι μὲν ὡς| ἐν [στήλ]ηι μέ[ν]ει τοῖς κρι|τικοῖ[ς], βλεπο[μ]ένην δ' ἔχει τὴ[ν ἐ]υηθί[α]ν ἐκ τῶν εἰρημένων. See Porter 1995a for discussion.

[225] Phld. *De poem.* 5 col. 24.31 Mangoni: "Crates and the critics value the sound that appears on (the surface of) the *sunthesis* [of the *lexeis*] (τὴν ἐπιφαινομένην | [α]ὐ[τῆι] [sc., τῆι συνθέσει] φωνὴν ἐπαιν[οῦσι])." (ἐπαιν[οῦσι] Delattre and Monet: ἐπαιν[εῖ] Jensen).

something that is unique but also evanescent (as perceived by the ear); it also designates an emergent synthetic feature of sounds in combination.

Though the term *idion* understood in this sense is rare in ancient aesthetics, it may derive ultimately from Aristotle, who uses it widely as a logical designator both in his *Poetics*, where it stands for "proper function," and in his *Topics*, where he defines it, significantly, as what is "real for one subject [viz., possessor of the function or feature] alone."[226] And in his *De anima* we find another, no less significant component of the term. Here, the *idion* is whatever a sense faculty is infallibly right about in its judgment. It defines the proper sphere of judgment of that faculty (things heard for hearing, which cannot be judged by vision, and so on for the other faculties).[227] Both senses of the term are fully active for the critics discussed by Philodemus. For them, euphonious sound is treated as *idion*, which is to say, as *phenomenally unique* to the *place* where it appears (ἐπιφαινομένη, "on the surface" of the composition of the letter-sounds it supervenes upon), but also – logically (though they don't quite press the point) – it ought to be phenomenally unique to the *time* when it appears and for the *subject* to whom it appears, while meanings and diction (word choice) are treated as belonging to the public domain (as *koina*), virtually as universals shared by all users of the same language and which can be transferred from one context to another without making any discernible aesthetic difference to those users. *Koina*, we might say, are not experienced as such by speakers or readers: they are the data of communication – the ideas and meanings – that language conveys, ideally in a transparent form.[228]

Beauty, on the alternative view I am sketching, while radically *idion* in the ancient vocabulary, can be called "radically empirical" in the language of William James, which means that it is radically rooted not only in the materiality of an object but also, and equally importantly, in a subject's experience of that object. James's conception might at first sight seem surprising in the current context. But as I hope to show, the convergences between the modern pragmatist and the ancient aesthetic empiricists on

---

[226] Reesor 1983, 129, with reference to Arist. *Top.* 6.5.154b23.
[227] *De an.* 2.6.418a11–18. The contrast is with common objects of sense: movement, rest, number, shape, size; these are, so to speak, universals shared by the senses in common. Thus, movement is common to touch and to vision (as with a pen twirling in your hands), but you can't see the very thing you feel as felt when you touch it (viz., the *sensum* that is felt): that is reserved for touch alone. Gorgias makes similar points in *MXG*; see Ch. 5 below.
[228] *Koina* can nonetheless carry a connotative feeling as a secondary association, and these can, of course, be experienced. On such feelings, see Porter 2006b.

this question are all but inevitable, given their starting assumptions. First, consider the following quotation from James's posthumous collection of essays, *Radical Empiricism*:

I give the name of "radical empiricism" to my *Weltanschauung*. Empiricism is known as the opposite of rationalism. Rationalism tends to emphasize universals and to make wholes prior to parts in the order of logic as well as in that of being. Empiricism, on the contrary, lays the explanatory stress upon the part, the element, the individual, and treats the whole as a collection and the universal as an abstraction. My description of things, accordingly, starts with the parts and makes of the whole a being of the second order. It is essentially a mosaic philosophy, a philosophy of plural facts.

James perhaps overstates his critique of rationalism in order to avoid falling into contradictions of his own. For there is obviously a form of rationalism intrinsic to any analysis of parts and wholes, of orders of being, and of facts made philosophical. What distinguishes James's, as it were, rational empiricism from its modern predecessors, what approximates it to the ancients, and finally what makes it *radically* empirical, is the way in which it grasps the "elements" or "parts" (*stoicheia*) of experienced reality: it grants these an essential experiential value in addition to a certain non-negotiable primacy. In radical empiricism, parts are won (grasped) through experience, and it is this latter process which confers on them their essential dignity. As James goes on to explain his novel conception,

to be radical, an empiricism must neither admit into its constructions any element that is not directly experienced, nor exclude from them any element that is directly experienced. For such a philosophy, *the relations that connect experiences must themselves be experienced relations, and any kind of relation experienced must be accounted as "real" as anything else in the system.* . . . In other words: Everything real must be experienceable somewhere, and every kind of thing experienced must somewhere be real.[229]

In other words, unlike in idealist systems, which appeal to some "extraneous trans-empirical" instance so as to connect the parts of the whole and "the relations between things," radical empiricism seeks no higher unifying agency than the apprehension of things and their relations from within experience itself.[230] In rendering experience "the *materia prima* of everything," James is far from adopting some form of reductive materialism pure and simple: that would be to adopt the very sort of

---

[229] James 2003 [1912], 22; 83; emphasis in original.
[230] James 1987, 826–27 (*The Meaning of Truth* [1909]).

dualism he is striving to overcome by making experience an indistinguishably psychical and physical (material) event in its own right.[231] Nevertheless, bodily experience is an essential ingredient of radical empiricism even
if materialism as a metaphysical dogma, let alone a spiritual abstraction, is
not.[232] The same holds for the emphatic materiality of experience. Experience for James is decidedly "thick," not "thin": it is not colorless or, in his
own description, "diaphanous." It comes tinged with all kinds of affections and interests, pleasures and pains, and passions; it works itself on our
bodies in "alterations of tone and tension, of heartbeat and breathing, of
vascular and visceral action."[233] And, finally, experience of rich particulars,
without any resort to bloodless abstractions, is where James's philosophy
begins but also ends.[234]

Beauty is one of the perturbations that colors experience and gives it
texture and density. Indeed, one of James's generic labels for the "thickness" of experience is what he calls "the aesthetic factor," though *aesthetic*
is doubtless to be understood in its widest sense, whereby it includes the
domain of sensuous perception and individual feeling (experience).[235]
And though James does not elaborate on this particular phrase, he does
offer a careful assessment of aesthetic beauty, which it will be worth
contrasting with Plato's view of beauty from the *Cratylus* witnessed earlier:

> The various pleasures we receive from an object may count as "feelings" when we
> take them singly, but when they combine in a total richness, we call the result the
> "beauty" of the object, and treat it as an outer attribute which our mind
> perceives. We discover beauty just as we discover the physical properties of
> things. Training is needed to make us an expert in either line.[236]

Beauty is something like a *sunthesis*, or aggregate, of individual sensations
experienced as pleasures. On the other hand, beauty is not necessarily a
property of objects or of our experience of them. Rather, it is a label
conferred by us – here, on an object – by dint of habituation or convention,

---

[231] James 2003 [1912], 72; cf. ibid., 110–14; 135–36.

[232] On materialism as being due to a "materiality-effect," see Brown 2001, 8. The notion that
materialism is itself an idealism was launched by Baudrillard in the 1970s against the Parisian
Tel Quel school.

[233] James 2003 [1912], 15; 78–79; cf. 109–10; cf. James 1987, 757–58: "All the thickness, concreteness,
and individuality of experience exists in the immediate and relatively unnamed stages of it," in its
peculiar "richness" (*A Pluralistic Universe* [1909]).

[234] Platonism might fall under what James calls "Absolutism," which is the antithesis of
"Empiricism," and about which he tellingly writes, "the one *fundamental* quarrel Empiricism
has with Absolutism is over this repudiation by Absolutism of the personal and aesthetic factor in
the construction of philosophy" (James 2003 [1912], 146; emphasis in original).

[235] James 2003 [1912], 146; see previous note.   [236] James 2003 [1912], 75.

though on another day and upon further reflection we might confer the
label *beauty* on the experiences (the relations) that mediate between an
object and ourselves. These experiences (pleasures and feelings), while
radically empirical, are themselves relational. For, as James adds, "single
sensations may also be ambiguous" (we can speak of the pleasurable
warmth of the fire or the pleasure caused by the warm fire),[237] and so it
may be that the source of beauty is the pleasure we take in an object rather
than a feature inhering in the object itself. Or it may be that *beauty* applies
ambiguously to both the object and the feeling. In Santayana's terms,
whose discussion James invokes, "beauty ... is pleasure objectified" – quite
literally so.[238] Pleasure, the sensation, comes first; beauty – the attribute
and label (or judgment) – follows, if and when it does, as a synthetic
judgment.

More fundamentally, experience is itself essentially ambiguous, because
it is the *prima materia* of the world we know and the common coin into
and out of which all attributes must be cashed: "There is no original
spirituality or materiality of being, intuitively discerned, then; but only a
translocation of experiences from one world to another; a grouping of
them with one set or another of associates for definitely practical or
intellectual ends."[239] The conferral of the label *beauty* on one or the other
object or both – the object that is experienced and the object *as* experienced (what we might call the object *of* our experience) – would be an
instance of such a translocation. And translocation seems inevitably to
draw in its train what Kant calls a "subreption," namely the misattribu-
tion of a quality.[240] *Beauty* would always seem to be at risk of being a
misnomer, forever lacking a proper object. What is more, under a different convention or in a different mood, the label conferred by us might not
be *beauty* but something else altogether – *sublimity*, or *rarity*, or *brilliance*.[241] The link is frail, being but a convention and a habit. And after
all, beauty is but a name. Be this as it may, the point that most matters
here is that for James *beauty is a function of experiences*, and those experiences are *of concrete particulars*.[242] If radical empiricism implies an aesthetics, as it plainly does, then it also implies a *radical aesthetics of the*

---

[237] James 2003 [1912], 75.   [238] Santayana 1988 [1896], 35.   [239] James 2003 [1912], 77.
[240] *CJ* §27; Ak. 257.
[241] In defense of "rarity," cf. Polyclitus' definition of the sculptural criterion: "the good [sculptural
work] comes about through many numbers, just barely," i.e., only with difficulty, and *rarely*. And
compare the proverb, "Beautiful [or "fine"] things are *difficult*" (χαλεπὰ τὰ καλά, e.g., Pl. *Hp.
mai.* 304e8).
[242] On the materialist undertone of James' radical empiricism, see n. 84 above (this chapter).

particular. And to this extent, James's concept compares favorably with the ancient concept that contrasts so markedly with Plato's. One difference, perhaps, is that the ancient concept of the *idion* is less concerned with the synthetic judgment of particular feelings than with the singular effect of the particular feelings themselves and then their overall cumulative impact. A fine poem will consist of many such fine moments, whether to a greater or lesser quantitative degree. (The rules by which one arrives at a comprehensive judgment of a poem are anything but clearly marked out on this alternative poetics from the Hellenistic era.)

The effect that this pre- and post-Platonic conception of aesthetics achieves is to undo the notion of teleologies by obliterating them: a sense perception overwhelms any concern we might have for longer-term gratification; it gives us all the grounds we need to cast a judgment of aesthetic value here and now. Such a conception of aesthetics at the same time grounds aesthetic evaluation in the materiality of an object and its perception, or more precisely, in the materiality of the experience of an object. Attaching itself to *this* experience *here*, beauty (or aesthetic value under some other name) becomes a concrete thing, non-transferable, non-generalizable, and non-universal: it is truly idiosyncratic (an *idion*). In its purest form, then, we should expect to find a sensuous aesthetics of the material particular grounding itself in the sensation that is had at the very moment the sensation is had (whether with pleasure or pain). And this is what we in fact find, for instance in Hellenistic criticism.

This kind of attentiveness to the material detail ought to have lain behind the Democritean title *On Euphonious and Harsh-Sounding Letters.* It is the principle that later compels Dionysius of Halicarnassus to write,

Now the most powerful [of the vowels], and those which produce the most attractive (ἡδίστην) sound, are the long vowels, and those common ones which are lengthened in utterance, and this is because they are sounded for a long time, and do not arrest the strong flow of the breath .... Of the long vowels, the one with the best sound (εὐφωνότατον) is *alpha*, when lengthened .... Of the short vowels neither [*omicron* nor *epsilon*] is beautiful (εὔμορφον), but *omicron* is less ugly than *epsilon*: for the former causes the mouth to open wider than the latter .... *Lambda* gives [the ear] pleasure (ἡδύνει), and is the sweetest (γλυκύτατον) of the semi-vowels. [etc.][243]

---

[243] *Comp.* 14; trans. Usher.

Similar remarks can be found in Dionysius and elsewhere applied to syllables and then to rhythms and larger clausulae and finally whole periods – in a word, to what continues to be called the *harmonia* (fitting-together, harmony) of verbal composition.[244] As if by natural attraction, the focus on the material "density" of the elements – the materiality they contribute to the whole – remains fixed and unwavering as the critic's eye (or ear) moves up the ladder of organizational complexity.

It would be a mistake to reduce attention to individual *stoicheia* like this to an obsession merely with sound effects or euphony, though it is this too. Rather, what we have before us is an aesthetic obsession with the *particular* and the *detail*, with the *concrete* and the *material* (here) of linguistic expression. And for the same reason, this kind of aesthetic analysis never rises above the level of the sentence *even when it seems to be passing judgment on larger-scale units*. As unorthodox as it may sound to us, this view eschews works viewed as complete wholes. The Longinian sublime, which is indexical (it transpires *here* and *now*), consumed by the moment (καιρίως ἐξενεχθέν), and never a matter of the whole, is a case in point, though there are explicit parallels in the euphonists attacked by Philodemus.[245] Indeed, it is the quintessence of this aesthetics of the momentary particular, of the evanescently experienced bit of material that is glimpsed and, once glimpsed, fades out only to remain a burning trace in memory. I don't want, at least not here, to press the connections between the aesthetic materialism of the particular and the sublime beyond the observation that the sublime transpires at the intersection of the contingent particular and its momentary (and hence, too, eternal) abstraction: its particularity is, so to speak, absolute. In William James's terms, the sublime's material counterpart is not coarsely empirical, but rather *radically* empirical. Longinus' stance is, in this regard, typical of materialist aesthetics.

The contrast with what I have been calling formalist aesthetics should be plain. Whenever a proponent of aesthetic materialism takes up a passage or author for consideration, what he sees, at least in the first instance, is a concatenation of sentences, not larger units of signification, and certainly nothing rivaling the Aristotelian idea of a (well-)composed plot, let alone Plato's notion of an organic totality. The materialist dwells in the microscopic, in bits of (sublime) matter. And the synthetic unities

---

[244] *Subl.* 39.4–40.1; cf. Dion. Hal. *Isoc.* 2: "[Isocrates] avoids hiatus, on the ground that this breaks the structure of the sounds" (τὰς ἁρμονίας τῶν ἤχων). See below for further examples.

[245] *Subl.* 1.4; see Porter 2001a for parallels.

he constructs are themselves just further material wholes – a sound or a (collective) impact on the senses, qualitatively assessed on a scale of, say, beauty or sublimity. One does not have to wait until the modern era to notice that aesthetic properties are anchored in "an absolutely specific quality which cannot be reduced to verbal description."[246] In fact, it is completely wrong to suppose, as Terry Eagleton does, that "the assumption that all art is vividly particular is of fairly recent vintage."[247] There were at least some schools of thought in antiquity and a great many tendencies besides for which this very assumption was possible and even a matter of course. The modern radical aesthetics of the particular, familiar from Roland Barthes and others, marks a rediscovery, knowing or not, of the ancient version of the same.[248]

10 BEAUTY'S MATERIAL CAUSES

If the foregoing stands any chance of being halfway right, we have succeeded in demonstrating that aesthetic materialism was not only conceivable, but it was also put to work as a critical practice in antiquity. Further instances will be provided below. But neither did this perspective on art and aesthetics appeal universally. Aesthetic materialism was generally spurned by anyone who took a Platonic or Aristotelian approach. Which is not to say that a critic like Aristotle was entirely insensitive to the materialism of art. One brief exception comes in chapter 4 of the *Poetics*, when he suddenly drops his mimetic criterion of aesthetic pleasure and allows for the possibility of another kind of pleasure, a non-cognitive pleasure, whereby the beholder of an object stands, as it were, blindfolded, intellectually speaking, before what he beholds. Unable to recognize the object before him, he fails to identify it (this is a prerequisite of successful mimesis), and so he must fall back on his senses, on a bare sensuous perception of the object.

The passage begins with the familiar, if somewhat gory, account of pleasures that are taken in the mimetic details of cadavers. The level

---

[246] Bann 1989, 29.

[247] Eagleton 2003, 75. But this claim may have to do with the way Eagleton links equality (which he believes must likewise be modern) with particularity (ibid., 147).

[248] Cf. Barthes 1985, 259: "'listening' to a composition (taking the word in its etymological sense) by John Cage, it is each sound one after the next that I listen to, not in its syntagmatic extension [as meaning], but in its raw and as though vertical *signifying* (*signifiance*).... This is valid, *mutatis mutandis*, for many other forms of contemporary art, from 'painting' to the 'text'...." As Barthes also recognizes (*pace* Eagleton), this model ultimately derives from ancient rhetoric (Barthes 1975, 66–67).

of accuracy in the details of such objects allows onlookers to identify the depiction as this or that object in real life: here, it is the identification more than the depiction proper that is the source of the pleasure, which is one of "learning" or "understanding" – of "getting it" (μανθάνειν). But what happens if the depiction is of something you've never seen before? Aristotle's answer comes in a brief and uncharacteristic statement:

> If you happen not to have seen the original, the picture will not produce its pleasure *qua* instance of mimesis (ἤ μίμημα), but because of its workmanship [viz., *facture* or "finish," or simply "craftsmanship" (ἀπεργασίαν)] or colour or for some such other reason (αἰτίαν).[249]

Aristotle knew how to posit, abstractly, a "purely" material or sensuous realm distinct from one informed by thought. But he nowhere makes the concession to literary objects that he makes to visual or plastic objects here, namely that they can be enjoyed, never mind conceptualized, *qua* "the forms, textures, patterns [and sounds] of art, apprehended in and for themselves and not as the medium of mimetic significance."[250] There was simply no room for such a conception in his theory of poetics. Quite the contrary, the material causes of art, named fleetingly yet expressly here, are on Aristotle's view suppressed throughout the *Poetics*, as we saw earlier, while the formal and final causes are promoted at their expense. Another possible exception to this rule comes at the tail end of chapter 24, where he momentarily and uncharacteristically considers the idea of style (*lexis*) as abstracted from, and at the expense of, all considerations of plot and character:

> Homer completely disguises [lit., "makes disappear," "obliterates": ἀφανίζει] the absurdity [of narrative, e.g., the fairytale circumstances of Odysseus' conveyance by the Phaeacians] by his sweetness (ἡδύνων). It is in the parts that involve no action and no mimesis of character or intellect that one should be most elaborate

---

[249] *Poet.* 4.1448b17–19; trans. Hubbard, slightly adapted.

[250] Halliwell 1986, 67; my bracketed addition. The same concession is made in identical language at Arist. *Pol.* 8.5.1340a25–28, though with the opposite point – this time in the name of *mimēsis*: "If someone enjoys contemplating (χαίρει θεώμενος) the image of something [or 'of someone,' τὴν εἰκόνα τινος] for no other reason (μὴ δι' ἄλλην αἰτίαν) than the very shape [or 'appearance,' 'form,' or 'beauty,' διὰ τὴν μορφὴν αὐτήν] of it, he will necessarily take pleasure in contemplating the thing itself whose image he is contemplating" (trans. Kraut 1997; my brackets). The two positions, that of the *Politics* and that of *Poetics* ch. 4, needn't be contradictory. For Aristotle, however, they are. Whence the recommendation in the immediate sequel that the young focus on the works of Polygnotus, who specialized in the representation of superior characters, rather than on those of Pauson, who specialized in the depiction of inferior characters (cf. *Poet.* 2.1448a5–6). The *Politics* passage is clearly espousing a representationalist view of art, whereas the *Poetics* passage is momentarily casting representational considerations aside.

(διαπονεῖν) in verbal expression; when character and intellect are being represented, too brilliant a style often conceals them (ἀποκρύπτει γὰρ πάλιν ἡ λίαν λαμπρὰ λέξις τά τε ἤθη καὶ τὰς διανοίας).[251]

A telltale clue that Aristotle is departing from his standard practice is his advice that a poet should take refuge, at certain moments, in style, which is something he normally (and here, self-evidently) considers a ἥδυσμα, or mere "sweetener." "Elaborate" (διαπονεῖν) sounds like a possible technical term for poetic elaboration, one that could be further bound up with "pleasure" and verbal "brilliance" (this latter term frequently often associated with sound) irrespective of content – though διαπονεῖν is in fact rather rare in literary critical contexts.[252] The connections between this passage and that from chapter 4 earlier in the same text are evident. In both cases the beholder/reader suppresses his representational instincts in favor of another kind of attention, one we might call an aesthetic form of attention in a materialist vein: of exclusive interest now are the phenomenal and phenomenological effects of craftsmanship, labor, and finish. Just to underscore the point, consider what Aristotle might have said in the earlier chapter (ch. 4), namely that we appreciate the *art* (*technē*) even if we are ignorant of the intentions in the artist's *mind*. Putting things like this, he could have held that we appreciate the efficient cause of the artifact but not its formal and final causes.[253] But Aristotle does not say this. Instead he speaks of "color" and "finish," making it clear that he is talking about the work not *qua* mimetic art (process of production) but rather *qua* sensuously palpable and aesthetically pleasing artifact (product or object). And that is what is so unusual about the passage.[254]

---

[251] *Poet.* 24.1460b1–5; trans. Hubbard, adapted. The passage is not to be outdone, of course, by ibid., 24.1460a18–19: "Homer taught the rest of the poets how to lie," which is promoted in the teeth of Plato *et al.* Gudeman 1934, 418 points to the parallels in *Subl.* 15.11 and in Plut. *Mor.* 41c.

[252] Cf. Isoc. 5.85 (διαπονεῖν), an inexact parallel; *Subl.* 14.1; and Dionysius of Halicarnassus' general extolling of the virtues of literary *ponos*, as in *Lys.* 11, describing Lysias' skill in *lexis*, "whether it is to be called natural gift or skill and art" (εἴτε φύσεως αὐτὴν δεῖ καλεῖν εὐτυχίαν εἴτε πόνου καὶ τέχνης ἐργασίαν).

[253] See Frede 1992, 95–96.

[254] A third apparent exception is not really one at all. At *Poet.* 6.1450b1–2 we read, in an analogy between plot and visual art, how "the most beautiful colours, if smeared on at random, would give less pleasure than an uncoloured outline that was a picture of something." According to Aristotle, "the most beautiful colours" do not by themselves warrant aesthetic attention unless they are part of some intentional totality. It would be asking a lot of Aristotle to bend towards an appreciation of paint for paint's sake. Whether he would appreciate a Jasper Johns is another question! (Probably not; see Gudeman ad loc.: "Es klingt dies wie eine Vorahnung unserer heutigen Expressionisten.") On the other hand, Aristotelian plot is more like an outline than a patchwork of colors; see below.

While these are two of the very few moments when Aristotle breaks his own rule about the primacy of mimesis, possibly the only two moments, a slight but significant revision in what I said earlier is necessary about Aristotle's concessions to the senses. It is not only the case that Aristotle knew how to posit, in theory, a "purely" material or sensuous realm. He knew how to do this *because others had done so before him.* Indeed, it looks as if in chapter 4 Aristotle must be admitting as valid, albeit begrudgingly, someone else's position on visual pleasure, perhaps a theorist of painting or sculpture or of the visual arts generally who would have taken a primary interest in the techniques of image-making and in "the material-ity of the image."[255] There is no need to cast our net very far in search of likely candidates. Xenophon has already furnished us with one of the more significant instances: Parrhasius the painter, who professed that his only interest lay in depicting visible objects (τὰ ὁρατά) in their "shape [and] color [and] the other qualities" that were mentioned by Socrates in their dialogue, namely, "hollows and heights, darkness and light, hard and soft, rough and smooth," by means of his palette (διὰ τῶν χρωμάτων).[256] The story of Apelles and Protogenes competing over a mere brushstroke, described in the Introduction (pp. 11–12), is another, even more striking example, as it involves no representational content in any way, but is merely a showcase for refined workmanship (*subtilitas*). There were surely other artists working in the same vein around this time and earlier. If such clues and anecdotes are not convincing enough, there is always the art as evidence of itself (see Chapter 8 below). But there are still further considerations to add.

Aristotle's *Poetics* is by no means a disinterested theoretical treatise on art, nor is it a work made up of unprecedented insights. It is an interested *prise de position* that draws heavily on and is directed against any number of forerunners in the field, from the sophists to Plato to others, though these are for the most part left unnamed by him and, thanks to the vicissitudes of historical transmission, sadly lost to us today. As a result, this fact about Aristotle's treatise and its inheritances is too often ignored today. There are, for instance, definite traces in the *Poetics* of a debate around the central theory of (surprisingly enough) plot construction, the heart and soul of Aristotle's treatise, precisely where one might have

---

[255] Gudeman 1934, 119 (ad loc.) hints vaguely at such a connection without making any. The quotation is from Rouveret 1989, 389 (addressing *Poet.* ch. 4).

[256] See Ch. 3, at n. 176 above.

expected Aristotle to be absolutely original. In a word, plot theory – the theory of *muthos* – was richly elaborated at some point before Aristotle, whose *Poetics* is polemically engaged with this earlier theory. This was already touched on at the end of Chapter 2, but the point can be backed up with further concrete details now.

At the beginning of *Poetics* chapter 8, we read how "unity of plot is not, *as some think*, achieved by writing about one man."[257] Unless we take this as an inference drawn from the practice of past poets (so Hutchinson),[258] this offhand reference has to be a remarkable clue to a lost prehistory in poetics, something that most scholarship since Gudeman fails to appreciate.[259] What it shows, then, is that someone (possibly from within the sophistic circle – so Gudeman) had already anticipated Aristotle's theory of the structural unity of plot, however crudely in Aristotle's eyes. The very conception of plot (*muthos*) as a formal organizing principle marks an enormous achievement in poetic theory. Plato already presupposes such a theory, one that closely resembles Aristotle's own, as the following exchange from the *Phaedrus* establishes:

SOCRATES: Now suppose someone went up to Sophocles or Euripides and said he knew how to compose lengthy dramatic speeches about a trifling matter, and quite short ones about a matter of moment, that he could write pathetic passages when he chose, or again passages of intimidation and menace, and so forth, and that he considered that by teaching these accomplishments he could turn a pupil into a tragic poet.

PHAEDRUS: I imagine, Socrates, that they too would laugh at anyone who supposed that you could make a tragedy otherwise than by so arranging (συνισταμένην) such passages as to exhibit a proper structural relation (σύστασιν) to one another and to the whole of which they are parts.[260]

Whatever else the earlier theory of plot entailed is anyone's guess, but it would be wrong to imagine that the anticipation of Aristotle stopped here. As Gudeman rightly infers, and as a later passage in the *Poetics*

---

[257] *Poet.* 8.1451a16–17 (ὥσπερ τινὲς οἴονται).
[258] Hutchinson 2006, 109 n. 9: "probably a barbed reference to the poets."
[259] Gudeman 1934, 199 (ad loc.). The reiterated verb, οἴονται γάρ, in 1451a21, would have to refer to the selfsame critics on this view, as Gudeman suggests (ibid., 200–1).
[260] καὶ οὗτοι ἄν, ὦ Σώκρατες, οἶμαι καταγελᾶν εἴ τις οἴεται τραγῳδίαν ἄλλο τι εἶναι ἢ τὴν τούτων σύστασιν πρέπουσαν ἀλλήλοις τε καὶ τῷ ὅλῳ συνισταμένην (Pl. *Phdr.* 268c5–d5; trans. Hackforth, slightly adapted); not cited by Gudeman. The repetition of τινὲς οἴονται in *Poet.* 8.1451a16 and 21 could either refer to this passage by Plato, or else (what is more likely) it points to the same thing that it points to in Plato: the prevalence of an earlier belief about the structural nature of plot.

proves (with the occurrence of "some claim" in a discussion of single and double plots),[261] the argument about plot rejected by Aristotle "cannot possibly be an isolated point of contention, but is rather conceivable only if the entire set of questions intimately connected with it had been drawn into these very kinds of investigations too."[262] The whole of Aristotle's discussion of plot, in other words, is polemically bound up with earlier theorizing. Certainly one index antedating both Plato and Aristotle appears to be found in an undated fragment of Cratinus (though a date shortly before 430 BCE has been proposed[263]), who, as Rosemary Harriott notes, "said that the tragic poet Acestor would deserve a beating if he failed to achieve unity and economy of incident, ἐὰν μὴ συστρέφῃ τὰ πράγματα, and a similar dislike of unwieldy length is noticeable in the *Frogs* [911–15]." Cratinus may well be reflecting contemporary sources.[264] Nor should we forget that tragic theory had evolved already in the mid-fifth century, starting at least with Sophocles' (lost) treatise, *On the Chorus*.[265] This does nothing to detract from the brilliance of Aristotle's achievement. If anything, it highlights it. Plainly, Aristotle seized on the earlier discussions, which may have been well advanced in their own right, and then he reshaped them in his own image, possibly eclipsing them forever.

[261] Arist. *Poet.* 13.1453a13: ὥσπερ τινές φασι. This can in no way be attributed to poets.

[262] Gudeman 1934, 199.

[263] Geissler 1925, 23.

[264] Harriott 1969, 136; Cratinus fr. 92 K–A; Ar. *Ran.* 911–15; "συστρέφειν τὰ πράγματα significare videtur actionem et argumentum fabulae rotundare et suis finibus circumscribere, ne temere diffluat et extra terminus vagetur" (Meineke in the app. crit. to K–A). Stohn 1955, 67–81 makes the same point in a more elaborate exploration of Cratinus, Aristotle, and their context, and (following Gudeman) states, "Es scheint so, als ob Aristoteles hier polemisiert" (70). Stohn concludes (77–79) that Cratinus is drawing on contemporary poetic (especially tragic) criticism, some of which may overlap with Gorgias.

[265] *Suda* s.v. "*Sophoklēs*"; cf. Plut. *Mor.* 79B, which may derive from this same source; see Bowra 1940 and n. 14 above (this chapter). Moreover, see Pohlenz 1920, 145 (followed by Dover 1993, 301) on Ar. *Ran.* 862 (τάπη, τὰ μέλη, τὰ νεῦρα τῆς τραγῳδίας): Pohlenz sees a progression, not an apposition, which leads to the "sinews," viz., structure ("*Gesamtkomposition*") of tragedy – in Greek, its σύστασις. At Ar. *Nub.* 1367 Aeschylean tragedy is criticized as ἀξύστατος (see Dover ad loc.); plot structure is further discussed at *Ran.* 911–15 (see prev. note) and 945–46; and Aristophanes already knows how to describe plot as *pragmata* (*Eq.* 39; *Ran.* 1122, if this is not an interpolation – see Dover, ad loc.). Aristotle's reaction was discussed in Ch. 2 above. Further, one might point to Soph. *Ant.* 1111 (Creon): ἔδησα . . . καὶ ἐκλύσομαι, "I imprisoned her . . . and I shall release her," or more figuratively (which is in fact the more appropriate way to construe the passage, as Antigone has not literally been "bound"), "I caused the tangle, and I shall untie it" (so Griffith ad loc.), which has obvious resonances with Aristotle's theory of *dēsis* and *lusis* (*Poet.* ch. 18). Another pair of examples are Aesch. *TrGF* 392: ἢ βαρὺ φόρημ' ἄνθρωπος εὐτυχῶν ἄφρων ~ *Poet.* 13.1452a34–36; Aesch. *TrGF* 398: κακοὶ γὰρ εὖ πράσσοντες οὐκ ἀνασχετοί ~ *Poet.* 13.1452a36–37. It would be useful to scour extant drama for such anticipations of Aristotle – or rather, for such terms and concepts that Aristotle later took over into his own theory (and not only in connection with Aristotle; see Ch. 5, n. 16 below on Protagoras).

We should not be surprised, then, if Aristotle's momentary and quite remarkable concession to sensuous aesthetics in *Poetics* chapter 4 turned out to be a nod to pre-existing theory too, especially when we have clear evidence of activity in this area, unlike in the area of *muthos*, where we have so very little. But if so, then Aristotle's concession to the material causes of beauty looks much more like a backhanded criticism than a ringing endorsement. Aristotle is prepared to acknowledge the impact of sensuous factors only once the more significant mimetic factors have given out. Material causes for him remain decidedly minority causes of beauty in art, criteria of the last resort, and applicable to the cognitively handicapped alone.

On the opposing view, of course, the Aristotelian proviso would appear absurdly restrictive. There is no reason why unfamiliarity with an object should be a prerequisite to taking pleasure in its sensuous features. It is not even clear that willful cognitive blindness needs to be a prerequisite to sensuous aesthetics. (Meaning, content, or contextual value can be enhanced by surface properties, if one wished to divorce these for the sake of the argument.[266]) On the other hand, there is no denying that sensuous enjoyment may well lead to an exclusion of cognitive enjoyment, whether momentarily (owing to an immediate absorption in the sensuous features of an object) or as a matter of principled refusal to attend to meaning, content, or reference (as is the case for anyone who zealously observes "the irrational criterion" [τὸ ἄλογον κριτήριον] in assessing art).[267] An interesting parallel to Aristotle, but also one that supplies a counterargument to his own, is found later on in Lucian. In history writing,

there are some who leave out or skate over the important and interesting events . . . and dwell very fully and laboriously on the most insignificant happenings [lit., "the entirely smallest things" (τὰ μικρότατα πάνυ)]. This is like failing to observe and praise and describe for those who do not know it the entire grandeur and supreme quality (τὸ μὲν ὅλον κάλλος τοσοῦτο καὶ τοιοῦτο ὄν) of the Zeus at Olympus, and instead admiring [or "marveling at": θαυμάζοι] the "good workmanship" (τό τε εὐθυεργές) and "good finish" (τὸ εὔξεστον) of the

---

[266] See Saito 2007, 10. n. 1, an eminently sane position: "By emphasizing the sensuous and design as the focus of the aesthetic, I am not denying the aesthetic relevance of the conceptual. On the contrary . . . I am not committed to the formalist aesthetics that excludes the cognitive from the realm of the aesthetic" (where *formalist* has a sense opposite to that which I give it in this study, following different precedents, as noted in the Introduction and in Ch. 2).

[267] Appearances, however, can be deceiving. See Porter 2006b on this criterion, which is more complex (and more rational) than it first seems.

footstool and the "good proportions" (τὸ εὔρυθμον) of the base, and developing all this with great concern.[268]

Lucian appears to be mocking unnamed connoisseurs of a (now classical) materiality, who are, moreover, prepared to ignore the grand whole in favor of the – seemingly no less sublime, and at any rate fetishized – part. Evidently, such a posture was coherent with classical feeling in later antiquity.

Plato's disparaging remarks in various places directed against the same "material causes" of art – shades and variations in color, rhythm, sound, and motion – and of the sensuous pleasures derived from them, likewise suggest an identical opponency against anonymous targets of a similar aesthetic persuasion to those singled out by Lucian. Some of the antagonists can be named or adumbrated in the areas of music and in linguistic analysis, where language and music were brought into mutual proximity, and this will be the subject of Chapters 6 and 7. Otherwise, we are for the most part left groping in the dark with the barest of clues to aid us (though we can be fairly certain that the earlier adorers of aesthetic materiality were not moved by classicism). In cases like the following, there is no trouble identifying a target: "Well then, if one stripped away from the whole composition (τῆς ποιήσεως πάσης) [sc., of a tragedy] the melody, the rhythm, and the meter, does it turn out that what's left is only speeches (λόγοι)?" "Necessarily."[269] Even without knowing the title of this dialogue, *Gorgias*, one would be able to identify the source of this view and recognize how it has been not so subtly turned against its original purpose. Gorgias had claimed, in what is usually considered one of the early milestones in poetic theory, that poetry is "speech (λόγος) with meter," which is to say it is ordinary language with aesthetic features superadded to it (a position we will be exploring more closely in the next chapter). There is a potential weakness in this view, and Plato is perhaps right to exploit it. Nonetheless, it is characteristic of Plato to want to strip away the aesthetic accretions as so many inessential layers obscuring the foundational content of any linguistic message, and in the case of the poets to find nothing at the foundational layer once he reaches that point (as in the *Ion*). Poets, in Plato's eyes, are intellectually vacuous. Consequently, their works are *nothing but* melody, rhythm, and meter masquerading as conveyors of ideas and useful contents – in Protagoras' terms, their works are nothing but appearances.

---

[268] Lucian *Hist. conscr.* 27; trans. Kilburn.   [269] Pl. *Grg.* 502c; trans. Zeyl, adapted.

II AESTHETIC PLEASURES OF THE SENSES

But what about the notion, rejected by Socrates in the same vicinity of the *Gorgias*, that music furnishes its hearers with pleasure and nothing more? "But consider whether you don't think that all singing to the lyre and composing of dithyrambs has been invented for the sake of pleasure," he asks.[270] We do not know whether Plato is reciting a specific view from among a repertoire of received opinions on music, though the mention of "dithyramb" is a tip-off that we are in the ambit of a cultural polemic, indeed of a wider culture war in which the frivolousness of the intricate dithyramb was decried as a degenerate source of pleasures, especially after the introduction of the so-called New Music in the later fifth century. The opponents of the newly liberated dithyramb were an austere and puritanical rear-guard, and their arguments pretty much followed the same lines as Aristophanes' *Frogs*, with its stark juxtaposition of the virtuous Aeschylus and the turpid Euripides (though it is not inconceivable that Aristophanes was happy to embarrass this entire cultural polemic).[271] But Plato's attack here is of a broader nature: it encompasses singing to the lyre and the hedonic goals of music generally, just as the attack on tragedy to come locates in the materials of that medium the engines of "irrational" pleasure and the final, deplorable goal of tragedy. Thus, tragedy is "bent upon giving pleasure and upon gratifying the spectators."[272]

Discrediting hedonism is a signature feature of Plato's attack on the arts.[273] Often, the attack is more specifically aimed against base, sensual pleasure as the criterion of art, as in the *Laws*.[274] But there is no clear indication that Plato has in mind specific opponents there, any more than he does in *Republic* 5 when he disparages "the lovers of sights and sounds (φιλήκοοι καὶ φιλοθεάμονες) [who] like beautiful sounds, colors, shapes, and everything fashioned out of them, but [whose] thought is unable to

---

[270] Pl. *Grg.* 502a; trans. Zeyl.

[271] The literature on the New Music is vast. A good introduction, with texts in translation, is to be found in Barker 1984, 93–116. More recently, see Martin 2003; Wilson 2003; Csapo 2004; Franklin forthcoming.

[272] Pl. *Grg.* 502c.

[273] Hence, aesthetic pleasure is "irrational" (Pl. *Tim.* 47d).

[274] Cf. *Leg.* 2.658e (pleasure is "a proper criterion in the arts, but not the pleasure experienced by anybody and everybody"; trans. Saunders); ibid., 2.667e (downplaying mere pleasure as "play," παιδία – a sophistic association); ibid., 2.668ab (repeating and qualifying the claim from 658e); ibid., 3.700d–701a (decrying *theatrokratia*).

see and embrace the nature of the beautiful itself."[275] Plato may only be imagining the natural impulses of common individuals based on his own experiences, and he may also be right to fear the spontaneity of this kind of response to art, given his own aesthetic puritanism. Or, conceivably, for a very brief moment, Plato and Shklovsky join hands in a common wariness of the habits of sensuous reactions to works of art, which can lead to two very different kinds of superficiality – either mindless seduction (Plato) or automatic familiarization (Shklovsky). Whatever the case may be, it stands to reason that sensualism, phenomenalism, and materialism should go hand in hand with a kind of hedonism in aesthetics. This is, after all, their later fate; Plato and Aristotle are on their guard against this collusion of interests in their own writings. And it is inconceivable that earlier thinkers would have resisted this obvious connection.

Gorgias is a good case in point, though he brings complications of his own that will warrant separate discussion below. Gorgias, Hippias, and Democritus aside, or the various tribes of musicians (*harmonikoi* and *rhuthmikoi*), about whom we know only too little, I am unaware of any direct evidence that would point to this exact fusion of interests outside of the poets (who are by no means negligible, but we are looking for theorists working in prose now) and the very few examples of painters mentioned above, though indirect evidence exists. One such clue involves the sophist Prodicus of Ceos, active at the time of Socrates and Gorgias, who was something of a stickler for words, and who also evidently held a theory of linguistic meaning that, when applied to sensation, comes out looking rather like Aristotle's later theory of spheres of sensation. According to the Prodicean theory, each sphere of sensation was coordinated with a pleasure that had to be designated by its own proper name. The term associated with propriety here is none other than *idion*. Whether the term was originally used by Prodicus is hard to say. There may be some terminological contamination (the two witnesses to this theory come late in the tradition). But in any case, the general conception is clear enough, and it is roughly corroborated by Plato and Aristotle. Here is a first text:

Prodicus tried to assign to each of these words [for pleasure] some essential significant characteristic (ἴδιόν τι σημαινόμενον), just as the Stoics [later] did, saying that *joy* (χαράν) is rational elation (εὔλογον ἔπαρσιν), *pleasure* (ἡδονήν)

[275] *Rep.* 5.476b; trans. Grube; rev. Reeve. These spectators are introduced at 475d. Nightingale 2004, 78 ties them to a new kind of *theōros*, but, apart from the question whether such a spectator existed at the time, the reference seems to have a generic, *ex hypothesi* character. Cf. ibid., 476a10; 548e5.

irrational elation (ἄλογον ἔπαρσιν), that gladness (τέρψιν) is the pleasure which has its source in *hearing* [lit., "in the ears"], and *enjoyment* (εὐφροσύνην) is the pleasure which has its source in discourse [or according to another version, "that has its source *in vision* (lit., "in the eyes")].[276]

This parsing of pleasures into the categories of rational and irrational, and sensuous and non-sensuous, shows more than a passion for lexicography.[277] It shows a definite interest, on the part of a philosophical mind from the second half of the fifth century, in coming to grips with the vast realm of pleasures. Leaving aside the intriguing and counterintuitive assignment, in one instance, of "elation" to the rational half of things, what ought to impress us here is the frank confrontation of sensual pleasures and their admission into a logical taxonomy. We do not know how Prodicus stood on the question of sensual pleasures, and his taxonomy of pleasures does not appear to have won a following in later centuries. If anything, terms for pleasure continue to be as haphazard and variable in their usage as they always were. That pleasure, as a phenomenon, is fundamentally haphazard may well have been one of Prodicus' desired lessons. For present purposes, the testimony is valuable as a record of the particularizing tendency discussed above and its application to the pleasures of the senses: for every sphere of sensation there must correspond a different pleasure, each named according to its kind.

If the aesthetic relevance of this exercise in conceptual and linguistic tidiness isn't obvious yet, it will be so once we look again to Plato. Plato appears to be referring to the Prodicean theory in the *Hippias Major*, which turns on an inquiry into the meaning of *to kalon*, or "the fine." Socrates suggests one approach to the problem of a definition, in a passage quoted earlier in Chapter 2 above:

If whatever makes us be *glad* (χαίρειν), not with all the pleasures, but just *through hearing and sight* – if we call *that* fine, how do you suppose we'd do in the contest? Men, when they're fine anyway – and everything decorative, pictures

---

[276] Πρόδικος δὲ ἐπειρᾶτο ἑκάστῳ τῶν ὀνομάτων τούτων ἴδιόν τι σημαινόμενον ὑποτάσσειν, ὥσπερ καὶ οἱ ἀπὸ τῆς Στοᾶς, χαρὰν μὲν λέγοντες εὔλογον ἔπαρσιν, ἡδονὴν δὲ ἄλογον ἔπαρσιν, τέρψιν δὲ τὴν δι' ὤτων ἡδονήν, εὐφροσύνην δὲ τὴν διὰ λόγων (Alex. Aphrod.: τὴν διὰ τῶν ὀμμάτων Herm. *in Phdr.* 239.1–2) (Alex. Aphrod. *in Top.* 181.2–5 Wallies = DK 84A19); trans. Reesor 1983, 124–25, adapted. For a confirmation of the alternative reading, cf. Xen. *Symp.* 4.22: ἡ μὲν αὐτοῦ ὄψις εὐφραίνειν δύναται, ἡ δὲ τοῦ εἰδώλου τέρψιν μὲν οὐ παρέχει, πόθον δὲ ἐμποιεῖ. Cf. Pl. *Prt.* 337c; Arist. *Top.* 2.6.112b22–24.

[277] It is a passion that Alcidamas would, moreover, not share. Cf. Alcidamas *Soph.* 19: "Now, there are only a few arguments in speeches and they are important, but there are many words and phrases that are unimportant and differ only slightly from one another" (trans. Gagarin and Woodruff).

and sculptures – these all *delight* (τέρπει) us *when we see them,* if they're fine. Fine sounds and music altogether, and speeches and storytelling have the same effect.[278]

Appearances notwithstanding, Plato is tilting the argument against aesthetic pleasures. To lump together pictures and sculptures under "things decorative" (τὰ ποικίλματα) is scarcely flattering to the arts, and Plato's concessions have a hidden sting. A bit further on, pursuing the same line of argument, Socrates poses a question that leads to the obvious conclusion that each sense must govern its own sphere of sensual pleasure. And it is here that the connection with Prodicus may be lurking in the background again – or else Plato is confronting the same kind of issue that Prodicus was wrestling with in turn: "Then is the pleasant through sight (τὸ δι' ὄψεως ἡδύ) pleasant through sight and hearing? Or is the pleasant through hearing pleasant through hearing and through sight?"[279] The answer proves to be No. This leaves the problem that if both senses (and their pleasures) can give a glimpse of what is fine in some singular sense, then sensual pleasure (being a constitutively plural activity and, so to speak, divided by the organs of sensation) and the fine (which must be one) cannot coincide, and a typically Platonic disparagement of sensual pleasure follows.[280] Nor would renaming the various pleasures solve the problem that Plato has identified but that Prodicus would not have seen. Prodicus, after all, was content to identify each of the pleasures with a different sense object and activity, whereas Plato is in search of a single transcendental pleasure that could embrace all the many pleasures under its wings. What is there to prevent Prodicus from running out of ink? Does he even have a guiding principle?

Plato's conclusion naturally follows from his refusal earlier in the same dialogue to equate "the fine" with material values, such as gold or ivory: Phidias' Athena Parthenos, though chryselephantine in every other respect, was fitted out with pupils of stone, not with precious materials, a choice that must be considered a flaw on the materialist view of what is "fine," or so Plato says. And isn't a well-turned pot fine, or any finely

---

[278] Pl. *Hp. mai.* 297e5–298a5; trans. Woodruff; emphasis added.   [279] Ibid., 299c.

[280] Ibid., 299d–300b. Hence the claim by Socrates, voicing that of an imagined objector, "'I don't suppose pleasure through sight is fine because of *that* – namely, through sight. Because if that were the cause of its being fine, the other – the one through hearing – wouldn't ever be fine. It's not a pleasure though sight.' Shall we say that's true?" Hippias: "We'll say it" (ibid., 299e; trans. adapted). Here, the two sense faculties are being played off against each other in a mutually eliminative way, leaving only the fine intact.

made utensil, for that matter?[281] But then, Plato is caricaturing materialism in art, or rather its advocacy, which again ought to encourage us to look for further signs of its theorization elsewhere in the ancient sources. But not without first venturing a quick reply to Plato. A materialist aesthetic *can* discover beauty and sensuous satisfactions in the simplest and smallest of material objects – in Lucian's terms from above, *ta mikrotata panu*. It can even find hidden depths of grandeur there, though it needn't. (Lucretius finds an image of sublimity in a puddle that lies between the stones on a paved street and that offers a mirror below of the gaping heavens above, *mirande*.[282]) Grandeur and the sublime are not necessary coefficients, even if beauty and sublimity often are in antiquity. There may be a secret thrill that runs through any sensuous encounter with any material object framed as aesthetically pleasing or interesting, no matter how banal the object may be. A mere *stoicheion* will often serve the purpose, whether in its visual appearance or in the sound that it gives rise to (the open-mouthed echoing of an *ō-mega*), as will brush strokes, scratches on a surface, or a well-joined corner stone, all of which testify to the impress of an artist's hand or his process, while the same can hold, *mutatis mutandis*, for natural objects, as any of the accounts of nature's marvelous details can show, from Homer's snowflake-similes to Posidippus' epigrams about stones.[283] And that thrill is frequently the first inkling of greater, if not grander, things to come.

---

[281] Ibid., 290b–c; 288d–289a.
[282] Lucr. 4.414–19; Porter 2007b, 169.
[283] More on Posidippus in Ch. 9 below.

CHAPTER 5

The evidence of Aristophanes and Gorgias

Aristophanes is a priceless witness to contemporary literary criticism and aesthetics. This is true even if his testimony comes filtered through comic exaggeration and hostile distortion, as he pokes fun at the rationalizing efforts of sophists and poets, all of which he finds outrageous and an embarrassment to common sense. While Aristophanes' concerns are visible elsewhere in his preserved writings, particularly in the opening of *Thesmophoriazusae* (about which more below) and in *Acharnians*, as well as in fragments, no other single document we have by him comes as close as *Frogs* to opening a small crack of light onto the evolving discourses of aesthetic description and evaluation in late fifth-century Greece.[1] To be sure, any connections that can be made to aesthetic developments outside the play must remain speculative: apart from Socrates and Euripides, Aristophanes names no names. But it makes little difference if we cannot pin Aristophanes' notions on anyone in particular, since we can always as a last resort pin them on Aristophanes himself. The dean of Old Comedy might appear to be the first ancient literary critic, but this is an honor he does not entirely deserve: he is best seen as a symptom of the age.[2] But there is far more to *Frogs* than literary criticism. Indeed, in *Frogs* we find excellent confirmation of the very kinds of concerns that we have been tracking so far in this study, as a few quick examples will make abundantly clear.

---

[1] See Dover 1993, 24–37, despite his reservations about the evidentiary value of the play (similarly, Clayman 1977). Further, Pohlenz 1920 (succinctly, 153); Denniston 1927 (e.g., 119: "technical jargon is being satirized"); Griffith 1984; O'Sullivan 1992; Rosen 2008 (on authorial intentionality and characterization).

[2] Sommerstein 1996, 14 ("earliest sustained piece of literary criticism surviving in the Western tradition") is closer to the truth. Cf. Ch. 4, §1. For a good contextualizing analysis, see Nagy in Kennedy 1989, 67–77; also, Pfeiffer 1968, 47–48. Further, Stohn 1955; Taillardat 1962, 467–70.

I MEASURING VALUES IN 'FROGS'

The central and culminating scene of the play is the contest between Aeschylus and Euripides, in which the relative merits of the two play-wrights are assessed by Dionysus, who acts the part of the judge. What is striking here are the kinds of metaphors for critical evaluation that are put into play by Aristophanes as he ridicules the technical languages of criticism, or at least their pretenses to scientificity, particularly in the location of criteria of judgment (*krisis*). Consider the exchange between Dionysus' companion to the underworld, Xanthias, and a slave of Pluto's as they relish the anticipated battle between the two tragic worthies, which has all the earmarks of a final Judgment Day of Art itself:

XANTHIAS: So the thing is really going to happen?
SLAVE: Indeed it is, and very soon. And *then* something really awesome will be set in motion. Art will be weighed in the balance (ταλάντῳ μουσικὴ σταθμήσεται) –
XANTHIAS: What do you mean? Will they be treating tragedy like an Apaturia sacrifice?
SLAVE: – and they'll bring out word-rulers (κανόνας) and word-measures (πήχεις ἐπῶν), and folding frames (πλαίσια ξύμπτυκτα) –
XANTHIAS: What, are they going to be making bricks (πλινθεύσουσι)?
SLAVE: – and set-squares (διαμέτρους) and wedges (σφῆνας); because Euripides says he's going to put plays to the proof word by word (κατ' ἔπος).
XANTHIAS: Aeschylus must surely, I fancy, have found that distasteful (βαρέως ... φέρειν).[3]

The clash between crude dimensional measures and refined poetic values is both shocking and comical. Surely one of the absurdities being mocked by Aristophanes is the bare fact of trying to decide between Aeschylus and Euripides, both of whom had already achieved canonical stature by the end of the fifth century: the play is a dramatization of this absurdity.[4] The play achieves this end by mocking the very procedure by which one might arrive at such a decision. Hence, Aristophanes seems to be saying, *sotto voce*, if you want to compare aesthetic values among these near-equivalences (or else incommensurabilities), you are going to have to quantify poetic quality, which is likewise absurd. Modern-day equivalents might be the Research Excellence Framework in the UK or the NRC Assessment of Research Doctorate Programs in the US, both of which are

---

[3] *Ran.* 795–803; trans. Sommerstein.
[4] See Rosen 2004; Porter 2006b, 301–5.

committed to producing quantitative assessments of (in this case, academic) quality.

But what were the methods available for estimating aesthetic value in Aristophanes' day? The entire measuring scenario, built around elaborate scales designed to weigh the heft and therefore the value of poetic verses, is in one sense nothing but a large-scale metaphor or allegory for critical judgment gone awry. Taken by itself, one might suppose there is not much to be surmised from Aristophanes' text about contemporary practice, save the possible fact that some such critical evaluation was ongoing at the time of Euripides' death in 405, and that Aristophanes found the practice objectionable. But as Aristophanes pursues the metaphor of critical measurement, there seems to be a consistency to it that goes beyond the logic of ridicule, and that chimes with other known aesthetic practices from the time, including the verbal arts. Could there be a reflection here, and not just a distortion, of actual literary criticism behind the persiflage? Despite the paucity of evidence and the reservations of some scholars, there are good arguments to think there is. For starters, we might reason along the following lines: with quantification comes an inevitable concretization of the terms of comparison. Language is literally reified: words are placed on scales and weighed. As one of the characters remarks, it is "as if [the parties involved] were selling cheese."[5] Perhaps. But we can also turn this around and demonstrate how Aristophanes' play throws a precious light on late fifth-century views of poetic and aesthetic perception, according to which objects of art enjoyed a material and sensuous character: they were palpable, they had a heft to them, were felt to be light or heavy, angled or four-square, and so on. (One is put in mind of Simonides and his concretizing language, not least in his poem in praise of the virtuous man: "It is difficult for a man to be truly good, | in hands, in feet, and in mind, | four-square (τετράγωνον), fashioned (τετυγμένον) without flaw . . ."[6]). And as D. A. Russell observes, "Many words – ἁδρός and ἰσχνός, 'fat' and 'thin,' for example – appear to be transferred directly from their literal and physical uses to serve as descriptions of speech," adding that "ancient theorists understood that ἁδρός and ἰσχνός were so derived and that χαρακτήρ meant 'bodily habit' before it meant 'style.'"[7] The same pattern of extension is observable

---

[5] Ar. *Ran.* 1369.
[6] Simonides fr. 542.1–3 *PMG*; trans. Campbell, adapted.
[7] Russell 1964, xxx–xxxi with n. 1 (citing Phoebammon in *Rhet. Gr.* 14.383–84 Rabe).

outside the domain of speech. Only, the literal and physical connotations were never entirely lost in any of these areas.

Seen from this perspective, Aristophanes is arguably opening a window onto a wider discourse of aesthetic evaluation, one that intersected with other art forms. I say art forms, being careful not to reduce the field of comparisons to a level lower than art, which has been the temptation in the past. Thus, Rosemary Harriott, whose book *Poetry and Criticism Before Plato* (1969) remains the best general study of the language of poetic description before Plato (with a good discussion of Aristophanes), refers to the "tendency [in comedy] to express ideas and abstractions in visual, concrete terms" by way of what she calls "craft-metaphors."[8] This is too restrictive. It gives the impression that criticism at the time was of a primitive nature, being unable to lift itself above the level of crude analogies to, say, building or carpentry. It also places the focus of such thinking in the wrong place. While craft-thinking may well turn tragedies into "solid objects with weight and dimension," the emphasis in such thinking falls on the perceptual aesthetic character of tragic language and effects, and not only on the craftsmanlike (product-like, manufactured) quality of the form, as we shall see. Nor is it correct to align craft-metaphors with "the new criticism" and then to align Euripides with this development, to the exclusion of other poets, above all Aeschylus.[9] What is more, the tendency to get at the aesthetic aspects of art and experience by way of attention to the craftsmanly nature of objects, which inevitably brought with it attention to process, materials, details, finish – in other words, all that would later be celebrated (or disdained) under the label of *(ex)ergasia* – reaches back to Homer, with Indo-European roots that reach farther back still.[10] The extension of this form of attention to language is likewise nothing substantially new, though the level of intensity it achieves in the late fifth century perhaps is – aligned, no doubt, with a newfound focus on the analysis of language, grammar, and the arts of meaning. But let us take up the question of the neighboring arts, which is to say, those arts whose languages of evaluation can be shown to have intersected with those of comedy.

Consider the mention of "word-rules" (κανόνες) in the quotation from *Frogs* above. The term instantly calls to mind Polyclitus' contemporary

---

[8] Harriott 1969, 97; cf. Denniston 1927, 114.
[9] Harriott 1969, 149; see below on *Ran.* 818–25.
[10] E.g., *Il.* 11.24–44 (Agamemnon's armor); *Od.* 23.184–204 (the bed: τέτυκται, etc.). Further, Frontisi-Ducroux 1986. For disdain, see on Arist. *Poet.* 4.1448b17–19 at Ch. 4 §10 above. On the Indo-European roots of craft terms for art, see Ch. 9, n. 201 below.

treatise and its exemplifying statue, the *Canon*. There, the notion of a calculus of beauty was pursued to the absolute limit of rigor, and was felt by its author and maker to be anything but absurd. Only a few reminiscences of Polyclitus' own language have been preserved, but they suffice to show that at least in this case quantification and beauty went hand in hand: "[Polyclitus claimed that] the good [sculptural work] comes about through many numbers, just barely" (τὸ γὰρ εὖ παρὰ μικρὸν διὰ πολλῶν ἀριθμῶν ἔφη γίνεσθαι).[11] The final and much bedeviled tag, "just barely," probably indicates the level of difficulty that is involved in achieving aesthetic perfection in sculpture,[12] and as such it is comparable to the parallel quotation from the *Canon* preserved by Plutarch and later used by Horace in his *Ars poetica* as a model of artistic perfection: "The work is most difficult for those for whom the clay comes to the nail" (*ad unguem*), which is to say, down to the finest detail, at the point where the workmanship is the most difficult to perfect – originally, at the outermost reaches of the casting process in the manufacture of bronze statues (Polyclitus' preferred medium).[13]

What is more, Polyclitus famously espoused a theory of proportions, or *summetria*, in his treatise. As it happens, this theory further exemplifies the componential method of analysis that I described above in the context of the first-generation sophists:

Beauty, [the Stoic philosopher Chrysippus] thinks, does not reside in the proper proportion of the elements (στοιχείων) but in the proper proportion of the parts (ἐν τῇ τῶν μορίων συμμετρίᾳ), such as for example that of finger to finger and of all these to the hand and wrist, of these to the forearm, of the forearm to the whole arm and of everything to everything else, just as described in the *Canon* of Polyclitus.... Polyclitus supported his theory (λόγον) with a work of art, making a statue according to the tenets of the theory and calling it, like the treatise itself, the *Canon*. So then, all philosophers and doctors accept that beauty resides in the due proportion of the parts of the body.[14]

Once again we find an equivalence of rational or component parts and material counterparts – an abstract proportional grid that is being mapped

---

[11] Ph. *Bel.* 4.1.49.20 (= DK 40B2). Trans. after Huffman 2002 (see next n.).

[12] See Huffman 2002, who definitively ousts the Pythagorean interpretations as well as the irrationalist line, according to which παρὰ μικρόν is taken to mean "almost" and perfection is taken to be unreachable in principle.

[13] Hor. *Ars. P.* 294; cf. Plut. *Mor.* 86A; *Mor.* 636c. See D'Angour 1999.

[14] Gal. *De plac. Hippoc. et Plat.* 5.448–49 Kühn = 308.17–26 De Lacy; trans. Stewart 1978, 125 n. 23; slightly adapted.

onto an articulated body – with beauty emerging from their relations.[15] The theory represents a radical confrontation of logic and matter, of formalized aesthetic principles and their material embodiment, just as the treatise, along with its theory (*logos*), was embodied in the eponymous statue, the *Canon* (also known as the *Doryphorus*). From this painstaking clash of enumerated contraries ("through many numbers"), ramified through the many parts of the whole, an aesthetic excellence (τὸ εὖ), was said to arise.

Such interest in rational mensuration was a commonplace in sophistic circles (whose motto might as well have been Protagoras' "Man is the measure"), and I believe we can catch a further reflection of it in the Aristophanes passage above, and in the entire conceit of "weighing" verses.[16] The idea of resorting to calipers, square rules, and other calibrated instruments in order to scrutinize the aesthetic particulars of the two tragedians' verses[17] strikes the old-fashioned Aeschylus as abhorrent, while Euripides, representing trendy newfangled techniques, just as naturally leaps at the chance to undergo this kind of scrutiny – to his undoing, it turns out. In his commentary on the passage, Dover refuses to countenance anything resembling a sophistic influence (he mentions only builders and "mathematicians"),[18] but Kerferd corrects this reluctance: sophists were keenly interested in mathematical problems (Hippias was said to have discovered a curve function useful for attempting to square the circle, a problem that preoccupied Antiphon too), and so "it is probable that the word" – namely *diametros*, found at *Frogs* 801, which was quoted above – "was actually invented by one of the sophists."[19] We do not know who first reapplied these terms to literature, but Aristophanes' ridicule has more bite if he is producing Euripides as a representative of a much wider trend instead of himself coining a strange new vocabulary out of the blue and asking his audience to marvel at its

---

[15] Chrysippus' polemic against *stoicheia* in favor of larger bodily parts (*moria*) is Chrysippan and needn't reflect anything in Polyclitus.

[16] Sophocles' *Oedipus Rex* reflects the tragic dilemmas of the Protagorean-style pursuit of numerical rigor, of "mensuration and calculation"; see the brilliant analysis by Knox 1957, 147–58. The play culminates with Oedipus having to face the fact that in age (and in other respects) he is "commensurate" (*summetros*) with the criminal he has been searching for (*OT* 1113).

[17] I take "particulars" to lie behind the meaning of κατ' ἔπος ("word by word"). Its culmination is the verse-by-verse examination in the scale scene, which Aeschylus finally tires of (repeating the phrase κατ' ἔπος at 1407).

[18] Dover 1993, 290 (at 801).

[19] Kerferd 1981a, 39; cf. ibid., 38; and cf. Pl. *Prt.* 318d–319a. Philostratus records that Hippias wrote or lectured on geometry and astronomy in addition to music and rhythm (DK 86A2 = Philostr. *VS* 495).

unheard-of strangeness.[20] The same would apply to his fooling around with the language of rhythm and meter in *Clouds*, which the wannabe initiate Strepsiades blockheadedly finds newfangled and strange, and likewise insists on literalizing – for instance, by turning *metra* ("measures") into "quarts" (Socrates: "I'm not asking you about that; I'm asking you what you consider the best measure aesthetically" [ὅ τι κάλλιστον μέτρον | ἡγεῖ]), and by turning "dactylic" rhythm (κατὰ δάκτυλον) into the more comprehensible gesture of the middle finger ("Like this!" [οὑτοσί]).[21] Aristophanes is indeed a precious window onto some of the earliest formalized literary and aesthetic criticism known to us from the Graeco-Roman traditions.

A confluence of influences in Aristophanes is most probable, not only from the side of the sophists but also from that of builders and sculptors (like Polyclitus), and of course earlier poets as well. Before considering this last likelihood, let us look at a few more instances of related critical terminology from *Frogs*. In the immediate sequel to the passage quoted earlier, the Chorus mimic the salivations of Xanthias and his fellow slave at the prospect of the contest to come:

There will be flashing-helmeted struggles of lofty-crested (ὑψιλόφων) speech,[22]
there will be slivers of linchpins (σχινδάλαμοι) and shavings (σμιλεύματα) from
    the chisel (παραξονίων ... ἔργων),
as the man [sc., Aeschylus] fights off the galloping words
of a master craftsman of the intellect (φρενοτέκτονος)
... with a roar he will utter
words coupled together with rivets (ῥήματα γομφοπαγῆ), tearing them off like
    ship-timbers
with his gigantic gusting (γηγενεῖ φυσήματι).[23]

Words and verses are being likened to the materials of building and construction again, this time less with an eye to precise measurement than as a reminder of feverish composition (as suits Aeschylus, the *poeta furens*). The language is copiously paralleled in later critical discourse,

---

[20] Cf. Ar. *Ran.* 956–57 for similar terminology applied to Euripidean subtleties. The aforementioned skepticism of Dover (at 801) is unnecessary, even if it is provoked by the overconfident assertions of Radermacher 1921, 257–58, which presume a simple, linear process of borrowings from the plastic arts to rhetoric to literary criticism. The borrowings were much more likely to go in various directions at once. See further Muecke 1982, 45.

[21] Ar. *Nub.* 640–41; trans. Sommerstein; ibid., 652; 654.

[22] ὑψιλόφων is a variant known to ancient scholia and one MS and is printed by Sommerstein 1996 and also by Wilson in the 2007 OCT in place of ἱππολόφων (so, e.g., Dover), which is carried by four MSS but known to no scholia.

[23] Ar. *Ran.* 818–25; trans. Sommerstein.

starting with the Hellenistic euphonists reported by Philodemus and then in Dionysius of Halicarnassus, Quintilian, and Longinus. And there are precedents in earlier, archaic poetry, for instance in Hesiod, who makes a metapoetic comment, or so it has been argued, in a much-discussed passage from *Works and Days* celebrating his victory with a hymn after a sea-voyage from Chalcis to Euboea. In metaphorical terms, Hesiod is describing a voyage in song that rivals the Homeric epic quest:

This [tripod, won in the competitions,] I dedicated to the Heliconian Muses, where they first set me upon the path of clear-sounding song. This is as much experience of many-bolted ships as I have acquired (τόσσον τοι νηῶν γε πεπείρημαι πολυγόμφων); yet even so I shall speak forth the mind of aegis-holding Zeus, for the Muses taught me to sing an inconceivable hymn.[24]

Epic poetry (if that is what it is) is vast, "many-bolted," "manifold," even "monumental."[25] The metaphor is reinforced a few lines earlier with the boastful claim, which is again self-reflexively aimed, "I shall show you the measures (μέτρα) of the much-roaring sea (πολυφλοίσβοιο θαλάσσης), I who have no expertise (σεσοφισμένος) at all in sea-faring or boats" (648–49).

Overtly, Hesiod is contrasting his own minor genre of poetic fashioning with the larger-scale poetics of Homer – whence the two contrasting "measures" of poetry, made visible in a concrete metaphor of a constructed vessel for song. But if we look away from the Achaean ships for a moment and think about the act of building itself (as in the parable of the two kinds of Eris at *Works and Days* 25–26, where potter vies with potter, builder with builder (τέκτων), beggar with beggar, and poet with poet (ἀοιδός)), another Homeric parallel comes to mind. For arguably one of the earlier reference points for Hesiod was the construction of the raft by Odysseus on Calypso's island, a scene that is itself reminiscent of poetic elaboration:

[Calypso] gave him a great ax that was fitting to his palms (ἄρμενον ἐν παλάμῃσι) and headed
With bronze, with a double edge each way, and fitted inside it
A very beautiful handle of olive wood, well hafted (περικαλλὲς ἐλάϊνον, εὖ ἐναρηρός);
Then she gave him a well-finished (ἔυξοον) adze, and led the way onward

---

[24] Hes. *Op.* 656–62; trans. Most.
[25] Rosen 1990, 103, n. 16, whose article is a seminal reading of the entire Nautilia passage along the lines followed here.

To the far end of the island where there were trees, tall grown (δένδρεα μακρὰ
πεφύκει),
Alder and black poplar and fir that towered to the heaven (οὐρανομήκης),
But all gone dry long ago and dead, so they would float lightly.
. . .

He threw down twenty in all, and trimmed them well with his bronze ax,
And planed them expertly (ἐπισταμένως), and trued them straight to a chalkline
(ἐπὶ στάθμην ἴθυνε).
Kalypso, the shining goddess, at that time came back, bringing him
An auger, and he bored through them all and pinned them together (ἥρμοσεν
ἀλλήλοισι)
With dowels (γόμφοισιν), and then with cords he lashed his raft together (ἄρα
τήν γε καὶ ἁρμονίῃσιν ἄρασσεν).
And as great as is the bottom of a broad cargo-carrying ship,
When a man well skilled in carpentry fashions it (τίς τ' ἔδαφος νηὸς
τορνώσεται ἀνὴρ | ... εὖ εἰδὼς τεκτοσυνάων), such was
The size of the broad raft made for himself (ποιήσατο) by Odysseus.[26]

In the next few verses, Odysseus further fashions (ποιήσατο, ποίει)
deckboards and a mast. The entire scene is one of fabulous artifice, a
virtual fairy-land of aesthetic production: the tools, themselves already
beautifully fashioned and well fitting (*fitting* being one of the key operative terms in the passage, repeated in various verb and sound forms),
encourage further fine craftsmanship. Even the surrounding natural world
is prone to art, much as in a Theocritean landscape. The timbers are
marvels of creation, monumental in size and pointing to the heavens, but
ready for the sea. These verses, incidentally, contain the one recorded
occurrence of γόμφος ("dowel" or "rivet") in Homer and the Epic Cycle.
The reoccurrence of the term in Hesiod can be no accident – never mind
the reverberation of carpentry and building analogies for poetry in later
poets.[27] Quite plainly, Aristophanes is but a relay in a much longer
tradition, one to be discussed below under the rubric of "sublime
monuments."

    Readings of this kind in Homer could be multiplied almost at will, for
the simple reason that all the objects found in Homer are aestheticized
(and so treated and described): the world of Homer is an enchanted one,
aesthetically speaking. Add to this the characteristically Homeric *Lust am*

---

[26] Hom. *Od.* 5.234–51; trans. Lattimore. See further *Od.* 8.246–53, with the ingenious reading of Rosen
    1990, 103–04, n. 19; also Dougherty 2001, esp. 19–37.
[27] For the Indo-European ancestry of such terms see Ch. 9, n. 201 below.

Material, or "pleasure in materials,"[28] and you have a built-in recipe for a materialistically slanted aesthetics and a window onto something like an aesthetics of the everyday (despite the presentational mode of a *Kunstsprache*), all rolled into one.

A particularly interesting echo, in part because it is so precise and so rare, is the repetition of γόμφος in a column from Philodemus' *On Poems*, where in play is the question, what binds sounds together, and the answer given is, consonants: these act like "glue" or "rivets" by holding together the vowel sounds in the "composite" (the *sunthesis*) of sound clusters. The analogy of materials being glued or riveted together is then extended to include more complex elements of diction, whose σύμπηξις ("framing" or "putting together") as a whole can be considered successful if the texture of the whole is made "firm" (εὐπαγές).[29] Sounds made firm are further likened to a body (σῶμα), the parts (μέρη) of which "are uniform [or 'harmonious'] and symmetrical in their linear dimensions (τοῖς μήκεσι) and in their volumes (τοῖς ὄγκοις)."[30] A clear predecessor to both the passage from *Frogs* and this piece of Hellenistic critical ecphrasis is the account of Agathon's poetic activity in *Thesmophoriazusae*:

Agathon of the beautiful verses (ὁ καλλιεπής) is about to ... set the pegs on which to frame the play (δρυόχους τιθέναι δράματος ἀρχάς). He is bending new curves for his verses (κάμπτει δὲ νέας ἁψῖδας ἐπῶν): he is chiseling some bits (τὰ δὲ τορνεύει), fixing some with song-glue (τὰ δὲ κολλομελεῖ), knocking up maxims, making periphrases, wax-moulding, rounding, casting ...[31]

A similar theme, the idea of poetry as a gluing or riveting of material, appears in a fragment by Teleclides: "Euripideses ... riveted together [i.e., poetically or conceptually patched together] by Socrates" (Εὐριπίδας σωκρατογόμφους).[32] Gluing crops up again in Plato as a way of demeaning the efforts of rhetoricians who compose written speeches (πρὸς ἄλληλα κολλῶν τε καὶ ἀφαιρῶν), where "gluing [the parts] to each other" is a virtual calque on *sunthesis* (συνέθηκε), which brings out the literal and concrete senses of "composition" and offers a more colorful alternative to "writing" (ἔγραψεν).[33]

[28] See Ch. 3, at n. 179 above.
[29] Phld. *De poem.* 2, *P. Herc.* 994 col. 34 Sbordone.
[30] τοῖς τε μήκεσι καὶ τοῖς ὄγκοις ὁμολογο[ύ]μενά τε καὶ σύμμετρα ὄντα (ibid., col. 34.22–25).
[31] Ar. *Thesm.* 49–57; trans. Barker 1984, 109, adapted.
[32] Teleclides fr. 42 K–A = D.L. 2.18 (Εὐριπίδας Cobet: Εὐριπίδης MSS: Εὐριπίδας ⟨τοὺς⟩ Kaibel). Cf. Conti Bizzarro 1999, 185–86 for discussion and parallels.
[33] Pl. *Phdr.* 278d8–e1.

Plato's conceit is in the same vein as its Aristophanic ancestor: both belong to the tradition that tends to visualize poetic and rhetorical language as a kind of matter possessed of weight, dimensions, angles, detachable parts, seams, and the like. In the Philodemean columns, bits of language are being treated microscopically, whereas in Plato it is words or larger-scale entities, not sounds, that are being held together. Elsewhere, the same analogizing tendency goes off in the opposite direction, and the objects of language assume magnificent and even monumental proportions. *Stoicheia*, or elements, become *ogkoi*, or massy solids in their own right. Indeed, the very terms for dimensionality witnessed here, *mēkos* and *ogkos*, "length" and "solid mass," and several others ("weight," "breadth," "quantity," "magnitude," and so on) lend themselves to this more sublime connotation.[34]

Aeschylus tends to attract analogies of the latter kind in *Frogs*, as one might only expect of a poet whom antiquity considered the exemplar of the grand, if (at times) slightly fustian, style of tragedy. Aristophanes contributed powerfully to this judgment. Among the more extended stylistic evaluations of Aeschylus from antiquity is the *Life of Aeschylus*, which borrows heavily from Aristophanes. Here, Aeschylus is deemed to be remote from the "lean" style (ἡ λεπτότης) and notable for his "weighty" diction and characterization and for the archaic majesty of his stylistic effects. In Greek, the salient terms are *to megaloprepes, to hērōikon, to archaion, to baros,* and *ogkos*.[35] This same judgment later comes out as a way of accounting for aspects of Aeschylean dramaturgy: "he equipped the actors with gloves and dignified (ἐξογκώσας) them with long robes and elevated (μετεωρίσας) their stance with higher (μείζοσι) buskins."[36] The combination of bulk, magnification, and height already points towards a judgment that the Aeschylean *Life* all but names: Aeschylus is sublime.[37] Aristophanes, a prominent source of this view, would only concur. Two terms that we encountered just above are the sort that will eventually

---

[34] It is an intriguing fact about dimensional terms like "quantity" that they can be utterly neutral or suggestive of large, but never small, dimensions. Greek aesthetic language seems to exploit this coincidence of semantics.

[35] *Vit. Aesch.* 332. 9; 331.15–19 Page.

[36] *Vit. Aesch.* 333.10–11 Page; trans. Lefkowitz 1981, 159. Philostr. *VS* 492, plainly indebted to the same tradition, uses the synonym ὀκρίβαντι ὑψηλῷ, as is Dion. Hal. *De imit.* fr. 6. (*Opusc.* 2:206.2–3; 21–22 U–R): "Aeschylus was the first sublime (ὑψηλός) [poet] possessing grandeur" (μεγαλοπρεπείας), while Euripides "is neither sublime nor plain" (οὔτε ὑψηλός . . . οὔτε λιτός).

[37] Niall Slater points out (*per litt.*) that the tragic mask was equipped with a hair spike called an *ogkos*. Pollux (4.133), who describes this, adds that the spike points upwards (εἰς ὕψος) in the shape of a *lambda* – make of this what one will.

come to typify sublime discourse, as later echoes in the same play will soon confirm. "Lofty-crested (ὑψιλόφων) speech," attached to neither poet in particular, can only be said with reference to Aeschylus.[38] The same holds for "gigantic gusting" (γηγενεῖ φυσήματι), which would be ill-suited to Euripidean slenderness and subtlety. The phrase, incidentally, clearly points ahead to a much-used topos of the sublime, that of Gigantomachy and cosmic themes.[39]

The judgment that Aeschylus is sublime predates Aristophanes. Sophocles reportedly attributed *ogkos* – grandeur that results from bulk or weightiness – to Aeschylus, though the judgment may have originated in Ion of Chios.[40] And in *Crapataloi*, Pherecrates has Aeschylus, likewise in Hades, describe himself as one who "built to perfection a big art" the way one builds houses (τέχνην μεγάλην ἐξοικοδομήσας).[41] To think of art in this way, one has to be a φρενοτέκτων ἀνήρ, someone who "builds with his mind," as Aristophanes puts it in *Frogs*.[42] Building large structures with words seems to be Aeschylus' hallmark in Old Comedy. In *Peace* (421 BCE), Aristophanes reinforces the same theme, probably quoting Pherecrates, and introducing a new verb: "he built up a tower (ἐπύργωσε) ... with big words and thoughts" (ἔπεσιν μεγάλοις καὶ διανοίαις).[43] The same expression, "building up towering structures of majestic words" (πυργώσας ῥήματα σεμνά), appears again in *Frogs* in connection with Aeschylus, along with other comparable terms designating language, thoughts, or art that are out of the ordinary in size, height, weight, and mass.[44] Aeschylus even affirms his own artistic principle in the same play: "It's absolutely imperative, you wretched fool, when

---

[38] See n. 22 above.

[39] See Innes 1979.

[40] Plut. *Mor.* 79B. See Ch. 4, n. 14. On the contemporary imitation by rhetors of "die erhabene Würde des Vortrags der tragischen Bühne," see Krumbacher 1920, 22.

[41] Pherecr. 100 K–A.

[42] Ar. *Ran.* 820 (though, to be sure, the reference here is to the intellectualism of Euripides as a poet).

[43] Ar. *Pax* 749–50. Compare Aristophanes' ἐποίησε τέχνην μεγάλην ἡμῖν κἀπύργωσ᾽ οἰκοδομήσας with Pherecrates' ὅστις γ᾽ αὐτοῖς παρέδωκα τέχνην μεγάλην ἐξοικοδομήσας. On the relative dates of the two poets, see O'Sullivan 1992, 15.

[44] Ar. *Ran.* 1004; "oxhide words" (ῥήματα ... βόεια), ibid., 924; "sheer massive mounts of words" (ῥήμαθ᾽ ἱππόκρημνα), ibid., 928 (cf. *Eq.* 628); Euripides complains that Aeschylus' art was "swollen (οἰδοῦσαν) with bombast and overweight (ἐπαχθῶν) vocabulary," ibid., 940; "words the size of Parnassus" (σὺ λέγῃς ... Παρνασσῶν ἡμῖν μεγέθη) (trans. Sommerstein); "débite ... 'des altitudes de Parnasse'" (Taillardat 1962, 281), ibid., 1057. Taillardat (ibid., n. 1) compiles a useful list of places where the later synonyms, ὑψηλὰ ῥήματα, τὸ ὕψος τῶν λόγων, etc. appear, from an Epicurean writer (*P. Herc.* 831) to Dionysius of Halicarnassus to Plutarch, with a possible origin in Soph. *Aj.* 1230: ὑψήλ᾽ ἐφώνεις (ὑψήλ᾽ ἐκόμπεις cett. mss.); but cf. Aesch. *PV* 360–61: τῶν ὑψηγόρων | κομπασμάτων, and the Homeric ὑψαγόρης (lit., "speaking from on high," i.e., "boasting").

expressing great (μεγάλων) thoughts and ideas, to create (τίκτειν) words that measure up (ἴσα) to them."[45]

The desideratum of equivalence looks directly ahead to the final judgment scene, in which the words of the two poets are placed on measuring scales and their art is weighed one against the other, "as if [they] were selling cheese."[46] The poets are instructed to speak their verses into the scales, and the audience watch with bated breath as each new verse is added. Weightiness is evidently a good thing on the older aesthetic, which the play ultimately appears to vindicate, though not without extreme reservations. In contrast, Euripides, with his slender, anorexic style, looks ahead to the slender style seemingly embraced by Hellenistic poets and critics alike: "I began by reducing [Aeschylus'] swelling and removing its excess weight with a course of bite-size phrases, walking exercise and small white beets, while dosing it with chatter-juice strained off from books."[47] But while Aristophanes' play is a precious archive of critical attitudes and practices at the end of the fifth century, it is of course much more than this. It is a deliciously distortive allegory of what it represents. It achieves its ends by literalizing and materializing metaphors that were themselves already of a materialistic cast, and in all probability by combining a heroic and mythological motif from a play by Aeschylus (*Psychostasia,* or *Weighing of Souls*) with a debasing critical practice that ironically targets Aeschylus himself. In doing so, *Frogs* marks a pricelessly comic and, above all, a self-conscious and self-critical moment in the history of aesthetic judgment.

Aristophanes was probably not the first to bring literary criticism to such radical (or radically debasing) heights. There is evidence of an entire comic tradition devoted either to dead poets resurrected from the under-world or else to the figure of Poetry itself, with a number of these plays, as it happens, clustering around the year 410.[48] Cratinus, one of Aristophanes' early rivals, is a case in point, and possibly the first to bring Poetry (and himself as poet) on stage. What is more, Cratinus is known to have played with the metaphorics of scale well before *Frogs*, in his *Putine* (*The Wineflask*) from 423 BCE. There, Cratinus is arraigned on stage by

[45] Ar. *Ran.* 1059.
[46] *Ran.* 1369.
[47] Ar. *Ran.* 939–43. Cf. Reitzenstein 1931, 25–40; Ambühl 1995, on Callimachus' adoption of the slender and sweet sounding style (the λιγὺς ἦχος) of the cicada over against the swollen noisy style (the ὄγκος) of the braying ass (Callim. *Aet.* fr. 1.29–32 Pf.; 31: ὀγκήσαιτο; see Hopkinson 1988, 96, ad loc., on the pun).
[48] See n. 56 below.

the allegory of Comedy, who is introduced as his "wife," and who threatens to leave him for his infidelity (he has been seeing another woman: Drink). In this play of allegorical mirrors, designed to repudiate Aristophanes' charges of incompetency from the previous year's competition, Cratinus appears to present himself as firmly rejecting the poetics of the small and the refined (the *leptos*)[49] in favor of the grand, the (comically) sublime, and the Bacchicly (alcoholically) inspired:

> Lord Apollo, what a flood of words (τῶν ἐπῶν τοῦ ῥεύματος)
> the springs are pouring forth (καναχοῦσι πηγαί); truly he [sc., Cratinus] has a
>   twelve-fountained mouth;
> he has an Ilissos in his throat. What more could I say?
> For unless someone puts a bung in his mouth,
> he'll overwhelm (κατακλύσει) everything with his compositions.[50]

The language of rushing streams, unstoppable flows, and cataclysm will become commonplaces of the later sublime tradition, as will the pointed rejection of the small and reduced in scale.[51] Cratinus, too, knew how to exploit the long-standing imagery in which song and carpentry were fused together, as in a two-line fragment that talks, in mock-Pindaric tones, about "artificers of dexterous songs" (τέκτονες εὐπαλάμων ὕμνων).[52] Aristophanes, who quotes these words in *Knights* (424 BCE), proceeds to dismantle the conceit, nearly word by word, by turning the person into a thing:

> As it is, you don't take pity on him, although you see him in the grip of
>   dementia, with his pegs falling out, his tunings gone, and his joints gaping.
> νυνὶ δ᾽ ὑμεῖς αὐτὸν ὁρῶντες παραληροῦντ᾽ οὐκ ἐλεεῖτε,
> ἐκπιπτουσῶν τῶν ἠλέκτρων καὶ τοῦ τόνου οὐκέτ᾽ ἐνόντος
> τῶν θ᾽ ἁρμονιῶν διαχασκουσῶν.[53]

In doing so, however, Aristophanes unwittingly set the stage for Cratinus' reverse trick of personifying that thing called Comedy in *The Wineflask* a

---

[49] Fr. 205 K–A (= Ath. 3.94f): "How slim (ὡς λεπτός) is the sausage slice!" The dietary reduction recommended and rejected in this fragment thus anticipates the dietary regimen imposed on poetry by Euripides in *Frogs*. Similarly, Cratinus fr. 206 K–A ("little" pitchers and jars, which he presumably disdains).

[50] Fr. 198 K–A; trans. Ruffell 2002, 158. See the scholia ad loc. for commentary on this fragment.

[51] Consider the much-discussed pure stream/muddy waters motif from archaic poetry found in Aristophanes (e.g., *Eq.* 526–28 [to which Cratinus could be responding with the verses just quoted]; *Ran.* 1005), in Callimachus, and at Rome (cf. Asper 1997, 108–34; Hor. *Sat.* 1.4.11–12, citing "Eupolis, Cratinus and Aristophanes" in verse 1); *Subl.* 8.1 (the five "springs" [πηγαί] of the sublime); and 12.4 (on Cicero and Demosthenes).

[52] Fr. 70 K–A (= Ar. *Eq.* 530); trans. Sommerstein.

[53] Ar. *Eq.* 531–33; trans. Sommerstein.

year later, a clever comeuppance that won him first prize at the Lenaea –
though to say that Comedy had been made into a person is really to beg
any number of questions, for in point of fact Cratinus was parading a
thing (once abstract, now made concrete and palpable)[54] in the guise of a
woman throughout his play.

It may be that Old Comedy, with its debasing instincts and its *nostalgie
de la boue*, was inclined to go looking for objective correlatives of criticism
in natural and above all in material metaphors. But the echoes of the same
kinds of language in the adjacent discourses of art criticism and aesthetics,
both earlier (as in Homer and the lyric poets) and contemporary (as in
Polyclitus), tip the scales, so to speak, against this likelihood. It would
seem, rather, that the language of aesthetics was at least in part born out of
a confrontation with the materials of the world – not out of any deficiency
or impoverishment, but out of a curiosity, a need to explore, and a desire
to make contact with things.[55] In the case of comedy, this attention to
things combined all too happily with a desire to deconstruct them into
their absurdly material parts again. Be that as it may, while Cratinus,
Pherecrates, and Teleclides are a sobering reminder of just how much
sophisticated criticism prior to Aristophanes has gone missing, Aristophanes
is undeniably a superb instance of the genre he exemplifies and invaluably
represents as its most complete survivor.[56]

2 GORGIAS' "CRITICAL" MATERIALISM

With this broad background established we can return now to Gorgias
(who was discussed earlier in the context of the sophists),[57] with the
renewed assurance that, as a seeming proponent of a *kind* of materialism
in aesthetics, this colorful figure of the Greek Enlightenment was not
operating in a vacuum by any means. He adopted a qualified position
towards materialism, which led him to embrace some of the potentials of
contemporary materialist thinking while criticizing other aspects of it.
In doing so, Gorgias did contribute to the evolution of materialism in the
areas that are of concern to us here (art, language, and sensation), not least

---

[54] The same may hold true of the wineflask itself and all its surrogates in the play (e.g., "pitchers . . .
wine-buckets and all the other vessels," fr. 199 K–A), if they stand for containers/sources of his
Bacchic inspiration.

[55] Cf. Russell 1964, xxx–xxxi (on literary critical terms for speech).

[56] See Dover 1993, 26–27 for a list of such predecessors in comedy known as titles only or from small
scraps.

[57] Ch. 4, esp. §§3 and 6 above.

by giving all three areas a firmer foundation in the analysis of cultural contingency that was prevalent at the time (typically in the debates between nature and culture). But he was by no means the reductive materialist he is frequently made out to be in current scholarship.

This should come as no surprise. Reductionism is usually the last thing that comes to mind when one thinks of Gorgias. Gorgias often seems to stand outside his own projects and to look back on them with a detached irony. One way of making sense of Gorgias from the perspective of the present study is to see him as commenting critically on the values that the concepts of matter, nature, and physicality ("body") could assume in his contemporary intellectual scene. Like much else in Gorgias, matter and its workings are made by him into a problem rather than something to be safely taken for granted, or so I want to suggest. As in his aporetic treatise *On Not Being*, Gorgias' positions in his epideictic and other writings are hard to pin down, and more often than not they are premised on a series of hypotheticals whose truth-value he refuses to commit himself to unequivocally. Given that this is so, it is all the odder that one should find unqualified arguments in the recent literature in favor of a reductive and near mechanical materialism at work in Gorgias' writings.[58] All of Gorgias' hesitations notwithstanding, his writings remain a unique source of information for late fifth-century views about art and materialism. As with so much ancient evidence, a certain amount of extrapolation will be necessary to arrive at these views.

Materiality or autonomy?

We may begin by examining Gorgias' *Encomium of Helen*. The *Helen* is universally assumed to embrace the exceptional powers of *logos* and persuasion, which in turn appear to be achieved through the immediate, physical nature of language. By manipulating language in its materiality, a speaker on Gorgias' theory is able to manipulate the psychology of his listeners, which is likewise said to be of a material nature – and he is able to do so with an irresistible command at that.[59] Several obstacles stand in the way of this standard view of Gorgias. I will first list these

---

[58] E.g., Mazzara 1983; Ford 2002, 165; 179–84. For strong qualifications, see Porter 1993, from which much of the following is adapted in heavily revised form; also Halliwell 2003, 179.

[59] Apart from the references given in the previous note, see also Rosenmeyer 1955; Segal 1962; Guthrie 1971; Kerferd 1981a; Kerferd 1981b; Cassin 1980; Mourelatos 1987.

(they are in fact interlocking) and then develop them in the remainder of the present chapter:

(i) language has a materiality of a kind, but it is not the only materiality there is on Gorgias' theory: outside of *logos* there is the materiality of bodies and things;

(ii) the gap between the realm of *logos* and what lies beyond does not form an unbridgeable chasm, despite the overwhelming consensus of Gorgias' modern readers;[60] that is, *logos* and what he calls *to ektos* ("the outside") are not obviously made of incommensurable stuffs: the two realms are in communication – at the very least causal communication – whenever sensation and human communication about the world occur (and Gorgias' own writings are the pragmatic counterexample to his apparent claims here and to the theory that is conferred upon him in their wake); indeed, *logos* simply *is* another object in the world once it becomes an object of sensation – as a thing seen, heard, or (in written form) touched;

(iii) the thesis about linguistic autonomy ("the autonomy thesis" for short) requires that *logos* be self-contained and all-controlling, and that it account for the whole of human action once it is engaged; but there is considerable evidence to show that for Gorgias language is *not* autonomous in this sense.

If all of this is correct, then Gorgias' theory will exhibit a far richer view of the materiality both of language and of the external world, as well as a more complex view of the problem of autonomy than has been attributed to him in the past. Gorgias may be shown to hold a version of linguistic materialism, but not one in which the matter of language is irreducible to the matter of worldly things, or vice versa. Quite the contrary, their materiality will be shown to be of a shared and communicable nature. Language is vulnerable to what lies outside itself for the same reasons that it participates in the world; but this is not to say that the nature of matter is for Gorgias self-evident or unproblematic: matter is partly natural, a thing of the world, while the concept and its applications are vague, being of human and cultural extraction. Insights like this are what make Gorgias so intriguing a materialist: he can appear to be both an exponent of the

---

[60] Cf. Kerferd 1981a, 81, characteristic of this consensus: "Gorgias is introducing a radical gulf between logos and the things to which it refers," viz., between *logos* and the reality that is "irretrievably *outside* [*logos*] itself" (emphasis in original). For important qualifications to the consensus view, see Mansfeld 1985a.

doctrine and one of its subtler critics. With all this in mind, let us turn
to his various writings.

The *Helen* is the privileged body of evidence for the view that speech is
an autonomous and self-subsisting substance. *Logos*, after all, is a "powerful master," a δυνάστης μέγας, and it carries out its effects "with the
smallest and least evident body" (§8); Helen can be absolved, by words,
from charges of crime (which are themselves mere words).[61] The linguistic
theory implied by Gorgias' philosophical writing appears only to certify
the powers of *logos*. There is, for instance, the claim from *On Not Being*
that language is self-contained and can convey nothing of what exists
outside itself. Since this is so, the argument runs, *logos* enjoys absolute
mastery in its own realm (the sphere of verbal communication); it
exists autonomously, in self-confirming isolation, and in a world apart.
Autonomous and therefore utterly given over to the logic of persuasion,
logos dominates our psychological reality.[62]

A reading such as this contains unsuspected and possibly insuperable
difficulties. The first of these has to do with the status of deception. For
suppose that language, by virtue of its disjunction from reality, is systematically deceptive, that we are already deceived thanks to the linguistic
mediation of our experience (the fact that our experience is irremediably
colored by language).[63] What would second-order deception consist in,
and how would it differ from being existentially deceived?[64] The idea of
a second-order deception seems incoherent: there would be no baseline
from which to assess a condition like this. Nor is it clear why linguistic
deception should be fundamentally different in kind or degree from
the deception that comes with sensation in each of its five realms: the
deception lies in the gap between a faculty and its objects, not in the
faculty or in its objects taken by themselves. That is, deception ought to
be a matter not of language, but rather of embodiedness. And, by the way,
through what faculty does a subject take in *logos*? (More on this below.)

---

[61] Paragraph sections of *Helen* follow those in DK B11. Translations of the Gorgias material in what
follows are either from or after Gagarin and Woodruff 1995, 190–209, except for the quotations
from 82B3 (Sextus), which I have translated myself.

[62] See esp. Rosenmeyer 1955, 232–33; Segal 1962, 119–20.

[63] Segal 1962, 111–12; Kerferd 1981a, 81; Cole 1991, 148; see at nn. 120–25 below on Gorgias'
contemporaries for the same view.

[64] Though the perfect conflation of *logos*, deception, and persuasion is not strictly warranted by
Gorgias' writings, *Hel.* §11 does underscore the native weakness of the human mind, which dwells
constitutively in a state of *doxa* (belief). A crueler version of this position, which is one of radical
apatē, is given by Jean Baudrillard: "Art is everywhere, because artifice lies at the heart of reality"
(Baudrillard 1976, 117).

Such difficulties aside, there is the genuine problem that Gorgias' view of persuasion is, in itself and from all that can be gleaned about it from antiquity, glaringly unpersuasive. Gorgias' individual arguments in his best-preserved writings, including even those that concern persuasion, tend to unravel one another. And if he enjoyed a reputation in antiquity, it was not for the persuasiveness of his arguments, but for his cleverness and his ability to construct absurd but entertaining (or irritating) paradoxes – what was called his *paradoxologia.*[65]

This is nowhere truer than in the *Helen.* If the speech is a demonstration of the overwhelming powers of *logos*, it is a curiously self-defeating one. In it, Gorgias offers not one but four possible explanations for Helen's elopement with Paris. As in *On Not Being*, these are presented in a chain of concessive, disjunctive, and hypothetical arguments, and then negated (rather than refuted) each in turn, only to melt away in a dazzling if numbing blur that establishes nothing but the playfulness of Gorgias' own speech, which he calls a *paignion* – a "plaything," "diversion," or "amusement" – in the very last word of his discourse: "... Helen's encomium, and my amusement" (ἐμὸν δὲ παίγνιον) (§21). If anyone is persuaded by Gorgias' claims on behalf of persuasion, this will not be thanks to any power intrinsic to the speech itself. Gorgias' *Defense of Palamedes* fares little better. The speech cannot be heard without the knowledge that it, too, will fall miserably short of its hoped-for suasive end: Palamedes crucially *fails* to convince the audience he is addressing (against Odysseus' trumped up charges of treason), and he pays for this failure with his life. This is surely an ironic complication, and a part of what deserves to be called Gorgias' *dissuasive* strategy. Indeed, the gap between assertion and application in Gorgias is precisely one of the least analyzed features of his claims to persuasiveness, and their greatest barrier.

A second problem with the conventional view of Gorgias has to do with the way a contradiction in his own thinking is quietly smoothed off. It may be that language can convey nothing of what exists outside itself, but this is, properly speaking, a *limitation* on language. It points to a fundamental incapacity of *logos*, which is difficult to square with the theory of language as power put forward in the *Encomium of Helen.*[66] Language cannot, without further argument, be both autonomous (cut off from reality) and effective in the realm of persuasion. How does language

---

[65] Philostr. *VS* 492. See DK 82A1–5; 9; etc.
[66] Cf. Calogero 1977, 262–65. Newiger 1973, 183 likewise recognizes "the impotence" (*die Ohnmacht*) of *logos* in *On Not Being*.

impinge on a real, listening subject? The very means of linguistic efficacy are entirely uncertain on this theory. This is where Gorgias' alleged linguistic materialism is brought in to fill the void left by his theory. But it is precisely this void that cannot be filled by an appeal to the external world of matter – certainly not if *logos* is to remain an absolute "dynast" in its own realm. That is, *logos* requires the agency of the physical, non-linguistic world in order to have efficacy. But then it is no longer autonomous. Take away the "outside," and language vanishes too (just as the ways of being and appearance are mutually dependent, as he says in another fragment).[67] Linguistic materialism and linguistic autonomy cannot both be true without running into mutual contradiction.

Gorgias' claim that *logos* impinges quasi-physically upon a realm – the soul – that (presumably) is not constituted by language but is only "moulded" by it (τυποῦται, §15), flatly goes against the assumption of the autonomy of *logos*, which requires that language be cut off from everything that lies externally to it. It may be that Gorgias had two theories of language. Or perhaps he was confused. Alternatively, Gorgias' presumed theory of persuasion might be usefully viewed instead as the embodiment of a paradox. The theory cannot be about the self-containment of language without falling into either self-contradiction or self-conscious subversion. In other words, the theory cannot be true without being self-canceling.

To make matters worse, the view that language is autonomous of reality, "the creator of its own reality," becomes confused with an argument about aesthetic autonomy, and from there is made into a "literary principle," one that can be thought to anticipate Aristotle's own theory of literary and aesthetic autonomy – if only Aristotle held such a view (I doubt that he did).[68] Gorgias' *Helen*, for instance, can be said to be "a free imaginative creation ... consciously literary and artificial, without [any] sense of reality and immediacy."[69] So conceived, the speech is a

---

[67] "[Gorgias] says, 'Being is invisible if it lacks appearance, while appearance is strengthless if it lacks Being'" (τὸ μὲν εἶναι ἀφανὲς μὴ τυχὸν τοῦ δοκεῖν, τὸ δὲ δοκεῖν ἀσθενὲς μὴ τυχὸν τοῦ εἶναι; B26 = schol. Hes. *Op.* 760–64).

[68] Rosenmeyer 1955, 232; 233. The second quote is said of *apatē* (deception), but these are fused for Rosenmeyer, because *logos* just is *apatēlos* (deceptive) by virtue of its disconnection from reality. Cf. ibid., 231; and 237: "the word is its own master, and ... *apatē* is at the very heart of the dramatic [viz., literary] experience." For a few different reasons why autonomy fails to make sense of Aristotle and most other aesthetic theories, see p. 34 above. For the opposite view, see Ford 2002. For two critiques of autonomy along similar lines to mine, see Halliwell 2003 and Papaioannou 2003.

[69] Segal 1962, 119–20.

perfect playground for *logos*, which can be shown to act as "almost an independent external power which forces the hearer to do its will."[70] The *Helen*, even more so than the *Palamedes*, is thus taken to typify an exponential tendency of art at the end of the fifth century. According to this view, which is in some ways rationalistic and in others irrationalist, art gradually emancipates itself from extra-aesthetic dictates over the course of the fifth and into the fourth centuries, and, so to speak, discovers itself *as* art: literary production becomes literature, literary criticism becomes "an independent and distinct branch of knowledge," mimesis is enjoyed for its own sake, and the visual arts follow the same path.[71] As this view about the autonomy of art is one of the motivating sub-texts of the standard approaches to Gorgias' *logos*, all I wish to do for now is to flag this view about art and culture in order to mark it for discussion in the section on the cultural dimensions of Gorgias' critique below. Instead, let me make the simpler point that the thesis of aesthetic autonomy need not follow from any of Gorgias' extant writings, nor is it compatible with the thesis of linguistic autonomy. Gorgias' theory of aesthetics, in other words, can be shown to be fully engaged with questions of matter and experience without falling prey to a reductive and sterile thesis about aesthetic autonomy. As we shall see, his reflections on aesthetics are ultimately inquiries into the cultural pressures on experience and on the *lack* of autonomy from those surrounding pressures that experience can only ever display. But in order to see why this is so, we will need to explore more closely Gorgias' arguments about language, sensation, and communication.

As we saw, the problem of linguistic autonomy is crucially, but problematically, bound up with the problem of how language impinges physically and irresistibly on the mind and soul of the hearer. Given that this is so, we need to ask just how much of a materialist Gorgias was in his theory of language. His flirtation with linguistic materialism of a reductive and mechanical stamp is most pronounced in the central sections of the *Helen*. In fact, his thesis about the materialism of language is strikingly limited to this one speech. There are no traces of it in the *Palamedes*. And any hopes for such a view are cut off in the theory of language found in the pseudo-Aristotelian treatise that contains a synopsis, to an unknown degree of fidelity to the original, of Gorgias' treatise *On Nature, or On Not*

---

[70] Ibid., 121.
[71] Ford 2002, 22 (quotation); cf. ibid., 171. For a parallel argument about the visual arts, see most recently Tanner 2006.

Being (*De Melisso, Xenophane, Gorgia* [*MXG*]). The theory given there effectively isolates language from outer physical reality, rendering the two domains mutually opaque and mutually untranslatable: "Even if [things] were knowable," Gorgias is reported as saying, "how could someone express in words what he has seen? . . . Therefore, <if anything is knowable>, no one could make it evident to another *both because things* (τὰ πϱάγματα) *are not logoi* and because no one has the same thing in mind as another."[72] If things are not words, then presumably words are not things: they must be made of some unthinglike substance. A similar point about the chasm between things and our inner reality is made in the *Helen*: "*The things we see do not have the nature we would want them to have, but what each happens to have*" (§15), and this fact ought, in principle, to hold good for each of the senses and the imprints they leave on the mind.[73]

Can *logos* effectively and durably annul these imprints? Gorgias nowhere suggests they can. Physical compulsions like drugs or sight (*opsis*) enjoy an immediacy of effect that no amount of speech can alter. The constant appeals to an extra-linguistic realm, in the form of analogies (*logos* is like a drug, or like vision), do nothing to confirm the intrinsic power of *logos*; they only advertise the fact that we lack the words to describe what it is that *logos* "does." The question to ask, however, is not, What are the relevant analogies, but, What does *logos* in fact do? The answer typically given is that "*logos* persuades," but all that Gorgias gives us in his speech are a series of evasions rather than an answer to the question, let alone a persuasive argument about *logos*.

This is especially true of the *Helen*, which goes into considerable quasi-scientific detail, seeming to offer in its central sections (§§8–17), through sheer assertion, a theory of persuasion based on some kind of particle theory of matter and a theory of impressions. *Logos* carries out its effects either "by means of the smallest and least apparent (or 'most invisible') body" (σμιϰϱοτάτῳ σώματι ϰαὶ ἀφανεστάτῳ, §8). His most recent translators assure us that "Gorgias has a materialist theory of speech, derived perhaps from Empedocles."[74] Democritean atomism likewise

---

[72] *MXG* 980a21; 980b26; angle brackets restored to the translation; emphasis added.

[73] The language of imprinting is used in §17, though no other sense faculty is discussed *per se* in *Helen* apart from sight and hearing; but see below on *to ektos* in *On Not Being*, which includes senses like taste. In *Hel.* §17, sight is being addressed as the medium of the fourth cause of Helen's abduction – namely, love, which conventionally transmits its powers through the eyes.

[74] Gagarin and Woodruff 1995, 192, n. 188. Contrast MacDowell 1982, 36 (*ad Hel.* §8): "it is not safe to deduce from [what] may just be a figure of speech" "that [Gorgias] really believed that speech was a material substance."

springs to mind, and it too has been proposed as a model.[75] Unfortunately, the quoted phrase does not take us very far, and similar language can be used of macroscopic bodies in natural philosophical description (for instance, of pores, which would indeed match Empedoclean physics) and of other kinds of large-scale agencies in later medical writing (where such phraseology is used to describe unspecified causal agents acting on a body).[76] Most of the *Helen*, however, drifts off into a vaguer kind of physics, and pinning Gorgias' thought down to any particular framework is hard going.

No sooner are "invisible bodies" mentioned than they disappear from Gorgias' text, giving way to more visible bodies, only to hover somewhere between medicine, magic, and psychology. It is perhaps safest to say that Gorgias means to refer to no physicalist or materialist framework in particular, nor to exclude any either. Indeed, he seems to be willing to invoke, and to take on, all contenders, from poets to mythographers and rationalists of myth (§2), to natural scientists, speech-writers, and philosophers (§13). He indulges in a bit of medical wisdom (§14), optical physiology (§15), and psychology (§§16–17), and he knows something about painting and color theory (§18). Most of these references enjoy a strongly physical tint, and together the instances do suggest that materialism of some kind or other is their underlying feature, and an attraction. If so, what is striking is not so much any materialism of language that might be on display in one section of Gorgias' *Helen* (though not elsewhere in that work), but rather the generic, if somewhat noncommittal, materialism coursing through the various spheres of expertise that Gorgias wheels out in his defense of Helen.

In the catholicity of his thinking and his method (if we wish to call it this), Gorgias is fully symptomatic of his age. Nevertheless, even the allusion to invisible factors – a kind of watchword of contemporary science, always boastful of its capacity to penetrate beyond the visible

[75] See Cassin 1980, 95–103; cf. ibid. 506 *ad* 980a15; Mazzara 1984; Ford 2002, 161–87, who occasionally invokes Anaxagoras as well. For a strikingly close piece of atomistic doxography, see Phlp. *in Ph.* 25.7 (not in DK): ἀτόμους δὲ ἔλεγε [sc., Democritus (?)] σώματά τινα διὰ σμικρότητα ἀφανῆ καὶ ἀδιαίρετα.

[76] καὶ εἶναι πόρους ἀφανεῖς διὰ σμικρότητα δι' ὅλου τοῦ σώματος (Phlp. *in GC* 181.23; ἀφανὲς δ' ἐστὶ διὰ σμικρότητα (Gal. *De loc. aff.* 8.28.14 K); see also next note. Further parallels in the Hippocratic writings (esp. *Flat.*) are given by Jouanna 2003, 13–17, which indicate how symptomatic of the age Gorgias' language is, without establishing any substantive or dogmatic allegiances. Further, Dion. Hal. *Isoc.* 1: "Isocrates took [the study of oratory] over from [Gorgias, Protagoras, and their associates] and was the first to set it on a new course, turning away from treatises on dialectic and natural philosophy (τῶν φυσικῶν) and concentrating on writing political discourses," etc. (trans. Usher).

into the unseen – is probably best taken as a mark of Gorgias' claiming (or rather, pretending) to be up to the minute and on the cutting edge of contemporary science.[77] If the role played by magic in his speech stands out in curious contrast to the appeals to scientificity, there are a few possible explanations available. The appeal to the invisible is as much a leap of faith as it is a badge of rationalism: Gorgias could be parodying rather than endorsing the hyperconfidence of science.[78] Alternatively, magic could be a genuine sign of his recalcitrance towards the spirit of late fifth-century rationalism. Or, finally, Gorgias' stance could reflect the fact that magic and rationalism coexisted, however oddly to us, in late fifth-century minds.[79] Whatever the case, materialism was a strong methodological attractor at the time, and the *Helen* seems to be a collecting point for materialist discourses put into the service of rhetoric and aesthetics, however unstable the combination of rational and irrational factors Gorgias' resulting synthesis may have been. And Helen, the exemplar of aesthetic seduction and beauty *par excellence*, is the product and symptom of this synthesis.[80]

Helen, *or, what is not (but erotically is)*

How much of a body is required to produce a seduction? Evidently only "the smallest and least visible body." Perhaps Gorgias is a minimalist materialist, to the extent that he is a materialist at all. In ways, seduction has everything to do with the body – for instance, Helen's: "With *one body* she brought together *many bodies* (ἐνὶ δὲ σώματι πολλὰ σώματα συνήγαγεν) full of great ambition for great deeds; some had abundant wealth, some the glory of an old noble lineage, some the vigor of personal valor, and some the power of acquired wisdom" (§4), all properties which are not Helen's, but which she attracts to her person. Gorgias is of course reversing the habitual one/many cliché that attaches to Helen from

---

[77] Cf. "Appearances (phenomena) are the sight of things unseen" (Anaxagoras, DK 59B21a; Democritus, DK 68A111); Hippoc. *Vict.* 11.1; *Flat.* 3.3; Gorg. *Hel.* §13: "astronomers [or possibly 'natural philosophers'] made the invisible apparent to the eyes of opinion" (τὰ ... ἄδηλα φαίνεσθαι τοῖς τῆς δόξης ὄμμασιν ἐποίησαν); Eur. (incert.) *TrGF* 5.2.913, a blistering critque of the same profession put in the mouth of an unknown character: "Beholding these things, who is not conscious of god? Who does not cast far from him the deceitful wiles of the star-gazers (μετεωρολόγων), whose mischievous tongues, void of sense, babble at random of matters unkown (περὶ τῶν ἀφανῶν)?" (trans. Guthrie 1971, 233).

[78] Even Democritus could waver about truth in "the depths," and was later taken for a skeptic rather than a dogmatist about reality (and sometimes still is). See Barnes 1982, 559–64.

[79] See Lloyd 1979, 99 on this precise point; and *passim*. Further, Collins 2003.

[80] See Porter 1993, 274–75.

Homer onwards.[81] But it pays to take heed of the peculiarly abstract qualities of Gorgias' language, its immediate echoes in his own speech, and its possible resonances with his other writings.

We may begin by asking the question, how *visible* is Helen's "one body"? The echoes with the psychagogic "body" of *logos* (σώματι, §6) are striking, and these set up the obvious expectation that Helen should be something like an emblem or analogue for Gorgias' own art of *logos*, and consequently for his speech and *its* seductions, the *Helen*. But if so, then the question of visibility regarding both Helen and *logos* suddenly becomes rather complex. At one level, Helen has the exact status of the iconic, painterly and "composite" image depicted in §18: "Whenever painters perfectly create a *single body and shape from many colors and bodies* (ἐκ πολλῶν χρωμάτων καὶ σωμάτων ἕν σῶμα), they delight the sight." As earlier, in §4, Gorgias presents the image of an attractive "single body," one that (here) is manifestly made up, whether of body parts, as in the famous parable about the painter Zeuxis combining the features of the five most beautiful women of Croton in order to render his *Helen*,[82] or of paint pigments, said by Empedocles to produce a deceptive appearance (ἀπάτη).[83] Both images (Helen and the painter's icon) furnish visual delight; both can be seductive and pleasurable (but also painful [§18] or painfully pleasurable [§9]); both embody a kind of unrivaled and irresistible perfection; both resemble the illusions of rhetoric,[84] but also those of poetry.[85] Images (εἰκόνας) engraved in the mind are the explicit topic of the fourth "cause" (§§15–19), whose aim is to acquit Helen of any guilt entailed by an erotic, visual compulsion beyond her powers of control (Alexander's "body" overpowering her "eye" [§19]). But we have already heard about Helen's irresistible powers of attraction, and there is no way to dissociate the painter's construction of a delightful body from the powers of Helen's own image, which is to say, her own multiply

---

[81] *Od.* 11.438; 14.69; Aesch. *Ag.* 62; 1456.

[82] Jex-Blake 1896, lxi–ii; Reinach 1921, §§214–23. An ideal of female beauty, Zeuxis' Helen is thus virtually a Platonic Form *avant la lettre*.

[83] DK 31B23.9. See Ch. 3, §4 above. For a later echo (one of many), see Lucian, *Dom.* 21, where "colors, shapes, and place" enjoy the double connotations of painting and of rhetorical embellishment (Goldhill 2001a, 165); but so too does the very verb for composition: "You see the difficulty of the challenge, to put together (συστήσασθαι) so many images (εἰκόνας) without colour, form, or space" (χρωμάτων καὶ σχημάτων καὶ τόπου) (trans. Harmon, adapted) – where in question is again a verbal ecphrasis underlain (quite possibly) by no visual referent at all.

[84] Cf. Pl. *Soph.* 234c; *Rep.* 9.586b–c.

[85] Cf. *Hel.* §§8–9; Aesch. *Ag.* 242.

constructed, multiply imagined, worshipful body (she too is an *agalma*, an *eikōn*, or else an *eidōlon*).[86]

If visual images produce desire (πόθον ἐνεργάζεται) and the desire of – or just *for* – desire (προθυμία ... ἔρωτος) in the mind of the beholder (§19), the image of Helen worked this very effect on whoever beheld her (ἐπιθυμίας ἔρωτος ἐνειργάσατο, §4).[87] There is thus a fundamental confusion of agency at work in Gorgias' *Helen*: the seduced is at the same time the seducer. But even more devastatingly, in dissolving Helen's agency, Gorgias also dissolves her consistency: she first becomes an image, and then a mere collection of elements. As she dissolves into a welter of parts, so too does the speech that produces and contains her – and that simultaneously fails to contain her, so manifold and inconsistent an entity is she. Dematerialized as an ideal projection, she rematerializes as a construction of, as it were, "smallest and least visible bodies," whether these are sculptural, painterly, or the elements of *logos*, which is itself now threatening to come apart. Which version of Helen exerts the greater attraction, or rather *fascination*, on her audience: Helen, her iconic image (or images), or the *Helen*?

As a composite figure, literally as a product of poetic and material making and construction (ποίησις and ἐργασία, §18), Helen is, at another level, not what she is, but both more and less. She is bound up with the logic of the one and the many, but elusively so. Like the Helen of *Odyssey* Book 4 who assumes multiple identities, mouthing the words and miming the voices of every woman belonging to the men crouched within the Trojan horse, Gorgias' Helen, if she is anything at all, represents something for everyone. As a figure of desire, Helen is also a figure of projection; she (or the tradition that embodies her) may be nothing more than the sum of her projected identifications in literature, myth, and cult.[88] Accordingly, Helen, as she appears in Gorgias' speech, is not a stable identity. She is viewed, instead, as a series of superimposed layerings of a historical and poetic tradition, like the plaster that Euripides' Helen

---

[86] Cf. Eur. *Hel.* 34, where Helen's *eidōlon* is the result of one such *sunthesis* (ξυνθεῖσα).

[87] Indeed, the two passages are mirror images of each other: πολλὰ δὲ πολλοῖς πολλῶν ἔρωτα καὶ πόθον ἐνεργάζεται πραγμάτων καὶ σωμάτων (§18); πλείστας δὲ πλείστοις ἐπιθυμίας ἔρωτος ἐνειργάσατο (§4). Cf. the further parallels between §18 and §§8–9: ποίησις/ποίησιν; ποθεῖν/πόθος; λυπεῖν/λύπην; χρωμάτων καὶ σωμάτων/πραγμάτων καὶ σωμάτων.

[88] The erotic, bewitching effects of Helen's speech or her association with *pharmaka* are likewise a traditional facet of her personality since Homer (cf. esp. *Od.* 4, but also *Il.* 3: her capacity to "name"), which Gorgias does not suppress so much as he quietly alludes to these things, by appropriating them to *logos* as an analogue for the *Helen*/Helen herself.

would like, impossibly, to have now removed from her comely face (ἐξαλειφθεῖσ' ὡς ἄγαλμα) – which is the face of a phantom.[89]

Helen in Gorgias' *Helen* is nothing more than a phantom-object upon which have been inscribed traits that tell us more about their source than about her, much like the alternative mythological tradition, known from Stesichorus and Herodotus, that Helen never went to Troy because only her image (her *eidōlon*) did.[90] Helen, in other words, is a figure for something that is not. More like void than a body, Helen is more like Not Being than Being. So viewed, the status of her materiality cannot but fall prey to suspicion: she seems less a figure for matter than a figure for the seductive attractions *of* matter ("with one body she brought together many bodies"), whether its appearances (as an image without substance), or whatever else it has to offer. To possess Helen is to materialize an insubstantial desire (as the object of a *pothos*). A quick side-glance at Gorgias' other fragments will help bear out the suspicion that he is playing with the concept of matter and its discursive limits in a philosophical sense, both here in the *Helen* and in his other writings, with one important difference: in the *Helen*, he is *eroticizing* those meanings.

Logos *without* aisthēsis

We can make some sense of Helen's status – her odd (lack of) identity – in terms of Gorgias' views about Parmenidean logic. Indeed, it can be understood as the ultimate consequence of Gorgias' *On Not Being*, which argues that (a) if anything is, it is nothing; (b) if something were, it would be unknowable; (c) if it were knowable, it could not be made manifest to others (because *logos* exists in its own sphere and cannot communicate reality). From this argument it is usually concluded that all language, just by functioning autonomously and inventively (by creating its own realities), must be deceptive to the core. But restore Gorgias' conception in all of its radical stringency, and not only must we imagine how *logos* screens us from the world in a massive veil of ignorance, which would be tantamount to a Heraclitean or Parmenidean nightmare;[91] we have to imagine something far more insidious, and possibly unimaginable: a *logos* that is without echo or resonance, without access to its audience, without

---

[89] Eur. *Hel.* 262.
[90] See Porter 1993, 277–80.
[91] See Rosenmeyer 1955, 229, for the parallel with Heraclitus, and see below at n. 150; Verdenius 1981, 127, for the parallel with Parmenides.

persuasive effect, utterly lacking a corresponding physiology or psychology, but which simply exists in the realm of its own literal "tautology":
λέγει ὁ λέγων, "the speaker speaks."[92] The speaker speaks, perhaps – but
then speaking takes place in isolation from any contents that can be
specified, let alone revealed. For nothing guarantees that the same thing
will appear alike to different people or be thought in the same way, and
everything suggests that it won't.[93] "So that scarcely would anyone [else]
perceive the same thing as another," and "no one has in mind (ἐννοεῖ)
the same thing as anyone else."[94] Nothing guarantees the identity of
mental representation across the gap between two individuals, and least
of all (it would follow) *logos*, which is not equivalent to, nor yet clearly
commensurable with, that representation either. In principle, communicating inner states will be just as problematical as conveying information
about the "outside." It is not even clear that the speaker can communicate
what he has to say *to himself*, never mind to others. The speaker is mute,
the communicant deaf.

The questionable nature of communication on this outlandish theory is
partly captured by Calogero's observation that in Gorgias' *On Not Being*,
"the identification, or essential coincidence, between verbal content and
cognitive content does not hold good, because concrete and immediate
sensible experience is one thing, and the *logos* with which one attempts to
designate and to express this experience is quite another."[95] At issue is the
speaker's *control* over what is spoken (the "*incapacità* espressiva"),[96] but
also the logical identity of *logos*, which would have the status of a parodic
counter to Parmenidean monism (which likewise calls for the absolute
autonomy of Being, but, Gorgias felt, with disastrous results).[97] Grant
absolute autonomy to *logos*, and you end up with a *logos* that has to be

---

[92] *MXG* 980b3–4.

[93] Cf. *MXG* 980b11–14, answering the question in b9, "But how will the hearer have in mind the same
thing [as the speaker]?": "Even if in fact the same thing were in many persons [at the same time],
there is no reason why it should appear the same to them" (οὐδὲν κωλύει μὴ ὅμοιον φαίνεσθαι
αὐτοῖς) – more literally, "nothing prevents it from appearing differently to [each of] them."
Cf. Aristotle, who has learned this lesson well: "for things do not appear either the same to all men
or always the same to the same men" (*Metaph.* Γ 6.1011a31–32).

[94] *MXG* 980b16–17; b19; cf. b9 (quoted in the foregoing note).

[95] Calogero 1977, 255; cf. also Cassin 1980, 551–52.

[96] Calogero 1977, 254, 259.

[97] Gorgias can, in other words, and perhaps should be associated with an "ultra-Parmenideanism"
(Guthrie 1971, 196) gone purposely askew. Cf. Cassin 1980, 67–68, who however goes to an
extreme in reductionism (ibid., 98). Alternatively, Gorgias is not countering Parmenidean logic,
but is reenacting Parmenides' antilogies of reason (on which, see Mackenzie 1982). Gorgias did not
invent this kind of parasitical argument; see Cherniss 1970, 22–27.

severed from its materializations (Calogero calls this an "objective λόγος"), one that cannot be heard or seen, and only doubtfully can make itself understood even to one's self.[98]

The claim from *Helen* about the colorful (aesthetic) features of poetic *logos* stands in a different light now ("I call poetry *logos* that has meter," §9), as does the claim about persuasion, which is something "super-added to *logos*" (§13), much like the "reasoning" (*logismos*) that Gorgias wants to bring to the "discussion" or "debate" (*logos*) of Helen's guilt (§2).[99] In each of these cases, there is *logos*, and then there is something else. These "something else's," I want to suggest, are equivalent to the various manifestations – phenomenalizations and materializations – of *logos*. Finally, to take the least obvious but most celebrated case of all, strictly speaking, *logos* cannot, on this view, be reducible to the σῶμα (body) it activates, either as its instrument or its locus: it achieves its effects *by means of* or perhaps *in* the smallest body (σμικροτάτῳ σώματι ... ἔργα ἀποτελεῖ), without being identical with its instrument or its place of activity. *Logos*, in other words, seems to have an identity all its own prior to any of these colorations or additions. But then, what is *logos*? Stripped bare of its materializations, *logos* will never be equivalent to its effects, its contents, its form, its sensible attributes, and the rest, but instead will occupy the place of some unknown and unknowable object, one that goes beyond comprehension or even imagination. As Kerferd writes, "Unfortunately no account survives of how Gorgias supposed the transition occurs from sense-impression to related λόγος" – or, it must be added, *back again*, from language to sensible or psychic impressions.[100] And with no route mapped either way, persuasion and *psuchagōgia* cannot come about.

Thus, paradoxically, instead of locating linguistic autonomy in some comprehensible way, the link with persuasion opens up the question of its status all over again. More than that, posing the question of *logos* in the way that Gorgias does puts the problems of matter and experience in an interesting and urgent light. What does it really mean to call language self-contained? We can begin by considering what Gorgias may have

---

[98] Calogero 1977, 258. See Mansfeld 1985a, 256 and Mourelatos 1987, 138, 150 for different views on the problem of self-communication raised by Gorgias.

[99] §2: ἐγὼ δὲ βούλομαι λογισμόν τινα τῷ λόγῳ δούς; cf. §13: "persuasion, *when added to* [or: 'when it comes towards'] *speech*" (ἡ πειθὼ προσιοῦσα [AX : προσοῦσα, Blass] τῷ λόγῳ). This "confusion" caused Guthrie 1971, 50, more honest here than most, to postulate *two* "forces" acting on Helen, speech and persuasion.

[100] Kerferd 1985, 605.

meant by it, starting with an excerpt from the report of *On Not Being*
given by Sextus Empiricus: "For that by which we reveal [our thoughts] is
logos, but *logos* isn't the underlying realities and beings; therefore, we don't
reveal to our fellow creatures what is, but [only] *logos*, which is different
from the underlying realities."[101] *Logos* travels in its own circuit, without
touching the ground, so to speak. This is not because *logos* is incommensurable with all that is foreign to itself, whether we designate this foreign
world with "non-linguistic reality" (thus creating the impression of some
autonomous linguistic reality, the validity of which I am contesting)
or whether we designate it with the sensible world that lies "outside"
language, as is sometimes assumed on the basis of the two reports of *On
Not Being*, and especially that by Sextus, where the phrase "the outside"
(*to ektos*) originates.[102] The first reading is simply wrong, while the second
reading stands in need of qualifications (see below). On the contrary,
Gorgias is thinking along early Presocratic lines here. His claim, accordingly, is that given a world endowed with true Being, conceived as
underlying *both* language and sensation, *logos* would be incommensurable
with this underlying reality. Hence, on this assumption, "things (*pragmata*)
would be unknowable by us."[103]

But Gorgias is not content to let things stand there. His position is not
just that language is out of touch with a reality it cannot even reflect.
It is that all objects in the world are utterly incommensurate with their
perception in any form whatsoever, because our sensory contact with the
world is forever divided by the complexity of sensation: "The same person
plainly *does not perceive things which* [appear] *the same for himself at a given*
[self-same] *moment, but* [only] *things which are different for the ear and
the eye,* [and these same things are perceived] differently both now and
earlier."[104] Objects can never be "known" in some stable way for the
selfsame subject, either by way of sensation or through thought: what one
perceives is divided by the senses into competing sense data (objects as
seen cannot be matched up with the same objects as heard), nor can they
seemingly enter into the stream of thought (never mind the complexities

---

[101] DK 82B3 (84) = Sext. Emp. *Math.* 7.84.
[102] DK 82B3 (85) = Sext. Emp. *Math.* 7.85.
[103] *MXG* 980a18. The fuller context reads: "if just as what we see is not the more because we see it, so
     also what we think is not the more for that (and, were it otherwise, just as in the one case our
     objects of vision would often be just the same, so in the other our objects of thought would often
     be just the same) ... but of which kind the true things are is uncertain. So that even if things are,
     they would be unknowable by us" (ibid., 980a12–19; trans. Loveday and Forster).
[104] *MXG* 980b14–15.

of perception and thought over time). When these results are applied to language, the results are again disastrous.

The results of these musings cohere well with Calogero's observation, which was quoted above, that for Gorgias there is no intrinsic or necessary correlation in *logos* between verbal content (presumably, meaning) and cognitive content (thought). Calogero fails to draw out the implications of Gorgias' position, which has not been entirely correctly stated by him. *Logos* is not only the referring and the expression; it is also the expressed, both *qua* sound and *qua* meaning.[105] Therefore, and what is worse, there can be no intrinsic or necessary correlation between "the concrete and immediate sensible experience" of language itself and "the *logos* with which referring and expression are attempted." These sundry aspects of *logos* are not just joined by an arbitrary link; they point to a radical gap between *logos* and its own contents. This is where the autonomy thesis and its implications finally meet: if *logos* (as defined according to Gorgias' strictest prescriptions) cannot communicate the contents of an outer reality, it is not just because the two realities are incommensurable, as is standardly assumed, but because *logos can only fail to communicate the inner reality of logos, its very own contents*, since in the final analysis *logos* has no measurable relationship either to its own material expression (its outer distortion) or to its undistorted intentional reflex (whatever that might be). The *logos* that exists prior to its attributes – a so-called "objective" *logos*, a *logos* that is literally lacking all aesthetic attributes – is the only *logos* that can be said to function autonomously. But its very idea is manifestly incoherent.[106] Gorgias' analysis would appear to invite this rigorous isolation of *logos* from its contents in order to provoke the paradox that we have just reached, and the incoherencies that ensue from it. In a word, *logos*, left to itself, is a cul-de-sac.

It is tempting to see in Gorgias' *logos* an implied commentary on the implausibility and inconceivability, not to say incommunicability, of Parmenidean Being, the consequences of which Parmenides either sought to evade or else knew but failed, in Gorgias' eyes, to expose sufficiently in all its painful *aporia*. If so, then Gorgias is in a sense merely closing the

---

[105] Sound: "For just as vision does not recognize sounds, so hearing does not hear colors, but sounds (φθόγγους); and he who speaks, speaks, but does not speak a color or a thing" (*MXG* 980b1–3). Meaning: "for it is not at all <sound> or color [or any phenomenal object] but *logos* that is communicated, with the result that it is not possible to think color, but [only] to see [it], nor [to think] noise (ψόφον), but [only] to hear [it]" (*MXG* 980b6–8; text of Wilson 1893, 38, on which see Newiger 1973, 152 and 153 n. 13).

[106] The term "objective *logos*" is Calogero's (see above at n. 98).

gap that Parmenides had already opened by inviting speculation on the relation between truth and persuasion (for the true way of Being is that of Persuasion, Πειθώ, who "attends upon" Truth[107]), which in turn opens a provocative gap between conceptuality and conceivability.[108] *Logos* is situated somewhere in their midst, a troubling, nagging *question* mark, like Helen.

The seductions of sensation: logos with aisthēsis

It ought to be evident that language is not Gorgias' sole preoccupation, nor is accounting for its capacities necessarily his primary objective either. The remains of his theory of language from *On Not Being* point unanimously to the limitations of language, not to its powers. There, Gorgias repeatedly shows how language is circumscribed by the spheres of sensation; not a word is said about the powers of language within its own domain. There is even a hint, in Sextus' version, that language can be the passive recipient of outer sensations, and therefore is emphatically not cut off from them, though Gorgias' language is so vague (at least in the way it is reported) that perhaps we had better restrict ourselves to the more modest assertion that *logos* is somehow susceptible of an outer determination, while the exact mechanism by which this occurs is nowhere spelled out:

Logos is composed (συνίσταται) of things that strike us from the outside (ἀπὸ τῶν ἔξωθεν προσπιπτόντων ἡμῖν πραγμάτων), that is, from things perceived (τῶν αἰσθητῶν). From the incursion (ἐγκυρήσεως) of [sensation] there arises within us (ἐγγίνεται ἡμῖν) the *logos* [i.e., the expression] that concerns this quality (ὁ κατὰ τῆς ποιότητος ἐκφερόμενος λόγος).[109] If this is so, then *logos* is not exhibitory (παραστατικός) of [i.e., does not display, make manifest] the outside; the outside is revelatory (μηνυτικόν) of *logos*.[110]

---

[107] Parmenides DK 28B2.4, cf. B1.29–30.

[108] In Parmenides, four aspects of Being are enumerated (compulsion, fate, justice, and persuasion); the fact of their seductiveness (*eros*) is implied (cf. Mourelatos 1970, 160–63). These features are repeated in distorted form in Gorgias.

[109] The examples given are juice, viz., taste (χυλός), and color, which I have generalized both for the sake of the argument and for clarity. In the case of color, the word used for "incursion" is ὑπόπτωσις.

[110] DK 82B3 (85) = Sext. Emp. *Math.* 7.85. Because this admission appears to undermine Gorgias' earlier claims about the absolute insulation of *logos* from outer *pragmata*, one has to ask whether Sextus is acting as a reliable witness here. Calogero 1977, 260, who raises this question, concludes that the passage contains "a remnant and deformed fragment" of Gorgias' thought, specifically from the second argument in *On Not Being*. (Similarly, Newiger 1973, 167.) There are, however,

Our words gesture vaguely towards their objects without being able to deliver truth claims about them: the statement that "*logos* is not exhibitory of the outside" rules out the latter possibility definitively. Just so, the process by which words come into existence is left half-lit by Gorgias' description. But we can say this much: *logoi* arise as a result of (which is to say, are caused by) incursions from the outside, whether from tastes or colors or other sensations.[111] For the causal connection to occur, there has to be a physical communication between things and *logoi*. If *logos* is susceptible to physical external pressures, that is because it is itself a physical structure. And yet what the example teaches us once again is that it is *sensation* that dominates language by setting limits to it, not the other way round.

The speech on Helen only confirms this thesis, though the speech is typically looked at from the wrong end, that is to say, from the perspective of language and its supposed potency.[112] There, for example, *logos* is not so much incommensurable with what lies "outside" as it is powerless before the realm of the body and its attendant sensations (§§15–17):

Through sight (δι' ὄψεως) the soul (ἡ ψυχή) is moulded (τυποῦται) even in its character (τοῖς τρόποις) .... Some indeed, who have seen fearful things, have lost their present purpose [or else: "thought" or "mind" (φρονήματος)] in the present moment, so thoroughly does fear extinguish (ἀπέσβεσε) and expel thought (τὸ νόημα) .... In this way sight engraves (ἐνέγραψεν) upon the mind (ἐν τῷ φρονήματι) images (εἰκόνας) of things that are seen.

no signs whatsoever that Sextus is tampering with Gorgias' testimony: the report seems to be straightforward in nature, not designed to entangle Gorgias in self-contradictions or incoherences. Since this is so, the burden is on our getting all of the report to cohere as best we can before we go looking for interference. The challenge that Gorgias' admission presents is less difficult than one might imagine. For starters, the claim in the preceding sentence (84) that "*logos* is different from the underlying realities" (λόγος ... ἕτερος ἐστι τῶν ὑποκειμένων) should not be understood to mean "irreducibly different," nor in general should *logos* be thought of as radically other than the outer world of objects: there are a variety of ways to effect a *rapprochement* between *logos* and *pragmata*. Thus, David Sedley suggests (*per litt.*) that συνίσταται ἀπό "expresses causal, not constitutive, origin, 'gets its structure/content from'" (contrast Calogero 1977, 256: "costituito"). This would block the possibility of a reductive identity of language and things, while also leaving open the likelihood that *logos* is impacted in a directly physical way by outer things. See further Newiger 1973, 164–70 (who mistranslates the μηνυτικόν clause). Contrast Mourelatos 1987, 160–62, who invokes a stimulus-response model that, however, skirts half of the issue by assuming the closed circuit of a linguistic context: the stimulus he assumes is the utterance "sweet!" after tasting honey, not the taste itself (*pace* Sextus' own testimony). Even so, on this rendering the word is a heard thing, which brings us back to *logos* as a *pragma* again.
[111] Obviously, *logoi* are not made up of juice and color molecules, so they presumably reflect the change in their own structure, whatever that consists of.
[112] Even Calogero (Calogero 1977, 264) subscribes to this view.

Logos is less cut off from "things" (*pragmata*), as one might expect it to be on the autonomy thesis, than it is helplessly *vulnerable* to them, being itself a thing, and a minority member of their class at that.[113] Overwhelmed by outer reality as it is, *logos* (implicit in the rational elements of "purpose" and "thought" above) is in no condition to communicate what it "sees," or rather transmits. We might say that upon such jarring exposures to material reality as these, *logos* is incapable of expressing, commensurably, what the mind and body feel. But that is, I want to suggest, because *logos* is itself not qualitatively different in make-up from those sources of feeling.

Consequently, *logos* in such cases is not turned into another sensory faculty of sorts, as one commentator suggests, utilizing the desperate image of a "language-pore"(!).[114] Instead, it becomes another sensible object, one more *pragma* among others, perhaps (to use the language from Sextus) "made up" of outer objects, or (in our own language) contingent upon them, causally and otherwise, and communicating with them. As such, *logos* is susceptible to pressures from without – and here, Gorgias is no longer likening *logos* to the featureless Not Being of Parmenides (*logos* without *aisthēsis*), but to its phenomenally rich counterpart, the world of Being, of material appearances, and of *doxa* (*logos* as dependent upon *aisthēsis*). The mind's rational features, when they are "blinded" by sensation, are said to be "driven out" before the invasion of outer *pragmata*. In such a state (which is one of panic), *logos* is no longer causally operative, and so it ceases to be a factor at all. It thereby approaches the impotence of *logos* in *On Not Being*, but for the opposite reasons now.

This insight into the psychological sections of the treatise has implications for how we read the treatise as a whole. On any reading of the *Helen*, one would have to agree that describing *pragmata* and their appearances – colors, shapes, beautiful or frightful objects – is often of as much interest to Gorgias as are the effects of *logos*. But if I am right that language becomes describable only to the extent that it has become in its own way a kind of *pragma*, then we would have to say that the *whole* of the *Helen* is taken up with the description of *pragmata*, of which *logos* just happens to be one instance. And so, rather than putting the accent on the psychology of *logos*, as is the norm in studies of Gorgias' *Helen*, one ought to focus

---

[113] This is not contradicted by the statement that "things (*pragmata*) are not *logoi*" in *MXG* 980b 18–19: they obviously are not. Both are kinds of *pragma*, just in different ways, and at times in the same way (see also Newiger 1973, 165).

[114] "*Sprachpore*" (Buchheim 1989, xviii; cf. xii).

instead on the *sensations* that *logos* gives rise to – or else transmits from the outer, physical world – while also simply recognizing that for much of the treatise Gorgias is not talking about *logos* at all, but rather about the world of the senses. In Gorgias' eyes, *language is a sensory realm* while *sensation just is its very own seduction.*[115] Even if this does not warrant calling Gorgias a "pragmatist," it does make him into a kind of radical empiricist.

Gorgias, after all, is as curious about the empirical world of the senses as he is keen to invest *logos* with all the traits of seductive sensuousness: meter, rhythm, the eponymously named "Gorgianic figures" for which he was famous in antiquity (more on these below), intricate formal organization, or *taxis* (§14), and elaborate formal workmanship, or *ergasia* (§18). And he is as keen to pursue all these, whether in the name of momentary diversion or provocative pleasure, as he is eager to demystify the workings of *logos* and to pull the rug out from under his façade of illusionism. He does this latter spectacularly by admitting that his pretenses are merely a "game," but this is only the crowning blow in a long list of insults to the pretense of illusionism, which collectively make up the sum and substance of his speech. Perhaps Plato was not far off after all when he said of rhetoricians that they "bewitch" (γοητεύειν) the ears of their audiences, "rendering things said about everything into mere *phantoms* (εἴδωλα), and so making it appear that it is the truth they are telling."[116] In one sense, rhetoricians produce "phantoms" simply by distorting truth. In another, they produce phantoms by reproducing false images of reality itself. In that sense, they are like painters and other artists.[117] But rhetoricians can be understood to create phantoms in a further sense, insofar as they create *an enhanced world of sensations,* one that echoes the empirical world of experience but also acts as its embellished doublet. Rhetoric here works to intensify the effects or simply to extend the reach of sensible reality just by reverberating its images and sensations both in and through language. In Plato's eyes, rhetoric is guilty of "copying" sense data for consumption by the ears and the imagination much the way an artist is guilty of copying the colors, shapes, and forms of empirical objects. Gorgias would have to confess to being guilty on this score – not of illusionism and deception *per se*, nor even of persuasion, but rather of a kind of seduction by virtue of extending the reach of sensation available to his audience. Gorgias' greatest weapon, on this view, is that he can divert

[115] See also Buchheim 1989, 198–99 on the general role of seduction in Gorgias.
[116] Pl. *Soph.* 234c5–6.
[117] Pl. *Soph.* 233e–235a; cf. *Rep.* 10.596d–e. Cf. Cornford 1957, 195.

his hearers' minds and souls – which is to say, can cause them to be detained and absorbed in the play of surfaces that his language is both made of and projects in turn.

The cultural dimensions of Gorgias' critique

In manipulating language, Gorgias is doing little more than manipulating cultural signs. If so, then he is advertising one further aspect of the materialism of language: its materiality as a cultural practice. Culture is itself an unstable blend of inner and outer sensations, of fantasies, facts, and fictions, of physical objects, of structures of language that can be inward and inaccessible or outer and sensible, which is to say part of *to ektos* (the external world) and equivalent to any other physical sensation. But in no way is language an all-dominant force, nor do the seductions of culture have any obvious single agency that can be "blamed." Above we saw how for Gorgias to live in a world informed by language, which means to inhabit culture and its conventions, is to be deceived. Simply to use language is to participate in this deception. Gorgias' *bon mot* about deception, typically taken to apply only to tragedy, has a much broader reach that is relevant to linguistic and cultural deceptions alike: "The deceiver is more just than the one who fails to deceive, and the one who is deceived is wiser than one who fails to be deceived."[118] The continuation of the text, which is supplied by Plutarch but could easily be Gorgianic, runs: "For whatever is not stupid [or "insensible," τὸ μὴ ἀναίσθητον] is easily enthralled [or "easily ensnared," εὐάλωτον] by the pleasures of discourse" (ὑφ' ἡδονῆς λόγων). Pleasure, in other words, is what permits communication across sensory divides to take place; it effectively *short-circuits* reason and acts as the conduit for communication in lieu of rationality.[119] The sensible phenomenon of language is one of the many ways in which cultures organize their pleasures.

    Gorgias' view was not an aberration in its day, nor was it merely an expression of sophistic cleverness. On the contrary, his view about the predominantly deceived condition of human nature was gaining currency in the fifth century as a considered view about the nature of human communication across any medium whatsoever, from language to painting to plastic art. When asked why he deceived everyone but the Thessalians, Simonides' reply, at least apocryphally, was similar to

---

[118] DK 82B23 = Plut. *Mor.* 348c = *Mor.* 15D (part).
[119] In this respect, pleasure is analogous to, but the obverse of, pain, as described in *Hel.* §§15–17.

Gorgias': "Because they are too stupid (ἀμαθέστεροι) to be deceived by me."[120] (Simonides is also reported to have written that "appearance does violence even to truth," that is, it "overwhelms truth with its compulsions."[121]) The author of the *Dissoi Logoi* made similar assertions about painting: "In tragedy and in painting, whoever deceives most ... is best."[122] And Aeschylean dramaturgy was associated with deception by the end of the fifth century.[123] Conventionalist (*nomos*-based) theories of language, such as those held by Anaxagoras, Empedocles, and Democritus, were strictly entailed by the view that the human cognition of reality is false: language is the codification of this deep-seated error.[124] Even Plato would agree: to be deceived just is the nature of human consciousness, at least in its unenlightened state. The view had a good Parmenidean pedigree.[125] On this point, materialists and their opponents could concur: language, deception, and sensation tended to go hand in hand. Their only difference lay in how they were willing to characterize the nature of revealed truth, and its points of entry.

To assume that *logos* names something above and beyond this fundamentally constitutive state of mind is to enter into a new level of mystification, but it is not to exit from the "vicious" circle of deception. The pretense that *logos* can point beyond deception to a condition in which one can exercise control over deception is one of the many lures and traps held out by Gorgias' writing. We should try instead to view Gorgias' speech as I think he would have us view it, namely as a microcosm of the conditions of knowing, opining, and desiring, which is to say, as a model of the power that is promised but not necessarily granted by cultural habits and assumptions. *Logos* can no more be grasped or controlled than can the cultural coordinates that may turn out to define its position. Positioned as much as positioning, communication will always bear the signs of its imperfectness (just as *logos* is "conditioned," συνίσταται, by what it is not, which is to say, by external sensibilia,

---

[120] Plut. *Mor.* 15D. The proximity and similarity of the two sayings has led some scholars, such as Wilamowitz-Moellendorff 1913, 143 n. 3, to assign both to Gorgias. Further, Carson 1999, 48–52.

[121] Fr. 598 *PMG*.

[122] *Dialex.* 3.10.

[123] Ar. *Ran.* 909–10.

[124] See Kahn 1973, 154–55. As a rule, *doxa* needn't be the product of *logos*. It can be the product of a false belief about the world, based on sensation and perception generally, as in Parmenides (see next note).

[125] DK 28B8.51–52: "From this point on learn about the false opinions (δόξας) of mortals as you listen to the deceptive order (κόσμον ... ἀπατηλόν) of my words," viz., those concerning the false world of sensation and appearances.

αἰσθητά); and these signs, which are situational indices and moments of powerlessness, can be read or ignored. Choosing one or the other is tantamount to choosing demystification or mystification. Gorgias' starting assumption, which he everywhere advertises, is that to take a stance is to occupy a position, to enter into a game (a παίγνιον), to invite others to join complicitously in this enterprise, and to risk control over its stakes.[126] The stakes are culturally defined, like the positions that Gorgias sketches in. But by rhetorically inhabiting these positions, and by flaunting this occupancy, Gorgias directs attention to the logic of their relations, and to their reversibility. His argument is vulnerable, like Helen, and blatantly false besides. Herein lies, I would suggest, its ultimate seductive power: the speech absorbs all meaning through a kind of attraction; meaning is drawn to its limit-conditions as if by a vacuum, and then returned to its users as a shared, complicitous illusion – in the aesthetic public sphere defined by the realms of sensation and communication.

3 GORGIAS AND THE 'STOICHEION': STRUCTURE, SIGN, AND PLAY AT THE END OF THE FIFTH CENTURY

One last point about Gorgias' materialism deserves to be made. The strongest arguments in favor of his mechanically reductive linguistic materialism draw their greatest hope from a single phrase in *Helen* §8, namely that *logos* carries out its effects "by means of" (or is it "in"?) "the smallest and most invisible body" (σμικροτάτῳ σώματι καὶ ἀφανεστάτῳ). As I mentioned, all manner of philosophical and scientific precursors have been proposed as models for this claim, from Empedocles to Anaxagoras, Democritus, and the Hippocratics. None of these candidates is particularly convincing, and the very breadth of the options on offer attests to the true nature of the problem: the absence of a smoking gun, due not least to the glaring lack of clarity in Gorgias' terminology.[127] Any kind of "body" could be meant, so what kind did he mean? The precise mechanism by which the effects of *logos* are achieved is left untold and obscure. Just how is the unapparent body of matter related to appearances and sensations, which are the foundation (I am arguing)

---

[126] Cf. DK 82A1a (= Philostr. *VS* 482): κινδύνευμα.

[127] To the several parallels adduced above (nn. 75–76), one might add another (given by Buchheim 1989, 164, ad loc.): "Even if [intellect] be small in bulk, much more does it in power and worth surpass everything" (εἰ γὰρ καὶ τῷ ὄγκῳ μικρόν ἐστι, δυνάμει καὶ τιμιότητι πολὺ μᾶλλον πάντων ὑπερέχει, Arist. *Eth. Nic.* 10.7.1178a1–2; trans. Ross; rev. Urmson).

of Gorgias' aesthetics of seduction? The very difficulty of the question ought to be an index not of its potential for solution but of its critical force: what if the gap between invisible body and visible consequences is meant to provoke reflection on the very dilemmas of Gorgias' own explanatory model, the terms it invokes, and the models and terms it calls to mind from contemporary discourses?

One possibility yet to be considered has to do with what, in my mind, is the likeliest proposal to date for making sense of the problematic phrase in *Helen* §8, namely that the body in question is not Democritean or some other esoteric Presocratic matter, but the linguistic material from which speeches are made.[128] This is surely more plausible than the suggestion that Gorgias has in mind the human tongue![129] But the tongue at least has the advantage of being unapparent – some of the time. In what way is linguistic material this too? A direct connection with sound might look promising, were it not for the same objection: sound, the matter from which speeches are made, is anything but "unapparent," because it appears to the senses.[130] I believe we can press the proposal of linguistic material a step further in a more promising direction by reverting to the componential model of material parts which was discussed earlier and which was seen to be a common way of analyzing all kinds of material compounds, including language, at the end of the fifth century. One could, in other words, try to line up "the smallest and least visible body" directly with "the smallest and least divisible" parts of language (its "atoms"), to wit, its *stoicheia*, the letters of the alphabet. But letters are not exactly invisible or unapparent, so it is not at all clear that this can provide a solution. Or can it?

Though it is true that the letters from which Gorgias' speeches were composed are not invisible on the page, they are invisible – unapparent as letters – whenever those speeches are being read aloud or recited. Spoken language, *qua* language, is after all comprised of the very same stuff, the very same *stoicheia*, as written language. But this linguistic matter will be neither visible when it is spoken nor audible as *stoicheia* at *any* point if *stoicheia* are by definition prior to sound – that is, if they are analytical elements to which sound is diversely attached in the act of phonation. (These diverse realizations in sound would in this case be what we saw

---

[128] Buchheim 1989, 164.
[129] Immisch 1927, 23: "*lingua humana est.*"
[130] Cf. [Arist.] *De audib.* 803b37: "sound appears to us (ἡμῖν ... φαίνεται) to be united and continuous." See Ax 1986, 114, who (rather extremely) sees in *On Not Being* a lesson in the reducibility of language to sound (*psophos*, a meaningless object of hearing) as opposed to sense.

come to be called the various *dunameis*, or phonetic "values," of the letter-elements.) Such an entity, the *stoicheion*, would truly be "smallest and least apparent," though it would only metaphorically speaking be a "body."[131]

Neither would an entity of this kind have resembled a Democritean atom if the entity in question was meant to represent the analytical *stoicheion* of language that was circulating in the last decades of the fifth century, as was discussed earlier in Chapter 4.[132] There, we saw how the spread of writing naturally raised questions about the status of letters and sounds, and about the relationship between texts as taken in with the eye and the ear, or about the nature of texts as spoken, sung, read, or seen. The concept of the *stoicheion* was introduced, in turn, as a partial answer to questions like these. I have been arguing that Gorgias, in pressing to the point of aporia the problem of the identity of *logos*, was probing exactly the same issue. I now want to consider the possibility that Gorgias had in mind the theory of the *stoicheion* in his speech on Helen.

That Gorgias would have been aware of the compositional model of analysis founded on the *stoicheion* as its building block seems likely enough. There is evidence pointing in this direction from within the *Helen* speech itself, for instance at *Helen* §18: "Whenever painters perfectly create a single body and shape from many colors and bodies (ἐκ πολλῶν χρωμάτων καὶ σωμάτων ἓν σῶμα ... ἀπεργάσωνται), they delight the sight." The mere allusion to the fabrication of color hues from individual pigments is an allusion to the process of *mixis* that, as we saw, was an early forerunner of the *sunthesis* model and that Gorgias could easily have learned about from his teacher Empedocles, if not elsewhere.[133] As a rhetorician, Gorgias could not have failed to come across the theory of *stoicheia* that was all the rage in sophistic circles in his day. Above, in Chapter 4, I discussed the *stoicheion* as an ingredient of the componential model, which, I argued, had a general role to play in aesthetic thought in antiquity. I want to focus now on the *stoicheion* as a hinge in the dynamics of the visible and the invisible in view of the specific nature of the puzzle of Gorgias' *Helen* §8, which, as we shall see, draws on wider contemporary issues in the realm of language towards the end of the fifth century.

---

[131] See Ch. 4, n. 138 above.

[132] Contrast Ford 2002, 166, who invokes Democritus, for whom "words were arrays of invisible sound atoms." However, no such atoms exist for Democritus.

[133] Cf. *MXG* 974a 25–974 b1, where a process of generation (of a hypothetical "One") is described in terms of a mechanical *mixis* and *sunthesis* of many moving elements (πράγματα) into one. The model here is Melissan.

This treatment will naturally be somewhat speculative. We cannot pin the *stoicheion*-model of language on Gorgias with any certainty. But the possibility is worth exploring just the same, if only for the resonances that his inquiries into language would have had in the minds of his scientifically attuned peers, if not in his own as well. As will be seen, Gorgias' view of language seems well suited to exploring the problem of language as an abstract system and as a literal phenomenon (as a source of appearances), while both avenues raise important questions about the nature of aesthetic materialism generally. But in order to make this connection, we will need to make some general remarks on how works of art, and texts in particular, can be thought and said to appear.

Language as phenomenal

Now, if language has a structure that is invisible to the eye or ear, part of the purpose of linguistic science is to show how this structure comes to be made phenomenally apparent, but also how its different arrangements (through rearrangement, or *metathesis*) produce variable phenomena, whether at the level of individual sounds, rhythms, or syntax. Even Aristotle would apply the principle on a much larger scale to plot construction, likewise in the tradition of inquiry into generation and corruption, and likewise invoking the criterion of phenomenal difference as the proof of structure and its variation, as when he holds that the plot ought to be a mimesis of a single whole action, "with the different parts (μέρη) so arranged that the whole is disturbed (κινεῖσθαι) by the transposition (μετατιθεμένου) and disrupted (διαφέρεσθαι) [or 'destroyed': διαφθείρεσθαι[134]] by the removal of any one of them; *for if it makes no visible difference* (μηδὲν ποιεῖ ἐπίδηλον) whether a thing is there or not [lit., 'if the presence or absence of a thing makes nothing manifest'], that thing is no part of the whole."[135] The logic of mechanical change is Presocratic, perhaps above all atomistic, and there are medical overtones besides.[136] Now, the structure of, say, a sentence, is not quite the same thing as its form, its shape, or the sum of its parts. We might say that

[134] For this variant, confirmed by the Arabic translation, see Gudeman, ad loc.
[135] Arist. *Poet.* 8.1451a 32–35; trans. Hubbell, adapted; emphasis added.
[136] See pp. 154–56 above (Empedocles); Arist. *Gen. corr.* 1.1.315b 14–15 (= DK 67A9), quoted at Ch. 4, n. 196 above, for the atomistic language; and see Ch. 2 at n. 203 above for the medical overtones. Discussion in Porter 1989, 170 n. 114, to which add Lucr. 3.513: *addere enim partis aut ordine traiecere aequumst.* The earliest example of the *metathesis*-model applied to language known to me is *Dialex.* §§11–13 (*c.* 400 BCE).

a sentence's structure exists in a quasi-formal and quasi-material way, as do its elements. *Logos* is more complex still. Parsing *logos* into its constituent parts is a lot like a dog chasing its own tail: because the parts are relative to sought-for structures, one is never quite sure when to stop, or even what one is after. The task is no easier today than it was when it was in its infancy in the age of the first professors of Greek.

Modern approaches to texts know how to postulate these very sorts of ambiguity, which can at times rival the paradoxes of Gorgias. G. Thomas Tanselle, a contemporary textual theorist, describes how "arrangements of words ... can exist in the mind, whether or not they are reported by voice or in writing." Consequently, "literary works do not exist on paper or in sounds," while "the medium of literature and other pieces of verbal communication is language, not paper and ink" or sound.[137] This radical restatement of the "ontology" of texts is premised on the fact that all texts, be they verbal or visual, "consist of arrangements of [their constituent] elements," where "arrangements" stands for the work's current (textual) realization – in this edition, this performance, this moment of hearing, and so on. Elements, we could say, are defined in a relational way, that is, relative to whatever whole (work) one wants to analyze in whatever realization the whole happens to have assumed. In construing the elements of an object (in reading it, interpreting it, giving voice to it, taking it in visually), one is simultaneously reconstructing the work that "lies behind" that object.[138] One is, hermeneutically speaking, attempting to reveal its structure. *Logos* would be this structure in Gorgias' terms.

One way of viewing Tanselle's approach is to accuse it of a kind of Platonism in postulating a work "that lies behind" its manifestations in the text.[139] The charge won't entirely stick, inasmuch as Tanselle's project is guided by a radical uncertainty about what the identity of a work is. A more interesting way of reading Tanselle's approach, it seems to me, is to see how it arrives at its concept of a "work," wittingly or unwittingly, through a form of radical empiricism *à la* William James. That is, to approach a work in this way, aesthetically speaking, is to approach it as something that is radically contingent: "for in each interval between encounters the unruly forces of time will have altered the work (or its

---

[137] Tanselle 1989, 17–18; 40.
[138] Tanselle 1989, 18.
[139] Tanselle 1989, 18. For this reason, a textual materialist like Jerome McGann calls Tanselle a "textual idealist" (McGann 1991, 7), though not at ibid., 69.

physical embodiment), the present context of the work, and our own attitudes" towards the work.[140] "We can never know exactly what such works consist of and must always be questioning the correctness – by one or another standard – of the texts whereby we approach them."[141] In this respect for contingency lies a respect for the materiality of the text and the "varieties of experience" that it engenders.[142]

The most intriguing upshot of this approach to the question what works are is not that the question is left in a state of radical uncertainty in the end. It is that the process of construal produces uncertainty *out of its respect for* the material conditions of textuality itself. The "text" is, in effect, really another way of stating what the material contingency of the work is. But by the same token, each and every material contingency *alters* the *experience* of the work, the way the conditions of lighting alter the colors of a painting or the way the variable tuning of an instrument can alter a melody – nor is there any way to measure colors or melodies against some invariable original: *they can only be measured against other alterations*, the same picture or score seen or heard under different conditions.[143] The net effect of this aesthetic encounter is that of a *divided* materialism: a highly specified materiality for the text, and, in direct proportion to that, an equally uncertain materiality and identity for the work. Once again, the parallel with Gorgias ought to be evident: there is *logos* in its manifestations, each radically contingent and experienceable, and then there is the puzzle of *logos* apart from these. *Stoicheia* would be one of the *loci* of this division: they are the elements in which the division replicates itself, being (as we saw) the site of a double articulation of system and physical embodiment, while the structures they build in their

---

[140] Tanselle 1989, 24–25.

[141] Tanselle 1989, 25.

[142] Tanselle 1989, 24, with a nod to William James. Cf. Saito 2007, 25: "the temporal character of our experience ... affords numerous possibilities of differing experiences, even regarding the same 'object.'"

[143] Thus, Sextus Empiricus (*Pyr.* 1.130; 1.118; *Math.* 7.208) notices how "patches of Taenarum marble, which, on their own, looked white when polished, might be perceived as yellow when viewed in the context of a whole column. The colour of buildings could change, as the position of the sun seemed to shift or the viewer moved around a space. Towers appeared both round and square, according to the angle or distance from which they were seen" (Thomas 2007, 210). The Peripatetic work *On Colors* similarly notes the variability of colors according to whether objects are seen in full light or in the shade ([Arist.] *Col.* 793b12–19; cf. Thomas, ibid., 209). And one of Lucian's narrators in *On the Hall* observes (8; 11) how the changing conditions of the ambient light changes the aesthetic effects of the building, whether at sunset or in low light (Thomas, ibid., 232). Cf. Clark 2006 and Saito 2007, 25 for two contemporary confirmations of the same principle.

mutual (and mute) relations are another such *locus*, and the resulting realizations, visual or aural, form a third, one last time.[144]

If this parallelism is correct, then by pointing to the smallest "invisible" constituents of language, Gorgias is advertising the *gap* that exists between the phenomenality of language and its non-phenomenal sources, not any continuity. And this would be entirely in keeping with the kinds of maneuvers we witnessed him performing in *On Not Being*, a text that was at worst evasive and at best dialectical. *Logos* is once again being reduced to a condition prior to its materializations. But unlike in *On Not Being*, what is left incoherent, and painfully puzzling, is the curious phrase about the "smallest and least apparent *body*" from the *Helen*. We can, I believe, demystify both our image of Gorgias and this phrase by bringing them both in line with contemporary fifth-century linguistic analysis.

Gorgias needn't be stating anything other than a simple and obvious fact about language: that its workings are extraordinarily remarkable, even "divine," and the more so since they are founded on primary elements that can be understood to be either letters of the alphabet and so "invisible" when they are spoken aloud, or the same letters (or, more abstractly, the *stoicheia* that represent them) that combine into syllables, rhythms, words, and sentences and are used in speech and poetry but that have no phenomenal correlate in themselves. *Logos* names this transparent or non-apparent aspect of language, language in its invisibility to the eye or ear, as it goes about its everyday business, clothed in materiality. But above all, *logos* names that which the materiality of language must clothe, the abstract skeleton or structure on which language is founded, in the same way that meter represents a sensuous feature that *logos* can, but need not, have. Once it has acquired this or any other feature, *logos* will resound, as it does in the very sentence that announces the principle of *logos* (*Hel.* §9) and that, like the rest of his speech, exemplifies the area of style for which Gorgias was famous in antiquity – that of poetic sound effects.

Gorgias did not invent such figures of sound as antithesis, isocolon, homoeoteleuton, and parisosis, but he experimented in them and pushed them to such an extreme that they later became known simply as "Gorgianic figures." To modern ears these jingles may sound frigid, even

---

[144] The problem of what counts as a total result – the totality of a work – carries the dilemmas to another degree and on another level. This is more strictly a hermeneutic question. To be sure, Gorgias was well attuned to this too. The reference in *Hel.* §21 to "the beginning" of his speech, implying as it does a beginning of a whole, seems deliberately vague: does it refer to the first word in §1, or to "the beginning of my future speech" in §5?

if they did not to every ancient ear (though they were controversial).[145]
As techniques for achieving euphony, these figures of sound were also
acknowledged by literary critics in antiquity who could legitimately be
called materialists of language insofar as they privileged sound over other
aspects of language (above all, sense).[146] Gorgias' speeches are filled with
such ringing turns of phrase. But that is because those speeches are
embodied *logoi*, not "non-apparent" *logoi*. If Gorgias in the *Helen* is
toying with a kind of reductionism, this time that reduction can be argued
to exhibit a coherent rationale because it appears to be conducted in the
name of linguistic science. At the very least, the reduction of speech – not
to a body, but to a *logos* conceived as an abstraction minus its materializations – can be seen to mimic one of the enigmas that contemporary
Greek linguistics (or its logic) had produced, that of the uncertain status
of language organized around its component *stoicheia*.

Yet at the same time, and by the same token, if Gorgias appears to be
drawn to the sensuous surface of language or of images, he seems no less
drawn to the hidden element, to a kind of *je ne sais quoi*, that might or
might not lie behind these. Rhetoric, after all, is as much an art of silence
as it is an art of speaking.[147] As the following possible relic of Gorgias'
writings indicates (it is given among his *Spuria* by Diels – Kranz, but for
no good reason), Gorgias found a special beauty in what is "hidden" in
art, in that which painters, and presumably poets and speech-writers like
himself, struggled to capture "with their tried and true colors," but which
resisted depiction and expression:

Gorgias said, "The outstanding beauty of something that is hidden – this is what
you have when clever painters are unable to paint it with their tried and true
colors. All their great labor and their great effort testify marvelously to how
splendid a thing it is in its concealment. And once the [individual] stages of their
work have reached an end they bestow on it a [final] victory wreath: their silence.

---

[145] After Plato, Philostr. *VS* 492 is one of the dissenting views (though contrast id., *Ep.* 73 = DK
82A35: "Gorgias' admirers were noble and numerous," etc.), as is Dion. Hal. *Lys.* 3 (and elsewhere).
For a damning critique of Gorgias' cacophony, see Cole 1991, 72–74. For a sampling of positive
ancient judgments, see Norden 1971 [1909–18], 1:51–52 (and ibid., 65, on the inevitable clash of
modern and ancient sensibilities).

[146] See Diod. Sic. 12.53.4 and Dion. Hal. *Lys.* 3 (both DK 82A4, and both possibly on the authority
of the third-century BCE historian Timaeus, who was branded an Asianist in stylistic terms).
Cf. Norden 1971 [1909–18], 1:15–79 on the Gorgianic figures and their influence on Greek prose;
and ibid., 251–70 for a quick overview of Asianism, with which Gorgias was, and often still is,
associated.

[147] The orator must know how "to say what is required in the required moment, and when to be
silent" (σιγᾶν) (DK 82B6).

But that which no hand touches and no eye sees – how can the tongue say it or the ear of the hearer perceive it?"[148]

One is reminded of Susan Stewart, who writes, "Whenever art makes visible it does so by referring to the invisible from which the visible emerges."[149] But there are closer analogues to hand. Gorgias is perhaps to be aligned with Heraclitus, who, we may recall, wrote that "an unapparent structure is stronger [or 'better'] than an apparent one" (ἁρμονίη ἀφανὴς φανερῆς κρείττων) and that "nature [or 'reality': φύσις] tends [or 'prefers,' or 'loves'] to hide itself."[150]

This hidden structure is not an abstraction: it, too, has a physical and material existence, just one that is not phenomenally apparent. *Harmoniē*, after all, means a "fitting together." If the constituents of this structure are left somewhat uncertain on Heraclitus' ontology (these seem to be primarily fire, then earth and water), their materiality is not.[151] So understood, Heraclitus' insight into the material structure of reality would match his philosophy of nature. His own theory of *logos* is a relevant predecessor to Gorgias', if it is understood along these lines, and as Kirk, Raven, and Schofield take it, namely as "the unifying formula or proportional method of arrangement of things, what might almost be termed their structural plan."[152] While a more fully developed analysis of this potential parallel would lead us astray, the essential notion of *logos* as denoting a *material structure* – a form made up of material components and thus consisting entirely of relations between material entities – is all we need to retain at this time.

Now, in describing this structure, one is describing the *materiality of the form* of reality (its material shape or organization), and the same holds for works of art. In this, Heraclitus and Gorgias are in complete agreement. Where they stand apart is in the fact that for Heraclitus, reality's form exists objectively in the realm of nature, whereas for Gorgias, the very idea of such a realm will always be inflected by our experience of it: such is the nature of cultural co-determinacy, which is a two-way street. None of this

---

[148] DK 82B28; translation after Buchheim 1989, 99, who has in turn adapted Ryssel's German translation from the original Syrian, as reproduced in DK. DK list the fragment as "Schlechtbezeugtes." See Buchheim 1989, 200–01 for arguments in favor of authenticity. I personally see no reason to doubt that we have in B28 a filtered transmission of a genuine Gorgianic fragment.
[149] Stewart 2005, 24.
[150] DK 22B54; trans. K–R–S, adapted; B123.
[151] DK 22B30; B31.
[152] Kirk *et al.* 1983, 187.

cancels out the fact that for Gorgias there are hidden recesses even within the realm of culture, recesses in the outer and inner worlds of nature and language within which human subjects live their lives as partially knowing subjects and as partially subject to their environments. Thus, while it may be true for Gorgias that subjects have, as it were, private ("personal") experiences they cannot communicate to others if others have not had the same experience,[153] I take it that for Gorgias they also have experiences of the world of nature or of culture that are equally unfathomable to *themselves*.[154] And in this respect, they resemble artists who stand before a beauty they cannot quite name.

And so it is that in the end the best artists, Gorgias felt, must bow to the inevitable beauty of what, in the most interesting of cases, they may themselves have produced – for it is just as likely that the enigma they are trying to express is one they create while trying to express it – and then seal it with the greatest rhetorical act there is: "their silence." If the sensible world contains a parallel enigma, and this hidden element is the world's "art," then we can only admit that Gorgias, who has to have been one of antiquity's most ardent theorists and practitioners of language, was also one of the great lovers of the world's beauty, and that his paradoxical writing *On Not Being* and his other accounts of sensation, especially in the *Helen*, are the ultimate testament to this love.

---

[153] So Mansfeld 1985a, 252–55, softening, and relativizing, the harshness of Gorgias' position in *On Not Being*.

[154] Cf. Assmann 1991, 16: "It seems to me … that culture is always both: what is taken for granted *and* what is demanded of one, the implicit *and* the explicit, the unconscious *and* the conscious." Much the same follows, it seems to me, from Gorgias' assumptions about the cultural implications of his argument; see "The Cultural Dimensions of Gorgias' Critique" (p. 296) above.

CHAPTER 6

The music of the voice

The science of civil oratory is, after all, a kind of musical science (μουσική), differing from vocal and instrumental music in degree, not in kind. In oratory, as in music, the phrases possess melody, rhythm, variety and appropriateness; so that here too the ear delights in the melodies, is stirred by the rhythms, welcomes the variations, and all the time desires what is appropriate to the occasion. The distinction is simply one of degree.

Dionysius of Halicarnassus[1]

How musical was ancient poetry and prose? Probably we shall never really know. We have no direct access to the way Greek and Latin sounded, and no reason to suspect our criteria of euphony would match those from antiquity. Difficult as it is to answer the question, we can approach it through another pair, namely, how aware of the question were the ancients, and how did this awareness evolve? Our current knowledge of these matters is at best partial. So far as I know, there exists no comprehensive survey of the poets' programmatic and others' casual opinions as to what constitutes poetic sound, though a collection of this sort is badly needed.[2] The critics are better studied, but a comprehensive survey of their views and especially of the historical development of their teachings has yet to be undertaken.[3] The lion's share of attention has been directed at the Hellenistic era, when euphonism was already flourishing as a critical doctrine. But we know that the Hellenistic critics did not invent their teachings from scratch: they were building on earlier traditions in poetics, which has been the primary target of the modern study of literary

---

[1] *Comp.* 11 (40.8–16 U–R); trans. Usher.
[2] For some hints, see Norden 1971 [1909–18], 1:24 n. 1 and Stanford 1943, Stanford 1967. Kaimio 1977 offers a useful taxonomy of terms for sounds of all kinds in Greek poetry down to around 400 BCE (see her Introduction for earlier treatments). Also useful, but more directed towards Greek musical practices, is Barker 1984. See further on the Greek language: van Groningen 1953; Sommerstein 1973; Allen 1987; on Latin: Wilkinson 1963; Allen 1978; Traina 1999; on Greek and Latin: Edwards 2002.
[3] Continuities of a sort are implied by van Groningen 1953 and by Rispoli 1995.

criticism (though not in the areas of euphony or musicality *per se*), and on earlier traditions in music, which offered its own poetics of sound but remains sadly underexamined as a source of information about literature and its critical appreciation. What is more, it seems likely that if we go back far enough in time we will find that the study of poetic sound – which is to say, of the musical sound of the poetic voice – was central to the ways in which literary theory and criticism began to take shape as discourses of their own, as distinct from, and rivaling, other branches of ancient science and learning. Nevertheless, those discourses of literature were drawing heavily on adjacent areas, notably in music – and to such an extent that the phrase "the music of the voice" (τὸ τῆς φωνῆς μέλος) could be used to capture the two traditions at their exact point of intersection.[4]

I will attempt to justify these last remarks in the present chapter. In the first section, I want to focus in particular on a brief passage from Aristotle's *Rhetoric*, which appears to map out some of the prehistory of the way in which the voice was treated as a source of music – in short, the early history of the (musical) voice. Indeed, the analysis by Aristotle is in many ways a brief and selective history of literary theory and criticism, though it has not been exploited as one until now.[5] I will show how this is the case, and how Aristotle's analysis is a very particular kind of literary history as well. But before continuing, a few definitions will be needed. The word *euphonism*, I take it, can be understood in two senses. First, euphonism is the practice of poets that corresponds to the commonplace intuition (which it is probably a mistake to say we no longer share to the degree that the ancients did) that qualities of sound contribute to the overall effect of poetry and of literary prose, and indeed to that of communication generally. (All of these elements would have fallen under the general rubric of *hellēnismos*, or pure Greek expression, and its Latin counterpart, *Latinitas*.) Secondly, and derivatively, euphonism is the doctrine, found among some of the rarer strands of ancient literary criticism, according to which poetic excellence is to be located solely in the euphonic properties of a text, which is to say, in its aesthetic properties as sounded (its musicality), even if, as I believe, this second, reductive approach to euphony is ultimately just another way of referring to the role

---

[4] For the phrase, see Ch. 4, at n. 26 above (Dion. Hal. *Comp.* 11, p. 43.5–6; and *Comp.* 11, *passim*). μελίχροος ("honey-sweet") is a good gauge of the musicality (and mellifluousness) of speech, as in μελιχρᾷ τῇ φωνῇ ἀπαγγέλλειν said of the second-century CE sophist, grammarian, and Atticist Pollux of Naucratis in Philostr. *VS* 593. See also μουσικῶς εἰπεῖν (Alcid. *Soph.* 31; Isoc. 13.16) and Antisthenes, fr. 51 Decleva Caizzi (quoted in nn. 116 and 117 below).
[5] A predecessor to this analysis of Aristotle appeared in Porter 2004b.

played by the voice in a text, which in turn opens the door to a much wider range of issues, both aesthetic and ideological or cultural, and above all their intersection.

The intuition that sound has aesthetic properties is so firmly rooted in Greek thinking that it overrides the medium of writing in which sound was felt to be contained and transmitted. It does this by rendering the voice audible no matter how many layers of writing, transmission, quotation, or time have intervened. "Let us hear how he speaks" (ἀκούσωμεν δὲ αὐτοῦ, πῶς λέγει) is a standard way of introducing a written quotation from a classical author in the postclassical era. The conflation of voice and text is felt to be entirely natural. But above all, it is the attitude of eager anticipation, the expectation of sheer aural pleasure and of an immediate contact with the past, that is remarkable in this kind of gesture. The example just given is from the Augustan literary critic Dionysius of Halicarnassus,[6] whom we on occasion find waxing poetic, and nearly becoming ecstatic, at the prospect of recovering a classical author's voice (in this case, Plato's), as, for instance, in the following passage from the same treatise: "If, then, the spirit (πνεῦμα) with which Demosthenes' pages are still imbued after so many years possesses so much power and moves his readers in this way, surely to hear him delivering his speeches at the time must have been an extraordinary and overwhelming experience" (ὑπερφυές τι καὶ δεινὸν χρῆμα).[7] The epithets are all Longinian. But the sentiment is broadly felt.

What Dionysius shows beyond any doubt is the way the line between written texts and these same texts as deposits of sound is typically blurred in the ancient sources. When Dionysius writes, "Let us hear how Plato speaks," he is not using a mere turn of phrase. He is quietly announcing a theme, which has to do with the aural qualities of Plato's diction (*lexis* and *phrasis*),[8] in contrast to his ideas, and which he finds paralleled in the poets. Like Plato at his finest, Pindar, too, "was more concerned with the music and rhythm (τὰ μέλη καὶ ῥυθμούς) of the words than with what they said" (τὴν λέξιν).[9] We needn't be confused by this last choice of term. *Lexis* usually stands for expression, but it also touches the thing expressed. Music and rhythm are in fact part of *lexis*, but they are, so to speak, its deepest and most essential components: they are at the heart of

---

[6] *Dem.* 26; trans. Usher (as with all passages from Dionysius of Halicarnassus below).
[7] *Dem.* 22.   [8] *Dem.* 25.
[9] *Dem.* 26. Cf. ibid., 25: "Everyone knows ... that the philosopher [sc., Plato] prided himself more on his powers of expression (περὶ τὴν ἑρμηνείαν) than upon his subject matter (τὰ πράγματα)."

the way language sounds, comprising those reaches of language which are farthest removed from the silence of meaning.[10]

In contrasting musicality with meaning, Dionysius is reenacting a division that had first emerged in purely formal terms during the time of Gorgias and the sophists, namely between sound and sense, a distinction that could be couched in terms of a division between expression and delivery on the one hand, and meaning and intention on the other.[11] We have already seen how Gorgias developed the distinction in various ways, notably through his stringent isolation of thought from sound, and of *logos* from its phenomenal characteristics. In the critical tradition, this insight was best remembered in the form of Gorgias' groundbreaking observation in his *Helen* (§9) that "poetry is *logos* plus meter." We might partially transpose the distinction of sound and sense into one between texts in their quality as declaimed and the same texts as read without florid vocal inflections (μεταβολῶν).[12] The more familiar opposition between the spoken and the written styles is a third way of capturing some of the distinction between musicality and meaning, though we would probably do well to avoid reducing this last contrast to one between improvisational speech and calculated writing, for reasons that will emerge below. A more productive issue to focus on has to do with a more generic problem, or better yet, tension. For behind all these models stands another, namely the view that within all linguistic expressions, oral or written, lies buried a voice that animates them. This voice is musical, and more often than not a source of senselessness.

This is the "voice" whose emergence I will be tracing in the present chapter. As I hope to show, the focus on the role of the voice in ancient sources provoked reflection about poetics proper, that is, about language as an aesthetic phenomenon, in contrast to speech and rivaling music. It helped bring attention to poetry as an artifact of a craft or art (*technē*), and consequently to poetic technique. This focus on sound posits – if not reductively and absolutely, then at least provisionally – the possibility of

---

[10] On the ancient commonplace that language has an intrinsic musical element, one that reflects an innate sensibility to rhythm and music, see Norden 1971 [1909–18], 1:55 and Norden 1928 (here purveying the doctrine as a linguistic, if not cosmic, universal that is not only a Greek conceit, but also independently true).

[11] The tripartite distinction between speech (*logos*), sound (*melos, harmonia*), and rhythm (*rhuthmos*) discussed by Plato in various places may be traditional, but there is no evidence that it reaches back into the late sixth century or to Lasus of Hermione (*pace* Privitera 1965, 40–42). It is, in any event, reducible to a more primitive distinction, or better yet, tension (ibid., 40), between sound (musicality) and sense which does predate Plato.

[12] Cf. Isoc. 5.25–29.

an analysis of language as a material substance with claims to relative autonomy. At its most extreme, focusing so intently on speech and writing as aesthetic phenomena could work to suspend considerations of logical structure, meaning, content, and morals altogether, clearing the way for a different kind of apprehension, one that depended upon an irrational grasp of the perceived phenomena of language through the ear (ἡ ἄλογος αἴσθησις). But more on this below. First we must turn to the rise of the voice.

I ARISTOTLE ON THE ASCENDANCY OF THE "VOICE"

The emergence of the formal distinction between language as an aural phenomenon (equivalent to a "music" of sorts) and as a conveyer of meaning is at best dimly lit, but from Aristotle we can grasp the outlines of a general picture. The information comes from the opening of the third book of the *Rhetoric*, which proves to be quite revealing, not least because it teasingly hints at how much information about the early study of the Greek language we have in fact lost. The passage reads like a short speculative history of rhetoric in one of its more prominent aspects. In a word, rhetoric emerges here as a theory and practice of the voice, of speech directed πρὸς τὸν ἀκροατήν ("to the listener"), whereby language comes to be viewed as a resource of sound worthy of independent speculation and treatment. Aristotle traces this development along two lines, that of style (*lexis*) and that of delivery (*hupokrisis*), in each case starting with the poets, who instigated both tendencies.[13] The lessons of the poets, he says, were then generalized by being transposed into the sphere of prose. Subsequently those lessons were developed in more abstract and theoretical terms.[14] Let us follow Aristotle's argument, bearing in mind its selectivity and even its tendentiousness – two traits which are driven by logical and practical choices on Aristotle's part and which are worth analyzing in their own right.[15]

---

[13] Arist. *Rh.* 3.1.1404a20.

[14] Cf. Dion. Hal. *De imit.* fr. 9 (*Opusc.* 2:215.10–15 U–R: "Gorgias transferred poetic expression (τὴν ποιητικὴν ἑρμηνείαν) over into political discourse, because he considered the rhetorician to be different from lay people. Lysias did the opposite: he strove to produce a style that was evident to all and commonly used, in the belief that ordinary language and simplicity were likeliest to persuade lay people."

[15] I would therefore agree to an extent with Düring 1966, 152 n. 164, who calls Aristotle's history here "reine Gedankenkonstruktionen," valuable less as a comprehensive archival source than as a logical reconstruction, which is not for that reason devoid of historical fact.

The rise of lexis

First, Aristotle says, there came something like a poeticization of speech and writing, in the figure of Gorgias.[16] Subsequently, attention was drawn to the question of what Gorgias had added to his language in order to make it poetic (ποιητική), and the answer seemed to lie in language itself: *lexis* (style, diction, expression).[17] For just as "the poets, while speaking sweet nothings (λέγοντες εὐήθη), seemed to acquire their reputation through their *lexis*, it was through this [viz., through the emphasis on *lexis*] that a poetic style (ποιητικὴ λέξις) first came into existence [in prose as well], for example, that of Gorgias."[18] Emphasis on style produced a style of writing the virtues of which were palpably detached from sense.

So far, we are still in the region of practice, but not yet of theoretical articulation. Practice followed undeveloped intuitions – for instance, the intuition that poets, as we just saw, were gathering fame through their mere use of a distinctive language (quite apart from anything they had to say). How common was this perception? Aristotle doesn't say, but at the very least it was assumed and nourished by the earliest rhetoricians, and has since become (for Aristotle) a regrettable truth about rhetoric.[19] It is regrettable, not least because language for Aristotle is inevitably (but not essentially) tied up with voice and utterance. "Discourse is *meaningful* voice" (λόγος δέ ἐστι φωνὴ σημαντική), he affirms in *On Interpretation*.[20] And in *On Sense and Sensibles*, he adds, "For rational discourse is a cause of instruction [or "learning"] in virtue of its being audible (ἀκουστὸς ὤν), which it is, *not in its own right, but incidentally*" (οὐ καθ' αὑτὸν ἀλλὰ κατὰ συμβεβηκός).[21] D. A. Ross's gloss on this last passage (ad loc.) gets things only half right, but for the wrong reasons: "For meaning is not inherent in speech but attached to it only by convention." This ignores Aristotle's resistance to the audible component of meaning in language and to the gradual detachment of sound from sense, which is palpable throughout the early chapters of *Rhetoric* Book 3 (and not only there). To complete the paraphrase, one would have to add: "Sound is not inherent in language, but attached to it only as a matter of contingency." At any rate, theoretical attention gradually came to focus on this sundering of expressiveness and sense as an abstract idea, indeed

[16] *Rh.* 3.1.1404a26. [17] Compare his definition of rhetoric as "speech plus meter" (*Hel.* §9).
[18] *Rh.* 3.1.1404a24–26. Translations are after Kennedy 1991. [19] *Rh.* 3.1.1404a1–8; 18–19.
[20] Arist. *Int.* 1.4.16b26. [21] *Sens.* 1.437a11–17; trans. Beare; emphasis added.

on the very fact of its possibility, which produced yet another abstract idea, the category of style or *lexis* itself, at whatever point this happened (the term is not attested prior to the comic poet Plato, active between 420–390 BCE).[22]

The rise of the voice

(i) Licymnius of Chios and the New Music

It fell to Gorgias' pupil Licymnius of Chios to recognize, somewhere around 400, that "verbal beauty (κάλλος ὀνόματος) lies either in the sounds (ἐν τοῖς ψόφοις) or in the sense (τῷ σημαινομένῳ), and ugliness the same."[23] This feat, obvious to us, paved the way in later centuries for a theoretical justification of euphony as a self-sufficient criterion of verbal beauty, unless this step was not already being taken by Licymnius himself. Licymnius, a mere shadow, seems to have specialized in crossing rhetoric with poetry, disastrously according to both Plato and Aristotle.[24] His dithyrambs, Aristotle says, are more suited to reading aloud than to enacting. Whence Licymnius numbers among the *anagnōstikoi* as opposed to the *agōnistikoi*.[25] I take it that *anagnōstikos* is a

---

[22] Fr. 99.2 K–A, from *The Little Child*: οὐκ ἂν παρέβην εἰς λέξιν τοιάνδ' ἐπῶν, "I wouldn't have stepped forward to deliver such a profusion of verses." LSJ (λέξις s.v. 1) wrongly dates the first occurrence of the term *lexis* to the philosopher Plato (but cf. s.v. παραβαίνω IV). It is odd that we should have entire books devoted to *hupokrisis* (Zucchelli 1962), but no studies, so far as I am aware, devoted to the origins of *lexis* as a category of criticism. Equally odd, however, is the way the category seemingly appears out of the blue and is taken for granted by ancients and moderns alike. The fact that Plato Comicus wrote a play called *Sophists*, probably disparaging contemporary innovations, suggests that he may have found the term in use among his sophistic contemporaries.

[23] Arist. *Rh.* 3.2.1405b6–8.   [24] *Phdr.* 267c; Arist. *Rh.* 3.13.1414b17.

[25] Arist. *Rh.* 3.12.1413b14; see frr. 768–73 *PMG*. There is some debate about whether the former term (*anagnōstikoi*) means "writers who mean to be read" and so are "readable" ("easy to read" or "suitable to be read") or whether it means those who are "fondly read," "a favourite choice for private reading" (Allan 1980, 244–46 favors the latter meaning, while excluding the former as "an illusion"). I do not see much of a difference in the end, since readers welcome texts that lend themselves to being read. Nor is the point about the nonequivalence of *anagnōstikos* and *euanagnōstos* ("readable" and "easily read") sustainable in the light of the author *On Style*, who states that the *graphikē lexis* (written style) is *euanagnōstos* (easy to read [aloud]): Demetr. *Eloc.* 193; *pace* Allan, ibid. See further at n. 48 below. Holding positions similar to my own are Blass 1887–98, 1:86; Cope 1970, III:145; III:146–47; III:154; and Hunter 2003, 219. It is worth remembering that originally "ἀγώνισμα [declamation] can mean either the public reading of an epideictic λόγος (as in Thuc. 1.22.4) or the public performance of a play (as in Arist. *Poet.* 1451b37)" (Hudson-Williams 1949a, 65–66). Further, Crusius 1902. Peter Bing suggests (*per litt.*) that Chaeremon is called *anagnōstikos* by Aristotle at *Rh.* 3.1.1413b13 because he designed his works to be read; he is known, for instance, for an acrostic (see Kannicht in Snell 1971, 159–60, 166–68). I find this unconvincing for some of the reasons just stated (as does Sifakis 2002, 157 n. 23, who adduces evidence that Chaeremon's plays were eminently suitable to performing). After all, Alcidamas, a fellow culprit, does not use acrostics, but he does use urbane and *obscurissima verba* (as Aristotle complains).

synonym for a writer of *lexis graphikē*,[26] or rather of *lexis graphikōtatē*, the function (*ergon*) of which is to be read, which is to say, read aloud (this is built into the meaning of ἀνάγνωσις).[27] Plato further notes that Licymnius' innovations were aimed at aesthetic decoration (πρὸς ποίη-σιν εὐεπείας)[28] – certainly not at meaning (Licymnius' metaphors, some of them involving coinages, troubled the ancients and are still obscure today). Consequently, Licymnius must have been aiming in the first instance at euphony in the broadest sense, namely the aesthetic effects of language when sounded out (as the surviving traces of his writing suggest).[29]

I do not mean to suggest that Licymnius was by any means the first to articulate the distinction between sound and sense, but only that he was the first to give the distinction an abstract and theoretical expression, possibly in his manual, the *Art* [sc., *of Rhetoric*]. He was preceded by Gorgias, but Gorgias was doubtless following earlier precedents in poetry and adapting them to prose. Prose is the realm where the distinction was most likely to be expressed anyway, because prose has a utilitarian cast to begin with: separating off the "musicality" of the voice from what the voice means semantically is an easy trail to follow in the prose world. The examples prior to Gorgias happen to be somewhat disguised, as they all occur either in poetry or in music, where musicality obtains all the time. But this shouldn't put us off the trail: musicality for the sake of sound, salient for its irrationality, can even within these realms be distinguished from music that follows clear patterns and conveys evident sense (see below on Pratinas).

(ii) Hupokrisis *(Delivery)*

A parallel development appears to have taken place in the realm of *hupokrisis*, or delivery, which gradually detached itself from its origins in drama (*hupokrisis* in its primary sense is "acting") and became part of the art of rhetoric. The pressure for this change seems to have come from changing dramaturgical practices: dramatists at first acted in their own

---

Reading aloud and declaiming can be ways of disambiguating or else merely calling attention to textual and aural complexity and virtuosity, a point Crusius makes (ibid., 384). There is no reason why the two elements of textuality and aurality should be at odds: if they are, this is our modern hang-up, not the ancients'. See further Wehrli 1946, 23, tying Licymnius to Democritean teachings on euphony; and Quadlbauer 1958, 59, linking him to a theory of the sublime.

[26] *Rh.* 3.12.1413b8–9.   [27] *Rh.* 3.12.1414a18–19.   [28] Pl. *Phdr.* 267c3.

[29] See Radermacher 1951, 118–19 (§§4–7). See further Dion. Hal. *Dem.* 26 on Licymnius' rhyming jingles and *Thuc.* 24 on his Gorgianic figures of sound. *Dem.* 26 likewise involves a preferential contrast between aesthetically pleasing language (εὐεπεία and καλλιλογία) and ideas (αἱ νοήσεις) – in favor of the former.

plays,[30] but owing to the increasing complexity of the stage and, no less importantly, to the powerful appeal of delivery (to which Aristotle's *Poetics* bears witness),[31] they then turned these roles, and their voices, over to professional actors. One example is a certain Theodorus, who is singled out for his superior acting abilities: his voice "seems to be that of the speaker [viz., the character's], while the others' are those of somebody else."[32] The need for practical manuals arose (Theodorus may have written one himself),[33] and eventually parallels to rhetorical delivery were noticed, for instance by Thrasymachus in his *Eleoi* (*Appeals to Pity*), a work devoted to the elicitation of emotions.[34] But apparently no substantive technical treatise on rhetorical *hupokrisis* existed down to Aristotle's day,[35] even if handbooks on acting and uses of the voice and vocalization in poetic contexts (for instance, tragic and rhapsodic recitations) had been developed, like that by Glaucon of Teos.[36] Theophrastus would fill the gap in the next generation.[37]

Aristotle is a reluctant witness to the phenomenon he retails: duty-bound, he offers valuable clues to the way in which the study of style and sound came to be conceived, even though he remains dismissive of the final value of vocalization in rhetoric despite its immense and undeniable powers.[38] Aristotle's phrase, a virtual sigh, ἀλλ᾽ ὅμως μέγα δύναται, "But nevertheless, [delivery] has great power," seems to echo Gorgias' famous statement in his *Helen* (§8), λόγος δυνάστης μέγας ἐστίν, "speech is a

---

[30] Arist. *Rh.* 3.1.1403b23–24.

[31] Compare *Poet.* ch. 26 on the rising popularity of delivery and other crowd-pleasing devices in the evolution of drama, and *ibid.*, 1461b32–1462b14, for the same bias against delivery on the stage (where, interestingly, Aristotle favors reading plays aloud).

[32] Arist. *Rh.* 3.2.1404b22.

[33] Cf. D.L. 2.103 on a certain Theodorus (§4) οὗ τὸ φωνασκικὸν φέρεται βιβλίον πάγκαλον. See Cope ad loc. The D.L. reference is not mentioned by Burkert 1975, who usefully collects the prosopography on this once famous actor. That Theodorus could have written such a manual seems reasonable if we compare the material on vocal training gathered in §9 ("Cultures of the voice") below. Whether parallel developments in the culture of the sung voice took place is hard to say but likely, especially given such evidence as [Arist.] *Pr.* 19.15.918b12–16: "Why were *nomoi* not composed with responsion, while choral songs were? Is it because the *nomoi* were performed by professional musicians who were already capable of acting and sustaining their voices, so that what they sang *could* be long and complicated?" (trans. D'Angour 2006, 280).

[34] *Rh.* 3.1.1404a14–15.   [35] *Rh.* 3.1.1403b21; b35.   [36] *Rh.* 3.1.1403b26.

[37] See Diels 1886, 32–34; Fortenbaugh 1985; frr. 712–13 FHS&G (from *On Delivery* [= fr. 666.24]; but note, too, how delivery merges with questions of "the pitch of the voice," τὸν τόνον τῆς φωνῆς, in fr. 712); frr. 681–92 on euphony and frr. 698–704 on rhythm (from, or reflecting, his work *On Style* [frr. 666.17a–b]); fr. 707 (= Quint. *Inst.* 10.1.27) on the virtues, for orators, of reading poets for sublime inspiration, pleasure, and reinvigoration. For a good collection of primary materials pertinent to the profession of acting, see Csapo and Slater 1994, 221–74.

[38] *Rh.* 3.1.1403b20; 3.1.1404a15–19; 3.1.1403a24–26, quoted above.

great dynast."[39] The passage from acting (gesturing) to vocalization (delivery) in the meaning of *hupokrisis* is in one sense not a transition at all, since the two activities are mutually co-involved, at least in the arts of language: actors and rhetors gesture and speak at the same time. But there was also a sequence historically speaking, and Aristotle's *Rhetoric* passively mirrors these developments in its very organization, with its third book, originally a separate work, being devoted entirely to *lexis* and *taxis*, and appended (whether by Aristotle himself or by some later redactor) onto another work in two books on thought or invention (*dianoia*), with these now comprising the first two books of the *Rhetoric*.[40] The *Rhetoric* thus participates in a chain of deferrals that is initiated in the *Poetics*: there, in chapter 19, he had declined to investigate the art of delivery (ἡ ὑποκριτική), "since it belongs to another field [meaning, rhetoric] and not to poetry"[41] – oddly so, given the obvious links, genetic and other, between the art of delivery (ἡ ὑποκριτική) and acting (ὑπόκρισις). Here, in the *Rhetoric*, he is reluctant to delve too deeply into the same topic of delivery.

But even more telling is Aristotle's seeming conflation of delivery and language: he seems incapable of making up his mind which of these two items comprises the final subject matter of his treatise; he announces the topic of Book 3 first as *lexis* but then redescribes it as *hupokrisis*.[42] One suspects a bad conceptual join, as it were, an infelicitous transition in the synthesizing of Aristotle's earlier treatment, whether that synthesis is the work of Aristotle or a later redactor. But while critics have puzzled over this patchiness in the flow of the argument, there is a logic to the apparent mistake.[43] Though mutually irreducible in other respects, what

[39] *Rh.* 3.1.1404a27. But cf. Aeschin. 2.34 on the audience expecting to hear Demosthenes' "extraordinary power of speech" (ὑπερβολάς τινας δυνάμεως ἀκουσόμενοι λόγων). On Aristotle's reluctance, see further Diels 1886, 32; Fortenbaugh 1986, 246.

[40] See D.L. 5.24; Diels 1886; Düring 1966, 121; Düring 1968, 226–27; Burkert 1975, 71; Fortenbaugh 1986; Kennedy 1991, 216–17 and 304–05 (who favors viewing our *Rhetoric* as the product of Aristotle's own revisions). See further n. 43. A weakness in many of these accounts is an inability to state clearly the relationship between delivery and style. Cope 1970, III:2 suggests that style includes delivery (followed somewhat bemusedly by Kennedy 1991, 219 n. 7, but Aristotle does not say this, presumably because for him *lexis* has connotations that are irreducible to *hupokrisis*, and vice versa. Düring 1968, 226 gets it right (though he feels Aristotle failed to deliver on his promises): "Er spricht hier, als ob es seine Absicht ware, die Frage von Grund aus zu behandeln: über die menschliche Stimme, die Tonlagen, die Sprachmelodie, den Rhythmus, die Wörter als Elemente der Sprache, die Satzbildung," etc., as does Fortenbaugh 1986, 246: "the important point is that Aristotle recognizes the fundamental role that voice plays in communication." Cf. n. 99 below.

[41] *Poet.* 19.1456b10; 1456b18–19.   [42] *Rh.* 3.1.1403b14–15; 20–22.

[43] This is the case regardless of who did the synthesizing. When the reorganization of *Rhetoric* 3 occurred is unclear (it may have been the handiwork of a late Hellenistic editor, possibly Andronicus). The thought, however, is all Aristotle's. See Düring 1966, 125, and n. 40 above.

language and delivery share in common is, in fact, the voice, be it written or spoken: they both lie ἐν τῇ φωνῇ, in the realm of the voice, broadly conceived;[44] their domain is that of "volume, pitch, and rhythm" (μέγεθος ἁρμονία ῥυθμός);[45] and both are ultimately a kind of "impression" (φαντασία) that is directed "at the hearer" (πρὸς τὸν ἀκροατήν),[46] which helps to account for the fact that "written speeches owe their effect not so much to the sense as to the style" (*lexis*), which is to say, to the way they sound – a Licymnian point.[47] For the same reason, "what is written should generally be easy to read (εὐανάγνωστον) and easy to speak (εὔφραστον) – which is the same thing."[48] The essential orality of Greek writing naturally leads to this kind of presumption, as it does to the continuous focus, early and later in Book 3, on rhythm,[49] which is a property distinctive neither of *lexis* nor of *hupokrisis*, but only of voice (φωνή). And it was equally natural that with the development of written forms, increasing attention should have been paid to discovering just where their vocal properties lay and how these might be enhanced, and so made euphonic. Luckily, euphony was less lethal to writers than to singers. A speech by Antiphon, *On the Chorister* (419/418 BCE), tells of a certain unfortunate Diodotus, a youthful chorus singer who died from a potion that, according to the hypothesis, promised to improve his voice and make it euphonic.[50]

Indeed, the breathy substance of voice for Aristotle lay at the source of the language arts that would eventually culminate in an exclusive attention to the voice: "Voice (φωνή), the most mimetic of all our parts, *was there to start with* (ὑπῆρξεν). Thus, the [verbal] arts were established: rhapsody and acting and the others."[51] At a lesser extreme, writers of prose would realize the fruitfulness of the conjunction of delivery and *lexis*, treating them nearly as functions of each other, as in Dionysius of Halicarnassus: "Here the style itself (λέξις) shows what kind of delivery (ὑποκρίσεως) is needed for it,"[52] while at the same time preserving a space for the virtues of reading aloud without declamation (as in the passage from Dionysius about "listening to Plato speak" quoted at the start of this chapter). Aristotle, going the other way, would define the true virtue of *lexis* not in terms of its subservience to sound, but in its

---

[44] *Rh.* 3.1.1403b27. Cf. Arist. *Int.* 1.16a3–4 (n. 144 below).
[45] *Rh.* 3.1.1403b31.   [46] *Rh.* 3.1.1404a11; cf. *Poet.* 7.1451a6–7: πρὸς τὴν αἴσθησιν.
[47] *Rh.* 3.1.1404a18–19. *Hupokrisis* and *lexis* are intimately linked again in *Poet.* ch. 19, which has as its basis an analysis of voice (φωνή, ibid., ch. 20).
[48] *Rh.* 3.5.1407b11–12.   [49] A point well remarked on by Fortenbaugh 1986, 243.
[50] εὐφωνίας χάριν (Antiph. 6, *Hypoth.*); see Krumbacher 1920, 15; Blass 1887–98, 1:194 n. 1.
[51] *Rh.* 3.1.1404a21–24.   [52] Dion. Hal. *Dem.* 54; cf. ibid., 22 (177.15–16 U–R).

transparency of meaning: with clarity (τὸ σαφές)[53] and naturalness (the seeming artlessness) defining the goals of expression,[54] and the final aim of rhetoric lying in persuasion and demonstration. And he would cling to the genre boundaries between poetry and prose, resisting their virtual conflation and the tide of popular opinion, which was bewitched by the new poetic qualities of rhetoric (as in the case of Gorgias) – by insisting, "but the *lexis* of prose differs from that of poetry"[55] – even as he recognized the essential rhythmic quality of all well-turned *lexis*, rhythm being (as we saw in the case of Dionysius above) one of the deepest features of language.[56]

In his very resistance to the power of the voice and in his attempt to contain its effects, Aristotle supplies us with evidence of its separation in theory and in practice, as had Plato before him.[57] Aristotle's account is incomplete, but we can fill in some of the gaps ourselves. Noticing these differences will help bring out what is distinctive, and in ways deeply true, about Aristotle's picture of τὰ ἐν τῇ φωνῇ, the domain of the voice, as well as what he neglects to mention, chiefly out of philosophical antipathy.[58]

2 EUPHONY AND THE NEW SCIENCE OF AESTHETIC SOUND

To summarize: the distinction between sound and sense was captured early on in the realm of language, whereby language in its senseless materiality, and considered as sheer vocality without reference to meaning, was felt to be musical and songlike. Once sundered and so justified, the idea of language *qua* sound, voice, or song took on a life of its own. It seems to have attracted independent attention among theoreticians, as in Democritus' studies *On Sounds* (Περὶ φωνῶν), *On the Beauty of Words* (Περὶ καλλοσύνης ἐπέων), and *On Euphonious and Harsh-Sounding Letters* (Περὶ εὐφώνων καὶ δυσφώνων γραμμάτων),[59] or in Plato's *Cratylus*, where, however, sound was explored intensively for its

---

[53] *Rh.* 3.2.1404b1–2; similarly, τὸ σαφὲς τῆς λέξεως *Poet.* 22.1458b1; ibid., 1458a18.
[54] *Rh.* 3.2.1404b18–19.   [55] *Rh.* 3.1.1404a28–29.
[56] It is in the nature of *lexis* to be rhythmical: *Rh.* 3.9.1409a22–24; cf. ibid. 3.7.1408b30–31.
[57] See the passages from Pl. *Rep.* 3 to be cited below; and Fortenbaugh 1986, 246; 250.
[58] The phrase [τὰ] ἐν τῇ φωνῇ recurs in *Int.* 1.16a3–4 (n. 144 below).
[59] D.L. 9.48. The titles are generally taken to be authentic. At the very least, they point to their plausibility in antiquity, which is significant by itself.

immediate mimetic characteristics, and thus not quite independently of meaning. Eventually, much later, an entire branch of literary criticism would come to be devoted to the way language sounds,[60] not to mention the subdivision of grammar into a special topic devoted to the voice (περὶ φωνῆς, *de voce*).[61] Rhetoric was once again involved in this increasing isolation of the voice. We might compare Cicero: "For on the question of voice (*de voce*) I am not yet speaking of points that concern delivery, but about a matter that seems to me to be connected with utterance as such," by which he means the mechanics of utterance – the regulation of the "tongue and breath and actual tone of voice" (*vocis sonus ... ipse*).[62] Plainly, to isolate the voice was to concentrate on its aesthetic qualities.

But the later technical language must have had roots in late fifth- to mid-fourth-century predecessors, as we saw. That it did, and that it had already filtered into the minds of practicing rhetoricians in Aristotle's day, is further indicated by the example of Aeschines in his speech *Against Ctesiphon* from 330 BCE.[63] Indeed, Aeschines and Demosthenes are precious but little-examined witnesses to the degree to which literary aesthetics had become practically second nature by the mid-fourth century. Aeschines here is castigating Demosthenes for both the harshness and the excessive musicality and seductiveness of his speeches. Combing through his speeches with the variegated arsenal of a literary critic – κατὰ τὸ λεκτικόν, as Dionysius later noticed[64] – he singles out Demosthenes' delivery, which is enhanced by his exploitation of pitches (ὁ τόνος τῆς φωνῆς)[65] and by his compositional technique (τὴν τῶν ὀνομάτων σύνθεσιν).[66] Demosthenes could repay the compliment, labeling Aeschines "euphonious," as though this were a dubious distinction, at least in the hands of a corrupt user like his opponent.[67] These are two of the

---

[60] The experiments by musicians and especially by poets, such as Sacadas of Argos, Lasus of Hermione, Pindar, Lysander of Sicyon, Pratinas, and others, can only have prompted these later critical theories. See Ch. 7 below.

[61] See Ax 1986.   [62] *De or.* 3.40–41; trans. Rackham.   [63] Aeschin. 3.142; 209–10; 229.

[64] *Dem.* 35. In addition to places in Aeschin. 3, Dionysius mentions Aeschin. 2.34 and 40, which are more specifically devoted to criticisms of *lexis* (fondness for obscurity, neologisms or arcane terms, etc.). He could have added Aeschin. 2.157 (Demosthenes' harsh and ungodly voice).

[65] Aeschin. 3.210 (cf. 3.209), a phrase that would later be picked up by Theophrastus (see n. 98 below). Cf. Cic., *Orat.* 56–59, e.g. 59: "Certainly natural excellence of voice is to be desired, and the superior orator will therefore vary and modulate his voice; now raising and now lowering it, he will run through the whole scale of tones" (*omnis sonorum ... persequetur gradus*) (trans. Hubbell).

[66] Aeschin. 3.142.

[67] Dem. 18.285; 19.126; 19.337–39, where 338 praises the qualifications of any herald who is capable of euphony (who is εὔφωνος), while 339 likewise praises euphoniousness (δεινότητ᾽ ἢ εὐφωνίαν ἢ τι τῶν ἄλλων τῶν τοιούτων ἀγαθῶν) – though not in Aeschines' case.

handful of recorded instances of the terms εὐφώνως and εὐφωνία (*euphoniously* and *euphony*) down through the fourth century BCE, the earliest being found in Pindar (twice) and then in Aeschylus (once) and thereafter not again until Aristophanes, Critias, and Xenophon. The last of these passages by Demosthenes starts off with a technical-sounding disquisition, as it were, *On the Voice*: "And indeed, it is perhaps necessary to say something about his voice [or more abstractly, 'about the voice'] as well ..." (καίτοι καὶ περὶ τῆς φωνῆς ἴσως εἰπεῖν ἀνάγκη). We might recall Cicero above: "For on the question of voice (*de voce*) ..." The same applies to other similar aesthetic qualities of the voice, the terms for which have a long afterlife in criticism, but which can be traced in fourth-century Attic orators: brightness, strength, clarity, loudness, liveliness, its capacity for being well acted or well delivered, and the like.[68]

Similarly, Isocrates shows himself to be fluent in what looks like the vocabulary of literary criticism, for instance in his mention of the accessories of "voice and the variations" (μεταβολῶν) of delivery,[69] and in his general awareness of the proximities of literary prose and poetry: he describes his output as being "closer to works composed with rhythm and music than to court-room speeches," and as affording his audience (οἱ ἀκούοντες) pleasures akin to those of poetry.[70] That is, there seems to have existed already by this time a kind of theoretical reflection on the subject to which Dionysius of Halicarnassus, possibly in imitation, would later devote a treatise – using the very same phrase ("the composition of words") as is found in Aeschines (and nowhere else earlier) for his title and in his writings, and in various permutations: περὶ συνθέσεως ὀνομάτων, ἡ τῶν ὀνομάτων σύνθεσις, etc.[71] If so, then none of this literature has survived, and we have only the scarcest trace elements of this kind of activity in the surviving works of such writers as the orators. Meanwhile, reflection on delivery, especially as this pertained to the voice, became an accepted element in rhetorical handbooks once delivery was

---

[68] Dem. 19.199: λαμπρᾷ τῇ φωνῇ; 206: τίνα δὲ φθέγγεσθαι μέγιστον ἁπάντων καὶ σαφέστατ᾽ ἂν εἰπεῖν ὅ τι βούλοιτο τῇ φωνῇ; 216 (the answer is, "Aeschines"): μηδέ γ᾽ εἰ καλὸν καὶ μέγ᾽ οὗτος φθέγξεται (where "fine" and "loud" qualify each other); 18.313: νεανίας ("vigorous, lively": Jebb, ad loc.), λαμπροφωνότατος, ὑποκριτὴς ἄριστος; cf. 18.259.

[69] Isoc. 5.26.   [70] Isoc. 15.46–47; cf. *Ep.* 1.2; fr. 12.

[71] The closest parallel is ἡ τοιαύτη σύνθεσις ἔκ τε ῥημάτων γιγνομένη καὶ ὀνομάτων (Pl. *Soph.* 263d); but even this could postdate Aeschines' texts. Cf. also Anaximenes, *Rh. Al.* 22.8; 25.1; 25.3–4 (late fourth century). The point I am making here is slightly different from the one I made earlier (p. 238) about the presence of technical linguistic and musical vocabulary in the fourth-century courtroom, though the two developments are obviously related.

canonized by Theophrastus.[72] It is worth noting two final continuities: Aeschines studied under Alcidamas, while Demosthenes was influenced by Alcidamas;[73] and both cultivated ties to the stage, whether by training as an actor (Aeschines) or by studying under actors (Demosthenes).[74]

Sunthesis, mousikoi, harmonikoi

Aristotle fingers the poets as the culprits for the developments he charts, but that can't be the whole story. As the language in the examples from the orators begins to suggest, and as Aristotle's own language betrays, musical terminology could be interchanged with literary-critical terminology. Does the idea of *sunthesis onomatōn*, or the composition of words, owe a debt to the musical tradition?[75] Quite possibly. Music seems to have been in the minds of anyone reflecting on the uses of the voice in non-musical contexts, even if that is not the picture Aristotle would have us see, charting as he does developments in the arts of language without directly mentioning the musical inheritance. The connection would seem obvious: reflection on the voice as a resource of sound, and one that obeys pre-rational criteria, inevitably points to the musical voice, by which we should understand that which in the voice evades rational analysis and creates irrational effects on the hearers.

A case in point is the hyporcheme fragment attributed to Pratinas, the dates of which are disputed (either late sixth or early fifth century). Controversies of dating aside, what matters here is the heart of the polemic it purveys (or mocks – a satyr chorus is "speaking"):

What is this din? (τίς ὁ θόρυβος ὅδε;) What are these dance-steps? What outrage has come to the noisy altar of Dionysus? Mine, mine is Bromius: it is for me to shout and stamp ... singing a song of flashing wings like the swan. *Song* (ἀοιδάν) *was made queen by the Pierian: so let the pipe dance in second place* (ὁ δὲ αὐλὸς | ὕστερον χορευέτω): *he is the servant* .... Beat the one with the mottled toad-breath, burn the spittle-wasting reed with its prattling growl (λαλοβαρύοπα), striding across melody and rhythm (παραμελορυθμοβάταν), its body fashioned under the auger! Look this way! Here is how to fling out hand and foot! Thriambodithyrambus, lord with ivy in your hair, hear, hear my Dorian dance-song.[76]

---

[72] E.g., Dion. Hal. *Dem.* 54–56. On Theophrastus' innovation, see Diels 1886, 32–34.
[73] Alcidamas T4–6 Avezzù.   [74] See at nn. 255 and 257 below.
[75] As Dionysius suggests in other contexts, e.g., *Lys.* 11: "The advice which teachers of music (οἱ μουσικοί) give ...."
[76] Fr. 708 *PMG* = *TrGF* 1.4 fr. 3; trans. Campbell.

The opposition of song and music is clear, and within that opposition, the subordination of the *aulos* to the sung voice is being laid down as firmly as a law. The terms are identical to those later enforced by Aristotle, and they reappear in the debates around the New Music (which, on one dating of the fragment, they may reflect). In each case, sheer and senseless musicality, here represented by the supple tones of the *aulos*, is being criticized for encroaching on the domain of meaning (represented in part by the orderly symmetries of melody and rhythm, and in part just by what the chorus has to say). The voice here is taking on the role of the signifier – and establisher – of orderly meaning.

In the New Music, musicality could be represented by the *aulos*, but also by the non-semantic features of language itself: sound for its own sake (sound figures),[77] violation of pitch accent and other melodic and rhythmic contours associated with speech, syntax fitted to musical rhythm as opposed to sense divisions (word and phrase breaks), and sensuous, imagistic, and riddling expressions, devolving into "sweet nothings" and "empty sounds."[78] Some of this account we owe to the third book of Aristotle's *Rhetoric*, and some of it to his reflection of what has been nicely termed the "collective problem with the *aulos*," as in the *Politics*: "Let us add that the *aulos* [which is orgiastic] prevents the player from using words; and this is another fact about it that militates against education."[79] The bias was widespread, early and late, and it usually took the form of a reminder that playing the *aulos* physically distorted the mouth, the natural organ of rational speech. Melanippides, a dithyrambic poet and representative of the New Music from the mid-fifth century, paradoxically had Athena disparage the art of the aulos in his *Marsyas*: "Athena threw the instruments from her holy hand and said, 'Away, shameful things, defilers of my body (σώματι λύμα)! I do not give myself to ugliness (κακότατι)'."[80] In the same vein, the aulete Pronomus of Thebes (*fl.* 400 BCE) was famous because he "drove his audiences wild with his facial contortions and the gyrations of his body."[81]

As a dithyrambic poet reminiscent of the New Music and as a rhetorician, Licymnius was exactly the kind of verbal artist in whom the two areas of Aristotle's anxieties coincided. The sheer senseless materiality of

---

[77] Antisthenes would call these *tropoi* (fr. 51 Decleva Caizzi = fr. 187 Giannantoni). See n. 117 below.

[78] Arist. *Rh.* 3.1.1404a24; 13.1414b17. Excellent discussion of all these features of the dithyramb in Csapo 2004, 218–29 and in D'Angour 2006; also Martin 2003.

[79] Wilson 2002b, 45 (quotation); Arist. *Rh.* 3.3.1406b1–2; 3.9.1409b23–29; 3.15.1415a10; *Pol.* 8.6.1341a24–25; trans. Barker 1984, 177–78.

[80] Ath. 14.616e–f; trans. Barker.   [81] Paus. 9.12.6; trans. D'Angour 2006, 272.

sound cannot for Aristotle be allowed to take primacy over meaning, any more than it could for Pratinas (or his satyr personae). But with the premise that meaning takes precedence over sound, a series of entailments follow: pleasure, seduction, and rapture are all code names in the earlier traditions for meaningless (musical) sound, which contrasts with (unmusical) sense. One of the earliest instances of this pairing is the enchanting and deadly song of the Sirens in Homer, which promises an unstable combination of aural pleasure and deep knowledge.[82] This is the beginning of the *dulce* and *utile* paradigm, or rather split, that continues into Xenophanes, then later poets, and which is found in the reaction against the dithyrambists, in the *Dissoi Logoi*, in Plato, then in Eratosthenes of Cyrene, and thenceforth makes its way into the broader streams of literary criticism.[83] How disconcerting it must have been for Aristotle to find the voice – that rational signature of the human animal – infected by convention with all the traits of irrational matter.[84]

Aeschines' speech against Ctesiphon cannot be understood in any other way except against such a background: Demosthenes is himself "a man who has been compacted of words" (ἐξ ὀνομάτων συγκείμενος) .... If you took away his tongue, as with flutes, there would be no remainder."[85] That is, Demosthenes' language is all show with no substance, all *lexis* and delivery, all *voice* and no meaning. His critique of Demosthenes' exploitation of musical pitches is of a piece with this assault. Aristotle's account of voice in the *Rhetoric* betrays some of the same technical language (not to speak of the paired activities of selection and combination he mentions: "selecting ... one combines," ἐκλέγων συντιθῇ),[86] which could stem from the musical tradition, but also from the researches of Hippias, Prodicus, and Thrasymachus, who may have been picking up on the cue of a wider scientific and medical tradition, though Aristotle is here referring specifically to the field of poetry (if not also that of poetics): "It is a matter of how the voice should be used in expressing each emotion, sometimes loud and sometimes soft and [sometimes] intermediate, and

---

[82] Hom. *Od.* 12.185–92. Demosthenes apparently tarred Aeschines with the same brush, by comparing him to the Sirens and their music (τὴν τῶν Σειρήνων μουσικήν), or so Aeschines claims (Aeschin. 3.228; see Easterling 1999, 154).

[83] Xenoph. fr. 81 DK: "the fictions (πλάσματα) of former [poets] ... in which there is nothing useful (χρηστόν)"; *Dialex.* 3.17: "and the poets make poems, not aiming at truth (ἀλάθειαν), but aiming at pleasures (τὰς ἀδονάς) for people"; Pl. *Rep.* 10.607d: poetry ideally should not only give pleasure, but also be useful; Eratosthenes *ap.* Strab. 1.2.3: "the poet aims at entertainment (ψυχαγωγίας), not at instruction (διδασκαλίας)."

[84] Arist. *Int.* 1.16a; *De an.* 2.8.420b.   [85] Aeschin. 3.229.

[86] *Rh.* 3.2.1404b25. Cf. Pl. *Symp.* 198d5–6: ἐκλεγομένους ... τιθέναι.

how the pitch accents (τόνοι) should be used, whether as acute, grave, or circumflex (οἷον ὀξεία καὶ βαρεία καὶ μέση), and what rhythms should be expressed in each case: for [those who study delivery in poetry] consider three things, and these are volume, change of pitch, and rhythm" (μέγεθος ἁρμονία ῥυθμός).[87]

Though Aristoxenus gives us the first clear attestation of the analogy between the two kinds of *sunthesis*, musical and linguistic, he was probably preceded by Hippias and others.[88] For, if Plato can speak of the elements (*stoicheia*) of music, this can only presuppose their *sunthesis* in a composition.[89] The componential (*stoicheion*) model, inherited by Plato, *ipso facto* implies a compositional (*sunthesis*) model. Thus, in his *Elements of Harmony*, Aristoxenus writes, "the nature of continuity in melody (ἐν τῇ μελῳδίᾳ) seems to be similar to that which in speech (ἐν τῇ λέξει) relates to the putting together of letters" (περὶ τὴν τῶν γραμμάτων σύνθεσιν).[90] The idea of notes standing in a *sunthesis* is a commonplace of the treatise. Another section of this same work treats of the phenomenon of "voice" generally, including its "movements" ("relaxation," "tension," "pitch," etc.).[91] The analogy between music and literature is found again in Theophrastus, and it later becomes a foundational axiom in both areas of analysis, for instance in Philodemus' *On Music*, where it is allowed that there is a congenital similarity between music and grammar, and then in the literary criticism of Dionysius of Halicarnassus, as the epigraph to this chapter shows.[92]

In literature, the analogy could take on a more technical or a more associative aspect, depending on the context – the former usually denoting an Aristoxenian heritage, the latter a grander rhetorical heritage that stretched back at least to Isocrates. For Isocrates, Greek eloquence produces "discourses which, as everyone will agree" – presumably, at least since Gorgias – "are more akin to works composed in rhythm and set to music (τοῖς μετὰ μουσικῆς καὶ ῥυθμῶν πεποιημένοις) than to the speeches which are made in court.... All men take as much pleasure (χαίρουσιν) in listening to this kind of prose as in listening to poetry" (τῶν ἐν τοῖς μέτροις πεποιημένων).[93] Ironically, in the judgment of

[87] *Rh.* 3.1.1403b27–31. For the wider intellectual background, see Griffith 1984, 287.
[88] Aristox. *Harm.* 27.19–20, 37.1–8; see Ch. 4, §7 above.   [89] Pl. *Tht.* 206b.
[90] Aristox. *Harm.* 27.18–20; trans. Barker.   [91] Ibid., 1.3.
[92] Phld. *De mus.* 4 col. 22.35–38 Neubecker = col. 136.35–38 Delattre: κατὰ μέντοι τὸ γρά[φεσ]θαι καὶ ἀνταποδιδόναι τ[ὸ] μέλος ἔστω τι παραπλήσι[ο]ν αὐ[τ]ῆς [sc., τῆς μουσικῆς] καὶ τῆι γραμματι[κῆι]; Dion. Hal. *Comp.* 11, *passim*, and esp. 40.17–41.1 U–R. Further, Kroll 1907, 93; Koller 1963, 174–79 (thanks to D. Schenkeveld for reminding me of this last work).
[93] Isoc. 15.46–47; trans. Norlin. Cf. Isoc. *Ep.* 1.2, to be quoted below at n. 185.

posterity, Isocrates' straining after the musical qualities of euphony (τὴν εὐφωνίαν ἐντείνων μουσικήν) was misguided, and it distracted him from achieving a genuinely lively style – and genuine euphony.[94] After Isocrates and before Hieronymus of Rhodes, there is Ephorus of Cyme, Isocrates' pupil, who treated prosodic features in his work *On Style* (Περὶ λέξεως), and who was remembered in the later euphonist tradition for his contributions.[95] Because Ephorus also strongly advocated the medium of writing over oral performance, it is reasonable to conclude that his work on prosody explored the vocal possibilities of writing, probably along the lines of Isocrates and against the overt position taken by Isocrates' arch-rival Alcidamas (on whom more below). Prose has virtues of its own and must not imitate the qualities of poetry.[96] Ephorus' refusal to measure metrics in terms of intervals of time aligns him with the *metrikoi* against the *rhuthmikoi*, and may be a further sign of his literary puritanism. But his explorations were not, for all this, strictly negative. He made positive contributions to the understanding of prosody, and at an early date. Nor was he alone. There was also Theodectes, the Athenian tragic poet, orator, and rhetorical theorist on whom Aristotle composed a study. And Theopompus the historian shared some of Ephorus' views and held others of his own.[97] Aristotle was clearly pointing to an entire region of activity around Ephorus in the area of music and the voice.

Significantly, Aristotle's emphasis is on voice, not on gesture (an element that Theophrastus would bring back into the picture).[98] Once again, *hupokrisis* understood as delivery is of interest for what it shares with *lexis*, even if the two are irreducibly different elements of rhetorical speech.[99] Aristotle's emphasis on *hupokrisis* as quintessentially vocal is a salutary reminder of the difference not only between rhetoric as delivery and as acting with gestures, but also more generally between expressiveness (for example, reading aloud) and declamation.[100] (The same associations will persist in

---

[94] Dion. Hal. *Isoc.* 3; ibid., 13.

[95] *FGrHist* 70F6 and 107–08; §33 Radermacher; Phld. *De poem.* 2(?) *P. Herc.* 994, cols. 36.25–37.1 Sbordone. Further, Janko 2000, 183 n. 1, on Ephorus; Janko, ibid., 183–84 and Porter 2001a, on this prosodic tradition.

[96] *FGrHist* 76F1. See esp. the mentions in Cic. *Orat.* (*FGrHist* 70F107), which suggest that Ephorus explored prosody in order to set limits on its use vis-à-vis poetry.

[97] See Ch. 2 at n. 144 above.

[98] Cf. Fortenbaugh 1985, 271. Theophrastus defines delivery as the coordination of bodily motion and "the pitch of the voice" (τὸν τόνον τῆς φωνῆς)" (fr. 712 FHS&G).

[99] Cf. Krumbacher 1920, 15: "dem stimmlichen Moment kam dabei [sc., in delivery] die Hauptrolle zu"; Calboli 1983.

[100] *Rh.* 3.12.

Rome.[101]) But this move also serves to contain the voice, at least for Aristotle: it limits the perceived value of the voice as a gesture in its own right, a point revealingly made in *Rhetoric* 3: "*hupokrisis* (τὸ ὑποκριτικόν [acting understood as gesture generally, not vocality in specific]) is a matter of natural talent and largely not reductive to artistic rule (ἀτεχνότερον); but insofar as it involves how things are said (περὶ δὲ τὴν λέξιν), it has an artistic element" (ἔντεχνον).[102] The same point is developed at greater length in the *Poetics*.[103]

Here it is worth recalling Plato's strictures on the correct speaker (ὁ ὀρθῶς λέγων) in *Republic* 3, that is, on the narrator of poetry and how he manipulates his voice, in a passage that serves as an appendix to the more famous distinction between kinds of narrative voice (*mimēsis* and *diēgēsis*). The strictures arise in the course of an attempt to outline a theory of kinds (*eidē*) of style (*lexis*) and of narrative (*diēgēsis*) that must surely be novel, to judge from Adeimantus' seeming unfamiliarity with the distinctions.[104] The upshot for Plato is that variations (*metabolai*) in the voice of the "correct" speaker "are not to be great": harmonic and rhythmic modulations, accomplices of mimetic effects, are to be reduced to a bare minimum.[105] Similar restrictions are laid on the musical voice in the same work, for instance in Book 3, where polyharmonic modalities and modulations of the voice (presumably of pitch) are criticized.[106] Is Plato bucking a new tide? It often seems as if he is.[107] At times, Plato's text reads like an excerpt from a musical treatise on "the movement of the voice" (Aristoxenus),[108] and Plato does in fact refer later on in the same work to a group of theoreticians called "harmonicists." These are quite likely the very same group whom Aristoxenus mentions as his own predecessors in the study of "harmonic motion," presumably dating from the end of the fifth century.[109] But there are further and earlier hints pointing to the musical analysis of rhetorical speech.

[101] "*Pronuntiatio* is called *actio* by many people. It seems to have acquired the first name from its voice-element (*a voce*), the second from its element of gesture. Cicero in one passage [*De or.* 3.222; cf. *Orat.* 55] calls *actio* a 'sort of language,' and in another 'a kind of eloquence of the body.'... So we are free to use both names indifferently" (Quint. *Inst.* 11.3.1; trans. Russell).

[102] *Rh.* 3.1.1404a.15–16.

[103] Cf. *Poet.* 6.1450b17 (disparaging *opsis* on the same grounds) and *Poet.* ch. 16; and see n. 31 above.

[104] Pl. *Rep.* 3.396c2.   [105] *Rep.* 3.396b–397c.

[106] E.g., Pl. *Rep.* 3.399a8–9: πρεπόντως ἂν μιμήσαιτο φθόγγους τε καὶ προσῳδίας. See 399a–d generally.

[107] See Pl. *Rep.* 3.410a–412b; Pl. *Grg.* 501e–502c; and D'Angour 2006, esp. 282 on Pl. *Rep.* 3.400a1: "Over a century after Pratinas lamented the subordination of song to melody, Plato complained that modern music had attained a new nadir in its subordination of *logos* to *melos*."

[108] Aristox. *Harm.* 3.5–6. For the same phrase, cf. Pl. *Leg.* 2.672e.

[109] Aristox. *Harm.* 2.6–3.4 (where it appears that Aristoxenus devoted a now lost treatise to this group, possibly called *On the Harmonicists*). See further Barker 1989, 55 n. 5; Barker 2007, ch. 2.

The Hibeh Papyrus

One of these is the tantalizing Hibeh musical papyrus, which is of interest not only for the light it sheds on musical theory and practice in the early fourth century, but just as importantly for the way it documents the contestation over authority in the public sphere among two rival discourses, rhetoric and music.[110] The anxiety of the speaker, who is plainly himself an orator,[111] has to do with professional boundaries (claims to critical judgment and expertise). The opponents he has in view are musical theorists who happen to call themselves "harmonicists" (these must be the same group identified by Plato) and who claim to excel in the domain of the trained ear.[112] The speaker is "surprised at the way [they] construct demonstrations not belonging [to their own areas of expertise]," namely in instrumentalism and song, while they lay claim only to (empirical) "theory" (τὸ θεωρητικὸν μέρος). And so, "they waste [their entire life] on strings" making their demonstrations of theory, "they do everything worse than any orator one might come across ... and they beat the rhythm all wrong."[113] Orators can only have been sensitive to their debts to the musicologists and to the inevitable similarities between oratory and musical practice. Alcidamas, to whom Brancacci intriguingly attributes this papyrus fragment, is aware that improvised speechmaking, in distancing itself from writing, necessarily approaches other forms of presentation, such as acting and rhapsodic performance (*hupokrisis* and *rhapsōidia*),[114] the same pair of terms that Aristotle singles out in *Rhetoric* 3.1,[115] but also, in some respects, music (compare Alcidamas' emphasis on speaking opportunely and musically[116]). Antisthenes, who noted that the orator's skill

---

[110] *P. Hib.* 1.13, cols. 1–2. See Barker 1984, 183–85; Brancacci 1988; Avezzù 1994; Barker 2007, 69–73.

[111] Col. 1.1–3.

[112] Cf. Pl. *Phdr.* 268d–e where a similar criticism is lodged against a similarly self-appointed *harmonikos*.

[113] Trans. Barker 1984, 184–85.   [114] *Soph.* 14.

[115] *Rh.* 3.1.1403b22; 1404a23. Cf. ibid. 3.12.1414a15–17: "Where there is most need of performance (ὑπόκρισις), the least exactness (ἀκρίβεια) is present. This occurs where the voice is important and especially a loud voice" (μεγάλης [sc., φωνῆς]), a passage that strongly recalls Alcidamas' *On Sophists*. One suspects there is a good deal of Alcidamas lurking behind Aristotle's presentations in Book 3. (Cf. also O'Sullivan 1992, 43 n. 107; 74.) I am assuming that these terms for performance are positive traits for Alcidamas, as does O'Sullivan 1992, 47 and 59, but not at 49 n. 148. Tragic vocal performance must have paved the way for this positive evaluation of the booming voice (cf. schol. Dion. Thrax 17.29–34 Hilgard, linking the "loud voice" with "solemnity" and grandeur [*ogkos*]).

[116] τὸ εὐκαίρως καὶ μουσικῶς εἰπεῖν (*Soph.* 31).

is music-like,[117] seems to have written a work called *On Music*.[118] Possibly Alcidamas did too.[119]

If the analysis of rhetorical speech had not yet progressed to the same degree of sophistication as the theory of the voice in music and poetry, Aristotle, who would do little to advance this progress, was nonetheless right to predict that this development was just around the corner.[120] What he perhaps could not foresee was the form this progression would take. Poetic language was changing; it was approaching the language of speech. The language of prose, for its part, was seemingly going in two directions at once: it was taking its cues from the earlier poets, and it was following the natural progression of poetic *lexis* as this began descending to the level of the everyday.[121] Aristotle was critical of the first tendency, which seemed anachronistic and absurd.[122] But what about the second tendency? It would be up to later generations to decide, and to attempt a genuine poetics of prose.[123] Sound (φωνή, the voice) might appear too reductive and narrow a category to fulfill as many promises as all of this, but the limitations of the category are precisely where its generative power lay.

From here lay unlimited aesthetic possibilities awaiting discovery: sound as a material object of art and technique with a claim to attention equal to that of poetic meaning; and the irrational allures of sound. Standing, therefore, in a direct line of descent and at the end of the progression was one of the more extreme forms of euphonic criticism, which devoted itself exclusively to the resources of sound while scanting the remaining features of literary language, whether in prose or poetry, as so many accessories to the true object of aesthetic experience, namely, aural pleasure. Our main witnesses to this trend are the so-called *kritikoi*, a motley assemblage of Hellenistic euphonist literary critics (probably assembled by Crates of Mallos, the Pergamene Homerist and critic from the mid-second century BCE) who are attacked vehemently, and so too

---

[117] χρῆται τῷ τρόπῳ καὶ ἐπὶ φωνῆς καὶ ἐπὶ μελῶν ἐξαλλαγῆς (fr. 51 Decleva Caizzi = fr. 187 Giannantoni).

[118] D.L. 6.17.

[119] Brancacci 1988, 79 n. 41. Alcidamas rejects the analogy between rhetoric and poetry in *On Sophists*, but his own writing is highly poeticized and frequently dwells on poetry. More than that, it strongly recalls many of the features of the dithyramb signaled at n. 78 above – at least in Aristotle's (sharply critical) view, which may contain a grain of truth. See further Solmsen 1932.

[120] *Rh.* 3.1.1404a12–14: "Whenever delivery comes to be considered it will function in the same way as acting, and some have tried to say a little about it, for example, Thrasymachus."

[121] *Rh.* 3.1.1404a29–39; 3.2.1404b24–25.   [122] *Rh.* 3.1.1404a35–36.

[123] Cf. Dion. Hal. *De imit.* fr. 9 (Lysias). See further Whitmarsh 2006.

ironically preserved for us, by the Epicurean from the Bay of Naples, Philodemus of Gadara.[124] Like Aristotle and other philosophers after him (including Epicurus and the Stoics), Philodemus puts a premium on clarity of expression and the conveyance of meaning, but not so the group he opposes himself to. A later echo of this one-sided critical tendency is found in the stylistic essays of Dionysius of Halicarnassus. The flowering of euphonist literary criticism *pure* is intense but short-lived. After the first century BCE, euphonism returns to the fold of literary criticism as one more component among others, but never again quite as preeminent among them.

3 THE VIVACITY OF THE VOICE

The intimate association of *hupokrisis* and the voice is borne out by one further piece of evidence, which will help backdate the phenomenon, but will also add to it another vital dimension that has yet to be named in the present context. The evidence comes in the form of an Athenian inscription from the early fifth century, originally belonging to an *ex voto* bronze statuette (now lost), which reads:

> To all men I answer (*hυποκ|ρίνομαι*) the same thing (ἴσ'),
>   whoever asks (ἐ[ρ|ο]τᾶι) me
>   which man dedicated me: "Antiphanes, as a tithe."[125]

Adducing the inscription as an example of archaic "speaking objects," and discussing the usage of the (originally Ionic) verb form and its Attic congener ἀποκρίνομαι, Svenbro suggests that the verb ὑποκρίνομαι carries connotations beyond merely "answering": it picks out the object *as* a speaking object, and thus designates the "vocal implications" of the statue. "A strong theatrical connotation" is also inevitable, he claims, given the institutionalization of tragic contests in 534 BCE by Thespis in Athens and the role of the same verb in that context. Unhappy with "I answer" as a translation for ὑποκρίνομαι, Svenbro suggests, as an alternative paraphrase, that the statue "interprets" the enigmatic writing on its base: it "'deciphers itself' before the eyes of the spectator-reader, who does not have to make the effort of vocalizing the written word,

---

[124] See Porter 1995a on Crates' role in this organization of the literary critical past.
[125] πᾶσιν ἴσ' ἀνθρόποι|[ς] *hυποκ|ρίνομαι, hόστις ἐ[ρ|ο]τᾶι*| *hός μ' ἀνέθεκ' ἀνδρõν·* "Ἀντιφάνες δεκάτεν." *IG* I³ 533 = *CEG* 286. I follow the text of D. Lewis and L. Jeffery, not the translation or text of Svenbro 1993, 172, who cites Lazzarini 1976, no. 658.

for the simple reason that here the writing 'vocalizes' itself." [126] This seems both over-elaborate and patently false: it is the reader who ventriloquizes the statue. Nevertheless, if one wished to reach beyond the question-and-answer scenario in order to bring out additional connotations, a simpler and better translation of the term might be "I enact" (or "give voice to") "my response." And if one compares other inscriptional uses of ὑποκριν-verbs, it appears that Svenbro's general point about vocality is reinforced by these examples, though not his particular justification.

When Svenbro goes on to note that the Antiphanes inscription is "our earliest clear example of an inscription using, with regard to itself, the metaphor of the voice," he is on firmer ground, especially if one takes into account the entire genre of inscriptions to which it appears to belong: those that turn manufactured objects into "speaking objects," or better yet, "speaking artifacts," of which the monument to Phrasicleia is only one of the best known:

> I am the grave [or "monument"] (σῆμα) of Phrasicleia. I shall
>   always be called (κεκλέσομαι) "girl" (κόρε),
> having received this name from the gods in place of marriage.
> Aristion the Parian made me. [127]

The role of the voice in the metaphorical tug of war between poetry and sculpture will be underscored once again in the final chapter on "sublime monuments" below, and we shall see later in this chapter (§4) how the same nexus of motifs is activated again around the turn of the fourth century in debates over the primacy of speech and writing. The prescient anticipation of Plato's (or else Alcidamas') critique of the fixity of writing in the Antiphanes inscription ("I answer the same thing to all who ask me") is probably no accident, especially if Plato was, so to speak, merely giving voice, in turn, to a well-worn topos, of which the Antiphanes inscription may well be the earliest recorded instance. [128] In any event, one point of this brief glance back has been to show how the explicit

[126] Svenbro 1993, 173. cf. *IG* II² 429: ... ὑποκρινο[μ - - -], apparently similar, but lacking context (and likewise Athenian, but post 336/5). The only other early examples of inscriptions framed by the dialogue (question and response) form known to me are *CEG* 110 (only hinting at the form), 120, 429, and *AP* 16.23 (Simonides?), the latter of contested date – though subsequently the dialogue form becomes a common feature of the latter genre.

[127] Svenbro, ibid. Phrasicleia: *IG* I³ 1261 = *CEG* 24 (*c.* 540 BCE, Attic), in stoichedon. On Phrasicleia, see Svenbro 1993, ch. 1; Steiner 2001, 258–59.

[128] Alcidamas *Soph.* 28: "a written speech, which has just one form and arrangement (ἑνὶ σχήματι καὶ τάξει κεχρημένος), may have some striking effects when viewed in a book, but for a particular occasion is of no help to those who have it because it cannot change (ἀκίνητος)" (trans. Gagarin and Woodruff 1995). Even if Alcidamas anticipated Plato in his critique of writing's fixity,

connection between *hupokrisis* and the voice is attested early on, while their co-implication would only tighten over the next century or so. But there is another theme that comes to the fore in the early inscriptional record, and it is on this connection that I want to dwell a while longer, as it also happens to point to one of the earliest uses to which writing was first put in the Graeco-Roman world.

Grave markers that "respond" to passers-by display the quality of aliveness that only a living speaker has. Those that cannot respond in this way instead pointedly play upon the melancholic associations of death's disruption of speech. But votive and other inscriptions frequently participate in a similar dynamic by bringing materials to life in much the same way, as in the case of the Antiphanes dedication, which takes the form of a lively exchange with the reader. As we can see from the Phrasicleia inscription, one of the main attractions of the voice was its immediate connection to life. To speak was to breathe and literally (or figuratively) to give expression to the soul. But to do so was simultaneously to quicken matter, literally to animate it, rendering it palpable, audible, sensible, and aesthetic, and in a way that short-circuited (and often eventually enhanced) appeals to meaning. Here we return to a theme that was raised in Chapter 1, and that, as we saw, runs through so much of aesthetic speculation, albeit with different accents, from Aristotle to Epicurus to Hume, Kant, Shklovsky, and Dewey: the connection between aesthetic activity, the feeling of life, and the vivacity of sensation. Only here we find that connection being expressed in poetic and intuitive form. The depth of this insight and its implications for the verbal and musical arts were realized early on, as the Aeschylean fragment from the satyr play *Theoroi* or *Isthmiastai* shows:

Look hard and tell me if [you can spot the difference between this image of me and me] ... This [votive] image (εἴδωλον) full of my form, this imitation of Daedalus, *lacks only a voice* (φωνῆς δεῖ μόνον).[129]

Give the statue a voice and it will come to life, indistinguishably real, being nearly that now, a copy lacking only breath and voice, the satyr seems to be saying.[130]

Plato's treatment of writing's inability to reply save in one way (*Phdr.* 275d) recalls the Antiphanes inscription even more closely than it does Alcidamas. Cf. also Fantuzzi 2004, 322.
[129] Aesch. *TrGF* 78a, col. 1.5–8.
[130] Steiner 2001, 46–47 gets the emphasis right (in the wake of Morris 1992, 219–20): at stake in the fragment is "not so much the artist's skill in exactly replicating nature as his ability to create a semblance of life," indeed, "to mimic life." Nevertheless, the fragment never stops pointing to the ineluctable gap between the artifact and life, which is occupied by the missing element of the voice. See Ch. 3, at n. 180 above.

The connection between life and voice was nothing new. It was well established among the Presocratics. We might compare a fragment in which Empedocles retails an early stage of evolution when human creatures were mere "shapes" (τύποι) lacking "the desirable form of limbs or voice (ἐνοπήν), which is the part proper to men": perhaps they were alive after a fashion, but they lacked the specific *differentiae* of mankind.[131] Trusting in the same set of associations, Parmenides held a bizarre – and probably deliberately materialist and reductionist – view about the sentience of corpses. Reasoning by the principle of opposites, he claimed that a corpse "does not perceive (αἰσθάνεσθαι) light and warmth and sound (φωνῆς), but does perceive cold and silence (σιωπῆς) and the other contrasting qualities." Whatever else we may wish to say about this view, it stands to reason that Parmenides is revamping conventional wisdom while giving it an unconventional, macabre twist.[132] On the same grisly note, another (possibly) early text, the Hippocratic writing *Fleshes*, likewise affirms *e contrario* the connection between life and voice, this time adopting a simple and grim logic. Here we find a physiological account of language in which breath features centrally as the source of utterance (πνεῦμά ἐστι τὸ φθεγγόμενον), which when present gives rise to speech and when cut off causes speech to cease. To make the point, the author resorts to a graphic proof: "Having taken note of this, suicides cut their throats," with predictable results.[133]

By the time we reach Plato and Aristotle, reason has been restored to Greek writing, and voice is once again the unproblematic possession of a living creature: ζῷον and ἔμψυχος, "living thing" and "ensouled," are the operative terms here.[134] Subsequently, beyond their value as a cliché of the vivacity of art in general, life and breath enjoyed a close if not quite independent existence in the verbal arts, where the link between voice and breath was all but inevitable. For the cliché, we might compare Theocritus' fifteenth *Idyll*:

Lady Athena! what spinning women wrought them, what painters designed those drawings, so true (ἀκριβέα) they are! How naturally (ὡς ἔτυμα) they stand and move, like living creatures (ἔμψυχα), not patterns woven! What a clever thing is man![135]

---

[131] 31B62 DK; trans. K–R–S.
[132] 28A46 DK (= Theophr. *Sens.* 4) with Kirk *et al.* 1983, 262. See Ax 1986, 65 for cogent arguments for taking φωνή here as "voice" (and not merely as "sound"), φωνή being the antonym of human (linguistic) silence (σιωπή).
[133] Hippoc. *Carn.* 18.   [134] E.g., Arist. *De an.* 2.8.420b5–13.   [135] *Id.* 15.80–83; trans. M. Carroll.

Conjuring up similar themes is an epigram of unknown date on Myron's bronze victory statue for Ladas, in which the statue mimics the runner, their two breaths in synchrony first with each other and then with the ambient air, as the statue threatens to lift off its pedestal and take wing:

Just as you were in life (ἔμπνοε) Ladas ... breathing hard (πνεῦμά θ' ἱείς) ...

And on his lips is seen the breath (ἄσθμα) which comes from the hollow flanks. Soon the bronze will leap forth to gain the crown, and the base will not hold it. O art swifter than the wind (πνεύματος)![136]

A fragment from a lost play by Euripides runs in the same vein: "All these Daedalic statues seem to move / and to see. That man was so clever!,"[137] as is the recently discovered epigram by Posidippus on a statue of Philitas,

moulded accurately ([ἀ]κ[ρ]ιβὴς [ἔπλ]ασεν) ... down to the toenails ..., moulded with all his skill, holding fast to the straight canon of truth (ἀληθείης). He seems about to speak, so characterful is he – the old man's [alive] ([ἔμψυχ]ος), though he's made of bronze.[138]

I suspect that the Aeschylean fragment quoted above is *already* a cliché too, even though it is frequently taken to be the sign of a new, startled awareness of art's heightened mimetic or naturalistic capacities.[139] The innumerable instances of kinetic ecphrases in Homer and the stylized response of astonishment that accompanies them give the lie to this quasi-anthropological and quasi-art-historical insight.[140]

Restoring texts to life was a concern and a problem in later, postclassical times, which were reliving a crisis that was felt in the classical era at the time of Aristophanes: in both cases, reading a classical text comes to be fundamentally tied to re-experiencing a classical past, a point to which we will return in the final sections of this chapter.[141] But the problem must have been sensed even earlier than Aristophanes. After all, the theme of literary vivacity had already asserted itself as one of literature's essential

---

[136] *Anth. Plan.* 4.54 (Anon.); text and trans. as in Hallett 1986, 79. ἐπ' ἀκροτάτῳ ... ὄνυχι in the second verse must be a pun on the accuracy of the casting technique first introduced by Polyclitus; see D'Angour 1999 for discussion of the phrase *ad unguem*; and see "down to the toenails" in the next epigram to be quoted.

[137] Eur. *Eurystheus TrGF* 372.

[138] Posidipp. AB 63; trans. Stewart 2005, 196. On the suitability of the conjecture [ἔμψυχ]ος, see Scodel 2003 with *Anth. Plan.* 16.120.3–4 = Asclepiades 53 G–P, another "speaking statue" epigram. Further, Mosch. *Eur.* 107: μούνης δ' ἐπιδεύεται αὐδῆς. For further Hellenistic parallels, including Erinna on Agatharchis (*Anth. Pal.* 6.352 = Erinna 3 G–P), see Gutzwiller 2002, 88–92.

[139] So Hallett 1986.

[140] See Himmelmann 1969, a leitmotif of which is "*Lebendigkeit*." Similarly, Webster 1939, 176–79.

[141] See Porter 2006b.

features long before the fifth century, thanks in no small part to the sepulchral epigraphic tradition and to the Homeric epics themselves. Hence, the recuperative gesture of reviving the voice of the past in later literature was not merely a matter of superimposing a frivolous metaphor on a long-cherished but inert canon. It was a matter of *reviving* a *once-active* metaphor, and possibly *reliving* an ancient debate over the role of the voice as well. The (inevitably) speculative example of Alcidamas, for whom the voice is matter vivified, can help us catch a brief glimpse of this debate in its formative stages.

4 SPEECH-WRITING: ALCIDAMAS OF ELAEA ON THE SPOKEN AND WRITTEN WORD

Alcidamas of Elaea, who flourished in the early fourth century and was a contemporary and rival of Isocrates, was one of Gorgias' two most famous pupils (the other was Isocrates). His brilliance earned him a chapter in Aristotle's *Rhetoric*, though not Aristotle's unstinting approval: Aristotle finds his style excessive in its metaphors and obscure in its diction, and he uses these pages from the *Rhetoric* to take Alcidamas to task for his faults.[142] Nonetheless, few writers could boast the distinction of having captured Aristotle's attention for so long under any circumstances, and anyway not all of antiquity would agree with Aristotle.[143] His works have all but vanished, and today he is known principally as an advocate of improvisational rhetoric. A treatise preserved under his name, *On the Writers of Written Speeches, or, On Sophists* (dated to around 391), provides the conventional grounds for this reading of him, and on its basis entire edifices of argument have been erected, implicating at times the whole of the late fifth and early fourth centuries in a culture war that divided along similar polemical lines in an acrimonious debate over the virtues of speech versus writing. I believe this line of argument rests on too stark a series of contrasts, but I won't contest it at length now. Instead I want to draw upon two facts that are untouched by the controversy. The first is that Alcidamas in *On Sophists* is concerned to bring out what it is that is speechlike in written texts (his own text being the most immediate example). Qualities that he admires, as does Plato in the *Phaedrus* (whose

---

[142] *Rh.* 3.3.

[143] See T6–9 Avezzù on Aeschines as Alcidamas' pupil, and esp. T7 on the powerful qualities of Aeschines' language (its *megethos* and *semnotēs*), which (as Avezzù rightly notes ad loc.) match well the features of Alcidamas' own language; T14, Cic. *Tusc.* 1.48.116: *Alcidamas ... rhetor antiquus in primis nobilis.*

argument *On Sophists* superficially resembles), include a speech's being animated (ἔμψυχος) and alive (καὶ ζῇ), supple and mobile ([οὐκ] ἀκίνητος), opportune, accomplished, and harmonious, or musical (εὐκαίρως καὶ μουσικῶς), and showing signs of energy.[144] For according to Alcidamas, underlying every written text is a voice that animates it:

I do not even think it is right to call written texts *speeches* (λόγους); rather, they are like images (εἴδωλα) or outlines (σχήματα) or representations (μιμήματα) of speeches, and it would be reasonable to view them in the same way as bronze statues (ἀνδριάντων) or stone sculptures (ἀγαλμάτων) or pictures of animals (γεγραμμένων ζῴων). Just as these are representations of real bodies – they are a joy to look at but of no real use in people's lives – in the same way a written speech, which has just one form and arrangement (σχήματι καὶ τάξει), may have some striking effects when viewed in a book, but for a particular occasion is of no help to those who have it because it cannot change (ἀκίνητος ὤν).... A speech spoken extemporaneously from one's own mind (ἀπ᾽ αὐτῆς τῆς διανοίας) is animated (ἔμψυχος) and alive (καὶ ζῇ) and corresponds to actual events, just like a real body, whereas a written text by nature resembles the image (εἰκόνι) of a speech and is totally ineffective (ἀπάσης ἐνεργείας ἄμοιρος καθέστηκεν).[145]

This might seem a blanket condemnation of written texts. But it is not, for reasons that will soon become apparent. To begin with, the speech turns on a paradox, for how effective is an attack on writing when that attack is itself made through writing? Alcidamas confronts the point head-on. The next line anticipates and disarms the objection: "Perhaps someone might say it is illogical (ἄλογον) that I criticize the ability to write while I present my case by this very means, and that I cast aspersions on that very activity through which one procures a good reputation among the Greeks."[146] And in the next sentence Alcidamas pungently adds, "Let me first say that *I have uttered this speech* (τούτους εἴρηκα τοὺς λόγους) not because I do entirely reject the ability to write, but because ...," upon which follows a series of sophistic arguments, or else prevarications, that culminate in his own stated desire "to leave behind a memorial (μνημεῖα) of myself and ... [to] gratify my ambition,"[147] before the speech dissolves

---

[144] Alcid. *Soph.* 28; 31. Cf. Pl. *Phdr.* 276a8–9: "You mean no dead discourse, but the living speech, the original of which may fairly be called a kind of image" (τὸν τοῦ εἰδότος λόγον λέγεις ζῶντα καὶ ἔμψυχον, οὗ ὁ γεγραμμένος εἴδωλον ἄν τι λέγοιτο δικαίως); trans. Hackforth. Also Arist. *Int.* 1.16a3–4: "vocal phenomena ([τὰ] ἐν τῇ φωνῇ) are symbols of affectations in the soul, and written phenomena are symbols of vocal phenomena"; Mich. Psell. *Opusc.* 2:57: "Voice [unlike meaningless sound] has as its *telos* the indication of some condition and desire of the soul."

[145] *Soph.* 27–28; trans. Gagarin and Woodruff 1995; Greek text after Radermacher.

[146] *Soph.* 29.

[147] *Soph.* 32; trans. slightly adapted; emphasis added.

into playful self-deconstruction smacking of Gorgias' "plaything" or
παίγνιον (Alcidamas uses the terms παιδία and παρέργον)[148] – thus
circling back to where the speech had anyway begun ("I think one ought
to practice writing as an incidental side-line" [ἐν παρέργῳ]).[149]

The arguments against writing, quite different from Plato's in his own
written dialogue the *Phaedrus*, are about as slippery as the claim to "have
spoken a written speech,"[150] and it seems best to read them as a defense
not only of extempore speechmaking but also of *the speechlike elements of
writing*, which Alcidamas' speech, a piece of *Kunstprosa* in itself, has been
deemed to share.[151] The suspicion, invited by Alcidamas himself, is that
his own piece is in imitation of improvised speeches, just as "people who
write speeches for the law courts [the *logographoi*] avoid great precision of
expression and imitate instead the style (τὰς ἑρμηνείας) of extempor-
aneous speakers; and their writing appears finest when they produce
speeches least like those that are written."[152] This impression, which has
not escaped the notice of some modern readers (the speech has, in
consequence, been called "blemished"), has led one scholar to wonder
whether Alcidamas hasn't "intentionally given this work a spontaneous
appearance, including in it apparent repetitions, inconsistencies, and
arguments which look haphazard."[153] But it is not clear whether the thesis
about simulation (or dissimulation) widens or narrows the gap between
the form and the content of Alcidamas' speech. And anyway, opinions
vary. Another scholar assures us that "this work of Alcidamas is no
improvisation, but is carefully written with an eye to style and artistic
effect ... to show that he too, when he wishes, can distinguish himself
in the more leisurely form of composition."[154] Can we even tell the
difference?

It has been suggested that Alcidamas more or less invents a contrast
between two styles of writing, the written and spoken styles.[155] But, given
the formal contradictions of his own speech, perhaps what he is attempting
is not to best his opponents on their own terms by simulating improvised

---

[148] *Soph.* 34: τοῦ δὲ γράφειν ἐν παιδιᾷ καὶ παρέργῳ ἐπιμελόμενος εὖ φρονεῖν κριθείη παρὰ
τοῖς εὖ φρονοῦσιν.

[149] *Soph.* 2; trans. adapted.

[150] Cf. O'Sullivan 1992, 31: "The idea of writing a speech to attack the writing of speeches is itself a
paradoxical idea," which is true, though this is no more than a paraphrase of Alcidamas.

[151] Blass 1887–98, II:355–59; and esp. O'Sullivan 1992.   [152] *Soph.* 13; cf. ibid., 4.

[153] Liebersohn 1999, 11, in reaction to van Hook 1919, 90.   [154] Hudson-Williams 1949b, 30.

[155] O'Sullivan 1992, 23–62. O'Sullivan acknowledges the difficulty of extracting a notion of "style"
from Alcidamas' position (e.g. 46–47 n. 138; 56; 59), and notes that the difference between the
written and unwritten styles is hard to maintain in ancient theory and practice (ibid., 43).

speechmaking in writing, but something far more interesting. I suspect
instead that he is trying to bring out in a vivid way *the paradox of the voice
that lies buried in written language*. In Alcidamas' own words, "a written
text has the same nature as the image of a [spoken] speech" (ὁ δὲ
γεγραμμένος [sc., λόγος] εἰκόνι λόγου τὴν φύσιν ὁμοίαν ἔχων).[156]
The point is obviously double-edged: written texts lack vital energy; "they
lack all but a voice," as Aeschylus would put it, which is to say, they lack
just about everything there is to the art of language.[157] But on the other
hand, written texts *are a kind of image* – are copies, semblances, representations – of speech, which *do* capture, or render, the movements of the
soul: they merely capture them in one pose, in one recollected "arrangement" (*schēma* or *taxis*), or in a series of such poses. As Alcidamas says at
the end of his speech, writing is like a "mirror" of one's self: "In written
speeches one can most clearly see (ἐναργέστατα κατιδεῖν) signs of the
probable improvement in one's thinking" (ἐν τῇ διανοίᾳ), unlike in
extempore speeches. And so, "by looking at something written one can
view (as if in a mirror [ὥσπερ ἐν κατόπτρῳ]) the improvement of the
mind" (τῆς ψυχῆς).[158]
    This is a remarkable concession to writing! It also invites comparison
with another of Alcidamas' famous sayings. For, he once called Homer's
Odyssey "a beautiful mirror of human life," as Aristotle preserves the
record.[159] Whatever else Alcidamas had in mind with this *aperçu*, he at
least knew very well that Homer was a singer of tales, not a writer of
prepared speeches.[160] If written speeches can act as mirrors in the same
way epic poetry can do this, the comparison ought to make us suspicious
of any one-to-one, let alone reductive, correlation between writing as a
process of fixation and what a written text *does*. The most animated of
texts will be those that display the lively features of spoken discourse as
enumerated by Alcidamas above, and as displayed in his own ably written
treatise. It is these very features that later critics, from Aristotle to Longinus, will seize upon whenever they want to describe in words what it is

---

[156] *Soph.* 28; trans. adapted.
[157] Diels 1886, 28–29 stands in need of revision, as he grants too much originality to Aristotle for
    introducing "der Begriff der Lebendigkeit der Darstellung" and a consideration of the "ἐνέργεια
    des plastischen Wortes" into rhetorical theory. Alcidamas is the innovator here. Note Alcidamas'
    anticipation of the term ἐνέργεια of Arist. *Rh.* 3.11 at *Soph.* 27 (ἐνεργείας).
[158] *Soph.* 32; trans. slightly adapted.
[159] Arist. *Rh.* 3.3. Aristotle finds this and other metaphors by Alcidamas to be flamboyant and
    "unpersuasive."
[160] To judge from the *Certamen* at least, which showcases Homer in improvised verse-making
    (however literate a poet he may also appear to be in that same work).

that moves readers, or auditors, of literature. "Generally, what is written should be able to be easily read and easily spoken, *for these are the same thing.*" So Aristotle, who is very likely in Alcidamas' debt for this insight into the twofold nature of speech-writing.[161]

To sum up then, Alcidamas' *On Sophists* is a playfully evasive and sophistical speech, and not to be taken at face value.[162] It is, after all, a contradiction in terms, being a written defense of extemporized speech; the speech itself simulates extemporaneity; and it was doubtless designed to be read aloud, and even declaimed, before a public (δεικνύναι).[163] Finally, Alcidamas was best known in later antiquity for the body of writing he left behind, and not only for his defense of orality, for the very same reasons that he predicted in his speech: he wished to leave behind a memorial (μνημεῖα) of himself, and so he did.[164]

5 HIERONYMUS OF RHODES ON THE ANIMATED VOICE

A later echo of Alcidamas is found in a fragment by the philosopher Hieronymus of Rhodes (first half of the third century BCE), probably from his treatise *On Isocrates*, in which he launched a devastating critique of the great Athenian rhetorician. The preserved fragment in two versions closely parallels Alcidamas, whose treatise *On Sophists* has been understood since Vahlen (1864) to be an attack on Isocrates. Isocrates' fondness for writing and his diffidence towards public appearances (ostensibly because of his *ischnophōnia*, or weak and shrill voice) were seen as vulnerable points. Seizing on this vulnerability, Hieronymus criticized Isocrates on the grounds that his diction is "lifeless" (ἄψυχος in one version, and lacking in "life," τὸ ἔμψυχον, in another):[165] it cannot be spoken or delivered; it can only be read. The best preserved report is by Dionysius of Halicarnassus:

---

[161] Arist. *Rh.* 3.5.1407b11–12.
[162] One should not forget that Alcidamas was capable of writing such sophistic works as an *Encomium of Death*, which is called "paradoxical" (παράδοξα) by Menander Rhetor along with two other such writings by him (T14 Avezzù = Men. Rhet. 3.346.17 Spengel; cf. Cic. *Tusc.* 1.48.116; Stob. 120.3).
[163] *Soph.* 31. See Hudson-Williams 1949a, 68–69 on this sense of the verb.
[164] Apart from his speeches, which are among the longest documents to be handed down from the age of the sophists, and the important writing, the *Museum* (to be discussed below), there were also his writings on physics, about which little is known, except that they dealt with the Eleatic and Zenonian philosophical heritage in a serious fashion (see frr. 8–9 Avezzù; see Dušanić 1992).
[165] The first term is from Philodemus' report (see next note): Isocrates' diction is ἄψυχον ... καὶ ἀνυπάκο[υσ]τ[ο]ν, "lifeless ... and not suited to hearing [or 'delivery']."

Hieronymus the philosopher says that one could read his discourses effectively, but to declaim them in public (δημηγορῆσαι) with modulation of the volume and the pitch of the voice (τήν τε φωνὴν καὶ τὸν τόνον ἐπάραντα), and with the appropriate techniques of delivery that are used in live oratory, would be quite impossible; for he has neglected the orator's most important instrument for moving (κινητικώτατον) a crowd – intensity of feeling and animation (τὸ παθητικὸν καὶ ἔμψυχον). He is always the slave of smoothness, and has sacrificed the advantages of the moderation and variety (τὸ δὲ κεκραμένον καὶ παντοδαπόν) that are achieved by the increase and relaxation of tension (ἐπιτάσει τε καὶ ἀνέσει), and has not divided up his speeches by means of emotional climaxes. He concludes that the reader of Isocrates' prose must assume the monotonous voice of a child, because it cannot accommodate inflection (τόνον), expression (πάθος) or animated delivery (ὑπόκρισιν). Many other critics have passed this and similar judgments, and there is no need for me to comment on these.[166]

The passage demonstrates just how detailed and how musically informed the literary examination of rhetorical prose could be in early antiquity. Hieronymus was a learned Peripatetic from a generation or so after Theophrastus. Even so, nothing in his vocabulary would have been unavailable to Aristotle, as a glance at *Rhetoric* 3 combined with the following from chapter 20 of the *Poetics* indicates:

The elemental letter-sounds (*stoicheia*) . . . can be further classified according to the shape of the mouth, the place of contact [of the lips and teeth], rough or smooth [breathing], length or shortness [of quantity], and acute, grave, or intermediate [pitch or accent]. One can investigate the subject further in works on metric.[167]

Presumably, *metrikoi* and others prior to Aristotle would have had similar analytical tools, as the case of Hippias suggests.

Nevertheless, the ancient prejudice against Isocrates, which was repeated widely beginning with Plato, does him an injustice.[168] In point of fact, Isocrates' position is closer to Alcidamas' than either of them would care to admit, while both were anticipated by Gorgias in most of the essentials. To anticipate myself, the view that casts Isocrates as the first genuine writer from antiquity who turned his back on orality with an easy conscience goes wrong for a few different reasons, not the least of which are the clear signs of defensive awareness everywhere visible in Isocrates'

[166] Dion. Hal. *Isoc.* 13 (= fr. 52b Wehrli); trans. adapted; closely similar: Phld. *P. Herc.* 1423 cols. 16ª. 13–17ª.9 (pp. 198–99) Sudhaus (= fr. 52a Wehrli).
[167] *Poet.* 20.1456b31–34; trans. Hubbard, adapted.
[168] Other critiques: Pl. *Euthphr.* 305c; Demetr. fr. 169 Wehrli = Phld. *Rh.* 4 col. xviª 9–11 Sudhaus; Plut. *Mor.* 837A.

self-positioning throughout his writings, and, related to this, his frequent resort to a *simulated* orality.[169]

What this kind of picture wrongly frames is a cultural revolution that positions writing on one side or another of a technological divide (orality/literacy), and then views Isocrates from one side or the other – either as the consummate writer who banished orality or as the failed orator who fled, disgraced, into writing. That this divide was less well marked in practice than it was once thought to have been has recently become the new majority view in classical cultural historical studies, and with good reason.[170] What has not been sufficiently appreciated, perhaps, is that writing is not a sign of literacy, but is rather a domain in which the crossing over of differently placed activities can occur, whether these are a matter of production and consumption or of reading and speaking. That is, the written word is a *neutral* territory in phenomenological terms. Like Gorgias' *logos*, it has no clear features, which is to say, none that would mark it as belonging either to orality or to literacy. Written texts can function like spoken texts, like fixed monuments, like paintings or calligraphy, like sonograms, or even like written texts. But mostly they are neutral between these options, and how they are read is as much a matter of just that – the way in which they are read.[171] To be sure, how they are written can enhance these potentialities, though other factors count for as much or more, such as setting, context, display, use, and so on. (We might call these conditioning factors a part of writing's materiality.) Isocrates was by no means the first to have had this insight into the fluid nature of writing. He merely had a problem to contend with: a physically weak voice, whether resulting from the debility of age or natural reserve, as he was more than prepared to admit.[172]

6 ISOCRATES ON THE WRITTEN VOICE

If Isocrates was sensitive to criticisms of the kind lodged against him by Alcidamas and others, it is doubtless because he had first raised them against himself.[173] His writings are dotted with confessions, apologies, and defenses, as in his *Address to Philip*:

---

[169] *Pace* Lentz 1989, 124–28.
[170] See Thomas 1989; Lentz 1989; Thomas 1992; Yunis 2003. Cf. *Auct. ad Her.* 3.15.27, explaining how "to express physical movements in words and imitate vocal intonations in writing."
[171] See now Bakker 2005, 38–43, developing Ong 1982; see below.
[172] E.g., Isoc. 12.10; 5.81; *Ep.* 1.9, 8.7. Cf. Philostr. *VS* 505; *Vit. Isoc.* ap. *Schol. graec. in Aeschin. et Isoc.* Dindorf 102.26–27 (= Mandilaras 1:212).
[173] Cf. Usener 1994, 91.

And yet I do not fail to realize what a great difference there is in persuasiveness between discourses which are spoken (οἱ λεγόμενοι) and those which are to be read (τῶν ἀναγιγνωσκομένων)…. For when a discourse is robbed of the prestige of the speaker, the tones of his voice, the variations which are made in the delivery (καὶ τῆς φωνῆς καὶ τῶν μεταβολῶν τῶν ἐν ταῖς ῥητορείας γιγνομένων), and, besides, of the advantages of timeliness and keen interest in the subject matter; when it has not a single accessory to support its contentions and enforce its plea, but is deserted (ἔρημος) and stripped (γυμνός) of all the aids which I have mentioned; and when someone reads it aloud (ἀναγιγνώσκῃ) without persuasiveness and without putting any personal feeling into it, but as though he were repeating a table of figures (ἀπαριθμῶν) – in these circumstances it is natural, I think, that it should make an indifferent impression (φαῦλος εἶναι δοκεῖ) upon its hearers.[174]

And yet, Isocrates' confession here is intensely personal, even passionate, and affecting, at least in its overt intention: it strives to convey everything it might at first sight appear to lack. This is, to be sure, not a speech made for public declamation, though at issue is not public oratory, but the question whether a text, detached from its author and circulating abroad (ἔρημος can have this connotation too), can nevertheless recuperate enough of the author's voice to animate itself in the presence of its intended audience and thus overcome the apparent handicaps of distance, textuality, recitation, and so on. Is this a sign of irony, of a "politics of the small voice" designed to align the author against the new generation of loud-voiced orators after the age of Pericles and thus a device that is being exploited to the full before a knowing audience?[175] Probably not. A booming voice was not universally held in disrepute in the fourth century, and if anything a large voice was a desirable quality in an orator, as it had been for Homer.[176] One need only recall Aristotle's emphasis on the "volume" of the voice as one of its captivating qualities, quoted earlier.[177] Politics are indeed involved, but in other ways. And besides, other factors are more immediately at work.

[174] Isoc. 5.25–26; trans. Norlin; cf. 13.12–15 (and the whole of that speech).
[175] Too 1995, 74–112.
[176] E.g., *Il.* 3.221–22: "But when [Odysseus] let the great voice (ὄπα τε μεγάλην) go from his chest, and the words came | drifting down like the winter snows …."
[177] Arist. *Rh.* 3.1.1403b31, quoted at n. 45 above. See also Ch. 7, nn. 64 and 66 below, for later examples (the tradition is, in other words, consistent). Demosthenes sought to overcome a handicap similar to Isocrates'. And his positive remarks on Aeschines' "fine and loud voice" at Dem. 19.216–17 and elsewhere (cf. n. 255 below) likewise contradict Too's thesis, which is thinly documented in any case. Further, Easterling 1999, 156–60, and *passim*. Cf. also schol. Dion. Thrax 17.29–34 Hilgard (n. 115 above).

Isocrates is, after all, banking on the obvious, namely that his text can "speak" for itself. And this is characteristic of his position towards the false dilemma of speech versus writing generally, as others have noticed too. His writings are everywhere marked by their oral, "live" character, and possibly overmarked, as if by way of compensation, for instance in the *Panathenaicus*.[178]

I sense how a feeling is coming upon me (αἰσθάνομαι δὲ πάθος μοι συμβαῖνον), the opposite of what I felt when I was speaking earlier (τοῖς πρότερον εἰρημένοις). Then I fell into uncertainty, bafflement, and forgetfulness, but now I realize clearly that I am not keeping to the mild tenor of speech (lit., "discourse": τῇ πραότητι τῇ περὶ τὸν λόγον) that I had when I began writing.... But since the impulse to speak out freely (τὸ παρρησιάζεσθαι) has struck me and I have loosened my tongue (καὶ λέλυκα τὸ στόμα) ... there's no keeping silent (οὐ κατασιωπητέον).[179]

This feature (it is in fact a cultivated *style*) of approximating or affecting speech in writing is hardly restricted to Isocrates. Dialogism is detectable in Plato (obviously), but also in Aristotle, in Roman literature, and, arguably, in all forms of communication (so Bakhtin).[180] Whether or not the related phenomenon of subvocalization, or reading by articulating the words with one's lips accompanied by a barely audible sound, encourages orality in writing (and it conceivably might), it does "contribute to the aesthetic enjoyment of a text."[181] The next rung up from subvocalization is the pleasure of "quiet murmuring" (*lepido susurro, murmure,* I am unaware of any Greek equivalents).[182] In any event, the Isocratean ideal is not "writing well" but *speaking* well (τὸ εὖ λέγειν), very much in line

---

[178] As Gregory Hutchinson reminds me, because the terms *oral* and *orality* have two distinct senses, positive (vocal performance, vocality) and negative (absence of writing), I should perhaps stress that I am using the terms in their positive connotations here and in what follows.

[179] Isoc. 12.95–96; trans. Norlin. Similarly, id., 10.29: "But I am at a loss about how to approach what remains to be said ... But, on the other hand, I perceive I am being carried beyond the proper limits of my theme"; trans. van Hook, adapted.

[180] On Isocrates, see Hudson-Williams 1949a; Lentz 1989, esp. 131–33 ("The Oral Style of Written Composition"); Usener 1994, *passim*; Too 1995, 74–150; on Plato and Aristotle ("d[ie] Mündlichkeit in der Schriftlichkeit"): Dirlmeier 1962, 5–24; on Hippocratic writings, see Jouanna 1984; on Greek literature from Euripides to the Hellenistic era, see Cameron 1995, e.g. 84–90; for Rome, see Desbordes 1990; Vogt-Spira 1990; Starr 1991; Vogt-Spira 1993; Gunderson 2000, 29–57; for Greece and Rome, see Dupont 1999. On the sociology of reading (aloud) in antiquity, see Johnson 2000, 607–10; Johnson 2003 (both articles contain good hints on "the aesthetics of reading production and apprehension"); Johnson and Parker 2009. Bakhtin 1981; Bakhtin 1984.

[181] Gavrilov 1997, 61.

[182] *lepido susurro*: Apul. *Met.* 1.2 with Dupont 1999, 208; *murmure*: Plin. *Ep.* 9.34.1; cf. Quint. *Inst.* 11.2.33.

with traditional rhetoric: "for the power to speak well is taken as the surest index of a sound understanding, and speech (λόγος) which is true and lawful and just is the outward image (εἴδωλον) of a good and faithful soul" – Alcidamas' point, exactly.[183]

The point is made again in a parallel passage to the *Panathenaicus* quoted just above, now in a personal letter of advice to Dionysius of Syracuse. There, Isocrates once again cites the deficiencies of writing as compared to speaking. But in this case, the decisive factor is not orality, but rather proximity and immediacy (standing face to face, παρὼν πρὸς παρόντα). For, as he says, people "listen[184] to the [orally delivered word] as they would to a practical proposal and to the [written word] as they would to an artistic composition."[185] While there are obvious differences between the two forms of communication, and while the advantages of face-to-face communication include the opportunities for defending one's meaning against misunderstanding (or worse), the key point is that readers and auditors *both listen*. In either case, they are attuned to the *logos* with their ears, and if anything rather more so in the case of carefully wrought prose than with personally delivered advice. If Isocrates makes the allowance here that prepared prose is more like poetry than is impromptu rhetoric, it is typical of his views elsewhere too. This happens to be Alcidamas' view as well, and for identical reasons: "In fact, when speeches are fashioned with verbal precision, resembling poems more than speeches, having lost spontaneity and verisimilitude, and appearing to be constructed and composed with much preparation, they fill the minds of the listeners with distrust and resentment."[186]

With Alcidamas and Isocrates agreeing on so much, one might wonder just where their differences lie. The answer is likely to be irrecoverable, given our lack of independent evidence, but it is also not likely to lie in the nature of rhetoric itself. For if Alcidamas' writings approximate to living speech, and his oratory is both prepared and rehearsed but also left open to last-minute alteration (and hence, to appearing lively but not scripted),[187] the *formal* difference between the two kinds of verbal production is likely to be minimal. Isocrates' prepared writings are perhaps more polished, more given to periods and flourishes,[188] but they cling purposefully to their oral character, and they attempt to disarm every suspicion in advance by conceding these openly – *too* openly, perhaps.

---

[183] Isoc. 15.255; trans. Norlin, slightly adapted. 　[184] ποιοῦνται τὴν ἀκρόασιν.
[185] Isoc. *Ep.* 1.2; trans. van Hook. 　[186] Alcidamas *Soph.* 12; trans. adapted.
[187] See Hudson-Williams 1949b. 　[188] See Dion. Hal. *Isoc.* 2; Blass 1887–98, II:145–81.

Longinus would later fault him for this very tendency: "The encomium on the power of speech [in the *Panegyricus*] is equivalent to an introduction recommending the reader not to believe what he is told!"[189] Where the differences between these two rhetorical titans of the early fourth century most seem to lie, unsurprisingly, is in the *rhetoric* of their positions on rhetoric. One represents the older ideology of sophistic culture, while the other is attempting to carve out for himself a market niche and to label himself as somehow "other" – as the *non*-sophist, the alternative, the philosopher, the New Greek Educator, reaping the fruits of Greek *paideia* from earlier generations and wresting these fruits from the hands of the corrupt generation of sophists around him. Aesthetically speaking, their differences, which are rhetorical at best, may come down in the end to the difference between Coke and Pepsi. And in case you have any doubts about any of this, just ask Plato . . . .

In fact, from the fourth-century perspective, Alcidamas and Isocrates might appear to be rehearsing a debate from the previous generation, one that played itself out in nearly identical terms between Gorgias and Prodicus, with Gorgias taking up the banner of improvisation against Prodicean exactitude and memorization.[190] The trouble with this view is that it conceals Gorgias' keen interest in writing. Gorgias, after all, was famous for having introduced poetic and musical rhythms and figures of sound into prose, and his best-preserved writings are full of speechlike gestures (all in the name of vivacity, seductiveness, and euphony – in a word, *aesthetic* effects) – the very same figures that both Alcidamas and Isocrates, Gorgias' two best-known pupils, would avail themselves of and that Isocrates would even boast about at the start of his *Panathenaicus*.[191] The battle lines are less clearly drawn than they might first appear to be.

Isocrates does seem to be responding to Alcidamas when he claims that statues (εἰκόνες), while they make "fine memorials" (καλὰ μνημεῖα) and have an immediate palpability, remain fixed in place; publications circulate widely; they can, moreover, easily "imitate the character [of men] and their thoughts and purposes which are embodied in the spoken word."[192]

---

[189] *Subl.* 38.2.

[190] Philostr. *VS* 483 (= 82A24 DK); cf. 82B6 DK, extolling "correctness of speech" over "the precision of law." See O'Sullivan 1996, 122–23.

[191] ". . . a style rich in many telling points, in contrasted and balanced phrases not a few, and in the other figures of speech (οὐκ ὀλίγων δ' ἀντιθέσεων καὶ παρισώσεων καὶ τῶν ἄλλων ἰδεῶν) which give brilliance (διαλαμπουσῶν) to oratory and compel (ἀναγκαζουσῶν) . . . the audience" (Isoc. 12.2; trans. Norlin). Dionysius of Halicarnassus did not find these embellishments compelling, but only "juvenile" (*Isoc.* 13–14); but cf. Cic. *Orat.* 176 (*moderatius*).

[192] Isoc. 9.74; trans. van Hook, adapted. The last bit of argument recalls Xen. *Mem.* 3.10.1–8.

But it could easily be the other way round, with Alcidamas attempting to turn the tables on Isocrates when Alcidamas refused to call written texts speeches because they are more like fixed images. After all, Isocrates makes the monumentality of writing a topos of his writings. In the *Panegyricus*, he exclaims, "For who that is skilled to sing or trained to speak will not labor ... to leave behind a memorial ... for all time to come" (μνημεῖον εἰς ἅπαντα τὸν χρόνον)?[193] And in the *Antidosis*, Isocrates fantasizes a discourse that would serve as "a true image (εἰκών) of my thought and of my whole life ... and, at the same time, as a monument (μνημεῖον) after my death, more noble than statues of bronze."[194] (The fantasy is, or will be, Horatian.)

Isocrates could easily be, and doubtless is, alluding to Pindar,[195] in which case Alcidamas, if he is responding to the image, could be attempting an exegetical correction. And anyway, in praising the advantages of verses' mobile circulation over fixed monuments, was Pindar defending song or writing, or both? (Isocrates plainly sees no material difference between these in the passage from the *Panegyricus* just quoted.) As Pindar sings/writes in *Nemean* 5,

> I am no maker of statues,
> no producer of figures who stand
> motionless on their pedestal (ἐπ' αὐτᾶς βαθμίδος ἑσταότ');
> rather, on every ship, every bark
> set sail, sweet song, going from Aegina
> to say that Pytheas,
> the mighty son of Lampon,
> won the victor's crown in the pancration at Nemea.[196]

What is more, in acknowledging that writing imitates speech, Isocrates is gesturing at the speechlike character of writing, in the same way that Pindar was by no means simply set on disparaging the fabricators of hard and immovable forms (and we have already seen how Alcidamas stands on this theme – which is to say, identically to Pindar and Isocrates both). It is interesting to see how behind this fourth-century debate between the proponents of speech and writing lurks the older debate between the poets and the plastic artists (to be explored in Chapter 9 below). The terms are identical; they have merely accumulated new associations without quite shedding their older symbolic values. There may even be a hermeneutic

[193] Isoc. 4.186; trans. Norlin.   [194] Isoc. 15.7; trans. Norlin.
[195] Cf. Gentili 1988, 163; Thomas 1992, 114–15.
[196] Pind. *Nem.* 5.1–5; trans. Cole in Gentili 1988, 163.

tug of war running in the background as each side attempts to reinterpret the sayings of the poetic prophets to his own polemical ends. Possibly, fourth-century writers found the poets' words just ambiguous enough to support arguments in favor of either speech or writing or even speechlike writing. Whether the poets were that ambiguous by intention or whether their verses simply admitted the fluidity of such distinctions as these is hard to decide (more on this in Chapter 9 below). In the end, what is impossible to distinguish in any hard and fast way are not the arguments for or against speech or writing, but the very formal and structural differences and effects of these two technologies of communication (of capturing and transmitting the poet's voice), at least starting with the age of Isocrates, if not in Pindar's own. At issue in every case is the question, What effect does writing or speaking have on the materiality – the sensory aesthetics – of the author's voice? As we saw with Alcidamas, the differences between the extremes melt away whenever one considers the case of a possibly simulated *tertium quid*. And by the way, do the transmitted texts of Homer bear the marks of an oral poet with no access to literacy, or of a literate poet at the end of an oral tradition?

7 HEARING AND PUNCTUATING THE VOICE: INCIPIENT CLASSICISM

Much later, Longinus would reassert the value of the impromptu "agonistic" style in its written form, for instance in celebrating the deepest virtues of apostrophe, rhetorical questions, asyndeton, anaphora, hyperbaton, and so on. Such tricks of the trade accomplish two things at once, depending on where you stand. From the perspective of the original audience, they help "cheat [the audience] into believing that all the points made … are being put into words on the spur of the moment" or else "convey the impression of an agitation" and of a "sudden inspiration."[197] From the perspective of a postclassical audience gazing nostalgically on Athens in its golden prime, figures of speech help revivify the past, bringing it back to life with an immediacy that is sublime.[198] Alcidamas is plainly among those who helped pave the way for this kind of attentiveness by labeling these most unlocatable of virtues of writing and style in his treatises.

---

[197] *Subl.*, chs. 16–22. More insipid is the commonplace found in, e.g., Dion. Hal. *Isoc.* 13: "the most effective style [of oratory] is that which most resembles natural speech," retailed in the vicinity of the criticism by Hieronymus of Rhodes (fr. 52b Wehrli), to which it is linked.

[198] *Subl.*, *passim.*

Later writers, including some of those just named, will turn to these virtues in a classicizing vein, desperate as they were to revivify a distant, frozen past, and especially by reanimating the sound of the past and so make audible again the original voices of classical authors, as in the case of Longinus. Alcidamas shows no signs of classicism in *On Sophists*, in which he merely provides an *instrumentarium* for later classicizers in search of markers of orality, and perhaps an impetus and a certain amount of solace, to the extent that he validates the primacy and originality of the voice, but also excuses its inaccessibility in preserved writing. But what about his other writings? *The Contest of Homer and Hesiod* (*Certamen*), an indeterminate amount of which stems from Alcidamas' *Museum*, stages a contest between the two great founding poets of the Greek tradition. It, too, has been read as being symptomatic of the speech/writing controversy in which Alcidamas is somehow implicated.[199] But it is likely that the Alcidamantine elements of the *Contest* are not taking sides in that controversy, but are instead doing a variety of other things, from commenting on the slipperiness of the distinction between speech and writing to mocking the nascent traditions of biographical and literary historical criticism (this would require separate comment).[200] A recent proposal aligns the two categories of speech and writing with Homer and Hesiod, respectively, but I doubt this can be made to stick.[201] Homer, after all, is said by the Colophonians to be a teacher of reading and writing (φασὶν αὐτὸν γράμματα διδάσκοντα), and he has the chance to compose the epigraph to his own tomb – apparently in writing (a new reading of the Michigan papyrus gives the verb γράφει) – before he slips in the mud and dies.[202] And the *Museum* was in any case, again, a *written* text. Clearly, a different approach to the problem is necessary. Here, the overall context of Alcidamas' work gives us a clue. The *Museum* is a literal museum: it has a classicizing and canonical function (one that could easily have inspired the Alexandrians a century or so later). In parading the two arch-poets before his readers, each of them reciting or inventing their verses, Alcidamas is doing nothing other than satisfying the very same kind of desire that

---

[199] See O'Sullivan 1992, for a recent overview of the literature and a contribution to it.

[200] Some of the traces of this predominantly, but not exclusively oral tradition have been pointed to earlier in this study. See too Halliwell 2003, 178: "There must have been widespread oral discussion of song in the archaic age, carrying with it many ways of praising and blaming that do not show up in our extant sources," a remark that recalls Dover's in the epigraph to Ch. 1, §1.

[201] O'Sullivan 1992. *Contra*, Rosen 2004.

[202] *Cert.* 16 Allen; *P. Mich. Inv.* 2754.10: γράφει for Winter's *princeps* reading of π[οί]ει, perhaps suggested by ποίει in *Cert.* 333 (I read this with Nikos Litinas in July of 2002, and intend to publish the complete set of readings which I made at the time).

Aristophanes was responding to in *Frogs* when he paraded his two arch-tragedians on the stage in a mock contest for the Chair of Tragedy.[203] In both cases, the past has literally come to life again in a retrospective *fantasy* about the literary and historical past.

Alcidamas' authorship places the *Museum* in the fourth century. But it is likely that he was also hijacking a pre-existing contest-tradition, if not also passing a critical judgment on this tradition the way a sophist might. Whether or not it took the form of oral performance or consisted in texts that were written and read, the tradition, which may date to the sixth century, suggests an interesting mixture of popular entertainment (the desire to hear Homer and Hesiod performing – and improvising σχεδιάσαι [*Cert.* 279] – "live") and reflection on the oral traditions that in itself comprises an early form of criticism: it must have offered a reflection on the relative value of the two poets and on the veracity of their transmitted *vitae*.[204] Indeed, the mere fiction of the two poets in mutual dialogue is a sign of a sophisticated, second-order connoisseurship of literature, one degree removed from a simple enjoyment of the two poets individually (which was doubtless never "simple"). Did literary criticism have a popular source? Quite possibly. Still, the point worth stressing is that the two strains, one pressing for the reperformance of the author's unsurpassed, fully embodied voice, the other critically aware of the fictionality of this premise, seem to belong to the same tradition from which classicism will eventually spring, while criticism is born of the same confluence as well. Literary classicism rests on the premise – the fiction or fantasy – of the resuscitation of the poet's voice. Indeed, much of the apparatus of ancient literary criticism is devoted to capturing the aesthetic qualities of this experience.[205]

How ingrained in the rhapsodic tradition was the prospect of hearing or overhearing the voice of Homer? Wasn't the singing of Homer's verses in its own way classicizing? Plato's Ion felt he was in direct touch with Homer's mind, if not with his very sounds. Surely Ion's listeners felt the same way too, just as earlier audiences of rhapsodes must have. Lyric poets did not enjoy rhapsodic guilds like Homer's, but some did enjoy cult status, like Archilochus. On one reconstruction at least, the cult of Archilochus on Paros, which from the sixth century into later antiquity

---

[203] Porter 2006b, 301–07.
[204] This is possible irrespective of whether one has to posit an "Ur-*Certamen*" (Heldmann 1982). Further, Richardson 1981.
[205] This is argued at greater length in Porter 2006b.

may have "involved ritual readings of the poet's work written on his funerary monument," must have worked in much the same way as Ion's performances of Homer's verses had done.[206] One piece of the confirming epigraphical evidence, the Mnesiepes inscription, first unearthed in 1949 and dating from the latter half of the third century BCE, explicitly mentions Archilochus as an improviser: "they say that Ar[chilochus], when improvising ([αὐτο]|σχεδιάσ[αντα]) ... taught some of the c[iti-zens] [poems (?) that] had been handed down ... adorned ... of a herald to P[aros] ... and they followed [him]."[207] The inscription describes a passage from improvisation to instruction and transmission. It is therefore con-ceivable that the fixation of an oral tradition is being described as a literary history, which would be of interest to anyone, including the author of a *Museum*. It may be a bit more than a coincidence that the one non-epigraphical notice from antiquity to mention the Archilocheion on Paros stems from Alcidamas, seeing how improvisation was so central to the latter's rhetoric and to his poetics.[208]

The habit – the request for the voice – is as old as writing itself. The earliest inscriptions, when read, play off the fiction of re-animation, whether in question was the animation of the object or its owner or the owner's voice. "One epitaph actually salutes the traveler in thanks for lending his voice to the name of the deceased."[209] Later on, orators when composing speeches regularly broadcast the qualities of their own declaiming voices, like so many virtual cues meant for their readers.[210] For they knew that the style and *ductus* of their voices could be gathered from their writings, as Cicero observes in the cases of Quintus Catulus and Scaevola: "the simple directness of his oratory is adequately known (*habemus cognitam*) from the speeches which he left."[211] In a more tech-nical language, that of the professional grammarians, writing is "inscribed" or "lettered voice" (ἐγγράμματος φωνή), in the sense that it is the transcription of "voice capable of being articulated into letters."[212]

---

[206] Dupont 1999, 63, citing the argument of Svenbro 1990 (esp. p. 15).

[207] *SEG* 15. 517, E₁ III.19–24 (D. Clay's supplement). See Clay 2004 for a reevaluation of the evidence for the hero cult (with no discussion of Svenbro).

[208] Arist. *Rh.* 2.23.1398b11 (= Alcidamas fr. 10 Avezzù).

[209] Thomas 1992, 64; *IG* VII 2852 (from Haliartos; date unknown).

[210] Cic. *Brut.* 313.

[211] Cic. *Brut.* 163; cf. 133: "concerning his voice and the charm of his enunciation ..." (*de sono vocis et suavitate appellandarum litterarum*); trans. Hubbell.

[212] Schol. Dion. Thrax 120.37 Hilgard, and *passim*; *P. Osl.* 2.13 (text of Janko 2000, 185 n. 2); Crates of Mallos (schol. Dion. Thrax 316.24–6; cf. Porter 1989, 171–74); D.L. 3.107 (τῆς τοῦ ἐμψύχου φωνῆς ἡ μέν ἐστιν ἐγγράμματος, ἡ δὲ ἀγράμματος. ἐγγράμματος μὲν ἡ τῶν ἀνθρώπων); ibid., 7.56 (attributing the view to Diogenes of Babylon); *Div. Arist.* 30 [24], p. 38, cols. 1.4 and 2.6

Renewing a practice of the later fifth century (for instance, Hippias of Thasos' discussions of alternative voicings of Homer, such as accentuation and breathing, or Empedocles' repunctuation of Homer's verses, and their implications for appreciating his poems),[213] the Alexandrian scholars could make similar points about the Homeric poems: recovering details such as breathing and intonation in the stacks of papyrus manuscripts (punctuating pauses and stops, as well as pitches and other prosodic features) was a way of recovering some of Homer's original voice itself.[214] Reading in this way made the texts aesthetically palpable, and as intimate as the act of breathing. Little has changed, as the editorial debates raging today over the needed presence or absence of commas or semicolons in Jane Austen's texts demonstrate nicely, and dramatically.[215]

To recover original sounds was felt to be a feasible goal simply because this kind of familiarity with texts was widely assumed: to read an author was to recognize his or her voice and its qualities. Tellingly, in Greek the preferred synonym for the verb ἀναγιγνώσκειν ("to read") is ἀκούειν, "to hear"; *audire* in Latin has a similar, though more restricted, range.[216] To read in antiquity is to read aloud, or rather to *audition* a text that

---

Mutschmann; [Plato], *Definitions* 414d1; Sext. Emp. *Math.* 1.100; but see *GL* IV:525.19 (given at n. 280 below): voice is sound that can be written (*scriptibilis*); etc. ἐγγράμματος φωνή technically implies but does not require writing: in itself, ἐγγράμματος φωνή conjures up the thought of transcription into written letters (*Schreibbarkeit*), whereas articulation of the voice in a purely physiological sense (in the act of phonation) is covered by the parallel term, φωνὴ ἔναρθρος (cf. Ax 1986, 192–93; for some reservations: Schenkeveld 1990, 304–05). But if *grammata* merely means "letter-sounds," or "discrete units of *speech*-sound," the nuance may be moot, especially given the synonymy of *grammata* and *stoicheia*. Cf. Zirin 1974, 24–25; Lo Piparo 1988, 93. Ambiguities and grey zones are bound to result, and not only redundancies. For Aristotle, certain kinds of birds can utter *grammata*, though not yet in a fully developed language (Arist. *Part. an.* 660a29–33). Ax (ibid., 192 n. 213) claims that the expression ἐγγράμματος φωνή is a later (evidently Hellenistic) coinage, though what of [Plato], *Definitions* 414d1, a list thought to be a product of the fourth-century Academy? Then there is Xenocrates, Plato's disciple, who seems to have inaugurated the idea that the spoken voice can be divided into letters, in contrast with the musical voice, which is divided into intervals and notes (fr. 10 Heinze = fr. 88 Isnardi Parente = Porph. *Comm. in Ptol. Harm.* 8.22–27 Düring; cf. Blank 1998, 155). Nevertheless, the more general idea that writing is encoded voice has its origins in the sophistic movement (Alcidamas) and in tragedy (Eur. *Erechtheus TrGF* 369), but is also the premise of the epigraphic tradition of *oggetti parlanti*.

[213] Arist. *Poet.* 25.1461a21–25; see Gudeman 1934, ad loc.; further, Stanford 1967, 9; 23 n. 33.

[214] See Porter 1992, 80–82.

[215] See Sutherland 2005, 266–313, a revealing chapter entitled "Speaking Commas."

[216] For some striking examples, the earliest dating from Herodotus, see Hendrickson 1929; Hudson-Williams 1949a; Chantraine 1950; Allan 1980; Schenkeveld 1992. Chantraine 1950 notes how ἀναγιγνώσκειν ("to read") means in effect "to recognize" the letters and to decipher them; but as Carson 1999, 83 suggests, what is involved is in fact the recognition of *sounds* and their translation from the stone or page to the ear and mind (similarly, Rohde 1963, 294).

(in Roland Barthes' phrase) was originally *written aloud*.[217] Barthes also calls this kind of writing a "vocal writing" (*écriture vocale*), because what it conveys is a voice that reaches beyond meaning and content to more tangible qualities, such as breath, tonality, "the grain of the voice," and the like. To read in this way was quite literally to be aware of an author's "breath" (πνεῦμα, *spiritus*), or its lack. In effect, texts were conceived as congelations of breath that simply needed the articulation of a reader to be stirred, dissolved, released, and heard again.[218] Given the circumstances of ancient writing (for instance, the absence of word division and the infrequency of accents, even after their invention in the third century, to mark pitches and of interpunction to mark clausulae and breathing places),[219] this conceit is hardly far-fetched.

Strength of breath is a sign of power that makes itself felt over the centuries. For the same reason, it becomes an aesthetic criterion. Lysias, for all his charms, is not full of breath or spirit for Dionysius of Halicarnassus (οὐδὲ θυμοῦ καὶ πνεύματός ἐστι μεστή),[220] nor are the generation of historians prior to Thucydides, save Herodotus,[221] while Demosthenes does enjoy these powers.[222] Isocrates "lacks breath" for Hieronymus of Rhodes and others, as we saw. According to Arcesilaus, head of the Middle Academy in the mid-third century BCE, Pindar was "terrific at filling one's voice to the brim."[223] On one of the meanings of *voice* canvassed by the scholia to Dionysius Thrax, voice is equated with breath: "*Voice* is defined this way: voice is a bit of breath (πνεῦμά τι) that is fetched up (ἀναφερόμενον) from the whole organism and the blood until it reaches the tongue."[224] According to the same scholia, all voice is pitched, presumably because voice comes about "when breath strikes the air," which results in a pitch (τόνος), possibly due to the compression or collision involved, because "pitch is an intensifying

---

[217] Barthes 1975, 66. See further Theon *Prog.* 61.28–65.25 Spengel. Cf. also Svenbro 1990, 14 ("la voix dans l'écrit"), citing *Anth. Pal.* 7.193 = Simias 2 G–P and the funerary inscriptional tradition as a whole; ibid., 17 (citing Xen. *Mem.* 1.6.14); Gunderson 2000, 38 ("the written style forms a special subset of the speaking voice"); Webb 2001, 308–09; Porter 2006b; Bakker 2005, 41: "The discourse produced by the reader's voice is a reenactment of the writer's voice that was transcribed in the act of writing."

[218] This is more complex than viewing written letters (γράμματα) as "elementary sounds" (φωναὶ πρῶται), as was frequently done (see Ch. 4, §7 above), because there is more to language and to reading than the mere phonation of individual letters, or even their euphonious combination.

[219] Cf. [Dion. Thrax] *Ars Gramm.* §4: the middle-height interpunction mark is a "sign made for the sake of [taking a] breath" (πνεύματος ἕνεκεν).

[220] Dion. Hal. *Lys.* 13.   [221] Dion. Hal. *Thuc.* 23.

[222] Dion. Hal. *Dem.* 22.   [223] δεινὸν εἶναι φωνῆς ἐμπλῆσαι (D.L. 4.31).

[224] Schol. Dion. Thrax 181.37 Hilgard; cf. ibid., 483.17–18.

(τάσις) of the breath."[225] Musicality is thus a physical consequence
of uttered language. Written language is breath transcribed, or inscribed.
And so too, "voice articulated in letters is the final state [viz., "culmination"]
of the breath that is stored within us."[226] Language is in effect being
defined by the scholia, remarkably, as a divided continuum of *breath*.

In visual terms, this is exactly what an ancient text represented. *Scriptio
continua*, the ancient practice of writing without punctuation, accents,
and breathing marks, gave a visual translation or even transcription of the
vocal stream minus sense-making pauses. Dividing and articulating the
breath was an all-important tool of understanding; but it was inevitably
tied to the very kinds of aesthetic features that were traced earlier in this
chapter.[227] So, for instance, in a discussion of the paean, a prose rhythm
that Aristotle claims arose with Thrasymachus and then gradually became
widespread, Aristotle argues in the *Rhetoric* that clause endings should
be marked off "not through the action of a scribe or the presence of a
marginal mark [i.e., through what would later become interpunction], but
through the rhythm," that is, through the sound alone.[228] The distinction
between writing as written and writing as voiced is plainly weak, and if
anything the latter carries more weight, or rather brings out the essential
character of the former.

For the same reason, Isocrates finds it distasteful in the extreme when
his competitors mispunctuate his speeches in order to put them in the
worst possible light, making them harder to read aloud as compared with
their own speeches in public demonstrations before students.[229] The
Homeric oral tradition may have given rise to some of this practice,
especially if the tradition was a way of preserving or interpreting the
musical "intonation units" that became "stylized into metrical properties"
punctuating longer syntactical combinations of words.[230] Later on,
Aristarchus perpetuated the tradition in his own way by paying special
heed to the "melodic contour" of the Homeric verses and by parsing the

---

[225] Schol. Dion. Thrax 478.25–28 Hilgard.
[226] ἐγγράμματος δὲ φωνή ἐστιν ἀποτέλεσμα τοῦ ἐν ἡμῖν ἐντεθησαυρισμένου πνεύματος
(schol. Dion. Thrax 212.23–24; 353.4–5 Hilgard).
[227] See generally Saenger 1997; also, Nagy 2000, for the intriguing argument that *scriptio continua* in
ancient poetic texts actually *enforces* aesthetic attention to melodic contour (rhythm, pausing, cola,
accentual responsion, etc.), while the modern system of word division "strips" the texts of these
features and imposes on them anachronistic criteria (e.g., periodic structures that are textual and
compositional cues rather than aural, oral, or performative cues).
[228] Arist. *Rh.* 3.8.1409a19–21. Cf. ibid., 3.9.1409b13–22 on breathing as the means of articulating prose.
[229] Isoc. 12.17: παραναγιγνώσκοντες ὡς δυνατὸν κάκιστα τοῖς αὑτῶν καὶ διαιροῦντες οὐκ
ὀρθῶς καὶ κατακνίζοντες καὶ πάντα τρόπον διαφθείροντες. Cf. Usener 1994, 55.
[230] See Bakker 2005, 48–55 (quotation at p. 48).

texts according to the way they sounded as they were read aloud.[231] The operative verb here is, once again, "to read (aloud)" (ἀναγιγνώσκειν). In fact, twice we hear of a professional reader (ἀναγνώστης) "of Aristarchus," a certain Posidonius, who may have been called upon to supply the Attic-trained Aristarchus with an insider's dialectal informa- tion (for instance, Ionic) about prosody (accentuation, pitch, rhythm, melodic contours), but also about the basic articulation of phrases.[232] Given that so many of Aristarchus' readings of Homer are presented as a "reading" (ἀνάγνωσις) of Homer, one has to wonder whether oral "performance" wasn't the accepted practice for Aristarchus and for the Alexandrians generally, and not only in restricted questions of melody and pronunciation, but as a basis for comprehending the transmitted text of Homer.[233] If so, we can be fairly certain that the practice reached back to well before Aristotle,[234] just as it lived on in the Roman era.

The same principles were extended to professional authentication: what better criterion of authorship could there be than the signature left behind by an author in the way his or her words sounded, of the sort that the empirical sense of hearing can alone detect (with *aisthēsis* standing in for *hearing*)? Not for nothing would the act of criticism define itself by the two poles of its procedures: it began in reading, correctly and aloud, with attention to the aural features of diction – melody, expression, and the punctuating pauses (ἀνάγνωσις ἐντριβὴς κατὰ προσῳδίαν, καθ᾽ ὑπόκρισιν, κατὰ διαστολήν, ἀδιάπτωτος προφορά) – and it culmin- ated in *krisis*, or evaluation, "the finest part of all in the art of grammar."[235] If connoisseurship was grounded in the most immediate and most sensuous properties of texts, the apprehension of which was modeled on the handling of a multi-dimensional art object, then criticism, pedagogy, and reading practices generally were modeled on the discriminating connoisseur. Examining a text was a lot like examining a vase, holding it up to the light, feeling its heft, turning it this way and that.

---

[231] Nagy 1996, 132, rephrasing Scheller 1951, 9 n. 3.

[232] So Nagy 2006; schol. *Il.* A 6.511a; schol. *Il.* A 17.75a. See Nagy 2000, for parallel insights into the Bacchylidean scholia and papyri.

[233] See Nagy 2006 for illuminating suggestions regarding "the common reading" or "text" (ἡ κοινὴ ἀνάγνωσις), one of the technical expressions among the Alexandrian scholars for granting textual authority to some variants.

[234] See Nagy 1996, 121–32, reviving arguments by Lehrs 1882, Wackernagel 1969–79, II:1072–1120, esp. 1103–06 [1909], and West 1970 (in *OCD*[2] s.v. "Rhapsodes") about an unbroken oral tradition preserving, *inter alia*, the musical characteristics of Homeric verses into the Alexandrian era.

[235] [Dion. Thrax] *Ars Gramm.* §1. Cf. Quint. *Inst.* 1.8.1; 11.3.35–39.

8 THE VOICE VISUALIZED

Comparison of the two kinds of art – verbal and visual – and their respective judgments are a commonplace in the critical tradition, as in the following passage from Dionysius of Halicarnassus:

I should recommend all those who wish to understand the style of Demosthenes to do this: to form their judgment from several of its properties, that is to say the most important and significant of them. He should first consider its melody, of which the most reliable test (κριτήριον) is the instinctive feeling (ἡ ἄλογος αἴσθησις); but this requires much practice and prolonged instruction (τριβῆς). Sculptors and painters without long experience (ἐμπειρίαν) in training the eye by studying the works of the old masters (τῶν ἀρχαίων) would not be able to identify (οὐκ ἂν διαγνοῖεν) them readily, and would not be able to say with confidence that this piece of sculpture is by Polyclitus, this by Phidias, this by Alcamenes; and that this painting is by Polygnotus, this by Timanthes and this by Parrhasius. So with literature (λόγων).[236]

Elsewhere, Dionysius points out the analogies between the mixing of sounds and the mixing of pigments, two practices whose terminologies and analytical procedures are so close one can only suspect some sort of filiation:

I hold the view that there are very many distinct forms of composition, which can be included neither in a comprehensive view nor in a detailed reckoning. I also think that, as in personal appearance (ὄψεως), so in literary composition, an individual character is associated with each of us; and I find not a bad precedent (παραδείγματι) in painting. As in that art all painters mix their pigments together in a variety of shades, in the same way in poetry and all other literature, though we all use the same words, we do not put them together in the same manner.... The first [style I shall call] *austere* (αὐστηράν), the second *polished* (γλαφυράν), the third *well-blended* (εὔκρατον).[237]

As it happens, the three styles named here are attested from painting, and it has been argued that Dionysius is deriving his terminology from professional treatises by painters possibly from the fourth century, such as Euphranor's *On Colors*, which Pliny likewise knew.[238] The point, however, is not simply that Dionysius was borrowing terms from a neighboring specialization, a striking innovation if it is one (though the general move to analogy was hardly unprecedented, as we have seen already).[239] It is that

---

[236] Dion. Hal. *Dem.* 50; trans. Usher.   [237] Dion. Hal. *Comp.* 21; trans. Usher, adapted.
[238] Pollitt 1974, 322–25; 374–75.
[239] "Polished" appears as a "character" or style in the author of *On Style* (ch. 36). The analogization to painting occurs as early as Gorgias (see above).

he found it fitting to translate the experience of sound into the experience of vision and color. Hearing sounds, he was in a sense *hearing colors*. What is more, in another sense Dionysius is merely rediscovering the common roots of the *sunthesis*-model all over again, as if for the very first time. For, if the analysis given earlier in Chapter 4 is right, that model was originally designed to apply to phenomenal appearances *tout court*, but above all those in the realms of sound, sight, and touch.

Analogies of sound to visual and physical structures are found elsewhere in Dionysius and in the Hellenistic euphonist critics reported by Philodemus, and these will be explored in Chapter 9 below. The boundaries between the visual and verbal arts were plainly felt to be permeable, and not just parallel. One might speculate that at the origin of these metaphors lay not only the nascent aesthetic languages of the Greek fifth century or earlier, but also the practice of writing on objects.[240] In both cases, that of the euphonists and the euphonistically inclined Dionysius of Halicarnassus, at issue was the proper evaluation and judgment (*krisis*) of the materials of language. The tradition of *enargeia*, or vividness of expression, according to which language, whether heard or read, was felt to come alive before the senses and especially before one's eyes (*ad oculos*), was a strong contributing factor. This can be traced from the first stirrings of literature in Homer (so-called Homeric "vividness").[241] A good example from later in the same tradition comes from the ancient scholia to Homer. Here, we can see how easily auditory and visual signals cross over, though one suspects that visuality among the grammarians is obtaining on two levels, that of *mental imagery* and that which accompanies the *physical act of reading* a voice inscribed on a page: "*One can actually see* (ἔστιν ἰδεῖν) the huge surf of the sea being thrown against the current of the river and *roaring* as it is beaten back, with the beaches on either side *echoing the noise* (ἠχούσας) .... In this way [Homer] has presented *the thing heard even more vividly* than something actually seen."[242] Designed to illustrate a visual experience (ἔστιν ἰδεῖν), the comment demonstrates, almost inadvertently, the triumph of the ear in the end – or else proves that *enargeia* is a function, at least some of the time, of *hearing in reading*.

Evaluation implied a judgment not only about quality, but also, and above all, about authenticity.[243] The two criteria, and so too their associated

[240] For a suggestive analysis, see Carson 1999, 92–93. [241] See Bakker 2005.
[242] Schol. bT *Il.* 17.263–65; trans. Bakker 2005, 159.
[243] As is evident from the ancient practice. Cf. also schol. Dion. Thrax 170.5; 303.28; 471.34–35; 568.15 Hilgard.

pleasures, were evidently linked. If to read gave pleasure, to read aloud the genuine voice of a treasured author gave this pleasure a completeness that could not be rivaled. In later antiquity, the highest esteem went to those authors whom we would call classical but who for the most part were known simply as the "best" and the "purest" of the "ancient" writers, from Homer to Plato and Demosthenes. These were the writers who were worth emulating and whose sentences were worth analyzing, microscopically and in endless detail, in order to see how they achieved the effects they did. (Hellenistic and later authors didn't make the grade.) The aesthetic value of literary objects was indissociable from the ideology of classicism, which is to say, from the ideology of Hellenism. A similar bias existed on the Latin side as well, as authors from Cicero to Aulus Gellius show.[244] Authentication in another vein, of the sort that issued from literary evaluation, could cash in on all of this too: euphonist literary criticism sought to capture the extra dimensions of the voice contained in and implied by writing. Such criticism provided a way of accessing – literally, of touching – the past. The habit persisted into the post-oral era of writing, and it is not clear that with all of our technological sophistication we have ever quite managed to free ourselves from the spell of listening for the music of the voice buried in written texts today. Roland Barthes' explorations of this very quality of writing, of "vocal writing," which conveys traces of a voice that reach beyond meaning and content to its more tangible and sensuous qualities, whether heard or made visual in the mind's eye, despite the warnings of Derrida and others, is an outstanding example from the contemporary world, nor is he alone.[245]

9 CULTURES OF THE VOICE IN GREECE AND ROME

A brief comparison with Rome will be useful to indicate both the continuities and differences in practices vis-à-vis Greece. Romans were unabashed logocentric offenders.[246] "Thus Pliny, in one of his famous letters to Tacitus, declared that a written speech (the word he used was *oratio*) was the archetype or paradigm of an oral speech (here the word used was *actio*): '*Est enim oratio actionis exemplar et quasi* ἀρχέτυπον.'"[247] Cicero

[244] See Porter 2006b.   [245] Cf. Rée 1999; Smith 1999; Stewart 2002; Bruns 2005.
[246] At least from a Derridean perspective. For a critique of Derrida's view of the voice, from a Saussurean perspective, see Porter 1986b.
[247] Plin. *Ep.* 1.20.10; Dupont 1999, 232.

had earlier claimed that writing is the best training for speaking (though he was also taking up a stance against extempore speechmaking).[248] Though the logic might appear to suggest that writing takes formal precedence over speech, in functional terms writing is in both cases approximating to speech. *Recitatio*, the public and often theatrical reading of works to a small coterie of social peers, ensured that writing and delivery kept equal pace.[249] Persius describes how public recitation becomes a musical spectacle, as the reader, like a veritable Ion, is supposed to come "decked out" in costume, stand "on a lofty rostrum," and hold forth

> in a flowing *recitativo*,
> from nimble, liquid gullet, and roll
> over the audience an orgastic eye.
> Soon, you can see enormous Toms and Dicks
> off good behaviour: their voices fog over,
> they begin to flutter as the chant enters
> via their backsides and their insides are tweaked by twitching verses.[250]

As Florence Dupont notes, the Roman *recitatio* "calls for a musical and sensuous reception of the text," but to such an extent that overpowering seduction looms near: the audience is easily "led astray by the musicality and vocal play of [the] *lector*. The pleasure of the audience is thus [the] musical pleasure of a body both abandoned and possessed" – an anxiety that Persius is flippantly exposing.[251] It made little difference that all this display and seduction was enacted under the thin veil of a fiction, be it the simulation of speech in written form or the construction of an authorial voice for readerly consumption often under imaginary pretexts (as in *controversiae* and *suasoriae*).[252] If Romans were logocentric offenders, they were at least complicit in their crimes.

Greece inaugurated a culture of the voice, one that thrived thanks to the cultivation of the voice. Rome pursued this same culture with a new passion, even an obsessiveness.[253] The Greek name for vocal training was *phōnaskia*. The Latin term for vocal trainers was *phonasci*, and one name for the art was *ratio* or *exercitatio declamationis*.[254] The art covered

---

[248] Cic. *De or.* 1.150. Cf. Quint. *Inst.* 1.4.3, 12.10.51, and 12.10.55 (all echoing 1.7.31, quoted earlier) on the co-implication of writing and speaking, owing in fact to the primacy of speech.

[249] See Dupont 1997; Dupont 1999, 204–57.

[250] Pers. 1.15–21; trans. R. E. Braun, as in Dupont 1997, 51.

[251] Dupont 1997, 51–52.   [252] On which, see Imber 2001.

[253] Indispensable still: Krumbacher 1920. See also Rousselle 1983; Gleason 1995, 88–130 (especially on gender anxieties connected with vocal performances).

[254] As in *Auct. ad Her.* 3.20. (The voice is the topic until 3.30.)

everything from practicing before mirrors to diet and hygiene to physical exercise to vocal regimens. Only one textbook on the subject is mentioned in antiquity, *On Vocal Training*, by an otherwise unidentified Theodorus (Diogenes Laertius calls it "very fine"), but there must have been hundreds of such manuals: the idea and the terminology of *phōnaskia* is widely attested from an early date.[255] Aelius Dionysius relates how "Pericles was the first to reject as ungainly and wide the shape of the mouth that results from the letter *s*, and that he used to practice all the time before a mirror."[256] Demosthenes also trained before a mirror, and he is said to have paid the actor Neoptolemus 10,000 drachmas to teach him to speak entire periods in a single breath.[257] Nero used to strengthen his thin and husky voice by declaiming with a leaden plate on his chest, taking emetics and purgatives, and avoiding constipating fruits and other foods harmful to the voice.[258] Inscriptions openly attest to the ongoing value of vocal training to winners of citharodic competitions, so customary and uncontroversial a part of vocal culture was this focus. (These are signaled with such stock phrases as "under the vocal trainer So-and-So," or "first among those with vocal training."[259]) Burial inscriptions could boast the skill of professional reader as well, as in, "I was a grammarian and a professional reader, but a reader who used the pure method of those who pleased through the sound" (*Grammaticus lectorque fui, sed lector eorum | more incorrupto, qui placuere sono*).[260] Affording pleasure through the sound of one's voice was plainly as much a part of the aim as anything else.

The powerful conjunction of reading, hearing, and recognizing vocal sound held possibilities that were easily and quickly realized. Pedagogy was one of the more immediate beneficiaries. School children were drilled in word division and punctuation (which is to say, in vocal management), and they also trained their ears and their tongues in the more properly musical inflections of textual sounds.[261] Unmusical sounds, in the form

---

[255] D.L. 2.103 (§4). See n. 33 above. Cf. Dem. 19.336 on Aeschines, himself a former actor: "at other times he will raise his voice (ἐπαρεῖ τὴν φωνήν) and appear well-trained" (πεφωνασκηκὼς ἔσται). Cf. Dem. 19.255; 18.259–60, 280, 291, 308. Also, Quint. 2.17.12.

[256] Eust. *Il.* 10.385–89.

[257] See Plut. *Dem.* 11; [Plut.] 844E–F; Phot. *Bibl.* Cod. 265, 493a Bekker; Krumbacher 1920, 23. Demosthenes seems to have studied with several actors. Other names mentioned in the tradition are Andronicus ([Plut.] 845A; Quint. *Inst.* 11.3.7) and Satyrus (Plut. *Dem.* 7).

[258] Suet. *Ner.* 20.1.

[259] E.g. (ranging from the mid-third century BCE to the imperial period and from across all Greece), *IG* II² 3169/70; *IG* IV 591; *IvO* 237; *EKM* 1. Beroia 373; *I.Smyrna* 659 (cf. Robert 1938, 94–95).

[260] *CIL* vi.2.9447 = *ILS* 7770.

[261] On division and punctuation in ancient school texts, see Cribiore 1996, 81–88; Cribiore 2001, 189–92.

of tongue-twisters and other hard-to-pronounce bits of language, were likewise put into the service of drilling children in the mastery of speech and the voice. The purpose of exercises like these is best given by Quintilian:

It would be a good idea, at this age, in order to develop the vocal organs and make the speech more distinct, to get the child to rattle off (*volvant*), as fast as he can, words and verses designed to be difficult, formed of strings of syllables which clash with one another (*asperimme coeuntibus inter se*), and are really rocky (*confragosos*), as it were: the Greeks call them χαλινοί [tongue-twisters; literally, "bits" or "curbs"]. This sounds no great matter (*modica dictu*), but leads to many faults of pronunciation which, unless removed in early years, persist through life as an incurable bad habit.[262]

Examples of the drills, not given by Quintilian but found elsewhere in papyrus fragments and in other remnants of teaching materials are combinations of letters such as *gxbg, idb, zibz*.[263] Here, disagreeability of sound is being exorcised in the name of euphony: in place of stones in the tongue, the way Demosthenes had practiced, students are being asked to roll (*volvere*) the very letters of the alphabet on their tongues. The letters have turned into clashing rocks, hard bits of ugly matter, the aural equivalents of toy letter-shapes given to children to play with "so as to stimulate them to learn," and to habituate them in the literal palpability of sound-shapes: there is a pleasure to be had (*iucundum sit*) in "handling, looking at, and naming" objects like these.[264] Indeed, a further irony of this pedagogical "primal scene" is that it replicates the terrors and confusions of illiteracy that it is designed to help overcome: to a novice unskilled in the arts of lectional signs or self-guided punctuated breathing, the texts of Greek and Latin written out in *scriptio continua* were a mere jumble of letters and a phonic blur.[265]

Sometimes, the lessons came by utter negation, in the form of unpronounceable, unpunctuatable, and indivisible clusters of letters and sounds that do not even merit the name of tongue-twisters, as with the following from an Egyptian papyrus of the first century CE:

---

[262] Quint. *Inst.* 1.1.37; trans. Russell.
[263] Quoted by Krumbacher 1920, 57 from Wessely 1904–08; cf. Ziebarth 1913, 5 and *passim*; Cribiore 2001, 166.
[264] Quint. *Inst.* 1.1.26.
[265] See the *Shepherd of Hermas*, Vision 2.1[5]:4 (second century CE), which plays on this kind of confusion. (It is discussed by Cribiore 2001, 175.)

κναξζβιχθυπτηςφλεγμοδϱωψ
βεδυζαψχθωμπληκτϱονσφιγξ.[266]

As has been noticed, this piece of text contains all twenty-four letters of the alphabet in each line. It is therefore built on two (nearly unsayable) pangrams.[267] Long and short vowels roughly alternate in each line, a further drill in vocal gymnastics.

When schoolboys' tongues were not being put through the paces, they were being obliged to practice more standard vocal training, and even to sing: they were taught

when to take a fresh breath, where to make a pause in a verse, where the sense ends or begins, when the voice is to be raised or lowered, what inflection should be given to each phrase, and what should be spoken slowly or quickly, excitedly or calmly [without] degenerating into sing-song or the effeminate artificiality that is now so popular.[268]

Simply by pressing linguistic competence to such radical limits, exercises like these walked a fine line between competence and incompetence, and ultimately between culture and its lack. Anxieties attended the very act of performance, given the disrepute that attached to acting and, when carried out in the wrong places or with the wrong emphasis, to song culture itself.[269] Whence the impossible double bind of the dictum quoted by Quintilian, which he finds "an excellent remark": "If you are singing, you are singing badly; if you are reading, you are singing" (*si cantas, male cantas: si legis, cantas*).[270] Similarly, Cicero: "I want neither excessive precision nor yet slackness in the pronunciation of the letters, neither faintness and feebleness nor yet excessive fullness and volume in the utterance of the words ... [neither] a soft or effeminate tone of voice [n] or one that is unmusical and out of tune."[271] Best is to start off the reading regime with Homer and Vergil: epic is manly and virtuous, a safe ground for the sung voice. Here, too, the mind can "be uplifted by the sublimity (*sublimitate*) of the heroic poems, and inspired and filled with the highest principles by the greatness of their theme."[272] But this last remark by

---

[266] Wessely 1904–08, XLV; cit. Krumbacher 1920, 57. I have inserted Krumbacher's correction of μ for the text's original ιγ, a student's error, which mars the pangram of the second line. The same sequence is repeated in Clem. *Strom.* 5.8.48.5 (correctly there).

[267] The final three syllables happen to spell out two Greek words. More on pangrams and lipograms in the next chapter.

[268] Quint. *Inst.* 1.8.1–2; trans. Russell. Cf. Krumbacher 1920, 69 (quoting Stadelmann 1891, 106): such introductory syllabic exercises played the role of, "as it were, a kind of musical instruction."

[269] See esp. Gunderson 2000; Habinek 2005.   [270] Quint. *Inst.* 1.8.2.   [271] Cic. *De or.* 3.40.

[272] Quint. *Inst.* 1.8.5.

Quintilian shows a certain guardedness towards the vocal tradition, which generally put less stock in sense than in sound and its attendant pleasures, and which at the extreme could achieve a sublimity all its own without a thought for high-minded principles and heroic themes.[273] Therein lay its danger. The tradition was double-edged.

With so much staked on the voice in an oral culture, and with so much anxiety flowing freely around the question of vocality, it is inevitable that the medical tradition, which from the first had a hand in vocal culture, should be the ever-diligent handmaiden of the same culture into the later periods as well.[274] We have already heard the sad story of Diodotus, the youthful chorister who apparently died from a potion while seeking to improve his voice and to render it euphonic. The cultivation of the voice could at times verge on hypochondria or neurosis, and it is a fair question whether the presence of medical opinions helped assuage or intensify these tendencies. Fronto once panicked at the thought of losing his voice from colic, which disease and symptoms he describes in intense medical detail. He later thankfully regained his voice in all its clarity.[275] Oribasius records a surgical procedure that was used to correct a patient's inability to pronounce the letters *d*, *l*, and *r*: the lingual frenulum was incised at the middle to free its movement (freedom of movement always carrying ideological connotations, whether in speech or elsewhere).[276] A different operation on both sides of the same membrane was performed to correct the mispronunciation of *ph*, *p*, *k*, or *x*.[277] (An identical procedure, called frenulectomy, is fashionable today among South Koreans eager to learn fluent English, according to news reports from 2002.[278]) At the other extreme, the risks of overtraining the voice, whether to the point of

---

[273] So too Krumbacher 1920, 60: reading for the meaning had "the least importance" in the tradition of vocal ascesis. Cf. [Plut.] *Mor.* 848B: Demosthenes said that actors should be judged by their voices, rhetors by their minds.

[274] E.g., Plut. *Mor.* 349A (more dietary than medical). In addition to Krumbacher 1920, see Schöne 1930; Finney 1966; Rousselle 1983; von Staden 2002.

[275] Fronto, *Ep.* 5.55 van den Hout (to Marcus Aurelius).

[276] Cf. Arist. *Part. an.* 2.17.660a17–23: "It is in man that the tongue attains its greatest degree of freedom (ἀπολελυμένην ... ἔχει ... μάλιστα τὴν γλῶτταν), of softness, and of breadth; the object of this being to render it suitable for ... the articulation of letters and for speech" (trans. Ogle). Aristotle goes on to contrast the behavior of the disadvantaged, "tongue-tied" speaker who lacks this degree of lingual movement.

[277] Orib. *Coll. Med.* 45.16.5. Cf. Quint. *Inst.* 1.11.5 on the difficulties of getting *lambda* and *rho* straight in pronunciation, evidently a widespread worry.

[278] See "Koreans Take a Short Cut on the Road to English," *The Independent*, 9 April 2002: "Now, after decades of cruel jokes about 'rice' and 'lice,' South Korean doctors claim to have found a surgical operation which improves English pronunciation." The ten-minute, US$300 procedure reportedly was part of a then US$3 billion-a-year industry in English-language instruction.

effeminacy or exhaustion, were no less dire.[279] These anecdotes from antiquity reflect the pressures of a profession, and possibly more. But they also reflect the place that the voice had in medical therapy, both as an end in itself and as a means to curing physical ailments of all kinds.

Voice was first and foremost a physiological function: it was an exhalation of the lungs. This produces something of a paradox for aesthetics. Language, reduced to its character as voice, is tantamount to language in its character as something bodily, physical, and material. It becomes "thingly," a pulsation of air, what Galen and others call "the matter of the sound" or "of the voice" (ἡ ὕλη τῆς φωνῆς; *materia*).[280] But the reduction of language to this most basic material and physiological level – to its breathy substance – is also the way in which language most approximates to music, as opposed to its serving as a vehicle of meaningful discourse. Here, language becomes *aesthetic*, as opposed to its being an expression of a bodily organ. And yet, this last opposition is hardly tidy. For the musical aesthetic qualities of language are those that derive, precisely, from its thingly qualities: pitch, melodiousness, rhythm, and the rest are modulations of *breath*, and nothing else. Nor is this all. For, when language is reduced to its materiality and tied to its intimate relationship with the breath and the body, it simultaneously reveals itself to be an index of *life* and of *vitality*, of the very essence of animate being, as we saw. "Voice (φωνή) is a kind of sound (ψόφος τις) characteristic of what has soul in it" (ἐμψύχου), Aristotle writes in *On the Soul*. "Nothing that is without soul utters voice, it being only by a metaphor that we speak of the voice of the flute or the lyre or generally of what (being without soul) possesses the power of producing a succession of notes which differ in length and pitch and timbre. The metaphor is based on the fact that all these differences are found also in voice."[281]

Aristotle and others will want to bring the voice, so conceived, back into the ambit of meaningfulness once again.[282] But aestheticians in antiquity need not, and often do not, follow this logic. They linger, instead, in the delicious and indeterminate zone between the animate and the inanimate, the material and the immaterial, sound and voice, the literal and the metaphorical (or oral). It is here that sound can signify

---

[279] Quint. *Inst.* 11.3.23–26.
[280] ἡ ἐκφύσησις δ', ἣν ὕλην τῆς φωνῆς ἐδείξαμεν (Gal. *De usu part.* 3.611.12 K). Cf. Varro, *De serm. Lat.* fr. 83, p. 213. 3–4 Goetz–Schöu (= *GL* IV:525.19): *materia esse ostenditur vox, et ea quidem qua verba possunt sonare, id est scriptibilis.*
[281] Arist. *De an.* 2.8.420b5–9; trans. J. A. Smith.
[282] As he does soon afterwards at *De an.* 2.8.420b32: "voice is a sound with meaning" (σημαντικός).

differently, can be meaningful without meaning anything in particular, can echo and be sung, and can even on some accounts be sublime. Meaning, after all, can be wrung from irrational criteria without being vested with meaning in some constraining sense of the term. Sound, as a signifier of value, for instance of canonical and classical value, reigns supreme in much of the ancient world, and it can at times supplant the value of morals and meaning in the conventional sense. But this is not to say that sound is therefore meaningless. Quite the contrary, the voice, whenever it comes to signify its own materiality, presents connotations that poets and others can harness, be this a sense of harsh contingency and finality (as in burial inscriptions, to be discussed in the final chapter), or an irrational and erotic blissfulness (as in ecstatic, sympotic, or any other countless number of contexts found in antiquity), or a complex atmospherics resting on a *je ne sais quoi* that conjures up ineffable past glories – though the list of aesthetic possibilities is in principle endless.

And so, to complete our cycle, with breath taken to such lengths of appreciation and removed from the constraints of day-to-day meaning (or else finding its original significance there), voice – as mere breath – also begins to detach itself from matter and the body again, like that of the cicadas who, so the myth goes, were once sprung from men who sang and sang, and were so struck with pleasure in the course of their singing that they quite forgot to take in food or drink and eventually died, unaware even of their own deaths. Cicadas repeat this ancestry, requiring nothing but air and dew for sustenance, and releasing a song that is enchanting in the extreme, a song that is seductive to others and fatal to themselves. Consequently, they live on as pure voice and pure spirit, as the sheer music of the voice, embodying a nearly breathless breath that is "dedicated to a spirituality beyond the contingencies of matter."[283] And yet, they remain audible, a voice that is sung and heard, and therefore lying not beyond but within the realm of matter, the senses, and experience.

---

[283] See Pl. *Phdr.* 258e–259d; Aesop. *Fab.* 1; cf. Porph. *In Harm.* 76 on the lightness of the breath and voice of the cicada, which lacks *ogkos* (bulk), moisture, quantity, density, etc; Svenbro 1990 (quotation at p. 9).

CHAPTER 7

The voice of music

Music is in many ways one of the most widely attested but least recoverable of all the ancient aesthetic practices in Greece and Rome.[1] Without pretending to offer anything like an exhaustive history of musical theory and practice, which would in any case be pointless (several excellent studies already exist, many of them book-length, and all of them formidably learned), I will simply mark out a few of the steps in the evolution of musical discourse from the sixth to fourth centuries BCE as this pertains to the kinds of questions we have been following in this study.

I MUSIC IN ITS ANCIENT CONTEXTS

The absolute relevance of music to performance contexts (dance, theater, festivals, contests, symposia), and especially to the performance of poetry (epic, lyric, tragedy, dithyramb, comedy, mime), ensured that musical vocabulary and musical thought would remain deeply entrenched in the ancient world and a central part of its aesthetic reflexes. Music lay closer to the verbal arts than did either painting or sculpture: it shared the same aural space, deployed the same rhythms, and last but not least, musical production appears to have been primarily geared to vocal accompaniment, to judge from the surviving evidence.[2] The mutual proximity of music and verbal artistry continued to flourish in the realm of criticism and rhetoric, and eventually not even the domain of prose would remain untouched, as we saw in the foregoing chapter, and as Cicero nicely

---

[1] Cf. M. L. West's comment about Greece: "Ancient Greek culture was permeated with music. Probably no other people in history has made more frequent reference to music and musical activity in its literature and art" (West 1992, 1).

[2] See West 1992, 154; 197.

encapsulates in a later phase of the rhetorical tradition: "What music is sweeter (*dulcior*) than a well-balanced speech?"[3]

While the verbal arts were the primary beneficiaries of this exchange, they were by no means the only ones. Vase painting is richly illustrative of music.[4] But so, too, was architecture engaged in dialogue with music. One need only think of the Odeion in Athens, purpose-built for performances, or the circular theater-shaped spaces designed on acoustic principles and renowned even today for their superior acoustics. Ancient architects went so far as to install bronze or clay sounding vessels (*echea*) and wooden floorboards under the seats in order to ensure the full resonance of the acting and singing voices throughout the theatrical space. (These have long vanished, but the archaeological record preserves their traces.[5]) Vitruvius is our most detailed source of information on this practice. His account, if it is to be trusted, is truly remarkable, because it illustrates the extraordinary measures ancient architects will have taken, not merely to accommodate the musical aspects of performance, but actually to model their designs on principles culled from treatises in musical harmonics. The pages of *On Architecture* from which this account comes are in themselves an object lesson in the ancient disregard for disciplinary boundaries, while the actual built theaters are the physical embodiment of this attitude (and the material evidence does appear to bear Vitruvius out). Vitruvius devotes an entire chapter to sounding vases. The chapter follows a short lecture on harmony and introduces two further chapters on theater construction, which is followed by a short chapter on vocal acoustics in the theater from a design perspective.[6] A brief glimpse of the details that Vitruvius provides about sounding vessels will give a taste of his account.

Bronze vessels, preferred for their resonant qualities over cheaper clay, were actually manufactured so as to produce enharmonic chords when touched (*cum tangantur*), whether by hand or by the voice, simultaneously: "the sound of a fourth, a fifth and so on to the second octave."[7] But that is only the beginning of the story. Their arrangements at the sites were unusually complex, and these varied with the size of the theater:

Mark off a horizontal area at the mid-point of the theater's height. In this area thirteen cavities (*cellae*) separated by twelve equal intervals (*intervallis*) are to be

---

[3] *De or.* 2.34.
[4] See Paquette 1984.
[5] See Thielscher 1953, Canac 1967, which combines modern acoustical analysis with ancient architectural data, and thus, as it were, updating the theories found in Vitruvius; further, Shankland 1973; and see below. Thanks to Kate Bosher for some of these references.
[6] Vitr. 5.5.1–8.   [7] Vitr. 5.5.1; trans. Granger.

arched over, so that the vases referred to above, giving the note of the *nētē huperbolaeōn*, may be placed at each end; second from the end, vases of the *nētē diezeugmenōn* at an interval of one fourth (*diatessaron*) from the last; third from the end at the *paramesē* (another fourth), [and so on].[8] . . . By this calculation the voice poured forth from the stage, as if from the center (*vox a scaena uti ab centro profusa*), and circling outward, will strike the hollows (*cava*) of the individual vessels on contact, stirring up an increased clarity and a consonance harmonizing with itself.[9]

All this applies only to smaller-sized theaters. Larger theaters should be arranged to encompass all three traditional harmonic tunings – the enharmonic, chromatic, and diatonic – with the hollow vases arranged in three concentric zones corresponding to each tuning and around the center of the stage. And in case the reader is puzzled by any of this, Vitruvius accompanies his account with a diagram (reconstructed in modern translations) "drawn in accordance with the method of music" (*musica ratione*) of Aristoxenus. Follow these instructions, and you will "easily be able to erect theaters adapted to the nature of the voice and the pleasure of the audience."[10]

So conceived, the theater was a veritable harmonium, an instrument more than a building, and a production site of literal *symphonies* (*habet symphoniarum communitates*). Unlike his pages on temples, baths, or porticoes, the Vitruvian account of theaters is entirely spatial *because it is entirely aural.* But the nature of the space it describes is that of an *emptiness*, of an evacuated, resonant, three-dimensional space that is adapted to capture sound. Not only are the vases in Greek called *echea* ("containers"); they are also set out as a visual analogue of a musical scale, at *intervals* (*intervallis distantes*), waiting to receive their notes. What is more, their emptiness is doubled – it is *itself* surrounded by emptiness: "they have an empty space (*locum vacuum*) around them and above."[11] In other words, *the theater is itself one vast empty sounding vessel* composed,

---

[8] The notes named are the two highest standing notes of the so-called Greater Perfect System familiar from Greek musical theory (and discussed in the immediately preceding brief lesson in harmony of 5.4.1–9). Thanks to John Franklin for help in understanding the physical layout of the vases and their harmonic values. There are peculiarities to the arrangement described. One of these was noticed by Franklin (*per litt.*): "Why is the *proslambanomenos* [another standing note] not used? Perhaps because the theatre itself, as a whole, is intended to resonate at that frequency. That explanation also has the advantage of explaining why Vitruvius does not specify a given *tonos*: that pitch value would be given by the theatre itself. But again, pure speculation!" This inadvertently chimes well with the image of the whole theater as a sounding vessel, to be proposed below.

[9] Vitr. 5.5.2–3; trans. after Granger and Rowland, adapted.
[10] Vitr. 5.5.6.   [11] Vitr. 5.5.1.

as it were, of micro-intervals that musically articulate and enhance the sound as it pours forth from the stage.[12] There is, in this remarkable scheme, a final, striking absence that needs to be noted: that of the viewer, who is all but missing (and, oddly, not only here, but everywhere in Vitruvius' accounts of the theater). The only trace of spectatorship left, on this skewed account, lies in the peculiar, almost surreal image of the sounding vases that have to be wedged up to face the front of the theater (*in parte, quae spectat ad scaenam*) in order to act as receptacles of sound, like virtual viewers.[13] The theater, that preeminent "place of seeing," has been reduced here to a place for sound, a *locum vacuum*. And yet, to stand in a theater with an architect's eyes is to see and to hear nothing: it is to *see* the intervals of sounds, and to await the arrival of the notes.

Vitruvius describes a Greek practice that was literally transferred to Italian soil. (When Lucius Mummius destroyed the theater at Corinth in 146 BCE, he brought back with him to Rome the bronze vessels he found there. He dedicated them in the temple of Luna, but other Italic theaters sported this architectural feature, Vitruvius says.[14]) But as peculiar, and in other respects as exemplary, as the case described by Vitruvius is, the influence of music across all the arts was long and lasting. Homer provides ample accounts of musical settings and performances, as do his successors, and the Roman tradition is equally rich, if diverse from the Greek.[15] The Pythagorean tradition is a whole other avenue of influences that has barely been touched on in the present study, though it has been extensively covered elsewhere. To take just one example, modern archaeologists have speculated on the proportions of building structures in southern Italy, for instance those of the Temple of Zeus (the Olympeion) at Acragas, modern-day Agrigento in Sicily, or at the temple of Athena at Paestum. What they have found is that the temple dimensions display possible configurations of Pythagorean ratios (proportions), which in turn could possibly reflect musical intervals, likewise in accordance with Pythagorean number theory.[16] If this were the case, then we would indeed have concrete instances in which architecture represented "frozen music."[17]

---

[12] For a detailed analysis of the musical harmonics produced by this system of resonances, see Landels 1967.

[13] Vitr. 5.5.1.

[14] Vitr. 5.5.8. Evidently the practice of sounding vessels was perpetuated into post-Carolingian northern Europe. See Gros 1997, 1:689 (thanks once again to Kate Bosher for this reference); Baumann 1990; more detailed still: Arns and Crawford 1995.

[15] See Wille 1967; Wilson 2002b, 64–67; and now Habinek 2005.

[16] Bell 1980; Nabers and Wiltshire 1980.   [17] See Ch. 8, §8 below.

But such speculations aside, and to reinforce the larger point, what remains of interest is that the descriptive traditions inaugurated by the poets encouraged a specialized language for naming sounds, instruments, techniques, subjective effects, and the like, many of these suggestively spatial and architectural, which could then flourish in their wake: musical theory had in a strong sense already been in motion long before the first known glimmerings of musicology come into view for us. Even dating these latter can be difficult, so finely does practice shade off into the first theorizing about practice, let alone theorizing for theory's sake alone.

Leaving aside the earliest descriptive language, some of which was discussed in previous chapters, let us turn instead to a moment that is on the cusp of musical theory. In the Homeric *Hymn to Hermes*, of disputed date but usually placed at the end of the sixth century,[18] we encounter the following description of Hermes' invention of the lyre:

He cut stalks of reed to measure and fixed them, fastening them by the ends through the back of the tortoise's shell. Then he stretched oxhide over it by his skill, and added arms, with a crossbar fixed across the two of them; and he stretched seven harmonious [lit., "concordant"] strings of sheep-gut (ἑπτὰ δὲ συμφώνους ὀΐων ἐτανύσσατο χορδάς).[19]

One scholar writes about the final line that "it could come straight out of a music theory textbook."[20] Whether or not it could, the verse may well supply us with the first attested occurrence of *sumphōnos*, while the surrounding verses do read like the assembly manual of a craftsman. It is no doubt thanks to passages like these that the image of Homer and other poets as gifted with extraordinary powers of knowledge arose, at times only to be subjected to critical scrutiny or worse. Here, one can imagine the performer carrying out his "lesson" through ostension, nodding at the lyre in his hands, much like the later *harmonikoi*. In the verses that follow, one sees how easily the self-description of an art could merge into self-advertisement for that art, while both simultaneously, if inadvertently, could advance the causes of aesthetic and technical description along the way:

When he had made it, he picked up the lovely toy and tried it in a tuned scale (κατὰ μέλος) with a plectrum. Under his hand it rang out awesomely (σμερδαλέον κονάβησε). Then the god sang to it beautifully (ὑπὸ καλὸν

---

[18] See Crudden 2001, 116 for the usual dating and West 2003, 14 for a fifth-century dating.
[19] *Hom. Hymn Merc.* 47–51; trans. Barker.   [20] Richter 1974, 266.

ἄειδεν), trying out improvisations (ἐξ αὐτοσχεδίης), like young men mocking each other with taunts at a feast. He sang of Zeus, son of Cronos, and Maia ....[21]

While the language of the Hymn is more technical and of a later date than the Homeric poems, and indeed is considered to be among the latest of the *Homeric Hymns*, the basic rhetorical gesture is entirely Homeric. All of Homer's descriptions of minstrelsy, from Demodocus at the Phaeacian court to Phemius, who figures prominently at the *Odyssey*'s close, to Achilles strumming his lyre in a brief moment of reflexive tranquility in the *Iliad*, are self-descriptive and self-advertising. They also act as virtual cues for the audience, modeling aesthetic reactions for them: when we listen to a singer singing about a singer who "sings beautifully" and who provides his audience unsurpassed *terpsis* (pleasure), we naturally transfer the praise back to the song we actually hear. And so, in this way the languages of aesthetic and technical description could take off, in parallel with the descriptive language applied to other aesthetic objects and aesthetic effects in the poems.[22] Indeed, theoreticians of music would later draw on the rich store of terminology that had evolved over the centuries when they set about developing technical terms for their hand-books. *Orthios* (high-pitched), *oxutonos* (shrill-pitched), *ligus* (clear), *krou-mata* (strummings), *sēmata* (signals marking times or beats), *euphōnos, sumphōnos, harmonia, psuchagōgos*, not to speak of the various song types (*nomos, humnos, skolion, dithurambos, ailinos*) and instrument names (*luros, kithara, surinx, phorminx, salpinx, aulos, tumpanon*), or the very umbrella term for music, *mousikē* ("of the Muses"), are all derived from the earlier epic and lyric poets.[23] In the absence of such foundations, the musicologists would have had nothing to build on at all.

A later, similarly technical-sounding set of verses is the epigram on the eleven-stringed lyre by Ion of Chios, dated to no later than 421 BCE (his death), and which once again provides the audience with a thick description of his instrument's "ten-step arrangement and (?) concordant road-junction(s) of *harmonia*."[24] Ion was proudly trumpeting his innovation of

---

[21] Ibid., 52–57; trans. Barker, adapted.

[22] For a useful collection of Homeric (and later) passages about music in poetry, with indispensable annotations, see Barker 1984. On bards in Homer, see Segal 1994, esp. ch. 6.

[23] This list is not meant to be complete by any means. Further examples may be found in Barker 1984. The term *mousikē* first appears in Ibycus (*SLG* 255.4), *pace* West 1992, 225 (awarding the coinage to Lasus).

[24] ἑνδεκάχορδε λύρα, δεκαβάμονα τάξιν ἔχουσα | †τὰς συμφωνούσας ἁρμονίας τριόδους†, fr. 32 West; trans. West 1992, 227, who notes a correspondence with the terminology of Aristoxenus' later *Elements of Harmony*.

having added four strings to the seven-stringed lyre: "Formerly Greeks plucked you at seven pitches, two tetrachords (?), raising a scanty Muse."[25] But he also seems to have had a general penchant for reflexive self-depiction. Athenaeus reports how in his *Omphalē*, Ion called Lydian girls "pluckers of strings," and how in his *Second Phoenix*, he wrote (and doubtless sang) the verse, "'Playing a loud deep-pitched *aulos* in running rhythm,' referring in this way to the Phrygian kind. For it is deep in pitch."[26] Athenaeus' technical gloss on a compressed verse description is notable by itself: it reads like a response to an invitation from the side of Ion. On the other hand, consider how in his original Ion has literally *voiced* his instrument, which underscores but also goes beyond the point made earlier about how so much of the surviving early Greek music, including musical scores, is vocal in nature. Such self-depiction is nothing new, and neither is the convergence of technical and practical vocabularies: we have already witnessed the same kinds of moves in Homer and the Homeric Hymns, and we shall see more of the same presently in the case of Pindar and Lasus. Only the heightened sophistication in the technical language appears to be new (in fact, it is not). But the key point is that both of these vocabularies are simultaneously being taken under the wing of an aesthetic language (visible, for instance, in the evaluative tag, "scanty Muse"), the effects of which it is possible at times only to imagine, so fragmentary are the remains that have come down to us.

2 LASUS OF HERMIONE AND THE NEW POETICS OF SOUND

Before leaving the sixth century, we need to examine one tantalizing cluster of clues concerning the close intimacy of musical theory and practice in its early phases, especially as these pertain to the shadowy but clearly impressive figure of Lasus of Hermione. Lasus' *floruit* is put in the last quarter of the sixth century BCE, and he is said in later sources to have been Pindar's teacher. If we can trust the ancient record, he was a musical innovator on several fronts: he wrote the first treatise on music and conducted empirical acoustic experiments; he introduced the dithyrambic competitions in Athens at around 508 after the death of his patron Hipparchus, and was himself a composer and innovator in the genre; he also innovated in auletic technique, in choral arrangements

---

[25] πρὶν μέν σ' ἑπτάτονον ψάλλον διὰ τέσσαρα πάντες | Ἕλληνες, σπανίαν μοῦσαν ἀειράμενοι (fr. 32.3–4 West; trans. West 1992, 357).

[26] Ath. 14.634e, 185a; trans. Barker.

372 *The voice of music*

(having invented the circular chorus), and in the sounds of choral songs.[27] This is an impressive list of achievements, but it only begins to hint at their boldness.

Let's start with the last-named of these. From various sources we know that Lasus wrote at least two compositions for the voice in which he suppressed the *sigma*, which is to say, the sound "*s.*" To suppress the *s*-sound in Greek – "one of the commonest sounds in the Greek language"[28] – is no easy feat, and it puts one in mind of the contemporary French author Georges Perec (1936–82), whose ludic achievements included lipogrammatic novels that deliberately leave out one or more vowels, for instance *La Disparition* (1969; English trans. *A Void*, 1994), which abjures the vowel *e* and in fact turns on the mysterious disappearance of that letter from the alphabet (and of many other things from reality as well). Perec also wrote a short story whose only vowel was *a*. But if Perec had no obvious reason to do what he did, he at least had a precedent in Lasus (as he was well aware), and in fact he was working in an entire tradition of lipogrammatic writing.[29] But what could have motivated Lasus' proto-Oulipian gesture, the earliest known of its kind?[30] No reason is given in the direct testimonies, but inferences can be drawn from adjacent contexts. According to Aristoxenus, earlier unnamed musicians rejected the *sigma* because it was "difficult to pronounce" or "harshsounding" (σκληρόστομον) and ill-suited to the *aulos.*"[31] Aristoxenus is echoed by Dionysius of Halicarnassus, who in *On the Composition of Words* finds the *s*-sound to be "neither charming nor pleasant." It can even "cause pain" when used excessively, for it produces a "hiss," a *surigmos*, like that of "an irrational beast."[32] And while language, Dionysius believes, can be irrational to the extent that it is musical (it affects the *alogos aisthēsis*, or irrational faculty of the ear, giving rise to pleasure and even ecstasy), he also implicitly believes that language must, so to speak,

---

[27] See Privitera 1965, a full-length study; Barker 1984, s.v. "Lasus" in the index; West 1992, 342–43, for a convenient summary of Lasus' achievements; and D'Angour 1997, for a striking reappraisal of some of the key evidence.

[28] West 1992, 40.   [29] See Perec 1988, esp. 77–78 (on Lasus).

[30] "Oulipo" is an acronym for "Ouvroir de Littérature Potentielle" ("Workshop of Potential Literature"), a literary movement founded in 1960 by R. Queneau and F. Le Lionnais in the name of the unlimited production of literature under limiting constraints. (An Oulipian author is defined by Oulipians as being like a "rat who constructs his own labyrinth in order to attempt to escape it.") Other members have included M. Duchamp, I. Calvino, and G. Perec. See their website: http://www.oulipo.net/ (accessed March 2010).

[31] Ath. 11.467a (= fr. 87 Wehrli). Cf. Eust. *Il.* 10.385–89 (quoted at Ch. 6, n. 256 above).

[32] *Comp.* 14; trans. Usher.

be *rationally* irrational: its unreason knows constraints and conventions of all kinds. As a result, "some of the ancient writers used the *sigma* sparingly (σπανίως) and with caution, some even composing entire odes without *sigmas*." As proof, Dionysius adduces the first two verses of a dithyrambic fragment from Pindar that is partially completed by an Oxyrhynchus papyrus (the papyrus fragment goes on for another thirty-one lines):

Formerly the singing of dithyrambs crept along (ἕρπε), stretched out like a rope (σχοινοτένεια),
and the 's' (τὸ σὰ[ν]) came out [sounding] base-born (κίβδηλον) to men.[33]

Both Aristoxenus and Dionysius, then, hint at the existence of asigmatic composition prior to Pindar. Neither names Lasus, but further sources do. A drama begins to unfold, pitting Pindar against his predecessor, and rather unremorsefully at that. If Lasus suppressed the *sigma*, Pindar foregrounds it with a vengeance: the opening salvo bristles with sibilants; it literally hisses like a snake – an image that is also conjured up by the phrases "creeping along" and "stretched out like a rope" (if that is the meaning of the much-disputed word σχοινοτένεια). Nor is Pindar's practice in the remainder of the ode any different: there is even a mention of "the hissing (κλαγγαῖς) of ten thousand snakes," as though the intention were to take the initial imagery to an unheard-of limit.[34]

3 CLEARCHUS AND THE RIDDLE OF 's'

The exact meaning of Pindar's verses and their polemical intent, if that is what we have, is probably irrecoverable. The closer the ancient sources come to fingering Lasus as the recipient of Pindar's presumed attack, the more confusing the details grow. According to Athenaeus, Clearchus of Soli, a learned Peripatetic and pupil of Aristotle's, called the first two verses of the dithyrambic fragment, or at least these two verses, "a kind of riddle set forth in lyric composition" (ἐν μελοποιίᾳ) – unless he meant "a kind of riddle set forth *in the area of* musical [or "lyrical"] composition." The phrase ἐν μελοποιίᾳ is peculiar, and it appears only here: it smacks of academicism on the part of Clearchus, which could lend support to the second alternative.[35] Unfortunately, Clearchus' detection

---

[33] Pind. *Dith.Oxy.* 2.1–3 = fr. 70b Snell–Maehler; trans. Barker 1984, 59–60.
[34] Cf. also D'Angour 1997, 338 and 342.
[35] "In song" is surely wrong; that would be ἐν μέλει, *vel sim.* See also Privitera 1965, 31: "fu usata nella melopea."

of a riddle in Pindar's dithyramb is itself somewhat enigmatic, and rather enigmatically preserved.

His report comes in two different versions in Athenaeus. The first is a direct quotation, which shows that the original seat of the fragment was a book, *On Riddles*. Much like W. K. Wimsatt, Clearchus counted seven kinds of riddles in the world, the first of which "depend[s] on a letter" (of the kind, "Tell me the name of a fish that starts with an *a*"), one sub-species of which is named after letters present or missing, "like the so-called ἄσιγμοι-riddles [those lacking a *sigma*]; whence even Pindar wrote an ode with reference to the letter *s*, as if a kind of riddle were being set forth in [better still: "in the area of"] lyric composition (μελοποιία)."[36] The second report is more expansive (unlike the first, it offers the example of Pindar's two verses, as in Dionysius); and it appears to be interlarded with Athenaeus' own comments (or paraphrases from whatever further sources Athenaeus may have culled his information). Deciding on where to draw the exact lines between Clearchus' words, their paraphrase, and external information is probably an impossible task. But even so, given the direct report, which was centered on the special case of the missing *sigma*, we can be quite certain that the kernel of the second report is genuine: "Pindar composed these verses [from *Dithyramb 2*] with reference to the ode composed without a *sigma*" (πρὸς τὴν ἀσιγμοποιηθεῖσαν ᾠδήν),[37] presumably Lasus' ode *Centaurs*, which is mentioned by Athenaeus by title in the immediate sequel.[38] This is about all that *is* clear. The rest is a hopeless tangle.

Before moving on, we need to pause a moment and take stock of Clearchus' report. One of its oddities is that it attributes "a kind of riddle" to Pindar, *just when we would expect him to attribute it to Lasus*. Recall how Pindar gets introduced, namely on the heels of the riddles of the "missing *sigma*" type. But Pindar's ode has no missing *sigmas*, while Lasus' ode did. D'Angour is the only scholar to parse the problem correctly: "Clearchus may have been alluding to a particular γρῖφος [riddle], whose riddling terms were *echoed* in Pindar's lines."[39] But D'Angour's solution, while plausible as an account of musical practice, is less plausible as an account of a riddle. The musical solution he proposes has to do with Lasus' discovery that the disturbing hissing

---

[36] Ath. 10.448c–d (= fr. 86 Wehrli). See Appendix to this chapter for the text in translation.
[37] *Pace* Privitera 1964, 167, the second statement accurately reflects the first.
[38] By title and title alone – possibly because it no longer existed in his day (as it does not for us).
[39] D'Angour 1997, 331–32; emphasis added.

of the *sigma* could be minimized by reorganizing the chorus into a circular formation around the conducting aulete: in this way the chorus' singing could be coordinated, and trailing sibilants could be made to vanish. Somewhere *en route* to this formal solution Lasus decided to test out the effects of *sigma*-suppression by composing an asigmatic ode (in addition to an asigmatic hymn to Demeter, some of which is preserved).[40] Satisfied with the euphonic results of these experiments, he somehow hit upon a superior way of enforcing them across a wider spectrum of sounds, which involved rearranging the chorus in a circle, and abandoned the asigmatic experiments as being, in the long run, impracticable.

This is all well and good – more than that, it proposes a neat reconstruction of Lasus' musical reforms – but wherein lies Lasus' riddle? Unable to discover one in this scenario, D'Angour has to invent one: "What crawls like a snake but does not hiss?" Answer: "An asigmatic dithyramb."[41] One problem with this *ersatz*-riddle is that it is not asigmatic (*asigmos*), it is merely *about* asigmatism (it is a description rather than an instance).[42] But surely Clearchus, who must have adduced the asigmatic ode *Centaurs* mentioned by Athenaeus (and also by Dionysius of Halicarnassus),[43] has in mind an entire class of lipogrammatic riddles that suppress the *s* ("the so-called *asigmoi* riddles"); it is hard to imagine what class of riddles could *refer to* asigmatism. If Lasus presented his ode in a riddling fashion, we would expect it to be of this class.[44] Pindar's riddle, by contrast, is adduced as a quasi-member ("as if it were a kind of riddle") of the class that *contains* (that is, whose members comprise) *asigmoi* riddles (riddles that hang on the presence or absence of a letter), which is quite different from riddles that refer to *s*-sounds, for instance, by way of hissing noises or other sibilants. Nothing prevents Lasus from having presented his ode by way of an additional riddle that referred to *s*-sounds. But the explicit mention by Clearchus of *asigmoi griphoi* and then of "asigmatic ode," and Clearchus' own definition of a riddle (which we happen to have), suggest that this extra step is unnecessary, as I will try to show.

---

[40] *PMG* 702 = Ath. 14.624e–f.   [41] D'Angour 1997, 342.

[42] See the Greek version supplied *exempli gratia* at D'Angour 1997, 342 n. 68.

[43] *PMG* 704.

[44] As would, necessarily, any asigmatic ode written by any author. Dion. Hal. *Comp.* 14 assures us some ancients "composed whole odes without sigmas" (ἀσίγμους), before quoting the Pindaric verses. Lasus' songs would have stood out as special cases if they were novelties, which is likely.

Athenaeus gives us Clearchus' definition of what a riddle is in the same context as the first of the two reports about Pindar. According to Clearchus in his *On Riddles*, "a riddle is a problem (πρόβλημα) put in jest (παιστικόν), requiring, by searching the mind, the answer to the problem (τὸ προβληθέν) to be given for the sake of saving or losing face."[45] The ludic character of riddling as a practice is reemphasized a few pages later: "Like Theodectas, according to Clearchus, Dromeas of Cos and Aristonymus the harp virtuoso used to play at riddles" (ἔπαιζε γρίφους).[46] Riddles are keenly intellectual games. In their "most archaic" and purest form, they are sheer logical conundrums, meant to embarrass or reward the players. That Lasus, a kind of proto-sophist and author of witticisms that later were collected under the name of *Lasismata*, should have been drawn to riddles, particularly of the linguistic sort that turned on amphibolies and plays on words, seems only natural.[47] A delightful example was recorded in a book on Lasus by Chamaeleon of Heracleia, another Peripatetic. Once Lasus stole in jest (παίζων) a fish from some fishermen and handed it over to bystanders. When asked, "he swore [to the fishermen] he did not *have* (ἔχειν) it himself nor did he know of anybody else who had *taken* (λαβόντι) it, because he had *taken* it himself, but somebody else *had* it, and this person he had instructed to say on oath, in turn, that he had not *taken* it himself nor did he know of anyone else who *had* it. For Lasus had *taken* it, but he himself *had* it."[48] He seems to have been a kind of Oulipian after all.

With this example in mind we can turn back to Pindar and Lasus. A simpler scenario for Lasus' original riddle suggests itself, one that need not involve any references to snakes, or indeed to anything at all. Let us imagine that Lasus merely composed an asigmatic ode, and then a hymn, each quite possibly the first of its kind, but also that he failed – deliberately – to note the absence of the *sigma* in each. The puzzle, or the joke, would have lain *in the very absence of the designation that each song was demonstrating an absence.* They would have been true lipograms. Lipograms generally do not call attention to the fact that they are lipograms: they

---

[45] Ath. 10.448c; trans. Gulick, adapted. Note the words πρόβλημα, τὸ προβληθέν, which reoccur in the second version of the Clearchean report at 456c: "posing, as it were, a kind of riddle in (the area of) lyric poetry" (οἱονεὶ γρίφου τινὸς ἐν μελοποιίᾳ προβληθέντος).

[46] Ath. 10.452–53.

[47] Cf. Privitera 1964, 47–60. Brussich 2000, 16–9 is incomplete.

[48] Ath. 8.338cd; trans. Gulick. Did Lasus suggest Heraclitus' riddle about Homer, the fisherboys, and the lice, which likewise turned on a play between two similar words, *getting* (λάβειν) and *carrying back* (φέρειν)? (DK 22 B56 ~ *Cert.* 328 Allen).

conceal their secrets out in the open. That is, *their riddle lies in their very form, not (or only secondarily) in what they say.* "Ils ne le disent pas." They don't say what they are, they simply are.[49] That is their whole point, and the source of their pleasure (or sting): one has to discover the code in order to appreciate the technique of their construction. For this reason they are closely related to cryptograms.[50]

An example cited by Perec, but also by E. G. Turner, who edited a papyrus that turned out to be the remains of either a fifth-century or a Hellenistic lipogrammatic (asigmatic) satyr-play, is the rewriting of the *Iliad* by Nestor of Laranda under Septimius Severus: in the first book there were no *alphas*, in the second no *betas*, in the third no *gammas*, and so on.[51] Triphiodorus of Sicily (third century CE) is known to have followed the same procedure for the *Odyssey* (neither poem has survived). The inverse of a lipogram is a pangram, a sentence or other unit that contains every letter of the alphabet.[52] There are quasi-pangrams that are also lipograms (suppressing one or more letters of the alphabet).[53] To determine or verify whether you have a lipogram before you, and then what kind it is, you simply have to start counting the letters. And what is more, Perec warns, any phrase you like has every chance of being lipogrammatic. (My last sentence has no *z*'s, *q*'s, or *v*'s. *Iliad* 7.364 contains no *sigmas*.[54]) Taking a swipe at literary history and philology, Perec notes that the terms for lipogram have themselves been suppressed from academic discourse and its apparatuses (including lexicons), and treated as non-serious outsiders, "aberrations," "pathological monstrosities," tricks of cleverness, or signs of madness. "Literary history seems deliberately to ignore writing as a practice, as work, as play."[55] Nevertheless, he writes at the close of his essay, the lipogram has a genuine power, in that it operates somewhat "like the zero degree of constraint, *on the basis of which*

---

[49] Perec 1988, 74: "la plupart du temps, ils ne le disent pas." There are exceptions, of course, such as Jacques Arago's *Voyages autour du monde sans le lettre A* (1853) – which is only a partial exception, however, for just what is a "voyage around the world *without the letter A*"?

[50] Perec 1988, 77. A master of encryption, Lasus was also known as a master of decryption, for as Herodotus relates (7.6.3), he famously exposed a forgery by Onomacritus, catching him as it were *in flagrante*, by showing how the latter had surreptitiously slipped his own poetry (ἐμποιέων), in oracle form, into the words of Musaeus. Exile by Hipparchus followed as a punishment for this literary crime.

[51] Perec 1988, 78–79; Turner 1976, 20 (= Adesp. *TrGF* 2.655); on Nestor, see now Ma 2007.

[52] E.g., "The quick brown fox jumps over the lazy dog." See also p. 361 above.

[53] At least according to Perec 1988, 86–87.

[54] Detecting asigmatic verses like this and other alphabetic anomalies in Homer was evidently a (proto-Perecian) literary pastime at some point in antiquity, according to Athenaeus (10.458a–e).

[55] Perec 1988, 75.

everything becomes possible." I believe that something of the same spirit must have infused Lasus' lipogrammatic experiments. It was through a suppression of sound – here, an individual sound – that Lasus discovered how to *enable* and *unleash* sound, in the name of musical reform. And I believe we can demonstrate this through Pindar's example, on the reasonably safe assumption that Pindar was following in Lasus' wake.

4 PINDAR'S RHETORIC OF INNOVATION AND THE NEW POETICS OF SOUND

Let's turn one last time to Pindar's second *Dithyramb*, and attend to it a bit more closely, this time as a whole poem. I quote the first five verses for starters: [56]

> Formerly (πρίν) the singing of dithyrambs crept along (εἶρπε), stretched out like a rope (σχοινοτένεια),
> and the 's' came out from human mouths (ἀπὸ στομάτων) [sounding] base-born (κίβδηλον) to men,
> [but now] youths[57] are spread out wide [in well-centred?] circles.[58]

In the sequel, Pindar proclaims himself the "chosen" and "appointed herald" of a new style of poetry for all Greece – a style that is Bacchic, frenzied, and above all, *noisy* and *loud*. The verses that follow are in fact chock-full of sound terms, with an effect that can be elevating, terrifying, baroque, and even grotesque all at once: whirling tambourines, clattering castanets, "loud-sounding wails and frenzies and shouts," lightning bolts "breathing fire," "the strong aegis of Athena [that] resounds (φθογ-γάζεται) with the hissing (κλαγγαῖς) of ten thousand snakes," pile up, then comes a transitional section (in the preserved portion) to a mythological invocation of Cadmus' bride Harmonia, whose name inevitably takes on an acoustic overtone here, and not least of all given her immediate surroundings (her name stands adjacent to the phrases, "the report ([φ]άμα) goes" and "harkened to the voice of Zeus" (Δ[ιὸ]ς

---

[56] Text after Snell–Maehler. The bracketed words reflect the new readings, supplements, and renderings by D'Angour 1997, who reads εἶρπε for ἔρπε (corr. Schroeder, 1900) in 1 along with the majority of ancient testimonia in addition to the MSS, as does Lavecchia 2000.

[57] νεαγ[ίαι D'Angour ("youths"): νέαι [Snell–Maehler.

[58]] πύλα[ι κύ]κλοισι Grenfell–Hunt: εὐο]μφάλ[οις κύ]κλοισι D'Angour, who renders the last line "but now youths are spread out wide in well-centred circles." At 4 in his text, Lavecchia 2000, 30 reads διαπεμ[.].[, where D'Angour follows the earlier editions' διαπέπ[τ]α[νται; and at 5 (p. 133, ad loc.) he entertains [ἐπ' ὀ]μφαλ[ὸν κύ]|κλοισι, "[but now] let us send forth a new [cry] to the altar in circles," while his more conservative text leaves dotted and unrestored 4–5 spaces in the place of μφαλ.

δ' ἄκ[ουσεν ὀ]μφάν). All of which is to say that Pindar's poem, charged though it may be with ritual motifs, is heavily programmatic in literary terms: it deliberately takes a proud polemical stand on the poetics of sound; it broadcasts that position "loudly"; and it weaves its poetics into the poetry itself. Whatever else the first few verses may be doing (and these are the subject of unresolved dispute today), Pindar's poem as a whole is a literal *celebration of the open mouth*: it opens the floodgates of sound in an absolute torrent. That torrent is not only announced in the opening verses, but it is also performed by them. The first two verses, we saw, bristle with the sibilants they denounce as *passé*, while the prominent if elusive word σχοινοτένεια, in combination with τ' ἀοιδά, makes for a striking if unseemly phonic cluster that simultaneously names and caricatures the forbidden σάν (*sigma*) of the second verse.[59]

Remarkably, it is these same aural qualities in Pindar's ode which are singled out for comment in a papyrus fragment of late date, which looks to be either a commentary on Pindar and his dithyrambs or else a general treatise on the ancient dithyramb, but in either case belonging to the Peripatetic school and probably stemming from the fourth century BCE.[60] The anonymous author quotes precisely the "obstreperous" verses from Pindar's second *Dithyramb* (8–18), setting them off as such ("the poet says the following," [λέ]γει γ(ὰρ) οὕ[τως·]), and tagging the lemma with his own words, "full ... and noises [or "sounds"]" (πλήρ[ει]ς καὶ ψόφους), as if expressing part of a comment that described Pindar's verses as containing loud noises or sounds. There is more at stake here than "Bacchic noise."[61] For the remark appears to be of an aesthetic and literary-critical cast, given the context, which is aimed at metrical details and powerful psychagogic effects. This is not, in other words, a piece of religious history or the like.[62] An earlier parallel might be the characterization of Aeschylus, by Aristophanes in *Clouds*, as "full of noise [or

---

[59] For another "noisy" ode, see Pind. *Pyth.* 12.4–27, this time celebrating the mythical birth of the *Polukephalos nomos*, which likewise "wove into [the] music [of the *aulos*] the deathly dirge of the fierce [ophidian] Gorgon" (ibid., 7–8). For an analysis, see Martin 2003, 162–63.

[60] *P. Berol.* 9571ᵛ, ed. Schubart 1941 (dated by the hand to the early third century CE). The suspicion of its genre (as commentary) was raised by Lobel (*ap.* Schubart).

[61] Schubart 1941, 29.

[62] One lesson of the anonymous author of *P. Berol.* seems to be that Pindar's second dithyramb is capable of "powerfully changing the inner states" of its listeners through excitation; by contrast, his or another's (Simonides'?) song, in a different style, can "calm down the mind" (col. 2.52–57), though by what means is unclear – perhaps through a more "static" rhythm (Lavecchia 2000, 130). The metrical comment about "sculpting a verse" (col. 2.55) will be discussed in Ch. 9 at n. 10).

'sound']" (ψόφου πλέων).[63] And later echoes in a similar vein, in Aristotle, in Dionysius of Halicarnassus, and elsewhere, confirm that this observation had its origins in a specifically aesthetic context.[64] With one crucial difference. In this tradition of aesthetic criticism, the sonorities of the earlier dithyramb would be assimilated to the later manifestations of the New Music, which were roundly censured.[65] Thanks to these and similar verses Pindar may have seemed like a precursor of the New Music to later historians of music and literature, but he was no Timotheus. We should bear in mind that the pseudo-Aristotelian *Problems* called the Aeolian tuning in which Lasus innovated "magnificent and stately," while Sacadas was said to have clung to the "nobility of style" that Terpander first introduced into music. Lysander's style, inspired by these predecessors, is called *euogkos*, "full" and "rich," for all its sigmatic whistling (*surigmos*).[66] One should be wary of importing back into the earlier material anachronistic assumptions about genre and value, a point whose full significance will emerge below.[67]

The contrast Pindar draws in the second *Dithyramb* between a poetic, voluble "now" and a quieter "then" is similar, moreover, to one he draws in another fragment where he sets himself up against a Locrian rival, a certain Xenocritus from a century earlier (so the scholia inform us): "Hearing him playing his few notes (παῦρα μελ[ι]ζομεν[), and busying myself with my loquacious [art] ([γλώ]σσαργον ἀμφέπω[ν]),[68] I am roused to rival his song ([ἐρεθίζ]ομαι πρὸς αὐτά[ν]), like a dolphin of the sea, moved by the lovely melody (μέλος) of *auloi* in the flood of the waveless ocean."[69] And elsewhere, too, Pindar is happy to sing out his

---

[63] Ar. *Nub.* 1367. The comment is doubtless in part aimed at capturing cacophony, in addition to capturing meaningless "bombast." A scholiast glosses the phrase with ταραχώδη, "baffling," but this looks more like a paraphrase of the next part of the same verse, ἀξύστατον στόμφακα. See further Griffith 1984, 287 n. 23.

[64] Arist. *Rh.* 3.3.1406b1: dithyrambic poets are "full of sound" or "noisy" (ψοφώδεις); Dion. Hal. *Dem.* 7, equating a style (Plato's, in the *Phaedrus*) that is full of "sounds" (ψοφοί) with one that is full of "dithyrambs"; cf. Csapo 2004, 228–29. Cf. Ch. 6 at n. 223 (Arcesilaus).

[65] See generally Csapo 2004; also Martin 2003, who also notes that Pindar's *Pythian* 12, on the polycephalic nome, is attentive to "sounds and their echoes" (163).

[66] Sacadas: [Plut.] *De mus.* 1134C; cf. Proclus *ap.* Phot. 320b12–18 (describing the early nomos generally as "stately": ἀνεῖται τεταγμένως καὶ μεγαλοπρεπῶς); [Arist.]: n. 94 below; Lysander: Ath. 14.637f–638a. Incidentally, to the ancient ear poetic obstreperousness and loftiness can go hand in hand, for instance in Homer (and epic poetry generally); further, Ch. 6, n. 177 above. See Plin. *Ep.* 9.26.6, affirming the sublime style and quoting as examples three verses from Homer which are descriptive of loud, crashing sounds on a celestial or supernatural scale (*Il.* 21.38, 5.356, 14.394).

[67] For the general point, see Franklin forthcoming.

[68] Grenfell–Hunt supply μελ[ι]ζομέν[ου τέχναν], i.e., "art."

[69] Fr. 140b.11–17 Snell–Maehler; trans. Barker 1984, 60–61.

projects in loud and ringing tones.[70] In retrospect, it looks as though Pindar may have coined a rhetoric of innovation that would reappear two generations later in the poetry of Ion of Chios, as we saw above, one pivoting on the renunciation of the musty, dated old-timers ("formerly," πρίν) and their narrow bandwidth of sound ("scanty [σπανίαν] Muse," "few [παῦρα] notes").[71] But it is even more probable that Pindar inherited this rhetoric rather than inventing it, just as Ion did, the rhetoric of invention being the most suspect cliché there is in poetry. And in fact, this kind of contrast, which was by no means just a matter of rhetoric, would recur repeatedly over the next few centuries, as music restlessly expanded its scope and found new ways to break through old forms.[72]

An extreme culmination of the same tendency is described by Polybius and then put into anecdotal form by Athenaeus.[73] In 167 BCE, the Roman general Lucius Anicius celebrated his victory over the Illyrians with musical contests in which he deliberately perverted Greek musical performances. A large stage was built in the Circus and the most distinguished musicians from Greece were summoned to perform, the catch being that they were to perform *all at once*. *Aulos*-players, dancers, and choristers appeared, and then were directed to play not *together*, but *against one another*, combat-style. Confusion (σύγχυσις) reigned, licentiousness was encouraged, notes were blown "unintelligibly" and "at odds with one another," warlike gestures were mimed, and a veritable concerto for *auloi* against orchestra was waged. Even boxers were finally led onto the stage to the accompaniment of trumpets and horns. "The result was unspeakable" (ἄλεκτον), Polybius concludes, unable to conceal his displeasure.[74] Polybius' account is already anticipated by Plato in his *Laws* (unless the Platonic critique isn't in fact being alluded to).[75] Lasus of Hermione certainly deserves a place in this story, as we shall see, even if the exact details must of necessity remain shrouded in speculation.

Nonetheless, one suspects there is some particular innovation lurking behind Pindar's *Dithyramb* 2. Putting the two Pindaric fragments together, it might be thought possible to construe "stretched out like a rope" as

---

[70] E.g., Pind. *O.* 1.7–9: αὐδάσομεν; ὁ πολύφατος ὕμνος; κελαδεῖν.

[71] Cf. Lavecchia 2000, 131.

[72] See West 1992, 327–85, for a historical survey; also Privitera 1965, 77; Wilson 2002b; Csapo 2004.

[73] Polyb. 30.22; Athen. 14.615a–e.

[74] The symbolism of the event is nicely described in Musti 2000, 41.

[75] Pl. *Leg.* 3.700d1–e1, not least the idea of musical pandemonium: "The result [of radical musical innovations frowned upon by the Athenian, viz., Plato] was a total confusion of styles" (πάντα εἰς πάντα συνάγοντες) (trans. T. J. Saunders).

characterizing an earlier simplicity and austerity that contrasts with Pindar's embracement of a new aural complexity and abandon.[76] Lasus' avoidance of the *sigma*, a simplification of the aural spectrum under any description, could perhaps count as a simplicity of sorts. Therefore, it would naturally seem to follow (and there are ancient sources to promote and corroborate the suspicion) that Pindar must have been attacking Lasus of Hermione in *Dithyramb* 2.[77] But there are problems with this conflation of the two polemics, and possibly with this version of musical evolution: Lasus was an older contemporary, Xenocritus lived much earlier, and there is little to connect them. "In earlier times" (or "formerly" [πρίν]) ill-suits Lasus, unless Pindar was attempting to put some distance between himself and the man later reputed to have been his teacher, or unless Lasus was exacerbating an older tendency – which is not unlikely in itself, though it *is* unlikely that he was exacerbating a tendency to musical austerity.[78] To make matters worse, Lasus was an innovator and exponent of, precisely, a *new* kind of music. And Pindar might be thought to have borrowed as much from Lasus as he was reputed to have objected to him.[79] It is far safer to assume, then, that Pindar in both poems has joined forces with Lasus, but with a Lasus who has surmounted, in whatever way he did, the inhibitions regarding the *sigma*.

To anticipate the argument in what follows: the words εἷρπε σχοινοτένεια, translated above as "crept along, stretched out like a rope," *could* be understood to support the view that Pindar is rejecting a prior musical austerity – just not one that was practiced by Lasus. On the other hand, the hypothesis of an earlier austerity seems forced and unnecessary. Is it even true? Even if we do not understand σχοινοτένεια to mean "stretched out like a *pleated* rope," which would bring out one of its root senses,[80] we can nevertheless suppose Pindar means to say that in the past, intricately composed, possibly extended, "creeping" dithyrambs – or songs that Pindar is calling dithyrambs – were discouraged, as was the

---

[76] For the hypothesis of earlier simplicity, see Barker 1984, 59 n. 20, doubtless with [Plut.] *De mus.* in mind and the entire tradition he represents (e.g., 1133B, 1135D, 1141C, 1142C). But we need to be on our guard here, as the hypothesis is something of an ancient and, subsequently, a modern construct (see Ps.-Plutarch at n. 160 below) and a cultural bias that is evidenced in other areas, such as the visual arts (see below).

[77] So, e.g., Barker 1984, 59 n. 20.

[78] West 1992, 344 ("before the time of Lasus"); contrast D'Angour 1997, 333: "Pindar's πρὶν μέν is too general to refer solely to the dithyrambs of the unnamed Lasos." A further possible understanding of πρίν is implicit in Wilson 2002a (more developed than Wilson 2000 314 n. 32); see n. 160 below.

[79] Cf. also Pind. fr. 107a1–3 with *Pyth.* 1.4 (cit. Franklin forthcoming at n. 57).

[80] See LSJ s.v. σχοῖνος, II: "anything twisted or plaited of rushes, esp. rope, cord."

sigma-sound.[81] That music before Pindar could be complex, even experimentally so, is an attested fact. Pseudo-Plutarch knows this.[82] And the details surrounding the otherwise shadowy figure of Sacadas of Argos, the early sixth-century pioneer of the *aulos*, confirm it. They also happen to make for a remarkably close fit to the present circumstances, a fact that has been noticed previously but never fully appreciated.

5 SACADAS, LASUS, AND THE NEW POETICS OF SOUND

Sacadas, who thrice took the prize for his performance on the pipes at the newly reorganized Pythian games between 586 and 578, is known for having established the *Puthikos nomos*, an instrumental piece that portrayed, and mimed, the religious myth of Apollo's slaying of the serpent at the Pythian sanctuary.[83] The composition was structured in five sections, each named according to the stage of action represented, and culminating in a joyous celebration of victory. It was clearly an intricate work, and it must have required an extended performance as well. It was also a showpiece for the virtuoso aulete, who used his instrument to create all manner of sound effects, from a trumpet-call to a tooth-gnashing sound (achieved by pressing the tongue or reed against the teeth), both of these in the central combat segment, to a *surigmos* sound mimicking the hissing of the dying serpent.[84] Then along came Lasus, who embraced both the intricate dithyrambic style and, I want to suggest, the *s*-sound developed by Sacadas a generation or two earlier, whether by directly transposing Sacadas' innovations for the *aulos* to the chorus or else by suggesting them. Pindar followed in his wake, singing a dithyramb that re-Joyces in both of these things. However murky the details of this story may be, our best clue to understanding Lasus' reforms and Pindar's reflection of them in his second *Dithyramb* may well lie in their common approach to the possibilities of poetic sound. But it is to Lasus that we must now turn.

---

[81] This would be compatible with D'Angour's proposed choreographical and euphonic interpretation of εἶρπε σχοινοτένεια, "proceeded in a straight line." For the association of σχοινοτενής with a marked length of colons or periods and with consequent troubling effects for the breath, see the (admittedly late) testimony gathered in Lavecchia 2000, 126–27, nn. 72–73. (The scholia to the Aristotle passages, not cited by him, are more relevant still.) But the sense of extended length of poetic composition is also found, as at Philostr. *Her.* 55.4: καὶ ἄλλως σοφὸν ἐν τοῖς λυρικοῖς ᾄσμασι τὸ μὴ ἀποτείνειν αὐτά, μηδὲ σχοινοτενῆ ἐργάζεσθαι.

[82] [Plut.] *De mus.* 1138B, with the clarifying discussion in Franklin forthcoming.

[83] See West 1992, 212–14 for a full account; briefly, D'Angour 1997, 338.

[84] Poll. 4.83–84; Strab. 9.3.10; Hesych. s.v. ὀδοντισμός.

Let us start with a brief characterization of Lasus' new poetics of sound
as these can be grasped today. A fairly firm footing is given by the pseudo-
Plutarchan treatise *On Music*:

Lasus of Hermione, by altering his rhythms to the dithyrambic movement
[or "tempo"] (ἀγωγήν) and by pursuing the example of the multiplicity of
notes (πολυφωνία) belonging to the *aulos* (and so making use of more notes,
widely scattered about [διερριμμένοις]), transformed the music that existed
before him.[85]

Evidently, Lasus' revolution consisted in transposing the lively, melodic,
and polyphonic qualities of the *aulos*, which was a double-reed instrument
with multiple stops and capable of great range, of microtones, micro-
intervals, and extended techniques, onto vocal music. The impression is
confirmed by a fragment to be quoted momentarily (702 *PMG*). The
polyphony of the *aulos* had already been established by Sacadas of Argos,
as we just saw. And though Sacadas (or Clonas) is credited with a *trimelēs
nomos*, or three-mode song for the chorus, this appears to have been a
composition that modulated in successive strophes between the traditional modes (Dorian, Phrygian, Lydian) and so not to have been an
adaptation of Sacadas' revolutionary auletic technique to the voice.[86]
Adaptations for the cithara may have occurred before Lasus, as they surely
did after him (see below). But what evidence is there that Lasus either
adapted *Sacadas'* technique to the voice or else was inspired by it? This
is, to be sure, the most speculative element of my hypothesis. But the
hypothesis also makes provision for our ignorance as part of the history it
draws: that history was recorded by Pindar, albeit in a quasi-riddling
form, and then subsequently lost. In other words, the best (and only)
evidence we have for the transferral of *surigmos* to the vocal realm is
Pindar's dithyramb itself.[87] On this reconstruction, Lasus need not have
been the first to have experimented with vocal sibilance in the wake of
Sacadas' *aulos* techniques. Quite the contrary. Sibilance and sigmatism
would merely have served Lasus as a banner with which to flag his own

[85] *De mus.* 1141C; trans. Barker 1984, 235, slightly adapted.
[86] See West 1992, 342–43 on Lasus; ibid., 214 on Sacadas and Clonas (the ancient source is [Plut.]
De mus. 1134B).
[87] John Franklin has suggested to me that Lasus' own *On Music* (*Suda* s.v. "Lasus") may have
recorded this same history, and possibly supplied Heraclides of Pontus or another fourth-
century musicologist with the information. Even so, there is no telling whether Lasus would
have recorded his own position vis-à-vis Sacadas. The fate of Lasus' study, the very existence of
which is controversial, is unknown. For a defense of the authenticity of the notice, see Privitera
1965, 36–42.

promotion of a greatly expanded range of possibilities for the voice, above all in dithyrambic contexts.

The effects of Lasus' changes to vocal music must have been shocking. But the changes must also have entailed a wholesale transformation of existing music, as Pseudo-Plutarch suggests – and all the more so if Lasus was simultaneously adopting a dithyrambic rhythmical style in the totality of his choral productions, effectively endowing choruses with the *characteristics* of the dithyramb, and was not making changes only within the dithyrambic genre, as the text likewise suggests.[88] Vocal rhythms had to be altered, as did "movement" (ἀγωγή), whatever that is. *Agōgē* normally means "tempo," which is how the term is sometimes rendered here, but Privitera, who offers the most detailed analysis of this passage, is probably right to claim that its meaning here has a "comprehensive value": "it refers not only to rhythm and its stylistic realization, but also to the tempo of the diction, which in the case of choral songs was regulated by the music as well as by the rhythm."[89] Tessitura would have also required alteration, as well as the total character of the songs. And, given that Lasus seems to have been a citharode and not an aulete, it stands to reason that he would have sought to transpose the new music onto his own instrument. To do so would have necessitated changes of another kind, which appear to be substantiated elsewhere, and to which we now turn.

The only preserved verses by Lasus are from the hymn to Demeter mentioned by Heraclides of Pontus in the third book of his *On Music* and quoted by him in its *incipit*:

I sing (μέλπω) of Demeter and Kore, wife of Klymenos,
raising a sweet-crying (μελιβόαν) hymn
in the deep-resounding (βαρύβρομον) Aeolian attunement (ἁρμονίαν).[90]

It is easy to see why Heraclides took an interest in these verses: they too are programmatic, and they announce a proud new turn in the hymnic genre. That the Aeolian mode was uncommon at the time is confirmed by Pratinas of Phlius, a prominent and prolific poet active in the early fifth century, who urges its adoption, labeling it "fallow" and thus still underexploited.[91] As Lasus' language implies, the Aeolian *harmonia* was a "loud" and resonant one. "And," Heraclides continues, "in the sequel

<hr />

[88] So, too, Privitera 1965, 75–76; cf. Comotti 1989, 26–27. Others (Lasserre, Barker, West) construe the changes as limited to the dithyramb.
[89] Privitera 1965, 76 n. 15. Cf. Winnington-Ingram 1936, 60.
[90] Fr. 702 *PMG* = Ath. 14.624e–f; trans. Barker 1984, 282, adapted.
[91] Fr. 712 *PMG* = Ath. 14.624f–625a = fr. 163 Wehrli; West 1992, 342.

[Pratinas] says, more straightforwardly, 'The Aeolian *harmonia* is the song that suits everyone who is boisterous (λαβράκταις).'" This agrees with Heraclides' account of the tuning's *ēthos* in the earlier part of the passage, which in fact offers a kind of racialized taxonomy of Greek modes (Dorian, Aeolian, Ionian): like the Aeolians (i.e., Thracians), it displays elements of ostentation, fullness, and weightiness (τὸ ὀγκῶδες), "even conceit" (ἔτι δὲ ὑπόχαυνον); it is "lofty (ἐξηρμένον) and confident"; it has "a pretense of nobleness"; and it has a reach that goes lower than the Dorian mode, with which it shares some superficial characteristics, whence its nickname, the "Hypodorian" (which is best taken to mean "not Dorian, yet nearly Dorian," Heraclides or his epitomator assures us, the way *hupoleukon* means "not quite white, but whitish").[92]

Three features stand out in these accounts of Lasus' adoption of the Aeolian mode. First, once again we find Lasus promoting a highly *audible* modality of singing, conformable to the example set by Pindar above (and Pindar is the only other early poet to mention adopting the Aeolian *harmonia*[93]). Secondly, we get a first glimmering of the sublime entering into the language of musical description: *ogkos*, loftiness, nobility, and so on. The pseudo-Aristotelian *Problems* adds to this impression: it calls the Hypodorian (viz., Aeolian) mode "magnificent and stately" (μεγαλοπρεπὲς καὶ στάσιμον) and "hence [the] most suited of the *harmoniai* to *kitharōdia* [solo song accompanied by the cithara]."[94] And last but not least, βρόμος αὐλῶν ("brawl of the pipes") is used in the Homeric *Hymn to Hermes* (452), and so βαρύβρομον seems to underscore, like a kind of promotional book-jacket blurb, Lasus' transposition of *aulos*-sounds and melodic structures onto the voice.[95] Consequently, Pseudo-Plutarch's testimony that Lasus introduced auletic "polyphony" into vocal techniques is nicely confirmed in the *Hymn to Demeter*. So, too, is the likelihood that Lasus was eager to experiment with all elements of the vocal register, from deep brawling to shrill hissing sounds. Incidentally, one of the further musical forms mentioned by Pollux in his discussion of the *Puthikos nomos* is "the pipe-piece of the deep-toned kind (τῶν δὲ βομβύκων), the inspired and frenzied one, suitable for orgiastic

---

[92] Fr. 163 Wehrli = Ath. 14.624d–625a.
[93] *Pyth.* 2.69–71. But he is not the only other poet to celebrate the "loud deep-pitched *aulos*" (βαρὺν αὐλόν) (Ion of Chios *TrGF* 1.42 = Ath. 4.185a; trans. Barker); cf. Simonides(?) fr. 947b *PMG* (= Adesp. fr. 29b): τερπνοτάτων μελέων ὁ καλλιβόας πολύχορδος αὐλός; Pind. *Ol.* 3.8: βοὰν αὐλῶν.
[94] [Arist.] *Pr.* 19.48.922b14; trans. Barker 1984, 203.
[95] I owe this observation to John Franklin.

rites."[96] Nomoi, dithyrambs, and other ecstatic musical offerings are an orgy of sound effects that nearly exceed the boundaries of music altogether.

The *Hymn to Demeter* has one last feature that needs to be noted, and which we know attracted Heraclides' attention: it also happens to be the second of Lasus' two known asigmatic compositions.[97] If so, then the suppression of the *sigma* in a hymn otherwise conspicuous for its vocal reach cries out for a further explanation. That explanation already lies ready to hand. Recall the definition of lipogrammatic practice, the paradoxical aim of which is to unleash sound through the suppression of sound. This seeming contradiction at the level of musical form tells us everything about Lasus' self-presentation as a musician. And this in turn will lead us to an eventual solution of his riddle of sound as we find it in Pindar and Clearchus.

6 LASUS' THEORY OF THE MUSICAL NOTE

Lasus undoubtedly accompanied his *Hymn to Demeter* on the cithara. But in order to do so in the new "deep-resounding" Aeolian mode, it is likely that modifications in the tunings of his instrument would have been required, as they would have been for his new auletic style generally. Here, the sheer technical virtuosity of Lasus' theorizing of sound comes to the fore. The clues have been well assembled by Privitera, and they are worth repeating briefly. I also believe we can extract a bit more from them along the way.

Lasus' first step was to fractionalize the harmonic interval so as to obtain a greater number of notes ("and so making use of more notes, widely scattered about" [διεϱϱιμμένοις]), thus yielding a true variety of notes (πολυφωνία) closer to that of the *aulos*. Replicating the smaller intervals of the *aulos* entailed the production of semitones and quartertones previously unheard on the stringed instrument, most likely by modifying the cithara tuning itself.[98] A further possibility, suggested by Privitera, is an intriguing consequence of "the division of the interval": "in the moment in which a plurality of sounds (semitones and quartertones) was produced, the same interval lengthened [and "widened"], creating the

---

[96] Poll. 4.82. Cf. fr. 708.12 *PMG* (= *TrGF* 1.4 fr. 3), where Pratinas complains about the "deep-chattering mouth" (λαλοβαϱύοπα) of the *aulos*.

[97] Ath. 10.455c; Eust. *Il.* 24.1–2 (4:857.2–3 van der Valk).

[98] So Privitera 1965, 78–79; cf. Comotti 1989, 26–27 and West 1992, 343.

impression that the notes did not follow their natural order, but strayed apart from one another as a result of the interposed semitones and quarter tones."[99] While Privitera hangs this interpretation on a disputable under-standing of διεϱϱιμμένοις (taken in the sense of "distanced"), he needn't do so. The term's sense may be disputed, but the process of division and multiplication is not. And the possibility of a subjective impression that the intervals had been dilated just by being filled with so many notes remains valid, or at least worth considering. This is the line I want to pursue further.

Lasus' technical innovations in the scale are corroborated elsewhere. We know, for instance, that he developed a theory of micro-intervals. It is odd that Privitera, who spends some very interesting pages on this theory, fails to connect these two facets of Lasus' profile, because they are surely related to each other.[100] Aristoxenus is our primary source for this latter theory, which he introduces towards the beginning of his *Harmonic Elements* in its initial analysis of melody and the voice:

First of all, then, the prospective student of melody must analyse the movement of the voice, its movement, that is, with respect to place (*topos*), for there is not just one variety of this movement. The voice moves in the kind of movement I have mentioned both when we speak and when we sing (since high and low are obviously present in both of these, and movement with respect to place is that through which high and low come about), but the two movements are not of the same form. Up to now no one has ever carefully defined what the distinguishing feature of each of them is: and yet if this is not defined, it is not at all easy to say what a note (*phthongos*) is. Anyone who does not want to be forced into the position of Lasus and certain of the followers of Epigonus, who say that a note has breadth, must say something rather more precise about it: and once this has been defined, many of the subsequent issues will become clearer.[101]

We can only speculate about how Lasus defined a note as breadth (πλάτος), but the term immediately suggests a divisible space of sound that would lend itself to the very sorts of modification that he undertook in his alteration of the harmonic tunings. With sound so conceived – as a palpable entity, virtually as a kind of extended material body – its divisions could be empirically tested. And this seems to be just what Lasus did. A much later source, possibly dependent on another work of Aristoxenus', informs us that Lasus carried out acoustical experiments

---

[99] Privitera 1965, 79. Similarly, del Grande 1932, 89 (cit. Gamberini 1979, 250).
[100] For the undeveloped suggestion that they are, see West 1992, 343.
[101] Aristox. *Harm.* 3.5–26; trans. Barker.

using jars, and possibly strings and syrinxes, to test the effects of sound under different conditions. In the case of jars, these would be paired, one remaining empty as a control, the other variably filled with liquid, first half-way, then a quarter-way, then a third of the way, with their concords (συμφωνίαι) tested at each point. Strings and syrinxes were tested similarly for their concordances.[102]

One interesting feature of these experiments is the contrasting roles played by empty, subtracted spaces or "void" (κενόν), and the fullness of the body of sound, resonating in its "breadth." (We might think back to the Vitruvian theater, discussed earlier. There is every chance that such early experimentations on sounding jars and their consonances fed directly into the later architectural practice of "tuning" theaters harmonically through sounding vessels.) Another feature of these experiments is their reliance on phenomenalism, which is to say, on the way concords strike the ear. That is a natural corollary of their empiricism – and, one should think, of any interest in music, though the Pythagoreans and later Plato would beg to differ on this point.[103] Aristoxenus inherits, to some extent, both of these perspectives (empiricism – minus the experimentalism – and phenomenalism). Privitera disputes half of this inheritance, arguing that sound for Aristoxenus is immaterial, which motivates the latter's rejection of the Lasian theory of sound as *platos* (extension with magnitude).[104] A semantic and terminological confusion may be at play here, which it will be necessary to sort out.

That Aristoxenus has a technical appreciation of *notes* as immaterial points, or rather as formal boundaries marking off tonal intervals, is fairly evident. These points are probably extensionless.[105] But he also has a specific terminology for such limits: *topoi*.[106] Neither of these refinements would have been available to Lasus or Epigonus.[107] Aristoxenus is radically redefining the contemporary understanding of music, and probably also putting the accomplishments of the earlier century into a comprehensive system for the very first time.[108] We can only expect that some of his

---

[102] Theo Sm. 59.4–60.11 Hiller. Cf. Privitera 1965, 64–73; Barker 1989, 32 n. 11.

[103] *Pace* most scholars, Lasus' theory shows *no* traces of any Pythagorean influence or interest (so, too, Barker 1989, 31 n. 10; D'Angour 1997, 338).

[104] Privitera 1965, 66; cf. 68.

[105] Cleon. 180.5: *tonos* (note, or pitch) is "a range [or 'place'] (τόπος) of the voice, without breadth (ἀπλατής), capable of receiving a *systēma*" (trans. Barker 1989, 421 n. 117).

[106] Aristox. *Harm.* 3.20–24; 23.28–24.1.

[107] It may or may not be significant that in the reported definition of the note as possessing breadth, the operative term is *phthongos*.

[108] See Franklin 2002; Barker 2007, 144.

criticism is directed at the lack of sophistication his predecessors showed in failing to anticipate the subtleties of his own system. *Sound*, on the contrary, is "tracked" on Aristoxenus' system by following the progress of the voice as it moves across intervals. Indeed, tracking this movement of the voice is the first order of business in the *Harmonics*.

First of all, then, we must discuss the different kinds of movement with respect to place (τόπος), and try to understand what they are. . . . In the continuous form the voice *seems to perception* to traverse a space (τόπος) in such a way as never to stand still even at the extremities themselves, *at least so far as its representation in perception is concerned* (κατά γε τὴν τῆς αἰσθήσεως φαντασίαν), moving continuously to the point of silence; whereas in the other, which we call intervallic (διαστηματικήν), it seems to move in the opposite way. During its course it brings itself to rest at one pitch and then at another; it does this continuously . . . passing over the spaces bounded by the pitches, but coming to rest on the pitches themselves and sounding them alone, as is described as singing, and as moving in intervallic motion . . . Continuous movement is the movement of speech, for when we are conversing the voice . . . seems never to stand still. In the other form . . . it does seem to stand still, *and everyone says that the person who appears to be doing this is no longer speaking, but singing.*[109]

The last remark captures well the radical character of Aristoxenus' redefinition of what the singing voice is: a singer is not somebody who is singing, but *somebody whose voice everyone says appears to be standing still on one pitch and then on another*. The phenomenalism of Aristoxenus' position is repeatedly underscored in the above passage, with its frequent appeals to *aisthēsis* and *phantasia*. But it also comes to the fore in a part I did not quote, in which he dismisses the relevance of physics and of physical inquiry: whether or not the voice actually (physically) comes to a standstill on a note is irrelevant to harmonic inquiry, which traffics only in appearances.[110] For the same reason, Aristoxenus has no patience for the Pythagoreans (and others) who reduced notes and the voice to movement, which they sought and claimed to be able to measure: when the voice hits a note, Aristoxenus says, it stands on it and remains "at rest," much the way a string when tuned to a note is tensed until it becomes taut and stops moving when the note is finally reached.[111] Plainly, Aristoxenus' reservations are in the first instance directed against the physical inquiry *into* sound, not against a physical interpretation *of* sound. And while notes *formally* speaking are the dimensionless limits of an interval, *phenomenally*

[109] *Harm.* 8.13–9.29; trans. Barker.   [110] *Harm.* 9.1–11.   [111] *Harm.* 12.1–9; cf. 11.13–15.

speaking ("at least so far as its representation in perception is concerned") they are the place where the voice comes to a standstill, or rather *appears* to do so. So conceived, notes have a kind of breadth after all – which is why, in the Aristoxenian tradition, they are sometimes called a *topos* ("place").[112]

With musical sound so redefined, endless quibbles are possible. Aristoxenus knows that the voice is moving and it is not; that notes are formal limits but also audible sounds; that intervals are measurable but also inaudible *per se*, being the "space" through which the voice traverses, on the way to "coming to rest on the pitches themselves and sounding them alone." In point of fact, the relationship between intervals and notes is a fundamentally symbiotic one: neither has a self-sufficient identity, because each is defined in relation to the other. This is reflected, moreover, in the ambiguity of the term *tonos*, which can mean, among other things (both in Greek and for Aristoxenus), an *individual pitch* or the *interval* between two pitches. Strictly, notes *qua* limits of an interval are not immediately given to the ear, but have to be constructed (generated) by perception, nature, and convention as "the difference in magnitude between the first two concords," which is to say, as the difference between "the intervals of a fourth and a fifth."[113] Equally, intervals are constructed by their relationship to notes and to the system of the enharmonic tuning that encompasses both: their presence has to be *deduced* from the totality of the music.[114] One hears a spectrum of sounds (the voice in motion or standing still on "notes"), and one deduces a formal pattern (of intervals and notes) on that basis; but the elements of the pattern are not something one actually ever *hears* in themselves: they are audible only in their patterned interrelation. What is more, Aristoxenus is keen to suppress, in his theoretical description, the audition of the pattern itself as it is being formed: in song, the voice's "progress across the space of the interval which it traverses, whether relaxing or increasing tension, *must not be detected* (λανθάνειν αὐτὴν δεῖ διεξιοῦσαν), whereas it must give out the notes that bound the intervals clearly and *without movement*."[115] Only, the notes one hears are not quite the notes that bound intervals; they are the phenomenal equivalents of their non-phenomenal, formal counterparts:

---

[112] As in n. 105 above.   [113] *Harm.* 21.22–23; Barker 1978, 11.

[114] Whence a third ambiguity, whereby *tonos* in its less technical senses can mean tuning. On the ambiguities of the term, see Franklin 2002, 678 with n. 27.

[115] Aristox. *Harm.* 10.15–21.

they are a kind of aural *phantasia,* or impression.[116] For this reason, notes in a musical system are exactly comparable to *stoicheia,* which are intelligible only in relation to the system that contains them, and in relation to which they derive their phenomenal expression, whether aural or visual. Aristoxenus is well aware of the analogies that exist between the two compositional systems himself, as was previously noted.[117]

For all his petulance towards Lasus and Epigonus, Aristoxenus' theory of the note and of sound may not be so fundamentally different from his predecessors' in the end. Without more information, it is impossible to reconstruct the earlier theory in any detail. But some of its key features and especially its basic structure appear to have been shared by Aristoxenus: the common emphasis on the phenomenality of sound, which has to be won by comparing empirical sense data against an abstract formalized schema; the functional contrast between the fullness of sound and the empty space of an interval; the note's occupancy of a spatial plateau and its concordant relation to the variable ratios that define it;[118] and, finally, the synthetic power of *phantasia,* which is named in Aristoxenus and implied by the earlier method in the very idea of *sum-phōnia,* or concordance of sounds.[119] Obviously, the hands-on experimentalism of his predecessors is taboo for the armchair Aristoxenus, but the theoretical similarities are more striking than their differing attitudes towards empiricism.

Lasus' theories arguably paved the way for Aristoxenus' own theory of harmonics, however much the latter would resist this conclusion.[120] But what is more, two facts emerge from this ensemble of theorizing, both directly relevant to the problem of Pindar's second *Dithyramb.* The first is Lasus' emphatic emphasis on the subjective impression of sound as something phenomenally perceived, which has clear implications for the arrangement of the circular chorus, if that was indeed meant to eliminate vocal dissonances.[121] In this respect, Lasus would have anticipated Aristoxenus'

---

[116] Compare Barker 1989, 168n.110 on concordant and discordant intervals, classed by Aristoxenus as "'functionally' apprehended phenomena," for the reason that "they are not constituted by their magnitudes as such, but by the character under which they are experienced." Though Aristoxenus does not speak of notes in quite the same terms, he could have done so: they, too, are functionally apprehended phenomena.

[117] See Ch. 4, §8 ("*Stoicheia* and Perception," pp. 226–35).

[118] See Cleonides' somewhat tellingly contradictory definition of the note as "extensionless," and yet as a *topos* in n. 105 above.

[119] Cf. Lasserre 1954, 35, describing "consonance" as "un intervalle composé de deux sons différents dont l'émission simultanée éveille dans l'oreille une seule impression."

[120] Aristox. *Harm.* 3.5–24 (where Lasus and Epigonus or his followers are mentioned by name).

[121] See D'Angour 1997, 335, 340 (on sound as *heard*); 336 (on "poorly synchronized sibilants").

phenomenalism by nearly two centuries.[122] The second is Lasus' relentless drive to fractionalize the interval, creating new microintervals, ever smaller harmonic divisions, and finer grades of tonal variety. Plainly, the inherited musical sound palette was not broad or colorful enough to satisfy his aesthetic needs.

7 THE SEARCH FOR NEW SOUNDS

As in his more practical pursuits, Lasus gives the impression of a musician restlessly in search of new sources of musical sound and eager to expand the existing repertoire. In this, he is merely embodying the impetus of musical evolution in Greece from the sixth century into the fourth. Later sources remark upon this tendency, which is often treated as a passage from a simpler style characterized by a "narrowness of range" (στενοχωρία) and a "paucity of notes" (ὀλιγοχορδία) to a busier style characterized by "complexity" (ποικιλία), "many notes" (πολυχορδία), and being various or manifold (πολύτροπος), which is to say, modulating between different *harmoniai*.[123] Vases illustrate how musicians added strings to their lyres one by one from the traditional seven, presumably in order to reach beyond existing tunings and to attain new melodic possibilities, sometimes polyphonic. Timotheus' eleven-stringed lyre in the late fifth century lay at the extreme edge of this evolution.[124] A related development is the forty-stringed zither, possibly designed by Lasus' peer and contemporary, Epigonus, to map out divisions of the scales and intervals rather than for immediate performance.[125] Interestingly, both Epigonus and Lasus were quick to seize on the possibilities of expanding the harmonic and tonal range of the cithara.[126]

The Greek language corroborates this general historical trend. *Pamphōnos* ("all-sounding"), *poluphōnia* ("variety of tones"), and *poluchordia* ("using many strings" or "notes") all capture this search for an expansion in sound, and *poikilia* ("variety, subtlety, intricacy, coloration, ornament") is one of their congeners.[127] Pindar speaks of the "*pamphōnon* song of the

---

[122] See Barker 1978.   [123] [Plut.] *De mus.* 1137A–B. Cf. n. 76 above.

[124] West 1992, 62–64; Franklin 2002, 696.   [125] See West 1992, 78–79; 225.

[126] Epigonus and his circle were the "first" to adopt Lysander's auletic cithara techniques (Ath. 14.637d).

[127] *Poikilia* glosses *poluchordia* in [Plut.] *De mus.* 1137A. Cf. Pindar's use of *poikilia* in his epinicians beyond the dithyrambic genre (e.g., *O.* 3.7: φόρμιγγά τε ποικιλόγαρυν; *O.* 4.2: ποικιλο-φόρμιγγος ἀοιδᾶς; *O.* 6.86–87: πλέκων ποικίλον ὕμνον; *N.* 4.14: ποικίλον κιθαρίζων).

auloi," and an unassigned early fragment contains the striking catachresis, "*many-stringed aulos*."[128] This last expression seems like a virtual gloss on Lasus' polyphonic reforms, which involved transposing auletic techniques onto the *cithara* and from there to the voice. *Poikilia* is likewise associated with Lasus in a damaged column from Philodemus' second book of *On Poems*. That Lasus' name should surface in a discussion of euphony is not at all surprising; it is only a pity that the surroundings are so badly preserved. Euphonist critics, probably of the Hellenistic era, seem to have named Lasus to demonstrate how his very (or most) subtly wrought compositions (τὰ μάλιστα πεποικιλμένα [sc., ποιήματα]) produced pleasurable euphony, not a distressing harshness of sound.[129] Because sibilants and rough consonants are treated four columns earlier (ξ, ζ, σ, ϱ), Gomperz and others have suggested that Lasus' asigmatism was somehow involved in the discussion, though it is not at all clear how this should be so. (One awaits a fresh reading of these columns.) It is more likely that the whole of his euphonic practice and theory in their complexive totality was under scrutiny.[130]

To state this in terms that will become familiar from the later euphonist critics, Lasus was as much interested in the mechanisms by which euphony was produced (the *sunthesis*, or the arrangement of the sounds) as he was in the resulting sound itself as this presented itself phenomenally to the ear (the *euphōnia*, which was said to "appear" on the composition as its evanescent product).[131] And in general, it would be wrong to belittle Lasus' achievements by reducing them to the presence or absence of the *sigma*, even if he was at times remembered for his outlandish experiments in asigmatism.[132] His interests were far-ranging, and they obviously had an impact that reached well into the Hellenistic period and beyond.

---

[128] Pind. *Pyth.* 12.19; Adesp. fr. 29b (= fr. 947b) *PMG*, cit. in n. 93 above. Further examples in Franklin 2002, 696 n. 70.

[129] *P. Herc.* 994 col. 37.9–13 Sbordone: οὐδὲ τὰ Λάσου μάλιστα τοιαύτη πεποικιλμένα ποιεῖ (Janko: ποιεῖ[ν Gomperz) [τ]οιοῦτον οὔτε τὴν ἐσχ[ά]τὴν τ[ϱ]αχε[ῖ]αν ἀλγηδόνα φανεϱάν; "... nor do the compositions of Lasus which are wrought most subtly in this way [viz., euphonistically] produce [either] such [an effect(?), viz., aural pleasure; cf. ll. 6–7, 19–20], nor do [they make] manifest the most extreme harsh pain [resulting from the alleged harsh sounds of his compositions]." Both the text (after C. Romeo's readings) and the translation remain uncertain. With Janko's conjecture, it makes sense now to assume that Philodemus, true to form, is flatly rejecting claims on all sides of the debate, but other ways of construing the speakers are admittedly possible.

[130] So, too, Privitera 1965, 89 n. 5 (*pace* Gomperz 1891, 48 n. 2).

[131] The possible phenomenalism of Lasus' reforms is put to excellent use by D'Angour in his own reconstruction of that theory; see D'Angour 1997, 335; cf. ibid., 340.

[132] Thus, and rightly, Privitera 1965, 31; 89; 91.

Once again, his primary aim was to explore and ultimately to *emancipate* the full complexity of musical sound, not to restrict its range.[133]

It is this drive to *unleash* sound that paradoxically accounts for Lasus' *suppression* of the *sigma*, which is universally acknowledged to have been a miserable failure or at the very least an impracticable, but also only a momentary and experimental, measure. It lasted for no more than two pieces of music, even if it triggered a smallish vogue, or subgenre, of idiosyncratic composition under constraining conditions in antiquity. Still, the measure is an overly dramatic way of achieving its sought-for end, which surely could be achieved by other means (and ultimately was). As with Perec, lipogrammatism is meant to make a performative splash. So in order to understand better exactly why Lasus undertook asigmatism, we need to look at his performative practice.

As we saw, it cannot have been in order to underscore how the *sigma* vitiates the euphonies of musical sound. This explanation is surely wrong, and it is belied by Lasus' own rapid abandonment of the project. One possibility that to my knowledge has not been suggested in the past is that Lasus undertook the experiment not in order to banish the *sigma* from the aural spectrum, but as a *reductio ad absurdum* of any attempt to do so. In this case, the riddle of the *sigma* would have had a mocking, absurdist edge to it, by taking a pre-existing tendency – the stigma of the sigma – to an absurd limit. On the plus side, in its performative play of voluble silence, in suppressing a sound that it teasingly all but names, Lasus' riddle was embodied in his songs like a tacit reproach – of predecessors, but worse: of *sound itself*. It would also have been a way of signaling how the momentary reduction of sound to an inaudible minimum becomes, in Perec's later words, "*the basis of which everything becomes possible,*" which in Lasus' case would have meant everything that promoted a rich and fully realized sound. *This* would have made for a genuinely ludic (παιστικόν)

---

[133] It is tempting to see in a preserved fragmentary poem ascribed to Pratinas of Phlius (fr. 708 *PMG* = Ath. 14.617b–f) an averse reaction to the new Lasian poetics of sound ("What is this hubbub [τίς ὁ θόρυβος ὅδε;]? What are these dances? What loud-clattering arrogance [ὕβρις πολυπάταγα] has come upon the Dionysian altar?," etc.; trans. Barker), and not only to Lasus' reform of the dithyramb, as has long been suspected (see Pickard-Cambridge 1962, 29–32). But there are problems with this temptation. First, Pratinas makes no mention of the place of the voice *per se* on the opponent's program in this fragment. Consequently, he may be criticizing only the newly awarded prominence of the *aulos* itself due to the rearrangements instituted by Lasus in the dithyrambic chorus (D'Angour 1997, 342–43), and not Lasus' translation of the character of the *aulos* onto the voice. Secondly, elsewhere Pratinas seems to have embraced Lasus' promotion of the Aeolian tuning (fr. 712b *PMG*). We may not know enough about sixth-century musical polemics to be able to settle such complex matters. Or else the old suspicion that the author is a later, fifth-century Pratinas may be right (most recently, Csapo 2004, 214; Franklin forthcoming at n. 14).

riddle.[134] Likewise, when Pindar took up the banner of Lasian reform he could indulge in the same supercilious tone, hissing his disapproval of any puritanical predecessors who scourged the hateful letter *s*, vaunting his embrace of the complete register of sounds, by starting off gleefully with a word whose harsh sigmatism would have drawn hisses from the Hellenistic euphonists no less than from his predecessors: *schoinoteneia*.[135]

Who might these musical puritans have been? Though there are huge gaps in the evidence and we cannot properly fill them in with confidence, one possibility suggests itself immediately: musicians who reacted aversely to the music of Sacadas, or rather to the sibilant sounds that became musically conceivable for the voice thanks to Sacadas' innovations on the *aulos*. We can deduce this possibility directly from Pindar's own ode – and, indeed, from nowhere else – starting with his only explicit clue: "formerly . . . the 's' came out [sounding] base-born [or better yet: "counterfeit"] to men."[136] Such a scenario is not implausible, and it has quite a lot to recommend it. Sacadas' *Puthikos nomos* became part of the traditional repertory at the Pythian games. He also spawned emulators. In 490 BCE, Midas of Acragas won the Pythian contest with another element of the repertory, an auletic *Polukephalos nomos* ("many headed nome") that likewise involved the imitation of the hissing of a snake.[137] Midas won't have been the first exponent of the Sacadian technique – or the last. In 558 BCE, solo cithara contests were added to the Pythian competitions. Were these adapted to Sacadas' techniques and then extended still further to vocal songs?[138] If so, a general diffusion of Sacadas' innovations is conceivable, but also a conservative reaction, as the techniques grew increasingly adventurous and developed into a "free-form" style of musicianship. How, after all, do you imitate *s*-sounds on strings? The citharist Lysander of Sicyon (early fifth century) tried just this, and not just any *s*-sounds, but precisely those effects which were innovated by Sacadas

---

[134] Such a riddle would have been both lipogrammatic and cryptic at once.

[135] Richard Janko reminds me that the word *schēma* elicits similar responses from the euphonist critic Pausimachus. See Phld. *Poem.* 1 cols. 90–91 Janko, with Janko's comments ad loc. (a passage that concerns Euripides' much-mocked habit of sigmatism, here in the *Ion*).

[136] Thanks to Tim Whitmarsh for suggesting a convincing rationale for "counterfeit": "the *sigma* is proper to snakes, but 'fake' to humans." A pun on κίβδηλον meaning "straggling" (D'Angour) would still be possible on this interpretation.

[137] Schol. Pind. *Pyth.* 12 praef. 15b; 31a; 39a–b; 41; West 1992, 214. The meaning of "many-headed" is unknown, but it too is surely bivalent, referring to some musical character (such as *poluphōnia*, i.e., variety of musical sound, or the like) through the imagery of a many-headed snake.

[138] West 1992, 214 and 337 suspects they were.

on the *aulos*.[139] Imitation through vocal hissing, on the other hand, is a simple affair. What would have represented a distinct challenge would be to tame this sound effect musically along with other forms of sibilance in choral settings.

Lasus would have faced this problem, but he would have squared up to it in a more scientific fashion than his predecessors were able to do, with his background in harmonics and in acoustic experiments. The conservative reaction would have called for a ban on the overuse of sibilants; Lasus would have found a third way. He would have also, presumably, wanted to expand his repertory beyond the nome and to experiment with new harmonic possibilities in all musical settings (for pipes, strings, and voice). Perhaps he discovered how, given a wider spectrum of sounds, the circular chorus eliminated dissonances, as D'Angour has shown, and not just of the *s*-variety (and perhaps not only in the dithyramb). And so, if his asigmatic experiments were, as I suggested, merely a way of pointing up the absurdities of restricting the sound spectrum in music, we can now point to a culprit and a butt: those who opposed the new reforms in music made possible thanks to Sacadas in the sixth century.

8 SOLVING THE RIDDLE

In this light, some of the odder details of Pindar's second *Dithyramb* finally begin to fall into place as well, starting with his ophidian imagery. While it is true that this imagery would be appropriate to a Dionysian dithyramb sung before a Theban audience in their capacity as custodians of a cult of Dionysus,[140] we can now see that the imagery has added point if it is alluding to the very kinds of sibilant sounds that became musically possible thanks to Sacadas' Pythian poem and its operatic contents. If so, then Pindar must be referring to the snake that Apollo slays in Sacadas' poem – not the literal snake, but its literary and aesthetic emblem – while he is also conjuring up its sounds, or rather the *clamor* of its sounds, hyperbolized as "a thousand snakes"[141] – the

---

[139] Philochorus, *FGrHist* 328F23 = Ath. 14.637f–638a; see Barker 1982. The reconstructions of the two cases, of Lasus and Lysander vis-à-vis Sacadas, inevitably share similarities.

[140] See D'Angour 1997, 338 ("no less appropriate to Dionysos than to Apollo"); and Lavecchia 2000 in his commentary on the poem, which is strongly colored by his orgiastic (teletic) reading of this and other dithyrambs by Pindar.

[141] μυρίων φθογγάζεται κλαγγαῖς δρακόντων (18); the same term (ὁ δράκων) appears repeatedly in the key testimonies of Pollux and Strabo on Sacadas. Cf. D'Angour 1997, 338 (on the sounds of

sounds in their noisy aspect and diffused historically, or simply made baroque and hideous, a kind of taunt meant for those who despise the *s*, and something for Pindar to revel in. And if that is right, then Pindar is plainly directing his audience's mind to a Sacadian-like effect, even as he is proclaiming his allegiance to Lasus. Secondly, there is the ever-elusive term σχοινοτένεια itself. Surely, the most direct clue to its meaning is the one that has, as it were, been staring us in the face all along: the variety of the aulodic nome (a nome sung to the *aulos*) called the *Schoiniōn*, which was said to have been invented by Clonas (again), and whose name means something like "(twisted) like a rope" or "drawn out like a rope."[142] A connection between Pindar's word and the *Schoiniōn* nome (and name) has been mooted before, but only in passing.[143] The reason for this lack of interest is not far to seek: the *Schoiniōn* is barely mentioned by the ancients. But even more to the point, it is a *nome*, and Pindar refers to a *dithyramb*. Or does he?

"Formerly the singing of dithyrambs crept along (εἷρπε), stretched out like a rope" could easily be a kind of compressed musicological history in verse, albeit somewhat cryptically phrased, and equivalent to the statement, "formerly the singing of dithyrambs *had taken the shape of nomes*." So phrased, Pindar's statement could be intelligible, and true, in a few different ways. It might be possible that the Pythian nome had transformed itself into the dithyramb since Sacadas' day (some seventy-five years before Pindar), either in fact or in memory;[144] or that his nome had lent its *features* to the dithyramb, especially if we can count on the nome's wider diffusion, as sketched out above.[145] Or it may simply be that the difference between the nome and the dithyramb was not generically precise or even available until a much later date, as M. L. West has argued. West finds their distinction

---

these verses); Lavecchia 2000, 162 (ad loc.): "forse qui κλαγγά allude al suono dell'αὐλός, di cui i serpenti produrrebbero un'*immagine*" (with excellent parallels, none of which is Dionysiac).

[142] See Barker 1984, 252 ("rope-like"); West 1992, 216 ("drawn out like a rope"); [Plut.] *De mus.* 1132D, 1133A with Barker 1984, 209 n. 21 (on Clonas and the *Schoiniōn*).

[143] Wilamowitz-Moellendorff 1903, 90 n. 1; West 1971, 310 n. 6; West 1992, 216; Barker 1984, 252. The association is rejected by Zimmermann 1992, 44, on weak grounds ("zumal das Adjektiv [σχοινοτένεια] sich ausdrücklich auf den Gesang bezieht"; similarly, D'Angour 1997, 333 n. 18): all that is required is a verbal reminiscence in Pindar for the allusion to take effect. This rejection on verbal grounds further overlooks West's argument about what a nomos meant in musicological terms in Pindar's day (see below).

[144] "Perhaps a nomos was considered a solo dithyramb [i.e., in Pindar's day], as with Timotheus' *Persae*" later in the fifth century (D'Angour, *per litt.*). Cf. also Crusius 1888, 274; Fleming 1977, 224 (on Timotheus' proverbial confusion of dithyramb and nomos).

[145] For one borrowing from the nome by the dithyramb, viz., verbal concatenation, see Csapo 2004, 225.

"inapplicable to the early nomes," because nomes were merely "schemes used for the singing of all kinds of verse."[146] Thus, in West's view, Pindar is making a comment about "the traditional dithyramb *in the aulodic* σχοινίων νόμος."[147] I believe we can be more precise. But the conflation of nomos and *Schoiniōn* is attractive, insofar as it points us to the nomos genre, and from there to the most notorious innovator in nomos-sibilancy, Sacadas. The continuation in Pindar completes the evolutionary scheme: "and the 's' came out [sounding] base-born [or 'counterfeit'] to men."

This kind of picture fits well with what we know about Pindar, who evidently wrote a proemium about Sacadas, mentioning him by name, and who "often reflected on various aspects of musical history, including that of both *aulos* and dithyramb."[148] Speculatively, then, the picture looks like this: Sacadas originally made his musical innovations; these were propagated more widely and encouraged experimentation in other forms of vocal sibilance, which were then subjected to censure; Lasus intervened and rejected the purists' counterclaims; Pindar followed suit, both in his second *Dithyramb*, where his allusion to Lasus' emancipation of musical sound is couched in terms of an allusion to Sacadas' musically inspired practice, and in other places where he adopts sigmatism for the sheer sake of the sound.[149] (The presence or absence of the *sigma* is in fact only one small, principally symbolic, aspect of this new poetics and dynamics of sound, as we saw earlier.[150]) Later generations lost sight of the original allusions, and confusions set in over the nature of the polemics named only in Pindar's verses.

Two lingering clues to *Sacadas'* crucial role in this ancient squabble over musical aesthetics have to be the two pieces of evidence that are typically cited as evidence for *Lasus'* role in it, and which were mentioned earlier. Aristoxenus writes that earlier, unnamed musicians rejected the *sigma* because it was "harsh and ill-suited to the *aulos*," while Dionysius of Halicarnassus writes that the *s*-sound is aesthetically

---

[146] West 1971, 310.

[147] West 1971, 310 n. 4 (emphasis added). One might compare Telestes frr. 806 and 810 *PMG*, where "*hymnos* and *nomos* are used interchangeably to mean *harmonia*" (Fleming 1977, 222).

[148] Pind. fr. 282 (Paus. 9.30.2 + [Plut.] *De mus.* 1134A); Franklin forthcoming at n. 48 (quotation). The proemium must have included a physical description of Sacadas with his *aulos*, to judge from Pausanias' report.

[149] See D'Angour 1997, 334 n. 22; 338 (on *Isthm.* 1.22–25).

[150] Cf. also Dion. Hal. *Comp.* 22 and his virtual hymn to Pindaric phonic dissonance (ἀντιτυπία), exemplified with (and thus preserving for us) Pind. *Dith.* fr. 75.

ugly: it produces a "hiss," a *surigmos*, like that of "an irrational beast."[151] Aristoxenus has been taken to mean that the *s*-sound "presumably ... did not in his opinion sound distinctively against the aulos accompaniment."[152] But if we take the reference as being aimed at *Sacadas*, and not Lasus, Aristoxenus means just what he says (whether he knows it or not): hissing is harsh-sounding (one argument), and it is ill-suited to the *aulos* (another argument).[153] Dionysius' otherwise unintelligible outburst against hissing – why liken it to an irrational *beast* (θήρ)? – instantly becomes intelligible in the same light: Sacadas, after all, turned his *aulos* into an irrational beast. And *surigmos* is the precise term used in later accounts to capture the sound of the expiring serpent in Sacadas' mimetic nome.[154] Neither Aristoxenus nor Dionysius mentions Sacadas in this connection, most likely because that connection was already lost to them.

The original polemic as this was encapsulated in Pindar's second *Dithyramb* would have been obscured, and probably early on, by a few different factors. First, the connection with Lasus was remembered, but because of the tacit nature of Lasus' riddle there would have been no way of piecing together the various elements of this historical puzzle without an independent account of some sort. Evidently, that account never existed, or else it was lost (possibly being orally transmitted to begin with).[155] Secondly and relatedly, a confusion of genres and their genealogies was inevitable: we have sigmatic nomes, their offspring, Lasus' dithyramb and his hymn (both asigmatic), and Pindar's sigmatic dithyramb. If the Sacadian nome lent its features to the dithyramb, it also could have lent them to other musical genres[156] – which is exactly what Lasus' global reforms required.[157] Yet in the oversimplifying light of the fifth century, Lasus could appear as the precursor of the New Musicians, whose revolutionary musical activities were principally associated with the dithyramb.[158] Thirdly, thanks to the hostility with

---

[151] Both cited at nn. 31 and 32 above.   [152] West 1992, 40.

[153] D'Angour 1997, 335 likewise calls Aristoxenus' conflation "tendentious."

[154] Strab. 9.3.10; Poll. 4.83–84; Pind. *Pyth.* hypoth. 31.

[155] Presumably, Pindar would have come across Lasus' innovations by way of word of mouth.

[156] Sacadas himself composed lyrics and elegiacs, and had a circle of associates who composed in elegiacs as well ([Plut.] *De mus.* 1134A; 1134C). Note, too, Telestes' identification of the nome with the hymn (frr. 806 and 810 *PMG*).

[157] When Pseudo-Plutarch says of Lasus that he "chang[ed] his rhythms to the dithyrambic style" (ἀγωγήν) he means just this – not that Lasus adopted the dithyramb, but that his style became somehow dithyrambic, or if one likes, nomic, or Sacadic (the distinction may not have meant very much to Lasus, musically speaking).

[158] Privitera 1965, 82; D'Angour 1997, 339; Csapo 2004.

which the later dithyramb of the New Musicians was received, there was a tendency to rewrite the musical past in the light of the present. A musical "golden age" in the past was created, the traces of which we have already seen hinted at above: it was conceived as a time onto which the – now identifiably Greek – characteristics of simplicity, austerity, and purity, but also manliness and nobility, could be retrojected. The earlier period certainly showed a more relaxed attitude towards Asianism than later authors would suggest.[159] This fantasy of a simpler, quieter, more stately past took root in the conservative reaction to the new dithyramb: Aristophanes, Plato, Aristotle, Xenophon, and Aristoxenus were its more prominent exponents; the later work of Pseudo-Plutarch is a derivative crystallization of their and others' views.

Finally, because some of the features of the New Music resembled those of the earlier avant-garde, and in fact marked their prolongation and evolution, the idea that the past could have produced such "revolutionary" musicians was gradually eclipsed by the far more compelling ideal of a purer-sounding era when *sigmas* never hissed and instruments sounded out in clear and distinct tones. The fact that it was a feature of this radical tradition to revolutionize itself periodically from within and to claim more originality for itself at each new turn than was strictly warranted, led to overstatements ("the rhetoric of innovation" mentioned earlier) that, taken literally, only added to the historical confusion. It is a confusion that continues to plague us today – which is why we are only slowly coming to appreciate the complexity of music in its earliest forms, even with the occasional, if contradictory, testimony of an ancient source like Pseudo-Plutarch to assure us of the fact.[160]

---

[159] See Csapo 2004, 230–35, and *passim*.

[160] [Plut.] *De mus.* 1138B: "The forms of rhythmic composition used by ancient composers were *more complex* (ποικιλία οὔσῃ ποικιλωτέρᾳ), since they had a great respect for rhythmic complexity, and their patterns of instrumental idiom (τὰ περὶ τὰς κρουσματικὰς διαλέκτους) were also *more complicated*" (ποικιλώτερα) (trans. Barker; emphasis added). κρουσματικαὶ διαλέκτοι are rhythmic sounds lacking semantic content, one species of which is placed in the same ambit as Sacadas' innovations by later sources. See Lasserre 1954, 166 ("une sorte de vocalise sans signification réelle ... rythmique plutôt que mélodique"), citing Phot. s.v. νιγλαρεύων ("whistling, trilling"): τερετίζων; and cf. Poll. 4.83: μέρη δ' αὐλημάτων κρούματα, συρίγματα, τερετισμοί τερετίσματα, νίγλαροι. One possible trace of a polemic that has been lost could be a tussle in the regional politics of cult location between Athens, Thebes, and Argos, embodied (if it is) in the tension between Pindar, Lasus, and Sacadas. See Wilson 2002a for a suggestive argument about Athens and Thebes, along with Wallace 2003, 78–82.

APPENDIX: CLEARCHUS OF SOLI ON
PINDAR IN ATHENAEUS

Athenaeus twice quotes from Clearchus' *On Riddles* where Pindar's ode on the *sigma* (*Dith. Oxy.* 2) is mentioned. The overlapping (and I believe genuinely Clearchean) passages are italicized and set off in quotation marks in the following:

(1) Ath. 10.448c–d (trans. Gulick, adapted)

And again in the treatise *On Riddles*, Clearchus says there are seven kinds of riddles. "Depending on a letter, as when we are to tell, for example, the name of a fish or a plant beginning with *a*; similarly, when the propounder requires a word which contains or does not contain a certain letter, like the riddles called the *s*-less (οἱ ἄσιγμοι καλούμενοι τῶν γρίφων); *whence even* (i) *Pindar composed an ode with reference to* [Gulick: "against"] *the letter s* (πρὸς τὸ σ̄ ἐποίησεν ᾠδήν), *posing, as it were, a kind of riddle in (the area of) lyric poetry* (οἱονεὶ γρίφου τινὸς ἐν μελοποιίᾳ προβληθέντος)."

(2) Ath. 10.455b–c (trans. Gulick, adapted)

(ii) *With reference to the style of poem composed without an s in it* (πρὸς τὴν ἀσιγμοποιηθεῖσαν ᾠδήν), Pindar, to quote Clearchus again, wrote the following, *posing as it were a kind of riddle in (the area of) lyric poetry* (οἱονεὶ γρίφου τινὸς ἐν μελοποιίᾳ προβληθέντος), (a) since many had taken offence at him because he was unable to abstain from the letter *s* and they did not approve of it [*Dith.* 2.1–2]:

Formerly the singing of dithyrambs crept along stretched out like a rope, and the 's' came out from human mouths [sounding] base-born to men.

(b) One may make a note of this in answer to those who reject as spurious the song of Lasus of Hermione, entitled *Centaurs*, in which no *s* occurs. (c) So, too, the hymn to the Demeter of Hermione, composed by Lasus, has no *s*, as Heracleides of Pontus declares in the third book of his work *On Music*; it begins thus [= fr. 702.1 *PMG*].

A few comments are in order, first about text (1). The meaning of πρὸς τὸ σ̄ ἐποίησεν ᾠδήν is "composed an ode *with reference to* the letter *s*," not "*against* the letter *s*," as Gulick renders it. This has been a source of unnecessary confusion. Pindar has nothing against the letter *s*. Quite the contrary, he is defending it. Gulick's translation may depend on the assumption that Pindar composed his dithyramb against Lasus; cf. (ii), where πρός means the same as it does in (i). Clearchus writes, "posing, as it were, a kind of riddle in lyric poetry," to signal that Pindar has not actually posed a riddle with his verses, but that his verses constitute an apparent riddle, whether we are to understand by this the first two verses alone or the entirety of the *Dithyramb* 2, of which the opening two verses could have been taken to be emblematic by Clearchus. The clause is further best understood to mean: "as if a kind of riddle was being posed [by Pindar] in the area of *melopoiia*" (lyric composition), which is to say, about the problem of *melopoiia*. How much of the poem did Clearchus quote? Most probably, he quoted the opening first two verses only, given the citational tradition which appears to be limited to these verses and in all likelihood stems directly from Clearchus' discussion.

So far, nothing suggests that Pindar has alluded to a riddle by Lasus. The connection to Lasus comes in text (2). (ii) "With reference to the style of poem composed without an *s*" spells out (i) "composed an ode *with reference to* the letter *s*," but there is no reason to suppose a gloss by a later source. Clearchus went on to discuss Lasus' asigmatic ode *Centaur*, which in Clearchus' terms was a true riddle of the ἄσιγμος variety ("the riddles called the *s*-less"). Combining these two formulations, we can suppose that Clearchus originally wrote that Pindar posed a kind of riddle, or expressed something resembling a riddle, which performed two things at once: it alluded both to the asigmatic ode by Lasus and to the missing *sigma* of that ode, which we can now see means that Pindar's dithyramb referred to all that the missing *sigma* of Lasus' ode referred to, namely the prehistory of the *sigma*, from Sacadas to the conservative reaction against sigmatism. In this light, the academicism on Clearchus' part, mooted earlier, seems to have genuine point: Pindar's poem was written in a scholastic (musicological and historical) vein, pertaining as it did to problems of musical composition. And it did all this in the same spirit as Lasus, with the crucial difference that Pindar made *(quasi-)explicit* what was *implicit* in Lasus' (truly riddling, asigmatic) ode. But Pindar's riddle was not asigmatic. Only Lasus' riddle was. Whence Pindar's ode is labeled, "as it were, a kind of riddle."

Wedged in the midst of the second version of Clearchus' text comes some new information about Pindar's motives. But these are hardly clear, and their very lack of clarity is the surest sign that interpolation by a post-Clearchean source, possibly Athenaeus, is to blame. Pindar was referring to the asigmatic ode (a) "because many objected to him/it (τούτῳ) on account of the impossibility of avoiding the *sigma* and on account of his/its being viewed with disfavor."[161] The sentence is nearly

[161] Trans. after D'Angour 1997, 331, who construes τούτῳ as neuter (it is usually construed as referring to Pindar).

unintelligible, and nothing can heal its sense, not even changing the
pronominal referents. The reason must be that its author was trying to
discern what the riddle hinted at in Pindar's verses was. To be sure, the
author has been partly led astray by Clearchus, who will not have done
more than adduce Pindar's text as an example of a kind of riddle, and a
deviant one at that, and then mention Lasus' own original riddle – the
ode *Centaurs*, cited *by title only* – as a genuine example of the same kind
of riddle. Unless, that is, we postulate a transposition in Athenaeus'
report, which originally contained a reference to Lasus, thereby providing content, now missing, to τούτῳ.[162] Recall that one of the oddities
of this report is that it attributes "a kind of riddle" to Pindar, just when
we would expect him to attribute it to Lasus. Lasus does emerge as the
ultimate referent at the end of the day: the only question is how directly
and transparently he was meant to do so. At any rate, in response to
these alleged "objections" (a mini-drama has obviously been brewing in
the mind of an ancient scholar here), Pindar penned the two cryptic
verses "with reference to the ode that was composed asigmatically,"
which is to say, Lasus' ode *Centaurs*.

Athenaeus draws a moral in the sequel: (b) "Let this be a sign for
those who doubt the authenticity of the asigmatic ode of Lasus of
Hermione, entitled *Centaurs*." Evidently the poem's authenticity was
contested in his own day, though not in Clearchus'. Athenaeus then
goes on to name the second work by Lasus known to display asigmatism,
(c) a hymn to Demeter mentioned by Heraclides of Pontus in the third
book of his *On Music* and quoted by him in its *incipit*.[163] Here, it begins
to look as if Athenaeus is grasping at straws: unable to produce direct
evidence for the outlandish idea of a (possibly dithyrambic) ode called
Centaurs written *sans sigmas*, a poem that may no longer have existed in
his own day (as it no longer does for us), Athenaeus finally turns to the
one surviving clue to Lasus' asigmatic compositional output that he can
find, and quotes from it. Clearchus did *not* supply this piece of information or a host of other details about Pindar and Lasus: he was
compiling a study of riddles, not a work in literary history. And so,
Pindar's controversy with (but not clearly against) Lasus over the role of
the *sigma* can be taken as proof of the authenticity of a poem that may
have been attested for Athenaeus in title only.

---

[162] So the anonymous referee for Porter 2007c, the article on which this chapter is based.
[163] Repeated in expanded form at Ath. 14.624e.

CHAPTER 8

Visual experience

As was hinted at in various places above, a good deal of aesthetic interest was stimulated by visual objects and their representation in the visual culture or cultures of Greece from Homer into later centuries. "Visual culture" is a widely significant phrase.[1] Through it we can understand not only the direct presentation of visual objects in their cultural contexts (whether in the form of images or texts), but also their presentation alongside other media (for instance, spectacle and dance in drama) or else their evocation through non-visual art forms, primarily verbal, occasionally musical. In this chapter I want to focus on visual arts in their conventional sense – painting (chiefly vase painting), sculpture, and architecture – and their natural extensions (their translation as visual imagery in literature), and all this from the perspectives that are paramount in the present study.[2] Doing so will mean exploring viewing practices and habits, as well as discerning the different languages in which visual experience was expressed at different historical moments. The key question will be the following: To what extent did visual artists exploit, and did viewers register, the sensuous and phenomenal dimensions of their media from Homer to the fourth centuries? That is, how did visuality develop as a medium of palpable appearances? The question has been dealt with in the past, but on sometimes faulty premises, not least on the assumption that visuality underwent a gradual emancipation over time, in tandem with the growth of naturalism and idealism. A reexamination is in order, particularly with an eye to aesthetic materialism as this evolved in Greek antiquity.

Though there is no real dearth of visual artifacts or their remains from the period in question, finding ways to elicit confessions from the objects is an art unto itself, while contemporary statements about visual objects

---

[1] See, e.g., Evans and Hall 2007.
[2] Glyptic, metalwork, and jewelry will be touched on in Ch. 9.

and visuality are harder to come by. Nevertheless, my treatment will be relatively brief and selective, the aim being to touch on a few principal points relevant to the present study's themes. Beyond reappraising the thesis of emerging sensibilities, my purpose is emphatically *not* to separate off a domain unto itself that might artificially be labeled "visual culture," but rather to demonstrate the integral connections between the culture(s) of vision and other areas of aesthetic activity in this early, formative period from the classical world. The languages of materials, process, quality, evaluation, and subjective impact will claim our attention above all else, for it is here that we can find the greatest common denominators with other aesthetic undertakings.

As it happens, one way of locating commonalities is by confronting some of the impasses at their borders. Visual objects are in ways recalcitrant to discourse, existing as they do in seemingly separate ontological spheres (a complaint that Gorgias of Leontini was among the first to lodge, as we saw): on the one side there is the world of the – here, visual – senses, on the other that of the mind, ideas, and words, while a gap yawns in between. In point of fact, we can parse the equation into three disjunct spheres: the world of hard material objects, that of visual objects (appearances), and the mental or perceptual or linguistic world where everything is received and expressed. Experience occurs most richly at the borders between these spheres. And so, when we speak of languages and objects, we not only name the fundamental challenge of explaining how aesthetic judgments come about in the visual realm. We also name the productive sources of tension that, one might speculate, actually give rise to aesthetic reflection about visual objects and visual experience. For, conceivably, it is out of the seeming mismatch between orders of being posed by the very barest presentation of objects to the mind that reflection on the conditions of aesthetic experience comes about at all. Such self-awareness is of course true of all modes of sensation, and was felt even in antiquity, as we have had numerous occasions to witness above, from before Athenian theater to Gorgias, and as we shall have numerous occasions to witness again below.[3] But it is often dramatically true of vision, a realm of experience that presents itself with a kind of immediacy, however deceptively it may do so, and that makes demands upon the observer which are

---

[3] See Ch. 4, §§1–2 (on the arts); Ch. 5 (on Gorgias). For a philosophical articulation of this kind of self-awareness, see Arist. *De anima*, book 3 with Kosman 1975 and Gregoric 2007. The sophisticated, self-conscious plays on vision in tragedy and vases, which are legion, are proof of the same concept working at another level.

often equal only to the observer's inability to capture in words and thoughts what he or she sees. As a consequence, vision can at times be an overwhelming experience. That theory and reflection might arise out of a response to such a mismatch, or else might be a way of healing the jagged edges of experience, not to mention assuaging the abrupt confrontation with unyielding material realities, is an intriguing possibility. It was just this sort of embarrassment in the face of "objectality" – the quality of objects in their capacity (or incapacity) as dumb and mute matter – that troubles Phidias as he is recreated by Dio of Prusa in his *Olympian Discourse*. Though late, the speech is a useful point of departure for an examination of fifth-century aesthetic values, and is possibly a distant reflection of them. For now, it will simply serve as a useful illustration of the problem to hand, namely, visuality as a sensuous medium.

I THE MAJESTY OF PHIDIAS

Dio's speech is relevant in the present context for several reasons. First, ancient traditions at least since the Hellenistic period associated Phidias with aesthetic perfection – with majesty (*maiestas*) and the grand style – but also with massiveness of dimensions (which essentially amounted to the same thing). This is perhaps unsurprising, given the nature of Phidias' most famous works, the statue of Athena Parthenos on the Acropolis at Athens and that of Olympian Zeus in the Temple of Zeus at Olympia, which were colossal in scale and unrivaled in Greece.[4] Secondly, Phidias was particularly known for representing divinity. This reason is closely linked to the first: gods are naturally evocative of perfection, or perhaps we should say that the sheer difficulty of capturing divinity in earthly materials enhances the majesty, even sublimity, of divine representations.[5] But this second reason is also wrapped up with one of the central preoccupations of this study, namely the problem of presentation through phenomenalization, of rendering appearances sensuous and palpable. Divine appearances are an acute and special case of this problem: the divine can only ever be glimpsed through an appearance, given that

---

[4] Callim. *Ia.* 6; Demetr. *Eloc.* 12; Strabo 8.353–54; Dion. Hal. *Isoc.* 3; Quint. *Inst.* 12.10.9; Philostr. *VA* 6.19; Plin. *HN* 36.18; Paus. 5.11.9; etc.

[5] Cf. Sen. *Ep.* 31.10–11: *nemo novit deum . . . finges autem non auro vel argento: non potest ex hac materia imago deo exprimi similis;* similarly, Lucian *Pro imag.* 23. Further, Cic. *Orat.* 9; Sen. *Controv.* 10.5.8; Plotinus *Enn.* 5.8 (translations in Pollitt 1990, 223–24). According to these testimonia, Phidias did not actually have an epiphany of the divine. See Romm 1990, 77 n. 9 for one explanation of this skepticism, though conventional piety may be another reason.

divinity, the thing itself, is in classical terms more or less by definition
unpresentable, forever banished from the realm of appearances, or at most
dangerously available to the senses – a threat to the stability of the
apparitional realm and to the viewer's sense of intactness (a good example
of the latter being the famous Cnidian Aphrodite by Praxiteles, though
mythology furnishes any number of parallels).[6] Both sets of reasons are
basic to Dio's speech.

The speech, dating from 97 CE, is framed by a discussion of common
(virtually innate) conceptions of divinity,[7] and from there it detours into
one of the most extensive disquisitions on the powers and limits of
sculpture relative to language known from antiquity. Phidias' recreated
internal speech is an *apologia pro domo sua*. But it begins by delimiting the
boundaries of the sculptural art. Homer was free to imagine Zeus however
he wished. Not so the sculptor, whose imagination is bound by the nature
of matter and vision, but also by the constraints of time, which are, so to
speak, inscribed onto the surface of his product:

First we need a material substance (ὕλης), a material so tough (ἀσφαλοῦς) that
it will last (διαμεῖναι), yet can be worked without much difficulty and consequently not easy to procure.... In addition, the sculptor must have worked out for
himself a design that shows each subject in one single posture (ἐν σχῆμα) ... that
admits of no movement and is unalterable (ἀκίνητον καὶ μένον). [And while
poets can cast their inventions on the spur of the moment,] the execution [of the
sculptor] is laborious and slow (ἐπίπονον καὶ βραδύ), advancing with difficulty a
step at a time, the reason being, no doubt, that it must work with a rock-like and
hard material (πετρώδει καὶ στερεᾷ κάμνον ὕλῃ). [Finally,] the eyes are more
trustworthy than the ears ... yet they are much harder to convince and demand
much greater clearness (ἐναργείας).[8]

As an example of the last point Phidias mentions Homer's depiction of
Eris, head scraping the heavens and feet treading the earth – a pretty
image, but utterly impracticable for a sculptor who must obey the material
constraints of space and (let us not forget) of patronage as well: "I must be
content merely to fill up the space designated by Eleans or Athenians" (72).
Sculpture is the quintessential art of matter: the artist struggles with a
resisting object, and his own product cannot help but bear the signs of
that struggle, however refined it may appear in the end. Not for nothing
does Dio have Phidias quote with approval a pair of verses describing his

---

[6] See Stewart 1997, 97–106.
[7] Stoic, possibly Posidonian, *phantasia* theory may lie behind this idea; see Pollitt 1974, 61.
[8] Dio *Or.* 12.69–71; trans. Cohoon.

spiritual kin in the *Iliad*, Hephaestus, hard at work on his recalcitrant materials while fashioning the brilliant shield for Achilles: "The stubborn (ἀτειρέα) brass, and tin, and precious gold, | And silver, first he melted in the fire."[9] The general conceit, and the obsession with Phidias' creation in particular, may be a trademark of the Second Sophistic,[10] but the idea that highly valued aesthetic appearances emerge only from a harsh confrontation with stubborn materials is not. Indeed, as we just saw, that notion was already available to Homer.

The archaic age is full of such examples, of works of art that exhibit the stubborn resistance of matter. Indeed, its overall aesthetic, at least in its sculptural and plastic forms, arguably just is a proud foregrounding of this kind of resistance, whether in *kouroi* and *korai* assuming rigid stances, in thick-set columns, or in stiff archaic lettering.[11] Temple reliefs are a case in point. Consider a metope from Foce del Sele (near Paestum) which features Ajax leaning hard on his sword. Though unfinished, its final properties may be extrapolated by comparison with other reliefs from the same site, as Jeffrey Hurwit observes:

The edges would have remained sharp and the inner details would have been shallow, almost incised. The procedure was simply to draw an outline and cut straight back along it. Ajax is what was left after the excavation of the original surface of the block – a stone cutout, a silhouette with vertical walls for sides. The background of the relief is really an irregular trench dug into the stone, and here as elsewhere in early Archaic relief it is deeper in one spot than in another. The background does not, in fact, matter much. The figure of Ajax does not so much push out from the background as lie upon and behind a flat surface – the front plane.... Its existence is tangible and its force dictates the two-dimensional character of the relief. Not all early Archaic reliefs are as planar as the Foce del Sele metopes.... But all submit to the authority of the front plane. They are surface-bound and space-shy. They are like Black Figure vase paintings turned to stone.[12]

---

[9] *Il.* 18.474–75 *ap.* Dio *Or.* 12.83, as in the Loeb. Cf. Arnheim 1986, 679, on "the characteristic struggle of the artist with his or her medium, the exasperating discrepancy between the work as envisioned and its realization in the 'flesh.' The sculptor argues with the wood or stone, the dancer with his or her body," etc.

[10] See Overbeck 1868, nos. 692–754; Romm 1990, 76–90.

[11] For the general point, see Hurwit 1985, 227, etc., and more expansively, Neer 2010, ch. 1, both emphasizing that material rigidity is less a limitation than a consciously embraced aesthetic choice made by archaic artists. On the erotic attractions of the *kouros* form, which supports this view, or at the least suggests that the aesthetics of the *kouros* was motivated (willed and embraced), not haphazard or imposed by external limitations (a rather crude set of options in any event), see Stewart 1997, 63–70.

[12] Hurwit 1985, 293.

Moreover, as Hurwit notes, it is in "the nature of the Archaic ... in general" that it should "affirm the reality of the surface – its hardness, its flatness, its impenetrability."[13] Such, we might say, is the mark of archaic materialism in art, whereby all is – to adopt Riegl's vocabulary, which despite its progressivist overtones proves useful in this instance – haptic, tactile, and plastic.[14] Rather than seeking to overcome its materials, which is to say, to display and to transcend them as in the later classical era, the archaic aesthetic *flaunts* them, virtually *surrendering* to them.

Perhaps no stronger contrast to the archaic aesthetic, so described, can be found than in one of Phidias' successors, Paeonius of Mende. Paeonius is celebrated today for his technical sculptural achievements in a vein similar to Phidias', to judge from the mutilated remains of his Flying Nike (*c.* 420), which was prominently displayed before the temple of Zeus at Olympia atop a pillar. Carved from a single marble block, it presents a Nike with her gown fluttering in the breeze as if alighting on the pillar on which she stands. Triangular in form, the pillar stands 9 meters high, while the figure on top of it originally stood another 3 meters above the pillar's upper surface. Curtained drapery billowed in the rear.[15] Made of Parian marble, the complex is literally draped in illusion. But it also delights in the negation of this fact:

What Paionios therefore confronts us with is a "teasing duality of interest between a sort of pseudo-illusion of drapery and an insistent presence of the fact of [stone-] carving: the figure is equivocal as between representation on the one hand and material-*plus*-skill on the other. . . . Because one is suspended between representation and matter, the figure never lets one forget its mastery."[16]

Classical sculpture like this is the triumphant art of rendering intractable matter pliant and seemingly alive. But in the process, it renders visible two distinct kinds of materiality: (i) that of the raw material from which the sculpture is made – resistant, heavy, and endowed with other material properties, including color, density, and porosity; and (ii) the materiality

---

[13] Hurwit 1985, 227.

[14] Which is not to deny the role of the visual in the apprehension of the haptic (tactile); see Ch. 3, §2 above. Cf. also Riegl 1927, 28–29 on the earlier phases of art's perception, wherein objects are dense, "impenetrable," material, "the eye betrays only surface planes," and the figures in relief are themselves only further forms of the surface, "*denkbar flach gehalten*" (97). At one point he calls this early ("primitive") modality of aesthetic perception its "*Raumscheu*," or "space-shyness" (ibid., 30 n. 1; cf. ibid., 93–94: "*raumfeindlich*," "inimical to space"). The resemblances to Hurwit's language ("bound at the surface," "space-shy") are striking.

[15] Stewart 1990, 1:89.

[16] Stewart 1990, 1:91, quoting from Baxandall 1980, 191 (in a different context).

of the art that results from the artistic process itself, some of whose features inevitably draw on those of the object's primary material qualities themselves, while others do not – the flowing movement of the stone, both downward and outward, its luminosity, its polish, and so on.

Paeonius' Nike brings to the fore these two kinds of materiality in a further way, specifically in the way her form evokes a function that she does not in fact fulfill. The figure alighting on a parapet is herself a columnar fixture, being both part of the pillar she sets foot on and also an addition to it or an extension of it while standing apart from it – or else just *gracing* it. She therefore begs the question of where one draws the line between architecture and sculpture, somewhat in the same way that the Caryatids lining the southern portico of the Erechtheum in Athens or other *akroteiria* do (though these latter clearly have a weight-bearing function, while Paeonius' Nike is flamboyantly weightless and structurally superfluous, being free-standing and decoratively placed outside of and before the Zeus temple). Architecture generally enjoyed a sculptural quality in antiquity, even as its physical presence evoked utility and functionality. Hence, the aesthetic vocabulary that attached to architecture (*rhuthmos, eurhuthmia, summetria*, and the like), which was shared by the other plastic arts. But for all its sculptural character, architecture could stand in an interesting tension to sculpture, and the reverse could hold too, as the Flying Nike suggests, while both media sought to expand the range of visual experience.

Unable to surpass the physical limitations of space, sculptors nonetheless had at their disposal several ways of vying with the poets in the realm of *phantasia*. Strabo records how Phidias' Olympian Zeus was so constructed that, though sited and seated in a large temple, the god "nearly touches the roof with his head and makes the impression (ἔμφασιν ποιεῖν) that if he stood up he would unroof the temple."[17] The effect was clearly spectacular and worthy of the god, even if the proportions of the statue at first sight appeared somewhat miscalculated.[18] Pausanias adds a further description that parallels Strabo's. Framed by an impressive Doric temple, whose dimensions Pausanias sees fit to cite, the image of Zeus is by contrast huge beyond measure. Those who took the measure of its literal dimensions (ἐς ὕψος τε καὶ εὖρος) are to be faulted, he claims, "for even the measurements they mention fall far short of the impression (δόξα) made by the image

---

[17] Strab. 8.3.3.
[18] Strab. 8.3.3: δοκεῖν ἀστοχῆσαι τῆς συμμετρίας τὸν τεχνίτην.

(ἄγαλμα) on the spectator." The people of the place know the true measure of the statue, however. "For when the image was completed Phidias prayed that the god would give a sign if the work was to his mind, and straightway, they say, the god hurled a thunderbolt into the ground at the spot where the bronze urn stood down to my time."[19]

But what impression would such works of art have made in the golden age of the fifth and fourth centuries BCE? As mentioned, contemporary accounts are hard to come by for the classical and preclassical periods. After Aristophanes, who mentions Phidias only in connection with political scandals, Plato is the first author to discuss the sculptor again, once in rather glowing terms (Phidias made "conspicuously beautiful works," περιφανῶς καλὰ ἔργα).[20] More relevant to the present discussion is the treatment of perspectival illusion in the *Sophist*, which is sometimes thought to reflect Phidias' aesthetic principles as these were embodied in the Parthenon, whose construction he helped to supervise.[21] In the *Sophist*, Plato reveals a high degree of phenomenological awareness on the part of some observer (the source of the theory being reported is much debated):

ELEATIC STRANGER: One art that I see contained in [your division] is the making of likenesses (εἰκαστική)....

THEAETETUS: Why, is not that what all imitators try to do?

ELEATIC STRANGER: Not those sculptors or painters whose works are of colossal size. If they were to reproduce the true proportions of a well-made figure, as you know, the upper parts would look too small, and the lower too large, because we see the one at a distance, the other close at hand .... So artists ... make, not the real proportions, but those that will appear beautiful.[22]

The point being made on the perspectivalist view (represented by the Eleatic Stranger) is that monumental sculpture and painting require a tempering of their proportions in order to produce pleasing and effective optical results: the upper parts of the object on display must be made on a larger scale than the lower parts in order to offset the distances to the viewer's eyes. The lesson, and sting, that Plato draws from the principle is that the cause of pleasure in such cases is no longer the object itself but rather the appearance that the object gives off (τὸ φαινόμενον); and that

---

[19] Paus. 5.10.3 (the Dorian temple); 5.11.9 (quotation); trans. Farnell.

[20] Pl. *Men.* 91d.

[21] Though probably not in the executive sense that Plutarch's *Life of Pericles* assigns him (Stewart 1990, 1:60–61).

[22] Pl. *Soph.* 235d–236a; trans. Cornford.

to enter into this game of appearances is to exit from the realm of imitation proper and to slip into an inferior activity that deserves to be called *phantastikē*, or "appearance-making," which is to say, the production of elusive *phantasmata*.[23] Aristotle's worries in the *Poetics* about whether the eye can reasonably take in the whole of an oversize object are here effectively annulled – first by the perspectivalists, who cheerfully embrace illusionism at all costs, and then by Plato, who degrades images to mere appearances.

But Plato can hardly have been reacting merely to contemporary innovations, as has sometimes been thought. The kinds of optical refinements he is attacking in the *Sophist* were already in place in earlier architecture dating from the mid-sixth century, if not before.[24] And as a number of sources suggest, from Vitruvius to the few optical manuals that have survived, there was an entire science of such refinements, which involved swelling or tension (*entasis*) and curvature of design, especially in more colossal buildings, the purpose of which was to achieve harmonious or more impressive aesthetic effects, above all in the columns and entablature, as well as in the overall proportional appearances. At stake in such cases as these was the aesthetic presentation, and enlivening, of massive amounts of material. As Lothar Haselberger has written, in ancient testimonies

we find great pride and amazement at the new, truly colossal feats achieved [during the first half of the sixth century BCE] in dressed stone architecture, from the giant temples of Syracuse in the west to Ephesos in the east, described as wondrous, daring, divine works. Stone is the material now recognized in its mass and volume. And with it came the need to cope artistically with those huge surfaces and bodies, by giving "shape" to them and "expressing" their architectonic function [by means of] exuberantly bulging curves.... "Tension" (*entasis*) thus vividly describes the structural activity of a column body, brought to full conclusion in the elastic curves of the capital's echinus-bolster or spiraling volutes.[25]

The "great pride and amazement at the new, truly colossal feats" referred to here takes in such attestations as the inscription on the vertical face of the stylobate of the Temple of Apollo at Syracuse (*c.* 580–560 BCE), which, though weathered, appears to read:

---

[23] Pl. *Soph.* 235b–c. Cf. Schuhl 1952, 29; Schweitzer 1953, 86; Keuls 1978, 111–14; Rouveret 1989, 28–34; Haselberger 1999, 56–67.

[24] Coulton 1977, 111; Haselberger 1999, 16.

[25] Haselberger 1999, 64. Cf. Haselberger, ibid., with n. 236, commenting on the "corporeal aspect of Greek column architecture," after Gruben 1986, 8.

Κλεομ[..]ες : ἐποίεσε τόπέλονι : ℎο Κνιδιείδα : κἐπικ[λ]ε̄ στυλεῖα: κα[λὰ] ϝέργα.[26]

Cleom[en]es (or: "Cleom[ed]es"), son of Cnidieidas, made [the temple] for Apollo, and [he] also [made these] famous columns, beautiful works.

The inscription is said to be one of the most "imposing" of its kind found on an early Greek building. Its size alone is indeed imposing: the first line runs to nearly eight meters in length, which is to say, around a third of the width of the building, while the letters, deeply incised in the stone, run from 15 to 18 centimeters (about six to seven inches) in height (fig. 8.1).[27] Gottfried Gruben speaks of the extreme "*Künstlerstolz*" ("artist's pride") exhibited by the inscription, which in turn is matched by the impression the building makes in its heft and organization (he uses adjectives like "exorbitant," "extreme," "oppressive," and "Titanic").[28] The judgment about *Künstlerstolz* captures the spirit of the enterprise irrespective of whether the individual named on the inscription was the architect (now the minority view), whether he was the contractor or supervisor of the work, or whether he simply commissioned it.[29] The final tag, κα[λὰ] ϝέργα, "beautiful works," if correct, anticipates Plato's verdict about Phidias quoted above: Phidias made "conspicuously beautiful works," περιφανῶς καλὰ ἔργα. Though there is no trace of architectural refinement having been added to these columns for the sake of visual effects, the temple of Apollo was the first in a series of monumental buildings in Sicily and elsewhere that do show experiments with optical adjustments, and above all a concern for proportion.[30]

At any rate, optical refinements represented an attempt on the part of architects to achieve a kind of visual seduction or even deception on the part of the viewer, above all in the case of monumental buildings. And though the direction of influences is notoriously difficult to trace, it does appear as if one way in which Athenian architecture of the High Classical period was both pivotal and widely influential, "affecting all branches of

[26] *IG* xiv 1 (= *SEG* xxxi 841); Haselberger 1999, 64 n. 238 (with bibliography); Umholtz 2002, 263–64. The text is contested in several respects (see, *inter alios*, Dubois 1989). I have printed the text more or less as given by Engelmann 1981, but the translation supplements are mine. The proposed reading κἄ[λ(λ)α] ϝέργα (Engelmann 1981), like another by Calavotti (κα[τὰ] ϝέργα), has not found favor (see Dubois 1989, 91; Umholtz 2002, 264, n. 12).

[27] Kaibel and Lebègue 1890, 3; Umholtz 2002, 263; Engelmann 1981, 91.

[28] Gruben 1986, 266–67.

[29] See Marconi 2007, 42–45, with bibliography.

[30] See, generally, Gruben 1986, 266–69.

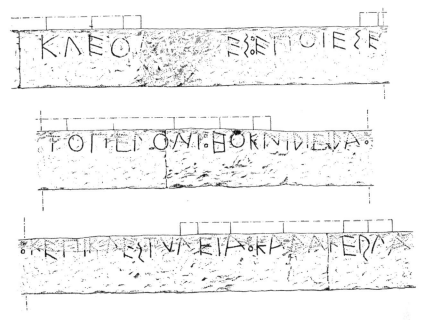

Fig. 8.1 Inscription from the Temple of Apollo at Syracuse, *c.* 580–560 BCE.
Line drawing after H. Engelmann, *Zeitschrift für Papyrologie und Epigraphik* 44, 1981,
p. 93. The inscription, running across the temple's base, is grand (ca. 8 m. long), befitting
the temple itself. It names either the temple's architect, builder, or sponsor: "Cleom[en]es
[or: 'Cleom[ed]es'], son of Cnidieidas, made [the temple] for Apollo, and [he] also
[made these] famous columns, beautiful works."

the visual arts, from painting to sculpture," had to do with experiments in appearances and perceptual effects.[31] Playing upon the illusory effects of visual appearances in the unrelenting medium of stone, Paeonius' parallel discoveries in the sculptural medium found contemporary echoes in Gorgias' *Helen* and in the sophists' rhetoric of deception. It also antici-pated by three-quarters of a century Lysippus' aesthetic of representing not reality *per se*, but the reality of appearances.[32] In all these cases, matter was being made to move.

[31] Haselberger 1999, 63.
[32] Plin. *HN* 34.65; Stewart 1990, 1:92, citing Gorgias *Hel.* §§18–19 (on statues); see Ch. 5, §2 above.

2 'TASTSINN' TO 'GESICHTSSINN'?

The resort to phenomenalism of the kind recorded by Plato has been held in some, but not in all, quarters to be a late evolution of Greek visual art.[33] Such was Alois Riegl's thesis, discussed earlier, which he couched as a progression from *Tastsinn* to *Gesichtssinn*, in other words, a progression from tactility to visuality.[34] The risks inherent in this kind of narrative, which have yet to be met head on, are evident from the terminology that controls it: are we to imagine that tactility simply goes away, or that the two forms of aesthetic sensation were not, and are not, somehow fundamentally co-involved? Contemporary philosophy suggests that they are mutually implicated, for instance, of the sort that descends from the French philosopher of perception and visual aesthetics Merleau-Ponty, who states that "vision is palpation by the gaze (*le regard*)" and that corporeality is constitutive of visuality: in his mind, there is a primordial interchange between these two spheres of sensation.[35] The thought is hardly anachronistic when applied to ancient optics, according to which seeing just is a kind of touching, or else its extension. This idea was an inheritance from Homer, for whom verbs of seeing transmit sensations through a kind of *actio in distans*,[36] as well as from the materialism of Presocratic thought. For as Aristotle says, "Democritus and most of the natural philosophers who treat of sense-perception (αἰσθήσεως) proceed quite irrationally, for they represent all objects of sense as objects of touch" (ἁπτά).[37]

A further problem with Riegl's model is the presumed disjunction it creates between the sensibility of the artist, be he a painter, sculptor, or architect, wrestling with his resisting material and fully immersed in its tactile qualities on the one hand, and the optical effects he strives to achieve on the other. Not only would one need to account for this split consciousness in the artist's own mind. One would also have to explain

---

[33] In favor of this evolution: Protzmann 1977, among others. I single out Protzmann's account here and below as a uniquely eloquent version of this story about evolving practice, and also because of its heavy but tacit use of Riegl's conceptual apparatus. The same apparatus underlies Schweitzer 1932 (see, e.g., 12–15) and even Pollitt 1999, 175 ("purely optical experience"). For critiques of progressivism from different perspectives, see Hallett 1986; Elsner 1995; Stewart 1997; Neer 2002; Elsner 2006. None of these quite takes on Riegl's apparatus or the progressivist thesis in the way I want to query them here.

[34] See pp. 135–37 above.

[35] Merleau-Ponty 1964, 177–78.

[36] See Snell 1980, 13–16.

[37] Arist. *Sens.* 4.442a29–31; trans. Beare.

how his tactile sense contributed to his visual sense, just as any visual "reading" of an object involves retracing the material signs of its production (*facture*). For what a beholder sees are not objects made by and for vision pure and simple but objects that were drawn, brushed, chiseled, scraped, polished, and so forth: what one takes in through the eye is the work of the *hand*. To quote Merleau-Ponty once more, "we *see* the depth, the smoothness, the softness, the hardness of the object; Cézanne even claimed that we see their odor."[38] On ancient theories of vision (though not on Riegl's), it would even be acceptable to say that we *touch* these features of objects with our eyes.[39] Finally, the progressivist narrative typified by Riegl assumes that visuality cannot have been as active a factor in the earlier (archaic and preclassical) periods as tactility would have been. This assumption can be shown to be false, if not altogether absurd. But it is also guilty of projecting tactility as a feature of primitivism or naïveté in Greek art and in earlier states of Greek consciousness generally, and of celebrating a disembodied ocularity in later art and culture (one that doubtfully ever existed in any event).[40] Such a view thus participates in the disgrace of matter that we encountered earlier in this study, for instance in Plato.

As it is often told, the story goes that Plato's critique of appearances in art presages a new turn in the arts towards a kind of phenomenalism that will come to full fruition with Lysippus in the later part of the fourth century. Plato puts his finger on the problem exactly: what is involved is a shift from the earlier world of self-enclosed objects to a strange new world of appearances that reside in the gap between objects and viewers. Henceforth, what one beholds is not a statue or temple *per se* but the appearances that these objects project (their *phainomena*); and the pleasures one takes

---

[38] "Cézanne's Doubt," in Johnson 1993, 65. See further Merleau-Ponty 1945, 243–44: "Le bleu est ce qui sollicite de moi une certaine maniére de regarder, ce qui se laisse palper par un mouvement défini de mon regard.... Le rouge 'déchire,' le jaune est 'piquant'...." Similarly, Collingwood 1938, 146. Cf. Scranton 1964, 18, defining sculpture as "an art of the sense of touch."

[39] Or even "kiss" them, on the Byzantine extension of this theory (Nelson 2000); further, Pentcheva 2007. For the extension of the haptic (possibly atomistic) model of vision into the Greek novel, see Morales 2004, esp. 130–40. Not even the Peripatetic view is an exception. According to Aristotle, vision receives the form (εἶδος) but not the matter of the object of vision (ἄνευ τῆς ὕλης), the way a seal leaves its imprint on wax, and similarly with all the other faculties of sense (*De an.* 2.12.424a17–424b3; 3.2.425b23–24, etc.). Aristotle strikes a compromise: he is keen, as ever, to stress that it is the *form* that impresses itself on the eye, but it nonetheless does so haptically (though he reserves this last term for the sense of touch). An atomist would naturally disagree with Aristotle on every point: *matter* is transmitted from the object to the eye, through an unabashed touching.

[40] Whence the unfortunate first section header of Protzmann 1972–73, "The End of Archaic Naïveté." But neither is Protzmann exceptional.

in them are pleasures of the eye, whereby *Augenlust* (visual pleasure) displaces an earlier *Körpergefühl,* or immediate bodily sensation.[41] *Illusionism* is another term that frequently comes into play here, not least thanks to Plato's denigrating association of phenomenalism with deception.[42] The invention of perspective in painting and corrective perspectivalism in architecture, the discovery of a middle space between viewer and object, and the projection of a dimensional space in sculpture into which the viewer can be drawn (as in the inviting dimensional images by Praxiteles, such as his Apollo *Sauroktonos,* where both of the figure's arms encircle the space before itself, invitingly, or the Lysippan *Apoxuomenos,* with its strigil held out at arm's length) – all this is felt to be part of the new advance in representational techniques and sensibilities of the early postclassical era.[43]

The culmination of these tendencies is said to be the Lysippan sculptural aesthetic, the essence of which is preserved by Pliny: "[Lysippus] used to say that his forerunners made men just as they were, while he made them as they appeared to be" (*dicebat ab illis factos quales essent homines, a se quales viderentur esse*), where appearance is physical, not ethical (as in Aristotle or earlier).[44] This suggestive remark seems to square well with a newfound interest in contemporary philosophical circles in phenomenalism, sensualism, materialism, subjectivism, and even skepticism: here, phenomena seem to be as real, if not more real, than reality itself. Among these currents in the neo-Hellenistic world, "all being is [now taken to be] corporeal."[45] "Facticity displace[s] all ideality. 'Positivistic' phenomenalism in art is sensualistic, trusting alone in the material of the world of the senses."[46] Strangely, it is claimed, to this preponderance of materialism in the Hellenistic worldview corresponds not the *tactile* sensibility one might reasonably expect to find, but its functional opposite, "the *optical* mastery of reality."[47] The eye has become – oddly – an instrument of sensuous and material phenomenalism. How consistent is this picture?

---

[41] Protzmann 1977, 173; cf. Pollitt 1999, 175.
[42] Pl. *Soph.* 240d2, labeling the art of producing *phantasmata* ἀπατητική. Illusionism is the one category that is thought to be the least vulnerable to critique even among those who would most contest progressivism (Neer 2002 is an exception).
[43] See also Schweitzer 1953, 84–87.
[44] Plin. *HN* 34.65.
[45] Protzmann 1977, 201.
[46] Protzmann 1977, 203.
[47] Protzmann 1977, 203.

Prima facie, there has to be something odd about a view of Greek aesthetics (or consciousness) that claims to want to distance itself from the naïve past and from the sophistic postclassical present, both of which were consumed by sensuous perception, when all this view has to offer in turn is a historical convergence, or rather collapse, of the naïve and the sophistic into a single aesthetic that is marked by *nothing but* sensuous perception – indeed, one that threatens to be swamped by a historical continuum of sensuous perception altogether, given the intermediary (classical) period's characterization as "haptic."[48] The easy confusion in aesthetic terms between the palpable sensuousness of the visually haptic and the (seemingly) same sensuousness of the optical suggests that somewhere along the line vision has incorporated, on the sly, something of the nature of the palpable within itself *and never released it.* That something has gone awry on this model of change is evident from further cracks in the same picture as it appears in other variants of it. Elsewhere, "'positivistic' phenomenalism" in early Hellenistic art is classified as "phenomenal *idealism*," while Lysippus' comment on his own practice is glossed as representing men in a "more or less *idealized* likeness."[49] "An ideal is a slippery concept," to be sure, and critics of the concept can often seem to be as justified as its exponents.[50] It is no great help that the terminology of idealism is a modern creation and that ancient equivalents are non-existent. But at issue here are not terms but conflicting assessments, which is to say, a seeming collapse of the modern rules for coming to grips with ancient works of art. Rather than try to sort out the confusion, let's simply add to it for a moment.

We might begin by acknowledging that no art is ever anything but an idealization of reality in some sense, which is to say, an embellishment or prettification. This is, admittedly, not quite the sense that the term *idealized* usually carries for us today (meaning, roughly, embodying traits of perfection beyond what reality permits), a sense that can, in fact, be found in ancient sources, for instance in Isocrates' assertion

---

[48] Protzmann 1968, 724. The archaic or early classical (austere) style is not clearly demarcated by means of this terminology, but it bears all the signs of the haptic nonetheless: "a tangible firmness, density, 'palpability,' and plastic pregnancy," rendering it "independent of the 'cooperation [*Mitarbeit*] of the eye'" (ibid., 722).

[49] Stewart 1990, 186; 80; emphasis added. Cf. Schweitzer 1932, 44, who describes "late Hellenistic idealism" as evolving out of the fourth century and its "painterly-[*malerisch*, i.e., optic (*optisch*)] idealistic art" (ibid., 7).

[50] Stewart 1990, 80 (quotation); see further Stewart 2005; Hölscher 1971 for one such critique.

that "no one can make the nature of his body resemble statues or paintings," whereas emulating the character of one's fellow-men, as this is found in their writing or speeches, is an attainable goal.[51] Isocrates may be recalling Alcidamas, who observed that "real bodies are less attractive in appearance than beautiful statues."[52] But statues and other works of art in antiquity were regularly conceded to transcend human beauty.[53] The ancient literary and critical traditions thus show an acute awareness of idealism in art, but also of its unreality and unattainability except as a fantasy, as does the visual tradition itself, to which we next turn.

3 LOCATING IDEALS: THE FOUNDRY CUP

An early example of this same insight into ideality is the red-figure Foundry Cup dating from the 480s, where at play is an image of image-making: depicted is a bronze-foundry in which artisans, smaller in scale (as befits their social status), are at work finishing a colossal nude hoplite in the archaic style (fig. 8.2). The contrast inevitably conjures up both the notion of a monumental object (a statue in bronze, larger than life and aesthetically more perfect than anything given in life), as well as the perhaps slightly farcical or caricatured but in any case knowingly constructed nature ("facticity") of this same object.[54] The Foundry Cup is a salutary reminder that one does not have to wait until the Hellenistic period for self-awareness to show itself in the visual realm, or for idealism to make an appearance either.

But we needn't focus on the nude hoplite to notice that idealism has taken hold of the images on the cup: to do so is to mistake the fundamental operations of idealization. The surrounding figures, the smaller-scale craftsmen involved in the production of this "ideal," are themselves no more real or any less idealized than the oversize warrior figure: they are all cut from the same cloth, being manifest

---

[51] Isoc. 9.75; trans. van Hook.

[52] Alcid. *Soph.* 27.

[53] Gorg. DK 82B11(§18); Xen. *Mem.* 3.10.2; Arist. *Pol.* 3.11.1281b10–15; *Poet.* 15.1454b10–11; Plin. *HN* 35.64; Lucian *Im.* 5–9 (e.g., 9 on a "spectacle transcending all human beauty" [πᾶσαν τὴν ἀνθρωπίνην εὐμορφίαν ὑπερπεπαικός]); Stewart 1997, 93 (reading such tales in the light of fetishism); Cic. *Inv. rhet.* 2.1; id. *Orat.*, *passim* (the work is premised on Demosthenes' being the closest approximation to a rhetorical ideal, the *summus et perfectus orator*), on which see Panofsky 1924; Philostr. *Her.* 52.2.

[54] See Porter 2006a. A superb reading of this object is to be found in Neer 2002, 77–85.

Fig. 8.2 Foundry workers at a bronze-foundry. Side B of the Foundry Cup (detail), by the so-called Foundry Painter, *c.* 490 BCE. Berlin, Staatliche Museen, Antikensammlung.

representations of human figures, and so too simplifications or sketches of the real thing. They share outlines of body parts, much like those of the hoplite warrior, even if the laboring craftsmen are not clearly improvements over real-life bodies, while their bronze products are meant to be this. Consider, for instance, the lines demarcating the breasts and abdomens of craftsmen on side A (fig. 8.3) with those of the hoplite on side B (fig. 8.2). Or consider the pose of the standing craftsman on side A, left arm akimbo and right arm supported on a hammer, but looking more like a statue with nothing to do – beardless and nude at that, exactly like the unfinished, headless bronze figure to his left (the viewer's right), whose dimensions he moreover shares identically.

On the other hand, the standing craftsman is perfectly symmetrical to the two bearded and clothed standing figures on side B flanking the hoplite to the right and left. These two are both equal to the hoplite in size, more propped up like objects than leaning on staffs, the one (on the viewer's left) balanced on his staff, the other (on the viewer's right) caught momentarily in the relaxed pose of a beholder, again like the standing craftsman, his near-double in stance but not in status or age. Are they onlookers, supervisors, patrons – or statues, like the hoplite they also

Fig. 8.3 Observers at the bronze foundry and workers casting a bronze statue of a nude
warrior. Side A (detail) of fig. 8.2.

resemble, at least in size? They seem too large to be real when measured
against the dwarflike craftsmen who are at work on the hoplite, unless we
resort to the criterion of social status as a justification of their elevated size
(for, being bearded and staff-bearing, they might be held to be socially
elevated).[55] In their symmetrical, near-mirrored pairing, they seem more
like decorative ornaments – serving as angular frames to the central scene –
than like realistic figures.[56] The circle of resemblances passes uncertainly
from "real" to manufactured to "real" again, and from manufacturer to
consumer to manufactured – without ever exiting from the orbit of the
ideal. Nor are these the only oddities on this literally self-consuming
artifact. In a brilliant reading of the cup, Richard Neer notices a series
of further uncanny similarities between bodies and bodies or bodies and
objects on the cup. So, for instance, "the craftsman who hammers [on
side A] is the same as the image he strikes: both are, in a way incomplete" –
as all idealizations are.[57]

---

[55] See Mattusch 1980, 440–41 (who calls them "enigmatic").

[56] Much more could be said about the decorative (and disruptive) function of the two onlooking figures
and the various framing devices on either side of the central bronze figure on side B (e.g., the spotlit
instruments and trailing fabric to either side of the central scene). See also Neer 2002, 83.

[57] Neer 2002, 81.

4 IDEALIZATION IN ART: A MATERIALIST PERSPECTIVE

So far, we have been skirting the edges of the problem of idealization, which as we saw occupies an uneasy place alongside aesthetic materialism. I now want to confront the problem more squarely in order to show how the two notions do not sit at opposite ends of a conceptual scale but are in fact frequently intertwined. Let's begin with the question of how ideals come to be generated in the first place.

Here, then, is one suggestion, which might be called a materialist theory of the ideal. We've seen how incompleteness can be as much an ingredient of the ideal in art as is the ideal's suggestion of completeness, and this is perhaps as one should only expect. Literary and visual representations of ideals are, after all, only suggestions of ideals, not their fulfillment. They arc cmblems of what could be, and thus are ideals twice over, the mere image of ideals (as it were, the image of an image). In this sense, they are twice deficient as well, being twice removed from the completeness they would figure, first as sign, then as potential embodiment. But if we press the point, we will find that the difference between any representation and any idealized representation is less substantial than may at first appear, just as the gap in representational quality between the craftsmen on the Foundry Cup and their artful products vanishes upon closer inspection: both kinds of figure are idealized in their own way, and in ways that are not entirely distinct from each other. Like Midas, representation idealizes whatever it touches, damning it to irreality, or to hyperreality.

If so, then the proper comparison between works of art, periods, representational strategies, and so on, should not be in terms of the *presence or absence* of idealization, because idealization will always be present in one form or another, but in terms of *kinds, uses, and styles* of idealization. The grand historical narrative of progressivism, built around a parabola of idealism that culminates in the fifth century, begins, on this view, to look rather suspect indeed.[58] True, idealization on such a narrative is usually made to coincide with the naturalism of the human form, but that is only because the differences between the two concepts tend to be conflated, with the end result that idealization becomes, as it were, naturalized: earlier instances of idealization disappear from view as if they never existed; and the occurrence of the human ideal in its so-called natural form no longer appears to be ideal but only as self-evidently

[58] See Neer 2010.

natural. It is this kind of reductionism (not to say anthropocentrism) that a materialist aesthetics can help to contest. Attention to the materiality of art, of the kind that is on full display in the Foundry Cup, works to change what it means to idealize a depicted object. And as I hope is becoming clear, materialism and idealism needn't be exclusive opposites: they simply point to different regions of the same objects, or rather to different ways of viewing them.

Even the earliest Protogeometric or full-fledged Geometric art, for instance the Dipylon Master's pots with their abstract figural forms (figs. 8.4 and 8.5), is manifestly idealizing – not because this art seeks to depict unchanging essences such as "humanness" or "horseness" lying behind appearances, but because they overtly subtract from the complex texture of appearances and present a blatantly minimalist mnemonic of reality that, even in their patterned repetitions and stark outlines, can be highly charged with expressiveness, if not emotion. What is more, strong hints of pictorial depth, which is to say, a "probing of virtual space lying behind the picture plane" (customary markers of fifth- to fourth-century naturalism), have been detected in vase painting from the seventh century.[59] It is not the case that these early artists were striving towards some naturalistic ideal of representation which they either failed to grasp conceptually or to master technically. Nor is it quite right to suggest that they had at their disposal every conceptual and technical capacity that later artists had. But neither should we underestimate the capacities that went into the making of the earlier art, which in various respects (it would be no exaggeration to say) *exceeded* those of later art, for instance in the areas of abstraction and geometrical patterning – achievements that required exceptional powers of conception and execution in their own right.[60] And if, say, a sense of recessive and projective space appears, however sporadically, centuries before this sort of practice becomes a regular convention, its sudden emergence in the seventh century is, of course, largely governed by the conditions of the art at the time. Nor would its effects be unintelligible to anyone habituated to the perceptual conditions of the later art. It may be that the artist's intent in the earlier case was "to enliven

[59] See Hurwit 1977, 29 on the Nettos amphora from the last quarter of the seventh century (NM 1002, Athens).
[60] Here, the views expressed by Laporte 1947, namely that classical art achieves a level of "abstraction" and pure "aesthetic quality" hitherto unseen, through a "slow emancipation of the representational design," all this expressed in the language of "quest" and "conquest" (143–45), while characteristic of the progressivist narrative, could be applied (minus the progressivist jargon) to much earlier Cycladic forms. See next section.

Fig. 8.4 Horses or "Horseness"? Late Geometric louterion of the Dipylon class. London, British Museum (1899.2–19.1). Line drawing after A.S. Murray, *Journal of Hellenic Studies* 19a, 1899, pl. VIII. S.

Fig. 8.5 Abstract geometric patterns. Detail from Late Geometric amphora by the Dipylon Master (Athens NM 805), *c.* 750 BCE. Photo courtesy of David Gill.

the surface, not to dissolve it with illusionistic space."[61] But then enlivening *is* a form of illusion – the entire Daedalic tradition rests on this premise, or at least it would be so read by the time of Aeschylus' *Theoroi* or *Isthmiastai* ("this [votive] image full of my form, this imitation of Daedalus, lacks only a voice"),[62] as does archaic ecphrasis – while no later art ever completely dissolves the material surfaces on which it is inscribed. Self-annihilation is

---

[61] Hurwit 1977, 29.

[62] See Ch. 6 at n. 129 above. On the Daedalic tradition: Frontisi-Ducroux 1975; Morris 1992. On animation, Daedalus, and art in the early poetic tradition, see Philipp 1968, 9–18; Himmelmann 1969.

inconceivable in the sphere of representation by virtue of the very fact of representation itself; at most, art can create the illusion of such a self-erasure. Even the intentionally broken surfaces of postmodern art create and willy-nilly assert a framing boundary at the edges of their own ruptured representational space, however much postmodernism may flout the conventions of the frame. Differently put, later art *projects* illusion – as something to enjoy (through utter absorption in the artifact) and to contemplate (as an effect of the artist's technique). Whether earlier art does the same remains to be seen – or speculated.

5 CYCLADIC MARBLE

We began this thread of argument with a reflection on idealization. Let us continue tracing the thread backwards, past Protogeometric art and into the brilliant if difficult Cycladic figures from the third millennium. Consider one of "the earliest known musical artifact[s] from the Mediterranean-Aegean area," the marble Harp Player from Keros (now in Athens; fig. 8.6).[63] The figurine is an example of a repeated type, all of which nonetheless transcend the limits of the form (or genre) through their individualizing touches, which is to say, through the specification of their formal features in their particular material arrangements.[64] Such particularization may be thought of as an expression of their form's matter or materiality. In a later idiom, one that would be employed by the Hellenistic euphonists, as was seen above, this quiddity of a work of art is the work's *idion*, which is specified in view of its material arrangement and the phenomenal effect – the appearances – that it radiates, rather than its conjunction of form and matter.[65] The so-called Harp Player conforms to the examples of ideality in art adduced so far, but also represents their essential complication in a heightened form.

Spare, possessing the barest of features (and no facial features, only a nose and the shape of a head), and not even holding a *stringed* harp but only (as today) the smooth outlines of a triangular harp (string fastenings

---

[63] Anderson 1994, 3.

[64] There are at least eight preserved harp players. See Getz-Preziosi 1980 for illustrations and discussion. I am grateful to the author, Pat Gentle, and also Peggy Sotirakopoulou, for further information about the Keros harp player and its context. For a fine appreciation of the harp-player type as a work of art, see esp. Mertens 1998, 11–15, with interesting speculations about the performative value of the same type at ibid., 16–20.

[65] See p. 116 above.

Fig. 8.6 Marble harp player from Keros. Early Cycladic (*c.* 2800–2300 BCE). Athens, National Museum.

are not so much even as contemplated on the object),[66] and thus *expressing* a harp more than representing one, he is an idealized figure of a musician *singing an idealized melody.* He is lost in a trance, fully rapt in his performance, face tilted upward, whether blind or gazing at the sources of his inspiration which he alone can see (it is not a shared vision, for it is not one we can see, but only one we can sense), or else singing through an open mouth that has to be imagined (he has no mouth and no lips – unless they were originally painted onto the marble, as was the case with

[66] See Aign 1963, 32: "Saiten oder deren Befestigung sind nicht einmal angedeutet." Thanks to John Franklin for this reference to Aign.

some but not all Cycladic marbles[67]), like the melody you cannot hear issuing from his unseen lips and strummed on the invisible strings of his harp. (The bard even lacks ears, as if to underscore the inaudibility of his song.[68]) In other respects, he is a monumental sculpture, as much marble as human. Though naked, he is attached to his chair, made of the very same stuff it is made of and polished to the same degree: the border where flesh meets imaginary wood is one, and it is all made of stone. While molding helps to set off the sides of the thighs from the seat of the throne, and paint may have further differentiated these, the boundary is smooth, not sharply drawn. But *no* distinction is visible from the frontal view: there, the flesh spills over onto and into the chair, merging with it, without molding or modeling of any kind at all.[69] The harp the figure holds rests, from the outside view, parallel to his leg and to the chair, its bottom bracket enlarged, possibly indicating a resonant sound box (though it too is a solid piece of marble),[70] while from the inside the harp blends into his torso where the instrument's curvature meets his flat-scraped front. The harp is thus as much a part of his body as it is a detachable instrument, and it too angles upward, repeating the tilt of the head. Not even decorative touches of paint would suffice to erase the impression of stoniness that the marble conveys or the massiveness of its contours, for all its diminutive dimensions (the piece measures 22.5 cm – just under 9 inches – in height).

[67] Unlike some other Cycladic heads, on this figurine the mouth and lips are not moulded in the marble. See next note. On the polychromy of Cycladic figures, see Hendrix 2003; Sotirakopoulou 2005.

[68] Ears could be added as part of the marble design of the harp-player type, but they are not so designed on our specimen: the figure is manifestly earless. This is in keeping with the most recent research on the dating of the remains, according to which molded features appear only on the very latest Cycladic figurines, chronologically speaking, of which the Keros harp player is not one (so Peggy Sotirakopoulou, private communication). Hendrix (ibid., 442) makes the intriguing observation that there is "a surprising absence of the mouth on most Cycladic figures," which lack she attributes to one of two possible explanations: either mouths were "somehow inappropriate on these works" (given their performative function; they may have been used ventriloquistically, like puppets), or else, "as a possible symbol of voice, story, song, channel, or port of nourishment, the mouth may have been painted in a changing variety of ways over the life-use of the figure." Obviously, other explanations are equally admissible.

[69] One thinks of Clement Greenberg's lovely comment about modernist sculpture, wherein "the stone figure appears to be on the point of relapsing into the original monolith, and the cast seems to narrow and smooth itself back to the original molten stream from which it was poured, or tries to remember the texture and plasticity of the clay in which it was first worked out" (Greenberg 1986–93 [1940], 1:36).

[70] "Das Instrument läßt eine als Resonanzkörper anzusprechende Verdickung erkennen, die über dem Knie des Spielers ansetzt und *ohne erkennbare Grenze* (Abstufung) in den senkrechten, am Oberkörper des Spielers anliegenden Rahmenteil übergeht" (Aign 1963, 30; emphasis added) – though, as I said, the sound box of the instrument merges indistinguishably into the singer's own body, which is (ideally) a sound box (*Resonanzkörper*) *in its own right*.

One of the most striking features of this artifact is its formal and material undecidability: the places where the form divides up the matter are uncertain along virtually every square inch of the object's surface. This uncertainty, whether it lies in the object or it exists only for ourselves, creates a difficulty when it comes to untangling the humanity of the figurine from the material out of which he is made. Consider on the one hand the contrast between the combined effect of the figure's massive haunches sinking into the chair and its flat, shapeless torso (absorbing the triangular harp that features curves running parallel but opposite to those of the chair's legs[71]), and on the other the harpist's shapely nose, which is his single most distinctive feature, but also his most humanizing feature. Yet even the harpist's nose is little more than a directional vector and a continuation of the upper compositional line of his forehead, which in turn runs off into two chiseled shapes not unlike the nose: the crown of the head, which is oddly pinched, then abruptly squared off on a plane parallel to the vertical rise of the chair's back, and the exquisitely rounded chin, which, set off from the neck and viewed in profile, likewise takes on a taper along the jaw line. Nevertheless, for all its kindred qualities to stone, the nose *is* the face: it is the solitary feature that transforms the oval marble of the head *into* a face, and so saves the figure as a whole from lapsing into the mute materiality of a marble Thing, or else into a human *manqué*: it marks the source and the site of the figure's activity.[72] Gazing up or else within, feet planted firmly on the ground yet with his music soaring ethereally into an inaudible abstract perfection, squat on his haunches but with a finely chiseled nose, somewhat feminized (steatopygous, he lacks all muscular definition, like other Cycladic fertility figures) and yet masculine (his slight bulge of a penis is unmistakable; it also happens to be aligned with the nose and to offer one more parallel to its shape), the singer/harpist, we would want to say, is *solidly* sublime. Here, both tactile and visual senses are not merely activated. They are *hyperactivated*, in coordination and in conflict, and to a dynamic and productive extreme: the marble constantly *moves*. But if so, then we have a very early, preclassical case of sublimity on our hands indeed, one that blends the material and the immaterial sublimes in a challenging mix.[73]

---

[71] These latter resemble nothing so much as four small harps; they repeat the harp's shape underneath his body; a fifth is repeated on the chair's back.

[72] Alternatively, or concurrently, the human merges *with* his activity: he is inseparable from the harp and from the stool that allows him to play the harp (and that repeats the harp motif; see previous note). The redundancy is therefore meaningful.

[73] On these two sublimes, see Introduction, n. 19. Of further interest is a continuation of the nose's profile in the harp itself, in a curious, tapered piece that curves upward and away from the instrument in the same direction as the harpist is facing. The piece may stand in for one of

6 THE NOLAN AMPHORA BY THE BERLIN PAINTER

The final object I would like to consider in this series follows on thematically from the last, and it will help us redirect along a more productive path the original problem of tactility and visuality from which we started out. It is the exquisite Nolan amphora by the Berlin Painter in the Metropolitan Museum, a red-figure painting set against a sheer black borderless background. The work dates from the early fifth century. On one side, a beardless citharist stands, singing – mouth open, face turned skyward, eyes fixed on some object that lies outside the visible plane of the vase, his left hand poised on the strings, his fingers spread over each string, and his right hand balancing the instrument (fig. 8.7). On the other side, his bearded tutor beats the time, staff in one hand and his other hand outstretched, index finger and thumb extended (possibly snapping his fingers or just waving his arm like a baton) (fig. 8.8).[74]

The citharist cuts a striking figure: his body curves in an *S*-shape that is accentuated by a fringed apron or decorative cloth that dangles from the instrument in the same rhythmic shape as his body. Both elements give a sense of flowing movement but also impart an extra dimensionality to the image, while the effects of motion and mass are further reinforced by the curvature of the vase itself. As Hurwit writes, in a significant study of image and frame in Greek art, "the bulging and retreating curves of the amphora are exploited, giving added corporeality to the youth who ... sways within an activated, boundless space."[75]

The figure is one of the variety called "spotlit," so named because it is free-floating, unframed, and seemingly liberated from the spatial confines of the vase in which it resides. One interesting consequence of spotlit figures is that, in their character as free-standing objects endowed with a kind of three-dimensionality, and set off against a background that, in

the several flanged notches that decorate some species of the trigonon: if so, then its function, too, is that of a formal abstraction from the viewpoint of design, though it rhymes with the compositional vectors of the nose and the face. Turned upward, it too faces the inspirational sources of the music, thus representing the harp's equivalent of the musician's own connection with some power outside of or within, himself. Some see this flanged piece as a swan's head and thus as a symbol of poetry's communing with divinity (Maas and Snyder 1989 I; 27; Getz-Preziosi 1990, 20; Cheney 1993, 70–71; Anderson 1994, 5).

[74] Beazley 1930, pl. 21. The tutor is often felt to be reprimanding the young musician (so Hurwit 1977, 17; Neer 2002, 72), but for no obvious reason. This may just reflect an anxiety over scenes of instruction rather than anything intrinsic to the image.

[75] Hurwit 1977, 16.

Fig. 8.7 Youthful singing cithara player, apparently in dialogue with his older time-keeper or teacher (depicted on side B; see fig. 8.8). Detail of red-figure amphora from Nola (Etruria), attributed to the Berlin Painter, *c.* 490 BCE. Side A. New York, The Metropolitan Museum of Art.

contrast, appears to have "dematerialized,"[76] they begin to resemble nothing so much as *sculpture*. That is, as the spatial dimensions and then the material qualities of the vases loan themselves to the images on their surfaces, the vases *as vases* recede quietly into invisibility (whether into the darkness of their black glaze or the blankness of self-effacement): the

---

[76] Hurwit 1977, 17.

Fig. 8.8 Side B of fig. 8.7.

surface of the painted object thus translates itself into an illusory surface and depth, while the spotlit image appears like a suspended sculptural work endowed with a *borrowed* corporeality.[77]

A first question, then: Does the image appeal to the eye or to the sense of touch? Plainly, the question is badly formed, which suggests that there

---

[77] There is, to be sure, a small sleight of hand at work here, since there is no "vase as vase" to speak of, or rather, defining what this is would be arduous. (What of the instrumental value of the vase? How can one isolate these functions?) I am speaking, however, of the vase as a physical object with minimal aesthetic properties, at least as it is treated on the dematerializing readings of it.

is something wrong with the conceptual scheme that has generated the question.[78] In its sculptural qualities, the image appeals to the sense of touch. Indeed, the image is in many ways *about* touch: the youth holding and plucking his cithara, the tutor holding his staff and possibly snapping his fingers, but at any rate pointing to his pupil on the other half of the vase – a communication that is thus installed across the two sides, but also forestalled by the black curve of space that intervenes and by the disregard of the strumming youth, lost in his own musical reverie. But in the visual intensity of the spotlight quality of the image, with its stark light and dark contrasts, and even in the projective dimensionalities of the sculptural image of the youth, the vase has an undeniable visual appeal.[79] The amphora confounds any simple categorization *à la* Riegl's categories. But it also confounds more modern categories.

A temptation with spotlit figures is to view their surroundings as void spaces and the figures as full bodies. One can make these bland propositions interesting, as Richard Neer does when he suggests that "the figure constitutes the void *as such*. Its mere presence transforms a black glazed surface into a depiction of empty space."[80] Perhaps this is what is meant by Hurwit when he describes "the visual interactions between figure and figure, between figure and contour, between spotlit image and activated, borderless and dematerialized blackness."[81] The problem with these formulations is that they capture only half of the visual experience offered by the amphora. While it is true that the black glaze of the surface dematerializes in proportion as the figure gains in corporeality, this dynamic of ground and figure is purely a function of a shift in focus by the viewer. It is very much a matter of "interaction," but one that takes place between the object and the viewing subject. A perfectly plausible and legitimate flip side to this interaction is another, whereby *the surface materializes*, while the figure *does not*. Here, the black glaze, instead of absorbing light and receding into blankness, reflects light and sends back fierce glints; its contours become visible as such (rather than being lent to the figure in its quasi-three-dimensionality); and as such they reveal themselves to be

---

[78] To be fair, Protzmann at least occasionally acknowledges the heuristic and tendential value of this schema, but insufficiently so. For instance, though admitting the initial, and indeed the theoretical, co-presence of the two poles (like Riegl), he continues to insist on the eventual "elimination" of one of them (e.g., Protzmann 1968, 726).

[79] See further Hurwit 1977, 16, esp. at n. 79.

[80] Neer 2002, 66; emphasis in original. See the similar point by Meyer Schapiro, quoted in Hurwit 1977, 16 at n. 76, namely that the figure "seems to incorporate the empty space around it as a field of existence."

[81] Hurwit 1977, 17.

lustrous and aesthetically pleasing in their own right, even as the red slip
or clay beneath shows through the occasional imperfections of the glaze.

On this view, the figure is anything but a three-dimensional statuesque
form. Quite the contrary, *it* is now rendered the dematerialized object, a
flat, contourless, decorative confection pasted onto the center of a three-
dimensional object for pure aesthetic effect. Far from "the figure constituting the void *as such*," we would have to say that here the figure is
"nothing but a configuration *of* the void":[82] it represents all that is left
when the surrounding void is mentally taken away in a momentary shift
of aesthetic focus, and when this red figure is deprived of the pseudo-
fullness it once enjoyed thanks to the contrastive presence of the surrounding black void (which in the manufacturing process was in fact
added last to the pot).[83] In this way, the figure returns to its original
materiality – not the illusory materiality of a body swollen with the
borrowed dimensionalities of the vase and so seeming to project from
the vase itself, but one that now (re)assumes the materiality of its making,
first as the "material trace" of the artist's hand,[84] and then (as we approach
the object more closely) as the actual surface and stuff of the vase – and
quite literally so, inasmuch as the red of the figure is the red of the clay
from which the vase, after all, was manufactured. A more traditional term,
which does not quite cover all that I have in mind, is *facture*.[85]

Which view is correct? Is the human form on the vase a figure or a
ground, a representation or a material surface? The real question is why
we should feel the need to choose between the alternatives. The choice
is in one way like that posed by a rabbit-duck illusion or a Necker
cube: all are perspectival effects that offer equally valid, if momentarily
exclusive, visual choices. Tactility and visuality, figure and ground,
materiality and formal features all seem to obey this same logic.
Perhaps their common point of collapse is found at those moments
when we can talk about the *materiality of the form*, when the formal
features of objects take on sensuous dimensions, as they always arguably do whenever they become phenomenally available, which is to say,
aesthetically actualized. At any rate, to take in the aesthetic features of

---

[82] I am paraphrasing Žižek 1999, 129 (discussing ancient atomism).
[83] The red figure is not only delineated in its outlines by the surrounding blackness, but is also
internally articulated by black lines within: here, it is as if the outer void has invaded the body and
divided it further into atomic parts. On the manufacturing process of red-figure pottery, see
Stewart 1997, 59 (and ibid., 58, on black-figure pottery).
[84] Neer 2002, 47.
[85] See Stewart 1997, 43–60.

the Nolan amphora on this expanded view of it is not to allow that its maker "refus[ed] to acknowledge the existence of the material surface by refusing to adorn it with flat decorative borders, choosing instead to explore the various viewpoints of a figure suspended in a more 'three-dimensional' space."[86] It is precisely to allow for this possibility *and* for its visual contradiction, and to acknowledge that both possibilities exist together on the selfsame vase. And it is to allow that the two views are proffered by the vase for aesthetic consumption. Perhaps it is time for art historians to *ignore* figures on vases, spotlit or not, and to explore backgrounds and grounds – their shapes and their shades, however black or blank – to the same degree that they explore the figures that decorate their surfaces. Perhaps, in other words, it is time to elaborate *an aesthetics of the surface* in the visual realm, and then to appreciate why, in Nietzsche's words, "those Greeks were superficial – *out of profundity.*"[87]

7 PHENOMENALITY

Appearing as he does in the late archaic period, the Berlin Painter undoes some of the neat chronologies that the progressivist approach to tactility and opticality would assert. Indeed, in the light of the series of objects we have just run (all too quickly) through, I hope it is clear why one has to be suspicious of any claims about the phenomenality of art being discovered and enjoyed only after the end of the fifth century.[88] Such perceptions are available wherever art exists, or so it would seem. And the same holds for any claims on behalf of the so-called emancipation of the visual, which is a commonplace of ancient art histories, and not only of the model that descends from Riegl. On the contrary, visuality is emancipated – or better yet, *released* – in the very act of beholding visual works of art. The eye roams unrestrictedly over its objects. It is *our* language that confines the gaze, setting limits to where it looks and what it is permitted to see.

What is more, visuality is a slightly dangerous concept: it is susceptible to different meanings. Riegl's analysis already indicates two poles within which visuality can be seen, in theory, to operate, namely between the haptic and the optical, though, to be sure, on his historical picture visuality evolves in the later, "dematerialized," direction. In another sense,

---

[86] Hurwit 1977, 16.
[87] *Gay Science*, Preface 4; trans. Kaufmann; emphasis (crucially) in original.
[88] E.g., Protzmann 1977, 187 and 201.

visuality can be understood to result from the emphasis on the play of formal relations along the surface, on the interplay between surfaces and surfaces, or between surfaces and depths (which are, from another point of view, merely further recessive surfaces) – with the accent placed here on the ludic element, as the eye travels pleasurably across the visual phenomena it takes in.[89] Such a perspective can easily translate into a lingering over visual sensuousness: curves become curvaceous, lines are almost erotically charged, or else (depending on the view) palpability may be enjoyed for the sheer pleasure of the sensation without any hint of eroticism. A further, seemingly inescapable connotation of phenomenality in art in the ludic sense is that of art's deceptive qualities – not necessarily in a mimetic sense, but in another, simpler sense, whereby the absorption in art's seemingly immediate qualities challenges the claims of one's immediate realities, displacing them momentarily, indeed for as long as one is rapt by an aesthetic experience. (We will want to return to this sense of "deception" below.) It is likely that Plato's resistance to art was motivated as much by this kind of psychological and phenomenological displacement as it was by art's occasional claims to epistemic authority. What constraints, if any, can be imposed on the gaze as it beholds its phenomena in all their material presence is an open question. Perhaps a longer look at our Greek sources prior to Plato will give us a better sense of an answer.

8 FROZEN MUSIC

The mind that is intent on plasticity often expresses in sculpture the sense of rhythm, the mental pulse. Plastic objects, though they are objects, often betray a tempo. Carving conception, on the other hand, causes its object, the solid bit of space, to be more spatial still. Temporal significance instead of being incorporated in space is here turned into space and thus is shown in immediate form, deprived of rhythm. (Adrian Stokes, *The Stones of Rimini* (1935))[90]

Pindar's eighth Paean: A founding myth of architecture

As a final test case for the various kinds of phenomenality that we have been exploring in this chapter and for the emergence of visual experience

---

[89] For one example, see the Nike sandal-binder (Nike temple parapet from the Acropolis, *c.* 410), a sculptural relief whose sensuous seductiveness is well noted in Osborne 1994, 85–86 and Stewart 1997, 148.

[90] Stokes 1978, 1:235.

in the aesthetic realm, let us consider Pindar's eighth *Paean*, which tells in a fragmentary way about the construction of the four mythical temples of Apollo at Delphi. The series begins with a first building that was made of laurel branches, then a second that was made of beeswax and feathers (as is known from Pausanias), followed by a third, built of bronze and gold by Hephaestus and Athena, and culminating in a fourth, built of stone by Trophonius and Agamedes, according to the story that was told about the building that burned down in 549 BCE.[91] A fifth, of marble, was said to have been built by the Alcmaeonids and dates to *c.* 510 BCE.[92] The sixth, which stands at Delphi today, is a later construction made of Corinthian *poros*, or black limestone. Traces of the fourth and fifth buildings are still visible today. Pausanias finds elements of the legends about the third temple dubious (though, ever the discerning skeptic, he is persuaded by the other three stories): "It cannot be improbable that Apollo should have had a temple made of bronze. However, as to the rest of the legend, I do not believe that the temple was a work of Hephaestus, nor the story about the gold songstresses [viz., wrynecks, the birds perched up on high on the temple] which the poet Pindar mentions in speaking of this particular temple [*Pae.* 8.68–71]. Here, it seems to me, Pindar merely imitated the Sirens in Homer." Pausanias goes on to ponder the stories of the temple's disappearance, this time without casting a verdict of his own: "Some say it fell into a chasm in the earth, others that it was melted down by fire."[93] The relevant verses from Pindar follow (they are preceded by a hiatus):

> Charmers [viz., wrynecks][94]
> temple. The one [viz., the second temple] a furious wind
> brought to the Hyperboreans ...
> O Muses. But of the other [viz., the third], what *rhuthmos*
> was shown (τίς ὁ ῥυθμὸς ἐφαίνετο)
> by the all-fashioning skills (παντέχνοις παλάμαις)
> of Hephaistos and Athena?
> The walls were of bronze and bronze
> columns stood in support (χάλκεοι μὲν τοῖχοι χάλκ[εαί
>   θ' ὑπὸ κίονες ἔστασαν),
> and above the pediment

[91] Cf. schol. Lucian *Dial. mort.* 77.10.1.
[92] Hdt. 5.62.
[93] Paus. 10.5.12; trans. Frazer.
[94] Following Maehler 1989, who prints Ἰυγ[γ (post Snell). Rutherford 2001, 211 prints τυ[.

sang six golden Charmers (Κηληδόνες).
But the children of Kronos split open
the earth with a thunderbolt
and hid (ἔϰρυψαν) that most holy of all works,

in astonishment at the sweet voice
because strangers were perishing
away from their children
and wives as they suspended their hearts
    on the honey-minded song ...
the man-releasing contrivance(?) (δαίδαλμα)
of undamaged ... to the virgin ...
and Pallas put (enchantment?)
into their voice and Mnemosyne
    declared to them
all the things that are
and happened before ...
... deception (δόλον)[95]

The verses present a (literally) charming set of myths about the arts of building and music-making, strangely intersecting in a poem that is itself sung, in all likelihood carefully architectonic, and by a poet eager to vie, as is well known, with monumental artists.[96] As Ian Rutherford drives home in his commentary on the poem, "No other poem in praise of a temple is known from classical Greece, but they are found in the Near East."[97] And so we have here a special poem indeed. The key verse for us is 67, τίς ὁ ῥυθμὸς ἐφαίνετο, "What *rhuthmos* appeared [on the temple's façade]?" For *rhuthmos* we may understand "arrangement" (Race) or "pattern, shape" (Rutherford) or, more in keeping with the musical surroundings of the verse and the root meaning of the word itself, "movement" as imparted by song and captured in stone.[98] Though the German Romantics are remembered for the apothegm, "Architecture is frozen music," the thought was first suggested by the Greeks, as we can now see.[99]

---

[95] Pind. *Pae.* 8.62–87; trans. Race, adapted: I have included verse 87, which is not given by Race.
[96] See Ch. 9 below.
[97] Rutherford 2001, 214.
[98] Rhythm in the technical sense of musical rhythm is not attested before the late fifth century. For *rhuthmos* as movement, see, e.g., Aesch. *Cho.* 797. On *rhuthmos* and its connection to *eurhuthmia* in architectural contexts, see Schlikker 1940, 81–95, esp. 83. On its dynamic meaning in Greek generally, see Petersen 1917, 11; Schweitzer 1932, 11; Fritz 1938, 25–26; Benveniste 1971; Thomas 2007, 209; Chantraine 2009, s.v. ῥυθμός. Slater (s.v.) gives "symmetry" (citing this passage, the only occurrence of the word in Pindar).
[99] The modern phrase first appears in F. Schlegel, evidently already as a quotation, and then in similar variants in Goethe, Görres, and Schelling. Its exact origins are untraceable. See Saleh Pascha 2004.

Exactly what Pindar meant by the expression is not entirely clear, nor need he have meant any one thing in particular: his language is suggestive, and that is all that may matter in a poem.

Hanna Philipp offers the following interpretation of the passage:

The accent of the word *rhuthmos* lies ... on the optical impression, [which is to say] on the way the columns rise up and bear the temple, and over which the gables rest, adorned with the sirens. That is, *rhuthmos*, understood here as 'quiet movement,' is being is referred not to a statue or a stationary image, but rather to the totality of a building, and thus points to its inner movement, to the way this movement lets itself be read off the interrelations of the individual parts of the building.[100]

Something like this may well be right. It may be true that with this verse Pindar is expressing what Dewey would later say about architecture, namely that "it expresses [the] characteristic effect [of 'natural forms, arches, pillars, cylinders, rectangles, portions of spheres'] upon the observer," and above all "the natural energies of gravity, stress, thrust, and so on."[101] The Greek language can capture this dynamic quality through a series of terms, one of which we encountered earlier under the rubric of *entasis* ("swelling" or "tension"), but which can also be described as "the most vigorous expression of the 'activity' produced by the individual parts of the structure, both the load-bearing parts and the sections that are themselves supported."[102]

Whether or not Pindar had such effects as these in mind, what seems clear enough is that for him the rhythm or pattern of the building's form is a function of its external visual appearance, much the way the term *rhythm* is used in architectural descriptions today.[103] His insight comes far too early to do anything but disturb the neat chronologies of the progressivist scheme, but soon enough to confirm the contrasting intuition that art and visual (as opposed to tactile) impressions go hand in hand.[104]

However, the parallelism between music and architecture was a going concern starting with the Renaissance, e.g., with Alberti, right through to Kayser 1958, a strange book that overenthusiastically attempts to read ancient harmonics off the architectural design of Paestum (but in passing documents the same obsession, historically, and usefully). Evidently, similar methods have been applied to the Parthenon (Bulckens 1999; *non vidi*). I owe the reference to Kayser to John Franklin.

[100] Philipp 1968, 47.

[101] Dewey 1989 [1934], 225.

[102] Haselberger 1985, 131. *Entasis* comes from the verb ἐντείνω, which means "to stretch, exert vigorously, strain," etc.

[103] See Wilson Jones 2001, 693: "the rhythm of the flank elevation"; similarly, ibid., n. 79.

[104] This passage does in fact force quick concessions in Protzmann 1972–73, 89 n. 132.

But visuality (Philipp's "*optisch*") is too restrictive a term by itself, and it conflicts with the powerful sense of movement that *rhuthmos* implies. Whether "gravity, stress, thrust, and so on" are involved in the perception evoked by Pindar is harder to say, though the strong sense of soaring verticality in his imagery is undeniable, given the bronze walls, the supporting bronze columns standing upright, with the pediment above, upon which perch the six golden Charmers, before all this plunges into an abyss below. The tactile sense is co-involved, activated along with the visual sense as the eye scans the monument in its built, material dimensions – presented as solid and palpable – and takes in its Daedalic rhythms. Those rhythms turn imperceptibly into music, the song of the six golden Charmers.[105] And just when they do, the monument comes crashing down, in one traumatic act of devastation, then disappears forever, only to be resurrected once again in song – Pindar's own.

There is a seductiveness to this kind of rhythming of the gaze, which also accounts, mythically, for the destruction of the second temple of Apollo. As if to counteract the overly seductive nature of the monument, which caused onlookers to suspend their movements and to come to a standstill, frozen by music into an architectural pose (caught "in astonishment" or "marvel" and "suspend[ing] their hearts on the honey-minded song"),[106] the Olympians caused the temple to fall into mysterious ruin. Thus does the temple, so long as it exists (or is held steady in the imagination), fulfill the third of the aesthetic criteria mentioned above, namely deception, in the sense described, by obliging absorption, rapture, seduction of the eye and ear (the songstresses are, after all, "Bewitchers," "Deceivers," or "Beguilers," and equated in later tradition to Sirens).

The interdisciplinary arts of measure

To be sure, all this remains on the level of myth and virtual description, which does not make it any less valuable as an index of late archaic sensibilities to spatial and visual phenomena in art. The striking phrase, "What *rhuthmos* was shown by the all-fashioning skills of Hephaistos and Athena?," suggests an attunement that would appear astonishingly

---

[105] The moment of transition is moreover marked, or rather disguised, by a verbal assonance that runs across 70–71: αἰετοῦ | ἄειδον ("pediment | sang").

[106] The effect is still stronger on another rendering: "hanging up their spirit as a dedication to the sweet voice" (...μελ[ί]φρονι αὐδ[ᾷ] | θυμὸν ἀνακρίμναντες, 78–79; trans. Rutherford 2001, 213).

"modern" (Philipp), were it not for the fact that there is a way of connecting the phrase back to the early language of architectural design, albeit speculatively. The basic building block of ancient architecture was the dactyl, a unit of measure (one-sixteenth of a Greek foot) upon which the underlying dimensions and proportions of buildings were constructed. It is unclear when this unit of measure first came into existence and even less clear what, if any, links it may have enjoyed with the dactyl of prosody, which was used to measure meter and rhythm (terms likewise of uncertain origin, though firmly attested by the latter half of the fifth century).[107] The archaeological evidence of the third century BCE points to a well-developed use of schematics by architects deploying dactyls to measure the proportions – the rhythms, so to speak – of buildings, for instance in the temple of Apollo at Didyma, the most spectacular example of its kind, where these designs were traced directly onto the walls of the construction site. (They are legible at Didyma primarily because the project remained unfinished.)[108] As in poetry, dactyls combined into "feet." It is notable that two metrological reliefs in marble, one probably from Samos in the fifth century BCE and another repeated at Salamis in the fourth century, show the figure of a man with his arms outstretched, palms open (palms being another measuring unit), and a foot impressed above his right arm (see figs. 8.9 and 8.10). He is plainly a kind of Vitruvian man *avant la lettre*.[109]

The prehistories of both sciences of mensuration, poetic and architectural, are murky, and both may reach back into the late archaic era.[110] Manuals and models by master builders are attested for the sixth and early fifth centuries, which is to say, pretty much as soon as Greek prose came into existence. Vitruvius records the names of architects who contributed to this early tradition: Theodorus and Rhoicus, Chersiphron, Metagenes, and others.[111] Two of these were also sculptors, and it seems likely, as J. J. Pollitt points out, that they would have translated their own concerns for architectural *summetria* (mathematical harmony) into or out of concerns for sculptural

---

[107] Cf. Ar. *Nub.* 638 (418–416 BCE): πότερον περὶ μέτρων ἢ περὶ ἐπῶν ἢ ῥυθμῶν; cf. ibid., 647–51: [ῥυθμὸς] κατὰ δάκτυλον; and Ar. *Ran.* 1323 (405 BCE): πούς; Dover ad loc.; Pl. *Lach.* 197d and *Rep.* 3.400a–c (on Damon's use of the term *pous* in Socrates' day); Cole 1988, 10–11; 220 at n. 309.

[108] See Haselberger 1980, Haselberger 1983, and Haselberger 1985 (an accessible account in English).

[109] For discussion and reconstruction of the Salamis figure, see Wilson Jones 2000, esp. 83–85.

[110] Haselberger 1983, 26 connects the discoveries at Didyma with the earliest known design markings on buildings from the seventh and sixth centuries. The practice was also known earlier in Egypt and possibly imported from there.

[111] Vitr. 7.praef.12.

Fig. 8.9 Detail from metrological relief, probably from Samos, mid-fifth century BCE. Oxford, Ashmolean Museum.

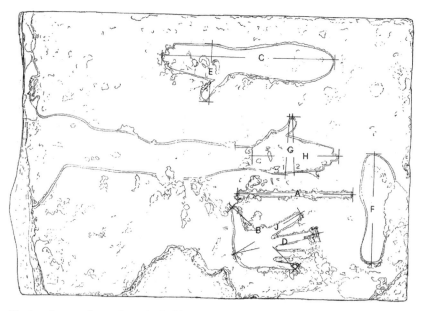

Fig. 8.10 Survey of metrological relief from Salamis. Fourth century BCE. Piraeus Museum no. 5352. Tracings and annotations by Manolis Korres and Mark Wilson Jones.

rhuthmos and *summetria*, terms that are attested, though late, for Pythagoras of Rhegium, an early predecessor to Polyclitus.[112] "The idea that there may

---

[112] Pollitt 1995; D.L. 8.47 (Pythagoras of Rhegium, as preserved by Xenocrates of Athens). On *summetria* as "mathematical harmony," see Wilson Jones 2000, 73 and Wilson Jones 2001, 695; 698. On this interconvertibility between sculptural and architectural mensuration, see generally Wilson Jones 2000 and Wilson Jones 2001, 699.

have been some connection between theories of design in architecture and sculpture is not at all implausible."[113] Nor, let us add, are the further connections between architecture and measured language or song all that implausible, as Pindar's eighth *Paean* already suggests, but not only there. In fact, starting with Pindar and Simonides, an entire tradition of "verbal architecture" and its associated metaphors comes into being, and it runs prominently through the rest of Greek and Roman literature, rhetoric, and criticism, from Cleobulus' Midas epigram to Horace's famous poetic *incipit*, *exegi monumentum aere perennius*. This aspect of material poetics will be developed in the next chapter.

For now, let us content ourselves with the observation that to contemplate the visual aspect of a monument is to appreciate its rhythm. But we needn't worry about whether putting the problem in this way is anachronistic. For there is good evidence that *rhuthmos* was indeed a term of art in ancient architecture, even if the attestations come late. *Eurhuthmia* is attested for the Hellenistic period, while verbs for motion can occur in architectural descriptions in later sources as well.[114] And *rhuthmos* itself is attested in a later fragmentary text on optics probably by Geminus (first century BCE), which must nonetheless reflect earlier architectural theory. (Note how especially the italicized portion – and, indeed, the whole passage – recalls both Plato's language in the *Sophist* and Lysippus' theory as reported by Pliny.)

Skēnographia is the part of optics that inquires into how one should draw images of buildings. *Since things do not appear as they actually are, buildings will display to beholders not the underlying rhythms* (μὴ τοὺς ὑποκειμένους ῥυθμοὺς ἐπιδείξονται), *but will be constructed as they will actually appear* (ἀλλ' ὁποῖοι φανήσονται ἐξεργάσονται). The goal of the architect is to make the work visually eurhythmic (τὸ πρὸς φαντασίαν εὔρυθμον ποιῆσαι τὸ ἔργον) and to discover what is needed to counteract the distortions [literally, "deceptions," ἀπάτας] of vision, not by aiming at [mathematical] equivalence or eurhythmy in accordance with truth, but at these things relative to [the way they appear to] vision.[115]

While the text helps to establish that *rhuthmos* sooner or later came to be a recognized technical term in ancient architecture, the parallel to Pindar might seem closer if the rhythms described were those displayed on the façade of a building. Instead, it looks as if *rhuthmos* here stands for

[113] Pollitt 1995, 20.
[114] See discussion in Schlikker (n. 98 above) for *eurhuthmia*.
[115] Gem.(?) *Opt.* 28.11–19 Schöne; emphasis added.

the underlying mathematical properties of a building, while their (corrected) appearances are its *eurhuthmia*. But in fact, Pindar's question, "What rhythm appeared on the façade of the temple?," is intelligible in terms of Geminus' framework: the temple's underlying rhythms could conceivably display themselves as eurhythmic on the superficies of the building, nor would their appearance by itself guarantee their mathematical equivalence to the temple's underlying architectural rhythms – how could you tell? This uncertainty could, moreover, be reflected in Pindar's question, which could be taken to have an anxious feel about it: "What *was* the rhythm that was shown on the temple's face?" Worse still, what if the building, which after all is divine and mysterious, had no other "rhythm" than the structure of a deception? At the very least, I would argue, that surface had (and continues to have) the structure of a perception.[116] And so too, either way we are confronted with a closely related topic that haunts any discussion of visuality in antiquity, namely that of appearance as deception or lure.

9 HIDING IN THE LIGHT: PERCEPTION, DECEPTION, ALLUREMENT

In tragedy and in painting, whoever deceives most ... is best. (*Dissoi Logoi* 3.10)

Pindar's eighth *Paean* brings to the fore the connection between phenomenality and deceptiveness that emerges so strikingly in the Platonic critique of appearances, whereby appearances are demoted to phantasms and the art concerned with their production is aligned with *apatē*. Deception is very much the hallmark of late fifth- and early fourth-century art and often said to be one of its greatest technical achievements, as the celebrated contest between the two Greek painters, Zeuxis and Parrhasius, was meant (or invented) to show. Let us recall the setting. Having learnt that Zeuxis had painted grapes so lifelike as to attract birds to his canvas, Parrhasius responded in kind by drawing a picture of a curtain. When Zeuxis requested that Parrhasius draw back the curtain to reveal the painting behind it, he soon perceived his error and declared Parrhasius the victor: for whereas Zeuxis had only deceived birds, Parrhasius had deceived an artist.[117]

---

[116] As such it would fall under a Lockean description; see Baxandall's account (n. 127 below).
[117] Plin. *HN* 35.4–6.

One point of the anecdote is of course that painting, while appearing to conceal something, in fact has nothing to conceal – apart from the fact that it has nothing to conceal. A further, related twist is that the truth of the image (its illusory status) is concealed by the absolute identity of the image with its own materiality, an identity that is normally interrupted by the conventions of painting: the curtain is the canvas on which the curtain is painted. As Jaś Elsner remarks, in Latin the word for both curtain and canvas is the same (*linteum*), and it is twice repeated in the passage from Pliny, first emphasizing the proximity of the surface of the curtain or canvas to, and then its distance from, the painting (*linteum pictum; remoto linteo ostendi picturam*). The surface is both the painting and the material condition of the painting which must be ignored ("removed") if the deception of the work of art as a work of art is to come about.[118] We may recall Socrates' thought-experiment in the *Gorgias à la* Gorgias: "Well then, if one stripped away from the whole composition [of tragedies] the melody, the rhythm, and the meter, does it turn out that what's left is only speeches?"[119] Here, in the case of the *linteum pictum*, we find as it were a response to this kind of separatism: the urge to strip away the materiality of the artwork would leave nothing behind, aesthetically and literally. In a sense, Parrhasius' gesture appears to enact Plato's urge and yet proves Parrhasius to be anti-Platonic at one and the same time: it proves the ultimate futility of the Platonic urge.[120]

Pindar's poem enacts a similar kind of hide-and-seek with its audience. For where the third temple to Apollo is said to disappear forever, only to be resurrected in song once again, Pindar hints at a connection between the song and the temple that needs to be teased out further. The temple is said to have been "hidden" (ἔκρυψαν), rather than "buried," by the Olympians, leaving ambiguous whether it was ever truly destroyed. To extract the true force of *hidden* here, one has to recognize that there is in fact nothing to hide, because in telling the story Pindar is both creating the hidden object and the place in which to hide it – namely, his poem (and all the more so if Pindar is creating the myth he tells out of whole cloth, as seems likely).[121] Or, to anticipate the Homeric stratagem concerning the Achaean wall as Aristotle would later construe it (see next chapter), one can say that, since it was Pindar who "made" the temple, he

---

[118] *Traditur ... ipse [Parrhasius] detulisse linteum pictum ita veritate ut Zeuxis ... flagitaret tandem remoto linteo ostendi picturam.* See Elsner 1995, 89–90.
[119] Pl. *Grg.* 502c; trans. Zeyl, slightly adapted.
[120] For a superb reading of the contest between Zeuxis and Parrhasius, see Bann 1989, 32–36.
[121] See Rutherford 2001, 217 for the suggestion that Pindar has created this myth, unknown from any other early source.

could make it vanish again – with Pindar (like Homer) all the while conceding between the lines that his construct never actually existed to begin with. The mention of *dolon* ("trick" or "deceit") in the same context, like the very idea of the Charmers luring men to their doom, reminds us that Pindar's tale is hardly an innocent one.[122] Pindar seems to be deliberately drawing on these lurid associations in order to color his own art of poetic creation. The question, "What *rhuthmos* appeared (on the temple's face)?" turns out to be not only difficult to translate, but a rather leading question with no clear answer after all – more of a teasing riddle than a self-evident description of an appearance, especially if the rhythm in question appeals to the ear and not only to the eye, or rather alludes to the poem's structure of appearances and not only to the building. But then, appearances in art are never entirely innocent, no matter what the medium.

Pindar's poem prompts the following general reflection on the connections between appearances and deception in art, which are rather more fraught than Plato's texts make them out to be, at least as these are conventionally read, and whenever they are narrowly historicized as pertaining to contemporary advances in artistic techniques. Above, I suggested that a seemingly inescapable connotation of phenomenality in art is not to be solved by the dilemma of the haptic or the visual but by that of art's deceptive qualities. *This* connotation of art was arguably available from as early as Homer. I want to show next how this was the case, but also how sensuous materiality played the role of co-conspirator, as it were, in this essential function of epic aesthetics.

Consider the brief description of Odysseus' brooch from the recognition scene in *Odyssey* 19:

> The pin ... was golden and fashioned (τέτυκτο)
> With double (διδύμοισι) sheaths, and the front part of it was artfully (δαίδαλον)
> done: a hound held in his forepaws a dappled (ποικίλον)
> fawn, preying on [or "gazing at": λάων] it as it struggled; and all admired (θαυμάζεσκον) it,
> how, though they were golden, it preyed on [or "gazed at": λάε] the fawn and strangled it
> and the fawn struggled with his feet as he tried to escape him.[123]

---

[122] For an aetiological reading of the Charmers as prefiguring the Pythian priestesses who continue to live on, literally "inspiring" the priestesses with vapors from the chasm at Delphi, see Rutherford 2001, 228–29.

[123] *Od.*19.226–31; trans. Lattimore 1965.

This ecphrastic moment has naturally attracted attention to itself: such is its self-designating purpose. But the passage stands out as an unusually intense and compressed example of its kind. Concerning itself with artistry *and* with the admiration of art, the passage is also oddly folded in upon itself, doubling the frames by which its imagery is taken in: we stand outside, identified with an internal admiring audience, while the whole image is organized by a string of gazes trained upon gazes, especially if the verb λάων is to be rendered as "gazing at" rather than "preying on," as Raymond Prier argues in a striking reading of the passage and as Joseph Russo's commentary confirms independently of Prier.[124] Building on the work of Snell, Reinhardt, and others, Philipp goes so far as to find in the passage evidence of "a new mode of visuality" in the *Odyssey* relative to the *Iliad*: for the first time, the viewer is directly faced with an object and drawn into its field of vision with a kind of immediacy that is unparalleled in the earlier *Iliad*.[125]

We would seem to be in the realm of the *optisch* again, or rather too soon. The liveliness of the image – it is Daedalic, after all – is a sure sign that visual and technical *apatē* is at work. But this sense of vivacity is belied by the deadliness of the act that is being described. Indeed, as Prier nicely puts it, "the hound strike[s] the fawn into a certain inactivity through the agency of his gaze." Visuality here is the realm of aesthetic pleasure, vivacity, and death all at once. These heightened contrasts and the complicity of gazes inside and out – the fawn's gaze meeting the hound's, the inner viewers', and our own voyeuristic gazes, and these last two both struck by wonder into a certain inactivity through the agency of the gaze (or at least this is the fiction of the scenario that we are being asked to subscribe to momentarily – wonderment, after all, is an active and participatory practice and a convention) – are themselves further evidence that deception is active in the splendid phenomenality of the work of art that is the brooch of Odysseus' and in the word artistry that is the poem of Homer's. Both objects are in one sense inanimate, yet both radiate *poikilia*. Their materiality is doubled, like the twofold (διπλῆν) cloak of Odysseus' onto which the brooch is pinned (225): they are inanimate lumps of matter (gold, sounds), and then they are shining textured things, capable of aesthetic effects.

---

[124] Prier 1989, 32; Russo in Heubeck *et al.* 1988–92, III:89.
[125] Philipp 1968, 10–11.

One did not have to wait, in other words, until Plato to realize that phenomenality could act as a lure, or that sensuous appearances and realities could come into conflict in their competitive solicitation of the viewer's attention.[126] For all the violent overtones of the imagery here in Homer or in Pindar's eighth *Paean*, there is nothing necessarily nefarious about visuality in art. There is something powerful, in each case, about the immediacy of the impact as the observer confronts the object in its sheer facticity, phenomenality, and luminosity. Appearances, *to phainesthai*, are coded as awe-inspiring in Homer and in much of archaic poetry, and the idiom persists into the classical era as well. But appearances are manifold, not simple, and their apparent immediacies are the end-product of an involved cultural process. Immediacy of impact is itself a deceptive effect of art and one of its oldest, if most varied, conventions. Generalizing, we can say that deception through sensuous appearances can occur on three levels of visual experience:

(i) the mere transformation of marks on a medium into recognizable shapes through the trained habit of visual and mental judgment enacts a fundamental "deception" of the eye that, once trained, becomes habitual and forgotten in the act (lines and colors become recognizable objects in the world while remaining mere lines and patches of color);

(ii) more advanced forms of graphic representation (perspective, shading, viz., *skēnographia, skiagraphia*, etc.) induce more refined forms of illusion tied closely to each of these techniques;

(iii) more generally, there is an aesthetic experiential component, what I am calling displacement of everyday reality through allurement and absorption (e.g., the "Daedalic" effects mentioned earlier).

Art historians in Riegl's wake too reductively attach "the optical" to deception in sense (ii) of visual experience. They thereby overlook the more basic significance of visual experience in sense (iii), and the still more primary significance of sense (i), which in turn can be related to a still more primary activity, and which therefore deserves to be numbered (i′):

[126] Gombrich 2000, 132–33 takes the same image from *Od.* 19 to be iconic of the beginning of "the rise of Greek art" and as a radical break from "the pre-Greek Orient" – a quite different point from my own.

(i′) translating the chaos of raw sense impressions into conventionally
understood representations of objects, a process that typically attracts
the attention of empiricist philosophers, for example Locke in his
analysis of perception, and virtually all the Presocratics, though not
necessarily under the rubric of deception, though sometimes it does
fall under this rubric, for example, in the eyes of Parmenides and
Heraclitus, both of whom label appearances (τὰ φαινόμενα) a form
of deception (ἀπάτη).[127]

It should be stressed that mimetic qualities are not highlighted in any of
these categories, apart, perhaps, from the second. But even there, mimesis –
copying reality – is not a primary concern. Perspectival effects wrought on
a statue, of the sort that are described in Plato's *Sophist* (235a–236c), do
not involve representation, copying, or mimicry. They involve compensation for the distortive effects of height and distance from a given viewing
position. And what the viewer finally sees is not the lifelike representation
of a natural object's qualities, but the truer representation of an object's
own qualities, or else a more harmonious representation of what a subject's perception ought to be. The same techniques translated into
painting are of course another matter, and are closer to mimesis in the
conventional sense. But what the two sets of techniques share, whether in
sculpture or in painting, is not mimesis *per se* but the deception of the eye,

---

[127] DK 28B23.9 (Parmenides); DK 22B56 (Heraclitus). Locke's account also covers senses (i) and (ii):
"We are further to consider concerning perception, that the ideas we receive by sensation are
often in grown people altered by the judgment, without our taking notice of it. When we set
before our eyes a round globe, of any uniform colour, e.g. gold, alabaster, or jet; it is certain that
the idea thereby imprinted in our mind, is of a flat circle variously shadowed, with several
degrees of light and brightness coming to our eyes. But we having by use been accustomed to
perceive what kind of appearance convex bodies are wont to make in us, what alterations are
made in the reflections of light by the difference of the sensible figures of bodies; the judgment
presently, by an habitual custom, alters the appearances into their causes; *so that from that which
is truly variety of shadow or colour, collecting the figure, it makes it pass for a mark of figure, and
frames to itself the perception of a convex figure and an uniform colour; when the idea we receive
from thence is only a plane variously coloured, as is evident in painting*" (*Essay Concerning Human
Understanding*, book 2, ch. 9, sec. 8). As Baxandall 1985, 95 so well puts it, on Locke's theory,
"a picture is thought of not as a representation of substance ... but as a representation of an act
of perception of substance." See Baxandall, ibid., 74–104 for a deeper analysis of Lockean ideas
as applied to painting. To be sure, in contrast to the ancients, some moderns (Constable;
Gombrich 2000, e.g., xxxiv–xxxv; 38) would reject the use of the term *deception*, especially in
aesthetic contexts, and would favor *illusion* instead. Others, however, readily embrace deception
(e.g., Nietzsche; Barthes; Kermode 1974, esp. 114–15).

blinded, as it were, by phenomena.[128] And here, Plato's analysis is apt. In a word, deception and mimesis need not inhabit the same universe of phenomenological experience: the feeling of being lured into a deception and that of being lured by a copy are not necessarily overlapping experiences. The former feeling is closer to the nature of perception generally, while the latter is a special case and, from the point of view of sensuous aesthetics, not even the most interesting one at that.

---

[128] Cf. Longinus: "As fainter lights disappear (ἐναφανίζεται) when the sunshine surrounds them, so the sophisms of rhetoric are dimmed when they are enveloped in encircling grandeur. Something like this happens in painting: when light and shadow are juxtaposed in colours on the same plane, the light seems more prominent to the eye, and both stands out and actually appears much nearer. Similarly, in literature, emotional and sublime features seem closer to the mind's eye .... Consequently, they always show up above the figures, and overshadow and eclipse their artifice" (*Subl.* 17.2; trans. Russell).

PART III

Broader Perspectives

CHAPTER 9

Sublime monuments in ancient aesthetics

> In my view, however, speaking well and writing well are one and the same thing, and a written speech (*oratio scripta*) is nothing but the record (*monumentum*) of a spoken pleading (*actionis habitae*).
>
> Quintilian, *The Orator's Education* 12.10.5 (trans. Russell)

> There [in the mystery of words],
> As in a mansion like their proper home,
> Even forms and substances are circumfused
> By that transparent veil with light divine,
> And, through the turnings intricate of verse,
> Present themselves as objects recognised,
> In flashes, and with glory not their own.
>
> Wordsworth, *The Prelude*, Book 5, 599–605 (1850 [1805], pp. 131–32)

The present and final chapter will trace the nexus between three themes in ancient aesthetic inquiry and reflection: verbal artistry, the art of building, and the sublime. Their conjunction produces a distinctive sort of monumentality, one that in its grandeur, in its material construction, and in its palpable and sensuous qualities is exemplary of what I have occasionally referred to in this study as the material sublime. Their concrete instances – be they sepulchral verse inscriptions, epinicians, historical commemorations, accounts, whether in rhetorical and literary criticism, of verbal structures or even of mere breath (what I will be calling "sound sculpture"), or finally images of structures on the verge of collapse or in ruin wherever these may appear – may be designated as *sublime monuments*. My starting point, however, will be on a more modest and programmatic level, namely the early convergence of poetry and objects, whereby poetry, conceived as something seen, heard, or imagined, takes on a thinglike character, while the object world proves to be closely bound up with the aesthetic functions of poetic language.

I 'LA PAROLE ET LE MARBRE'

Poetics and monumental architecture enjoy a close, but insufficiently scrutinized, relationship in classical thought. Poets and literary critics frequently describe literary works as a kind of monument, and architects repay the compliment by describing, whether through words or stone, what is in essence a kind of visual poetry. We might call this the theme of *la parole et le marbre*, following Jesper Svenbro's seminal and still unsurpassed work of the same title.[1] The connection highlights what Svenbro, in a key and concluding section of his book, labels "the 'materiality' of the poetic word."[2] Svenbro's thesis, in its broader implications for the history of aesthetics in antiquity, is powerful and attractive. It is that the lyric poet Simonides of Ceos (*c.* 556–468) ushered in a novel conception of poetics. According to Svenbro, the various features of this new poetics have to be taken as an ensemble. It was a distinctly literary, as opposed to oral, poetics, consciously organized around the written word and therefore around a sensitivity to the difference between the two diverging modalities of production and reception: orality and writing. It conceived its objects (written verses) as material products that vied for attention with those of craftsmen and artisans (painters and sculptors) – whence "the *'materiality'* of the poetic word." But it also conceived of poetry on an economic model, as works made for sale and (in a Marxist terminology) as commodities of the alienated labor of the poet, in contrast to the earlier and traditional system of gift-exchange which had governed relations between patrons and artists – whence an additional sense in which *materiality* is brought to bear in this new poetics of the late archaic and early classical eras. Henceforth, poems circulate in the public sphere as things endowed with fungible value but also with a value that would at times claim for itself a kind of autonomy. Always more and less than words, poems are *uncertain* objects, contesting the very notion of what a thing is or ought to be.

On this view, Simonides emerges as a highly self-conscious artist, occupying the transitional cusp between writing technologies, economies, and large-scale social changes (the rise of the *polis* and the decline of the older aristocracy).[3] Some of this self-consciousness can be used to explain his poetic self-awareness and to generate an account of his poetic inventions. Alienated from his own products, Simonides must stand in

[1] Svenbro 1976.   [2] Svenbro 1976, 186–212; "*la 'matérialité' de la parole poétique*," 188; cf. ibid., 155–57.
[3] Cf. Carson 1999; Kurke 1999b; Day 2000, 50–51.

a peculiar relation to them: poems are now for the first time truly "objects," even if – or because – their value is open to negotiation. Thus, Svenbro can say, "face à une culture étrangère, Simonide découvre la spécificité de sa parole."[4] That specificity is in the first instance material, but as we saw *material* has different senses here, whether pertaining to the qualities of an object, an artifact, or the circumstances of economic commoditization. But there is more. The ancient biographical tradition assigns a string of "firsts" to Simonides: the inventor of four letters of the Greek alphabet and of the arts of memory, he also seems to have added a third note (that is, eighth string) to the lyre.[5] And modern scholars have followed suit in awarding him various primary achievements in their literary histories. Thus, Simonides is "Western culture's original literary critic, for he is the first person in our extant tradition to theorize about the nature and function of poetry,"[6] "the first witness to the theory of the image,"[7] the discoverer of the literary epigram and therefore of literature in the proper sense of the word,[8] the first poet to sell his work, and the first materialist of language.[9]

Whether or not these attributions are right (the last of these is the most tendentious), there is no denying that Simonides does stand in a peculiar relationship to the material character of his words, while the parallels in Pindar (*c.* 518–*c.* 438) suggest that a new and distinctive mode of attention to poetic language was indeed emerging around the turn of the fifth century. A fragment tentatively assigned to Simonides by Lasserre, but in any case stemming from the ambit of early choral lyric, reads, "I sculpt a measure" (μέτρον διαγλύφω).[10] The thought is striking, but also

---

[4] Svenbro 1976, 186.   [5] See West 1992, 344 on this last innovation.   [6] Carson 1999, 46.
[7] Detienne, cited in Svenbro 1976, 156.   [8] Raubitschek 1968, 3; 5.
[9] Svenbro 1976, e.g., 198: "Si Homère n'attribue aucune 'matérialité' à son proper discours (comme le font les poètes choraux) . . . ," viz., in the wake of Simonides.
[10] *P. Berol.* 9571ᵛ col. 2.55 Schubart; Lasserre 1954, 48. The reading is in fact [μέ]τρον δ(ια)γλύφω. Simonides' name was conjectured by Schubart 1941 at line 53 (ibid., 28) and in col. 1.17 by Lobel, who hypothesized that the papyrus was a learned commentary on Pindar which also drew on other contemporary lyric poets. As Schubart explains (ibid., 28), "Das Zitat umfaßt nur μέτρον διαγλύφω; der Dichter wird durch διαγλύφω wie vorher durch ἀναπλάττειν mit dem Bildhauer verglichen." A precise parallel is to be found later in Ar. *Thesm.* 986: τόρευε πᾶσαν ᾠδήν, "Drill [or 'emboss'] all [parts] of your ode." Austin and Olsen ad loc. suggest "make elaborate" for τόρευε (and refer the expression to the accompanying dance rather than to the song) but recognize that the metaphor is drawn from metalwork (*toreutikē*). Cf. τὰ δὲ τορνεύει, "[Agathon] is chiseling some bits [of his verses]," ibid., 54 (cit. Ch. 5, at n. 31 above); and Ar. *Ran.* 819: "slivers [or 'splinters'] (σχινδάλαμοι) of linchpins [or 'audacious quibbles'] and carvings of works" (σμιλεύματά τ' ἔργων), said with reference to the contest brewing between Aeschylus and Euripides. An intriguing echo appears in [Plut.] *Vit. Hom.* 216: "He [sc., Homer] sculpted in the medium of language" (ἀνέπλασε δὲ τῇ ὕλῃ τῶν λόγων), which follows on the heels of Simonides' "silent poetry" dictum, quoted anonymously in the same passage.

ambiguous. Is the allusion to the incision of a (reed) pen on a writing surface, the appearance – the sculpted look – of a *metron* within a verse on a page, the visual impact of sculpted images projected by verses in the mind, or merely an analogy to the artisanal craftsmanship of poetry writing, laying claim to a value equal to that of a sculptor's own (and therefore demanding equal recompense, symbolic or other)? Any of these answers is possible, as further examples from the more secure parts of the Simonidean corpus can confirm. But there is no need to belabor the point: the ground has been gone over at great length since Svenbro.[11] What I want to do instead is to bring out a few additional features of this new, or rather newly heightened, materialist sensibility from the archaic era, especially those that will align it with developments to come in later periods.

I say "newly heightened," because as we have seen on several occasions already, and as others have noted (though more often in art-historical inquiry than in philology proper), there is abundant evidence of an attunement to the material dimensions of art and aesthetics from the Homeric poems onward. The single example of Odysseus' brooch from the recognition scene in *Odyssey* 19, discussed at some length in the previous chapter, should suffice to show this by itself, not to mention the long tradition of epigraphic verse inscriptions, to be discussed shortly. Further examples that might be adduced would include the introduction of inscribed poems, real and notional, during the archaic age – from signatures marking property and possession (as on the eighth-century cup of Nestor from Pithecusae) to the Theognidean *sphragis*, applied as if to seal "a physical object." The rise of the "poem as object" does indeed appear to have a traceable history during this era, long before Simonides.[12] The ecphrastic and epigrammatic traditions are exfoliations of the same phenomenon. And the lyric poets could feed off both traditions while giving them new force. What is more, scholarly attention to the poetic materialism of the lyric poets typically underestimates their achievement by neglecting their long-term impact. We have already seen how Isocrates sought "to leave behind a memorial ... for all time to come" (μνημεῖον εἰς ἄπαντα τὸν χρόνον), one that would serve as "a true image (εἰκών) of my thought and of my whole life ... and, at the same time, as a monument (μνημεῖον) after my death, more noble [or "finer": κάλλιον] than [votive] statues of bronze" (τῶν χαλκῶν

---

[11] Most recently by Carson 1999; Steiner 2001; Ford 2002, 93–112.
[12] This is the interesting subsidiary theme of Scodel 1992, who cites both these examples (quotations at pp. 75–76).

ἀναθημάτων).[13] Gorgias, Alcidamas, and Isocrates are all beneficiaries of the earlier tradition that Svenbro captured so well with his study of "*la parole et le marbre*," which is to say, the relationship between word-artists and sculptors which it would be an oversimplification to call a form of rivalry, even if this is how the lyric poets sometimes present matters.[14] That is, poets do appear to disparage the immobility of statues and the muteness of painting while vaunting the superiority of their own poetic medium, which, voiced and articulate, can travel unfettered across lands and seas. Thus, Pindar boasts in *Nemean* 5, as we saw,

I am no maker of statues,
no producer of figures who stand
motionless on their pedestal (οὐκ ἀνδριαντοποιός εἰμ', ὥστ' ἐλινύσοντα
    ἐργάζεσθαι ἀγάλματ' ἐπ' αὐτᾶς βαθμίδος ἐσταότ');
rather, on every ship, every bark
set sail, sweet song, going from Aegina
to say that Pytheas,
the mighty son of Lampon,
won the victor's crown in the pancration at Nemea.[15]

But as we shall see, their view is hardly as one-sided as it at first appears to be.

There is a further complication. On the one hand, though modern scholars are content to talk about a rivalry between lyric poets and sculptors, we have to reckon with the likelihood that this rivalry, if this is what it was, existed in the minds of the poets only – that it was a poetic fantasy useful for the purposes of self-promotion. On the other hand, no rivalry can have existed in those cases where the epigrammatist and the sculptor were identical, as in the case of three inscriptions from the mid-sixth century (*CEG* 14, 18, and 26), all by Phaedimus, a rather famous and self-assertive sculptor.[16] Not much given to modesty, he names his

---

[13] Isoc. 15.7; trans. Norlin. See Ch. 6 at n. 196 above.

[14] On Isocrates, see Steiner 2001, 278–81; on the same thematics surrounding Helen in Euripides and Gorgias, see ibid., 289. All three figures were discussed in Chs. 5 and 6 above. On this alleged rivalry, see esp. Svenbro 1976, 190–91; Segal 1986, 9–12, 153–64; Steiner 2001, 259–65, 280–1; Ford 2002, ch. 5.

[15] Pind. *Nem.* 5.1–5; trans. Cole in Gentili 1988, 163. Cf. Pind. *Isthm.* 2.45–46: "for I truly did not fashion [these hymns] to remain stationary [sc., like statues]" (trans. Race).

[16] On Phaedimus, see Dörig 1967; Deyhle 1969; Jeffery 1990, 63; 72–74; 111; Stewart 1990, 1:23; 1:120. Both Jeffery 1962, 151–54 (also Jeffery 1990 [1st edn. 1961], 63) and Deyhle (ibid., 51–53) observe that the signatures of Phaedimus, and so too the inscriptions on his works, seem to have been engraved by a professional or apprenticed letterer who also lettered others' works, not by Phaedimus himself – an intriguing finding, which does not, however, cancel out the sculptor as the effective author of his own works or epigrams.

Fig. 9.1 Inscription to a sculpture by Phaedimus, mid-sixth century BCE, from Vourva in Attica. (Athens, National Museum). Photo courtesy of David Gill. Only the plinth remains and the feet of the *korē* whose memory the monument preserves. The writing, preserved on a block of limestone marble, reads: "[…] had me built [as a monument] for his dear child, I a beautiful work to behold. Phaedimus made [me]" ([…] | με φίλες ː παιδὸς *vvvvv(v)* | κατέθεκεν ː καλὸν ἰδε̑ν | αϝὐτὰϱ ː Φαίδιμος ː ἐϱγάσαΙτο). (Text after *CEG* 18.)

handiwork "beautiful to see" (καλὸν ἰδε̑ν, fig. 9.1) and "beautiful" (καλόν) in two of these inscriptions, respectively (or else transfers the aesthetic quality of his own workmanship to that of the deceased). He was the first Attic sculptor to sign his work (another mark of self-esteem). And in one of these, he boasted, with good reason, that he was *sophos*, highly skilled in his work.[17] Could the coincidence of sculptor and poet within the epigraphic tradition, a rare but not unattested situation, have given rise to the poets' conceit to begin with? Or was it the sculptor who was encroaching on the poets' territory here (not that Phaedimus' verses amount to much more than a dedication posing as a poem), in which case the poets' outbursts have a defensive ring to them?[18] Even so, there is

---

[17] For discussion of Phaedimus' artistic production (all that can be inferred from it), see Richter 1961, 15; 24–25; Stewart 1990, 1:120; and previous note.

[18] We might note, too, the purely decorative function of so many early inscriptions, which suggests that writing could be co-opted *as lettering* for aesthetic purposes – another sign of encroachment. See below on the stoichedon style.

something futile about the dispute, however real or imaginary it may have been, for it appears that poets vied with one another and then sought lapidary fame in epigrammatic (elegiac) and possibly epitymbic contests, one reward for which was in fact monumental inscription.[19] Be that as it may, one of the most significant facts about this early classical motif (song versus stone) is also its most neglected aspect: its relative permanence in the ancient aesthetic and literary-critical traditions, well past the fourth century BCE and into the Roman imperial era.[20] We will want to explore these ramifications in later sections. But for now, let us return to the main purpose of the present chapter, which is to realign the innovation noted above – Simonides' so-called discovery of the object-oriented nature of poetry – with its traditionality, and then both of these with the materialist undercurrents of ancient aesthetic traditions and sensibilities. In the course of this realignment of tendencies we will inevitably encounter precursors to the Longinian sublime, read here in its materialist aspect.

In what must surely be Simonides' most discussed poem, his praise poem for the Thessalian dynast Scopas, which is partly preserved and analyzed in Plato's *Protagoras*, we find a monument in language that seems to meet all the criteria of the Longinian sublime in its stable (as opposed to its dynamic) aspect. The first three verses run as follows:

> It is difficult for a man to be truly good,
> in hands, in feet, and in mind,
> four-square, fashioned without flaw ...
> ἄνδρ' ἀγαθὸν μὲν ἀλαθέως γενέσθαι
> χαλεπὸν χερσίν τε καὶ ποσὶ καὶ νόῳ
> τετράγωνον ἄνευ ψόγου τετυγμένον ...[21]

Here, in the so-called Scopas poem, the virtuous man is fashioned (τετυγμένον) much as one would shape a statue, or the way Isocrates would project his image of himself in words. But what is significant in the poem, though it is not considered relevant to the Socratic discussion (which is concerned with meaning and not with artistry), is the way the verses reflect the statuesque qualities of the virtuous man. The verses are themselves statuelike, four-square, sturdy, and therefore, one suspects, they would meet with Longinus' approval, to judge from the criterion

---

[19] See Petrovic 2007, 18–19. Thus, Pindar's *Olympian* 7 was inscribed in golden letters and dedicated at the Hellenistic temple of Athena at Lindus on Rhodes (schol. Pind. *Ol.* 7) – an ironic wish-fulfillment of sorts.

[20] Though see Kassel 1991; and the glancing remark in Goldhill 2001a, 164.

[21] Simonides fr. 542.1–3 *PMG*; trans. Campbell, adapted.

of stability that is announced late in *On the Sublime* in the form of "a principle of particular importance for lending grandeur to our words":

The beauty of the body depends on the way in which the limbs are joined together (ἡ τῶν μελῶν ἐπισύνθεσις) ... Similarly the constituents of grandeur (τὰ μεγάλα) [viz., in language] ... if they co-operate to form a unity [lit., "if they form a body by their mutual association"] and are linked by the bonds of harmony (σωματοποιούμενα δὲ τῇ κοινωνίᾳ καὶ ἔτι δεσμῷ τῆς ἁρμονίας), they come to life and speak [lit., "they become speaking things"] (φωνήεντα γίνεται) just by virtue of the periodic structure [lit., "by virtue of being shut up in the very period"].[22]

Longinus goes on to cite a fragment from Euripides' *Antiope*:

> and where it could,
> [Dirce, being pulled about by the bull] writhed and twisted
>   round, dragging at everything,
> rock, woman, oak, juggling with them all.
> εἰ δέ που τύχοι
> πέριξ ἑλίξας ... εἶλχ᾽ ὁμοῦ λαβών
> γυναῖκα πέτραν δρῦν μεταλλάσσων ἀεί.[23]

He then comments on the architectural stability of the lines:

The conception [of the verses] is fine in itself, but it has been improved by the fact that the word-harmony [viz., the composition: τὴν ἁρμονίαν] is not hurried and does not run smoothly; the words are propped up by one another (στηριγμοὺς ἔχ[ουσι] πρὸς ἄλληλα τὰ ὀνόματα) and rest on the intervals between them (καὶ ἐξερείσματα τῶν χρόνων [sc., ἔχουσιν]); set wide apart like that, they give the impression of solid strength (πρὸς ἑδραῖον διαβεβηκότα μέγεθος).[24]

Elsewhere, too, Longinus compares words to statues:

The choice of correct and magnificent words is a source of immense power to entice and charm the hearer. This is something which all orators and other writers cultivate intensely. It makes grandeur, beauty, old-world charm [lit., "fine patina"], weight, force, strength (μέγεθος ἅμα κάλλος εὐπίνειαν βάρος ἰσχὺν κράτος), and a kind of lustre bloom (γάνωσίν τινα ... ἐπανθεῖν) upon our words as upon beautiful statues (ὥσπερ ἀγάλμασι); it gives things life and makes them speak (καὶ οἱονεὶ ψυχήν τινα τοῖς πράγμασι φωνητικὴν ἐντιθεῖσα).[25]

The concrete materiality of the image is striking: words all but sparkle in the light before one's eyes, and then they become enlivened, as if ensouled and endowed with a speaking voice (φωνητικήν). The convention of

---

[22] *Subl.* 40.1; trans. Russell, adapted.   [23] *Subl.* 40.4 = Eur. *Antiop. TrGF* 221; trans. Russell.
[24] *Subl.* 40.4; trans. Russell.   [25] *Subl.* 30.1–2; trans. Russell.

speaking objects is an ancient one. But so too is the image of vigorous and heavy-set language that is monumental in its presentation to the mind, the eye, and the ear. In order to connect up the dots that stretch over the centuries – for we are having to do with a conscious tradition here – we will need to go back to Simonides again.

The first three verses of the Scopas ode present a statuesque image of a virtuous man, as we saw. Indeed, they read like an illustration of the famous apothegm by Simonides, which announces an entire aesthetic outlook: "Words are an image [lit., an icon] of things" (ὁ λόγος τῶν πραγμάτων εἰκών ἐστιν).[26] The statement may be self-illustrating and itself iconic.[27] But it also anticipates Longinus' observation about the verses from Euripides' *Antiope*, with their clotted consonantal sounds (*perix helixas . . . heilch'* [πέριξ ἑλίξας . . . εἶλχ'] / *petran drun* [πέτραν δρῦν]) hindering the movement of the tongue and creating the impression (as he says) of foundational stones propped one on another:

andr' agathon/chalepon chersin
ἄνδρ' ἀγαθὸν/χαλεπὸν χερσίν

and especially

tetragōnon . . . tetugmenon
τετράγωνον . . . τετυγμένον.

Deborah Steiner's analysis of the Simonidean verses is spot-on: "First and foremost the poet calls attention to the object's fixed and unchanging nature as it stands firmly rooted to the spot where it is raised. The very sound and structure of the lines reinforce that impression of immobility: the assonant and ponderous *chi* in *chalepon* and *chersin*; the use of *t*'s and *g*'s (the one 'expressive of binding and rest in a place,' the other whose heavy sound 'detains the slipping tongue' [Plato, *Cratylus* 426d–427c])," and the balancing of two metrical blocks of echoing sounds on either flank of a stable base, *tetragōnon . . . tetugmenon*.[28] The apposite citation of Plato serves to remind us that the analysis by Longinus above is no mere whimsy of a later imperial writer: it has a pedigree that can be traced at least back to the time of Plato and Isocrates, and, in the light of Steiner's

---

[26] Simonides *ap.* M. Psellus, *De operatione daem. dialog.* 821B Migne = fr. 190b Bergk.
[27] For the statement as self-illustrating, see Carson 1999, 51–52. Adducing Herodotus 1.31, Svenbro 1976, 156 argues that *eikōn* includes statuesque and not only painterly depiction, while on p. 187 he adds a third connotation: "reflection" or "mirror image." (He might have added *CEG* 399(i) and 596: in inscriptions *eikōn* regularly connotes portrait sculpture.)
[28] Steiner 2001, 275.

euphonic analysis, a century earlier than that as well, if we accept as Simonidean the testimony from Psellus about words being an image (εἴκων) of things. Longinus could famously say about Simonides that he was unsurpassed in visualization (εἰδωλοποιία), and now we can see an additional reason why.[29] Longinus was doing more than paying tribute to a long-standing tradition that was encouraged by the sculptural and painterly program of Simonidean poetics ("Simonides calls painting silent (σιωπῶσαν) poetry and poetry a speaking (λαλοῦσα) painting").[30] With his comment, he was noticing the generally striking visual nature of Simonidean poetics: Simonides' verses are sculpted and hewn, and not only painted, a characteristic that Anne Carson has suggestively labeled his "iconic grammar."[31] And with his own advocacy of visual salience and architectural clarity in sentence structure, Longinus was himself drawing inspiration from the tradition that Simonides had helped to inspire.

I say "helped," because in fact Simonides was not alone in forging a new poetics of the material word. Pindar, as mentioned, was an energetic accomplice. Again, the ground has been carefully gone over before, and only a few details need to be highlighted here. Pindar frequently describes his own poetry in monumental terms, be these sculptural or architectonic. His poetry is a built edifice that resounds:

> A gold foundation has been wrought for holy songs.
> Come, let us now construct an elaborate
> adornment that speaks words ...
> κεκρότηται χρυσέα κρηπὶς ἱεραῖσιν ἀοιδαῖς·
> εἶα τειχίζωμεν ἤδη ποικίλον
> κόσμον αὐδάεντα λόγων[32]

Elsewhere, Pindar describes an ode as "a loud-sounding stone of the Muses," one he claims he knows how to "erect" (λάβρον ὑπερεῖσαι λίθον Μοισαῖον);[33] and in another poem he speaks (or rather sings) of "golden columns" of song:

---

[29] *Subl.* 15.7, where Simonides is singled out for having "depicted more vividly than anyone else (ἐναργέστερον εἰδωλοποίησε) the appearance of Achilles' ghost over his tomb at the departure of the Greek fleet" (trans. Russell, adapted).
[30] Plut. *Mor.* 346F.   [31] Carson 1999, 52 (in connection with Simonides).
[32] Fr. 194 Snell–Maehler; trans. Race.
[33] Pind. *Nem.* 8.46–48. For a defense of the reading, see Race's note ("Pindar compares his poem to a commemorative stele") and Ford 2002, 121 n. 35. Cf. Pind. *Pyth.* 6.7–17 for a comparable image – that of a "treasure house of hymns (ὕμνων θησαυρός) [which has been] built (τετείχισται) in Apollo's valley rich in gold" whose "front" (πρόσωπον) "will proclaim a chariot victory" "in clear light," etc. (trans. Race). Also *Nem.* 4.79–85, where Pindar likens his song once again to a (commemorative) stele "whiter than Parian marble."

Let us set up golden columns to support the strong-walled
   porch of our abode
and construct, as it were, a splendid [lit., "gazed at"]
palace; for when a work is begun, it is necessary to make
its front shine from afar.

Χρυσέας ὑποστάσαντες εὐτειχεῖ προθύρῳ θαλάμου
κίονας ὡς ὅτε θαητὸν μέγαρον
πάξομεν. ἀρχομένου δ' ἔργου πρόσωπον
χρὴ θέμεν τηλαυγές.[34]

These are bold architectonic analogies, thanks to which the poem becomes a
stand-in and a metonym for an imagined or actual object related to the
poem's occasion, present and future, and so (oddly) a metonym of a metonym: one can imagine the poem being performed before a temple, though the
poem *is* the temple that is being performed. The poem is thus literally
grounded in its circumstances of performance, while the truth of its image
of itself is renewed each time the poem is recited and reenacted. The poem
must, so to speak, be rebuilt on each occasion of its performance, while it
already looks ahead to its future performances throughout the Greek-speaking
world, as its "front" – its visible and audible "face" – "shines from afar."[35]

Pindar's poetry is full of such associations. Occasionally, these take on a
funerary character, as in *Isthmian* 8, where his encomium veers off into a
dirge for a certain Nicocles, a relative of the poem's *laudandus*, and the
poem thus momentarily becomes a virtual grave marker or monument
(μνᾶμα).[36] Simonides knew how to treat his verses in this way too, as in his
hymn to the dead at Thermopylae, where the poem is likened to a funeral
gift or burial shroud (ἐντάφιον) and then to a precinct (σῆκος) at a shrine
that encloses the glory (εὐδοξίαν) of the fallen.[37] Epitaphic poetry plainly
assumed this identification of words and objects as one of its conventions.
In Pericles' projective rhetoric, the tomb of the war-dead in Athens is both
"very conspicuous" (ἐπισημότατον) and also lastingly inscribed in the
"unwritten memory of their glory," namely as an echo of his own praise in
the Funeral Oration in which he said these things to be so in 430 BCE.[38] It
would seem that the very idea of monumental imagery creates the possibility for a further dynamic: that of writing as an echo chamber.

---

[34] Pind. *Ol.* 6.1–3; trans. Race. Further examples in Svenbro 1976, 190–91; Steiner 2001, 44–50, 251–94
(emphasizing sculptural monuments); Steiner 1993, 176; Ford 2002, 120–27.

[35] As Steiner 2001, 265 n. 52 notes, Pindar's songs did achieve this monumentality, at least some of the
time. See n. 19 above on the temple of Athena at Lindus on Rhodes.

[36] Pind. *Isthm.* 8.62. See Day 1989, 23–24.   [37] 531 *PMG*.

[38] Thuc. 2.43.2–3. Cf. Steiner 2001, 259.

2 VOICES MADE OF STONE: TOWARDS AN AESTHETICS OF EARLY SEPULCHRAL VERSE INSCRIPTIONS

The *epitaphios logos*, or funeral speech, is thus part of a tradition that reaches back into the archaic age. The high lyric and rhetorical genres are at the same time reflecting the lowlier practices of funeral inscriptions, a subset of *carmina epigraphica*, or inscribed poems, which are recorded from the middle of the seventh century onwards, which is to say, a century after the introduction of writing in Greece. These early inscriptions are marked by features that also mark the poems we have been examining so far. Both kinds of poem focus, above all, on presenting themselves as artifacts, indeed as monuments, that draw attention to their own visual and material presence. And they do so as objects that are intensely indexed by their individuality – which is to say, by their very indexicality (their quality of being "here" before a viewing subject). Whence the insistence, in sepulchral verse inscriptions, upon being "beautiful to behold" (καλὸν ἰδεῖν), "astonishing to look upon" (θαυμαστὸν προσιδῆν), "placed for all to see" (ἔθηκα ... τοῖς πᾶσι ἰδέσθαι), "far-shining" (τηλαυγές), as in Pindar, "made available (lit., 'manifest') for all to see" (τόδε τεῦξε ... | μνημεῖον θνητοῖς | πᾶσιν ὁρᾶν φανερόν), being "this (object) here" (τόδε), a "beautiful" (καλόν), "very beautiful" (περικαλλές), "pleasing" (χαρίεν, κεχαρισμένον), or "blameless" (ἀμενπhές [i.e., ἀμεμφές]) "dedicatory object," "ornament," or "(sculptural) image" (ἄγαλμα), an "artifact" (ἔργον), a "statue" (εἰκόνα), "monument," or "memorial" (μνῆμα), or a "gravestone" (σῆμα), one that is "beautifully made" (τουτ' [sc., σῆμα] ἐποίεσεν καλόν), "cunningly wrought" (τεχνήεσσα), and so on.[39]

An aesthetics of the archaic and classical verse inscription remains to be written.[40] The sepulchral verse inscription would be an ideal place to

[39] *CEG* 18; 19; 26; 67; 87; 93; 161; 165; 291; 311; 335; 348; 363; 399(i); 418; 422; 429 (τεχνήεσσα); 533; 624; 679; *IG* I³ 1214; *IG* XII Suppl. (1939), p. 100, no. 178 (χαρι-); cf. Karusos 1961, 18–19. Tombs placed on high ("on an acropolis," *CEG* 227) or "on the side of the road" (*CEG* 16; 28; 39; 74; etc.) or both (Croesus' monument, *CEG* 28; Day 1989, 22) likewise draw attention to their physical presence. (Note, however, that Croesus' monument does not call attention to its location, and surely many others do not either.) Cf. Wallace 1970, 100, nn. 14–15; Humphreys 1980, 103; Carson 1999, 78–85; Steiner 2001, 255–58.

[40] See Karusos 1972 [1941], lamenting the same lack. Karusos collects much the same data as here and combines them interestingly with adjacent arts, but his framework (according to which the καλὸν ἄγαλμα expresses a "mythical judgment," 96) and his overall historical thesis are to my mind unclear, in addition to suffering from a weakness still characteristic of work in this area, namely the desire to discern the "archaic mentality" of "archaic man." See more recently Robertson 1998, 109–13, investigating occurrences of καλός and χάρις (thanks to Dirk Obbink for this reference); Day 2000, 46–50.

start, for any number of reasons, some of which I will outline below. But whenever such a study comes into being, we can be sure that it will stand out thanks to its attention to material, sensuous, and phenomenal qualities, in agreement with Hanna Philipp's findings about archaic visual aesthetics as mentioned in Chapter 3 above – which is to say, it will be marked by a strong interest in the physical qualities of objects and their *facture*, as opposed to their formal organization. The reason lies partly in the nature of the genre, which was so heavily conditioned by the occasion, which, after all, revolved around life's brute materiality, and partly in the stark, thingly nature of the sepulchral epigram, as a pair of examples will make poignantly clear.

The first example dates from around 475 BCE, and it originally belonged to a bronze statue from Halicarnassus. While not a grave monument, it nonetheless sets the stage for the second example:

Voice wrought of stone (αὐδὴ τεχνήεσσα λίθο), say (λέγε), who
was it who erected this statue, gracing (ἐπαγλαΐ[σας]) the altar of Apollo?
Panamyes, son of Casbollis, if you urge(?) me on
to say it (ἐξειπἐν), dedicated this (as a) tithe to the god.[41]

The second example is of a much later date, and it was first paired with the above epigram as a comparandum by H. J. Rose in 1923.[42] The opening verses will suffice for our purposes, as they did for his. Unlike the previous epigram, which engages the passer-by in a dialogue, this poem is a kind of riddle in stone. It was composed by a *grammaticus* named Maximus, who was buried in Sebastopolis in Galatia (modern-day Anatolia), perhaps in the second century CE:

Earth bore me *voiceless* (ἄφων|ον) in the mountains, a virgin pure,
    formerly quiet (ἡσύχιον τὸ π|άροιθεν), *now chattering* to everyone
    (νῦν αὖ λαλέο[υ]|σαν ἅπασιν),
    telling (εἰ|ποῦσα) the heart of a dead man *through the chiseling arts*
    (σμιλιγλύ|φοις τέχνεσιν).[43]

Epigraphs point to the reification of objects and their revivification. Dead bodies are live bodies rendered as things. Grave monuments mark this

---

[41] *CEG* 429 (with different supplements and readings in the app. crit.).

[42] Rose 1923 = *IGR* 3.118 (1–11) = Peek 1955, no. 1184.

[43] *Epigr. Anat.* 13:71.15 = *IGR* 3.118 = Mitford 1991, 222 (no. 27). The grammarian was fairly learned, especially if κῆρ ε[ἰπ]οῦσα θανόντος is meant to echo Μενοιτιάδαο θανόντος | κῆρ ἄχεος μεθέηκα (*Il.* 17.538–39), a phrase that occurs once in Homer, and is embedded in an elusive syntax at that. Tim Whitmarsh suggests a possible allusion to the woodland nymph Echo and her chatter as well.

thingly quality of what a body now has become, but they also call to mind what the body once was.[44] The lettering on the stones and the aesthetic qualities of the monuments together endow the brute quality of the ensemble with another, memorable quality, which is what the voicings of the stones strain to capture, whether in a movement that passes from stone to voice, as in the case of Maximus, or the other way round, from voice to stone, as in the case of the Panamyes inscription. Either way, the movement is never one between outside and interior, for it always ends at the surface of a stone. Beauty, in this genre, is very much a matter of materiality.

As some of these examples already indicate, the emphasis in the inscriptions is frequently placed upon the labor and workmanship that went into the construction of the grave markers (τέτυκται, τεῦξε, ἐποίεσεν, πονέθε [= πονήθη], [ἀ]νέθηκεν ho τέκτον),[45] a fact that would have been visually underscored by the presence of striking ornamentation – "abstract floral designs, elaborate finials, sphinxes, bulls, lions, and other beasts, and unusually complex arrangements," not to mention the physical appearance of the inscriptions themselves. Sepulchral inscriptions would typically have been written in the so-called stoichedon style, which flourished from around the mid-sixth century to the end of the third century BCE. The style was notable for its grid pattern, which reinforced the lapidary qualities of the medium and the message and enhanced their overall aesthetic effect, though often at the expense of meaning, as the impression given was one of a stony mass of letters bordering on the indecipherable (fig. 9.2).[46] A question that is sometimes asked is what gave rise to this symmetrical lettering style, and the best answer available seems to be aesthetic considerations alone. The reasons advanced have tended to be of a purely formal, not material, sort: "feeling for beauty and order," "harmonious proportions and spacings," "clarity of the strokes," "roundness of the circles," and the like – all suspiciously familiar from

---

[44] On this quality of statues especially, adduced as examples of their "materialverhaftete Leblosigkeit," see Kassel 1991, 141 who cites the expressions "motionless," "impassive," "voiceless," "*taciturnius,*" "tickle a statue," and "wooden image: the insensate one" (βρέτας· ὁ ἀναίσθητος), all from Otto 1968, s.v. "*lapis* 2" (s.v. also "*statua,*" "*herma,*" etc.). (The last item, βρέτας· ὁ ἀναίσθητος, is a gloss by the Antiatticist on the comic poet Anaxandrides, fr. 11 K–A.) Cf. Kassel 1991, 151 on the later Hellenistic recrudescence of the same phenomenon of voiced objects, which as he rightly says has a tendency to emphasize "die Materialität und den Artefaktcharakter" of the objects in question.

[45] *CEG* 57; 106; 143; 152; 188; 548.8; cf. 778, etc.

[46] See Thomas 1989, 55 with n. 121; Walsh 1991, 96; Carson 1999, ch. 3; for background, see Austin 1938. The term *stoichedon* was apparently first applied by A. Boeckh in 1827 (*CIG* I, p. xviii; see Austin, ibid., 126, n.).

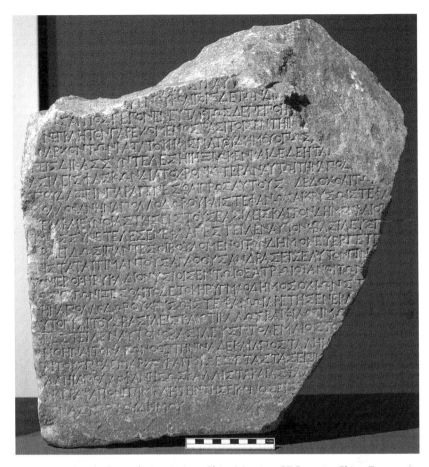

Fig. 9.2 Stoichedon-style inscription. Chios M006 = *SEG* 19 569. Chian Decree for Apollophanes, sent as judge by Ptolemy (Philadelphos?), first half third century BCE. Chios Archaeological Museum inv. 997. Photo courtesy of Charles Crowther.

inherited idealist classical aesthetics in loftier media.[47] Nevertheless, one could make a strong case for the materiality of these very same features: because the shapes of the letters are etched into the stone, their chiseled quality brings out the proximity of stone and letters, not the abstractness of the letter forms (see figs. 9.3–4). If so, then the stoichedon style merely brought out a feature that was inherent in all inscribed writing on stone – its

---

[47] See Austin 1938, 4–5; 5 n.; 8; 16; cf. 17; Hartel 1878, 161 cited ibid., 4. See also next note.

Fig. 9.3 Stoichedon-style inscription. *IG* I³ 19. Athenian proxeny decree for Acheloion,
c. 450/49 or 426/5 BCE.

pronounced palpability, a fact that the uses to which inscriptions were put
from the archaic period into the fourth century only served to underscore.[48]

A further outstanding feature of burial inscriptions was frequently one
of coloration: the letters could be painted in red or else in alternating red
and black lines, sometimes winding across the various faces of the larger

---

[48] See Thomas 1989, 45–57 on the (in her eyes, primary) iconic, material, visual, and symbolic
functions of public inscriptions in Athens, which, she argues, outweighed their semantic functions:
often, the "meer physical presence" of inscriptions as "material objects" – what we might call their
performative, material function – sufficed to convey their meaning, or rather their value (ibid., 49;
51; 57). Further arguments about the aesthetic origins and purpose of the stoichedon style: Turner
1952, 6 ("the best Athenian books might have been written in stoichedon," based on the oldest
known book, a copy of Timotheus' *Persians*; its letters are "epigraphic" in form); Raubitschek *ap.*
Immerwahr 1964, 45 ("calligraphic"); Immerwahr, ibid., about stoichedon lettering on vases
employed to aesthetic effect; Guarducci 1967–78, 1:447–51; Woodhead 1981, ch. 8; Thomas 1989, 51,
on stoichedon lettering's being endowed "with powerful non-written significance"; Thomas
1992, 88, on its "effect, especially in the high period of the Athenian empire, [being] highly
ornamental, impressive, and monumental"; see further Keesling 2003. One might compare
the aesthetic impact of Egyptian hieroglyphs (Assmann 1991, 25–26).

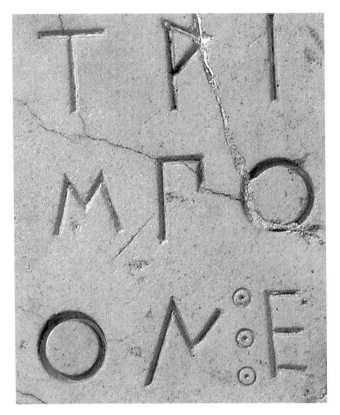

Fig. 9.4 Stoichedon-style inscription. Detail of the so-called Hekatompedon inscription (*IG* I³ 4), from the Athenian Acropolis, 485/4 (?) BCE. Photo by author.

monuments – all of which, combined with further aesthetic decoration, "betray[s] a desire to capture the eyes of wayfarers and overawe them with an impression of wealth and power."[49] We can recall how "inscriptions inherently emphasize the nature of the surface *as* surface,"[50] a point that, said of vase inscriptions, is no less true of their congeners on grave markers. Epitaphic sites are natural occasions for aristocratic displays and political manifestos, at least down to the 530s.[51] But they also are occasions for a harsh confrontation with a materiality of another sort. Life's terminus is here made manifest, and a tumulus is a constant

---

[49] Woodhead 1981, 27; Day 1989, 22 (quotation). To be sure, coloration of letters was not restricted to burial inscriptions.
[50] Hurwit 1990, 192.   [51] Wallace 1970.

reminder of this fact – not least of all for the living.[52] The rhetoric of the archaic funeral epigram is simple but insistent. On the other hand, the inscriptions do not need to be more elaborate than they already are: the physical presence of the monuments supplies all the referentiality that the relatively sparse epigrams on their faces would ever require to make a case for themselves, while the verses in turn render the monuments eloquent – quite often literally turning them into speaking objects (*oggetti parlanti*), as we saw.[53] The insistent materiality of sepulchral epigrams plays into this same rhetoric.

Inscriptions over the next two centuries markedly fall off from this pattern (the bulk of the quotations above are from the sixth century). The change is dramatic and striking. The language becomes tragic and rhetorical, higher-toned and moralizing, and decidedly more "literate." A simplification in the physical displays that provide inscriptions with their contexts is detectable.[54] But there is also a complete refocusing in the subject matter of inscriptions, directing attention away from the monument as an object in its own right (away from self-description) and towards the personalities involved (the family members and the personal or public circumstances of their death).[55] One could venture any number of speculations as to why this change occurs, many of these overlapping: the "discovery" of the individual and its alienation from the world of objects,[56] a newfound modesty towards human undertakings somehow paralleling a de-mythification of art since the archaic age,[57] the democratization of epitaphic discourse, its evolution as a literary form and possibly its specialization as a genre (wherein verses were no longer being produced by sculptors, as they may have been in the past,[58] but by paid

---

[52] See Sourvinou-Inwood 1995, 289–94 for arguments designed to temper reductionist explanations of the steady rise in archaic grave monuments to ideological (i.e., social and political) factors at the expense of emotional factors, e.g., "sadness" and heightened anxieties about death; but see also ibid., 143–44, 177–80, etc., on the undeniable significance of social considerations. Both kinds of consideration, to the extent they can be recovered, obviously matter. See, e.g., *SEG* 34 (Attic, *c.* 530 BCE, made by Aristion of Paros), more explicit than most: "Before the tomb of Antilochus, a good and prudent man, | shed [a tear], since death awaits you too."

[53] See Burzachechi 1962 for the term and for a collection of inscriptions (though with little analysis); Rasche 1910 (an early study); Svenbro 1993 (the classic modern study).

[54] Wallace 1970, 101–02.

[55] An odd but telling index: only one monument after the fifth century listed in *CEG* mentions its physical location "by the roadside" (§727, from 460–40(?), in Thrace), whereas six from the previous centuries invoke this formula.

[56] Philipp 1968, 21.   [57] Karusos 1972 [1941].

[58] See Wallace 1970, 100, referring to *CEG* 14; 18; 26, where the link between the sculptor's name and the author is a matter of inference, albeit a reasonable one.

professional poets[59]), its greater commodification and public role, but also the constraints in the post-Solonian era on funerary ostentation itself and the rise of a new civic-oriented austerity,[60] which inevitably would have shifted the focus away from the materiality of the monuments.[61]

Even if it is true that the aesthetic economy of grave monuments undergoes a change sometime towards the end of the sixth century, in another sense it appears to stay intact, while merely migrating over to other sets of objects. The lyric poets learn from the epitaphic tradition and they borrow heavily from it, absorbing its motifs, its tensions, and its pretensions (as we shall see momentarily). But they are not alone. From the few but significant glimpses available to us today, it emerges that architects or their patrons were participating in the same genre, borrowing identical dedicatory language and celebrating the aesthetics of display. One such dedication was cited in the previous chapter, an inscription prominently situated on the colossal Temple of Apollo at Syracuse from the early sixth century:

Κλεομ[..]ες : ἐποίεσε τὸπέλονι : ℎο Κνιδιείδα : κἐπικ[λ]ε̃ στυλεῖα: κα[λὰ] ϝέργα.[62]

> Cleom[en]es (or: "Cleom[ed]es"), son of Cnidieidas, made [the temple] for Apollo, and [he] also [made these] famous columns, beautiful works.

The term *kala* is misleading if it is construed narrowly: in question are not beautiful works, but *sublime* works, indeed sublime monuments – though even this may prove an insufficiently flat rendering of the word without more contextualization.[63] *Kalos*-words capture varying grades of aesthetic intensity, and it is to the process through which these values are produced and released that we should look if we wish to get a better sense of their meaning. As Dieter Mertens notes, what the inscription appears to celebrate is the successful "overcoming of the sheer masses" of material – all marble – that went into the construction of the temple, most likely at the

---

[59] See Wilamowitz-Moellendorff 1924, 1:123, Raubitschek 1968, 28 and Scodel 1992, 61–62, for the possibility that the more competently composed epigrams may have been furnished by rhapsodes; Sourvinou-Inwood 1995, 284, on the subsumption of private memorials by public collective epitaphs after 480 BCE.

[60] Wallace 1970, 101–03; Humphreys 1980, 101–02.

[61] Sourvinou-Inwood 1995, 293–94; cf. ibid., 385; but see Morris 1989.

[62] *IG* XIV 1 = *SEG* XXXI 841. See Ch. 8 at n. 26 above.

[63] The combination of *megethos* and *kalos* (or *kallos*) is a sure sign of sublimity in Homer and in the later periegetic tradition, in which the description of cities and especially of monuments is featured (see Thomas 2007, 116; 129; 139; 208; 302 n. 15 [μεγάλην καὶ καλήν, X. Eph. 5.1.1] – this last on the city of Syracuse, which continued to be renowned for both qualities). On Aratus' use of the phrase and its Homeric origins, see n. 119 below.

end of a period of economic consolidation by an outpost in the Greek West, and on a scale never before seen in Greece. The temple, in his words, embodies a "striving for monumentality" in stone.[64]

Soon after, the historians got in on the game, and they went the poets one better: in place of the individual deceased, they centered their attention on the passing of great historical figures, cities, and nations. History lends itself to a larger canvas by its very nature, with its sweeping view of space and time, and the temptation to hyperbole is for the same reason all the greater. Indeed, in the historical imagination, temporal events are easily spatialized, and therefore "monumentalized."

Thus, Herodotus famously equates the memory of human achievements with monuments, and implicitly equates history with an inscription that preserves the memory of the past against its being "blotted out by time" (ὡς μήτε τὰ γενόμενα ἐξ ἀνθρώπων τῷ χρόνῳ ἐξίτηλα γένηται). Such is the historian's task: to do this, and to ensure "that the great and marvelous deeds done by Greeks and foreigners should not lose their glory" (μήτε ἔργα μεγάλα τε καὶ θωμαστά ... ἀκλεᾶ γένηται).[65] As the preamble to the *Histories* already suggests, nor is this the only place in his text to do so, Herodotus has elevated the stuff of inscriptional memory to a level of stupendous "greatness" and "wonder." All of his choice phrases for this greatness – μέγας, θῶμα or θωμαστός (θωμάσιος), ὑπερφυής ("of extraordinary nature" or "size"), and μνήμης, θέης or λόγου ἄξια ("worthy of remembrance," "seeing," or "mention") – will come to characterize sublime grandeur – so much so that one has to suspect, on the part of Longinus and others, a conscious harking back to Herodotus, who in the view of the critical tradition was capable of achieving, if not always sustaining, sublimity.[66]

The sublime tradition consisted of multiple strands, and these could (and did) compound one another as time wore on, the more so as any given expression of the sublime could express itself in more than one medium and language at any given moment. From Homer and the poets, the tradition of the material sublime drew on images of poetic grandeur and ecphrastic possibilities of elaborate material description. From the Presocratics, it acquired a conceptual vocabulary and an array of cosmic and natural imagery. From the visual arts came other impulses, typically

---

[64] Mertens 1996, 25; 38.

[65] Hdt. 1.pr.; trans. Godley, adapted.

[66] Dion. Hal. *Thuc.* 5: Herodotus "enlarged the scope (ἐπὶ τὸ μεῖζον ἐξήνεγκε) and added to the splendour (καὶ λαμπρότερον) of the subject," viz., history (trans. Usher); ibid., 23; *Pomp.* 4.3 (Herodotus is sublime); *Subl.* 18.2; 31.2; 38.4.

incorporating influences from adjacent art forms (as in the sepulchral tradition, which combined poetry with architecture and statuary or relief sculpture). From Herodotus, who was aware of all these tendencies, the sublime tradition could draw on a vocabulary for an enlarged sense of space and time, one that was secular and of this world, which is to say, neither mythological nor cosmological, but rather empirical and anthropological. Like the sepulchral tradition, which Herodotus knew well (he supplies us with three epigrams later attributed to Simonides), Herodotus brought physicality near to hand.[67] In this genre of history-writing rooted in Ionian science, physical space and time enjoyed a powerful immediacy and proximity vis-à-vis the reader, albeit now in their immense capacities (in contrast to the more confining framework of private, individual death and the hard, immovable presence of a cold slab of marble). This new sense of sheer and at times overwhelming presence could act as a trigger of sublime thoughts. But our interest here is, in the first instance, in sublime monuments.

The architectural analogy in Herodotean history writing has been well noted by Henry Immerwahr:

The aesthetic enjoyment of monuments is an analogue to the sense of marvel aroused by great actions. Secondly, there is the idea of measuring buildings as an analogue to the evaluation of deeds ... Thus Herodotus, by *conceiving of greatness in spatial terms*, has a definite scale according to which he can judge the comparative greatness of different personalities in relation to each other. In the third place, the architectural metaphor expresses the permanency of a judgment which, based on tradition, is not liable to change.[68]

Philipp goes still further, noting in her quick survey of aesthetic sensibilities down to the fifth century that Herodotus is the first known Greek author to describe from autopsy individual works of art (often monumental in scale) in a "highly factual and informative way" and to reckon these

---

[67] Simonides *Epigr.* 6 and 22a–b Campbell (= Hdt. 7.228); on their likely authenticity, see Campbell 1982–93, III:519. These are epigrams for fallen Spartans at Thermopylae, and so they have a certain, as it were, world-historical significance that private inscriptions obviously lack. Herodotus' awareness of *oggetti parlanti* is evident from his several accounts of dedicatory objects, e.g. the tripods of 5.59–60 (cf. Vox 1975, 70). But as Dionysius of Halicarnassus says of his countryman, Herodotus stood out from his predecessors by virtue of the broad scope of his canvas: "He chose not to record the history of one city or of a single nation, but to gather together accounts of many different events which occurred in Europe and Asia, and assemble them in a single comprehensive work" (*Thuc.* 5; trans. Usher).

[68] Immerwahr 1960, 270; emphasis added. For a brilliant application of the principle of "spatialization," see ibid., 272 on Herodotus' account of the battle at Plataea, which also happens to be described by a contemporary Aeginetan observer as an ἔργον ... ὑπερφυὲς μέγεθός τε καὶ κάλλος, "a deed of extraordinary nature, great, and beautiful" (9.78.2).

(in his own words) "great and wondrous works" – epithets normally reserved for mythical or lost creations.[69] All that remains to add to these two sets of observations for now is that the buildings in question, just by virtue of their evidentiary value (by virtue of their being traces of history in danger of being effaced by time), are akin to monuments of a special kind – namely, sepulchral memorials – and that Herodotus' own writing is akin to the inscriptional writing that identifies and keeps alive the memory of these historical "monuments." In this way, the epigraphic tradition from the archaic period can be seen to have been displaced onto another discourse, while the lyric co-optation of archaic burial inscriptions in the name of individual and local fame can be seen to have been trumped by a perspective that is at once collectivizing and broad canvas in scope.[70]

In dilating the sepulchral motif to a grander scale and in rendering vanished events into memorials of themselves, Herodotus is already pointing ahead to the double-edged phenomenon that I am calling the tradition of sublime monuments. Monuments, after all, cast shadows of themselves just as much as they gleam in the light. Immerwahr is aware of this darker possibility, which is why he seems eager to save Herodotus from a kind of historical pessimism with the claim that "Herodotus emphasizes the preservation of monuments more than he does their destruction: he marvels at what remains rather than lamenting what is lost."[71] That may be, but to preserve a memory is to shore it up against its potential loss, as the first sentence of the *Histories* makes plain. And so I take it that the first half of Immerwahr's claim cannot possibly be valid as it stands. Herodotus does not emphasize the preservation of monuments more than he does their destruction. Indeed, the marvel with which he beholds the survival of historical monuments – which is to say, memorials of history – is strictly commensurate with and contingent on their possible non-survival. Herodotus' *Histories* needn't be elegiac in order to take in this sober fact about historical contingency. And as we shall see in the next section below, generally speaking, it is the juxtaposition of the hard monumentality of things with their vulnerability to time's passing that contributes to their sublime aura.

By the time we get to Thucydides, the pattern of hyperbole reaches new heights. In Pericles' Funeral Oration, "the whole earth" has become a "tomb" for the fallen soldiers of Athens, echoing their fame as it resounds forever into the future:

---

[69] Philipp 1968, 28–31 (quotation at 28–29).
[70] Cf. Immerwahr 1960, 271.   [71] Immerwahr 1960, 271.

So died these men as became Athenians. You, their survivors, must determine to have as unaltering a resolution in the field, though you may pray that it may have a happier issue. And not contented with ideas derived only from words of the advantages which are bound up with the defence of your country, though these would furnish a valuable text to a speaker even before an audience so alive to them as the present, you must yourselves realize the power of Athens, and feed your eyes upon her from day to day, till love of her fills your hearts; and then when all her greatness (μεγάλη) shall break upon you, you must reflect that it was by courage, sense of duty, and a keen feeling of honor in action that men were enabled to win all this, and that no personal failure in an enterprise could make them consent to deprive their country of their valor, but they laid it at her feet as the most glorious contribution that they could offer. For this offering of their lives made in common by them all they each of them individually received that renown (ἔπαινον) which never grows old (ἀγήρων), and for a sepulcher (τάφον), not so much that in which their bones have been deposited, but that noblest (ἐπισημότατον) of shrines wherein their glory is laid up to be eternally remembered upon every occasion on which deed or story shall fall for its com-memoration (αἰείμνηστος καταλείπεται). For heroes have the whole earth for their tomb (ἀνδρῶν γὰρ ἐπιφανῶν πᾶσα γῆ τάφος); and in lands far from their own, where columns with their inscription (στηλῶν ... ἐπιγραφή) declare it, there is enshrined in every breast a record unwritten (ἄγραφος μνήμη), with no monument [or "deed"] to preserve it (τοῦ ἔργου),[72] except that of the heart (τῆς γνώμης). These take as your model, and judging happiness to be the fruit of freedom and freedom of valor, never decline the dangers of war.[73]

To be sure, a curious inversion has taken place, as though owing to the limits to which Pericles (or Thucydides) has pressed the analogy between fame and epitaph. On the one hand, the analogy has been magnified to encompass the whole of the earth – echoing, but also exceeding, Simoni-des' terse line about the dead at Thermopylae who fell around their leader Leonidas of Sparta: "their tomb an altar, for lamentation remembrance, pity praise" (βωμὸς δ᾽ ὁ τάφος, πρὸ γόων δὲ μνᾶστις, ὁ δ᾽ οἶκτος ἔπαινος).[74] The rivalry (or just poignant contrast) between two kinds of media and their relative permanence or impermanence – language and stone – is being replayed again, now in darkened circumstances.[75] But in the process, a loss or a hollowness makes itself felt. Instead of highlighting

---

[72] On the contested meaning of this term, see Immerwahr 1960, 287.

[73] Thuc. 2.43.1–4; trans. Crawley, adapted.   [74] *PMG* 531.3.

[75] See Immerwahr 1960, 288: "In this passage and in the rest of the Oration, buildings are mentioned only to be contrasted with a higher spiritual reality.... Memorials are here mentioned in contrast to mere words of poets and prose writers, but again they are not actual memorials, for, as Wilamowitz saw, they stand for the memory of the successes and failures of Athens." On the other hand, the poets' monuments were not actual memorials either, and their contrasts were pseudo-contrasts too (more on this below).

the materiality of the monument and of the inscription that serves to identify it, the language backs off from the hard tangibility of what materially is: the inscription voiced by Pericles is avowedly "unwritten" because it is spoken, then memorized, and finally felt ("in the heart"). Perhaps what is felt is the hollowness and loss that stretch like a grave between what the speech promises and what little solace or truth it can actually deliver, the grave that the whole world has now become. Perhaps it is merely the prideful, global pretension of the trope that is felt. In ways, the trope merely captures what every epitaphic inscription implies as an assuagement of the living. But it does this *in extremis*, at the limits of language and emotion at a particularly hard moment in Athenian history.

What the Periclean epitaphic turn achieves is a transmutation of its own material conditions and surroundings, just as any epigraph does: death becomes immortality; youth is frozen into never-aging bloom; stone is made to speak; language is soldered to matter; and matter gives way to the immaterial, or rather to the *form* of matter etched in the memory of what matter is or once was. This transformation is distinctly aesthetic, as Vernant observes, taking a long view of the epitaphic genre:

In the course of the sixth century . . . death is no longer evoked by the brute stone that has no inscription, but by the visible beauty of a corporeal form that the stone fixes forever with a name, as death fixed it on the corpse of the young heroic warrior whom all admire, because in him, even or especially when he is dead, as Homer and Tyrtaeus say, "everything is fitting, everything is beautiful," *panta kala.* . . . [Later on,] glorious memorialization, inherited from epic, expresses in the form of the *enkōmion* (the eulogy) those new aspects that excellence and exemplary status have now acquired in the framework of the civic community.[76]

Nor does Thucydides stand at the end of the line in this progression, or rather this series of displacements and transformations, within the epigraphic tradition. But before looking ahead, it remains to glance back.

3 HOMER'S MONUMENTALIZING IMAGINATION

While the first recorded epitaphs date only from the mid-seventh century, the epitaphic genre is attested from the first beginnings of Greek literature. Homer is rich in epitaphic moments, which is to say, moments when the poem halts briefly and reflects on the future, in the form of so-called

---

[76] Vernant 1991, 162; 91.

"*tis*-speeches," statements of the form, "Somebody will say someday, 'So-and-so once fought here and died,'" sometimes using the overt formulas of τόδε σῆμα ("this grave marker") and (ὡς) ποτέ τις ἐρέει/εἴπῃσι ("(as) someone will say someday"), and sometimes not.[77] Such passages were singled out as epitaphic already in antiquity,[78] and recent discussion of what Ruth Scodel has suggestively called Homer's "monumentalizing imagination" has raised the question whether Homer was not in fact echoing an existing written genre of discourse, that of the sepulchral verse inscription.[79] Whether or not burial inscriptions antedated Homer, the so-called epigraphic habit (even if only in an oral form) was firmly in place whenever the Homeric poems were coming to be generated, as was the tendency to think of poetry as involved in the task of memorializing and monumentalizing the past.[80] Several consequences follow. One is that poetry, so conceived, stands in a direct relationship to the material traces of the past, and these are reflected in the self-conception of epic poetics.

The most obvious connection between epic poetry and its past is visible in the way in which epic supplements the material record by providing a voice for objects that renders them everlasting in memory. Epic here contrasts with its materials. Like all material things, monuments are in themselves mute things, and they can fade into insignificance. Is the turning-post described by Nestor in *Iliad* 23 a grave marker (σῆμα) of somebody long dead or a turning-post (νύσσα) set up by earlier generations?[81] The object is unclaimed by memory. A steep hill (κολώνη) called Batieia by men is a monument (σῆμα) known to the gods as Myrine: "the monument has evidently become generally an undifferentiated feature of the landscape, no longer a monument," but a mere tumulus of the sort that must have littered the Bronze Age landscape, no doubt puzzlingly and uncertainly.[82] And yet, rising above the plain (it is still visible today),[83] it is nevertheless a monument, a σῆμα, marking an all but obliterated past. Batieia points silently to this loss, and so it memorializes

---

[77] For the former kind, see *Il.* 7.89–91; for the latter, *Il.* 6.459–60. For the speech-form, see de Jong 1987.
[78] E.g., [Plut.] *Vit. Hom.* 135; schol. T; *Il.* 6.459–60. Cf. *CEG* 1.264 (*c.* 480 BCE?): --- [χ]τεάν[ον] --- | --- μνέμ' ἐπι]γιγνι[μένοις], a phrase that later became a stock formula (e.g., *CEG* 2.784).
[79] Lumpp 1963; Scodel 1992 (quotation at p. 59); contra, Raubitschek 1968, 6–8, and *passim*. Further, Vox 1975. The scholia regularly designate these instances as epigrams, which however proves nothing.
[80] The phrase "epigraphic habit" was first coined with Roman contexts in mind; see MacMullen 1982; Meyer 1990.
[81] *Il.* 23.331–32. [82] *Il.* 2.811–14; Scodel 1992, 66 (quotation).
[83] "... and a very obvious Batieia on the horizon," to the southwest of Troy (West 1995, 217 n. 43).

loss even more than it preserves a distinct memory. Epic is the antidote to mute materiality. Indeed, the very mention of such marginal cases of remembered pasts seems to reinforce the unique power of epic to sustain the past by keeping it alive on the lips of men in the form of *kleos aphthiton*, or imperishable fame. The immense heap of dirt that is Batieia may well conceal an unsung epic, as Homer teasingly reveals. How many such unsung epics does the *Iliad* contain? Its relic-strewn landscape suggests an answer: countless numbers.[84]

And yet, for all its self-assurance and seeming superiority over the constraints of matter, the physical, and the fixedly and perishably monumental, epic cannot sever its ties to these things; nor is the (faint) memory of the material past severable from epic's survival.[85] Epic, then, is mute materiality made audible, but not immaterial. Just as, in a later age, the twice-destroyed Phocian town of Parapotamii will no longer exist except in the memory of men, for as Pausanias writes, "no ruins of Parapotamii remained in my time, *and the very spot on which the city stood is forgotten,*" so too is epic acutely aware of its connection to the material past, above all in the form of its loss.[86] Parapotamii and Batieia are the ultimate kinds of remains, those which are denoted not by missing objects but by their absence, that is, by pure loss, a loss that thereby designates *the very loss of loss.* Remains like these, overwhelmingly oppressive in their felt material presence, are the most resistant to the project of description and therefore the most sublime sites of all. (Later tradition would call such sites "gaps," *diastēmata.* They have an obvious affinity to cosmic emptiness or void.[87])

With the fragile connection to the material past come the vexed problems of relation: an awareness of the transience of memory, the uncertain reliability of material objects in preserving the record of their own meaning without the aid of language, and the radical uncertainties of memorialization itself.[88] Whatever it was that caused Myrine to lapse into Batieia or a *sēma* to become a turning-post (if that is what happened) could as easily befall the heroes of *this* epic.[89] All the vaunting and boasting of gods and heroes, such as Hector's ("my fame [*kleos*] will never perish")

---

[84] See Kirk ad loc. for suggestive commentary on the passage.

[85] For the first perspective, see Ford 1992, 146: "The true epic, the total knowledge of every hero who fell before Troy, is not inscribed on any stone, far less on leather or papyrus; it has no authoritative physical form." For the latter, see n. 88 below.

[86] Paus. 10.33.8.   [87] Porter 1992; Porter 2007b.

[88] See Scodel 1992, 67: "The echoes of monuments from a more distant past indicate that without the epic Muse, memory is not guaranteed"; and Bassi 2005. For an early articulation of this same point, see Immerwahr 1960, 290.

[89] See Scodel 1992, 67 (previous note).

or an example of Poseidon's to be discussed below, seem like so many
desperate wishes held out against the knowledge that song is mobile
("winged"), in contrast to monuments fixed in place. A simile from *Iliad*
17 makes the point starkly: "But as a stele stays fixed in place, one that
stands over a tomb of a dead man or woman, they stood there [sc.,
Achilles' immortal horses]," mourning the death of Patroclus.[90] But the
greater mobility of song can cut two ways, either in the direction of
greater diffusion and longevity (thanks to oral tradition) or in the direction of obscurity and oblivion – in short, ephemerality (think of the
countless unsung epics contained in the *Iliad*). If contingency is an
element in epic's survival, the ephemerality of utterance brings this
contingency into the inner condition, as it were, of speech itself, which
suddenly looks like a chancy instrument. What is more, epitaphic
moments may be strangely out of place in epic for any number of reasons,
not least of all by being invariably premature in their predictions (and
sometimes wrong). From this it follows that through such moments "the
poet reveals," and so too casts in a critical light, "the inner impulse to
control future speech."[91] But then how does the poet escape the implications for his own genre of epic? It is not clear that he can or does – or that
he even wishes to do so, as we shall see when we turn briefly to the
problem of the Achaean wall. The poet's sense of the contingency and
fragility of song and memory may, in other words, turn out to be an
integral part of his poetic vision. With this, we have located yet another
sense of "the materiality of the poetic word," only now one that is fraught
with existential concern.

4 SONG 'VERSUS' STONE?

It is notable that Homer anticipates tensions that characterize the aesthetics of archaic lyric, and in particular the tussle between two kinds of
aesthetic imagery and perception as these are co-opted, assimilated, and
projected in Simonides and Pindar – essentially, the question framed by *la
parole et le marbre*. As poets tread upon the inscriptional territory of the
dedicatory object, rendering their poems into quasi-monuments, at issue
is the relative permanence of the two kinds of medium. Simonides'
critique of the monument erected by Cleobulus, the tyrant of Lindus on

---

[90] ἀλλ᾿ ὥς τε στήλη μένει ἔμπεδον, ἥ τ᾿ ἐπὶ τύμβῳ | ἀνέρος ἑστήκῃ τεθνηότος ἠὲ γυναικός
(*Il.* 17.434–35).
[91] Scodel 1992, 67.

Rhodes, to the Phrygian king Midas, is a case in point. The monument was fitted out with a haughty epigram, likewise by Cleobulus, which was much cited in antiquity – the so-called Midas epigram, which runs as follows:

I am a maiden of bronze (χαλκῆ παρθένος), and I stand on the tomb (ἐπὶ σήματι) of Midas.
As long as water flows and tall trees grow,
and the rising sun gives light or the bright moon,
and rivers flow and the sea boils,
here I shall remain on this sad tomb (τῇδε μένουσα πολυκλαύτῳ ἐπὶ τύμβῳ) and tell (ἀγγελέω) passers-by that Midas is buried here.[92]

In a move reminiscent today of the sculptor in Shelley's "Ozymandias," Simonides found the pretensions of this poet risible and "witless." Cleobulus, Simonides writes, pitted the "might of a statue" (μένος στάλας) against time and the elements (with a pointed echo of μένουσα in verse 5 of Cleobulus' poem). But "all things are less than the gods. Stone | is broken even by mortal hands. That was the judgement of a fool."[93] "The hand that mocked them, and the heart that fed," indeed.

Simonides' critique could be understood as expressing a rivalry between song and stone, with song enjoying the clear advantage. As further evidence of this reading, one could always marshal his dictum about painting being a silent form of poetry, which appears to be a critique of that second rival visual medium.[94] But things aren't quite so simple as they appear. First, the other half of the dictum, that poetry is a form of eloquent painting, is Simonides' way of laying claim, nonetheless, to the powers of that same medium, painting. Secondly, was Simonides attacking Cleobulus' monument or his poetry, or the welding of the one to the other (which is to say, the tying of the fate of the one to the other)? And in any case, in what medium was his own attack transmitted? Both Simonides' and Cleobulus' poems, after all, are species of recorded song, and both managed to circulate widely (Plato quotes the Midas epigram in the *Phaedrus*[95]). Thirdly, the examples from Simonides cited earlier deploy the very strategies that he mocks in the epigram by Cleobulus, for instance, his funeral ode to Leonidas and his men, which presents itself as a concrete monument (a "shrine"): Simonides' poem, too, can promise "a great adornment (κόσμον) of valour and

[92] 581 *PMG* (= D.L. 1.89–90); trans. Campbell. [93] Ibid.
[94] Thus Karusos 1972 [1941], 138–42; cf. Ford 2002, 105–11. [95] Pl. *Phdr.* 264d.

imperishable glory" (ἀεναόν τε κλέος).⁹⁶ Recall that Simonides was himself a master, and innovator, in the genre of epitaphic lyric.⁹⁷ Nor was he alone. Bacchylides followed suit, calling song "an immortal monument of the muses" (ἀθάνατον Μουσᾶν ἄγαλμα).⁹⁸ And the list goes on.

The tension between words and stones has been much discussed.⁹⁹ Of equal interest is the durability of the motif of poetry *as* a form of stone (or matter) itself. A thematic survey of later poetry and poetics would bear this relationship out, well beyond what Svenbro and others have shown for archaic Greece. I wish to illustrate the point with a brief detour into the Hellenistic period.¹⁰⁰

5 HELLENISTIC MONUMENTALITY: LITHIC 'LEPTOTĒS'

The most obvious extension of the thematics of song and stone after the archaic and classical periods in Greek literature is to be found in the Hellenistic epigram, which consciously harks back to the earlier epigraphic tradition and re-aestheticizes it anew. This later genre has been extensively studied, and I have no intention of repeating the findings of others here, except to recall what Peter Bing, who has explored the epigraphic sub-genre of the Hellenistic epigram perhaps as closely as anyone in recent years, has to say about the relationship between poems and stones – namely that "the boundaries between stone and scroll are quite permeable, and migration across them is easy," so much so that the distinction between inscription and quasi-inscription (or pseudo-inscription), that is, between real and fictional occasion, is impossible to determine.¹⁰¹ Of course, that boundary was already breached as early

---

⁹⁶ 531.9 *PMG*; cf. Steiner 2001, 259: "a tangible monument seems a necessary component."
⁹⁷ See Carson 1999, ch. 3, for a powerful appreciation. ⁹⁸ Bacchyl. 10.11.
⁹⁹ Karusos 1972 [1941]; Svenbro 1976, 187; 190–93; Steiner 2001, ch 5; Ford 2002, chs. 4–5. On the Egyptian counterpart, which points to the high antiquity of the motif, see Assmann 1991 (thanks to Dan Selden for this reference). Assmann's analysis brings out one important difference, however, which is worth underscoring briefly. Inscriptional writing on the Egyptian model, according to Assmann, is not intended to be vocalized (let alone seen). Rather, it is buried in an eternal muteness (26). Thus, monumental, material permanence is bought at the price of self-canceling constraints on material expression and realization (27–31; cf. 87). The parallel with *aere perennius* (29) is illegitimate: Horace's ode is *sung*.
¹⁰⁰ The few pages on Posidippus and *leptotēs* that follow are a greatly compressed version of Porter 2010a.
¹⁰¹ Bing 1998, 34 (citing the problem that was nominated by Wilamowitz-Moellendorff 1924, 1:119 with the catchphrase, "Aufschrift oder nicht"); cf. Bing 1995.

as the Homeric quasi-inscriptions,[102] but the Hellenistic epigrams are a genre unto themselves, free-floating, and very like actual burial inscriptions. What the link, real or fabricated, between a poem and its epigraphic context achieves is a connection between the poem "and its physical object," which is to say, between the poem as a poem and the poem as an inscription decorating an object (monumental in one or another sense of the term, that is, as "conspicuous" or as "memorializing"), occupying a physical context, and experienced as being read *in situ*. This situatedness of the epigram, its localization in a time and a place, and its immobility *qua* inscribed in that place, all contrast with the qualities of the free-floating textual life of the epigram *qua* poem, which lives on in the imagination and libraries of readers who, like the poems' authors themselves, may be miles and miles away from the original setting, assuming such settings ever existed to begin with. Real or not, the premise of the literary epigram is one of a physicality and immediacy that is being revived whenever the poem is being re-experienced by a reader.[103] In presenting themselves as inscriptions on monuments, Hellenistic literary epigrams do not merely evoke materiality: they embody it – inscribe it – in their very substance. Hellenistic poets were fond of exploiting these ambiguities. In doing so, they were playing with the materialities of poetry.

But this was not the only way in which materiality flourished in Hellenistic poetics, and if anything the recrudescence of the inscriptional epigram is but a symptom of a much larger tendency. In order to bring out this larger trend and the object-oriented character of Hellenistic aesthetics, its intense capacity to "think through things," but also in order to underscore how this aesthetic sensibility is to a great extent inherited from the archaic era, I want to turn now to another, broader way in which materiality made itself felt in Hellenistic poetry, a fact that, happily, is slowly dawning on contemporary scholarship, along with a growing awakening to the general usefulness of aesthetic perspectives in the field. Indeed, not only is aesthetics ever so slowly coming to be *à la mode* in Hellenistic literary studies again (displacing an older, more limited interest in poetics). What is more, or rather less, coming into fashion is – willy-nilly – an aesthetics of things or objects, what we might call a newfound aesthetic materialism, which I believe is peculiarly well suited to Hellenistic poetic

---

[102] This is evident from the quasi-epigrammatic character of the Homeric examples cited earlier and their specific poetic function in the Homeric poems. Cf. Gentili's comment about "epitafi fittizi, non reali" in Raubitschek 1968, 34.

[103] See Bing 1998, 33–35.

production. There are good and obvious reasons for this refocusing
of attention, the most recent being the discovery and subsequent publication in 2001 of the poetry book attributed with reasonable certainty to
Posidippus of Pella, the Macedonian epigrammatist and contemporary
of Callimachus. It is astonishing to see the terms *aesthetics, objects*, and
occasionally *materiality* and *material*, cropping up with such frequency
in Kathryn Gutzwiller's collection of essays on Posidippus from 2005
and the various art forms that his work implicates. And then there is the
2003 article by G. O. Hutchinson, likewise inspired by the discovery of
Posidippus, entitled, "The Catullan Corpus, Greek Epigram, and the
Poetry of Objects," in addition to other items in a rapidly growing
bibliography.[104] This new turn bodes well for interdisciplinary studies in
Hellenistic studies, which continue to remain underexploited, inexplicably for a field so rich in potential, given the then flourishing fields of
literature, philosophy, art, urban design, religion, and sciences. Aesthetics
would surely be one way of producing something like a unified field theory
for the Hellenistic era. My interest here is, however, in noting a particular
tendency of Hellenistic aesthetics: its materialist urges.

The table of contents of Posidippus' work tells us almost all we need to
know about the object-oriented nature of its subject matter: I. Stones(?)
(λιθι]κά); II. Omens; III. Dedications (ἀναθεματικά); IV. [Epitaphs
(ἐπιτύμβια)]; V. The Making of Statues (ἀνδριαντοποιικά); VI. Eques-
trian Poems; VII. Shipwrecks; VIII. Cures; IX. Turns (Characters?).[105] My
interest here lies in the first book, the *Lithika* (the title is virtually
guaranteed by the contents). Prior to this discovery it would have been
hard to imagine an entire set of poems devoted to kinds of stones, even if
treatises on stones and minerals are known to have existed at least since
Theophrastus' *On Stones*.[106] One might have thought one would have to
wait until the middle of the twentieth century before one could hit upon a
literary fascination with such simple objects, as in Francis Ponge's collection *Le parti pris des choses* (*Siding with Things* [1941]), which has its
fair share of sensuous accounts of stones and pebbles. Consider one poem
from that collection, "The Pebble," which begins:

[104] Gutzwiller 2002 on "art objects" and ibid., pp. 94–95 on "aesthetic objects"; Hutchinson 2003; cf.
Hutchinson 2002, 8. Even Callimachus was interested in material remains (Fantuzzi and Hunter
2004, 46). See further the essays collected in Rouveret *et al.* 2006, some of which draw on
Posidippus. See also Männlein-Robert 2007, ch. 4; Prioux 2007; Gurd 2007.
[105] From Nisetich's translation of the poems in Gutzwiller 2005b, 17–41. The tenth title is lost.
[106] See Bing 2005, 143 at n. 4; Gutzwiller 2005a, 301–02.

It isn't easy to define a pebble.
If you're satisfied with a simple description you can start out by saying
    that it's a form or state of stone halfway between rocks and gravel.
But this already implies a concept of stone that must be validated.
    So don't blame me for going back even further than the flood.[107]

Of course, Ponge's prose-poem is hardly concerned with the mere simplicity of pebbles, and neither is Posidippus' *Lithika*, an example of which is AB 15 (20 G–P), which is about a carving on a precious snakestone:

It was not a river resounding on its banks, but the head
    of a bearded snake that once held this gem (τόνδε λίθον),
thickly streaked with white. And the chariot on it
    was engraved by the sharp eye of Lynceus,
like the mark on a nail: the chariot is seen incised   5
    but on the surface (κατὰ πλάτεος) you could not notice
any protrusions.
And that's why the work causes such a great marvel (θαῦμα ... μέγα):
    how did the pupils
of the engraver's eyes not suffer as he gazed so intently.[108]

One of the striking features of the Posidippan book roll is the overall thematic progression it makes, especially when viewed against current conventional readings of Hellenistic literary aesthetics, which (I believe) are too much taken with *leptotēs*, or the conjunction of the refined with the poetics of the detail and the small scale. To what extent do these epigrams reflect a poetics of the small scale, of Callimachean, or rather Hellenistic λεπτός, and a rejection of the monumental, the epic, and the grand, as even the new scholarship on them has tried to affirm? I believe that the problem with the usual view of Hellenistic literary aesthetics lies in its one-sidedness, and my suggestion is that what is typically asserted about this aesthetics is correct, but only half-so: the other half of the picture needs to be brought back into view to complete the picture. In the case of the *Lithika*, this can be shown by appealing to any number of factors, which I will have to run through quickly.[109] The relevant point is that to shift the focus away from the slender, the polished, and the refined, and to include in our view of the Hellenistic aesthetic what is massive in

---

[107] "The Pebble" ("*Le Galet*"), in Ponge 1994, 91.

[108] Posidippus AB 15 (trans. Austin). On the other hand, the fascination with pebbles and their aesthetic properties is as old as human time itself. See the ongoing excavations into the Bronze Age patterned pebble beds in East Devon directed by archaeologist C. Tilley (http://www. pebblebedsproject.org.uk/poetics-of-pebbles.html; accessed April 2009). See further Tilley 2004.

[109] For a more detailed reading, see Porter 2010a.

scale, or rather in appearance, is to focus attention on the materiality of objects. For in the course of being magnified, objects in their sheer physicality are thrust to the fore as well.

Let us start with verse 7 of the Posidippus poem we began from, the "great marvel" (θαῦμα μέγα) caused by this little piece of workmanship on the snakestone. Plainly, the poem leaves us with an impression of magnitude, and not, or not only, of diminutiveness. Or rather, we should say that the stone object creates an impression of magnitude for all its smallness of scale. Aesthetically, it is the contrast of the two scales that is significant.

The rest of the stones follow the same pattern. Individually small and precious (at least some of them), the objects simultaneously involve large-scale themes, while their dimensions swell as the poems progress (especially from AB 16 to the end of the book). They come from the far-flung corners of the inhabited world (*oikoumenē*), and are, as it were, vomited forth from the bowels of the earth or from rugged geographies. They come from India ("Indian Hydaspes"), Persia, Nabataea, Arabia ("rolling yellow [rubble] from the Arabian [mountains]").[110] And they come from these exotic places with force and violence: "an Arabian stream rolls [a stone] along to the shore | of the sea, as it *constantly tears it from the mountains, | a lump in vast quantities*"; "*do [not] calculate*] how many waves have [cast] out [this] *great* [rock] | far from the raging sea ... | Polyphemus could not have lifted it.*"[111] One stone is nearly propelled by "a gigantic hurricane," another "uprooted by Mysian Olympus."[112] More-over, the stones sport immodest physical and aesthetic features to match their provenance. They are frequently described according to their bulk and mass (ὄγκος ["bulk"] appears thrice, possibly four times; βῶλος ["mass"] and πάχος ["thick"], once each) or with dimensional terms such as πλατύς ["wide"] and [τρισ]πίθαμον περίμετρον ["three spans in circumference"]). While the stones are occasionally colossal, many of their features are cosmic. "An engraved chariot is spread out *to the length of a span....* It defeats the rubies of India | when put to the test, with radiant beams of equal strength.... And this too is a marvel" (τέρας).[113] "A light spreads over the whole surface (ὄγκους), ... [a beguiling] marvel (θαῦμα), ... as it reaches for the beautiful sun."[114] "Bellerophon crashed into the ... plain | while his colt went up into the deep-blue sky," and so the stone that depicts the colt is said to be "aetherial."[115] There is nothing *leptos* here. Quite the contrary, "the result ... is a thematizing of nothing less than the physical nature of the universe" in all its parts.[116]

Ogkos, encountered several times already, is a key term in the *Lithika*, and it is significantly ambivalent: it denotes bulk, but bulk of any dimension. (Ancient atoms were called *ogkoi*, as we saw.) Austin at times astutely chooses to render *ogkos* with *surface* (not given in LSJ), and the rendering captures something that *mass* lacks: it picks out the perceptual or, more broadly, aesthetic dimension of Posidippus' poems on stones. For the stones are surface screens on which aesthetic effects appear and disappear, fleetingly, and then reappear. This play of appearances is a play of material surfaces. It occurs on and within the massy outer and inner dimensions of the poet's chosen objects, which is to say, their *ogkoi*, which are both large and small, aesthetically speaking. The net effect of this interplay of extremes is one of *thauma*, or marvel, as Epigram 13 illustrates again:

This stone is [deceptive] (κ[εϱδα]λέη): when it is anointed,
　[a light] spreads over the whole surface (ὅλους ὄγκους), [a beguiling]
　　marvel (θαῦ[μ' ἀπάτη]ς).
But when [the surface] (ὄ[γκων]) is dry, all at once an [engraved] Persian [lion]
　flashes as it reaches for the beautiful sun.[117]

Such extremes are typical of the Posidippan epigrams, as they are of so many other works in the same genre. (The Hellenistic epigrammatic tradition in its paradoxographical moods ranges over everything from volcanic eruptions to destructive floods to magnets to stranded monsters[118]). But in other respects, they are absolutely characteristic of Hellenistic poetry *tout court*, be it Callimachus' massive and massively learned *Aetia* (spanning some four to six thousand verses long, thus occupying an epic scale), or his aetiological *Iambs*, or Aratus' *Phaenomena*, a cosmic, "Hesiodic" work longer than either the *Theogony* or the *Works and Days*, and which combined both *leptotēs* and grandeur,[119] or Theocritus' *Idyll* 15, which luxuriates in exotic display at Arsinoe's palace, or his *Encomium of Ptolemy Philadelphus*, which again overtly participates in the Ptolemaic imperial project, or in Apollonius of Rhodes' *Argonautica*, just shy of six thousand lines,

---

[115] Posidipp. AB 14.　　[116] Gutzwiller 2005a, 302; cf. 303.
[117] Posidipp. AB 13; trans. Austin.
[118] See Wick 2000 (citing *Anth. Pal.* 6.222–23; 7.76; 7.299; 9.424; 9.568; 12.152). In art, there is the Hellenistic Baroque, of course.
[119] Aratus frequently invokes visual grandeur (*ta megala*: καλός τε μέγας τε, a Homericism, is one of his stock formulas); yet he famously wove a double acrostic into his verses with the word λεπτή (Arat. 783–87; Jacques 1960).

which combines large- and small-scale aesthetics, and is perhaps best termed mannerist, if not altogether baroque.[120]

I could continue listing examples but there is little point. Their underlying paradox has to do with the logic of scale itself, and indeed with the very nature of the detail or the small-scale object. A poet who dwells in the small scale invites us to entertain both ideas in our minds simultaneously (the miniature and the colossal) and, as we see in Posidippus, frequently invites us to confuse our points of orientation, hoping that we will forget whether the object before us stands at one end of the scale or the other. It is a natural impulse. Consider any tiny object, and view it from up close. As the object intrudes upon our field of vision, it also grows in a way that is disproportionate to its actual size. It becomes magnified, it fills our visual field, its details seem larger than life, and, finally, the object assumes colossal proportions. What was once tiny is now gigantic, even grand. And now all of our aesthetic descriptors have to change accordingly. Once again, we see how the mere confrontation with a material surface turns into an overwhelming experience and can be productive of intense aesthetic values, and even of sublimity. The very clash of scales and effects was itself a factor in this aesthetic process and sufficient to trigger a violent response. What is more, the Hellenistic detail was frequently an object endowed with sensuous features. In this way, Hellenistic miniaturism and pointillism could be put in the service of the senses, which in turn helped to magnify sensation itself. A range of aesthetic effects thereby resulted that exceeded the limits of *leptotēs* as this is currently understood (or so I would argue).[121] A good example of the materiality of the aesthetic detail irreducible to poetic refinement, at least in its current understanding, is to be found in the euphonic sound sculpture of the Hellenistic literary critics, which will be discussed in the next section.

There is, to be sure, a flip side to this same phenomenon that needs to be mentioned briefly, and which will remind us of an earlier discussion from Chapter 3 above. Focusing too intently on the materiality of an object does not always result in aesthetic pleasure, even in the case of

---

[120] See Stewart 2006 on *truphē*, the colossal, and the baroque.

[121] See Porter 2010a for extended arguments. A case in point are the bizarre *Tabulae Iliacae*, ascribed to a "Theodorean art" (arguably so named after the archaic miniaturist and architect, Theodorus of Samos; on this point, see further Porter ibid.). These twenty-two marble tablets present tiny, compressed versions of the Homeric epics and epic cycles in inscribed epitomes and in visual depictions. The writing is so miniscule that it is barely legible to the naked eye; yet the themes invoked are as grand as literature knows outside of cosmic themes. The clash in scales is part of the aesthetic experience, and indeed its essence. More on this in Porter, ibid.

objects conventionally considered beautiful or monumental. The Hellen-istic poets knew how to exploit this underbelly of the tradition, as when a terracotta Hermes admits, "I have been mixed with mud, I don't deny it,"[122] or when a statue (most likely aniconic) of the Milesian Apollo is addressed in a fragment by Callimachus, "Hail, polygon!" (πολυγώνιε, χαῖρε),[123] or another cult image is reminded, again by Callimachus, "You were a crude plank of wood."[124] As Kassel notes, these poetic ironies are doubtless meant to recall a specific prejudice that reaches back to Hera-clitus, who berated religious folk as "raving mad" for praying to the statues of their gods "as if one were conversing with houses," and for not recognizing gods and heroes for what they really were.[125] But such attitudes towards the materials from which divine icons were made also serve to expose a different, aesthetic prejudice that is at least as old as Heraclitus and that I referred to earlier as "the disgrace of matter." The two biases are here being merged into one, as they perhaps already are in the fragment from Heraclitus. Even Callimachus' detailed architectural measurements of the statue of Olympian Zeus in *Iamb* 6, covering nearly every cubic inch of its surfaces, seems an exaggerated eulogy of its material dimensions, and consequently a sacrilegious exposure of its cultic aura and its incalculable sublimity ("not to be reckoned, not even," [ο]ὐ [λ]ογιστὸν οὐδ. [.]; verse 47) – all done tongue in cheek.[126]

Matter and the divine consort badly together. Not even a materialist like Epicurus could evade this truth: the gods may have a human form, but "that appearance is not body (*nec tamen ea species corpus est*) but quasi-body (*sed quasi corpus*), and it does not have blood (*nec habet sanguinem*) but quasi-blood" (*sed quasi sanguinem*).[127] And if the gods' bodies are quasi-material, then their representations in statue form should be this too. That is what Artemidorus says in his *Interpretation of Dreams* at least.

---

[122] *Anth. Pal.* 16.191 (Nicaenetus).   [123] Callim. *Aet.*, fr. 114 Pf.

[124] Callim. *Aet.*, fr. 100 Pf. All three examples are discussed by Kassel 1991, 151–52, a learned and witty essay.

[125] DK 22B5; cit. Kassel 1991, 141.

[126] Pfeiffer 1941; Hutchinson 1988, 26–27; Acosta-Hughes 2002, 188–94.

[127] Cic. *Nat. D.* 1.49; trans. Long and Sedley 1987. Sanders 2004 argues that *corpus* renders σάρξ or τὸ σάρκινον, "flesh," rather than "body," and hence is not tantamount to a denial of the gods' corporeality. Nevertheless, Epicurus is squirming here, for we are still left, in that case, with a "quasi-flesh," and what is that? Cf. Gladstone 1858, iii:176–7: "The sentiment which craves for material representations of such objects [of divinity] in order to worship them, appears also commonly to exact that they should be somewhat materialized. The higher office of art, in connection with devout affection [viz., of the Christian persuasion] ... holds out the finger which we are to follow, not the hand which we are to kiss."

For if you are going to have a vision of a god, it will be either of "the Olympians themselves (αὐτούς), or statues of them that have been made out of an incorruptible material (ἐξ ὕλης [τῆς] ἀσήπτου πεποιημένα), cheerful, smiling, giving or saying something good." He later clarifies what he means by the oxymoron, "incorruptible material": "Statues that are fashioned from a substance that is hard and incorruptible as, for example, those that are made from gold, silver, bronze, ivory, stone, amber, or ebony, are auspicious. Statues fashioned from any other material, as, for example, those that are made from terra cotta, clay, plaster, or wax, those that are painted, and the like, are less auspicious and often even inauspicious."[128]

That engineering and the divine make for an odd mix is part of the point of Lucian's hilarious dialogue *Zeus Tragoedus*, in which Zeus convokes a departmental meeting of the cultic images of the gods, Greek and barbarian alike. The gods come scurrying together in order to get good seats, but he insists on seating them "according to their material or workmanship (ὡς ἂν ὕλης ἢ τέχνης ἔχῃ); gold in the front row, silver next, then the ivory ones, then those of stone or bronze."[129] Complications ensue, as the little particle "or" might lead one to expect. Hermes, the factotum, interjects a worry:

Suppose one of them is gold, and heavy at that, but not finely finished, quite amateurish and ill proportioned, in fact – is he to take precedence of Myron's and Polyclitus's bronze, or Phidias' and Alcamenes' marble? Or is workmanship to count most? (7)

Zeus plumps for material as the final grounds for deciding who gets to sit in the prized front row, with gold as the trumping criterion – never mind art. The upshot is that in the final analysis the Greek contingent fares the worst, as Hermes predicts, and as one might expect they would at the hands of the Graeco-Syrian Lucian, a master in exposing identity politics during the imperial era. Hermes' prediction runs as follows:

Zeus, the front row will be exclusively barbarian, I observe. You see the peculiarity of the Greek contingent: they have grace and beauty and artistic workmanship (χαρίεντες μὲν καὶ εὐπρόσωποι καὶ κατὰ τέχνην ἐσχηματισμένοι), but they are all marble or bronze (λίθινοι δὲ ἢ χαλκοῖ ὅμως) – the most costly of them only ivory with just an occasional gleam of gold, the merest surface-plating; and even those are wood inside (ὑπόξυλοι), harbouring whole colonies of mice.

---

[128] Artem. 1.5; 2.39; trans. White. I owe this reference to Platt forthcoming, ch. 5.
[129] Lucian *Jup. Trag.* 7; trans. Fowler.

Whereas Bendis here, Anubis there, Attis next door, and Mithras and Men, are all of solid gold, heavy and extremely precious (πολυτίμητοι). (8)

Upstaged by a "dog-faced Egyptian," Poseidon is told by his non-Greek counterpart, "Lysippus made you of paltry bronze." Aphrodite, though of white marble (λίθου τοῦ λευκοῦ), was merely "quarried" (λιθοτομηθεῖσα). And the Colossus of Rhodes, though of costly bronze, is too tall to sit in front, and so he must stand back and bend over, lest he block everyone's view (9–11). Kassel's comment on these theatrics is worthy of the Russian Formalists: "the requirement of finding criteria of rank provides a good opportunity for dwelling rather concretely on material and its manufacture," which is to say, if one likes, on what "makes the stone *stony*."[130] For *dwelling*, the original rather nicely resorts to a key verb of German classical aesthetics: *verweilen*.[131]

6 VERBAL ARCHITECTURE

So far, we have explored some of the ramifications of the interaction of poetry and sculpture or building around one point of commonality: their materiality (rather than, say, their form or structure). Behind this association lies the further fact that both kinds of art, poetry and visual art, are a form of *poiēsis*. Surely, it is both of these features that led poets to investigate associations with their kindred plastic art forms. And while statues provide a human connection, buildings and stones are of interest precisely because they *deprive* poetry of this upper semantic register: all that is left to compare are the bare qualities of materials in their individuality and in their synthetic totality and organization. The Colossus of Rhodes, treated with awe by both Posidippus and Longinus, is something of a limit case.[132] It is nominally a statue of a human form. But, given its sheer dimensions and overbearing materiality, whatever humanity it once possessed is perforce shed, leaving only the impression of a mass of bronze, stone, and iron, more a building than a sculpture, and ultimately more earthen than even a building – and all the more so after the structure collapsed into a magnificent heap of ruins, affecting its posthumous

---

[130] Kassel 1991, 152; Shklovsky 1965 [1917], 12 (cited in Ch. 2, n. 18 above). On *verweilen*, see Ch. 1, n. 93 above.

[131] See Ch. 1 at n. 93 above.

[132] Posidipp. AB 68; *Subl.* 36.3. With Posidippus' favorable (I would argue) attitude towards the grandeur of the Colossus, compare his epigram on the lighthouse of (Posidipp. 11 G–P = AB 115 = *P. Firmin-Didot*), which celebrates two features of the monument in particular: its height (5; ~ ὑψηλοῦ, Strab. 17.1.6); and its brilliant radiance (6–8; cf. also πῦρ μέγα καιόμενον, 8).

memory forever more. Longinus' comparison between the Doryphorus of Polyclitus and the "failed" Colossus of Rhodes is entirely apt: "statues are expected to represent the human form (τὸ ὅμοιον ἀνθρώπῳ), whereas, as I said, something higher than human (τὸ ὑπεραῖρον τὰ ἀνθρώπινα) is sought in literature" and in the sublime.[133] The reduction of anthropomorphic gods to their bare matter in Callimachus and Lucian is a further symptom of the same insight. Anything material is, finally, a thing. But a thing can in cases be sublimated into a Thing, something more than natural (*huperphues*) and more than material: in such instances, it becomes a sublime form of matter. What allows for this transformation is the way culture, habit, or convention impinges on perception.

Poets were naturally attracted to analogies with architecture. That poetry is a kind of architecture is easy to see from a purely formalistic perspective. Poems have shape and structure, symmetry and balance. But wrapping our minds around the idea that buildings, and in particular buildings of monumental stature, conjure up for the ancients something like a *poetics* of space and vision is a distinctly harder task, however right it may feel to our intuitions, and as schooled as we may be in contemporary discussions of aesthetics in which such connections are commonplace. Bachelard's study, *The Poetics of Space*, is a prominent example. Van Schaik's *Poetics in Architecture* is a more recent example, inspired, in fact, by Bachelard.[134] But the tradition is rich in such metaphorics, as Panofsky has shown for the Gothic age.[135] The reverse relationship, whereby poems or other literary works are viewed as verbal architecture on a page or in the ear, enjoying spatial and weight-bearing properties in the very form of the language in which they are composed, is also challenging to the modern imagination, but less so. The title alone of Cleanth Brooks's *The Well Wrought Urn: The Structure of Poetry* made this kind of poetic imaging conceivable for an entire generation of (close) readers, buttressed by claims like "the essential structure of a poem ... resembles that of architecture or painting: it is a pattern of resolved stresses."[136] T. S. Eliot's image of the canon as "a simultaneous order" of "monuments [that] form an ideal order among themselves," whereby with each newcomer "the relations, proportions, values of each work of art toward the whole are readjusted," anticipates the same sensibility on a vaster scale.[137] As it happens, there is a long list of predecessors in this same vein, stretching

---

[133] *Subl.* 36.3; trans. Russell.   [134] Bachelard 1969 [1957]; Van Schaik 2002.
[135] Panofsky 1957.   [136] Brooks 1947, 178.   [137] Eliot 1950 [1919], 4–5.

from the Middle Ages onward.[138] It is this latter phenomenon of verbal architecture that will be of interest to us below. Nevertheless, the two phenomena – the poetics of space and verbal architecture – are linked.

Buildings do appear to be a kind of visual poetry, a frozen music, as we saw in the previous chapter. The language of architectural aesthetics (say, that of Vitruvius), the sheer abundance of literary imagery drawn from the realm of built structures, and the fascination of poets and critics with monumental building in particular, are indeed of a piece, and they often converge around the sublime. The invitation to synaesthesia alone may by itself be sublime: the sheer strain of processing sensations across such diverse realms of experience can trigger a heightening of perception altogether. Horace's *exegi monumentum aere perennius*, "I have accomplished a work more lasting than bronze,"[139] echoed by Ovid at the end of his *Metamorphoses* (*iamque opus exegi, quod nec Iovis ira nec ignis | nec poterit ferrum nec edax abolere vetustas*; "Now I have accomplished a work which neither the anger of Jupiter nor fire nor iron nor devouring age can wipe out"[140]), is only a late version of a pretension that we find in early Greek lyric poets, and the same is true of the following from Tacitus' *Dialogue on Orators* (74 CE), which brings out the mutual coherence of the critical and poetic traditions:

I think of an orator as a family man of substance and taste: I don't want him to have a house that merely keeps wind and rain off, but one that catches the eye and pleases it. His furniture shouldn't be confined to necessities – he should have gold and jewels in his stores, so that one enjoys frequently taking him down and admiring him. Some things are out of date and smelly – let them be kept out: we want no word tarnished with rust, no sentences put together in a slow sluggish form (*tarda et inerti structura*) in the manner of the annalists: he must avoid tasteless and disagreeable pleasantry, vary his structure (*compositionem*), and use more than one kind of clausula.[141]

Here, the author and his style are fused together in the imagery of a building, from the overall structure to its inner workings: *structura* can apply to both levels of design.

Ancient literary critics resort with some frequency to monumental imagery as a fund of analogies and aesthetic parallels. The existence of the phenomenon is noteworthy in itself: it points to significant conversations

[138] See Cowling 1998 for examples from late medieval and early modern France; and Frank 1979 for Pater, Hopkins, Proust, and James, but also for pointers to the intervening ground, esp. in ch. 5.
[139] Hor. *Carm.* 3.30.   [140] Ov. *Met.* 15.871–72; trans. Fowler 2000, 196.
[141] Tac. *Dialog.* 22.6–7; trans. Winterbottom, slightly adapted.

that must have obtained within and across the larger sphere of aesthetic and critical discourses in antiquity, well beyond those that we know did take place.

By way of illustration, consider the following selection of terms, and then tote up mentally the number of objects to which they can be applied in antiquity, not only in literature and architecture, but also in music and painting (I leave aside common terms for beauty, size, color, surface texture, and other aesthetic values):[142]

akribeia ("precision"), *diathesis* ("arrangement"), *diastēma* ("gap"), *euruthmia* ("flow," "disposition"), *harmogē* ("fit"), *harmonia* ("structure"), *to megaloprepes* ("grandeur"), *ogkos* ("bulk"), *oikonomia* ("organization"), *poikilia* ("elaborateness"), *rhuthmos* ("rhythm"), *schēma* ("shape"), *summetria* ("proportionality"), *sumplokē* ("interwovenness"), *sunthesis* ("combination"), *tonos* ("tension"); *dispositio* ("arrangement"), *firmitas* ("firmness"), *forma* ("form," "shape"), *gravitas* ("weight"), *lineamenta* ("linear pattern"), *maiestas* ("majesty"), *nobilis* ("nobility"), *rigor* ("hardness"), *severitas* ("severity"), *simplex* ("simple"), *species* ("outer appearance"), *splendor* ("luminosity").

The author of *On Style* suggests that a transfer of vocabulary and ideas was easily made between music and the crafts of building: "Musicians are accustomed to speak of words as 'smooth,' 'rough,' 'well-proportioned' (εὐπαγές), and 'weighty' (ὀγκηρόν)." The presence of these terms in his own treatise confirms their transferability to a third domain: literary criticism.[143] While no preserved musical writing quite backs up Demetrius' claim (Aristides Quintilianus speaks of "ponderous masses (ὄγκων) of breath" in an account of *harmonia* in his *On Music*),[144] we have to take him at his word nonetheless. Gestures such as these point to integral dialogues in what was originally an interdisciplinary or else predisciplinary world. My interest in the topic of verbal architecture stems in part from this bare fact, but also from a few more specific reasons. One of these is the striking presence of architectural and other plastic analogies in a

---

[142] That all these terms can be found in philosophy and science in their various branches, and not least of all ethics, physics, and cosmology, goes without saying. This list is meant as a continuation of that given in Ch. 1 above at p. 59, where a similar point about cross-disciplinary influences was made (though not about architecture, specifically).

[143] Demetr. *Eloc.* 176; trans. Roberts.

[144] Aristid. Quint. 2.17. See, however, Phld. *De mus.* 4 col. 60.45–col. 61.1–6 Delattre, where Philodemus accuses Stoic opponents of having fallen victim to the ambiguities of such musical terms as "melody" and "rhythm," but also, presumably, "hardness" and "softness," as the discussion in col. 61 indicates – whereby bodily and especially moral ambiguities are meant. The exact details of this polemic are difficult to reconstruct, but they do further indicate the ways in which the language of music could not help but implicate adjacent fields for the Greek ear in different ways at different historical epochs – suggestively so for the Stoics, disastrously so in Philodemus' view. Many thanks to Linda Woodward for this reference (*per litt.*).

peculiar strain of ancient literary criticism that has uniquely to do with voice (φωνή), namely euphonist criticism, criticism that begins, and in cases ends, with an analysis of the way language sounds and is made to sound, above all musically. Euphonist criticism is strange by any standard, ancient or modern. I have already touched on this phenomenon at various points above, but there is more to say about it here.

7 SOUND SCULPTURE

My point of departure will be the best attested but also the most radical exponents of Hellenistic literary criticism, the euphonist critics known somewhat mysteriously from Philodemus as οἱ ὀνομαζόμενοι κριτικοί, "those who are called 'critics'."[145] I say mysteriously, because that is how they are introduced at one point, and there is a question whether they called themselves *kritikoi* or not (that is, whether Philodemus dubbed them with this label as a convenience) – and if so, why they did so, and what the etiquette means. But also, there is the very strange fact that we learn about their existence exclusively from Philodemus – or rather, that we learn about a number of critics, some of whose names appear only in his *On Poems* (mid(?)-first century BCE), while others appear as literary euphonists there but nowhere else (e.g., Heraclides of Pontus, Megaclides of Athens, Andromenides, Pausimachus, Crates of Mallos).[146] Why this should be so is unclear. Euphonism lives on in critics of the Roman era (Dionysius of Halicarnassus and Longinus both know this approach, as do Cicero, Quintilian, Plutarch, and others), and it is also a staple of much mainstream criticism after Aristotle, whenever critics (including scholia) turn their attention to attributes of sound.[147] What is more, the theory and practice of euphonism have a heritage that reaches back into the earlier musical tradition, then into the classical era, and finally back to Pindar and Lasus, as was discussed in Chapter 7.[148] We can be quite certain that the Hellenistic euphonists were aware of this continuity, which I believe they advertised through the metaphors, analogies, and images in which their theory is couched and through which significant

---

[145] Phld. *De mus.* 4 col. 22.25–26 Neubecker = col. 136.25–26 Delattre. See Porter 1995a. I find it increasingly unlikely that Philodemus should have awarded them this label, and I doubt that ὀνομαζόμενοι, as opposed to καλούμενοι, can bear this implication, as it is sometimes argued.

[146] Nowhere else apart from Demetrius of Laconia, a fellow Epicurean and near-contemporary of Philodemus' who also wrote a work *On Poems*. Both scholars were dipping into the same well.

[147] Cf. Richardson 1980, 283–87; Meijering 1987, 42–43; Nünlist 2009, 15 n. 55; 215–17. A simple search of εὐφων- in the *TLG* of all scholia brings up 62 hits alone.

[148] See also Porter 2001a; Porter 2004b.

aspects of that theory are conveyed. At any rate, as a rough first approximation we can say that the euphonist tradition sought to capture and explore through analysis the "music" of language, from pitch accents to complex patterns of rhythm and sound running across clauses and entire passages of both poems and prose works.

Concerned with language in its phenomenal aspect, with the way poetry sounds as opposed to what it means, this strand was materialist in tendency and decidedly un-Platonic and un-Aristotelian. The conceptual divisions effected here paved the way for a freer exploration of the intricacies of verbal arrangement, viewed as analyzable in its own right and without regard for meaning (the focus was "the text *qua* text," or τὸ ποήμα καθὸ ποήμα[149]), paralleling the Aristotelian isolation of the poetic work of art judged *per se* (αὐτὸ καθ' αὐτό), which in turn marked a nuance on the Platonic isolation of non-relative beauty (καλὰ καθ' αὐτά). In Hellenistic times, there was a veritable flowering of interest in the internal features of poetic artifacts, possibly in keeping, as we saw, with the miniaturism and pointillism of Callimachus and his followers. Isolated henceforth is no longer the plot, as in Aristotle, but the matter of poetry, the material support of an, as it were, immediately sensuous experience. Its pleasures are neither rational, as in Aristotle, nor discursive, as in Eratosthenes' defense of *psuchagōgia* (whereby poetic pleasure consists in a release from truth conditions), but somatic and inaccessible to the mind, which cannot take in the sensuous particularities of poems: the body provides the irrational criterion (ἄλογον κριτήριον) of poetic value.[150] Poetic materialism runs through much Greek literary theory and criticism, following the cue of the poets. But in this extreme reductionist form, whereby sound is all that matters, euphonism is virtually unparalleled.

Virtually, but not entirely. Plutarch at one point teasingly alludes to the practice, though we cannot tell from what he says how widespread the practice was:

Now just as in pasturage the bee seeks the flower, the goat the tender shoot, the swine the root, and other animals the seed and the fruit, so in the reading of poetry one person culls the flowers of the story, another rivets his attention upon

---

[149] *Poēma*, an aspectual distinction and untranslatable at that, is defined by the euphonists as any analyzable stretch of inscribed sound, though it is usually limited to individual words, a verse portion, a verse, or a handful of verses.

[150] Though the phrase "irrational criterion" appears in Dionysius of Halicarnassus (as discussed earlier), the very same criterion and equivalent phraseology first appears in the Hellenistic euphonists. See Phld. *De poem.* 1 cols. 27; 128; and 194 Janko; Phld. *De poem.* 5 cols. 27–28 Mangoni.

the beauty of the diction and the arrangement of the words (ὁ δ᾽ ἐμφύεται τῷ κάλλει καὶ τῇ κατασκευῇ τῶν ὀνομάτων), as Aristophanes says of Euripides,

> I use the rounded neatness of his speech [lit., "roundness of his mouth":
> χρῶμαι γὰρ αὐτοῦ τοῦ στόματος τῷ στρογγύλῳ, fr. 488 K-A];

but as for those who are concerned with what is said as being useful for character (and it is to these that our present discourse is directed) . . . [151]

The reference to Aristophanes betrays how the practice was consciously grounded in an earlier phase of the critical tradition. And though Plutarch's organic metaphor might suggest otherwise, it is plain that the euphonism he disparages was pursued for its own sake, just as his own, preferred utilitarian approach is meant to be. (Plutarch's treatise as a whole is a prophylactic against the hedonistic lures of poetry, not least of all in its sensual allurements.) A striking reappearance of the same doctrine of sweet sound comes in chapter 40 of *On the Sublime*. Here, euphony is a source of sublimity – which is one reason we can say with some immediate justification that this counter-aesthetics falls squarely within a tradition of the sublime that anticipates Longinus, though there are deeper reasons for making this kind of connection. These are all attractive grounds for looking more deeply at just what these odd critics from antiquity are about and at the kind of conceptual work the analogy to verbal architecture is performing in ancient aesthetic thought.

The euphonists are an odd bunch, but not completely so. In fact, connecting them up with larger aesthetic trends both before and after them can help throw much-needed light on their positions. Let me venture a first thesis that I won't argue for now: in this tradition of criticism, euphony stands not for the proposition that all poetry is reducible to the way it sounds, as it is commonly imagined to do, but rather for the fact that poetry cannot be grasped unless it is appreciated as it is *sensed and experienced*, which is to say, as a *felt phenomenon*. "Euphony" – εὐφωνία – stands for a kind of sensualism in art. And though the language of the reductionist euphonists is philosophically tinged, it refuses to slot into ready-made schools and labels, despite the widespread myth that they are Stoics.[152] On the contrary, they are philosophical mavericks, being sensualists of no particular bent who celebrate an existing current within Greek poetics. In fact, the euphonists are merely crystallizing a

---

[151] Plut. *Mor.* 30D; trans. Babbitt.
[152] Most recently, for example, Fantuzzi and Hunter 2004, 451; *contra*: Atherton 1989; Porter 1989, 150–51 n. 8; see Dion. Hal. *Comp.* 4; 22.3–14 U–R for ancient proof of the counterclaim.

tendency of all ancient literature, the appreciation of its aesthetic capacities whenever it is spoken or read aloud, which it almost always was. They simply do this with a single-minded zeal that appears to be unparalleled in our sources.

A text from Philodemus' *On Poems* will serve as a good *entrée* to the euphonists' critical theory, as it happens to act like a billboard for their views. It was quoted earlier, but it will now resonate differently in the present context:

The composition [alone, being ἴδια, viz., irreducibly particular] is the object of elaboration; and it stands as [engraved] in [stone] (ὡς | ἐγ [στήλ]ηι μέ[ν]ει) for all the *kritikoi* that "euphony, which is epiphenomenal (τὴν μὲν | [ἐπιφαι]νομένην [ε]ὐφωνί|αν), is to be considered *idion* [specific to a poem or its being heard], while the meanings and phrases [sc., the diction] must be considered external (ἐκτός) [to the poetic art] and common [or 'universal,' κοινά]"; but this is manifestly silly, as shown by my previous comments.[153]

Seeing how the language of the euphonists is rather idiosyncratic, let's try to translate it back into plain English. What Philodemus has in his sights is the main thrust of the euphonists' poetic program. The value of poetry for these critics lies not in what poetry means but in the way it sounds – its "musicality." Poems for them just are aggregates of sound – whence their favored term, *sunthesis*, which has to be taken literally: it stands for a "putting-together" of the *stoicheia*, the elements or letter-sounds, that make up, like building blocks, the syllables of the individual *lexeis* or words (or, at times, rhythmical "times" or "durations," *chronoi*). This much was discussed above in Chapter 4.[154]

Now, at stake in the present passage is nothing less than the value of the *idion*, which displaces the semantic aspects of poems, which includes meaning, moral effects, but also a poem's generic classification:[155] these are all sacrificed to the poem's material surfaces and to the way these latter appear to an auditor (whence ἐπιφαινομένη in the passage just quoted), which is to say, to the poem's acoustic appearances (its sounds). The *sole* preoccupation of poets, according to these euphonist critics, lies in what is *idion* to their own poetic productions, not in what is common to all other

---

[153] *P. Herc.* 1676 col. 6.1–11; text after Janko 2000, 125 n. 1 (part). (For the Greek, see Ch. 4, n. 224 above).

[154] See Ch. 4, §§7–9.

[155] See Walsdorff 1927, 33, to my knowledge the earliest recognition of this fact about the euphonists' indifference to genre boundaries. Cf. further Porter 1989, 171 at n. 119. Walsdorff was a doctoral student of Jensen, the first editor of Phld. *On Poems* 5 (1923); he was thus in an excellent position to know.

poems, or (as they also put it) what can be found "outside" their art (ἐκτός) – whence, too, the parallel phrase we find elsewhere in their teachings, ἔξω τῆς τέχνης.[156] These critics are consciously inverting Aristotle, who located the poetic essence – the "in itself" of poetry – in poetry's form: by contrast, they locate the essence of poetry in poetry's matter, in its sensation (*aisthēsis*), and in its appearance – *this* is their *in-itselfness* (καθ' αὐτό).[157] Poetic particulars (ἴδια), on this materialist and phenomenalist view, are deeply a part of the poetic "matter," the true *hulē* of the poet,[158] "original" to it and him: they are phenomena peculiar to their embedded context in a poem analyzed as a collection of sounds.[159] In the sample from Posidippus quoted above, these would include a range of effects, from word order to the role of pitches and accents to rhythms and meters, none of which would occur "naturally" in Greek prose, nor would they occur identically – that is, as a *koinon* – in any other poem either (except through quotation or plagiarism).[160] The various *meanings* that the sounds can be said to express (or can be said to reduce to) could, however, be found in any number of settings, from mineralogical hand-books to art catalogues to the simple gushing of a naïve onlooker, as the last verse implies: "How did its sculptor not blur his eyesight on the job!"[161] Hence, meaning is not *idion*: it is not rooted in the particular contingencies of this matter here at this moment of audition. It is common (*koinon*).

In an immediately preceding column from Philodemus, the particularity (τὸ ἴδιον) is claimed to reside not in the production of likenesses (for these are common, *koina*, just by virtue of being "alike," e.g. to painters and sculptors), but rather in the actual carving in metal and stone, which

---

[156] Phld. *De poem.* 1 cols. 132.27–133.1 Janko.

[157] Arist. *Poet.* 25.1460b15–16; ibid., 4.1449a8–9; ibid. 7.1451a6–7; Phld. *De poem.* 5 col. 25.30; ibid., *P. Herc.* 1676 col. 7.7–17 *N* = col. 18 Sbordone 1976. The resemblance in terminologies is striking and can hardly be haphazard. I suspect it points to a conscious harking back to Aristotle. There may be a further reminiscence (and inversion) in ἔξω τῆς τέχνης of Aristotle's key idiom in the *Poetics*, ἔξω τοῦ μύθου ("outside the plot"). See p. 116 above.

[158] My designation. ὕλη in its technical sense is reserved by the euphonists for its customary, presumably Peripatetically derived, usage, standing for plot, subject matter (*hupothesis*), and all that goes with this (meaning, *lexeis*, etc.). See Phld. *De poem.* 1 col. 74.8 Janko; *P. Herc.* 1081 col. 9.24; col. 13; *P. Herc.* 1676 col. 4.5–9 *N* = col. 15 Sbordone.

[159] For the connotation of *idios* as "original," "exceptional," "unique," see Pherecrates fr. 155.14 K–A; Eur. *Or.* 558; Antiph. frr. 207.1–3; 953.3 K–A.

[160] To be sure, euphonists will detect such effects in both prose and in poetry, as will Cicero (e.g., *Orat.* Book 3) and other stylistic critics.

[161] Posidipp. AB 15; trans. Nisetich (slightly adapted) in Gutzwiller 2005b, 20.

is specific to an instance of a given art (here, plastic art). The opponent committed a fallacy, Philodemus claims,

because, as I said, he adduced crafts that are different but have their goal in common. For just as it is not the peculiar function (ἴδιον) of the ring engraver to make a likeness – for this is common to the sculptor and painter – but [to make a likeness] in iron and gem stones through engraving (διὰ τῆς ἐγ[γ]λυφῆς), though the good does not lie in this [sc., in the engraving *qua* engraving] but in making a similarity, which is common to all, in like manner it is claimed that the poet [wants] his peculiar function (ἴδιον) [to lie] in the composition (*sunthesis*) [sc., of the sounds],[162] but hunts out the good in the common sphere, in meaning and diction – [a good] which this [critic] says does simply no [moral] benefit or harm at all, as he concluded from his examples, but not the opposite.[163] Therefore, poets (he claims) derive what is common from others [and make it their own (ἴδιον) by adding their own *suntheseis*].[164]

The analogies in this text make the same point as its sequel quoted above, only now they do so in a graphic way: if you fashion an image of a chariot in a gemstone and then reproduce the same image in bronze or paint, you will have produced something in common, a *koinon*; but what you will have lost in the translation from stone into bronze or paint is precisely the *idion*, the specific effect of the materiality of the likeness in this or that medium.[165] For the same reason, the most obvious element

---

[162] Cf. two columns prior: "according to the *sunthesis* of the rhythms and the diction" (*P. Herc.* 1676 col. 3.1–3 *N* = col. 14 Sbordone); and the subsequent column, which was quoted just above.

[163] I.e., presumably, not even a morally bad content ("the opposite") will result in either moral benefit or moral harm.

[164] διότι, καθάπερ ε[ἴ]Ιπον, δια]φεϱούσα[ς μὲν τέ]Ιχνας, ἐν δὲ τῶ⟨ι⟩ κοινῶι τὸΙτέ[λο]ς ἐχούσας παϱατέθηΙκεν. ὡ[ς] γὰϱ [δ]ακτυλιογλύΙφ[ο]ς ἴδιον ἔχων οὐ τὸ ποιΙεῖν ὅμο[ι]ον – κοινὸν γὰϱ ἦν Ι καὶ πλ[ά]στου καὶ ζωγϱ[άΙφου – Ι[τὸ δ'] ἐν σιδήϱω⟨ι⟩ καὶ λιΙθαϱίωι διὰ τῆς ἐγ[γ]λυφῆς,Ι τἀγ[αθὸ]ν οὐκ ἐν τούτωι κεί[με]νον, ἀλλ' ἐν τῶι ποιΙεῖν ὅμ[ο]ιον, ὃ πάντων κοιΙνὸν, ἔχει, παϱαπλησίως ἀξιοῦτα[ι] καὶ [ὁ] ποητὴς Ι τὸ μὲ[ν ἴδι]ον ἐν [τῆι συ]νθέσειβ[ούλε]σθαι, τὸ δ' ἀγα[ιθὸν δι[αν]οία[ι καὶ] λέ[ξει] κοιΙνῶ[ς] θηϱεύειν, ὅ φησιν οὗΙτος ἁπλῶς μηδὲ ἓν ὠφελΙεῖν ἢ βλάπτειν, ὥσπεϱ ἐκ τῶν παϱατεθέντωνΙ συνῆχε[ν, ἀ]λλ' οὐ τοὐνΙαντίον· [τὸ] τοίνυν τοὺς ποητὰς τὸ [κοιν]ὸν† παϱ' ἑτέϱων λαβόντας (*P. Herc.* 1676 col. 5.3–28 *N* = col. 16 Sbordone (rev. and trans. Asmis 1995, 160–61 (part); trans. adapted; final supplement mine, based on the subsequent column).

[165] By the way, we shouldn't be thrown off track by Philodemus, who seems to have introduced a second sense of *idion* into the discussion, viz., that of proper function, which is not part of the euphonists' vocabulary (*idios* for them means, practically, "original" to the artist and his product), though it is found in, say, Aristotle. Philodemus is taking a quality of the object, or the artist's contribution to the object, and making it into a function of the artist. But while we're at it, we might as well notice how the euphonists' point is rather different from Aristotle's, for instance when he states (*Poet.* 13.1452b33) that the *idion* of the poet is to *mimeisthai* (imitate or represent). For Aristotle, there is no real hint that the imitation is colored by the particularity of the medium, whereas for the euphonists the imitation is made distinctive by the medium in which it is made – indeed, its aesthetic value seems to lie not in imitation *per se*, but in this distinctive, material difference.

that gets lost in translation from one language to another is not the meaning, but the *sound* of the original. The euphonists are making just this point. Only, they are doing so in an especially emphatic way. For the truly radical thrust of their program is encapsulated in another text by Philodemus: "Good poets excel and they alone endure (διαμένουσιν) on no other account than the sounds," by which is meant "the sounds isolated in and of themselves" (οἱ ἦχοι αὐτοί) apart from their meanings, "the sound that appears on the surface of the composition" (ἡ ἐπιφαινομένη φωνὴ ἡ τῇ συνθέσει).[166]

This axiom, as it is usually understood, is taken to be a horrific inversion of all the hallowed values of classical poetics, at least as we grasp these today. I've recently tried to show how the euphonist critics have to be understood as in fact sustaining the ideology of classicism by appealing to the irrational mainsprings of the *habitus* that underlie it, which is to say, the sources of "feeling classical."[167] Nevertheless, there is something truly odd about the claim that poets excel and endure on account of their sounds alone, and this will turn out to provide a further key to understanding the euphonists' rationale. It will also give us a way of linking them up to their Hellenistic contemporaries, in addition to connecting them to the lyric and epigrammatic traditions of the archaic and early classical periods.

The verb διαμένουσιν above has an echo in the passage quoted earlier, which I doubt is accidental: "and it stands [or 'endures'] as [engraved] in [stone] (ὡς ἐγ [στήλ]ηι μέ[ν]ει) for all the *kritikoi*." The opinions of the euphonists stand as if written on stone (if the conjecture is right). Did they initiate, or at least suggest, the metaphor themselves? Even if they did not, and Philodemus was merely mocking them with the image, there would still be more to say about their possible connection to the epigraphical tradition. Behind everything lies a play of contraries: excellence endures thanks to sound, but sound is fleeting, epiphanic, and evanescent. Canonicity is a delicate, fragile thing: it lasts no longer than a breath, yet it lasts, optimally, forever. How can poems, read aloud, achieve this effect of eternality? If we can detect echoes of the archaic theme of *la parole et le marbre*, this is probably no accident. A kind of verbal architecture is in play in the euphonist critical program, whereby composition is felt to

---

[166] οἱ ἀγαθοὶ ποιηταὶ παρ' οὐδὲν ἄλλο πρωτεύουσίν τε καὶ μόνοι διαμένουσιν ἢ παρὰ τοὺς ἤχους (Phld. *De poem.* 1, col. 83.11–14 Janko); cf. ibid., col. 84.7; 84.12; 89.11–12: αὐτὸς ὁ ἦχος; ἡ ἐπιφαινομένη φωνή ἡ τῇ συνθέσει (*De poem.* 5, col. 23.38 Mangoni).

[167] Porter 2006b.

create sublime (verbal) monuments, as I want to show next. The effect of sublimity has everything to do with the contradictories that are enlisted in this interplay of metaphors.

Let us begin by observing one of the most pronounced features of the euphonist strain of ancient criticism: the way it regards poetry as process. Poetry here is viewed as a literal construction of materials. Only, the materials happen to be made of sound. In the architectural imagination of these literary critics, sounds are joined with sounds so as to build a pleasing edifice of euphonic effects (as it were, a wall of sound). The passage from process to materials to sound, with results both durable and transient, is an unstable one; and it is one that is in turn relived by the hearer or reader. As an initial example, consider the next bit of text from Philodemus' *On Poems*, reporting the views of an anonymous Hellenistic critic who is referred to simply as "the Milesian," but who may be a certain Pausimachus:[168]

For just as a kind of glue (κόλλα τις) or a bolt (γόμφος) or some such thing is used for joining wooden things (π[ϱὸ]ς τὴν τῶν ξυλίν[ω]ν σύν[θ]εσιν), so is the soundless element of language [viz., the consonant or mute, τὸ ἄφωνον], when it is aptly employed, used for binding the diction (πϱὸς τὴν τῆς λέξεως σύμπηξιν).

Another simile follows:

Indeed, just as in solid bodies (ἐπὶ τῶν σωμάτων) the compact (τὸ εὐπαγές) comes about when the whole body (τὸ ὅλον σῶμα) has all its parts arranged well (εὖ δι[α]κείμενα), [viz.,] when they are in agreement with the lengths (τοῖς τε μήκεσι) and with the massy constituents (τοῖς ὄγκοις) and are symmetrical (σύμμετϱα) ....[169]

The reference to architecture here, in the form of carpentry more than of heavy stonework, primarily serves to remind us that poems and speeches can be viewed as built structures, while their authors are comparable to builders or architects.[170] The things built don't have to be monumental to qualify for the analogy, though they sometimes do and are, as will soon be

---

[168] Phld. *De poem.* 2 (*P. Herc.* 994 col. 34.4–11); text after Janko 2000, 299 n. 8; see Janko ibid., 167 for the identification.

[169] Phld. ibid., col. 34.18–25 Sbordone.

[170] Cf. a euphonist quoted at Phld. *De poem.* 1 col. 55.2–9 Janko: "'Also, bad [poets] often presuppose the same [plots], and often even better ones than good [poets do]. But they are not able to build (οἰκοδομε(ῖ)ν) it, if it is a fine one.' He also writes, 'a prose writer too builds (οἰκοδομῆ[σαι]) [one], if p[...].'" Janko rightly compares *Subl.* 39.3, where *sunthesis* is said to be a kind of "building."

seen. Even without the comparison to a text like the following from Aristotle's *Metaphysics*, it is obvious that euphonists exemplify a kind of materialism in the area of literary poetics and aesthetics. They are treating poetry as *edifices (suntheseis) of sound*.

Now to Aristotle on the *differentiae* of matter:

> But evidently there are many differences [between things, viz., many *differentiae* of matter]; for instance, some things are characterized by (i) the mode of composition of their matter (οἷον τὰ μὲν συνθέσει λέγεται τῆς ὕλης), e.g. the things formed by mixture (ὅσα κράσει), such as honey-water; and others by (ii) being bound together (τὰ δὲ δεσμῷ), e.g. a bundle [sc., of sticks]; and others by (iii) being glued together (τὰ δὲ κόλλη), e.g. a book; and others by (iv) being bolted together (τὰ δὲ γόμφῳ), e.g. a casket; and others (iv) in more than one of these ways.[171]

Evidently, poetic texts qualify as material compounds in all four ways, if we apply Aristotle's criteria to the views of the later euphonists. Only mixture is missing in the passage from Philodemus, though even this term appears elsewhere in their vocabulary, in passages where sounds are being described as "mixed" in much the same way that primary physical substances are in, say, Empedocles.[172] The connection with Empedocles may not be as far-fetched as it seems. Empedocles may well be on Aristotle's mind above: he happens to make use of all the terms mentioned by Aristotle.[173] And the euphonists in one place resort to a technical term for the impact of sound (πρόπτωσις) that originates in Empedocles' theory of hearing.[174] I believe there is more than a hint of a direct connection between this one Presocratic and the later theory of poems as clusters of sounds. And there would have been plenty of intermediaries to help ensure the connection, from Democritus to the various sophists to Empedocles' pupil Gorgias to subsequent philosophical pathways.

At any rate, I hope it is clear by now that materialism in poetics follows as naturally for these critics as it does for any poet or critic who provisionally adopts a euphonist stance towards language – as many do, and not only in the Hellenistic period.[175] Sacrificing sound to sense, whether

---

[171] Arist. *Metaph.* H 2.1042b15–20; trans. Ross, adapted.

[172] E.g., Phld. *De poem.* 1 col. 114.16 Janko: "mixture [of sounds]"; cf. ibid., col. 89.19–20; Phld. *De poem.* 2, *P. Herc.* 994 col. 27.25 Sbordone.

[173] See the discussion of Empedocles in Ch. 3, §5 above. For "bolts" and "binding" see DK 31B33 (ἐγόμφωσεν καὶ ἔδησε) and B87 (γόμφοις).

[174] See Empedocles *ap.* Diels 1965 [1879], 406ª17; Phld. *De poem.* 1 col. 112.20 with Janko ad loc.

[175] See Fantuzzi and Hunter 2004, 456, for the suggestion that "contemporary poetry has here, in fact, influenced theory." On the practice of poets, see further Reitzenstein 1931; Van Groningen 1953; Krevans 1993; Ambühl 1995; Pendergraft 1995; Acosta-Hughes and Stephens 2002; Porter 2010a.

in principle or for the sake of momentary analysis, critics acting as euphonists have nothing left to describe but a poem's matter. By contrast, conventional criticism of the kind that is inspired by Plato and Aristotle for the most part eschews, or simply tolerates, questions of sound (as was seen earlier, the two philosophers were generally hostile to art as a sensuous phenomenon), and instead focuses on the finer and more intangible problems of form and meaning. And yet, how can *structure* and *form* fail to conjure up images of material building? How can anyone analyze verbal structure without falling into the metaphorical thinking of architectural form and the analogies to physical matter that this entails?

We have already seen how the very first accounts of verbal structure, from Homer to the archaic lyric poets to the comic poets in the fifth century, all tended to conceptualize poetic material in this way. In fact, the earliest Greek poets seem to have inaugurated and then perpetuated the tradition of what I am calling "sublime monuments" in poetry.[176] Plato escapes in part just by evading the problem of structure almost altogether: he has little interest in the concrete minutiae of poetic artistry – of "form" in this sense. Aristotle fares less well, as we saw, all but tumbling headfirst again into a materialism of sorts in the course of analyzing plot as a *sunthesis* or *sustasis*, whereby the "soul" of tragedy, subjected to a structural analysis, is revealed to be a unity of material parts. Formalists in the wake of these two grand philosophers could manage the dilemma by taking refuge in the very license of metaphor itself, which enabled them to treat form as a disembodied feature of objects and to discount the remainder as so much inessential dross. The Neoplatonists seem to have taken that route,[177] as do the Alexandrian critics, who focus mostly on formal and nearly immaterial plot structures *à la* Aristotle's conception of *praxis* whenever they attend to large-scale narrative shapes (*hupothesis, oikonomia, taxis*) as opposed to smaller, bite-sized *lemmata* and *zētēmata*.[178] An extreme but memorable example comes from the hypothesis to Sophocles' *Oedipus at Colonus*: "On the whole, the arrangement [of the action] in the play is *ineffable* (ἄφατος δέ ἐστι καθόλου ἡ

---

[176] See Ch. 3, §9 on Homer; this chapter, §1 on Pindar and Simonides; and Ch. 5, §1 on Old Comedy.
[177] Cf. Plotinus' famous account of beauty in *Enn.* 1.6.3, e.g., describing "the inner form (*eidos*) divided by [or 'distributed through'] the mass of external matter" (τὸ ἔνδον εἶδος μερισθὲν τῷ ἔξω ὕλης ὄγκῳ), where the form, akin to a Form, "antedates matter" ([τὸ] πρὸ σώματος), is "incorporeal" (or "unembodied," ἀσωμάτου), and is "invisible" (cf. τὰ μὴ ὁρώμενα, 1.6.4); trans. Armstrong; adapted.
[178] See Meijering 1987, chs. 3 and 4; Nünlist 2009, ch. 1.

οἰκονομία ἐν τῷ δράματι), almost like in no other play"! Plutarch, for his part, tends to blend both Platonic and Aristotelian positions syncretistically, as a glance at his treatise, *How the Young Should Listen to Poets* or his other comments on poetry would show.[179] But on the whole, form and structure in literary criticism (*eidos, sunthesis, sustasis, forma,* and *structura*) continued to signify concrete entities, as will be seen below.

More explicit examples of the architectural analogy come in *On the Composition of Words* by Dionysius of Halicarnassus, who stands at the far end of the Hellenistic tradition to which Philodemus' opponents belong somewhere near its beginnings and middle. Builders, he writes, pay "close attention to the following three questions": what materials (ὕλήν) will be put together (συντίθησι); "next how each of the materials should be fitted" (πῶς τῶν ἁρμοζομένων ἕκαστον ἑδράσαι), whether "stones, timber, tiling, or all the rest"; "and thirdly, if anything is seated badly (εἴ τι δύσεδρόν ἐστιν), how that very piece can be pared down and trimmed and made to fit well" (εὕεδρον ποιῆσαι).[180] And so "those who are going to put the parts of speech together effectively" (εὖ συνθήσειν τὰ τοῦ λόγου μόρια), he goes on, "should proceed in a similar way." The general term for the entire process he is describing, that of literary composition, is verbal *sunthesis.*

Dionysius calls this analogy an *eikōn* or image of the process of poetic making. But what is significant, though not immediately apparent from his language, is that the process he is describing has one goal in mind: the materials in question are *sounds,* and the aim of all this chipping and trimming of the material of sound is to produce a euphonious effect, one that will result in a *phantasia* that impresses itself upon the ear. Thus, consistent with the program of a sensuous aesthetics, the same chapter in Dionysius begins with an account of the functions of the science of composition (τῆς συνθετικῆς ἐπιστήμης), namely, (i) producing "a beautiful and attractive united effect" (καλὴν καὶ ἡδεῖαν συζυγίαν); (ii) judging "how each of the parts should be shaped (σχηματισθέν) so as to improve the harmonious appearance of the whole" (κρείττονα ποιήσειε φαίνεσθαι τὴν ἁρμονίαν); (iii) determining what modifications in "the material used (τῶν λαμβανομένων) – I mean subtraction, addition or alteration – " are necessary for "their future purpose."[181] These functions of composition revolve around the production of beautiful façades, which

---

[179] Further, Tagliasacchi 1961.   [180] Dion. Hal. *Comp.* 6; trans. Usher.
[181] Dion. Hal. *Comp.* 6; trans. Usher.

are a *sunthesis* at a higher level, this time of *perceptions*. Glancing back at Pindar and Simonides, with their language of beautiful poetic façades, one has to wonder whether they didn't have in mind exactly the same sort of phenomenon – not just the poem as a material object, but also as projecting a dimensional *appearance* in the mind (or ear) of the listener, and in cases (especially in Pindar) a magnificent one. Thus, when Pindar writes (or sings), "Come, let us now construct an elaborate | adornment that speaks words,"[182] how can he have anything else in mind than such an imaginary projection erected by way of the ear?

Let's simply footnote for now the emphasis placed in the passage from Dionysius on the causal relation, but also the distance, that lies between materials and their effect or appearance. At stake here is an *aesthetic* use of materials, the production of a unified aesthetic appearance (a *phainomenon*). And this, too, is a feature that is shared in common with architectural discourse, as a glance at Dionysius' contemporary, Vitruvius, can show:

1 Architecture consists of ordering (*ordinatione*), which is called *taxis* in Greek, and of design (*dispositione*) – the Greeks call this *diathesis* – and shapeliness (*eurythmia*) and symmetry (*symmetria*) and correctness (*decore*) and allocation (*distributione*), which is called *oeconomia* in Greek.

2 Ordering (*ordinatio*) is the proportion to scale (*commoditas*) of the work's individual components (*membrorum*) taken separately, as well as their correspondence to an overall proportional scheme of symmetry (*ad symmetriam*). It is achieved through quantity (*quantitate*), which in Greek is called *posotes*. Quantity, in turn, is the establishment of modules (*modulorum sumptio*) taken from the elements (*membris*) of the work itself and the agreeable execution of the work as a whole (*universi operis conveniens effectus*) on the basis of the elements' individual parts.

Next, design is the apt placement of things (*dispositio autem est rerum apta conlocatio*), and the elegant effect obtained by their *arrangement* according to the nature of the work (*elegansque compositionibus effectus operas cum qualitate*) ....

3 Shapeliness is an attractive appearance and a coherent aspect in the composition of the elements (*eurythmia est venusta species commodusque in conpositionibus membrorum aspectus*)....

5 Next, correctness (*decor*) is the refined appearance (*aspectus*) of a project that has been composed of proven elements and with authority.[183]

---

[182] See at n. 32 above.

[183] Vitr. *De arch.* 1.2.2–5; trans. Rowland and Howe. This same passage attracted the notice of Ben Jonson who annotated it with his own glosses and who likewise sought to align the architectural and verbal connotations of its various terms; see Turner 2006, 258. On the rhetorical background to Vitruvius' conceptual apparatus, see Callebat 1994.

A second, closely related use of monumental analogies in ancient literary criticism is to be found in stylistic analysis. When the styles in question are the grand style (*genus grande*) or else writing that exhibits archaic and archaicizing or severe and austere features (these needn't be exclusive categories), then for once the built structures in question most definitely are of a monumental stature, and we are put in mind of sublimity. That is the whole point of the analogy between words and grand buildings, which in part, due to the nature of classicism, equates exaltation with a reverence for the grand literary monuments of the distant past.[184] More simply put, classical structures in stone, on the page, and in the ear can take one of two forms: either by bulking large in the imagination as built structures *simpliciter*, or by presenting a hoary, jagged, somewhat worn, and somewhat primitive façade, and thereby evidencing their antiquity. Either way, they are truly sublime monuments.

I have not made a complete inventory of monuments in ancient literary criticism – far from it (though I would be grateful if somebody did). But my sense is that architectural metaphors in criticism tend to fall into one or the other of these two uses, which is to say, they serve as a reminder either of the built nature of the linguistic artifact or of its grander dimensions. In practice, these two considerations are closely allied, as for instance in Demetrius' *On Style*:

The members (τὰ κῶλα) in a periodic style may, in fact, be compared to the stones which support (ἀντερείδουσι) and hold together (συνέχουσι) a vaulted roof. The members of the disconnected style resemble stones which are simply flung carelessly together (διερριμμένοις ... λίθοις) and not built into a structure (οὐ συγκειμένοις). Consequently the older style of writing has something of the sharp, clean lines (περιεξεσμένον ἔχει τι καὶ εὐσταλές)[185] of early statues, where the skill was thought to lie in their succinctness and spareness.[186] The style of later writers is like the sculpture of Phidias, since it already exhibits in some degree the union of elevation and finish (ἔχουσά τι καὶ μεγαλεῖον καὶ ἀκριβές ἅμα).[187]

A parallel passage in Dionysius of Halicarnassus makes the same point about the austere style (ἡ αὐστηρὰ ἁρμονία). Only here, the description moves down a notch, away from the physics of the syntactical clause. The

---

[184] See Porter 2006b, 323–23.

[185] Chiron 1993, ad loc., renders περιεξεσμένον with "uni" ("united"). The word ought to mean hewn about, and so polished. In a parallel passage, *Comp.* 22 (to be quoted momentarily), Dionysius says the opposite: μὴ συνεξεσμέναι. Perhaps a negation has dropped from this troubled passage. For εὐσταλές of the MSS, Chiron reads εὐσταθές ("firm").

[186] Roberts renders these two terms ἡ συστολὴ καὶ ἰσχνότης with "severe simplicity."

[187] Demetr. *Eloc.* 13–14; trans. Roberts and Innes, adapted.

focus here is at the level of words (*onomata*), viewed briefly as "parts of a sentence" (though not exactly as clauses), and then as parts of words – namely, syllables:

The special character of the austere style of composition is this: it requires that the words shall stand firmly on their own feet (ἀσφαλῶς) and occupy strong positions (καὶ στάσεις λαμβάνειν ἰσχυράς ["like columns": Roberts]) and be seen on all sides (ὥστ' ἐκ περιφανείας ἕκαστον ὄνομα ὁρᾶσθαι); and that the parts of the sentence (τὰ μόρια) shall be at considerable distances from one another (ἀπέχειν τε ἀπ' ἀλλήλων), separated by perceptible intervals (διαστάσεις ἀξιολόγους αἰσθητοῖς χρόνοις διειργόμενα). It does not mind admitting harsh and dissonant collocations, like blocks of natural stone laid together in building, with their sides not cut square or polished smooth (μὴ εὐγώνιοι καὶ μὴ συνεξεσμέναι βάσεις), but remaining unworked and rough-hewn (ἀργαὶ καὶ αὐτοσχέδιοι). It has a general liking for expansion by means of long words which extend over a wide space (μεγάλοις τε καὶ διαβεβηκόσιν εἰς πλάτος ὀνόμασιν ὡς τὰ πολλὰ μηκύνεσθαι φιλεῖ), because restriction to short syllables is repugnant to it, except when necessity sometimes compels.[188]

The passage is remarkable for the way it visualizes a critical conceit about language – not only for the degree of vividness it imparts to the scenario, but also for the kinds of transformations it brings about. Words are turned into building materials, and then the gaps between them are magnified in such a way that they become three-dimensional objects jutting off the page and so too microscopically surveyable in their minutest textures. Needless to say, the gaps in question consist not of space, but of *time*.[189] The transformation thus wrought is twofold: a visualization of a text requires its (i) spatialization, which is to say, its translation into a spatial image. But that, in turn, requires, or rather is equivalent to, a (ii) temporalization, or translation of space into time. Finally, as this entire textual landscape is imagined under the sign of its being read aloud, in question at any moment are less whole words, with the gaps between them and their *chronoi* in the technical sense of the term in conventional (Aristoxenian) rhythmical theory (time-durations), than vocalic and intervocalic sounds, silences (pauses), and lengths of *breath* – "the speaker's breath" (τὸ πνεῦμα τοῦ λέγοντος).[190]

---

[188] Dion. Hal. *Comp.* 22; 96.10–22 U–R; trans. Usher, adapted.
[189] Cf. Dion. Hal. *Dem.* 38 for a less graphic and less extended version of the same metaphor: "Long words (ὀνόμασι μεγάλοις) with long syllables (μακροσυλλάβοις) are favoured, each with a broad, firm foundation (ταῖς ἕδραις αὐτῶν εἶναι πλατέως πάνυ βεβηκυίαις), and each separated (διορίζεσθαι) from its neighbour by a considerable interval of time" (χρόνων).
[190] Dion. Hal. *Comp.* 22; 97.16 U–R.

After all, "harsh and dissonant collocations" (τραχείαις καὶ ἀντιτύποις ταῖς συμβολαῖς) is a reference to effects of sound – and especially those that are productive of grandeur, or *megethos*.[191] Magnifying the micro-scopic as it does, Dionysius' analysis turns a soundscape into a palpable and visible landscape, strewn with stones, columns, and other three-dimensional objects. In spatializing and magnifying sounds as he does, he inspects these much like a tourist strolling about a temple precinct amid columns – columns that are made of sound.[192] His analysis thus marks a prolongation of the Hellenistic aesthetic of sublimely contrastive scales, wherein opposites coincide and grandeur is found in a grain of sand, as we saw in the case of Posidippus and company and then in the Philodemean *kritikoi*, to whom Dionysius in fact stands in a direct line of succession, being himself a latter-day *kritikos*. There may even be a nod to contemporary building practices, seeing how the trend towards vaulted architecture brought with it the increased likelihood of associating sound resonances with monumentality.[193] Sound sculpture, indeed … And we might further recall the analogous use of spatialization in Herodotus, where architectural metaphorics were put to similar ends, namely the creation of an aura of historical grandeur. Only there, the process went in the reverse direction, and time, large chunks of it, was being translated into space, in the form of a monument of extraordinary dimensions and on the brink of vanishing, like a ruin or a faded memory.

The tradition of blending architectural and literary vocabularies con-tinued to flourish in Roman circles, as a glance at the orators shows. Avoidance of hiatus is sometimes termed *coagmentare*, or "cementing,"[194] though smooth surfaces of sound are not always a desirable quality.[195] But often they are. Suetonius records how Caligula once criticized Seneca's style as lacking this binding quality: it is "like sand without lime."[196]

---

[191] Usher rightly references Demetr. *Eloc.* 48–49 and 68, which pick up on the same language as here; chs. 48–49 also concern the production of grandeur. ἀντίτυπος is a term of art in Dionysius for harshness or dissonance of sound. Cf. Dion. Hal. *Comp.* 22, *passim* (e.g., 101.13; 102.8 U–R; etc.).

[192] Thus confounding one's normal expectations, as expressed, e.g., by Stewart 1993, 102: "The miniature allows us only visual access to surface and texture; it does not allow movement through space."

[193] See Koenigs 1984, 63–64; Plin. *HN* 36.100; Paus. 5.21.17; Hor. *Sat.* 1.4.76: "the enclosed place gives a pleasing resonance to the voice"; Thomas 2007, 209–10; 220. This kind of effect is called "aural architecture" in Blesser and Salter 2007. The association appears to be perennial. Prehistoric decorated caves, such as those at Lascaux, display acoustic properties, which may have been deliberately exploited by the painters; see Scarre and Lawson 2006. Further, Tilley 2004, 35; 63; 99; 131.

[194] Cic. *De or.* 3.171.   [195] Cic. *Orat.* 77–78; *Brut.* 68.   [196] Suet. *Calig.* 53.2.

Words can be thought of as a *structura* when they are joined together (*iuncta, coniuncta, apta*). They need to be squared (*quadrata*) and polished (*polita*). (One is put in mind of Simonides' Scopas poem again.) They sit on foundations (*fundamenta*). And in general, to compose in language is to be like a "builder of words" (*architectus verborum*), the way the Stoics are in philosophical argument, though not in oratory.[197] It is to build a monument (*exaedificare*), though not always a splendid one.[198]

8 TAKING STOCK

Before moving on, it is worth summarizing the achievements of the radical euphonist critical tradition and situating it more firmly in the larger traditions of poetry and aesthetics that surround it. Several key points have emerged from the foregoing discussion:

1 In treating verbal artifacts as composites of materials, the euphonists enroll themselves in a long-standing tradition of "verbal architecture."
2 They hark back to the archaic lyric tradition of "verbal monuments" and even of "sublime monuments." This tradition is rooted in the epigraphic tradition, as we saw, which viewed texts as *objects inscribed with writing* rather than as *writing inscribed on objects*. Like their forebears, they are interested in how monuments *sound*.
3 By conceiving works of prose and poetry as potentially euphonious, these critics developed a general aesthetics of texts conceived as "speaking objects." As a rubric, *oggetti parlanti* is not a bad way to account for the entire phenomenon of ecphrastic things, whether poems or stones, early and late. Euphony is what happens to language when it is reduced to an object that is then made to speak – or better yet, to *sing*.
4 Drawing upon these sensitivities they compiled an aesthetics that was rooted in phenomenalism and sensualism, and that originated in technical vocabulary fifth-century materialism. Their language is heavily inflected with philosophical terms, but they are eclectics, not dogmatics, who flirt with various forms of Hellenistic hedonism, sensualism, and phenomenalism. They are a product of their age, even in their filiations with the past.

---

[197] Cic. *Brut.* 118; cf. Dion. Hal. *Comp.* 4; 22.3–14 U–R.
[198] Cic. *De or.* 1.164; 2.63; 3.175; *Brut.* 33; *Orat.* 149; 220; 224; Quint. *Inst.* 2.5.9 (*levis et quadrata*); Tac. *Dial.* 22.5 (ironically, with reference to Cicero). Cf. van Hook 1905, 40–42; Benediktson 2000, 105–08.

That the euphonist critics were attuned to the materialities of inscription is plain from their use of the engraver analogy, which serves their views well. It brings out the felt specificities of poetry. One has to imagine the phonic equivalent of a cut or scrape, unique to a given chiseled stone, and proper to its delectation as such. Such is the materialist aesthetic purveyed by the euphonist critics. Roland Barthes' theory of the "grain of the voice" and of "vocal writing" is a contemporary version of the same sensibility:

What it searches for ... are the pulsional accidents, the language lined with flesh, a text where we can hear the grain of the throat, the patina of the consonants, the voluptuousness of vowels, a whole carnal stereophony: the articulation of the body, of the tongue (*de la langue*), not that of meaning (*du sens*), of language (*du langage*).... A certain art of singing can give an idea of this vocal writing: ... it granulates, it crackles, it caresses, it grates, it cuts, it comes: that is bliss.[199]

Recent thinking on sculptural aesthetics in the postclassical period suggests that this kind of attention to sensuous detail – to material, tactile contingency, including *facture* – was one of the distinctive features of the early "Hellenistic Baroque," if not of the Hellenistic aesthetic as a whole.[200] If so, then the euphonists are at the very least entitled to an equally "baroque" theory of aesthetic contemplation.

9 MONUMENTS AND THEIR SHADOWS

Tracking down all the possible examples of architectural allusions in literary criticism would not be an endless task, but it would be a thankless one unless we could be guaranteed some interesting result at the end of the tallying. As it happens, I believe it is possible to note a convergence of motifs across the three areas of analogy and allusion which were discussed or else briefly alluded to in the previous section: (i) the analysis of sound; (ii) stylistic analysis; and (iii) the description of monuments by literary critics. To that end, let us turn to some general reflections about the third of these areas, namely the status of monuments, actual or fictional, in poetry and among the critics. Here critics and poets join hands in a common cause, fueled by a common imagination.

As mentioned, the initial attraction of monuments for poets is easy to fathom. Poets go reaching for metaphors of all kinds, many of them

[199] Barthes 1975, 66–67.
[200] Stewart 1993; Stewart 2006: 171–72 ("often regarded as the most characteristic and even the most important artistic innovation of the Hellenistic period").

material in nature (textiles, paintings, sculpture, carvings, and so on, most of these with close Near Eastern counterparts, and most with Indo-European roots),[201] but architecture supplies a material that is of a sturdier sort, a truly material metaphor, which ought to explain why poets so often turn to buildings for edification and analogies[202] – though this falls short of explaining why critics follow poets so persistently in the same pursuit. For all these reasons, I believe we can get closer to an understanding of this latter problem if we simply begin to look at the ways in which critics and poets join hands around descriptions of actual or fictional monuments and monumental structures, not infrequently *en route* to developing analogies to their poetic or critical enterprises. The terrain is a rich one, and just to investigate it will turn up answers.

Sublime Constructs . . .

On the one hand, the attraction of poets and critics to monuments is surely an attraction to the act of making, as we have seen. Poets are makers, generally on a small scale in material terms, but also in imaginative terms: at the extreme, they would like, in their fantasies and in the fantasies of their audiences, to rival the makers of the cosmos itself. This was apparent in the epic tradition, but then also to literary critics in the allegorical tradition who perceived parallels, for instance, between Hephaestus' making of the shield of Achilles, which in some quarters was held to be a *mimēma* or *eikōn* (symbol) of the cosmos, and Homer's making of his poem. Pseudo-Heraclitus follows this line in his *Homeric Problems*: "It was not implausibly that Homer made Charis [Grace, Pleasure] the companion to the architect of the universe (τῷ τῶν ὅλων ἀρχιτεκτόνι) [sc., to Hephaestus]. For the cosmos (τῷ κόσμῳ) was bound to be pleased (χαριεῖσθαι) by its own arrangement" (τὸν ἴδιον κόσμον).[203] Pseudo-Heraclitus' source here is Crates of Mallos, in his capacity as a Homerist and allegorical critic. Crates was particularly attuned to architectonic parallels in Homer's poetry, for he sought to show that Homer was

---

[201] For Mesopotamian parallels, see Winter 1995, 2570–72 (a reference I owe to Froma Zeitlin); for Indo-European prehistory, see Durante 1960; Schmitt 1967; West 2007, 35–40. For a recent cross-cultural comparison that tries to root poetic (sung) rhythmic patterns directly in the practices of textile weaving, whereby song patterns *encode* weaving patterns – an intriguing speculation – see Tuck 2006 (a reference I owe to Larissa Bonfante).

[202] Though not always. Wilamowitz observes how "the metaphors and imagery drawn from architecture by the Athenians go far beyond the measure that is familiar and agreeable to us" (Wilamowitz-Moellendorff 1969, III:256, *ad* verse 1261).

[203] [Heracl.] *Quaest. Hom.* 43.8.

everywhere illustrating the fact that the universe was spherically shaped.[204] In a case like this, where a parallel is being drawn between the *hoplopoiia*, or the "making of the arms of Achilles," and *kosmopoiia*, or "the making of the cosmos,"[205] it takes little imagination to bring the syllogism to its final step: poets are demiurges of a sort. A predecessor for this insight may have been Democritus, who was echoing but possibly also dilating an image that he received from Pindar: "Democritus says the following about Homer: 'gifted with a divine nature, Homer constructed a *cosmos* of multifarious verses' (Ὅμηρος φύσεως λαχὼν θεαζούσης ἐπέων κόσμον ἐτεκτήνατο παντοίων), since it is not possible to make verses as beautiful and as wise as those without a divine and daemonic nature."[206] Compare Pindar: "Come now, let us build an intricate speaking *cosmos* of words" (κόσμον αὐδάεντα λόγων) on "a golden foundation wrought for holy songs."[207]

On this view of things, poets are equal to their creations, which are as unbounded as the universe. A later expression of this same thought will come in Longinus' exuberant theory of the sublime, in which he is doubtless drawing on earlier tradition – a sublime literary tradition that treats literary works as sublime monuments. Briefly, in Longinus poets are celebrated for their capacity to encompass all that is with their minds. In each of his readings of Homer in *On the Sublime*, the monumental qualities of Homer's poetry are borrowed from those of the cosmos. There, Longinus speaks of Homer's using "a cosmic distance to measure" the speed of horses, which seem ready to vault beyond the limits of the universe.[208] That is, the language of criticism used by Longinus is shaped by an architectonic sense of how the universe has been imagined and structured by the poet. That Longinus shares this sense, which is either his own, his source's (for instance, Crates'),[209] or Homer's (as both Longinus and Crates of Mallos would have us believe), is evident from a passage that occurs towards the end of *On the Sublime*, which begins, "The universe therefore is not wide enough for the range of human speculation and intellect. Our thoughts often travel beyond the boundaries of our

---

[204] [Heracl.] *Quaest. Hom.* 43.10–14, in a context that is heavily indebted to Crates. See Porter 1992, 93–94.

[205] [Heracl.] *Quaest. Hom.* 43.1.   [206] DK 68B21 (= Dio Chrys. *Or.* 36.1).

[207] Pind. fr. 194 Snell–Maehler. Other parallels are Solon fr. 1.2 West (= Plut. *Sol.* 8.2: κόσμον ἐπ⟨έω⟩ν) and Parmenides DK 28B8.52 (κόσμον ἐμῶν ἐπέων), but both lack the architectural emphasis.

[208] *Subl.* 9.5.   [209] Porter 1992.

intellect," as Homer's clearly do in the earlier passage.[210] The sublime is a capacious tradition, capable of gathering together a number of different strands. Architectural and architectonic motifs do not stand all that far apart: they just seem to do so when the buildings in question are projected onto a cosmic scale. And, lest we forget, for most Greeks the cosmos, like a building and a poem, not only has a shape, but also a maker.

... and their Schattenseite

So far we have seen how poets and critics make use of architecture as a positive and pleasing analogy for poetry. But there is another, darker, though equally compelling side to monumental grandeur, and this was already hinted at in the hyperbolic gesture of the last two passages from Longinus. For poets are fascinated not only with buildings but also, and in particular, with the places where they give out, and above all with their total ruination. Longinus is again a good example of this, because in the lines immediately following his celebration of Homer's cosmic vision from ch. 9 he goes on to discuss an opposite kind of image, the apparent collapsing of the world in the course of a fearful theomachy, whereby "the earth is torn from its foundations" and its interior dimensions are exposed in a cosmic disaster:

Do you see how the earth is torn from its foundations, Tartarus laid bare, and the whole universe overthrown and broken up, so that all things – Heaven and Hell, things mortal and things immortal – share the warfare and the perils of that ancient battle?[211]

Or to return to his image of "the failed Colossus" (ὁ Κολοσσὸς ὁ ἡμαρτημένος), which may refer to the Colossus of Rhodes, is the monument's structure a failure because it physically collapsed or because of its formal (aesthetic) excessiveness? The difference is a fine one in the Longinian sublime, which is by nature pitched on the brink of disaster and ruin. Finally, we may think of the sublimity evoked by void in the architectonics of the Lucretian and, more generally, the atomistic universe (which was hinted at in Chapter 3).[212]

Here we see clearly how the sublime is generated at the nether ends of the spectrum that monuments can occupy – at their moment of greatest possible expansion (at the farthest reaches of the cosmos) and at the moment of their imminent collapse. The question is whether these two

---

[210] *Subl.* 35.3.   [211] *Subl.* 9.6.   [212] See Ch. 3, §§6 and 7.

thoughts are ever in fact separable. I doubt they are, at least not on the logic of sublime monuments in poetry and criticism, where, as with Longinus, *les extrèmes se touchent* in a kind of ecstasy of representation. Look beyond Longinus and you will find the same tension. The delicately balanced vaulted arch, structurally sound so long as its central keystone is not removed, is a recurrent theme in ancient philosophy, and not only among literary critics like Demetrius, as witnessed above (p. 506). Stoics could compare society to a vault (*fornix*). But if so, the image is a precarious one, and it inevitably led to the contemplation of society's ruin: "Our relations with one another (*societas nostra*) are like a stone arch (*lapidum fornicatione simillima est*), which would collapse if the stones did not mutually support one another, and which is upheld in this very way."[213]

The same principle is said to have been exploited by Phidias, who anecdotally inscribed his own portrait (and sometimes others', depending on the version of the story) at the peak of the shield of his Athena Parthenos on the Acropolis "with some invisible clever workmanship" as a permanent and threatening signature – lest anyone should try to remove it and, as a result, cause the statue to collapse. Here is the version that appears in the pseudo-Aristotelian treatise *On the Universe*:

> To use a somewhat humble illustration, we might with truth compare [God] to the so-called 'key-stones' in arches, which, placed at the junction of the two sides, ensure the balance and arrangement of the whole structure of the arch and give it stability. Moreover, they say that the sculptor Phidias, when he was setting up the Athena on the Acropolis, represented his own features in the centre of her shield, and so attached it to the statue by a hidden contrivance, that anyone who tried to cut it out, thereby necessarily shattered and overthrew the whole statue. The position of God in the universe is analogous to this, for he preserves the harmony and permanence of all things; save only that he has his seat not in the midst, where the earth and this our troubled world is situated, but himself pure he has gone up into a pure region, to which we rightly give the name of heaven, for it is the furthest boundary of the upper world.[214]

It is not entirely surprising that Democritus, who had a vested interest not only in material structures but also in their fragility, is said, apocryphally, to have discovered the arch form.[215] And we have already seen an example

---

[213] Sen. *Ep.* 95.53 = *SVF* 3.322; trans. Gummere, adapted. Cf. the similar thought in Chrysippus, according to Varro *Ling.* 10.59 = *SVF* 2.155.
[214] [Arist.] *Mund.* 399b29–400a7; trans. Forster. For other tellings, see Overbeck §§669–73. On the apocryphal nature of this story, see Preißhofen 1974.
[215] DK 68 B300.14 (= Sen. *Ep.* 90.32).

of this "motif of the dreaded collapse"[216] in operation in Demetrius, in his contrast between the periodic style, which is held together in a vaulting tension of clauses, and the disconnected style, which is not. In the latter style, he writes, "The members seem thrown upon one another in a heap without the union or propping, and without the mutual support, which we find in periods."[217]

The motif of collapse, though not quite the image of the keystone, recurs in Latin poetry, as Don Fowler has lately shown in his essay, "The Ruin of Time." Ausonius, in the fourth century CE, captured the melancholy overtones of faded inscriptions in an epigram that reads like the diary of a philologist who travels around the countryside squinting at epigraphic ruins and recording the faint traces of the letters as he finds them:

> 'Lucius' is one letter, but it is separated by twin points: in this way a single sign indicates the <entire> *praenomen*. After an 'M' is inscribed, at least I think so – it is not all visible. The top has been damaged by the stone breaking and has fallen off (*dissiluit saxi fragmine laesus apex*) .... The letters ... have perished in a confusion of signs (*omnia confusis interiere notis*). Are we surprised that men die? Monuments gape apart (*monumenta fatiscunt*), death comes even to stones and names.[218]

Ausonius might appear to embody a late antique wistfulness towards ruins, in the light of which ruins just are a kind of monument, and he may even be reflecting such an attitude[219] – though against this epigonal reading one has to factor in a passage like Thucydides 6.54.7 on the semi-obliterated and faded letters (ἀμυδροῖς γράμμασι) of the inscription dedicated to the younger Pisistratus from a century earlier but still legible in his own day.[220] But Ausonius is also continuing a topos that was well

---

[216] Schmidt 1968, 34. A curious parallel appears in Eur. *Tro.* 489, where Hecuba describes her personal ruin as the "final keystone" (τὸ λοίσθιον ... θριγκός) in the arch of evils piling up around her. Here, the keystone is a culminating moment in a series of collapses rather than a structural linchpin that prevents or triggers collapse.

[217] Demetr. *Eloc.* 12; cf. ibid., 13. On the prominence and symbolism of keystones in Antonine architecture, see Thomas 2007, 25; 40–43; 58–60, etc. Thanks to Tim Whitmarsh for this reference.

[218] Auson. *Epigr.* 37 Green; trans. Fowler 2000, 193.

[219] See Fowler 2000, 201 (a general commentary); Porter 2001b (the same insight, rooted in the Second Sophistic).

[220] Immerwahr 1960, 280 takes this notice as expressing Thucydides' "feeling for the transitory nature of monuments." See further on Simonides *PMG* 581 above (the Cleobulus inscription). See also Leonidas (*fl.* early third century BCE) *Anth. Pal.* 7.478 = Leon. 73 G–P on a roadside tomb monument pathetically exposed and scraped away by wagon wheels; similarly, in imitation, *Anth. Pal.* 7.479 = Theodoridas 16 G–P.

established at the origins of Latin literature, from Ennius to Lucan.[221] Indeed, in conceptual terms, the gamut runs from the paradoxical mortality of the very trace of mortality on the one hand, as in Juvenal's *Satire* 10.146 (*data sunt ipsis quoque fata sepulchris*) or in the final verse by Ausonius above (*mors etiam saxis nominibusque venit*), to the spectacular opposite extreme on the other, the sublime anti-matter of the monument about which it can be said that "*even the ruins have perished*" (*etiam periere ruinae*), as in Lucan (here, with Troy in mind).[222] Even Horace's proud *exegi monumentum* is tinged with the reminder of the potential for decay in its second verse, as Fowler insists, giving emphasis to a line of reading that the most recent commentary on Horace feels obliged to concede. *Exegi monumentum aere perennius*, "I have completed a monument more lasting than bronze," *regalique situ pyramidum altius*, "and higher than the regal site/decay (*situ*) of the pyramids ...."[223] As Fowler asks, "if real monuments decay, can we be so sure of metaphorical ones," such as Horace's?[224]

---

[221] Davis 1958; Häusle 1980, 136–39; Skutsch 1985, *ad* Enn. *Ann.* 404–06, citing Ausonius' epigram; Woolf 1996, 25–26, citing Pliny's reaction to the sadly neglected tomb of Verginius Rufus (*Ep.* 6.10.3–5).

[222] Luc. 9.969. Cf. Catull. 68.89–94; Ov. *Met.* 1.260–415; 15.424; Paus. 10.33.8 (Parapotamii, mentioned earlier).

[223] Fowler 2000, 197; see Nisbet and Rudd 2004, 369, ad loc. Given the strong Ennian influences in Horace's monumental imagery for his poetic undertaking (Hardie 1993; Barchiesi 1996), is there a possible allusion to his poetic forbear in *perennius*? See Feeney 1999, 16–17 with 17 n. 1.

[224] Fowler 2000, 198. Another, Antonine instance of a sublime monument is the tomb of the Flavii at Cillium in Tunisia (*c.* 150 CE), which bears an inscription that describes the magnificent monument-complex (*nobis operas descriptio magni*, 97), and which at one point reads:

> Honour stands sublime (*Stat sublimis*) and knocks at its neighbours, the clouds (*nubile pulsat*),
>   and measures the sun's path. If the eyes should choose by chance
> to join the mountains behind, these hills are surpassed (*vincuntur*) all in a line;
> if you look at the fields, the earth lies hidden beneath the monument.
> Not so is the colossus said to reach the heights of Rome
> or the obelisk in the circus reach into the middle of the sky
> Nor so does Pharos show the ways of sistrum-bearing Nile
> While it reveals its seas with visible flames.
>
> (*CIL* VIII 212–13 = *CLE* 1552, 78–85; text and trans. after Thomas 2007, 261)

This is a powerful piece of poetry, aggrandizing the tomb in cosmic language and dwarfing all earthly objects in the process. Indeed, earlier (16), it is said about the monument that it "surges through the highest airs" (*per quos* [sc., *divitias*] *aetherias surgunt monimenta per auras*), while its columns "hang in perfect balance (*pariter pendere*), agleam" (*lucentes*) (48). The poem is, however, undone by its own logic. Despite the tomb's pretenses to "everlasting newness" (*perpetua novitate*, 42), it remains a material thing, damned as much as all other things of the world are "damned by their own weight" (*momentis damnata suis*, 33, where *momentis* inevitably conjures up *monimenta* [16] in more ways than one), itself more of "life's accidents and labors [by which one may] measure man | by his own shortness" (35–36).

I think we can agree with Fowler's conclusion that "the essence of the monument is paradoxically its lack of monumental stability."[225] Nonetheless, not all monuments are created equal: there is a difference that needs to be underscored. The Latin examples Fowler and others cite refer to the object (poem or monument) as a completed and finished index of a poet's or erstwhile owner's fame, whether in a mood of hopeful projection (as with Horace) or of wistful backward-gazing (as in Ausonius); they do not reflect the mind of a poet in the workshop or that of a critic. These latter, by contrast, are interested in how things are put together. But as poets and critics alike know only too well, simply to detail the construction of a thing is to point to its elemental fragility. From the design perspective, an object is made of parts, and of necessity it can be analyzed back into those parts, even at the moment of their most compelling synthesis. This is the shadow-side to monuments.

In the *Protrepticus*, Aristotle claims that "architecture [is] the art of building houses, not of pulling them down."[226] Aristotle's assurances notwithstanding, one way to phrase the relationship between poets and monuments is to say that poets excel *in the building of ruins*. Another, more direct way is to affirm that poets are *destroyers* of what they make. Aristotle knows better himself, to judge from what he had to say about the problem of the Achaean wall by the ships described by Homer in Books 7 and 12 of the *Iliad*. The very presence of the wall has troubled ancient and modern readers alike (here, Strabo, Gottfried Hermann, and Denys Page are in fact indistinguishable): the Achaeans came to attack a wall, not to build one; why are they seemingly duplicating Troy on a smaller scale, rivaling the Trojans and their wall (ἀντιτειχιζόντων, in the words of one scholiast[227]), and all of this in the tenth year of the war?[228] The Greek wall disturbs, both in the way it suddenly appears, a monument looming strangely out of place on the Trojan plain (it begins as a grave [τύμβον] piled up and fashioned indiscriminately [ἄκριτον] from materials on the plain), and then in the spectacular way in which it disappears again, demolished vengefully by Poseidon and Apollo, along with Zeus, in a torrential flood of rivers, vanishing without a trace.[229]

Aristotle inaugurates the sanest line on the problem, but also one of the most daring: the wall is a non-problem, he says, or at least a self-effacing

---

[225] Fowler 2000, 211.   [226] Arist. *Protrept.* B12 Dühring.   [227] Schol. bT *Il.* 7.445.
[228] Strab. 13.1.36; Hermann 1827–77, VIII:387; Page 1959, 315–24. For a more elaborate discussion of the Achaean wall, see Porter forthcoming.
[229] *Il.* 7.433–53; 12.13–33.

one, because it never existed to begin with: "the poet who created it [viz., who made it up] (ὁ πλάσας) destroyed it (ἠφάνισεν; literally, 'obliterated it,' 'made it disappear')."[230] Thus, Aristotle read the episode as a twofold allusion. First, the traceless obliteration of the wall alludes to facts about the past that could no longer be verified by Homer or his audiences. But secondly, the very memory of what was no more – that is, poetic memory *tout court* – alludes to the poem's own poetics. In this ancient tradition, the destruction of the Greek wall is plainly emblematic of the traceless obliteration of Troy itself, by dint of the similarity between the two walls, but also thanks to either event's susceptibility to fictional manipulation. Thus, we find a conflation of the two kinds of making, the poetic fashioning of the *Teichomachia* (the Battle at the Achaean wall) and the construction of the wall itself (the *Teichopoiia*), to use the language of the scholia: "Now [Homer] wanted out of poetic necessity to shift the battle on the plain over to the wall. That's why *he made up* the *Teichopoiia* (ἀνέπλασε τὴν τειχοποιΐαν ὁ ποιητής), so as to shift the contests over to the *Teichomachia*" (ἐπὶ τῆι τειχομαχίᾳ).[231] "In order not to abandon his thought, he *made* the *Teichomachia* by the wall of the Greeks" (ἐπὶ τῷ τῶν Ἑλλήνων τείχει τὴν τειχομαχίαν ποιεῖ).[232] With this last comment, the two kinds of making come together: here, Homer, the poet, is held responsible for fashioning (ποιεῖ) an episode called the *Teichomachia*. We are put in mind of the similarities between *hoplopoiia* and *kosmopoiia*, two other kinds of fashioning, likewise emblematic of the poetic process, which were discussed above in connection with Crates and Homer.

The poet is the fashioner of a fashioning. And, as Aristotle adds, he is also, perforce, a great destroyer, even the maker of destruction (ἠφάνισεν). The problem this poses is a curious one, and it is most succinctly stated in a D-scholium to *Iliad* 12.4: in order to avoid having to explain away to later generations the embarrassing fact that the Achaean wall was a fiction of his own making, a *pseudos* about something that never was (ἵνα μὴ ἐλέγχηται αὐτοῦ τὸ ψεῦδος ὡς μὴ γενομένου ὑπὸ τῶν μεταγενεστέρων, καὶ τὴν ἀπώλειαν αὐτοῦ εἶπε),[233] Homer contrived to have its destruction retailed in all its needless splendor, in order to prevent anybody searching out the traces of the wall later on (εἰς τὸ μηδένα ἐπιζητεῖν ὕστερον τὰ τῶν τειχῶν ἴχνη), as another

[230] Fr. 162 Rose = Strab. 13.1.36.   [231] Schol. bT *Il.* 12.3–35.   [232] Schol. T *Il.* 12.3–35.
[233] Schol. D *Il.* 12.4. Cf. schol. bT *Il.* 12.3–35: οὐ δυνάμενος δὲ ἴχνος τι ἀπαιτηθῆναι τοῦ μὴ γενομένου.

scholium explains.[234] The first concession is remarkable, and here the ancients score higher marks than the moderns, who try to make the detail of the Achaean wall vanish: senseless and absurd, it must be an inter-polation (so Page).[235] The explanation the scholiasts finally offer is itself absurd; it is a way of pushing their own anxieties about the limits of fictionality onto the poet's shoulders. Of course, the problem that con-cerns the wall ought *a fortiori* to touch the greater wall of Troy, whose traces were likewise obliterated in antiquity.[236] That Troy was implicated in the problem helps to explain the powerful fascination this puzzle held for the ancients. In a word, the fate of the Achaean wall brings out the impermanence of things, and by implication, of the song that celebrates those things.[237] Like the watery obliteration imagined by Achilles at the hands of the river Scamander in *Iliad* 22, which would be an "anti-funeral" that produces an "anti-monument," the Achaean wall is itself a kind of anti-monument.[238] Its obliteration is not only absolute; it is also a great marvel that was never beheld.

10 SUBLIME MATTER

Of course, poets make nothing at all. They are builders, not of real things but of imaginary things. This was the thrust of Aristotle's point, and also of the scholia's explanations. Poets, we can say, build not actual but only sublime monuments, monuments grander than anything ever witnessed in history. This is something they seem to have sensed themselves. The monumental metaphors in Pindar and Simonides often stand in pointed contrast to the sturdy materiality they simultaneously evoke. Unlike stones, the poets' objects are voiced and they move; and they endure longer than any material object (as the euphonist critics also knew, as we saw: poets endure over time, διαμένουσιν, on account of their sounds alone). Whence Pindar's boast: "I am no statue maker, to fashion delight-ful objects that stand idle on their bases"; or, "I did not fashion these hymns to be idle. This is what you are to read out, Nicasippus, once you have reached my trusty friend"; or when he says that speech "lives longer

[234] Schol. bT *Il.* 7.445.   [235] Page 1959, 315–24.
[236] See Porter 2004a, 327 n. 14, now developed in Porter forthcoming.
[237] Cf. Lynn-George 1988, 257; Ford 1992, 147; 152 (this is the premise of Ford's discussion, though he assumes that the anxiety is over the textual permanence of Homer's poetry, not its permanence as song).
[238] The first term is from Redfield 1994, 167, 183, the latter from Ford 1992, 153 (who invokes Redfield's term and draws the comparison between *Iliad* 22 and 12).

than doings or makings," for example, epic songs that "wise craftsmen
(τέϰτονες) have fitted together from sounding words" (ἐξ ἐπέων
ϰελαδεννῶν).[239] Nor is Pindar alone. We might compare Simonides'
critique of inert crafted objects and their intrinsic silence, touched on
earlier. There are parallels in Bacchylides, for instance, his description of
the best kind of song:

> [The poet] has stirred the clear-voiced (λιγύφθογγον) bee into motion
> (ἐϰίνησεν) so as to make present an immortal *agalma* of the Muses, a joy to
> be shared among men as it proclaims your excellence to men on earth.[240]

And in a fragment from a satyr-play quoted earlier, Aeschylus confirms
the durability of this conceit:

> Look hard and tell me if [you can spot the difference between this image of me
> and me].... This [votive] image (εἴδωλον) full of my form, this imitation of
> Daedalus, *lacks only a voice* (φωνῆς δεῖ μόνον).[241]

In the imagination of poets, that lack was easily filled.

The monumental pretensions of Greek lyric poetry are a well-known
phenomenon, but they are also tricky to describe, combining as they do
both cool distance from the object-world and interested rivalry.[242] Exactly
how are we to read an analogy like the following, likewise from Pindar,
which advertises its faux-materiality through the very elaborateness and
excessiveness of the imagery in which it indulges:

> Let us erect golden columns
> for the well-built forecourt to our edifice, as if we were building a
>   palace to be looked at in awe.
> When a work is beginning, one must lay down a far-gleaming façade.[243]

---

[239] Pind. *Nem.* 5.1–3; *Pyth.* 3.112–15; *Nem.* 4.6; *Ol.* 4.10.
[240] Bacchyl. 10.10–14 Snell–Maehler. Trans. after Ford 2002, 125.
[241] Aesch. *Theoroi* or *Isthmiastai*, *P. Oxy.* 2162, *TrGF* 78a, col. 1.5–8. Sörbom 1966 and Hallett 1986
    view this fragment in a positive light, as an admiration for the vivacity of the revolution in
    depiction and in verisimilitude; Steiner 2001, 46–47 rightly points to the celebration of technical
    aspects that would qualify the celebration of naturalism and realism. My reading underscores the
    lack of voice that is noticed, both declaratively and performatively, by Aeschylus' choristers: they
    supplement this lack – all that the images cannot say about themselves – with their own voices. So
    viewed, the Aeschylean fragment fits into the critical perspective on visual art found in the lyric
    tradition. See Chapter 6 above, n. 130. It also points ahead to the euphonist tradition, which in
    turn harks back to the earlier ecphrastic tradition of "speaking objects," whose distinctive essence
    lies, precisely, in their ephemeral, but ever-renewed, possession of (a) voice.
[242] Segal 1998, 156; Steiner 2001; Ford 2002, 120–21.
[243] Pind. *Ol.* 6.1–3; trans. Ford 2002, 124.

Some scholars (such as Fränkel and Ford) talk about a "transcendence of material, visible constructions" or even of the "dematerialization" of poetic glory here, much, say, along the lines of Wordsworth in the fifth book of his *Prelude*, where the "proper home" of poetry, its "mansion," is "circumfused with light," and "even [its] forms and substances" are rendered seemingly weightless and so made to partake of a "glory not their own" (see the second epigraph to this chapter).[244] But the transcendence is only partial. The move is not from "material, visible constructions" to immaterial and invisible constructions; it is to *another* kind of materiality, one that never undoes its ties to the qualities of matter. It is, after all, to "a more secure *house* for the fame of those whom it celebrates" (Fränkel) that song takes itself. Song never sheds its associations with building materials even in its putative transcendence of them. Nor does it ever cease to be a material phenomenon. To exist at all, song must be heard and sung: it remains, in the end, a *voice* (and in cases – perhaps in every case – a text).[245]

Poetic monuments may gleam, but they do so with a kind of fierce resolve that betrays an underlying desperation: despairing in the permanence of things, they mimic things and what is most thinglike about them. Thus, they enjoy a productive tension with the world of things. And so, I propose, archaic poets do not discount matter and materiality, for all their seeming disparagement of architectural and statuesque immobility. Rather, they resort to a *sublime kind of matter*, or better yet, they invoke *the sublimity of matter itself*, which we may define as an aesthetic value that results from experiencing the very paradoxes of matter – its reliance on sensation, its resisting character, its firm yet uncertain place in the order of things, and its ineluctable relation to the human world. By this experience I mean, for starters, no more than what happens whenever one tries to describe matter and materiality, the things that seem most evident and obvious about the world. Simply to try and capture, through language

---

[244] Fränkel 1975, 430 n. 9; Ford 2002, 128. Cf. also Steiner 1999 in another context, concerning Simonides fr. 531 *PMG*, which "moves from the physical to the immaterial sphere" – a claim that can in principle be made of much if not all epitaphic poetry, with the qualifications that I am about to add.

[245] Similarly, Segal speaks of the "continuous dialogue within Pindar's work between song (poetry) on the one hand and monumentalization in statuary, architecture, and cult and religious celebration on the other. *Nemean 5* privileges one side of this dialogue, the poetic offering (*agalma*), but *without totally forgetting the value of the other*.... It is this more dynamic, breathing, yet more vulnerable glory that the Charites bestow; and it is with them that Pindar answers the statues' restful place on their bases in secure, but stony immortality" (Segal 1998, 178–80; emphasis added). Cf. also Steiner 2001, 258–59 (partially cited in n. 96, above); Halliwell 2003, 181–82.

and logic, the experience of the world is to encounter these paradoxes. There is nothing mysterious here. On the contrary, it is the beguiling simplicity of one's contact with the material world that generates all the paradoxes of matter there are. Philosophy, we might say, begins not in wonder, but *in the wonder of sensation*. The peculiarities that attend to the Greek experience, whether historical, cultural, or merely linguistic, color this insight in distinctive ways, as I hope to have captured to some extent in the foregoing pages. But it is an insight that we can still understand and even share today.[246]

For the same reason, to suggest that monuments exist only on a large scale of magnitude is to forget what is essential about their sublimity. Bigness in size and scale are merely figurative suggestions provoked by matter's features, which arises from a deeper crisis of representation that materiality brings about whenever it is made into an object of experience in its own right. This was the lesson of the early atomists, but it is also implicit in the allegorical tradition, at least from Metrodorus of Lampsacus in the fifth century onward, which adores drastic compressions and their resulting incongruencies (an image – say, a shield – or a single verse that evokes the whole of the cosmos), and it was also the lesson of Posidippus' radical juxtaposition of stones and massive boulders, or of monumental effects and little things, as we saw earlier in this chapter. What is sublime is the mere precipitation of this excess, irrespective of the size of the object, though perhaps not irrespective of the size of the perception, so to speak, which will always be magnified to an extreme. The sublime exists in the bare attention to "the matter of experience" on any scale, whenever this elicits a crisis in representation. And just as the sublime can be discovered at any moment of representational crisis at different cultural and historical moments, so too any object that is susceptible of such a crisis can become a monument, irrespective of its size. Atoms, those pure crystals of matter, little massy bits of being (ὄγκοι), are a case in point, as Lucretius knows[247] (and as the term suggests: ὄγκος, as is well known and as we have seen, is a standard

---

[246] In this, I am invoking a different concept from Žižek's concept of the sublime object and of sublime material, though they are ultimately linked. Dewey's views about sensuous experience, upon which I have been drawing from time to time throughout this study, are also highly relevant. On the other hand, in the second sentence of the *Metaphysics*, to which I am alluding here, Aristotle himself acknowledges that the desire to know, which leads to philosophy, originates in the pleasures of sensation, as is proven by "*the delight we all take in our senses*" (σημεῖον δ' ἡ τῶν αἰσθήσεων ἀγάπησις).

[247] Porter 2007b.

rhetorical name for grandeur), as is Aristotle's insistence on a tragic plot's being *eusunoptos*, graspable in a mental glance (he was warding off the threat of tragic sublimity, a concept he does not allow – as Longinus is eager to point out, though Aristotle does have a restrained sense of tragic grandeur).[248] As it happens, literary critics exploit the paradoxes of the sublime in questions of the voice, which, as we have begun to see, traditionally enjoyed associations with both monuments and materiality, or rather with *the monumentality of matter* – even if, or just because, *phōnē* is made up of the tiniest bits of linguistic matter there are, mere *stoicheia*, little elements of sound (or less than this), which last no longer than you can fetch another breath.

---

[248] "Some emotions, such as pity, grief, and fear (οἶκτοι, λῦπαι, φόβοι) are found divorced from sublimity and with a low effect" (*Subl.* 8.2; trans. Russell). Longinus carefully distinguishes these from factors of the sublime in his own treatise, which has no patience for plot-theory and the like, but only for epiphanic bursts of aesthetic brilliance.

PART IV

Aesthetic Futures

Epilogue

This study has initiated a process of recovering the traditions of aesthetic thought in Greek and Roman antiquity in a way has largely eluded scholarship. It has done so by examining the historical and universal root conditions of aesthetic reflection (matter, sensation, and experience), though to specify these is merely to invite further historical differentiation and contextualization, a process I have also merely begun. My account has been partial: it has been carried out with an eye to the evolving ancient traditions of aesthetic thought which placed the accent on works of art in their sensual, phenomenal, and material dimensions, in contrast to their formalist and idealist counterparts. And while much of the evaluative terminology in these two opposed strands of ancient aesthetics often ends up in the same place (beauty, sublimity, excellence, marvel, wonderment, pleasure), and while, indeed, the two tendencies can often appear to converge in their end-points, the accents, modes of attention, and overall feel are quite different in each, just as their trajectories – their ways of arriving – are markedly different too. They should not be confused.

A further source of potential confusion needs to be clarified. Single-minded attention to the materiality of an artifact might easily appear to be similar to an isolation of that object as self-standing, autonomous, and formally independent. But arguments in favor of aesthetic materialism need not be confused with arguments for aesthetic autonomy. These latter more properly belong to the comfortable, closed circuit of formalism, which is invested in ideal structures that fail, as it were, to touch ground in any way – which is one further argument in favor of aesthetic materialism. One need only think of the formal complicities of Cleanth Brooks's well wrought urn, which is self-enclosed, but also empty and immaterial, a mere formal structure in the mind. The sense my fingers have of a polished table puts me, so to speak, in touch with touch itself (cf. Arist. *De an.* 2.11.423b12–15), and occasionally in touch with the dilemmas of sensation. The formal pattern of a stanza or a vase closes me off from other forms: formal experiences are, by definition, experiences that are not propagated by the object, unlike those with palpable dimensions, which are, and which, in fact, can only come about because they are both derived and propagated from prior experiences of the same or a similar kind of object. In beholding a form abstracted from its material features, it is not clear that I am doing anything other than beholding an idea or its projection; in touching the object that is said to be inhabited by that form, I am in fact held by the object. There is much room, no doubt, for exploring the differences and relative virtues between these two modes of aesthetic experience in a more general and theoretical way, but this is not the place to do so.

By the same token, the present study is inevitably the starting point and not the end-point of its own inquiry. Much remains to be done. I have hinted throughout at my own outstanding interests. The Democritean heritage awaits exploration. The Hellenistic period has been barely discussed, and all that lays beyond it. And the theory of the sublime, both in the antecedents to Longinus (of the immaterial and material variety) and in its development in Longinus, has been touched on, but only indirectly at best. There is much else besides, above all in the visual arts, though not only in those media, that would be worth exploring both for their inheritance of the earlier materialist tendencies and for their negotiations with the canonical, non-materialist schools. The most exciting prospect of all is whether art theory in antiquity after the fourth century was ever truly idealizing and not, rather, inclined to examine the phenomena and materials of art as such. Nevertheless, these are all areas for true specialists to determine, be it in the standard forms of high art, in the intermediary decorative and ornamental arts, or in the more submerged but no less prevalent regions of material culture.

Then there is the vast realm of experience that lies outside art. What, for instance, might there be to say about the aesthetics of the everyday in antiquity, the commonest encounters with objects and experiences that fall outside the realm of art properly speaking, however we decide to define that boundary – encounters with the mundane, the lowly, the transient, encounters with nature or with hygiene (dirty, neat) and all other areas that captivate the eyes, the ears, and the other senses? The issue is rich and involved. It raises all kinds of theoretical and pragmatic problems about the reach and limits of aesthetic inquiry in a way that the present study would find most welcome. As things stand, I have done my best to seek out the existing commonalities not only among the individual arts and other areas of human thought and activity but also, as it were, between aesthetic experiences with a small a, approximating to the barest of sensations, and those with a capital A, typically associated with the nine Muses. But the aesthetics of the everyday presents challenges of another kind altogether.

The prospect of gains to be won from an expanded approach to the discourses and practices of ancient aesthetics by way of the everyday needs little defense. Much as in the study of popular morality, so too here the vocabularies, codified in language and by habit, which were used to describe encounters with forms, shapes, colors, and meanings, only stand to be enriched if we look beyond the recognizable but eminently challengeable realm of the arts. And yet, if I may venture a prediction, it is that these additional areas, once included, will fall under an enlarged view of aesthetic encounters in antiquity, and hence too under an enlarged domain of investigation by us today.[1] All this and more will have to wait for later occasions and for investigation by others. The mere fact that such questions exist at all and are ripe for discussion is a sure sign that aesthetic inquiry, while it had some of its most brilliant origins in the sensuous world of Greek antiquity, is not merely a thing of the past, but also a promise of the future.

---

[1] For a recent example of this kind of approach, see Saito 2007.

Bibliography

Abrams, M. H. (1989) "Art-as-Such: The Sociology of Modern Aesthetics," in M. H. Abrams, *Doing Things with Texts: Essays in Criticism and Critical Theory*, ed. M. Fischer. New York. 135–58.

Acosta-Hughes, B. (2002) *Polyeideia: The Iambi of Callimachus and the Archaic Iambic Tradition*. Berkeley, CA.

Acosta-Hughes, B., and S. A. Stephens (2002) "Rereading Callimachus' *Aetia* Fragment 1," *Classical Philology* 97: 238–55.

Addison, J. (1856) *The Works of Joseph Addison: Including the Whole Contents of B. Hurd's Edition, with Letters and Other Pieces Not Found in Any Previous Collection, and Macaulay's Essay on His Life and Works*, ed. G. W. Greene. 6 vols. New York.

Adorno, T. W. (1970) *Ästhetische Theorie*, eds. G. Adorno and R. Tiedemann. Frankfurt am Main.

Aign, B. P. (1963) "Die Geschichte der Musikinstrumente des Ägäischen Raumes bis um 700 vor Christus: Ein Beitrag zur Vor-und Frühgeschichte der griechischen Musik." Diss., Frankfurt am Main.

Algra, K. (1999) "The Beginnings of Cosmology," in *The Cambridge Companion to Early Greek Philosophy*, ed. A. A. Long. Cambridge. 45–65.

Allan, D. J. (1980) "ἀναγιγνώσκω and Some Cognate Words," *Classical Quarterly* 30: 244–51.

Allen, W. S. (1978) *Vox Latina: A Guide to the Pronunciation of Classical Latin*, 2nd edn. Cambridge.

(1987) *Vox Graeca: A Guide to the Pronunciation of Classical Greek*, 3rd edn. Cambridge.

Ambühl, A. (1995) "Callimachus and the Arcadian Asses: The *Aitia* Prologue and a Lemma in the London Scholion," *Zeitschrift für Papyrologie und Epigraphik* 105: 209–13.

Anderson, W. D. (1994) *Music and Musicians in Ancient Greece*. Ithaca, NY.

Armstrong, J. (2004) *The Secret Power of Beauty*. London.

Arnheim, R. (1986) "Art among the Objects," *Critical Inquiry* 13 (Summer): 677–85.

Arns, R. G., and B. E. Crawford (1995) "Resonant Cavities in the History of Architectural Acoustics," *Technology and Culture* 36, no. 1: 104–35.

Asmis, E. (1995) "Philodemus on Censorship, Moral Utility, and Formalism in Poetry," in *Philodemus and Poetry*, ed. D. Obbink. Oxford: 148–77.

Asper, M. (1997) *Onomata Allotria: Zur Genese, Struktur und Funktion poetologischer Metaphern bei Kallimachos*. Stuttgart.

Assmann, J. (1991) *Stein und Zeit: Mensch und Gesellschaft im alten Ägypten*. Munich.

Atherton, C. (1989) "Hand Over Fist: The Failure of Stoic Rhetoric," *Classical Quarterly* 38: 392–427.

Auerbach, E. (1929) *Dante als Dichter der irdischen Welt*. Berlin.
(1967) *Gesammelte Aufsätze zur romanischen Philologie*. Bern and Munich.

Austin, C. (1967) "De nouveaux fragments de l'Erechthée d'Euripide," *Recherches de papyrologie* 4: 11–67.

Austin, R. P. (1938) *The Stoichedon Style in Greek Inscriptions*. London. (Rpt. Arno Press, 1973.)

Avezzù, G. (1994) "Papyrus Hibeh I, 13: Anonymi fragmentum *De musica*," *Musica e Storia* 2: 109–37.

Ax, W. (1986) *Laut, Stimme und Sprache: Studien zu drei Grundbegriffen der antiken Sprachtheorie*. Hypomnemata, vol. 84. Göttingen.

Bachelard, G. (1969 [1957]) *The Poetics of Space*. Trans. M. Jolas. Boston, MA. (Translated from *La poétique de l'espace*. Paris 1957.)

Bakhtin, M. M. (1981) *The Dialogic Imagination: Four Essays*, ed. M. Holquist. Trans. C. Emerson and M. Holquist. Austin, TX.
(1984) *Problems of Dostoevsky's Poetics*, ed. C. Emerson. Trans. C. Emerson. Minneapolis, MN.
(1990) "Supplement: The Problem of Content, Material, and Form in Verbal Art," in M. M. Bakhtin, *Art and Answerability: Early Philosophical Essays*, ed. M. Holquist. Trans. V. Liapunov. Supplement translated by Kenneth Brostrom. Austin, TX. 257–325.

Bakker, E. J. (2005) *Pointing at the Past: From Formula to Performance in Homeric Poetics*. Washington, DC and Cambridge, MA.

Bann, S. (1989) *The True Vine: On Visual Representation and the Western Tradition*. Cambridge.

Barchiesi, A. (1996) "Poetry, Praise, and Patronage: Simonides in Book 4 of Horace's *Odes*," *Classical Antiquity* 15, no. 1: 5–47.

Barker, A. (1978) "Music and Perception: A Study in Aristoxenus," *Journal of Hellenic Studies* 98: 9–16.
(1982) "The Innovations of Lysander the Kitharist," *Classical Quarterly* 32, no. 2: 266–69.
(1984) *Greek Musical Writings. Volume 1: The Musician and His Art*. Cambridge.
(1989) *Greek Musical Writings. Volume 2: Harmonic and Acoustic Theory*. Cambridge.
(2007) *The Science of Harmonics in Classical Greece*. Cambridge.

Barlow, S. A. (1971) *The Imagery of Euripides: A Study in the Dramatic Use of Pictorial Language*. London.

Barnes, J. (1982) *The Presocratic Philosophers*, Rev. edn. London.

Barnouw, J. (1993) "The Beginnings of 'Aesthetics' and the Leibnizian Conception of Sensation," in *Eighteenth-Century Aesthetics and the Reconstruction of Art*, ed. P. Mattick. Cambridge. 52–95.

Barthes, R. (1975) *The Pleasure of the Text*. Trans. R. Miller. New York.

(1985) *The Responsibility of Forms: Critical Essays on Music, Art, and Representation*. Trans. R. Howard. New York.

Bassi, K. (2005) "Things of the Past: Objects and Time in Greek Narrative," *Arethusa* 38: 1–32.

Baudelaire, C. (1962) *Curiosités esthétiques, L'art romantique, et autres oeuvres critiques*, ed. H. Lemaître. Paris.

Baudrillard, J. (1976) *L'échange symbolique et la mort*. Paris.

Baumann, D. (1990) "Musical Acoustics in the Middle Ages," Trans. B. Haggh. *Early Music* 18, no. 2: 199–210.

Baumgarten, A. G. (1954 [1735]) *Reflections on Poetry: Alexander Gottlieb Baumgarten's Meditationes philosophicae de nonnullis ad poema pertinentibus*. Trans. K. Aschenbrenner and W. B. Holther. Berkeley, CA.

Baxandall, M. (1980) *The Limewood Sculptors of Renaissance Germany*. New Haven, CT.

(1985) *Patterns of Intention: On the Historical Explanation of Pictures*. New Haven, CT.

(1988) *Painting and Experience in Fifteenth-Century Italy: A Primer in the Social History of Pictorial Style*, 2nd edn. Oxford. (1st edn. 1972.)

Beardsley, M. C. (1981) *Aesthetics: Problems in the Philosophy of Criticism*, 2nd edn. Indianapolis, IN.

Beazley, J. D. (1930) *Der Berliner Maler, mit 32 Tafeln*. Berlin–Wilmersdorf.

Belardi, W. (1985) *Filosofia grammatica e retorica nel pensiero antico*. Rome.

Bell, C. (1981) *Art*. New York. (First published 1913; 2nd edition 1948.)

Bell, M. (1980) "Stylobate and Roof in the Olympieion at Akragas," *American Journal of Archaeology* 84, no. 3: 359–72.

Benediktson, D. T. (2000) *Literature and the Visual Arts in Ancient Greece and Rome*. Norman, Okla.

Benveniste, É. (1971) "The Notion of 'Rhythm' in its Linguistic Expression," in id., *Problems in General Linguistics*. ed. M. E. Meek. Coral Gables, FL. 281–313.

Bérard, C. (1989) *A City of Images: Iconography and Society in Ancient Greece*. Princeton, NJ.

Bergson, H. (1884) *Extraits de Lucrèce, avec un commentaire, des notes et une étude sur la poésie, la philosophie, la physique, le texte et la langue de Lucrèce*. Paris.

Berkeley, G. (1999) *Principles of Human Knowledge. Three Dialogues*, ed. H. Robinson. Oxford and New York.

Berleant, A. (1964) "The Sensuous and the Sensual in Aesthetics," *The Journal of Aesthetics and Art Criticism* 23, no. 2: 185–92.

Bernays, J. (1970) *Grundzüge der verlorenen Abhandlung des Aristoteles über Wirkung der Tragödie*. Hildesheim and New York. (1st edn 1858. Introd. 1970 by Karlfried Gründer.)

Bett, R. (1989) "The Sophists and Relativism," *Phronesis* 34, no. 2: 139–69.

Bing, P. (1995) "Ergängzungsspiel in the Epigrams of Callimachus," *Antike und Abendland* 41: 115–31.

(1998) "Between Literature and the Monuments," in *Genre in Hellenistic Poetry*, eds. A. Harder, R. F. Regtuit, and G. C. Wakker. Groningen. 21–45.

(2005) "The Politics and Poetics of Geography in the Milan Posidippus, Section One: On Stones (AB 1–20)," in *The New Posidippus: A Hellenistic Poetry Book*, ed. K. Gutzwiller. New York. 119–40.

Blank, D. L. (ed.) (1998) Sextus Empiricus, *Against the Grammarians (Adversus mathematicos I)*. Translated with an Introduction and Commentary. Oxford.

Blass, F. (1887–98) *Die attische Beredsamkeit*, 2nd edn. 3 vols. in 4. Leipzig.

Blesser, B., and L. -R. Salter (2007) *Spaces Speak, Are You Listening?: Experiencing Aural Architecture*. Cambridge, MA.

Bluck, R. S. (1975) *Plato's Sophist. A Commentary*, ed. G. C. Neal. Manchester.

Blumenthal, Albrecht von (1939) *Ion von Chios: Die Reste seiner Werke*. Stuttgart and Berlin.

Boardman, J. (2003) "'Reading' Greek Vases?," *Oxford Journal of Archaeology* 22, no. 1: 109–14.

Boersma, J. S. (1970) *Athenian Building Policy from 561/0 to 405/4 B.C.* Groningen.

Bohrer, K. H. (2000) "Das Ethische am Ästhetischen," *Merkur: Deutsche Zeitschrift für europäisches Denken* 54, no. 620: 1149–62.

Bosanquet, B. (1956) *A History of Æsthetic*, 2nd edn. London. (1st edn 1892; 2nd edn. 1904; rpt. 1956.)

Bostock, D. (2006) *Space, Time, Matter and Form: Essays on Aristotle's Physics*. Oxford.

Bourgeois, L. (1998) "Sunday Afternoons: A Conversation and a Remark on Beauty," in *Uncontrollable Beauty: Toward a New Aesthetics*, eds. B. Beckley and D. Shapiro. New York. 331–41.

Bowra, C. M. (1940) "Sophocles on his Own Development," *American Journal of Philology* 61, no. 3: 385–401.

Brancacci, A. (1988) "Alcidamante e *PHibeh* 13 'De Musica': Musica della retorica e retorica della musica," in *Aristoxenica, Menandrea, fragmenta philosophica*, eds. A. Brancacci, F. D. Caizzi *et al.* Florence. 61–84.

Broadie, S. (1999) "Rational Theology," in *The Cambridge Companion to Early Greek Philosophy*, ed. A. A. Long. Cambridge. 205–24.

Brooks, C. (1947) *The Well Wrought Urn: Studies in the Structure of Poetry*. New York.

Brown, B. (2001) "Thing Theory," *Critical Inquiry* 28 (Autumn): 1–16.

(2003) *A Sense of Things: The Object Matter of American Literature*. Chicago, IL.

Browning, R. (1963) "A Byzantine Treatise on Tragedy," *Acta Universitatis Carolinae Philosophica et Historica* 1 (*Studies Presented to George Thomson on the Occasion of his 60th Birthday*, eds. L. Varcl and R. F. Willetts): 67–81.

Bruns, G. L. (2005) *The Material of Poetry: Sketches for a Philosophical Poetics.* Athens.

(2008) "On the Conundrum of Form and Material in Adorno's Aesthetic Theory," *The Journal of Aesthetics and Art Criticism* 66, no. 3: 225–35.

Brussich, G. F. (ed.) (2000) *Laso di Ermione: Testimonianze e frammenti.* Pisa.

Buchheim, T. (ed.) (1989) *Gorgias von Leontini: Reden, Fragmente und Testimonien.* Hamburg.

Bulckens, A. M. (1999) "The Parthenon's Main Design Proportion and its Meanings." Diss., Deakin University.

Bürger, P. (1984) *Theory of the Avant-Garde.* Trans. M. Shaw. Minneapolis, MN.

Burkert, W. (1959) "Στοιχεῖον: Eine semasiologische Studie," *Philologus* 103: 167–97.

(1975) "Aristoteles im Theater: Zur Datierung des 3. Buchs der 'Rhetorik' und der 'Poetik'," *Museum Helveticum* 32, no. 2: 67–72.

Burnyeat, M. F. (1990) *The Theaetetus of Plato.* Trans. M. J. Levett. Introduction by M. Burnyeat. Indianapolis, IN.

(1997) *Culture and Society in Plato's Republic.* The Tanner Lectures on Human Values. Delivered at Harvard University, December 10–12, 1997. Accessed December 2007. <http://www.tannerlectures.utah.edu/lectures/documents/Burnyeat99.pdf>.

Burzachechi, M. (1962) "Oggetti parlanti nelle epigrafi greche," *Epigraphica* 24: 3–54.

Büttner, S. (2006) *Antike Ästhetik: Eine Einführung in die Prinzipien des Schönen.* Munich.

Calboli, G. (1983) "Oratore senza microfono," in [n.a.] *Ars rhetorica antica e nuova.* Genoa. 23–56.

Callebat, L. (1994) "Rhétorique et architecture dans le 'De architectura' de Vitruve," in *Le Projet de Vitruve: Objet, destinataires et réception du De Architectura. Actes du colloque international organisé par l'École Française de Rome, l'Institut de Recherche sur l'Architecture Antique du CNRS et la Scuola Normale Superiore de Pise (Rome, 26–27 mars 1993),* ed. n.a. Rome. 31–46.

Calogero, G. (1977) *Studi sull'eleatismo,* 2nd rev. edn. Florence. (1st edn. 1932.)

Cameron, A. (1995) *Callimachus and His Critics.* Princeton, NJ.

Campbell, D. A. (1982–93) *Greek Lyric.* 5 vols. Cambridge, MA.

Canac, F. (1967) *L'Acoustique des théatres antiques, ses enseignements.* Paris.

Capelle, W. (1912) "Μετέωρος – μετεωρολογία," *Hermes* 71: 414–48.

Carpenter, R. (1959) *The Esthetic Basis of Greek Art of the Fifth and Fourth Centuries B.C.* n.p. (1st edn. Bryn Mawr College: Bryn Mawr, PA, 1921.)

Carroll, N. (2001) *Beyond Aesthetics: Philosophical Essays.* Cambridge.

Carson, A. (1999) *Economy of the Unlost: Reading Simonides of Keos with Paul Celan.* Princeton, NJ.

Cassin, B. (1980) *Si Parménide: Le traité anonyme De Melisso, Xenophane, Gorgia.* Lille and Paris.

Cassirer, E. (1998 [1924]) "Eidos und Eidolon," in *Gesammelte Werke,* ed. B. Recki. 17 vols. Hamburg. xv: 135–63.

Chantraine, P. (1950) "Les verbes grecs signifiant 'lire' (ἀναγιγνώσκω, ἐπιλέγομαι, ἐντυγχάνω, ἀναλέγομαι)," *Annuaire de l'Institut de Philologie et d'Histoire Orientales et Slaves* 10: 115–26.

(2009) *Dictionnaire étymologique de la langue grecque: Histoire des mots*, ed. J. Taillardat, A. Blanc *et al.* Paris.

Cheney, P. (1993) *Spenser's Famous Flight: A Renaissance Idea of a Literary Career.* Toronto.

Cherniss, H. F. (1935) *Aristotle's Criticism of Presocratic Philosophy.* Baltimore, MD. (Rpt. 1964, New York)

(1970) "The Characteristics and Effects of Presocratic Philosophy," in *Studies in Presocratic Philosophy, Vol. I: The Beginnings of Philosophy*, eds. D. J. Furley and R. E. Allen. London and New York. 1–28.

Chiron, P. (ed.) (1993) Demetrius, *Du style.* Paris.

Clark, T. J. (2001) "Phenomenality and Materiality in Cézanne," in *Material Events: Paul de Man and the Afterlife of Theory*, eds. T. Cohen, B. Cohen *et al.* Minneapolis, MN. 93–113.

(2006) *The Sight of Death: An Experiment in Art Writing.* New Haven, CT.

(2008) "The Special Motion of a Hand: Courbet and Poussin at the Met," *London Review of Books* 30, no. 8 (24 April): 3–6.

Clay, D. (2004) *Archilochos Heros: The Cult of Poets in the Greek Polis.* Washington, DC and Cambridge, MA.

Clayman, D. L. (1977) "The Origins of Greek Literary Criticism and the *Aitia* Prologue," *Wiener Studien* 11: 27–34.

Code, A. (1982) "The Aporematic Approach to Primary Being in Metaphysics Z," *The Journal of Philosophy* 79, no. 11: 716–18.

Cole, T. (1988) *Epiploke: Rhythmical Continuity and Poetic Structure in Greek Lyric.* Cambridge, MA.

(1991) *The Origins of Rhetoric in Ancient Greece.* Baltimore, MD.

Collingwood, R. G. (1938) *The Principles of Art.* Oxford.

Collins, D. (2003) "Nature, Cause, and Agency in Greek Magic," *Transactions of the American Philological Association* 133: 17–49.

Comotti, G. (1989) *Music in Greek and Roman Culture.* Trans. R. V. Munson. Baltimore, MD.

Conti Bizzarro, F. (1999) *Poetica e critica letteraria nei frammenti dei poeti comici greci.* Naples.

Cook, B. F. (1984) *The Elgin Marbles.* London.

Cope, E. M. (1970) *The "Rhetoric" of Aristotle, with a Commentary*, ed. J. E. Sandys. 3 vols. Hildesheim. (First published 1877, Cambridge.)

Cornford, F. M. (1957) *Plato's Theory of Knowledge: The Theaetetus and the Sophist of Plato.* New York.

Coulton, J. J. (1977) *Ancient Greek Architects at Work: Problems of Structure and Design.* Ithaca, NY.

Cowling, D. (1998) *Building the Text: Architecture as Metaphor in Late Medieval and Early Modern France.* Oxford.

Cribiore, R. (1996) *Writing, Teachers, and Students in Graeco-Roman Egypt.* Atlanta, GA.

(2001) *Gymnastics of the Mind: Greek Education in Hellenistic and Roman Egypt.* Princeton.

Crönert, W. (1906) *Kolotes und Menedemos, Texte und Untersuchungen zur Philosophen-und Literaturgeschichte.* Studien zur Paleographie und Papyruskunde, vol. VI, ed. C. Wessely. Leipzig. (Rpt. 1965, Amsterdam.)

Crowley, T. J. (2005) "On the Use of *Stoicheion* in the Sense of 'Element'," *Oxford Studies in Ancient Philosophy* 29: 367–94.

Crudden, M. (2001) *The Homeric Hymns.* Oxford.

Crusius, O. (1888) "Über die Nomosfrage," in *Verhandlungen des 39. Versammlung der deutscher Philologen und Schülmmänner in Zürich vom 28. September bis 1. Oktober 1887,* Leipzig. 258–75.

(1902) "Die *anagnostikoi* (Exkurs zu Aristot. Rhet. III 12.)," in *Festschrift Theodor Gomperz: Dargebracht zum siebzigsten Geburtstage am 29. März 1902,* ed. M. v. Schwind. Vienna. 381–87.

Csapo, E. (2004) "The Politics of the New Music," in *Music and the Muses: The Culture of 'Mousikē' in the Classical Athenian City,* eds. P. Murray and P. Wilson. Oxford. 207–48.

Csapo, E., and W. J. Slater (1994) *The Context of Ancient Drama.* Ann Arbor, MI.

Currie, G. (2005) "Imagination and Make-Believe," in *The Routledge Companion to Aesthetics,* eds. B. Gaut and D. Lopes. 2nd edn. London. 335–45.

D'Angour, A. (1997) "How the Dithyramb Got its Shape," *Classical Quarterly* 47, no. 2: 331–51.

(1999) "*Ad Unguem,*" *American Journal of Philology* 120: 411–27.

(2006) "The New Music – So What's New?," in *Rethinking Revolutions through Ancient Greece,* eds. S. Goldhill and R. Osborne. Cambridge. 264–83.

Damon, P. (1961) *Modes of Analogy in Ancient and Medieval Verse.* University of California Publications in Classical Philology, vol. 15, no. 6: 261–334. Berkeley, CA.

Davidson, D. (1990) *Plato's Philebus.* New York.

Davis, H. H. (1958) "Epitaphs and Memory," *Classical Journal* 53: 169–76.

Davis, W. (1997) "Formalism in Art History," in *Encyclopedia of Aesthetics,* ed. M. Kelly. 4 vols. Oxford. II: 221–25.

Day, J. W. (1989) "Rituals in Stone: Early Greek Grave Epigrams and Monuments," *Journal of Hellenic Studies* 109: 16–28.

(2000) "Epigram and Reader: Generic Force as (Re-)Activation of Ritual," in *Matrices of Genre: Authors, Canons, and Society,* eds. M. Depew and D. Obbink. Cambridge, MA. 37–55.

de Jong, I. J. F. (1987) "The Voice of Anonymity: τις-speeches in the *Iliad*," *Eranos* 85: 69–84.

del Grande, C. (1932) *Espressione musicale dei poeti greci.* Naples.

DeMarrais, E., C. Gosden, and C. Renfrew (eds.) (2004) *Rethinking Materiality: The Engagement of Mind with the Material World.* Cambridge.

Denniston, J. D. (1927) "Technical Terms in Aristophanes," *Classical Quarterly* 21: 113–21.

Desbordes, F. (1990) *Idées romaines sur l'écriture*. Lille.

Dewey, J. (1989 [1934]) *Art as Experience*, in *John Dewey, The Later Works, 1925–1953*, eds. J. A. Boydston and H. F. Simon, vol. x: 1934. Carbondale, IL.

Deyhle, W. (1969) "Phaidimos," *Mitteilungen des Deutschen Archäologischen Instituts, Athenische Abteilung* 84: 46–57.

Diels, H. (1886) "Über das 3. Buch der Aristotelischen Rhetorik," *Philosophische und historische Abhandlungen der Königlichen Akademie der Wissenschaften zu Berlin* 4: 1–34.

(1899) *Elementum: Eine Vorarbeit zum griechischen und lateinischen Thesaurus*. Leipzig.

(1965 [1879]) *Doxographi Graeci, collegit recensuit prolegomenis indicibusque instruxit Hermannus Diels*. Berlin.

(1969 [1910]) "Die Anfänge der Philologie bei den Griechen," in H. Diels, *Kleine Schriften zur Geschichte der antiken Philosophie*, ed. W. Burkert. Darmstadt. 68–92. (First published in *Neue Jahrbücher für das klassische Altertum, Geschichte, deutsche Literatur und für Pädagogik* 25 (1910) 1–25.)

Dindorf, W. (1852) *Scholia Graeca in Aeschinem et Isocratem ex codicibus aucta et emendata*. Hildesheim.

Dirlmeier, F. (1962) *Merkwürdige Zitate in der Eudemischen Ethik des Aristoteles*. Heidelberg.

Dörig, J. (1967) "Phaidimos: Mit 13 Abbildungen," *Archäologischer Anzeiger. Beiblatt zum Jahrbuch des Deutschen Archäologischen Instituts* 1: 15–28.

Dougherty, C. (2001) *The Raft of Odysseus: The Ethnographic Imagination of Homer's Odyssey*. New York.

Dougherty, C., and L. Kurke (eds.) (1998) *Cultural Poetics in Archaic Greece: Cult, Performance, Politics*. Cambridge.

(eds.) (2003) *The Cultures within Ancient Greek Culture: Contact, Conflict, Collaboration*. Cambridge.

Douglas, M. (2002) *Purity and Danger: An Analysis of Concepts of Pollution and Taboo*. London. (First published 1966.)

Dover, K. J. (ed.) (1968) Aristophanes, *Clouds*. Oxford.

(1988) "Ion of Chios: His Place in the History of Greek Literature," in id., *The Greeks and their Legacy: Collected Papers Volume II: Prose Literature, History, Society, Transmission, Influence*. Oxford. 1–12.

(ed.) (1993) Aristophanes, *Frogs*. Oxford.

Dubois, L. (1989) *Inscriptions grecques dialectales de Sicile: Contribution à l'étude du vocabulaire grec colonial*. Rome.

Dupont, F. (1997) "*Recitatio* and the Reorganization of the Space of Public Discourse," in *The Roman Cultural Revolution*, eds. T. Habinek and A. Schiesaro. Trans. T. Habinek and A. Lardinois. Cambridge. 44–59.

(1999) *The Invention of Literature: From Greek Intoxication to the Latin Book*. Trans. J. Lloyd. Baltimore, MD.

Durante, M. (1960) "Ricerche sulla preistoria della lingua poetica greca: La terminologia relativa alla creazione poetica," *Rendiconti dell'Accademia dei Lincei* 17: 231–49 (= M. Durante, *Sulla preistoria della tradizione poetica greca* (Rome) 2: 167–84).

Düring, I. (1966) *Aristoteles: Darstellung und Interpretation seines Denkens.* Bibliothek der klassischen Altertumswissenschaften. Heidelberg.

(1968) "Aristoteles," *RE Suppl.* 11: 159–336.

Dušanić, S. (1992) "Alcidamas of Elaea in Plato's *Phaedrus*," *Classical Quarterly* 42, no. 2: 347–57.

Dyck, A. R. (ed.) (1986) M. Psellus, *The Essays on Euripides and George of Pisidia and on Heliodorus and Achilles Tatius.* Byzantina Vindobonensia, vol. XVI. Vienna.

Eagleton, T. (1990) *The Ideology of the Aesthetic.* Oxford.

(2003) *After Theory.* New York.

Easterling, P. (1999) "Actors and Voices: Reading Between the Lines in Aeschines and Demosthenes," in *Performance Culture and Athenian Democracy*, eds. S. Goldhill and R. Osborne. Cambridge. 154–66.

(2005) "*Agamemnon* for the Ancients," in *Agamemnon in Performance 458 BC to AD 2004*, ed. F. Macintosh. Oxford. 23–35.

Easterling, P., and E. Hall (eds.) (2002) *Greek and Roman Actors: Aspects of an Ancient Profession.* Cambridge.

Eco, U. (1970) *Il problema estetico in Tommaso d'Aquino*, 2nd edn. Milan.

(1994) *Arte e bellezza nell'estetica medievale*, 3rd edn. Milan.

Edwards, M. W. (2002) *Sound, Sense, and Rhythm: Listening to Greek and Latin Poetry.* Princeton, NJ.

Eldridge, R. (1992) "Form," in *A Companion to Aesthetics*, ed. D. E. Cooper. Oxford. 159–62.

Eliot, T. S. (1950 [1919]) "Tradition and the Individual Talent," in id., *Selected Essays.* 2nd edn. New York. (1st edn. 1932.) 3–11.

(1986 [1933]) *The Use of Poetry and the Use of Criticism: Studies in the Relation of Criticism to Poetry in England.* Cambridge, MA.

Else, G. F. (1930) "Lucretius and the Aesthetic Attitude," *Harvard Studies in Classical Philology* 41: 149–82.

(1938) "Aristotle on the Beauty of Tragedy," *Harvard Studies in Classical Philology* 49: 179–204.

(1967) *Aristotle's Poetics: The Argument.* Cambridge, MA.

Elsner, J. (1995) *Art and the Roman Viewer: The Transformation of Art from the Pagan World to Christianity.* Cambridge.

(1998) *Imperial Rome and Christian Triumph: The Art of the Roman Empire, AD 100–450.* Oxford and New York.

(2006) "Reflections on the 'Greek Revolution' in Art: From Changes in Viewing to the Transformation of Subjectivity," in *Rethinking Revolutions Through Ancient Greece*, eds. S. Goldhill and R. Osborne. Cambridge. 68–95.

Engelmann, H. (1981) "Die Bauinschrift am Apollonion von Syrakus," *Zeitschrift für Papyrologie und Epigraphik* 44: 91–94.

Erlich, V. (1975) "Modern Russian Criticism from Andrej Belyj to Andrej Sinjavskij: Trends, Issues, Personalities," in *Twentieth-Century Russian Literary Criticism*, ed. V. Erlich. New Haven, CT. 1–30.

Evans, J., and S. Hall (eds.) (2007) *Visual Culture: The Reader*. Reprinted edn. (First published 1999). London.

Falkner, T. (2002) "Scholars versus Actors: Text and Performance in the Greek Tragic Scholia," in *Greek and Roman Actors: Aspects of an Ancient Profession*, eds. P. Easterling and E. Hall. Cambridge. 342–61.

Fantuzzi, M. (2004) "The Epigram," in *Tradition and Innovation in Hellenistic Poetry*, eds. M. Fantuzzi and R. Hunter. Cambridge. 283–349.

Fantuzzi, M., and R. Hunter (2004) *Tradition and Innovation in Hellenistic Poetry*. Cambridge.

Farrar, C. (1988) *The Origins of Democratic Thinking: The Invention of Politics in Classical Athens*. Cambridge.

Feeney, D. (1999) "*Mea Tempora*: Patterning of Time in the Metamorphoses," in *Ovidian Transformations: Essays on the Metamorphoses and its Reception*, eds. S. Hinds, P. R. Hardie, and A. Barchiesi. Cambridge. 13–30.

Ferrari, G. A. (1981) "La scrittura invisibile," *Aut-Aut* 184–85: 95–110.

Ferry, L. (1990) *Homo aestheticus: L'invention du goût à l'âge démocratique*. Paris.

Feuerbach, A. (1855) *Der vaticanische Apollo: Eine Reihe archäologisch-ästhetischer Betrachtungen*, 2nd edn. Stuttgart and Augsburg. (1st edn. 1833, Nuremberg.)

Fine, G. (1995) *On Ideas: Aristotle's Criticism of Plato's Theory of Forms*. Oxford.

Finney, G. (1966) "Medical Theories of Vocal Exercise and Health," *Bulletin of the History of Medicine* 40, no. 5 (September–October): 395–406.

Fleming, T. J. (1977) "The Musical Nomos in Aeschylus' *Oresteia*," *Classical Journal* 72, no. 3: 222–33.

Ford, A. (1992) *Homer: The Poetry of the Past*. Ithaca, NY.

  (2002) *The Origins of Criticism: Literary Culture and Poetic Theory in Classical Greece*. Princeton, NJ.

Fortenbaugh, W. W. (1985) "Theophrastus on Delivery," in *Theophrastus of Eresus: On His Life and Work*, eds. W. W. Fortenbaugh, P. M. Huby *et al.* New Brunswick, NJ. 269–87.

  (1986) "Aristotle's Platonic Attitude Toward Delivery," *Philosophy and Rhetoric* 19, no. 4: 242–54.

Fowler, B. H. (1989) *The Hellenistic Aesthetic*. Madison, WI.

Fowler, D. (2000) "The Ruin of Time," in id., *Roman Constructions: Readings in Postmodern Latin*. New York. 193–217.

Frank, E. E. (1979) *Literary Architecture: Essays toward a Tradition: Walter Pater, Gerard Manley Hopkins, Marcel Proust, Henry James*. Berkeley, CA.

Fränkel, H. (1974) "Xenophanes' Empiricism and his Critique of Knowledge (B34)," in *The Pre-Socratics: A Collection of Critical Essays*, ed. A. P. D. Mourelatos. Garden City, NY. 118–31.

  (1993) *Dichtung und Philosophie des frühen Griechentums: Eine Geschichte der griechischen Epik, Lyrik und Prosa bis zur Mitte des fünften Jahrhunderts*, 4th edn. Munich. (1st edn. 1951.)

Fränkel, H. F. (1975) *Early Greek Poetry and Philosophy: A History of Greek Epic, Lyric, and Prose to the Middle of the Fifth Century.* Trans. M. Hadas and J. Willis. New York. (Translated from *Dichtung und Philosophie des frühen Griechentums,* 2nd edn. Munich, 1962.)

Franklin, J. C. (2002) "Diatonic Music in Greece: A Reassessment of its Antiquity," *Mnemosyne* 55, no. 6: 669–702.

  (forthcoming) "Dithyramb and the 'Demise of Music'," in *Song Culture and Social Change: The Contexts of Dithyramb,* eds. B. Kowalzig and P. Wilson.

Frede, D. (1997) *Platon, Philebos: Übersetzung und Kommentar.* Göttingen.

Frede, M. (1992) "On Aristotle's Conception of the Soul," in *Essays on Aristotle's De anima,* eds. M. C. Nussbaum and A. Rorty. Oxford. 93–107.

  (2004) "Aristotle's Account of the Origins of Philosophy," *Rhizai* 1, no. 1: 9–44.

Fritz, K. von (1938) *Philosophie und sprachlicher Ausdruck bei Demokrit, Plato und Aristoteles.* New York and London.

  (1971) *Grundprobleme der Geschichte der antiken Wissenschaft.* Berlin and New York.

Frontisi-Ducroux, F. (1975) *Dédale: Mythologie de l'artisan en Grèce ancienne.* Paris.

  (1986) *La cithare d'Achille: Essai sur la poétique de l'Iliade.* Rome.

Fry, R. E. (1990) *Vision and Design,* ed. J. B. Bullen. London and New York. (First published 1920.)

Gagarin, M., and P. Woodruff (1995) *Early Greek Political Thought from Homer to the Sophists.* Cambridge.

Gamberini, L. (ed.) (1979) *Plutarco, "Della musica".* Florence.

Gavrilov, A. K. (1997) "Techniques of Reading in Classical Antiquity," *Classical Quarterly* 47, no. 1: 56–73.

Geissler, P. (1925) *Chronologie der altattischen Komödie.* Berlin.

Gentili, B. (1988) *Poetry and its Public in Ancient Greece: From Homer to the Fifth Century.* Trans. A. T. Cole. Baltimore, MD.

Getz-Preziosi, P. (1980) "The Male Figure in Early Cycladic Sculpture," *Metropolitan Museum Journal* 15: 5–33.

  (1990) "Cycladic," in *Glories of the Past: Ancient Art from the Shelby White and Leon Levy Collection,* ed. D. von Bothmer. New York. 16–25.

Gilbert, K. E., and H. Kuhn (1953) *A History of Esthetics,* Rev. and enl. edn. Bloomington. (1st edn. 1939.)

Gladstone, W. E. (1858) *Studies on Homer and the Homeric Age.* 3 vols. Oxford.

Gleason, M. W. (1995) *Making Men: Sophists and Self-Presentation in Ancient Rome.* Princeton, NJ.

Glucker, J. (1968) "Notes on the Byzantine Treatise on Tragedy," *Byzantion: Revue Internationale des Études Byzantines* 38: 267–72.

Goldhill, S. (2001a) "The Erotic Eye: Visual Stimulation and Cultural Conflict," in *Being Greek under Rome: Cultural Identity, the Second Sophistic and the Development of Empire,* ed. S. Goldhill. Cambridge. 154–94.

  (ed.) (2001b) *Being Greek under Rome: Cultural Identity, the Second Sophistic and the Development of Empire.* Cambridge.

Goldhill, S., and R. Osborne (1994) *Art and Text in Ancient Greek Culture.* Cambridge.

Gombrich, E. H. (2000) *Art and Illusion: A Study in the Psychology of Pictorial Representation*, 2nd edn. Princeton, NJ. (1st edn. 1960.)

Gomperz, T. (1891) "Philodem und die ästhetischen Schriften der Herculanischen Bibliothek," *Sitzungsberichte der Kaiserlichen Akademie der Wissenschaften in Wien, philosophisch-historische Classe* 123, no. 6: 1–88.

Gordon, R. L. (1979) "The Real and the Imaginary: Production and Religion in the Graeco-Roman World," *Art History* 2, no. 1: 5–34.

Gourevitch, D. (1987) "L'esthétique médicale de Galien," *Les Études Classiques* 55, no. 3: 267–90.

Graham, D. W. (1999) "Empedocles and Anaxagoras: Responses to Parmenides," in *The Cambridge Companion to Early Greek Philosophy*, ed. A. A. Long. Cambridge. 159–80.

Grassi, E. (1962) *Die Theorie des Schönen in der Antike.* Cologne.

Green, J. R. (1991) "On Seeing and Depicting the Theatre in Classical Athens," *Greek, Roman and Byzantine Studies* 32, no. 1: 15–50.

Greenberg, C. (1986–93 [1940]) "Towards a Newer Laocoon," in C. Greenberg, *The Collected Essays and Criticism*, ed. J. O'Brian. 4 vols. Chicago. 1: 23–38. (First published in *The Partisan Review*, vol. 7, no. 4 (1940) 296–310.)

Gregoric, P. (2007) *Aristotle on the Common Sense.* Oxford.

Griffith, M. (1984) "The Vocabulary of Prometheus Bound," *Classical Quarterly* n.s. 34, no. 2: 282–91.

Gros, P. (ed.) (1997) Vitruvius, *De architectura.* 2 vols. Translation and commentary by Antonio Corso and Elisa Romano. Turin.

Gruben, G. (1986) *Die Tempel der Griechen*, 4th edn. Munich.

Guarducci, M. (1967–78) *Epigrafia greca.* 4 vols. Rome.

Gudeman, A. (ed.) (1934) Aristoteles, Περὶ ποιητικῆς. Mit *exegetischem Kommentar.* Berlin.

Guillory, J. (1993) *Cultural Capital: The Problem of Literary Canon Formation.* Chicago, IL.

Gumbrecht, H. U. (2004) *Production of Presence: What Meaning Cannot Convey.* Stanford.

Gunderson, E. (2000) *Staging Masculinity: The Rhetoric of Performance in the Roman World.* Ann Arbor, MI.

(2009) *Nox Philologiae: Aulus Gellius and the Fantasy of the Roman Library.* Madison, WI.

Gurd, S. A. (2007) "Meaning and Material Presence: Four Epigrams on Timomachus's Unfinished *Medea*," *Transactions of the American Philological Association* 137: 305–31.

Guthrie, W. K. C. (1971) *The Sophists.* Cambridge.

Gutzwiller, K. (2002) "Art's Echo: The Tradition of Hellenistic Ecphrastic Epigram," in *Hellenistic Epigrams*, eds. M. A. Harder, R. F. Regtuit, and G. C. Wakker. Leuven, Belgium and Sterling, VA. 85–112.

(2005a) *The New Posidippus: A Hellenistic Poetry Book.* New York.

(2005b) "The Literariness of the Milan Papyrus, or 'What Difference a Book?'," in *The New Posidippus: A Hellenistic Poetry Book*, ed. K. Gutzwiller. New York. 287–319.

Guyer, P. (2005) *Values of Beauty: Historical Essays in Aesthetics*. Cambridge.

Habinek, T., and A. Schiesaro (1997) *The Roman Cultural Revolution*. Cambridge.

Habinek, T. N. (1998) *The Politics of Latin Literature: Writing, Identity, and Empire in Ancient Rome*. Princeton, NJ.

(2005) *The World of Roman Song: From Ritualized Speech to Social Order*. Baltimore, MD.

Hahn, R. (2001) *Anaximander and the Architects: The Contributions of Egyptian and Greek Architectural Technologies to the Origins of Greek Philosophy*. Albany, NY.

(2003) "Proportions and Numbers in Anaximander and Early Greek Thought," in *Anaximander in Context: New Studies in the Origins of Greek Philosophy*, eds. D. L. Couprie, R. Hahn, and G. Naddaf. Albany, NY. 73–163.

Hall, E. (1996) "Is there a *Polis* in Aristotle's *Poetics*?," in *Tragedy and the Tragic: Greek Theatre and Beyond*, ed. M. S. Silk. Oxford. 295–309.

Hallett, C. H. (1986) "The Origins of the Classical Style in Sculpture," *Journal of Hellenic Studies* 106: 71–84.

Halliwell, S. (1986) *Aristotle's Poetics*. Chapel Hill, NC.

(2000) "Plato and Painting," in *Word and Image in Ancient Greece*, eds. N. K. Rutter and B. A. Sparkes. Edinburgh. 99–115.

(2002) *The Aesthetics of Mimesis: Ancient Texts and Modern Problems*. Princeton, NJ.

(2003) "From Functionalism to Formalism: Or Did the Greeks Invent Literary Criticism?," *Arion* 10, no. 3: 171–85.

Hamlyn, D. W. (1959) "Aristotle's Account of Aesthesis in the *De Anima*," *Classical Quarterly* n.s. 9, no. 1: 6–16.

Hannoosh, M. (1995) *Painting and the Journal of Eugène Delacroix*. Princeton, NJ.

Hardie, P. (1993) "*Ut pictura poesis?* Horace and the Visual Arts," in *Horace 2000: A Celebration. Essays for the Bimillennium*, ed. N. Rudd. London. 120–39.

Harriott, R. M. (1969) *Poetry and Criticism before Plato*. London.

Hartel, W. (1878) "Studien über attisches Staatsrecht und Urkundenwesen II," *Sitzungsberichte der Kaiserlichen Akademie der Wissenschaften. Philosophisch-historische Classe* 91, no. 1: 101–94.

Haselberger, L. (1980) "Werkzeichnungen am Jüngeren Didymeion–Vorbericht," *Istanbuler Mitteilungen* 30: 191–215.

(1983) "Bericht über die Arbeit am Jüngeren Apollontempel von Didyma–Zwischenbericht," *Istanbuler Mitteilungen* 33: 90–123.

(1985) "The Construction Plans for the Temple of Apollo at Didyma," *Scientific American* 253, no. 6: 126–32.

(1999) "Old Issues, New Research, Latest Discoveries," in *Appearance and Essence: Refinements of Classical Architecture—Curvature: Proceedings of the Second Williams Symposium on Classical Architecture Held at the University of*

Pennsylvania, Philadelphia, April 2–4, 1993, ed. L. Haselberger. Philadelphia, PA. 1–68.

Häusle, H. (1980) *Das Denkmal als Garant des Nachruhms: Beiträge zur Geschichte und Thematik eines Motivs in lateinischen Inschriften.* Zetemata, vol. 75. Munich.

Heath, M. (1987) *The Poetics of Greek Tragedy.* London.

Hegel, G. W. F. (1970) *Phänomenologie des Geistes*, eds. E. Moldenhauer and K. M. Michel. Frankfurt am Main.

   (1975) *Hegel's Aesthetics: Lectures on Fine Art.* Trans. T. M. Knox. 2 vols. Oxford.

Heldmann, K. (1982) *Die Niederlage Homers im Dichterwettstreit mit Hesiod.* Hypomnemata, vol. 75. Göttingen.

Heller-Roazen, D. (2007) *The Inner Touch: Archaeology of a Sensation.* New York and Cambridge, MA.

Hendrickson, G. L. (1929) "Ancient Reading," *Classical Journal* 25: 182–96.

Hendrix, E. (2003) "Painted Early Cycladic Figures: An Exploration of Context and Meaning," *Hesperia* 72, no. 4: 405–46.

Henrichs, A. (1995) "Why Should I Dance? Choral Self-Referentiality in Greek Tragedy," *Arion* 3, no. 1: 56–111.

Herington, J. (1985) *Poetry into Drama: Early Tragedy and the Greek Poetic Tradition.* Berkeley, CA and London.

Hermann, G. (1827–77) *Godofredi Hermanni Opuscula*, ed. T. Fritzsche. 8 vols. Leipzig.

Heubeck, A., S. West *et al.* (eds.) (1988–92) *A Commentary on Homer's Odyssey.* 3 vols. Oxford.

Hickey, D. (1993) *The Invisible Dragon: Four Essays on Beauty.* Los Angeles, CA.

Himmelmann, N. (1969) "Über bildende Kunst in der homerischen Gesellschaft," *Akademie der Wissenschaften und der Literatur. Abhandlungen der Geistes-und Sozialwissenschaftlichen Klasse (Mainz)* 7: 179–223.

Holford-Strevens, L. (2003) *Aulus Gellius: An Antonine Scholar and His Achievement*, Rev. edn. Oxford.

Hollander, J. (1996) "The Poetry of Architecture," *Bulletin of the American Academy of Arts and Sciences* 49, no. 5: 17–35.

Holmes, B. (2010) *The Symptom and the Subject: The Emergence of the Physical Body in Ancient Greece.* Princeton, NJ.

Hölscher, T. (1971) *Ideal und Wirklichkeit in den Bildnissen Alexanders des Großen.* Heidelberg.

Hölscher, U. (1974) "Paradox, Simile, and Gnomic Utterance in Heraclitus," in *The Pre-Socratics: A Collection of Critical Essays*, ed. A. P. D. Mourelatos. Garden City, NY. 229–38.

Hon, G., and B. R. Goldstein (2008) *From Summetria to Symmetry: The Making of a Revolutionary Scientific Concept.* Dordrecht.

Hopkinson, N. (1988) *A Hellenistic Anthology.* Cambridge.

Howes, D. (2003) *Sensual Relations: Engaging the Senses in Culture and Social Theory.* Ann Arbor, MI.

   (ed.) (2005) *Empire of the Senses: The Sensual Culture Reader.* Oxford.

Hudson-Williams, H. L. (1949a) "Isocrates and Recitations," *Classical Quarterly* 43: 64–69.

(1949b) "Impromptu Speaking," *Greece & Rome* 18, no. 52: 28–31.

Huffman, C. (2002) "Polyclète et les présocratiques," in *Qu'est-ce que la philosophie présocratique? What is Presocratic Philosophy?*, eds. A. Laks and C. Louguet. Villeneuve-d'Ascq. 303–27.

Humboldt, W. V. (1960–81) *Werke in fünf Bänden*, eds. A. Flitner and K. Giel. 5 vols. Stuttgart.

Humphreys, S. C. (1980) "Family Tombs and Tomb Cult in Ancient Athens," *Journal of Hellenic Studies* 100: 96–126.

Hunter, R. (2003) "Reflecting on Writing and Culture: Theocritus and the Style of Cultural Change," in *Written Texts and the Rise of Literate Culture in Ancient Greece*, ed. H. Yunis Cambridge. 213–34.

Hurwit, J. M. (1977) "Image and Frame in Greek Art," *American Journal of Archaeology* 81: 1–30.

(1985) *The Art and Culture of Early Greece, 1100–480 BC.* Ithaca, NY.

(1990) "The Words in the Image: Orality, Literacy, and Early Greek Art," *Word & Image* 6, no. 2: 180–97.

(1992) "A Note on Ornament, Nature, and Boundary in Early Greek Art," *Bulletin Antieke Beschaving* 67: 63–72.

(1999) *The Athenian Acropolis: History, Mythology, and Archaeology from the Neolithic Era to the Present.* Cambridge.

(2004) *The Acropolis in the Age of Pericles.* New York.

Hussey, E. (1999) "Heraclitus," in *The Cambridge Companion to Early Greek Philosophy*, ed. A. A. Long. Cambridge. 88–112.

Hutcheson, F. (2004 [1725; 2nd edn. 1726]) *An Inquiry into the Original of our Ideas of Beauty and Virtue in Two Treatises*, ed. W. Leidhold. Indianapolis, IN.

Hutchinson, G. O. (2006) "Hellenistic Epic and Homeric Form," in *Epic Interactions: Perspectives on Homer, Virgil, and the Epic Tradition. Presented to Jasper Griffin by Former Pupils*, eds. M. J. Clarke, B. G. F. Currie and R. O. A. M. Lyne. Oxford. 105–29.

(1988) *Hellenistic Poetry.* Oxford.

(2002) "The New Posidippus and Latin Poetry," *Zeitschrift für Papyrologie und Epigraphik* 138: 1–10.

(2003) "The Catullan Corpus, Greek Epigram, and the Poetry of Objects," *Classical Quarterly* 53, no. 1: 206–21.

Ierodiakonou, K. (2005) "Empedocles on Colour and Colour Vision," *Oxford Studies in Ancient Philosophy* 29: 1–35.

Imber, M. (2001) "Practised Speech: Oral and Written Conventions in Roman Declamation," in *Speaking Volumes: Orality and Literacy in the Greek and Roman world*, ed. J. Watson. Leiden and Boston. 199–212.

Immerwahr, H. R. (1960) "*Ergon*: History as a Monument in Herodotus and Thucydides," *American Journal of Philology* 81, no. 3: 261–90.

(1964) "Book Rolls on Attic Vases," in *Classical, Mediaeval and Renaissance Studies in Honor of Berthold Louis Ullman*, ed. C. Henderson. 2 vols. Rome. 1:17–48.

(1990) *Attic Script: A Survey.* Oxford.

(2007) "Nonsense Inscriptions and Literacy," *Kadmos* 45, no. 1–2: 136–72.

Immisch, O. (ed.) (1927) *Gorgiae Helena*. Kleine Texte für Vorlesungen und Übungen, vol. 158. Berlin and Leipzig.

Innes, D. C. (1979) "Gigantomachy and Natural Philosophy," *Classical Quarterly* n.s. 29: 165–71.

Inwood, B. (2001) *The Poem of Empedocles: A Text and Translation with an Introduction*, Rev. edn. Toronto.

Irmscher, J. (1981) "Warum die Byzantiner altgriechische Dramatiker lasen," *Philologus* 125, no. 2: 236–39.

Irwin, T. (1988) *Aristotle's First Principles*. Oxford.

Isenberg, A. (1973 [1955]) "Formalism," in *Aesthetics and the Theory of Criticism. Selected Essays of Arnold Isenberg*, ed. W. Callaghan, *et al*. Chicago, IL.

Jacobsthal, P. (1933) *Diskoi*. Berlin and Leipzig.

Jacques, J.-M. (1960) "Sur un acrostiche d'Aratos," *Révue des Études Anciennes* 62: 48–60.

Jaeger, W. W. (1931) *Das Problem des Klassischen und die Antike: Acht Vorträge gehalten auf der Fachtagung der klassischen Altertumswissenschaft zu Naumburg 1930*. Leipzig. (Rpt. 1972, Darmstadt.)

Jakobson, R. (1960) "Closing Statement: Linguistics and Poetics," in *Style in Language*, ed. T. Sebeok. Cambridge, MA. 350–77.

James, L. (1996) *Light and Colour in Byzantine Art*. Oxford.

(2004) "Senses and Sensibility in Byzantium," *Art History* 27, no. 4: 523–37.

(ed.) (2007) *Art and Text in Byzantine Culture*. Cambridge.

James, W. (1987) *Writings, 1902–1910*, ed. B. Kuklick. New York, NY.

(2003 [1912]) *Essays in Radical Empiricism*, ed. R. B. Perry. Mineola, NY.

Janko, R. (1984) *Aristotle on Comedy: Towards a Reconstruction of Poetics II*. London.

(ed.) (1987) Aristotle, *Poetics I*. Indianapolis, IN.

(ed.) (2000) Philodemus, *On Poems, Book 1. Introduction, Translation and Commentary*. Oxford.

Jeffery, L. H. (1962) "The Inscribed Gravestones of Archaic Attica," *The Annual of the British School of Athens* 57: 116–53.

(1990) *The Local Scripts of Archaic Greece: A Study of the Origin of the Greek Alphabet and its Development from the Eighth to the Fifth Centuries BC*, Rev. edn. with a supplement by A. W. Johnston. Oxford. (1st edn. 1961.)

Jenkins, I. (2001) *Cleaning and Controversy: The Parthenon Sculptures 1811–1939*. The British Museum Occasional Papers, no. 146. London.

Jennings, V., and A. Katsaros (eds.) (2007) *The World of Ion of Chios*. Leiden.

Jex-Blake, K. (1896) *The Elder Pliny's Chapters on the History of Art*. Translated by K. Jex-Blake. With commentary and historical introd. by E. Sellers and additional notes contributed by Heinrich Ludwig Urlichs. London. (Rpt. 1976, Chicago, IL.)

Joachim, H. H. (ed.) (1922) *Aristotle, De generatione et corruptione*. Oxford.

Johnson, G. A. (ed.) (1993) *The Merleau-Ponty Aesthetics Reader: Philosophy and Painting*. Evanston, IL.

Johnson, W. (2000) "Toward A Sociology of Reading in Classical Antiquity," *American Journal of Philology* 121: 593–627.

(2003) "Reading Cultures and Education," in *Reading Between the Lines: Perspectives on Foreign Language Literacy*, ed. P. C. Patrikis. New Haven, CT. 9–23.

Johnson, W. A., and H. N. Parker (eds.) (2009) *Ancient Literacies: The Culture of Reading in Greece and Rome*. New York.

Jouanna, J. (1984) "Rhétorique et médécine dans la collection hippocratique: Contribution à l'histoire de la rhétorique au Ve siècle," *Revue des Études Grecques* 97: 26–44.

(ed.) (2003) *Hippocrate: Oeuvres complètes. 2.1: L'Ancienne médecine*. Paris. (1st edn. 1990.)

Kahn, C. H. (1966) "Sensation and Consciousness in Aristotle's Psychology," *Archiv für Begriffsgeschichte* 48, no. 1: 43–81.

(1973) "Language and Ontology in the *Cratylus*," in *Exegesis and Argument: Studies in Greek Philosophy Presented to Gregory Vlastos*, eds. A. P. D. Mourelatos, E. N. Lee, and R. M. Rorty. New York. 152–76.

(1992) "Aristotle on Thinking," in *Essays on Aristotle's De anima*, eds. M. C. Nussbaum and A. Rorty. Oxford. 359–79.

Kaibel, G., and J. A. Lebègue (eds.) (1890) *Inscriptiones Italiae et Siciliae. Inscriptiones graecae*, vol. 14. Berlin.

Kaimio, M. (1977) *Characterization of Sound in Early Greek Literature*. Helsinki.

Kant, I. (1997) *Vorlesungen über Anthropologie*, in *Gesammelte Schriften*, eds. R. Brandt and W. Stark. vol. 25. Berlin.

Karusos, C. (1961) *Aristodikos: Zur Geschichte der spätarchaisch-attischen Plastik und der Grabstatue*. Stuttgart.

(1972 [1941]) "περικαλλὲς ἄγαλμα—ἐξεποιησ' οὐκ ἀδαής: Empfindungen und Gedanken der archaischen Griechen um die Kunst," in *Inschriften der Griechen: Grab-, Weih-und Ehreninschriften*, ed. G. Pfohl. Darmstadt. 85–152.

Kassel, R. (1991) "Dialoge mit Statuen," in id., *Kleine Schriften*. Berlin and New York. 140–53.

Kayser, H. (1958) *Paestum: Die Nomoi der drei Altgriechischen Tempel zu Paestum*. Heidelberg.

Keesling, C. M. (2003) "Rereading the Acropolis Dedications," in *Lettered Attica: A Day of Attic Epigraphy; Actes du Symposium d'Athènes, 8 mars 2000*, eds. D. R. Jordan and J. S. Traill. Athens. 41–54.

Kelly, M. (ed.) (1998) *Encyclopedia of Aesthetics*. 4 vols. New York.

Kennedy, G. A. (1989) *The Cambridge History of Literary Criticism. Volume 1, Classical Criticism*. Cambridge.

(1991) *Aristotle on Rhetoric: A Civil Discourse*. New York.

Kerferd, G. B. (1981a) *The Sophistic Movement*. Cambridge.

(1981b) "The Interpretation of Gorgias' Treatise περὶ τοῦ μὴ ὄντος ἢ περὶ φύσεως," *Deucalion* 36: 319–27.

(1985) "Gorgias and Empedocles," in *Gorgia e la sofistica: Atti del convegno internazionale (Lentini-Catania, 12–15 dic. 1983)*, eds. L. Montoneri and F. Romano. Catania. 595–605.

Kermode, F. (1974) "Novels: Recognition and Deception," *Critical Inquiry* 1, no. 1: 103–21.

Keulen, W. H. (2009) *Gellius the Satirist: Roman Cultural Authority in Attic Nights.* Leiden and Boston, MA.

Keuls, E. C. (1975) "*Skiagraphia* Once Again," *American Journal of Archaeology* 79, no. 1: 1–16.

(1978) *Plato and Greek Painting.* Leiden.

Kirk, G. S., J. E. Raven, and M. Schofield. (1983) *The Presocratic Philosophers: A Critical History with a Selection of Texts,* 2nd edn. Cambridge.

Knox, B. M. W. (1957) *Oedipus at Thebes.* New Haven, CT.

Koenigs, W. (1984) *Die Echohalle.* Berlin.

Koller, H. (1963) *Musik und Dichtung im alten Griechenland.* Bern.

Korsmeyer, C. (1999) *Making Sense of Taste: Food and Philosophy.* Ithaca, NY.

Kosman, L. A. (1975) "Perceiving that We Perceive: On the Soul III, 2," *The Philosophical Review* 84, no. 4: 499–519.

Kraut, R. (ed.) (1997) *Aristotle: Politics, Books VII and VIII.* Oxford.

Krevans, N. (1993) "Fighting against Antimachus: The 'Lyde' and the 'Aetia' Reconsidered," in *Callimachus,* eds. M. A. Harder, R. F. Regtuit, and G. C. Wakker. Groningen. 149–60.

Kristeller, P. O. (1990) "The Modern System of the Arts," in id., *Renaissance Thought and the Arts: Collected Essays.* Expanded edn. Princeton, NJ. 163–227. (First published in the *Journal of the History of Ideas* 12 (1951) 496–527 and 13 (1952) 17–46.)

Kroll, W. (1907) "Randbemerkungen," *Rheinisches Museum* 62: 86–101.

Krukowski, L. (1997) "Formalism: Conceptual and Historical Overview," in *Encyclopedia of Aesthetics,* ed. M. Kelly. 4 vols. Oxford. II: 213–16.

Krumbacher, A. (1920) *Die Stimmbildung der Redner im Altertum bis auf die Zeit Quintilians.* Paderborn.

Kuhn, H. (1931) *Die Vollendung der klassischen deutschen Ästhetik durch Hegel.* Berlin.

Kurke, L. (1999a) *Coins, Bodies, Games, and Gold: The Politics of Meaning in Archaic Greece.* Princeton, NJ.

(1999b) "Pindar and the Prostitutes," in *Constructions of the Classical Body,* ed. J. I. Porter. Ann Arbor, MI. 101–25.

La Piana, G. (1936) "The Byzantine Theater," *Speculum* 11, no. 2: 171–211.

Laks, A. (1999) "Soul, Sensation, and Thought," in *The Cambridge Companion to Early Greek Philosophy,* ed. A. A. Long. Cambridge. 250–70.

(2002) "'Philosophes présocratiques': Remarques sur la construction d'une catégorie de l'historiographie philosophique," in *Qu'est-ce que la philosophie présocratique? What is Presocratic Philosophy?,* eds. A. Laks and C. Louguet. Villeneuve-d'Ascq. 17–38.

(2006) *Introduction à la "philosophie présocratique".* Paris.

Lallot, J. (ed.) (1998) *La grammaire de Denys le Thrace.* 2nd, rev. edn. Paris.

Lanata, G. (1963) *Poetica pre-platonica: Testimonianze e frammenti.* Florence.

Landels, J. G. (1967) "Assisted Resonance in Ancient Theatres," *Greece & Rome* 14: 80–94.

Langdon, S. (2008) *Art and Identity in Dark Age Greece, 1100–700 B.C.E.* New York.

Lange, F. A. (1866) *Geschichte des Materialismus und Kritik seiner Bedeutung in der Gegenwart.* Iserlohn.

Laporte, P. M. (1947) "Attic Vase Painting and Pre-Socratic Philosophy," *The Journal of Aesthetics and Art Criticism* 6, no. 2: 139–52.

Lasserre, F. (ed.) (1954) Plutarque, *De la musique. Texte, traduction, commentaire, précédés d'une étude sur l'éducation musicale dans la Grèce antique.* Olten and Lausanne.

Lattimore, R., trans. (1951) *The Iliad.* Chicago, IL.

trans. (1965) *The Odyssey of Homer.* New York.

Lavecchia, S. (ed.) (2000) *Pindari dithyramborum fragmenta.* Rome.

Lazzarini, M. L. (1976) *Le formule delle dediche votive nella Grecia arcaica.* Rome.

Lefkowitz, M. R. (1981) *The Lives of the Greek Poets.* London.

Leftwich, G. V. (1987) "Ancient Conceptions of the Body and the Canon of Polykleitos." Diss., Princeton University.

(1995) "Polykleitos and Hippokratic Medicine," in *Polykleitos, the Doryphoros, and Tradition,* ed. W. G. Moon. Madison WI. 38–51.

Lehrs, K. (1882) *De Aristarchi studiis homericis,* 3rd edn. Leipzig. (1st edn. 1833, 2nd edn. 1865.) (Rpt. 1964, Hildesheim.)

Leibniz, G. W. (1965 [1704]) *Nouveaux essais sur l'entendement humain,* in *Die philosophischen Schriften von Gottfried Wilhelm Leibniz,* ed. C. I. Gerhardt. 7 vols. Vol. 5. Rpt. Hildesheim. (First published 1875–90, Berlin.)

Lentz, T. M. (1989) *Orality and Literacy in Hellenic Greece.* Carbondale, IL.

Lesher, J. H. (ed.) (1992) *Xenophanes of Colophon: Fragments. A Text and Translation with a Commentary.* Toronto.

Leszl, W. G. (2004) "Plato's Attitude to Poetry and the Fine Arts and the Origins of Aesthetics: Part I," *Études platoniciennes* 1: 113–97.

(2006) "Plato's Attitude to Poetry and the Fine Arts and the Origins of Aesthetics: Part II," *Études platoniciennes* 2: 255–351.

Leurini, A. (ed.) (2000) *Ionis Chii testimonia et fragmenta. Classical and Byzantine Monographs,* vol. 23. 2nd, updated edn. Amsterdam.

Levinson, J. (ed.) (2003) *The Oxford Handbook of Aesthetics.* Oxford.

Lewis, F. A. (2008) "What's the Matter with Prime Matter?," *Oxford Studies in Ancient Philosophy* 34: 123–46.

Liebersohn, Y. Z. (1999) "Alcidamas' *On the Sophists:* A Reappraisal," *Eranos* 97: 108–24.

Lippard, L. R. (ed.) (1973) *Six Years: The Dematerialization of the Art Object from 1966 to 1972: A Cross-Reference Book of Information on Some Esthetic Boundaries.* New York.

Lissarrague, F. (1987) *Un flot d'images: Une esthétique de banquet grec.* Paris.

Lloyd, G. E. R. (1979) *Magic, Reason, and Experience: Studies in the Origin and Development of Greek Science.* Cambridge.

(1987) *The Revolutions of Wisdom: Studies in the Claims and Practice of Ancient Greek Science.* Berkeley, CA.

Lo Piparo, F. (1988) "Aristotle: The Material Conditions of Linguistic Expressiveness," *Versus: Quaderni di studi semiotici* 54: 83–101.

(1999) "Il corpo vivente della *lexis* e le sue parti: Annotazioni sulla linguistica di Aristotele," *Histoire, épistémologie, langage* 21: 119–32.

Long, A. A. (1982) "Soul and Body in Stoicism," *Phronesis* 27: 34–57. (Rpt. in id. (1996) *Stoic Studies*. Cambridge.)

(ed.) (1999) *The Cambridge Companion to Early Greek Philosophy*. Cambridge.

Long, A. A., and D. N. Sedley (1987) *The Hellenistic Philosophers*. 2 vols. Cambridge.

Lotman, J. (1977) *The Structure of the Artistic Text*. Trans. R. Vroon. Ann Arbor, MI.

Lucas, D. W. (ed.) (1968) Aristotle, *Poetics*. Oxford.

Lüdtke, H. (1969) "Die Alphabetschrift und das Problem der Lautsegmentierung," *Phonetica* 20: 147–76.

Lukács, G. ([1920] 1971) *Die Theorie des Romans: Ein geschichtsphilosophischer Versuch über die Formen der großen Epik*. Neuwied.

Lumpp, H.-M. (1963) "Die Arniadas-Inschrift aus Korkyra: Homerisches im Epigramm—Epigrammatisches im Homer," *Forschungen und Fortschritte* 37, no. 7: 212–15.

Luther, W. (1966) "Wahrheit, Licht und Erkenntnis in der griechischen Philosophie bis Demokrit. Ein Beitrag zur Erforschung des Zusammenhangs von Sprache und philosophischen Denken," *Archiv für Begriffsgeschichte. Bausteine zu einem historischen Wörterbuch der Philosophie* 10: 1–239.

Lynn-George, M. (1988) *Epos: Word, Narrative and the Iliad*. Houndmills, Basingstoke, Hampshire.

Lyotard, J. F. (1991) "Presence," in *The Language of Art History*, eds. S. Kemal and I. Gaskell. Trans. M. Hobson and T. Cochran. New York and Cambridge. 11–34

Ma, J. (2007) "The Worlds of Nestor the Poet," in *Severan Culture*, eds. S. Swain, S. Harrison, and J. Elsner. Cambridge. 83–113.

Maas, M., and J. M. Snyder (1989) *Stringed Instruments of Ancient Greece*. New Haven, CT.

MacDowell, D. M. (ed.) (1982a) Gorgias, *Encomium of Helen*. Bristol.

(1982b) "Aristophanes and Kallistratos," *The Classical Quarterly* n.s. 32, no. 1: 21–26.

Mackenzie, M. M. (1982) "Parmenides' Dilemma," *Phronesis* 27, no. 1: 1–12.

MacMullen, R. (1982) "The Epigraphic Habit in the Roman Empire," *American Journal of Philology* 103: 233–46.

Maehler, H. (ed.) (1989) Pindarus, *Carmina cum fragmentis, Pars II: Fragmenta. Indices*. 8th edn. Munich and Leipzig.

Mandilaras, B. G. (ed.) (2003) Isocrates, *Opera omnia*. 3 vols. Munich.

Männlein-Robert, I. (2007) *Stimme, Schrift und Bild: Zum Verhältnis der Künste in der hellenistischen Dichtung*. Heidelberg.

Mansfeld, J. (1981) "Protagoras on Epistemological Obstacles and Persons," in *The Sophists and their Legacy: Proceedings of the Fourth International Colloquium on Ancient Philosophy Held in Cooperation with Projektgruppe*

Altertumswissenschaften der Thyssen Stiftung at Bad Homburg, 29th August–1st September 1979, ed. G. B. Kerferd. Hermes Einzelschriften, vol. 44. 38–53.

(1985a) "Historical and Philosophical Aspects of Gorgias' 'On What is Not'," in *Gorgia e la sofistica: Atti del convegno internazionale (Lentini-Catania, 12–15 dic. 1983)*, eds. L. Montoneri and F. Romano. *Siculorum Gymnasium*. n.s. 38, no. 1–2: 243–71.

(1985b) "Aristotle and Others on Thales, or the Beginnings of Natural Philosophy (With Some Remarks on Xenophanes)," *Mnemosyne* 38, no. 1–2: 109–29.

Marconi, C. (2007) *Temple Decoration and Cultural Identity in the Archaic Greek World: The Metopes of Selinus*. Cambridge and New York.

Martin, R. P. (2003) "The Pipes are Brawling: Conceptualizing Musical Performance in Athens," in *The Cultures within Ancient Greek Culture: Contact, Conflict, Collaboration*, eds. C. Dougherty and L. Kurke. Cambridge. 153–80.

Martindale, C. (2004) *Latin Poetry and the Judgment of Taste: An Essay in Aesthetics*. Oxford.

Marx, K. (1964) *The Economic & Philosophic Manuscripts of 1844*, ed. D. J. Struik. New York.

Mastronarde, D. J. (1990) "Actors on High: The Skene Roof, the Crane, and the Gods in Attic Drama," *Classical Antiquity* 9: 247–94.

Mattusch, C. C. (1980) "The Berlin Foundry Cup: The Casting of Greek Bronze Statuary in the Early Fifth Century BC," *American Journal of Archaeology* 84, no. 4: 435–44.

Mazzara, G. (1983) "Gorgia: Origine e struttura materiale della parola," *L'antiquité classique* 52: 130–40.

(1984) "Démocrite et Gorgias," in *Praktika tou Diethnous Synedriou gia ton Demokrito, Xanthe 6–9 Oktovriou 1983 = Proceedings of the 1st International Congress on Democritus, Xanthi 6–9 October 1983*, ed. L. G. Benakes. Xanthe. 125–37.

McGann, J. J. (1991) *The Textual Condition*. Princeton, NJ.

McLuhan, M. (1962) *The Gutenberg Galaxy: The Making of Typographic Man*. Toronto.

Meiggs, R., and D. M. Lewis (1988) *A Selection of Greek Historical Inscriptions to the End of the Fifth Century BC.*, Rev. edn. Oxford. (1st edn. 1969.)

Meijering, R. (1987) *Literary and Rhetorical Theories in Greek Scholia*. Groningen.

Mejer, J. (1972) "The Alleged New Fragment of Protagoras," *Hermes* 100: 175–78.

Meritt, B. (1936) "Greek Inscriptions," *Hesperia* 5, no.3: 355–430.

Merlan, P. (1960) *Studies in Epicurus and Aristotle*. Wiesbaden.

Merleau-Ponty, M. (1945) *Phénoménologie de la perception*. Paris.

(1964) *Le visible et l'invisible: Suivi de notes de travail*, ed. C. Lefort. Paris.

Mertens, D. (1996) "Die Entstehung des Steintempels in Sizilien," in *Säule und Gebälk: Zu Struktur und Wandlungsprozess griechisch-römischer Architektur. Bauforschungskolloquium in Berlin vom 16. bis 18. Juni 1994, veranstaltet vom Architekturreferat des DAI*, ed. E. -L. Schwandner. Mainz am Rhein. 25–38.

Mertens, J. R. (1998) "Some Long Thoughts on Early Cycladic Sculpture," *The Metropolitan Museum of Art* 33: 7–22.

Meskell, L. (ed.) (2005) *Archaeologies of Materiality.* Malden, MA and Oxford.

Métraux, G. P. R. (1995) *Sculptors and Physicians in Fifth-Century Greece: A Preliminary Study.* Montreal.

Meyer, E. (1962) "Weltanschauung," in *Herodot: Eine Auswahl aus der neueren Forschung,* ed. W. Marg. Darmstadt. 12–26. (= Ed. Meyer, *Forschungen zur alten Geschichte,* vol. 2: *Herodots Geschichstwerk.* Halle: Niemeyer, 1899, pp. 252–66.)

Meyer, E. A. (1990) "Explaining the Epigraphic Habit in the Roman Empire: The Evidence of Epitaphs," *Journal of Roman Studies* 80: 74–96.

Miles, M. (1998) "The Propylon to the Sanctuary of Demeter Malophoros at Selinous," *American Journal of Archaeology* 102, no. 1: 35–57.

Miller, D. (ed.) (2005) *Materiality.* Durham.

Miller, W. I. (1997) *The Anatomy of Disgust.* Cambridge, MA.

Mitford, T. B. (1991) "Inscriptiones Ponticae – Sebastopolis," *Zeitschrift für Papyrologie und Epigraphik* 87: 181–243.

Mitrović, B. (1993) "Objectively Speaking," Trans. I. Djordjević. *The Journal of the Society of Architectural Historians* 52, no. 1: 59–67.

Momigliano, A. (1929–30) "Prodico da Ceo e la dottrine sul linguaggio da Democrito ai Cinici," *Atti della Accademia delle Scienze di Torino, Classe di Scienze Morali, Storiche e Filologiche* 55: 95–107.

Morales, H. (2004) *Vision and Narrative in Achilles Tatius' Leucippe and Clitophon.* Cambridge.

Morgan, K. A. (2000) *Myth and Philosophy from the Presocratics to Plato.* Cambridge.

Morris, I. (1989) "Attitudes Toward Death in Archaic Greece," *Classical Antiquity* 8, no. 2: 296–320.

Morris, S. P. (1992) *Daidalos and the Origins of Greek Art.* Princeton, NJ.

Most, G. W. (1992) "Schöne (das) I. *Antike*," in *Historisches Wörterbuch der Philosophie,* eds. J. Ritter, K. Gründer, and G. Gabriel. 12 vols. Rev. edn. by R. Eisler. Basel and Stuttgart. vol. VIII: 1343–51.

(1999) "The Poetics of Early Greek Philosophy," in *The Cambridge Companion to Early Greek Philosophy,* ed. A. A. Long. Cambridge. 332–62.

Mourelatos, A. P. D. (1970) *The Route of Parmenides: A Study of Word, Image, and Argument in the Fragments.* New Haven, CT.

(1986) "Quality, Structure, and Emergence in Later Pre-Socratic Philosophy," in *Proceedings of the Boston Area Colloquium in Ancient Philosophy,* ed. J. J. Cleary. Lanham, MD. 2: 127–94.

(1987) "Gorgias and the Function of Language," *Philosophical Topics* 15: 135–71.

(2002) "La terre et les étoiles dans la cosmologie de Xénophane," in *Qu'est-ce que la philosophie présocratique? What is Presocratic Philosophy?*, eds. A. Laks and C. Louguet. Villeneuve-d'Ascq. 331–50.

Muecke, F. (1982) "A Portrait of the Artist as a Young Woman," *Classical Quarterly* n.s. 32, no. 1: 41–55.

Mukařovský, J. (1970 [1936]) *Aesthetic Function, Norm and Value as Social Facts.* Trans. M. E. Suino. Ann Arbor, MI.

Murdoch, I. (1978) *The Fire and the Sun: Why Plato Banished the Artists.* Oxford. (1st edn. 1977.)

Murray, P., and P. Wilson (eds.) (2004) *Music and the Muses: The Culture of 'Mousikē' in the Classical Athenian City.* Oxford.

Musti, D. (2000) "Musica greca tra aristocrazia e democrazia," in *Synaulía: Cultura musicale in Grecia e contatti mediterranei,* eds. A. C. Cassio, D. Musti, and L. E. Rossi. Naples. 7–55.

Nabers, N., and S. F. Wiltshire (1980) "The Athena Temple at Paestum and Pythagorean Theory," *Greek, Roman and Byzantine Studies* 21, no. 3: 207–15.

Nagy, G. (1996) *Poetry as Performance: Homer and Beyond.* Cambridge.
(2000) "Reading Greek Poetry Aloud: Evidence from the Bacchylides Papyri," *Quaderni Urbinati di Cultura Classica* n.s. 64, no. 1: 7–28.
(2006) "Reflexes of Aristarchean Methodology in the Homeric Scholia," Paper presented at the annual meeting of The American Philological Association, Montreal, January.

Neer, R. T. (2002) *Style and Politics in Athenian Vase-Painting: The Craft of Democracy, ca. 530–460 B.C.E.* New York.
(2010) *The Emergence of the Classical Style in Greek Sculpture.* Chicago, IL.

Nehamas, A. (1999) "Plato and the Mass Media," in id., *Virtues of Authenticity: Essays on Plato and Socrates,* Princeton, NJ. 279–99.
(2004) "Art, Interpretation and the Rest of Life," *Proceedings and Addresses of the American Philosophical Association* 78, no. 2 (November): 25–42.
(2007) *Only a Promise of Happiness: The Place of Beauty in a World of Art.* Princeton, NJ.

Nelson, R. S. (2000) "To Say and to See: Ekphrasis and Vision in Byzantium," in *Visuality Before and Beyond the Renaissance: Seeing as Others Saw,* ed. R. S. Nelson. Cambridge. 143–68.

Netz, R. (1999) *The Shaping of Deduction in Greek Mathematics: A Study in Cognitive History.* Cambridge.

Newiger, H. J. (1973) *Untersuchungen zu Gorgias' Schrift über das Nichtseiende.* Berlin.

Newman, B. B. (1947) "The First Man was an Artist," *The Tiger's Eye* 1, no. 1: 57–60.

Nietzsche, F. W. (1933–42) *Historisch-kritische Gesamtausgabe: Werke,* eds. H. J. Mette, K. Schlechta, and C. Koch, 5 vols. Munich.
(1988) *Friedrich Nietzsche. Sämtliche Werke. Kritische Studienausgabe in 15 Einzelbänden,* eds. G. Colli and M. Montinari. 15 vols., 2nd edn. Berlin.

Nightingale, A. W. (2004) *Spectacles of Truth in Classical Greek Philosophy: Theoria in its Cultural Context.* Cambridge.

Nisbet, R. G. M., and N. Rudd (eds.) (2004) *A Commentary on Horace, Odes, Book III.* Oxford.

Norden, E. (1928) *Logos und Rhythmus. Rede zum Antritt des Rektorats der Friedrich-Wilhelms-Universität zu Berlin am 15. Oktober 1927.* Berlin.

(1971 [1909–18]) *Die antike Kunstprosa vom VI. Jahrhundert v. Chr. bis in die Zeit der Renaissance.* 2 vols. Darmstadt.

Nünlist, R. (2009) *The Ancient Critic at Work: Terms and Concepts of Literary Criticism in Greek Scholia.* Cambridge.

Nussbaum, M. C., and A. Rorty (eds.) (1992) *Essays on Aristotle's De anima.* Oxford.

O'Brien, D. (1981) *Theories of Weight in the Ancient World. Volume I. Democritus, Weight and Size: An Exercise in the Reconstruction of Early Greek Philosophy.* Paris and Leiden.

O'Sullivan, N. (1992) *Alcidamas, Aristophanes, and the Beginnings of Greek Stylistic Theory.* Hermes Einzelschriften, vol. 60. Stuttgart.

(1996) "Written and Spoken in the First Sophistic," in *Voice into Text: Orality and Literacy in Ancient Greece*, ed. I. Worthington. Leiden and New York. 115–27.

Obbink, D. (2005) "New Fragments of Empedocles on Papyrus," Paper presented at the annual meeting of The American Philological Association, Boston, January.

Ong, W. J. (1982) *Orality and Literacy: The Technologizing of the Word.* London and New York.

Osborne, C. (1987) "Empedocles Recycled," *Classical Quarterly* n.s. 37, no. 1: 24–50.

Osborne, R. (1994) "Framing the Centaur: Reading Fifth-Century Architectural Sculpture," in *Art and Text in Ancient Greek Culture*, eds. S. Goldhill and R. Osborne. Cambridge. 53–84.

Osborne, R., and A. Pappas (2007) "Writing on Archaic Greek Pottery," in *Art and Inscriptions in the Ancient World*, eds. Z. Newby and R. E. Leader-Newby. Cambridge. 131–55.

Otto, A. (1968) *Die Sprichwörter und sprichwörterlichen Redensarten der Römer. Nachträge. Eingeleitet und mit einem Register herausgegeben von Reinhard Häußler.* Hildesheim. (1st edn. 1890.)

Overbeck, J. A. (1868) *Die antiken Schriftquellen zur Geschichte der bildenden Künste bei den Griechen.* Leipzig. (1st edn. Hildesheim, 1959.)

Owen, G. E. L. (1957) "A Proof in the Περὶ ἰδεῶν," *Journal of Hellenic Studies* 77: 103–11. (Rpt. in G. E. L. Owen, *Logic, Science and Dialectic*, ed. M. Nussbaum. Ithaca, NY, 1986.)

(1965) "Inherence," *Phronesis* 10: 97–105. (Rpt. in *Logic, Science and Dialectic*, ed. M. Nussbaum. Ithaca, NY: 1986.)

Page, D. (1959) *History and the Homeric Iliad.* Berkeley, CA.

Panofsky, E. (1924) *"Idea": Ein Beitrag zur Begriffsgeschichte der älteren Kunsttheorie.* Leipzig. (2nd edn. 1960. Rpt. of 2nd edn., Berlin, 1993.)

(1957) *Gothic Architecture and Scholasticism.* New York. (1st edn. 1951.)

Papaioannou, E. (2003) Review of A. Ford, *The Origins of Criticism: Literary Culture and Poetic Theory in Classical Greece* (Princeton, NJ, 2002). *Bryn Mawr Classical Review* 2003.06.07.

Papaioannou, S. (forthcoming) *Michael Psellos's Autography: A Study of Mimesis in Premodern Greek Literature.*

Paquette, D. (1984) *L'Instrument de musique dans la céramique de la Gréce antique: Études d'organologie*. Paris.

Pater, W. (1893) *Plato and Platonism: A Series of Lectures*. New York and London.
(1914 [1895]) *Greek Studies: A Series of Lectures*. London.

Paulson, R. (1996) *The Beautiful, Novel, and Strange: Aesthetics and Heterodoxy*. Baltimore, MD.

Pearson, L. (ed.) (1990) Aristoxenus, *Elementa Rhythmica: The Fragment of Book II and the Additional Evidence for Aristoxenean Rhythmic Theory*. Oxford.

Peek, W. (1955) *Griechische Vers-Inschriften. 1: Grab-Epigramme*. Berlin and New York.

Pendergraft, M. L. B. (1995) "Euphony and Etymology: Aratus' *Phaenomena*," *Syllecta Classica* 6: 43–67.

Pentcheva, B. V. (2002) "The Performative Icon," *Art Bulletin* 88, no. 4: 631–55.
(2007) "Epigrams on Icons," in *Art and Text in Byzantine Culture*, ed. L. James. Cambridge. 120–38.

Perec, G. (1988) "Histoire du lipogramme," in *La Littérature potentielle (créations, re-créations, récréations)*, ed. Oulipo (Association). Paris. 73–89.

Perusino, F. (ed.) (1993) *Anonimo (Michele Psello?), La tragedia greca: Edizione critica, traduzione e commento*. Urbino.

Petersen, E. (1917) "Rhythmus," *Abhandlungen der Königlichen Gesellschaft der Wissenschaften zu Göttingen, Philologisch-Historische Klasse* N.F. 16, no. 5: 1–104.

Petrovic, A. (2007) *Kommentar zu den simonideischen Versinschriften*. Leiden and Boston.

Pfeiffer, R. (1941) "The Measurements of the Zeus at Olympia: New Evidence from an Epode of Callimachus," *Journal of Hellenic Studies* 61: 1–5.
(1968) *History of Classical Scholarship from the Beginnings to the End of the Hellenistic Age*. Oxford.

Philipp, H. (1968) *Tektonon Daidala: Der bildende Künstler und sein Werk im vorplatonischen Schrifttum*. Berlin.

Pickard-Cambridge, A. W. (1962) *Dithyramb, Tragedy and Comedy*, 2nd edn. rev. by T. B. L. Webster, Oxford. (1st edn. 1927.)

Pippin, R. B. (2002) "What Was Abstract Art? (From the Point of View of Hegel)," *Critical Inquiry* 29 (Autumn): 1–24.

Platnauer, M. (1921) "Greek Colour-Perception," *Classical Quarterly* 15, no. 3/4: 153–62.

Platt, V. (forthcoming) *Facing the Gods: Epiphany and Representation in Graeco-Roman Culture*. Cambridge.

Podlecki, A. J. (1969) "The Peripatetics as Literary Critics," *Phoenix* 23, no. 1: 114–37.

Pohlenz, M. (1920) "Die Anfänge der griechischen Poetik," *Nachrichten von der Gesellschaft der Wissenschaften zu Göttingen* 2, ed. M. Pohlenz: 142–78.
(Rpt. in *Kleine Schriften*, ed. H. Dörrie, 1965, Hildesheim: 436–72.)

Pollitt, J. J. (1972) *Art and Experience in Classical Greece*. Cambridge.

(1974) *The Ancient View of Greek Art: Criticism, History, and Terminology.* New Haven, CT.

(1990) *The Art of Ancient Greece: Sources and Documents,* 2nd, rev. edn. Cambridge. (1st edn. 1965.)

(1995) "The *Canon* of Polykleitos and Other Canons," in *Polykleitos, the Doryphoros, and Tradition,* ed. W. G. Moon. Madison. 19–24.

(1999) *Art and Experience in Classical Greece.* Cambridge. (1st edn. 1972.)

(2002) "Περὶ χρωμάτων: What Ancient Greek Painters Thought about Colors," in *Color in Ancient Greece: The Role of Color in Ancient Greek Art and Architecture (700–31 B.C.). Proceedings of the Conference Held in Thessaloniki, 12th–16th April, 2000, Organized by the J. Paul Getty Museum and Aristotle University of Thessaloniki* = ΤΟ ΧΡΩΜΑ ΣΤΗΝ ΑΡΧΑΙΑ ΕΛΛΑΔΑ *[etc.],* eds. M. A. Tiberios and D. S. Tsiaphake. Thessaloniki. 1–8.

Ponge, F. (1994) *Selected Poems,* ed. M. Guiton. Trans. C. K. Williams, J. Montague, and M. Guiton. Winston-Salem, NC.

Porter, J. I. (1986a) "The Material Sublime: Towards a Reconstruction of Materialist Critical Discourse and Aesthetics in Antiquity." Diss., U. C. Berkeley.

(1986b) "Saussure and Derrida on the Figure of the Voice," *Modern Language Notes* 101 (Centennial Issue), no. 4 (September) 871–94.

(1987) "Putting Things into Perspective: *Scaenographia* and Vitruvian Aesthetics," Paper presented at the annual meeting of The American Philological Association, New York, December.

(1989) "Philodemus on Material Difference," *Cronache Ercolanesi* 19: 149–78.

(1992) "Hermeneutic Lines and Circles: Aristarchus and Crates on Homeric Exegesis," in *Homer's Ancient Readers: The Hermeneutics of Greek Epic's Earliest Exegetes,* eds. R. Lamberton and J. J. Keaney. Princeton, NJ. 67–114.

(1993) "The Seductions of Gorgias," *Classical Antiquity* 12, no. 2: 267–99.

(1995a) "οἱ κριτικοί: A Reassessment," in *Greek Literary Theory after Aristotle: A Collection of Papers in Honour of D. M. Schenkeveld,* eds. J. G. J. Abbenes, S. R. Slings, and I. Sluiter. Amsterdam. 83–109.

(1995b) "Content and Form in Philodemus: The History of an Evasion," in *Philodemus and Poetry: Poetic Theory and Practice in Lucretius, Philodemus, and Horace,* ed. D. Obbink. New York. 97–147.

(1996) "In Search of an Epicurean Aesthetics," in *Epicureismo greco e romano: Atti del congresso internazionale, Napoli, 19–26 maggio 1993,* eds. G. Giannantoni and M. Gigante. Naples. II: 613–30.

(ed.) (1999) *Constructions of the Classical Body.* Ann Arbor MI.

(2000) *Nietzsche and the Philology of the Future.* Stanford, CA.

(2001a) "Des sons qu'on ne peut entendre: Ciceron, les 'kritikoi' et la tradition du sublime dans la critique littéraire," in *Cicéron et Philodème: La polémique en philosophie,* eds. C. Auvray-Assayas and D. Delattre. Paris. 315–41.

(2001b) "Ideals and Ruins: Pausanias, Longinus, and the Second Sophistic," in *Pausanias: Travel and Memory in Roman Greece,* eds. S. E. Alcock, J. F. Cherry, and J. Elsner. New York. 63–92.

(2002) "φυσιολογεῖν: Nausiphanes of Teos and the Physics of Rhetoric; A Chapter in the History of Greek Atomism," *Cronache Ercolanesi* 32: 137–86.

(2003) "Epicurean Attachments: Life, Pleasure, Beauty, Friendship, and Piety," *Cronache Ercolanesi* 33: 129–51.

(2004a) "Aristotle and the Origins of Euphony," in *Mathesis e mneme: Studi in memoria di Marcello Gigante*, eds. S. Cerasuolo, G. Indelli, G. Leone, and F. L. Auricchio. 2 vols. Naples. 1: 131–48.

(2004b) "Homer: The History of an Idea," in *The Cambridge Companion to Homer*, ed. R. Fowler. Cambridge. 324–43.

(2006a) "Introduction: What Is 'Classical' about Classical Antiquity?," in *Classical Pasts: The Classical Traditions of Greece and Rome*, ed. J. I. Porter. Princeton, NJ. 1–65.

(2006b) "Feeling Classical: Classicism and Ancient Literary Criticism," in *Classical Pasts: The Classical Traditions of Greece and Rome*, ed. J. I. Porter. Princeton, NJ. 301–52.

(ed.) (2006c) *Classical Pasts: The Classical Traditions of Greece and Rome*. Princeton, NJ.

(2007a) "Hearing Voices: The Herculaneum Papyri and Classical Scholarship," in *Antiquity Recovered: The Legacy of Pompeii and Herculaneum*, eds. J. Seydl and V. Coates. Malibu. 95–113.

(2007b) "Lasus of Hermione, Pindar, and the Riddle of S," *Classical Quarterly* 57, no. 1: 1–21.

(2007c) "Lucretius and the Sublime," in *The Cambridge Companion to Lucretius*, eds. S. Gillespie and P. Hardie. Cambridge. 167–84.

(2009a) "Is Art Modern? Kristeller's 'Modern System of the Arts' Reconsidered," *British Journal of Aesthetics* 49, no. 1: 1–24.

(2009b) "Reply to Shiner," *British Journal of Aesthetics* 49, no. 2: 171–78.

(2010a) "Against λεπτότης: Rethinking Hellenistic Aesthetics," in *Creating a Hellenistic World*, eds. A. Erskine and L. Llewellyn-Jones. Swansea. 271–312.

(2010b) "The Materiality of Classical Studies," in *When Worlds Elide: Political Theory, Cultural Studies, and the Effects of Hellenism*, eds. Karen Bassi and P. Euben. Lanham, MD. 61–74.

(forthcoming) "Making and Unmaking The Achaean Wall and the Limits of Fictionality in Homeric Criticism." *TAPA* 141.1, 2011.

Potts, A. (1994) *Flesh and the Ideal: Winckelmann and the Origins of Art History*. New Haven, CT.

Prall, D. W. (1929) *Aesthetic Judgment*. New York.

Preißhofen, F. (1974) "Phidias-Daedalus auf dem Schild der Athena Parthenos? Ampelius 8, 10," *Jahrbuch des Deutschen Archäologischen Instituts* 89: 50–69.

Prettejohn, E. (2005) *Beauty and Art, 1750–2000*. Oxford.

Prier, R. A. (1989) *Thauma Idesthai: The Phenomenology of Sight and Appearance in Archaic Greek*. Tallahassee, FL.

Prins, Y. (1991) "The Power of the Speech Act: Aeschylus' Furies and Their Binding Song," *Arethusa* 24: 177–95.

Prioux, É. (2007) *Regards alexandrins: Histoire et théorie des arts dans l'épigramme hellénistique*. Leuven.

Privitera, G. A. (1964) "L'Asigmatismo di Laso e di Pindaro in Clearco Fr. 88 Wehrli," *Rivista di cultura classica e medioevale* 6, no. 2: 164–70.

(1965) *Laso di Ermione nella cultura ateniese e nella tradizione storiografica*. Rome.

Protzmann, H. (1968) "Objektive und subjektive Form im fünften Jahrhundert," *Wissenschaftliche Zeitschrift der Universität Rostock. Gesellschafts-und Sprachwissenschaftliche Reihe* 17, no. 7/8: 721–28.

(1972–73) "Zeugnisse zum Stilbewußtsein in der hochklassischen Kunst," *Jahreshefte des Österreichischen Archäologischen Instituts* 50: 68–93.

(1977) "Realismus und Idealität in Spätklassik und Frühhellenismus: Ein Kapitel künstlerischer Problemgeschichte der Griechen," *Deutsches Archaeologisches Institut* 92: 169–203.

Pucci, P. (2006) "Euripides' Heaven," in *The Soul of Tragedy: Essays on Athenian Drama*, eds. V. Pedrick and S. M. Oberhelman. Chicago, IL. 49–71.

Puchner, W. (2002) "Acting in the Byzantine Theatre: Evidence and Problems," in *Greek and Roman Actors: Aspects of an Ancient Profession*, eds. P. Easterling and E. Hall. Cambridge. 304–24.

Quadlbauer, F. (1958) "Die genera dicendi bis Plinius d. J.," *Wiener Studien* 71: 55–111.

Radermacher, L. (1921) *Aristophanes' 'Frösche': Einleitung, Text und Kommentar*. (= Österreichische Akademie der Wissenschaften. Philosophisch-historische Klasse. Sitzungsberichte, vol. 198, no. 4.), 3rd edn. Vienna. (Rpt. 1967, Graz–Vienna–Cologne.)

(ed.) (1951) *Artium Scriptores: Reste der voraristotelischen Rhetorik*. Österreichische Akademie der Wissenschaft, Philologisch-historische Klasse, Sitzungsberichte, vol. 227, no. 3.

Ramelli, I., and G. Lucchetta (2004) *Allegoria*, vol. 1: *L'età classica*. Milan.

Rancière, J. (2006) *The Politics of Aesthetics: The Distribution of the Sensible*. Trans. G. Rockhill. London and New York. (Translated from *Le partage du sensible: Esthétique et politique*, Paris, 2000.)

Ransom, J. C. (1941a) "Criticism as Pure Speculation," in *The Intent of the Critic*, ed. D. A. Stauffer. Princeton, NJ. 91–124.

(1941b) "Wanted: An Ontological Critic," in id., *The New Criticism*. Norfolk, CT. 279–336.

(1943) "The Inorganic Muses," *The Kenyon Review* 5, no. 2: 278–300.

Rasche, W. (1910) "De Anthologiae Graecae epigrammatis quae colloquii formam habent." Diss., Münster.

Raubitschek, A. E. (1968) "Das Denkmal-Epigramm," in *L'Épigramme grecque. Sept exposés suivis de discussions*, ed. A. E. Raubitschek. Vandoeuvres and Genève. 3–36.

Redfield, J. M. (1994) *Nature and Culture in the Iliad: The Tragedy of Hector*. 2nd, expanded edn. Durham, NC.

Rée, J. (1999) *I See a Voice: Deafness, Language, and the Senses—A Philosophical History*. New York.

Reesor, M. E. (1983) "The Stoic IΔION and Prodicus' Near-Synonyms," *American Journal of Philology* 104: 124–33.

Reid, T. (1846) *The Works of Thomas Reid: Now Fully Collected, with Selections from his Unpublished Letters*, ed. W. S. Hamilton. Edinburgh. (Rpt. 1983, Hildesheim.)

Reinach, A. (1921) *Textes grecs et latins relatifs à l'histoire de la peinture ancienne*. Paris. (Rpt. 1981, Chicago, IL.)

Reinhardt, K. (1959) *Parmenides und die Geschichte der griechischen Philosophie*, 2nd edn. Frankfurt am Main.

Reitzenstein, E. (1931) "Zur Stiltheorie des Kallimachos," in *Festschrift Richard Reitzenstein zum 2. April 1931*, eds. E. Fraenkel and H. Fränkel. Leipzig and Berlin. 23–69.

Renehan, R. (1980) "On the Greek Origins of the Concepts Incorporeality and Immateriality," *Greek, Roman and Byzantine Studies* 21, no. 2: 105–38.

Richardson, N. J. (1975) "Homeric Professors in the Age of the Sophists," *Proceedings of the Cambridge Philological Society* 21: 65–81.

   (1980) "Literary Criticism in the Exegetical Scholia to the *Iliad*: A Sketch," *Classical Quarterly* 30: 265–87.

   (1981) "The Contest of Homer and Hesiod and Alcidamas' *Mouseion*," *Classical Quarterly* 31, no. 1: 1–10.

Richter, G. M. A. (1961) *The Archaic Gravestones of Attica*. New York.

Richter, W. (1974) "ΣΥΜΦΩΝΙΑ: Zur Vor-und Frühgeschichte eines musikologischen Begriffs," in *Convivium Musicorum: Festschrift Wolfgang Boetticher zum sechzigsten Geburtstag am 19. August 1974*, eds. H. Hüschen and D. -R. Moser. Berlin. 264–90.

Riegl, A. (1927) *Die spätrömische Kunstindustrie, mit 23 Tafeln und 116 Abbildungen*, 2nd edn. Vienna. (1st edn. 1901.) (Rpt. 1987, Darmstadt.)

Rijk, L. M. D. (1986) *Plato's Sophist: A Philosophical Commentary*. Amsterdam and New York.

Rispoli, G. M. (1995) *Dal suono all'immagine: Poetiche della voce ed estetica dell'eufonia*. Pisa.

Rist, J. M. (1967) *Plotinus: The Road to Reality*. Cambridge.

Rivier, A. (1952) *Un emploi archaïque de l'analogie chez Héraclite et Thucydide*. Lausanne.

   (1956) "Remarques sur les fragments 34 et 35 de Xénophane," *Revue de philologie* 30: 37–61.

Robert, L. (1938) *Études épigraphiques et philologiques*. Bibliothèque de l'École des hautes études. Science historiques et philologiques, vol. 272. Paris.

Roberts, M. J. (1989) *The Jeweled Style: Poetry and Poetics in Late Antiquity*. Ithaca, NY.

Robertson, G. I. C. (1998) "Evaluative Language in Greek Lyric and Elegiac Poetry and Inscribed Epigram to the End of the Fifth Century B.C.E." Diss., University of Oxford.

Robinson, H. (1982) *Matter and Sense: A Critique of Contemporary Materialism*. Cambridge.

Robinson, H. M. (1978) "Mind and Body in Aristotle," *Classical Quarterly* n.s. 28: 105–24.

Rohde, G. (1963) "Über das Lesen im Altertum," in *Studien und Interpretationen zur antiken Literatur, Religion und Geschichte*, eds. I. Rohde and B. Kytzler. Berlin. 290–303.

Romm, J. (1990) "Wax, Stone, and Promethean Clay: Lucian as Plastic Artist," *Classical Antiquity* 9, no. 1: 74–98.

Rose, H. J. (1923) "The Speaking Stone," *The Classical Review* 37, no. 7/8: 162–63.

Rosen, Ralph M. (1990) "Poetry and Sailing in Hesiod's *Works and Days*," *Classical Antiquity* 9, no. 1: 99–113.

(2004) "Aristophanes' *Frogs* and the *Contest of Homer and Hesiod*," *Transactions of the American Philological Association* 134: 295–322.

(2008) "Badness and Intentionality in Aristophanes' *Frogs*," in *KAKOS: Badness and Anti-Values in Classical Antiquity*, eds. R. Rosen and I. Sluiter. Leiden.

Rosenblum, R. (1967) *Transformations in Late Eighteenth Century Art*. Princeton, NJ.

Rosenmeyer, T. G. (1955) "Gorgias, Aeschylus, and *Apate*," *American Journal of Philology*, no. 76: 225–60.

(1973) "Design and Execution in Aristotle, *Poetics* ch. xxv," *California Studies in Classical Antiquity* 6: 231–52.

Ross, W. D. (ed.) (1924) Aristotle, *Metaphysics*. 2 vols. Oxford.

Rossetti, W. (1866) *Swinburne's Poems and Ballads: A Criticism*. London.

Rousselle, A. (1983) "Parole et inspiration: Le travail de la voix dans le monde romain," in *Psicoanalisi e storia delle scienze: Atti del convegno, Firenze, 26–27–28 giugno 1981*, ed. M. Ranchetti. Florence. 129–57.

Rouveret, A. (1989) *Histoire et imaginaire de la peinture ancienne: Ve siècle av. J.-C.-Ier siècle ap. J.-C.* Bibliothèque des Écoles Françaises d'Athènes et de Rome, fasc. 274. Rome.

(2006) "Les yeux pourpres: L'expérience de la couleur dans la peinture classique entre réalités et fictions," in *Couleurs et matières dans l'antiquité: Textes, techniques et pratiques*, eds. A. Rouveret, S. Dubel, and V. Naas. Paris. 17–28.

Rouveret, A., S. Dubel, and V. Naas. (eds.) (2006) *Couleurs et matières dans l'antiquité: Textes, techniques et pratiques*. Paris.

Ruffell, I. (2002) "A Total Write-Off: Aristophanes, Cratinus, and the Rhetoric of Comic Competition," *Classical Quarterly* 52, no. 1: 138–63.

Russell, B. (1900) *A Critical Exposition of the Philosophy of Leibniz*. Cambridge.

Russell, D. A. (ed.) (1964) *'Longinus' on the Sublime*. Oxford.

Russell, D. A. (1981) *Criticism in Antiquity*. Berkeley, CA.

Rutherford, I. (2001) *Pindar's Paeans: A Reading of the Fragments with a Survey of the Genre*. Oxford.

Saenger, P. (1997) *Space between Words: The Origins of Silent Reading*. Stanford, CA.

Saito, Y. (2007) *Everyday Aesthetics*. New York.

Saleh Pascha, K. (2004) "'Gefrorene Musik': Das Verhältnis von Architektur und Musik in der ästhetischen Theorie." Diss., Technische Universität Berlin.

Sanders, K. (2004) "Cicero *De natura deorum* 1.48–9: *Quasi corpus?*," *Mnemosyne* 57, no. 2: 215–18.

Santayana, G. (1988 [1896]) *The Sense of Beauty: Being the Outlines of Æsthetic Theory. Critical Ed.*, ed. W. G. Holzberger. *The Works of George Santayana*, eds. W. G. Holzberger and H. J. Saatkamp. vol. II. Cambridge, MA.

Sartre, J. P. (1943) *L'être et le néant: Essai d'ontologie phénoménologique*. Paris.

    (1956) *Being and Nothingness: An Essay on Phenomenological Ontology*. Trans. H. E. Barnes. New York.

Sbordone, F. (ed.) (1976) *Ricerche sui papiri ercolanesi*. vol. II. Naples.

Scarre, C., and G. Lawson (eds.) (2006) *Archaeoacoustics*. Cambridge, MA and Oakville, CT.

Scarry, E. (1999) *On Beauty and Being Just*. Princeton, NJ.

Schapiro, M. (1994 [1966]) "On Perfection, Coherence, and Unity of Form and Content," in id., *Theory and Philosophy of Art: Style, Artist, and Society*. New York. 33–49.

Scheller, M. (1951) "Die Oxytonierung der griechischen Substantiva auf-ῐᾱ." Diss., University of Zürich.

Schenkeveld, D. M. (1992) "Prose Usages of ἀκούειν 'To Read'," *Classical Quarterly* 42, no. 1: 129–41.

    (1990) "Studies in the History of Ancient Linguistics, IV: Developments in the Study of Ancient Linguistics," 43, no. 3–4: 289–306.

Schiefsky, M. J. (ed.) (2005) Hippocrates, *On Ancient Medicine*. Translated with Introduction and Commentary. Leiden and Boston, MA.

Schlikker, F. W. (1940) *Hellenistische Vorstellung von der Schönheit des Bauwerks nach Vitruv*. Berlin.

Schlosser, J. (1924) *Die Kunstliteratur: Ein Handbuch zur Quellenkunde der neueren Kunstgeschichte*. Vienna.

Schmidt, E. G. (1968) "Antike und mitterlalterlich Schlußsteinsymbolik," *Das Altertum* 14, no. 1: 31–37.

Schmitt, R. (1967) *Dichtung und Dichtersprache in indogermanischer Zeit*. Wießbaden.

Schöne, H. (1930) "περὶ ὑγιεινῆς ἀναφωνήσεως bei Oribasius *Coll. Med.* VI 10," *Hermes* 65: 92–105.

Schubart, W. (1941) "Über den Dithyrambus," *Archiv für Papyrusforschung* 14: 24–30.

Schuhl, P.-M. (1952) *Platon et l'art de son temps (arts plastiques)*, 2nd, rev. and augmented edn. Paris. (1st edn. 1933.)

Schulz, D. (1955) "Zum Kanon Polyklets," *Hermes* 83: 200–20.

Schweitzer, B. (1932) *Xenokrates von Athen: Beiträge zur Geschichte der antiken Kunstforschung und Kunstanschauung*. Schriften der Königsberger Gelehrten Gesellschaft. Geisteswissenschaftliche Klasse, vol. 9, no. 1. Halle (Saale).

    (1953) *Platon und die bildende Kunst der Griechen*. Tübingen.

Scodel, R. (1992) "Inscription, Absence and Memory: Epic and Early Epitaph," *Studi italiani di filologia classica* 10: 57–76.

    (2002) *Listening to Homer: Tradition, Narrative, and Audience*. Ann Arbor, MI.

    (2003) "A Note on Posidippus 63 AB (*P. Mil. Vogl.* VIII 309 x 16–25)," *Zeitschrift für Papyrologie und Epigraphik* 142: 44.

Scranton, R. L. (1964) *Aesthetic Aspects of Ancient Art.* Chicago, IL.

Sedley, D. N. (1982) "Two Conceptions of Vacuum," *Phronesis* 27: 175–93.

(1998) *Lucretius and the Transformation of Greek Wisdom.* Cambridge.

(2003) *Plato's Cratylus.* Cambridge.

Segal, C. (1962) "Gorgias and the Psychology of the Logos," *Harvard Studies in Classical Philology* 66: 99–155.

(1986) *Pindar's Mythmaking: The Fourth Pythian Ode.* Princeton, NJ.

(1992) "Bard and Audience in Homer," in *Homer's Ancient Readers: The Hermeneutics of Greek Epic's Earliest Exegetes*, eds. R. Lamberton and J. J. Keaney. Princeton. 3–29.

(1994) *Singers, Heroes, and Gods in the Odyssey.* Ithaca, NY.

(1998) *Aglaia: The Poetry of Alcman, Sappho, Pindar, Bacchylides, and Corinna.* Lanham, MD.

Shankland, R. S. (1973) "Acoustics of Greek Theatres," *Physics Today* 26, no. 10 (October): 30–35.

Shapiro, H. A. (1992) "*Mousikoi Agones*: Music and Poetry at the Panathenaia," in *Goddess and Polis: The Panathenaic Festival in Ancient Athens*, ed. J. Neils. Hanover, NH and Princeton, NJ. 53–76.

Shiner, L. (2001) *The Invention of Art: A Cultural History.* Chicago, IL.

Shklovsky, V. (1965 [1917]) "Art as Technique," in *Russian Formalist Criticism: Four Essays*, eds. L. T. Lemon and M. J. Reis. Lincoln. 3–24.

(1965 [1921]) "Sterne's *Tristram Shandy*: Stylistic Commentary," in *Russian Formalist Criticism: Four Essays*, eds. L. T. Lemon and M. J. Reis. Lincoln. 25–57.

(1985 [1916]) "On Poetry and Trans-Sense Language," *October* 34 (Autumn): 3–24.

Sibley, F. (1959) "Aesthetic Concepts," *The Philosophical Review* 68, no. 4: 421–50.

(1965) "Aesthetic and Nonaesthetic," *The Philosophical Review* 74, no. 2: 135–59.

(2001) "Arts or the Aesthetic–Which Comes First?," in *Approach to Aesthetics: Collected Papers on Philosophical Aesthetics*, eds. J. Benson, H. B. Redfern, and J. Roxbee Cox. Oxford. 135–41.

Sifakis, G. M. (2001) *Aristotle on the Function of Tragic Poetry.* Herakleion.

(2002) "The Actor's Art in Aristotle," in *Greek and Roman Actors: Aspects of an Ancient Profession*, eds. P. Easterling and E. Hall. Cambridge. 148–64.

Simon, G. (1988) *Le regard, l'être et l'apparence dans l'optique de l'antiquité.* Paris.

Skutsch, O. (ed.) (1985) *The Annals of Q. Ennius.* Oxford.

Sluiter, I. (forthcoming) "Textual Therapy: On the Relationship between Medicine and Grammar in Galen," in *Medical Education: Proceedings of the XII Colloque Hippocratique*, ed. H. F. J. Horstmanshoff, *et al.* Leiden.

Smith, B. R. (1999) *The Acoustic World of Early Modern England: Attending to the O-Factor.* Chicago.

Smith, J. A. (2003) "Clearing up Some Confusion in Callias' *Alphabet Tragedy*: How to Read Sophocles *Oedipus Tyrannus* 332–33 *et al.*," *Classical Philology* 98, no. 4: 313–29.

Smith, P. C. (1997) "From Acoustics to Optics: The Rise of the Metaphysical and Demise of the Melodic in Aristotle's *Poetics*," in *Sites of Vision: The*

Discursive Construction of Sight in the History of Philosophy, ed. D. M. Kleinberg-Levin. Cambridge, MA. 69–91.

Snell, B. (1924) *Die Ausdrücke für den Begriff des Wissens in der vorplatonischen Philosophie.* Philologische Untersuchungen, vol. 29. Berlin.

(1926) "Die Sprache Heraklits," *Hermes* 61: 353–81.

(1971) *Szenen aus griechischen Dramen.* Berlin.

(1980) *Die Entdeckung des Geistes: Studien zur Entstehung des europaischen Denkens bei den Griechen,* 5th edn. Hamburg. (1st edn. 1946; Engl. translation 1953.)

Snell, B., *et al.* (eds.) (1955–2010) *Lexikon des frühgriechischen Epos (LfgrE).* 25 vols. Göttingen.

Snodgrass, A. (2000) "The Uses of Writing on Early Greek Painted Pottery," in *Word and Image in Ancient Greece,* eds. N. K. Rutter and B. A. Sparkes. Edinburgh. 22–34.

Solmsen, F. (1932) "Drei Rekonstruktionen zur antiken Rhetorik und Poetik," *Hermes* 67: 133–54.

Sommerstein, A. H. (1973) *The Sound Pattern of Ancient Greek.* Oxford.

(ed.) (1996) Aristophanes, *Frogs. The Comedies of Aristophanes,* vol. ix. Warminster.

Sontag, S. (1966) "Against Interpretation," in id. *Against Interpretation, and Other Essays.* New York. 3–14.

(ed.) (1982) *A Barthes Reader.* New York.

Sorabji, R. (1972) "Aristotle, Mathematics, and Colour," *Classical Quarterly* n.s. 22, no. 2: 293–308.

Sörbom, G. (1966) *Mimesis and Art: Studies in the Origin and Early Development of an Aesthetic Vocabulary.* Stockholm.

Sotirakopoulou, P. (ed.) (2005) *The "Keros Hoard," Myth or Reality?: Searching for the Lost Pieces of a Puzzle.* Los Angeles, CA.

Sourvinou-Inwood, C. (1995) *'Reading' Greek Death: To the End of the Classical Period.* Oxford.

St. Clair, W. (1999) *The Elgin Marbles: Questions of Stewardship and Accountability.* Oxford.

Stadelmann, F. (1891) *Erziehung und Unterricht bei den Griechen und Römern.* Trieste.

Staden, H. von (2002) "La lecture comme thérapie dans la médecine gréco-romaine," *Académie des Inscriptions & Belles-Lettres. Comptes rendus des séances de l'année 2002* avril–juin: 803–22.

Stanford, W. B. (1943) "Greek Views on Euphony," *Hermathena* 41: 3–20.

(1967) *The Sound of Greek: Studies in the Greek Theory and Practice of Euphony.* Berkeley, CA.

Starr, R. J. (1991) "Reading Aloud: *Lectores* and Roman Reading," *Classical Journal* 86, no. 4: 337–43.

Steiner, D. (1993) "Pindar's 'Oggetti Parlanti'," *Harvard Studies in Classical Philology* 95: 159–80.

(1994) *The Tyrant's Writ: Myths and Images of Writing in Ancient Greece.* Princeton, NJ.

(1998) "Moving Images: Fifth-Century Victory Monuments and the Athlete's Allure," *Classical Antiquity* 17, no. 1: 123–49.

(1999) "To Praise, Not to Bury: Simonides fr. 531P," *Classical Quarterly* 49, no. 2: 383–95.

(2001) *Images in Mind: Statues in Archaic and Classical Greek Literature and Thought.* Princeton, NJ.

Stewart, A. F. (1978) "The Canon of Polykleitos: A Question of Evidence," *Journal of Hellenic Studies* 98: 122–31.

(1979) *Attika: Studies in Athenian Sculpture of the Hellenistic Age.* London.

(1990) *Greek Sculpture: An Exploration.* 2 vols. New Haven, CT.

(1993) "Narration and Allusion in the Hellenistic Baroque," in *Narrative and Event in Ancient Art*, ed. P. J. Holliday. Cambridge. 130–74.

(1997) *Art, Desire, and the Body in Ancient Greece.* Cambridge.

(1998) "Nuggets: Mining the Texts Again," *American Journal of Archaeology* 102, no. 1998: 271–82.

(2005) "Posidippos and the Truth in Sculpture," in *The New Posidippus: A Hellenistic Poetry Book*, ed. K. J. Gutzwiller. New York. 183–205.

(2006) "Hellenistic Art: Two Dozen Innovations," in *The Cambridge Companion to the Hellenistic World*, ed. G. R. Bugh. Cambridge. 158–85.

(2008) *Classical Greece and the Birth of Western Art.* New York.

Stewart, S. (1993) *On Longing: Narratives of the Miniature, the Gigantic, the Souvenir, the Collection.* Durham. (1st edn. 1984, Baltimore, MD.)

(2002) *Poetry and the Fate of the Senses.* Chicago, IL.

(2005) *The Open Studio: Essays on Art and Aesthetics.* Chicago, IL.

Stohn, G. (1955) "Spuren voraristotelischer Poetik in der alten attischen Komödie." Diss., Freie Universität zu Berlin.

Stokes, A. D. (1978) *The Critical Writings of Adrian Stokes*, ed. L. Gowing. 3 vols. London.

Stolnitz, J. (1961) "On the Origins of 'Aesthetic Disinterestedness'" *The Journal of Aesthetics and Art Criticism* 20, no. 2: 131–43.

(1963) "Locke and the Categories of Value in Eighteenth-Century British Aesthetic Theory," *Philosophy* 38, no. 143: 40–51.

Strodel, S. (2002) *Zur Überlieferung und zum Verständnis der hellenistischen Technopaignien.* Frankfurt am Main.

Summers, D. (1989) "'Form,' Nineteenth-Century Metaphysics, and the Problem of Art Historical Description," *Critical Inquiry* 15, no. 2: 372–406.

(1990) *The Judgment of Sense: Renaissance Naturalism and the Rise of Aesthetics.* Cambridge.

Sutherland, K. (2005) *Jane Austen's Textual Lives: From Aeschylus to Bollywood.* Oxford.

Svenbro, J. (1976) *La parole et le marbre: Aux origines de la poétique grecque.* Lund.

(1990) "La cigale et les fourmis: Voix et écriture dans une allégorie grecque," *Opuscula Romana* 18: 7–21.

(1993) *Phrasikleia: An Anthropology of Reading in Ancient Greece.* Trans. J. Lloyd. Ithaca, NY.

Swain, S. (1996) *Hellenism and Empire: Language, Classicism, and Power in the Greek World, AD 50–250.* Oxford.

Tagliasacchi, A. M. (1961) "Le teorie estetiche e la critica letteraria in Plutarco," *Acme: Annali della Facoltà di Filosofia e Lettere dell'Università Statale di Milano* 14, no. 1–3: 71–117.

Taillardat, J. (1962) *Les images d'Aristophane: Études de langue et de style.* Annales de l'Université de Lyon. Troisième série: Lettres. Fascicule 36. Paris.

Tanner, J. (2006) *The Invention of Art History in Ancient Greece: Religion, Society and Artistic Rationalisation.* Cambridge.

Tanselle, G. T. (1989) *A Rationale of Textual Criticism.* Philadelphia, PA.

Taplin, O. (1995) "Opening Performance: Closing Texts?," *Essays in Criticism* 45, no. 2: 93–120.

Tatarkiewicz, W. (1937) "Art and Poetry: A Contribution to the History of Ancient Aesthetics," *Studia Philosophica* 2: 367–418.

(1963) "Classification of Arts in Antiquity," *Journal of the History of Ideas* 24, no. 2: 231–40.

(1970) *History of Aesthetics. Vol. 1, Ancient Aesthetics,* ed. J. Harrell. The Hague.

Taylor, A. E. (1928) *A Commentary on Plato's Timaeus.* Oxford.

Thielscher, P. (1953) "Die Schallgefässe des antiken Theaters," in *Festschrift Franz Dornseiff zum 65. Geburtstag,* ed. H. Kusch. Leipzig. 334–71.

Thomas, E. (2007) *Monumentality and the Roman Empire: Architecture in the Antonine Age.* Oxford.

Thomas, R. (1989) *Oral Tradition and Written Record in Classical Athens.* Cambridge.

(1992) *Literacy and Orality in Ancient Greece.* Cambridge.

(2000) *Herodotus in Context: Ethnography, Science, and the Art of Persuasion.* Cambridge.

Tilley, C. (2004) *The Materiality of Stone: Explorations in Landscape Phenomenology.* Oxford and New York.

Too, Y. L. (1995) *The Rhetoric of Identity in Isocrates: Text, Power, Pedagogy.* Cambridge.

Townsend, D. (1991) "Lockean Aesthetics," *The Journal of Aesthetics and Art Criticism* 49, no. 4: 349–61.

(1998) "Taste: Early History," in *Encyclopedia of Aesthetics,* ed. M. Kelly. 4 vols. New York. IV: 355–60.

Traina, A. (1999) *Forma e suono: Da Plauto a Pascoli,* Nuova edn. Bologna.

Tuck, A. (2006) "Singing the Rug: Patterned Textiles and the Origins of Indo-European Metrical Poetry," *American Journal of Archaeology* 110, no. 4: 539–50.

Turner, E. G. (1952) *Athenian Books in the Fifth and Fourth Centuries B.C.* London.

(1976) "Papyrus Bodmer xxviii: A Satyr-Play on the Confrontation of Heracles and Atlas," *Museum Helveticum* 33, no. 1: 1–23.

Turner, H. S. (2006) *The English Renaissance Stage: Geometry, Poetics, and the Practical Spatial Arts 1580–1630.* Oxford.

Umholtz, G. (2002) "Architraval Arrogance? Dedicatory Inscriptions in Greek Architecture of the Classical Period," *Hesperia* 71, no. 3: 261–93.

Usener, S. (1994) *Isokrates, Platon und ihr Publikum: Hörer und Leser von Literatur im 4. Jahrhundert v. Chr.* Tübingen.

Van Groningen, B. A. (1953) *La poèsie verbale grecque: Essai de mise au point. Mededelingen der Koninklijke Nederlandse Akademie van Wetenschappen, Afd. Letterkunde*, n.s. vol. 26, no. 4. Amsterdam.

van Hook, L. (1905) "The Metaphorical Terminology of Greek Rhetoric and Literary Criticism." Diss., University of Chicago.

——— (1919) "Alcidamas versus Isocrates: The Spoken versus the Written Word," *Classical World* 12, no. 12: 89–94.

Van Schaik, L. (ed.) (2002) *Poetics in Architecture.* London.

Vatilen, J. (1864) "Der Rhetor Alkidamas," *Sitzungsberichte der Wiener Akademie, Phil.-Hist. Cl.* 43: 491–528.

Verdenius, W. J. (1981) "Gorgias' Doctrine of Deception," in *The Sophists and their Legacy: Proceedings of the Fourth International Colloquium on Ancient Philosophy Held in Cooperation with Projektgruppe Altertumswissenschaften der Thyssen Stiftung at Bad Homburg, 29th August-1st September 1979*, ed. G. B. Kerferd. Hermes Einzelschriften, vol. 44. Wiesbaden. 116–28.

Vernant, J.-P. (1991) *Mortals and Immortals: Collected Essays.* Trans. F. I. Zeitlin. Princeton, NJ.

Versenyi, L. (1962) "Protagoras' Man-Measure Fragment," *The American Journal of Philology* 83, no. 2: 178–84.

Vlastos, G. (1991) *Socrates, Ironist and Moral Philosopher.* Ithaca, NY.

Vogt-Spira, G. (ed.) (1990) *Strukturen der Mündlichkeit in der römischen Literatur.* Tübingen.

——— (1991) "Vox und Littera: Der Buchstabe zwischen Mündlichkeit und Schriftlichkeit in der grammatischen Tradition," *Poetica* 23: 295–327.

——— (ed.) (1993) *Beiträge zur mündlichen Kultur der Römer.* Tübingen.

Vollgraff, W. (1948) "Elementum," *Mnemosyne* 2, no. 1: 89–115.

Vox, O. (1975) "Epigrammi in Omero," *Belfagor* 30: 67–70.

Wackernagel, J. (1969–79) *Kleine Schriften*, ed. B. Forssman. 3 vols., 2nd edn. Göttingen.

Wallace, M. B. (1970) "Notes on Early Greek Grave Epigrams," *Phoenix* 24, no. 2: 95–105.

Wallace, R. W. (2003) "An Early Fifth-Century Athenian Revolution in Aulos Music," *Harvard Studies in Classical Philology* 101: 73–92.

Walsdorff, F. (1927) *Die antiken Urteile über Platons Stil.* Bonn.

Walsh, G. B. (1991) "Callimachean Passages: The Rhetoric of Epitaph in Epigram," *Arethusa* 24, no. 1: 77–105.

Walter, J. (1893) *Die Geschichte der Ästhetik im Altertum ihrer begrifflichen Entwicklung nach dargestellt.* Leipzig.

Walton, K. L. (1993) "How Marvelous! Toward a Theory of Aesthetic Value," *The Journal of Aesthetics and Art Criticism* 51, no. 3: 499–510.

(1997a) "Spelunking, Simulation, and Slime: On Being Moved by Fiction," in *Emotion and the Arts*, eds. M. Hjort and S. Laver. New York. 37–49.

(1997b) "Listening with Imagination: Is Music Representational?," in *Music & Meaning*, ed. J. Robinson. Ithaca, NY. 57–82.

(2007) "Aesthetics—What? Why? and Wherefore?," *The Journal of Aesthetics and Art Criticism* 65, no. 2 (Spring): 147–61.

Ward, T. H. (1883) *The English Poets: Selections with Critical Introductions*, 2nd edn. 4 vols. London.

Warren, J. (2007) "Anaxagoras: Perception, Pleasure, and Pain," *Oxford Studies in Ancient Philosophy* 33: 19–54.

Webb, R. (2001) "The *Progymnasmata* as Practice," in *Education in Greek and Roman Antiquity*, ed. Y. L. Too. Leiden and Boston, MA. 289–316.

Webster, T. B. L. (1939) "Greek Theories of Art and Literature Down to 400 B.C.," *Classical Quarterly* 33: 166–79.

(1964) *Hellenistic Poetry and Art*. London.

Wehrli, F. (1946) "Der erhabene und der schlichte Stil in der poetisch-rhetorischen Theorie der Antike," in *Phyllobolia für Peter von der Mühll zum 60. Geburtstag am 1. August 1945*, O. Gigon, K. Meuli *et al.* Basle. 9–34.

Wessely, C. (1904–08) *Griechische Papyrusurkunden kleineren Formats. Ein Supplement zu den Sammlungen von Ostraka und Überresten griechischer Tachygraphie. Studien zur Paläographie und Papyruskunde*, vols. 3 and 8. 2 vols. in 1. Leipzig.

West, M. L. (ed.) (1966) Hesiod, *Theogony*. Oxford.

(1971) "Stesichorus," *Classical Quarterly* n.s., no. 21: 302–14.

(1992) *Ancient Greek Music*. Oxford.

(1995) "The Date of the *Iliad*," *Museum Helveticum* 52: 203–19.

(2003) *Homeric Hymns, Homeric Apocrypha, Lives of Homer*. Cambridge, MA.

(2007) *Indo-European Poetry and Myth*. Oxford.

Whitmarsh, T. (2001) *Greek Literature and the Roman Empire: The Politics of Imitation*. Oxford.

(2006) "Quickening the Classics: The Politics of Prose in Roman Greece," in *Classical Pasts: The Classical Traditions of Greece and Rome*, ed. J. I. Porter. Princeton, NJ. 353–74.

Wick, C. (2000) "'The Best of Nature': Naturphänomene und Naturkatastrophen in hellenistischen Epigrammen," Paper presented at The Fifth Groningen Workshop, "Hellenistic Epigrams," 30 August – 1 September.

Wilamowitz-Moellendorff, U. von (ed.) (1903) *Timotheus, Die Perser*. Leipzig.

(1913) *Sappho und Simonides: Untersuchungen über griechische Lyriker*. Berlin.

(1924) *Hellenistische Dichtung in der Zeit des Kallimachos*. 2 vols. Berlin.

(ed.) (1969) *Euripides: Herakles*. 3 vols. Darmstadt. (1st edn. 1889.)

Wilkinson, L. P. (1963) *Golden Latin Artistry*. Cambridge.

Wille, G. (1967) *Musica Romana: Die Bedeutung der Musik im Leben der Römer*. Amsterdam.

Williams, B. (1981) "Philosophy," in *The Legacy of Greece: A New Appraisal*, ed. M. I. Finley. Oxford. 202–55.

Wilson, C. (1893) "Apelt's Pseudo-Aristotelian Treatises," *Classical Review* 7: 33–39.

Wilson Jones, M. (2000) "Doric Measure and Architectural Design 1: The Evidence of the Relief from Salamis," *American Journal of Archaeology* 104, no. 1: 73–94.

(2001) "Doric Measure and Architectural Design 2: A Modular Reading of the Classical Temple," *American Journal of Archaeology* 105, no. 4: 675–713.

Wilson, P. (2000) *The Athenian Institution of the Khoregia: The Chorus, the City and the Stage*. Cambridge.

(2002a) Review of S. Lavecchia, *Pindari Dithyramborum Fragmenta* (Rome, 2000). *Bryn Mawr Classical Review* 2002.04.24.

(2002b) "The Musicians among the Actors," in *Greek and Roman Actors: Aspects of an Ancient Profession*, eds. P. Easterling and E. Hall. Cambridge. 39–68.

(2003) "The Sound of Cultural Conflict," in *The Cultures Within Ancient Greek Culture: Contact, Conflict, Collaboration*, eds. C. Dougherty and L. Kurke. Cambridge. 181–206.

Winckelmann, J. J. (1985 [1755]) "Thoughts on the Imitation of the Painting and Sculpture of the Greeks," in *Aesthetic and Literary Criticism: Winckelmann, Lessing, Hamann, Herder, Schiller, Goethe*, ed. H. B. Nisbet. Cambridge. 32–54.

Wind, E. (1983 [1932]) "Θεῖος Φόβος: (*Laws*, II, 671D): On Plato's Philosophy of Art," in E. Wind, *The Eloquence of Symbols: Studies in Humanist Art*, ed. J. Anderson. Oxford. 1–20.

Winnington-Ingram, R. P. (1936) *Mode in Ancient Greek Music*. Cambridge.

Winter, I. J. (1995) "Aesthetics and Mesopotamian Art," in *Civilizations of the Ancient Near East*, eds. J. M. Sasson, J. Baines, G. Beckman, and K. S. Robinson. 4 vols. New York and London. IV: 2569–80.

(2002) "Defining 'Aesthetics' for Non-Western Studies: The Case of Ancient Mesopotamia," in *Art History, Aesthetics, Visual Studies*, eds. M. A. Holly and K. P. F. Moxey. Williamstown, MA. 3–28.

Wismann, H. (1979) "*Atomos Idea*," *Neue Hefte für Philosophie* 15/16: 34–52.

Wohl, V. (2002) *Love among the Ruins: The Erotics of Democracy in Classical Athens*. Princeton, NJ.

Wollheim, R. (2001) "On Formalism and Pictorial Organization," *The Journal of Aesthetics and Art Criticism* 59, no. 2: 127–37.

Woodhead, A. G. (1981) *The Study of Greek Inscriptions*, 2nd edn. Cambridge.

Woodruff, P. (1985) "Didymus on Protagoras and the Protagoreans," *Journal of the History of Philosophy* 23, no. 4: 483–97.

Woolf, G. (1996) "Monumental Writing and the Expansion of Roman Society in the Early Roman Empire," *Journal of Roman Studies* **86**: 22–39.

Wordsworth, W. (1850 [1805]) *The Prelude, or, Growth of a Poet's Mind: An Autobiographical Poem*. London. 131–32.

Yunis, H. (ed.) (2003) *Written Texts and the Rise of Literate Culture in Ancient Greece*. Cambridge.

Zangwill, N. (1999) "Feasible Aesthetic Formalism," *Noûs* 33, no. 4: 610–29.

Zeitlin, F. I. (1994) "The Artful Eye: Vision, Ecphrasis and Spectacle in Euripidean Theatre," in *Art and Text in Ancient Greek Culture*, eds. S. Goldhill and R. Osborne. Cambridge. 138–196.

(1996) "Vision, Figuration, and Image from Theater to Romance." (TS, Sather Classical Lectures, UC Berkeley, 1996.)

Ziebarth, E. (1913) *Aus der antiken Schule: Sammlung griechischer Texte auf Papyrus, Holztafeln, Ostraka.* Kleine Texte für Vorlesungen und Übungen, vol. 65, 2nd edn. Bonn.

Zimmermann, B. (1992) *Dithyrambos: Geschichte einer Gattung.* Hypomnemata, vol. 98. Göttingen.

Zirin, R. (1974) "Inarticulate Noises," in *Ancient Logic and its Modern Interpretations: Proceedings of the Buffalo Symposium on Modernist Interpretations of Ancient Logic, 21 and 22 April, 1972*, ed. J. Corcoran. Dordrecht and Boston, MA. 23–25.

Zirin, R. A. (1980) "Aristotle's Biology of Language," *Transactions of the American Philological Association* 110: 325–47.

Žižek, S. (1999) *The Ticklish Subject: The Absent Centre of Political Ontology.* London.

Zucchelli, B. (1962) ΥΠΟΚΡΙΤΗΣ: *Origine e storia del termine.* Brescia.

Index locorum

General index

Achaean wall 445, 479, 517
  ancient scholia on 517, 518–19
Addison, J. 31, 49
Adorno, T. 2, 48, 49
Aeschines 238, 320–1, 322, 324–5, 335, 342, 359
Aeschylus 190
  and *scaenographia* 210
  as innovator in language and spectacle
    102, 106, 108, 379
  as sublime poet 271–3
  associated with deception 297
  in Aristophanes' *Frogs* 262–73, 455
  in Pherecrates' *Crapataloi* 272
  on *sunthesis* 237
  on vividness of plastic art 195, 332, 334, 338,
    425, 520
  plot criticized by Aristophanes 253–4
  Psychostasia (*Weighing of Souls*) 273
  Life of Aeschylus 108
aesthetic attention 13, 31, 48, 50, 53, 54–5, 64,
    70–1, 78, 79, 97–101, 100–1, 249, 254,
    426, 436, 440, 448, 510
  see also under aisthēsis; Aristotle, on
    contemplation; defamiliarization;
    Kant, on aesthetic contemplation;
    experience; *Verweilung*
aesthetic description and analysis (ancient)
  alleged or apparent impoverishment 6, 56
  borrowed and shared character 8–9, 62–3
  emergence 8–9
  rich abundance 6–7, 56–68
aesthetic experience
  complexity of 65
  shared across formal boundaries 49, 63–4,
    64–5, 65–6
  and impoverished nature of standard
    aesthetic labels for 65
  origins of (in experience of matter) 406–7
  phenomenological origins 155–6, 167, 250
  proto-theory of 16
  fundamental unity of 1, 36–7

social character 16–17
  see also aesthetics of experience
aesthetic form, *see* formalism
aesthetic function 49 (*see also* Mukařovský)
  of language (in Aristotle) 114
  of archaic lyric 453 (*see also* la parole et
    le marbre)
aesthetic inquiry (defined) 25–6
aesthetic materialism
  critical function 11, 71, 275–307
  in antiquity 7–8
  ineluctability 5–6, 9, 15, 32–3, 89
  modern rise 31–2, 31–2, 32–3
  see also materialist aesthetics
aesthetic particulars, *see* aesthetics, of the
    (sensuous) particular; *idion*;
    empiricism, radical
aesthetic pleasure
  mark of aesthetic value 39–40
  aural 246, 310, 324, 329–30, 360
    (*see also* euphony)
  belonging to larger economies of pleasure 47
  complexity of 63, 66
  in archaic poetry 172
  in Aristotle 53–4, 57, 114–15, 141–2, 248–51
  in Gorgias 296
  in Kant 54
  in Shklovsky 79
  enjoyed for its own sake 11
  of the senses (in sophists and Plato) 256–60
  shaped by social and cultural frameworks
    13, 34, 47
  see also beauty; intensities, aesthetic; sublime, the
aesthetic public sphere (in antiquity) 7, 193–6,
    298, 492–3
aesthetic reflection and inquiry (in antiquity)
  historical rise 1, 3–4, 179
  phenomenological rise 21, 406–7
  shared across (pre-)disciplinary boundaries
    41–2, 44, 195–6
  see also folk theories; aesthetic contemplation

586